W9-CIO-229

financial
management
and policy

financial management and policy

fifth edition

JAMES C. VAN HORNE

Stanford University

PRENTICE-HALL, INC., Englewood Cliffs, New Jersey 07632

Library of Congress Cataloging in Publication Data

Van Horne, James C
  Financial management and policy.

  Includes bibliographical references and index.
  1. Corporations—Finance. I. Title.
HG4011.V34–1980   658.1'5   79–18544
ISBN 0-13-315820-9

Editorial/production supervision by Ann Marie McCarthy
Interior design by Allyson Everngam
Cover design by Allyson Everngam
Manufacturing buyer: Anthony Caruso

Printed in the United States of America

10 9 8 7 6 5 4 3 2 1

Prentice-Hall International, Inc., *London*
Prentice-Hall of Australia Pty. Limited, *Sydney*
Prentice-Hall of Canada, Ltd., *Toronto*
Prentice-Hall of India Private Limited, *New Delhi*
Prentice-Hall of Japan, Inc., *Tokyo*
Prentice-Hall of Southeast Asia Pte. Ltd., *Singapore*
Whitehall Books Limited, *Wellington, New Zealand*

to mimi, drew, stuart, stephen

contents

2

concepts in valuation

16

3

valuation of a firm's stock

49

4

valuation from a relative standpoint

78

part **II**

investments in assets and required returns

5

principles of capital investment

105

6

risk analysis in capital budgeting
147

7

evaluation of risky investments:
required rates of return for projects
190

8

required rates of return for companies,
divisions, and acquisitions
220

preface

Financial Management and Policy has three major objectives. First, to develop an understanding of the rapidly evolving and exciting theory of finance so that the reader can evaluate the firm's investment, financing, and dividend decisions in keeping with an objective of maximizing shareholder wealth; second, to become familiar with the application of analytical techniques to a variety of problems in financial management; and third, to expose the reader to the institutional material necessary for a solid understanding of the environment in which financial decisions are made.

This edition has been substantively revised. All materials have been carefully screened in relation to new developments in the field and in relation to reviews and comments by individual professors. Every effort has been made to tie together concepts, not only within chapters but across chapters. In order to accommodate the new materials and to eliminate older, less-useful, and less-relevant materials, a good deal of pruning occurred. Important changes in this edition include the following:

1. The problems at the end of the chapters have been extensively revised. There are eighty-seven new problems; and over thirty less-useful

problems or those with difficulties have been eliminated. Solutions have been carefully checked and mistakes hopefully corrected. This emphasis is in keeping with comments by users.

2. Chapters 2 and 3 on valuation have undergone considerable restructuring so as to make the concepts more easily understood. The treatment of the time value of money has been expanded and substantially improved. In addition, certain newer ideas have been integrated into these chapters.

3. A new chapter presents option pricing valuation in a straightforward and understandable manner so that the reader can later apply the concepts to capital structure decisions, to mergers, to protective covenants, to the call feature, to bankruptcy, and to warrants and convertible securities.

4. There is a new section in Chapter 5 dealing with inflation and capital budgeting. A number of other changes occur in the chapter, including the introduction of capital formation, the scale of investment, the working-capital requirement, and the investment tax credit.

5. Chapter 6, "Risk Analysis in Capital Budgeting," has been consolidated so that it better flows into the chapters dealing with the required rates of return. In addition, the chapter has been simplified in places.

6. Chapters 7 and 8 on required rates of return have been revised in keeping with new developments on valuation. In addition, the examples as well as the overall exposition have been improved.

7. There is a new Appendix to Chapter 8 dealing with the adjustment of a company's beta for leverage.

8. Chapter 9, "Theory of Capital Structure," has been extensively reworked to reflect exciting new developments as well as to make it more understandable. New sections on the effects of agency costs and of personal income taxes, and on the need for "me first" rules in an option pricing context, have been added.

9. The treatment of leverage in practice has been improved. A new section focuses on coverage ratios and a new Appendix deals with inflation and debt.

10. An Appendix to Chapter 11 explores the double taxation of dividends and the effect of its elimination on corporate financial decision making.

11. The chapter on cash management has been reworked with a new emphasis on the goal of such management and on the use of electronic transfers. A number of other improvements occur as well.

12. The Appendix to Chapter 15 on the application of discriminant analysis to accounts receivable management has been substantially improved.

13. The chapter on short-term financing has been revised to bring in new conceptual considerations as well as to bring in money-market financing and spontaneous financing with accruals.

14. For richer insight into the motivation of various parties and into the value of protective covenants, lender-borrower relations are viewed in the context of the option pricing model.

15. The accounting treatment of leases is entirely new and comprehensive. A number of other improvements have been made in the lease-financing chapter.

16. A new section on venture capital appears in Chapter 20, and important improvements occur in the presentation of the call feature and of bond refunding in Chapter 21.

17. Chapter 22 on warrants and convertible securities has been integrated into concepts presented earlier in Chapter 4 on option pricing.

18. A new section on the effect of inflation on financial analysis appears in Chapter 25. The use of financial ratios to predict business failure and other events has been improved and a number of newer studies presented.

19. Substantive improvements have been made in the treatment of financial analysis, including collection matrix analysis, and common size and index analyses.

20. New and updated materials appear in other parts of the book in order to keep it abreast of recent developments. Indeed, this has been a motivating factor in all of my revisions, as I believe that students should be exposed to understandable concepts at the frontiers of our field.

21. Finally, the presentation has been simplified in a number of areas not mentioned above in order to make it more easily comprehended.

The appendixes at the end of certain chapters permit the reader greater flexibility in approaching the study of financial management. These appendixes deal with special topics related either to the chapter or to more advanced, usually mathematical, considerations. The book's continuity is maintained even if this material is not covered in the classroom. In the chapters themselves, the book assumes the reader is familiar with elementary algebra and with certain elementary probability concepts. Even without them, however, almost all of the quantitative material can be understood because symbols are carefully defined and used on a consistent basis throughout.

The order of the chapters reflects my preferences for teaching the course, but the professor is free to approach them in whatever order seems appropriate. Tools of financial analysis and control purposely appear at the end of the book, as many students have encountered them in courses in accounting. For those readers, Part VIII can serve as a review. If the reader has not previously had this background, the professor may wish to take up this material at the outset of the course.

A number of users of previous editions of *Financial Management and Policy* have offered comments which have been helpful to me in revising the book. These people are too numerous to acknowledge individually, but collectively I owe them a great debt of gratitude. Finally, I am grateful to Barbara Firpo, who typed this revision.

James C. Van Horne
Palo Alto, California

financial
management
and policy

part I

foundations
of finance

1
goals and functions of finance

The role of the financial manager in a modern company is everchanging. The responsibilities involved are broadening and becoming more vital to the company's overall development. Once these responsibilities were confined mainly to keeping accurate financial records, preparing reports, managing the firm's cash position, and providing the means for the payment of bills. When liquidity was insufficient for the firm's prospective cash needs, the financial manager was responsible for procuring additional funds. However, this procurement often included only the mechanical aspects of raising funds externally on either a short-, an intermediate-, or a long-term basis.

In recent years, the influence of the financial manager has expanded far beyond these limited functions. Now his concern is with (1) the investment of funds in assets and (2) obtaining the best mix of financing in relation to the overall valuation of the firm. The former determines the size of the firm, its profits from operations, its business risk, and its liquidity. The latter determines the firm's financial charges and its financial risk. As we shall see in this chapter, the financial manager needs a much broader outlook than he has ever needed before, for his influence reaches into almost all facets of the enterprise and into the external environment as well.

EVOLUTION OF FINANCE

In order to better understand the changing role of the financial manager and the evolution of his functions, it is useful to trace the changing character of finance as an academic discipline. In the early part of this century, corporation finance emerged as a separate field of study, whereas before it was considered primarily as a part of economics. By and large, the field encompassed only the instruments, institutions, and procedural aspects of the capital markets. At that time, there were many consolidations, the largest of which was the colossal formation of U.S. Steel Corporation in 1900. These combinations involved the issuance of huge blocks of fixed-income and equity securities. Consequently, there was considerable interest in promotion, and in consolidations and mergers. Accounting data and financial records, as we know them today, were nonexistent. Only with the advent of regulations did disclosure of financial data become prevalent.

With the era of technological innovation and new industries in the 1920s, firms needed more funds. The result was a greater emphasis on liquidity and financing of the firm.[1] Considerable attention was directed to describing methods of external financing, and little to managing a firm internally. One of the important texts of this period was Arthur Stone Dewing's *Financial Policy of Corporations*, which in a scholarly fashion, drew together existing thought, promulgated certain new ideas, and served to pattern the teaching of finance for many years to come.[2] During this period, there was widespread interest in securities, particularly in common stock. This interest became intense toward the end of the decade, and the role and function of the investment banker was particularly important in the study of corporate finance at this time.

The Depression of the thirties necessarily focused the study of finance on the defensive aspects of survival. A great deal of attention was directed toward the preservation of liquidity and toward bankruptcy, liquidation, and reorganization. The principal concern in external financing was how a lender could protect himself. Conservatism, naturally, reigned supreme, with considerable emphasis on a company's maintaining a sound financial structure. The large number of abuses with debt—particularly those that occurred in connection with public utility holding companies—were brought into the limelight when many companies collapsed. These failures, together with the fraudulent maltreatment of numerous investors, brought cries for regulation. Regulation and increased controls on business by government were quick to follow. One result of these regulations was an increase in the amount of financial data disclosed by companies. This disclosure made financial analysis more encompassing, because the analyst was

---

[1]See J. Fred Weston, *The Scope and Methodology of Finance* (Englewood Cliffs, N.J.: Prentice-Hall, 1966), Chap. 2.

[2]Arthur S. Dewing, *The Financial Policy of Corporations* (New York: Ronald Press, 1920).

able to compare different companies as to their financial condition and performance.

Finance, during the forties through the early fifties, was dominated by a "traditional" approach. This approach, which had evolved during the twenties and thirties, was from the point of view of an outsider—such as a lender or investor—analyzing the firm and did not emphasize decision making within the firm. The study of external financing was still largely descriptive. During this period, however, a greater emphasis on analyzing the cash flows of the firm and on the planning and control of these flows from within did develop.

In the middle fifties, great interest developed in capital budgeting and allied considerations.[3] This topic and the concurrent emphasis on present value served as a catalyst for the sweeping changes that subsequently occurred. With the development of new methods and techniques for selecting capital investment projects came a framework for the efficient allocation of capital within the firm. New fields of responsibility and influence for the financial manager included management of the total funds committed to assets and the allocation of capital to individual assets on the basis of an appropriate and objective acceptance criterion.

The Growth of Modern Finance

As a result of these developments, the financial manager had to come squarely to grips with how investors and creditors valued the firm and how a particular decision affected their respective valuations. Valuation models were developed for use in financial decision making. Interestingly enough, many of the dividend valuation models developed during the fifties for the valuation of the firm were offshoots of the classic 1938 work of John Burr Williams.[4] Unfortunately, the impact of this work was not felt in finance for nearly twenty years. With the concern for valuatiion in the fifties, however, came a critical evaluation of the capital structure and the dividend policy of the firm in relation to its valuation as a whole. The pathbreaking articles by Modigliani and Miller in 1958 and 1961 on these topics set the stage for extended theoretical inquiry which continues today.[5] Never before had academic and practitioner thinking been so jarred as when these authors argued that with efficient financial markets and no imperfections, the debt and dividend policies of a firm really did not matter from the standpoint of

---

[3]In the early fifties, Friederich and Vera Lutz expounded a comprehensive theory of the firm in their famous book *The Theory of Investment of the Firm* (Princeton, N.J.: Princeton University Press, 1951). Much of the work on capital budgeting owes its origin to Joel Dean's renowned book *Capital Budgeting* (New York: Columbia University Press, 1951). These works served as building blocks for subsequent theoretical and managerial development in finance.

[4]*The Theory of Investment Value* (Amsterdam: North Holland Publishing, 1964).

[5]Franco Modigliani and M. H. Miller, "The Cost of Capital, Corporation Finance and the Theory of Investment," *American Economic Review*, 48 (June 1958), 261–97; and "Dividend Policy, Growth, and the Valuation of Shares," Journal of Business, 34 (October 1961), 411–33.

valuation. Much of the subsequent work on these topics has tried to identify market imperfections that would give rise to a valuation effect.

A major event in the 1960s was the development of portfolio theory and its eventual application to financial management. First exposited by Markowitz in 1952, the theory was later extended and considerably refined by Sharpe, Lintner, Mossin, Fama, and a number of others.[6] Basically, this theory tells us that the risk of an individual asset should not be judged on the basis of possible deviations from its expected return but rather in relation to its marginal contribution to the overall risk of a portfolio of assets. Depending on the degree of correlation of that asset with other assets in the portfolio, the asset will be more or less risky. Concurrent with this development was considerable theoretical and empirical work on the functioning of financial markets. The simple notion that the firm's debt and equity instruments are traded in markets that may be more or less efficient depending on the circumstances was really never fully understood until much of the work on portfolio theory and efficient markets had been done.

The further refinement of Sharpe's capital-asset pricing model for valuing financial assets brought with it the application of these ideas to financial management in the 1970s. The model suggested that some of the risk of the firm was not relevant to the investor in the firm's stock, as this risk could be diversified away in the portfolio of stocks he held. It also brought an increased focus on market imperfections when judging decisions by the firm with respect to asset selection, financing, and dividends. In the ensuing chapters, we will devote considerable attention to the implications of these notions for financial management.

In a landmark contribution in the 1970s, Black and Scholes developed the option pricing model for the relative valuation of financial claims.[7] With a stock and an option on a stock, it is possible for an individual to establish a riskless hedged position by buying the stock and writing options. In efficient financial markets, the return on such a position should be the risk-free rate. If this holds, precise formulas for valuing various types of options are possible. With this basic notion, a number of scholars have valued convertible securities and warrants and have treated as options such things as the capital structure of the firm, the desire by lenders for restrictions on the borrower, and the call feature on corporate bonds. The application of the option pricing model to corporate finance is expanding and has been a rich lode of intellectual inquiry in recent years.

[6]See Harry M. Markowitz, *Portfolio Selection: Efficient Diversification of Investments* (New York: John Wiley, 1959); William F. Sharpe, "Capital Asset Prices: A Theory of Market Equilibrium under Conditions of Risk," *Journal of Finance,* 19 (September 1964), 425–42; John Lintner, "Security Prices, Risk and Maximal Gains from Diversification," *Journal of Finance,* 20 (December 1965), 587–616; Jan Mossin, *Theory of Financial Markets* (Englewood Cliffs, N.J.: Prentice-Hall, 1973); and Eugene F. Fama and Merton H. Miller, *The Theory of Finance* (New York: Holt, Rinehart & Winston, 1972).

[7]Fischer Black and Myron Scholes, "The Pricing of Options and Corporate Liabilities," *Journal of Political Economy,* 81 (May-June 1973), 637–54.

The use of the computer as an analytical tool added much to the development of finance from the 1950's on. With its advent, complex information systems have been developed that provide the financial manager with the data needed to make sound decisions. In addition, great strides have been made in the application of analytical tools to financial problems. Operations research and decision theory techniques have found widespread use, making possible more disciplined and fruitful financial analysis.

Finally, inflation has had an important influence on the way things are done. While inflation averaged only 2 percent in the 1950s and 1960s, it averaged 7–8 percent in the 1970s. Moreover, inflation has fluctuated widely, at times being "double digit." This change in inflation has caused a dramatic increase in interest rates from what prevailed in the earlier period. As a result, prices of existing corporate bonds have declined and there has been a sharp increase in the cost of debt financing by companies. With inflation, profits reported for accounting purposes are distorted. The sale of previously acquired low-cost inventories results in higher reported earnings. Moreover, depreciation charges on existing assets are less than the cost of replacing them. As a result, reported profits and the taxes paid on these profits are higher than the true economic profits of corporations and the taxes that would be paid on such profits. The increased volatility of inflation in recent years has increased the uncertainty that companies face. Forecasts of future demand, prices, and costs become ever so much more difficult. Capital investment and financing decisions are marked by a higher degree of risk than would occur in an era of stable and low inflation. In turn, these considerations have an adverse effect on the valuation of business firms. While one never knows what the future will hold, it is clear that if high and volatile inflation continues, corporate financial policy will need to be continually modified.

The evolution of finance described above has greatly impacted the role and importance of financial management. Finance has changed from primarily a descriptive study to one that encompasses rigorous analysis and normative theory; from a field that was concerned primarily with the procurement of funds to one that includes the management of assets, the allocation of capital, and the valuation of the firm in the overall market; and from a field that emphasized external analysis of the firm to one that stresses decision making within the firm. Finance today is best characterized as ever-changing, with new ideas and techniques. The role of the financial manager is considerably different from what it was twenty years ago and from what it will no doubt be in another twenty years. Academicians and financial managers must grow to accept the changing environment and master its challenge. In this regard, they must thoroughly understand the underlying objective of the firm.

OBJECTIVE OF THE FIRM

In this book, we assume that the objective of the firm is to maximize its value to its shareholders. Value is represented by the market price of the company's common stock, which, in turn, is a reflection of the firm's investment, financing, and dividend decisions.

Profit Maximization Versus Wealth Maximization

Frequently, maximization of profits is regarded as the proper objective of the firm, but it is not as inclusive a goal as that of maximizing shareholder wealth. For one thing, total profits are not as important as earnings per share. A firm could always raise total profits by issuing stock and using the proceeds to invest in Treasury bills. Even maximization of earnings per share, however, is not a fully appropriate objective, partly because it does not specify the timing or duration of expected returns. Is the investment project that will produce a $100,000 return five years from now more valuable than the project that will produce annual returns of $15,000 in each of the next five years? An answer to this question depends upon the time value of money. Few existing stockholders would think favorably of a project that promised its first return in one hundred years, no matter how large this return. We must take into account the time pattern of returns in our analysis.

Another shortcoming of the objective of maximizing earnings per share is that it does not consider the risk or uncertainty of the prospective earnings stream. Some investment projects are far more risky than others. As a result, the prospective stream of earnings per share would be more uncertain if these projects were undertaken. In addition, a company will be more or less risky depending upon the amount of debt in relation to equity in its capital structure. This risk is known as financial risk; and it, too, contributes to the uncertainty of the firm to investors in the marketplace.

For the reasons given above, an objective of maximizing earnings per share may not be the same as maximizing market price per share. The market price of a firm's stock represents the focal judgment of all market participants as to what the value is of the particular firm. It takes into account present and prospective future earnings per share, the timing, duration, and risk of these earnings, dividend policy, and other factors that bear upon the market price of the stock. The market price serves as a performance index or report card of the firm's progress; it indicates how well management is doing in behalf of its stockholders.

Management Versus Stockholders

In certain situations, the objectives of management may differ from those of the firm's stockholders. In a large corporation whose stock is widely held, stockholders exert very little control or influence over the operations of the company. When the control of a company is separate from its ownership, management may not always act in the best interests of the stockholders. Managements sometimes are said to be "satisficers" rather than "maximizers";[8] they may be content to "play it safe" and seek an acceptable level of growth, being more concerned with perpetuating their own existence than with maximizing the value of the firm to its shareholders. The most important goal to a management of this sort may be its own survival.[9] As a result, it may be unwilling to take reasonable risks for fear of making a mistake, thereby becoming conspicuous to outside suppliers of capital. In turn, these suppliers may pose a threat to management's survival.

Management of a company can be thought of as an agent for the owners. In essence, the stockholders delegate decision-making authority to the agent with the hope that he will act in their best interest. Jensen and Meckling have developed a comprehensive theory of the firm under agency arrangements.[10] They show that the principals, in our case the stockholders, can assure themselves that the agent (management) will make optimal decisions only if appropriate incentives are given and only if the agent is monitored. Incentives include such things as stock options, bonuses, and perquisites which are directly related to how close management decisions are to the interests of the stockholders. Monitoring consists of such things as bonding the agent, systematic reviews of management perquisites, financial-statement audits, and explicit limits on management decisions. These monitoring activities necessarily involve costs which are an inevitable result of the separation of ownership and control of a corporation. The less the ownership percentage of the manager, the less the likelihood that he will behave in a manner consistent with maximizing shareholder wealth, and the greater the need for outside stockholders to monitor his activities.

Maximization of shareholder wealth, then, is an appropriate guide for how a firm *should* act. When management does not act in a manner consistent with this objective, we must recognize this as a constraint and determine the opportunity cost. This cost is measurable only if we determine what the outcome would have been had the firm attempted to maximize shareholder wealth.

A Normative Goal

Because the principle of maximization of shareholder wealth provides a rational guide for running a business and for the efficient alloca-

---

[8]Herbert A. Simon, "Theories of Decision Making in Economics and Behavioral Science," *American Economic Review,* 49 (June 1959), 253–83. See also Weston, *Scope and Methodology of Finance,* Chap. 2.

[9]In a study of owner-managed and nonowner-managed firms, J. W. Elliott, "Control, Size, Growth, and Financial Performance in the Firm," *Journal of Financial and Quantitative Analysis,* 7 (January 1972), 1309–20, found a higher propensity by the nonowner-managed firms for liquidity. This may be some indication of greater risk aversion on the part of these managers.

[10]Michael C. Jensen and William H. Meckling, "Theory of the Firm: Managerial Behavior, Agency Costs and Ownership Structure," *Journal of Financial Economics,* 3 (October 1976), 305–60.

tion of resources in society, we use it as our assumed objective in considering how financial decisions *should* be made. The purpose of capital markets is to efficiently allocate savings in an economy from ultimate savers to ultimate users of funds who invest in real assets. If savings are to be channeled to the most promising investment opportunities, a rational economic criterion must exist that governs their flow. By and large, the allocation of savings in an economy occurs on the basis of expected return and risk. The market value of a firm's stock embodies both of these factors. It therefore reflects the market's tradeoff between risk and return. If decisions are made in keeping with the likely effect upon the market value of its stock, a firm will attract capital only when its investment opportunities justify the use of that capital in the overall economy.

Put another way, the equilibration process by which savings are allocated in an economy occurs on the basis of expected return and risk. Holding risk constant, those economic units (business firms, households, financial institutions, or governments) willing to pay the highest yield are the ones entitled to the use of funds. If rationality prevails, the economic units bidding the highest yields will be the ones with the most promising investment opportunities. As a result, savings will tend to be allocated to the most efficient uses. Maximization of shareholder wealth then embodies the risk-return tradeoff of the market and is the focal point by which funds should be allocated within and among business firms. Any other objective is likely to result in the suboptimal allocation of funds and therefore lead to less than optimal capital formation and growth in the economy as well as a less than optimal level of economic want satisfaction.

This is not to say that management should ignore the question of social responsibility. As related to business firms, social responsibility concerns such things as protecting the consumer, paying fair wages to employees, maintaining fair hiring practices, supporting education, and becoming actively involved in environmental issues like clean air and water. Many people feel that a firm has no choice but to act in socially responsible ways; they argue that shareholder wealth and, perhaps, the corporation's very existence depend upon its being socially responsible. However, the criteria for social responsibility are not clearly defined, making formulation of a consistent objective function difficult.

Moreover, social responsibility creates certain problems for the firm. One is that it falls unevenly on different corporations. Another is that it sometimes conflicts with the objective of wealth maximization. Certain social actions, from a long-range point of view, unmistakably are in the best interests of stockholders, and there is little question that they should be undertaken. Other actions are less clear, and to engage in them may result in a decline in profits and in shareholder wealth in the long run. From the standpoint of society, this decline may produce a conflict. What is gained in having a socially desirable goal achieved may be offset in whole or in part by an accompanying less efficient allocation of resources in society. The latter will result in a less than optimal growth of the economy and a lower total level of economic want satisfaction. In an era of unfilled wants and scarcity, the allocation process is extremely important.

Many people feel that management should not be called upon to resolve the conflict posed above. Rather, society, with its broad general perspective, should make the decisions necessary in this area. Only society, acting through Congress and other representative governmental bodies, can judge the relative tradeoff between the achievement of a social goal and the sacrifice in the efficiency of apportioning resources that may accompany realization of the goal. With these decisions made, corporations can engage in wealth maximization and thereby efficiently allocate resources, subject, of course, to certain governmental constraints. Under such a system, corporations can be viewed as producing both private and social goods, and the maximization of shareholder wealth remains a viable corporate objective.

DEVELOPMENT OF THE BOOK

The functions of finance can be broken down into the three major decisions the firm must make: the investment decision, the financing decision, and the dividend decision. Each must be considered in relation to the objective of the firm; an optimal combination of the three decisions will maximize the value of the firm to its shareholders. Because the decisions are interrelated, we must consider their joint impact on the market price of the firm's stock. We now briefly examine each of them and their place in the subsequent chapters of this book.

Investment Decision

The investment decision, perhaps, is the most important of the three decisions. Capital investment, a major aspect of this decision, is the allocation of capital to investment proposals whose benefits are to be realized in the future. Because the future benefits are not known with certainty, investment proposals necessarily involve risk. Consequently, they should be evaluated in relation to their expected return and risk, for these are the factors that affect the firm's valuation in the marketplace. Included also under the investment decision is the decision to reallocate capital when an asset no longer economically justifies the capital committed to it. The investment decision, then, determines the total amount of assets held by the firm, the composition of these assets, and the business-risk complexion of the firm as perceived by suppliers of capital. The theoretical portion of this decision is taken up in Part II. Fundamental to this decision is the appropriate acceptance criterion, or required rate of return, to employ. Because of the paramount and integrative importance of this issue, considerable attention is devoted to determining the appropriate required rate of return for an investment project, for a division of a company, for the company as a whole, and for a prospective acquisition.

In addition to selecting new investments, a firm must manage existing assets efficiently. The financial manager is charged with varying degrees of operating responsibility over existing assets. He is more concerned with the management of current assets than with fixed assets, and we consider the former topic in Part IV. Our concern in Part IV is with ways to manage current assets efficiently in order to maximize profitability relative to the amount of funds tied up in an asset. Determining a proper level of liquidity for the firm is very much a part of this management, and its determination should be in keeping with the firm's overall valuation. Although the financial manager has little or no operating responsibility for fixed assets and inventories, he is instrumental in allocating capital to these assets by virtue of his involvement in capital investment.

In Parts II and VII, we consider mergers and acquisitions from the standpoint of an investment decision. These external investment opportunities can be evaluated in the same general manner as an investment proposal that is generated internally. Also, in Part VII, we take up failures and reorganizations, which involve a decision to liquidate a company or to rehabilitate it, often by changing its capital structure. This decision should be based upon the same economic considerations that govern the investment decision.

Financing Decision

The second major decision of the firm is the financing decision. Here the financial manager is concerned with determining the best financing mix or capital structure for his firm. If a company can change its total valuation by varying its capital structure, an optimal financing mix would exist in which market price per share could be maximized. In Chapters 9 and 10 of Part III, we take up the financing decision in relation to the overall valuation of the firm. Our concern is with exploring the implications of variation in capital structure on the valuation of the firm. In Parts V and VI, we examine the various methods by which a firm obtains short-, intermediate-, and long-term financing. The emphasis is not only on certain valuation underpinnings but also on the managerial aspects of financing as we analyze the features, concepts, and problems associated with alternative methods. In Part III, on the other hand, the focus is primarily theoretical.

Dividend Decision

The third important decision of the firm is its dividend policy, which is examined in Chapters 11 and 12 of Part III. The dividend decision includes the percentage of earnings paid to stockholders in cash dividends, the stability of absolute dividends over time, stock dividends, and the repurchase of stock. The dividend-payout ratio determines the amount of earnings retained in the firm and must be evaluated in the light of the objective of maximizing shareholder wealth. If investors at the margin are not indifferent between current dividends and capital gains, there will be an optimal dividend-payout ratio that maximizes shareholder wealth. The value of a dividend to investors must be balanced against the opportunity cost of the retained earnings lost as a means of equity financing. Thus we see that the dividend decision must be analyzed in relation to the financing decision.

Financial Management

Financial management involves the solution of the three decisions of the firm discussed above. Together, they determine the value of the firm to its shareholders. Assuming that our objective is to maximize this value, the firm should strive for an optimal combination of the three decisions. Because these decisions are interrelated, they should be solved jointly. The decision to invest in a new capital project, for example, necessitates the financing of the investment. The financing decision, in turn, influences and is influenced by the dividend decision, for retained earnings used in internal financing represent dividends forgone by stockholders. With a proper conceptual framework, joint decisions can be reached that tend to be optimal. The important thing is that the financial manager relates each decision to its effect on the valuation of the firm.

Because of the importance of valuation concepts in understanding financial management, these concepts are investigated in depth in Chapters 2, 3, and 4. Thus the first four chapters serve as the foundation for the subsequent development of the book. Such key concepts as the time value of money, market efficiency, risk-return tradeoffs, valuation in a market portfolio context, and the valuation of relative financial claims using the option pricing model are presented, because they transcend discussion in the remainder of the book.

In an endeavor to make optimal decisions, the financial manager makes use of certain analytical tools in the analysis, planning, and control activities of the firm. Financial analysis is a necessary condition, or prerequisite, for making sound financial decisions; we examine the tools of analysis in Part VIII. This material appears at the end of the book in order to set it apart from the book's sequence of development. Depending on the reader's background, it can be taken up early or used for reference purposes throughout.

PROBLEMS

1. In what direction has the field of finance evolved in recent years?

2. Why should a company concentrate primarily on wealth maximization instead of profit maximization?

3. "A basic rationale for the objective of maximizing the wealth position of the stockholder as a primary business goal is that such an objective may reflect the most efficient use of society's economic resources and thus lead to a maximization of society's economic wealth." Briefly evaluate this observation.

4. Beta-Max Corporation is considering two investment proposals. One involves the development of ten (10) discount record stores in Chicago. Each store is expected to provide an annual after-tax profit of $35,000 for eight years, after which the lease will expire and the store will terminate. The other proposal involves a classical record-of-the-month club. Here much effort will be required to build an appreciation of classical music by the public. Management estimates that after-tax profits will be zero for two years, after which they will grow by $40,000 a year through year ten and remain level thereafter. The life of the second project is fifteen years.

   On the basis of this information, which project do you prefer? Why?

5. What are the major functions of the financial manager? What do these functions have in common?

6. Interest rates are said to embrace the real rate of interest for a given maturity plus a premium for inflation. What is the logic of this statement? What effect does continually fluctuating inflation have on corporate financing? On corporate planning overall?

7. Should the managers of a company own sizable amounts of stock in the company? What are the pros and cons?

8. In recent years, there have been a number of environmental, pollution, hiring, and other regulations imposed on businesses. In view of these changes, is maximization of shareholder wealth any longer a realistic objective?

9. As an investor, do you believe that some managers are paid too much? Do not their rewards come at your expense?

10. How does the notion of risk and reward govern the behavior of financial managers?

SELECTED REFERENCES

ANDERSON, LESLIE P., VERGIL V. MILLER, AND DONALD L. THOMPSON, *The Finance Function.* Scranton, Pa.: Intext, 1971.

BRANCH, BEN, "Corporate Objectives and Market Performance," *Financial Management,* 2 (Summer 1973), 24–29.

DAVIS, KEITH, "Social Responsibility Is Inevitable," *California Management Review,* 19 (Fall 1976), 14–20.

DE ALESSI, LOUIS, "Private Property and Dispersion of Ownership in Large Corporations," *Journal of Finance,* (September 1973), 838–51.

DONALDSON, GORDON, "Financial Goals: Management vs. Stockholders," *Harvard Business Review,* 41 (May-June 1963), 116–29.

ELLIOTT, J. W., "Control, Size, Growth, and Financial Performance in the Firm," *Journal of Financial and Quantitative Analysis,* 7 (January 1972), 1309–20.

FAMA, EUGENE F., "The Effects of a Firm's Investment and Financing Decisions on the Welfare of Its Security Holders," *American Economic Review,* 68 (September 1978), 272–84.

FINDLAY, M. CHAPMAN, III, AND G. A. WHITMORE, "Beyond Shareholder Wealth Maximization," *Financial Management,* 3 (Winter 1974), 25–35.

GERSTNER, LOUIS V. AND HELEN M. ANDERSON, "The Chief Financial Officer as Activist," *Harvard Business Review,* 54 (September-October 1976), 100–106.

HILL, LAWRENCE W., "The Growth of the Corporate Finance Function," *Financial Executive,* 44 (July 1976), 33–43.

JENSEN, MICHAEL C., AND WILLIAM H. MECKLING, "Theory of the Firm: Managerial Behavior, Agency Costs and Ownership Structure," *Journal of Financial Economics,* 3 (October 1976), 305–60.

LEWELLEN, WILBUR G., "Management and Ownership in the Large Firm," *Journal of Finance,* 24 (May 1969), 299–322.

MASSON, ROBERT TEMPEST, "Executive Motivations, Earnings, and Consequent Equity Performance," *Journal of Political Economy,* 79 (November-December 1971), 1278–92.

SOLOMON, EZRA, *The Theory of Financial Management,* Chaps. 1 and 2. New York: Columbia University Press, 1963.

WESTON, J. FRED, *The Scope and Methodology of Finance.* Englewood Cliffs, N.J.: Prentice-Hall, 1966.

2
concepts in valuation

Given the objective discussed in Chapter 1, we know that the firm should choose that combination of investment, financing, and dividend decisions that will maximize its value to its shareholders. These decisions affect the firm's value through their impact on its expected return-risk character. Because the return to stockholders is not known with certainty, risk necessarily is involved. It can be defined as the possibility that the actual return will deviate from that which was expected. Expectations are continually revised on the basis of new information about the investment, financing, and dividend decisions of the firm. In other words, on the basis of information about these three decisions, investors formulate expectations as to the return and risk involved in holding a common stock.

In this and the next two chapters, we take up the valuation of financial market instruments, with particular emphasis upon common stocks. These chapters form the conceptual groundwork on which the subsequent analysis of the investment, financing, and dividend decisions of the firm is based. Our concern will be with the expected return and risk associated with holding a security. Ultimately, we will be able to make some statements about the valuation of an individual firm under the assumption that investors are reasonably well diversified in their security holdings. Before we proceed, however, it is important to consider the time value of money and how one calculates the present value and the internal rate of return from an investment. The principles involved are used not only in Chapters 2, 3, and 4 but repeatedly throughout the book.

TIME VALUE OF MONEY

In any economy in which time preferences of individuals, firms, and governments result in positive rates of interest, the time value of money is an important concept. For example, stockholders will place a higher value on an investment that promises returns over the next five years than on an investment that promises identical returns for years six through ten. Consequently, the timing of expected future cash flows is extremely important in the investment of funds. In essence, the methods proposed allow us to isolate differences in the timing of cash flows for various investments by discounting these cash flows to their present value.

Compound Interest

The notion of compound interest is central to understanding the mathematics of finance. The term itself merely implies that interest paid on a loan or an investment is added to the principal; as a result, interest is earned on interest. In this section, we examine a class of problems that can be solved using the same concept; these problems will be illustrated with a number of examples. To begin our discussion, consider a person who has $100 in a savings account. If the interest rate is 5 percent compounded annually, how much will he have at the end of a year? Setting the problem up, we solve for the terminal value of the account at the end of the year (TV_1)

$$TV_1 = \$100(1 + .05) = \$105$$

For a deposit of two years, the $100 initial deposit will become $105 at the end of the first year at 5 percent interest. Going to the end of the second year, $105 becomes $110.25, as $5 in interest is earned on the initial $100 and $0.25 is earned on the $5 interest paid at the end of the first year. In other words, interest is earned on previously earned interest—hence the name compound interest. Therefore the terminal value at the end of the second year is $100 times 1.05 squared, or times 1.1025. Thus

$$TV_2 = \$100(1.05)^2 = \$110.25$$

At the end of three years, the individual would have

$$TV_3 = \$100(1 + .05)^3 = \$115.76$$

Looked at in a different way, $100 grows to $105 at the end of the first year if the interest rate is 5 percent, and when we multiply this amount by 1.05 we obtain $110.25 at the end of the second year. Multiplying $110.25 by 1.05, we obtain $115.76 at the end of the third year.

Similarly, at the end of n years, the terminal value of a deposit is

$$TV_n = X_0(1 + r)^n \tag{2-1}$$

where X_0 = amount of savings at the beginning

r = interest rate

While this equation may seem formidable, it is a simple matter to employ when using a calculator.

table 2-1
Illustration of compound interest with $100 initial deposit and 5 percent interest

Period	Beginning Value	Interest Earned during Period (5 percent of beginning value)	Terminal Value
1	$100.00	$5.00	$105.00
2	105.00	5.25	110.25
3	110.25	5.51	115.76
4	115.76	5.79	121.55
5	121.55	6.08	127.63
6	127.63	6.38	134.01
7	134.01	6.70	140.71
8	140.71	7.04	147.75
9	147.75	7.38	155.13
10	155.13	7.76	162.89

In Table 2-1, we show the terminal values for our example problem at the end of years 1 through 10. This table illustrates the concept of interest being earned on interest. Equation (2-1) is our fundamental formula for calculating terminal values. As can be visualized, the greater the interest rate r, and the greater the number of periods n, the greater the terminal value.

While our concern has been with interest rates, the concept involved applies to compound growth of any sort. For example, we might wish to determine the future earnings of a firm if they were expected to grow at a 10 percent compound rate. If earnings were $100,000 now, they would be the following at the end of years 1 through 5:

Year	Growth Factor	Expected Earnings
1	(1.10)	$110,000
2	$(1.10)^2$	121,000
3	$(1.10)^3$	133,100
4	$(1.10)^4$	146,410
5	$(1.10)^5$	161,051

Similarly, we can determine the level at the end of so many years for other problems involving compound growth. The principle is particularly important when we consider certain valuation models for common stock later in this chapter.

Tables of Terminal Values   Using Eq. (2-1), one can derive tables of terminal values (also known as future values). An example is shown in Table 2-2 for interest rates of 1 to 10 percent. For the 5 percent column, we note that the terminal values shown for $1 invested at this compound rate correspond to our calculations in Table 2-1 for $100. Also, it is seen that for any rows involving two or more years, terminal value increases at an increasing rate with increases in the interest rate. This is particularly apparent for one hundred years in the future, where $1.00 deposited today will be worth only $2.70 if the interest rate is 1 percent, whereas it will be worth $13,780.59 if the interest rate is 10 percent. Behold the wonders of compound interest!

Compounding More Than Once a Year

Up to now, we have assumed that interest was paid annually. While it is easiest to work with this assumption, we consider now the relationship between terminal value and interest rates for different periods of compounding. To begin, suppose that interest is paid semiannually. If one then deposited $100 in a savings account at 5 percent, the terminal value at the end of six months would be

$$TV_{1/2} = \$100 \left(1 + \frac{.05}{2}\right) = \$102.50$$

and at the end of a year it would be

$$TV_1 = \$100 \left(1 + \frac{.05}{2}\right)^2 = \$105.0625$$

This amount compares with $105.00 if interest were paid only once a year. The $0.0625 difference is attributable to the fact that during the second six months, interest is earned on the $2.50 in interest paid at the end of the first six months. The more times during a year that interest is paid, the greater the terminal value at the end of a given year.

table 2-2
Terminal value of one dollar at the end of *n* years

Year	1%	2%	3%	4%	5%	6%	7%	8%	9%	10%
1	1.0100	1.0200	1.0300	1.0400	1.0500	1.0600	1.0700	1.0800	1.0900	1.1000
2	1.0201	1.0404	1.0609	1.0816	1.1025	1.1236	1.1449	1.1664	1.1881	1.2100
3	1.0303	1.0612	1.0927	1.1249	1.1576	1.1910	1.2250	1.2597	1.2950	1.3310
4	1.0406	1.0824	1.1255	1.1699	1.2155	1.2625	1.3108	1.3605	1.4116	1.4641
5	1.0510	1.1041	1.1593	1.2167	1.2763	1.3382	1.4026	1.4693	1.5386	1.6105
6	1.0615	1.1262	1.1941	1.2653	1.3401	1.4185	1.5077	1.5869	1.6771	1.7716
7	1.0721	1.1487	1.2299	1.3159	1.4071	1.5036	1.6058	1.7138	1.8280	1.9487
8	1.0829	1.1717	1.2668	1.3686	1.4775	1.5938	1.7182	1.8509	1.9926	2.1436
9	1.0937	1.1951	1.3048	1.4233	1.5513	1.6895	1.8385	1.9990	2.1719	2.3579
10	1.1046	1.2190	1.3439	1.4802	1.6289	1.7908	1.9672	2.1589	2.3674	2.5937
11	1.1157	1.2434	1.3842	1.5395	1.7103	1.8983	2.1049	2.3316	2.5804	2.8531
12	1.1268	1.2682	1.4258	1.6010	1.7959	2.0122	2.2522	2.5182	2.8127	3.1384
13	1.1381	1.2936	1.4685	1.6651	1.8856	2.1329	2.4098	2.7196	3.0658	3.4523
14	1.1495	1.3195	1.5126	1.7317	1.9799	2.2609	2.5785	2.9372	3.3417	3.7975
15	1.1610	1.3459	1.5580	1.8009	2.0789	2.3966	2.7590	3.1722	3.6425	4.1772
20	1.2202	1.4859	1.8061	2.1911	2.6533	3.2071	3.8697	4.6610	5.6044	6.7275
25	1.2824	1.6406	2.0938	2.6658	3.3864	4.2919	5.4274	6.8485	8.6231	10.8347
50	1.6446	2.6916	4.3839	7.1067	11.4674	18.4201	29.4570	46.9016	74.3575	117.3907
100	2.7048	7.2446	19.2186	50.5049	131.5010	339.3014	867.7149	2,199.7569	5,529.0304	13,780.5890

The general formula for solving for the terminal value at the end of year n where interest is paid m times a year is

$$TV_n = X_o\left(1 + \frac{r}{m}\right)^{mn} \tag{2-2}$$

To illustrate, suppose that in our previous example interest were paid quarterly and that we wished again to know the terminal value at the end of one year. It would be

$$TV_1 = \$100\left(1 + \frac{.05}{4}\right)^4 = \$105.09$$

which, of course, is higher than that which occurs either with semiannual or with annual compounding.

The terminal value at the end of three years for the above example with quarterly interest payments is

$$TV_3 = \$100\left(1 + \frac{.05}{4}\right)^{12} = \$116.08$$

This compares with a terminal value with semiannual compounding of

$$TV_3 = \$100\left(1 + \frac{.05}{2}\right)^6 = \$115.97$$

and with annual compounding of

$$TV_3 = \$100\left(1 + \frac{.05}{1}\right)^3 = \$115.76$$

The greater the number of years, the greater the difference in terminal values that occur between two different methods of compounding.

If interest were compounded daily on the basis of a 365-day year, the terminal value of an X_o initial deposit at the end of n years would be

$$TV_n = X_o\left(1 + \frac{r}{365}\right)^{365n} \tag{2-3}$$

As m approaches infinity, the term $(1 + r/m)^{mn}$ approaches e^{rn}, where e is approximately 2.71828 and is defined as

$$e = \lim_{m \to \infty} \left(1 + \frac{1}{m}\right)^m \tag{2-4}$$

where ∞ is the sign for infinity. To see that e approaches 2.71828 as m increases, simply increase m in the above expression from, say, 5 to 10 to 20 and solve for e. The terminal value at the end of n years of an initial deposit of X_o where interest is compounded continuously at a rate of r is

$$TV_n = X_o e^{rn} \tag{2-5}$$

For our example problem, the terminal value at the end of three years would be

$$TV_3 = \$100(2.71828)^{(.05)(3)} = \$116.18$$

This compares with a terminal value with annual compounding of

$$TV_3 = \$100(1.05)^3 = \$115.76$$

and with semiannual compounding of

$$TV_3 = \$100\left(1 + \frac{.05}{2}\right)^6 = \$115.97$$

Continuous compounding results in the maximum possible terminal value at the end of n periods for a given rate of interest. As m is increased in Eq. (2-2), the terminal value increases at a decreasing rate until ultimately it approaches that achieved with continuous compounding.

Present Values

Suppose you wish to save for the future by putting aside a certain amount of funds today with the expectation that they will grow with interest to some larger amount in the future. To be more specific, suppose that you want to buy a stereo set which will cost $700 one year from now and that a local savings and loan association pays 6 percent on one-year deposits. How much must you put aside in order to have $700 one year hence? If we let A_1 represent the amount of money you wish to have one year from now, PV the amount saved, and k the annual interest rate, we have

$$A_1 = PV(1 + k) \tag{2-6}$$

For our example problem, this becomes

$$\$700 = PV(1.06)$$

Solving for PV, we obtain

$$PV = \frac{\$700}{1.06} = \$660.38$$

Therefore $660.38 would need to be saved now in order to have $700 one year hence. Stated another way, $660.38 is the *present value* of $700 to be received at the end of one year when the interest rate involved is 6 percent.

The present value of a sum to be received two years from now is

$$PV = \frac{A_2}{(1 + k)^2} \qquad (2\text{-}7)$$

which for our example problem would be

$$PV = \frac{\$700}{(1.06)^2} = \frac{\$700}{1.1236} = \$623.00$$

Thus $700 two years from now has a lower present value than $700 one year from now. Indeed, that is the whole idea of the time value of money.

In solving present-value problems, it is useful to express the interest factor separately from the amount to be received in the future. For example, our problem above can be expressed as

$$PV = \$700 \left[\frac{1}{(1.06)^2} \right] = \$623.00$$

In this way we are able to isolate the interest factor, and this isolation facilitates present-value calculations. In such calculations, the interest rate is known as the *discount rate,* and henceforth we will refer to it as such.

So far we have considered only present-value calculations for amounts of money to be received one and two years in the future. However, the principles are the same for amounts to be received further in the future. For example, the present value of $1 to be received at the end of n years is

$$PV = \frac{1}{(1 + k)^n} \qquad (2\text{-}8)$$

To illustrate, suppose we wish to determine the present value of $1 to be received five years from now when the discount rate is 10 percent. Setting up the problem, we have

$$\$1 \left[\frac{1}{(1.10)^5} \right] = \$0.62092$$

This tells us that $1 five years from now is worth approximately 62 cents today if the discount rate is 10 percent.

Fortunately, present-value tables exist that relieve us of having to make these calculations every time we have a problem to solve. Such a table is shown in Table A-1 in Appendix A at the end of the book. Here, present values of $1, known as discount factors, are shown for discount rates from

1 percent to 40 percent and for periods 1 through 25 in the future. We see in the table that for a 10 percent discount rate, the discount factor for five years in the future is 0.62092, just as we calculated. For one year, two years, and three years in the future, we see that the discount factors are 0.90909, 0.82645, and 0.75131, respectively. These discount factors are merely the result of the following calculations: $1/(1.10)$; $1/(1.10)^2$; and $1/(1.10)^3$.

If we had an uneven series of cash flows—$1 one year hence, $3 two years hence, and $2 three years from now—the present value of this series, using a 10 percent discount rate, would be:

PV of $1 to be received at end of one year	$1(0.90909) = 0.90909
PV of $3 to be received at end of two years	$3(0.82645) = 2.47935
PV of $2 to be received at end of three years	$2(0.75131) = 1.50262
Present value of series	$4.89106

Given a present-value table, we are able to calculate the present value for any series of future cash flows in the above manner.

Annuities However, the procedure can be simplified for a series if the cash flows in each future period are the same. A series of this sort is known as an *annuity*. Suppose that in a series of future cash flows, $1 was to be received at the end of each of the next three years. The calculation of the present value of this stream, using the above procedure, would be

PV of $1 to be received in one year	= 0.90909
PV of $1 to be received in two years	= 0.82645
PV of $1 to be received in three years	= 0.75131
Present value of series	$2.48685

With an even series of future cash flows, it is unnecessary to go through these calculations. The discount factor, 2.48685, can be applied directly. We would simply multiply $1 by 2.48685 to obtain $2.48685. Present-value tables for even series of cash flows have been developed that allow us to look up the appropriate compound discount factor. An example is shown in Table A-2 in Appendix A at the end of the book.

We note that the discount factor for an even series of cash flows for three years, using a 10 percent discount rate, is 2.4868—as we calculated. Thus, for an even series of cash flows, we simply multiply the appropriate discount factor times the cash flow. If we wish to know the present value, using an 8 percent discount rate, of a future stream of $5 cash flows to be received at the end of each year over a four-year period, the calculation would be

$$\$5(3.3121) = \$16.56$$

Using the present-value tables shown in Tables A-1 and A-2 at the end of the book, we are able to calculate the present value of various future streams of cash flows.

If we trace across any of the rows in Tables A-1 and A-2, we can see that the higher the discount rate, the lower the discount factor. However, we see that the relationship is not linear, but rather that the discount factor decreases at a decreasing rate with increases in the discount rate. Therefore the present value of an amount of money to be received in the future decreases at a decreasing rate as the discount rate increases. The relationship is illustrated in Figure 2-1. At a zero rate of discount, the present value of $1 to be received in the future is $1. In other words, there is no time value of money. As the discount rate increases, however, the present value declines but at a decreasing rate. As the discount rate approaches infinity, the present value of the future $1 approaches zero.

**Present Value When Interest
Is Compounded More Than Once a Year**

When interest is compounded more than once a year, the formula for calculating present values must be revised along the same lines as for the calculation of terminal value. Instead of dividing the future cash flow by $(1 + k)^n$ as we do when annual compounding is involved, the present value is determined by

$$PV = \frac{A_n}{\left(1 + \dfrac{k}{m}\right)^{mn}}$$

(2-9)

where, as before, A_n is the cash flow at the end of year n, m is the number of times a year interest is compounded, and k is the discount rate. The present

figure 2-1
**Relationship between
present value and the
discount rate**

value of $100 to be received at the end of year 3, where the discount rate is 10 percent compounded quarterly, is

$$PV = \frac{\$100}{\left(1 + \frac{.10}{4}\right)^{(4)(3)}} = \$74.36$$

The present value of $100 at the end of one year with a discount rate of 100 percent compounded monthly is

$$PV = \frac{\$100}{\left(1 + \frac{1}{12}\right)^{12}} = \$38.27$$

When interest is compounded continuously, the present value of a cash flow at the end of year n is

$$PV = \frac{A_n}{e^{rn}} \tag{2-10}$$

where e is approximately 2.71828. The present value of $100 to be received at the end of three years with a discount rate of 10 percent compounded continuously is

$$PV = \frac{\$100}{2.71828^{(.10)(3)}} = \$74.08$$

On the other hand, if the discount rate is compounded only annually, we have

$$PV = \frac{\$100}{(1.10)^3} = \$75.13$$

Thus the fewer times a year the discount rate is compounded, the greater the present value. This relationship is just the opposite of that for terminal values. To illustrate the relationship between present value and the number of times a year the discount rate is compounded, consider again our example involving $100 to be received at the end of three years with a discount rate of 10 percent. The following present values result from various compounding intervals:[1]

Compounding	Present Value
Annual	$75.13
Semiannual	74.62
Quarterly	74.36
Monthly	74.17
Continuous	74.08

[1]For semiannual compounding, m is 2 in Eq. (2-9) and mn is 6. With monthly compounding, m is 12 and mn is 36.

We see that the present value decreases but at a decreasing rate as the compounding interval shortens, the limit being continuous compounding.

Internal Rate of Return or Yield

The internal rate of return or yield for an investment is the discount rate that equates the present value of the expected cash outflows with the present value of the expected inflows. Mathematically, it is represented by that rate, r, such that

$$\sum_{t=0}^{n} \left[\frac{A_t}{(1 + r)^t} \right] = 0 \qquad (2\text{-}11)$$

where A_t is the cash flow for period t, whether it be a net cash outflow or inflow, n is the last period in which a cash flow is expected, and the capital Greek sigma denotes the sum of discounted cash flows at the end of periods o through n. If the initial cash outlay or cost occurs at time o, Eq. (2-11) can be expressed as

$$A_0 = \frac{A_1}{(1 + r)} + \frac{A_2}{(1 + r)^2} + \cdots + \frac{A_n}{(1 + r)^n} \qquad (2\text{-}12)$$

Thus r is the rate that discounts the stream of future cash flows—A_1 through A_n—to equal the initial outlay at time o—A_o. Implicitly assumed is that the cash inflows received from the investment are reinvested to realize the same rate of return as r. More will be said about this assumption in Chapter 5. Our purpose now is merely to alert the reader to this implication.

To illustrate the use of Eq. (2-12), suppose that we have an investment opportunity that calls for a cash outlay at time 0 of $18,000 and is expected to provide cash inflows of $5,600 at the end of each of the next five years. The problem can be expressed as

$$18,000 = \frac{5,600}{(1 + r)} + \frac{5,600}{(1 + r)^2} + \frac{5,600}{(1 + r)^3} + \frac{5,600}{(1 + r)^4} + \frac{5,600}{(1 + r)^5} \qquad (2\text{-}13)$$

Solving for the internal rate of return, r, involves an iterative procedure using present values. Fortunately, there are computer programs for solving for the internal rate of return; and these programs eliminate the arduous computations involved. To illustrate a manual method, however, consider again our example. The cash-flow stream is represented by an even series of cash flows of $5,600, to be received at the end of each of the next five years. We want to determine the discount factor that, when multiplied by $5,600, equals the cash outlay of $18,000 at time 0. Suppose that we start with three discount rates—14 percent, 16 percent, and 18 percent—and calculate the present value of the cash-flow stream. Using the different discount factors shown in Table A-2 at the end of the book, we find:

Discount Rate	Discount Factor	Cash Flow Each Year	Present Value of Stream
18%	3.1272	$5,600	$17,512.32
16	3.2743	5,600	18,336.08
14	3.4331	5,600	19,225.36

When we compare the present value of the stream with the initial outlay of $18,000, we see that the internal rate of return necessary to discount the stream to $18,000 falls between 16 and 18 percent, being closer to 16 than to 18 percent. To approximate the actual rate, we interpolate between 16 and 17 percent as follows:

	Discount Rate	Present Value
	16%	$18,336.08
	17	17,916.08
Difference	1%	$ 420.00

$$\frac{336.08}{420.00} = 0.80 \qquad 16\% + 0.80\% = 16.8\%$$

Thus the internal rate of return necessary to equate the present value of the cash inflows with the present value of the outflows is approximately 16.8 percent. It should be noted that interpolation gives only an approximation of the exact percent; the relationship between the two discount rates is not linear with respect to present value.

When, as above, the cash-flow stream is an even series, and the initial outlay occurs at time 0, there really is no need for trial and error. We simply divide the initial outlay by the cash flow and search for the nearest discount factor. Using our example, we divide $18,000 by $5,600, obtaining 3.214. The nearest discount factor on the five-year row in Table A-2 at the end of the book is 3.2743, and this figure corresponds to a discount rate of 16 percent. Inasmuch as 3.214 is less than 3.2743, we know that the actual rate lies between 16 and 17 percent and we interpolate accordingly. When the cash-flow stream is an uneven series, the task is more difficult; and here we must resort to trial and error. However, given practice, a person can come surprisingly close in selecting discount rates from which to start.

Actually, a present-value table is nothing more than a bond-yield table that takes account of compound interest. A more extensive discussion of the bond yields is found in the Appendix to this chapter. Given the rudiments of the time value of money and discounting a cash-flow stream to its present value, we are able to proceed with our examination of the valuation of financial instruments.

When an individual purchases a common stock, he gives up current consumption in the hope of attaining increased future consumption. His expectation of higher future consumption is based on the dividends he expects to receive and, hopefully, the eventual sale of the stock at a price higher than his original purchase price. The individual tries to allocate his wealth at a given moment in keeping with his desired lifetime consumption pattern, which includes any bequest he wishes to make. If the future were certain and the time of death known, the individual could apportion his wealth so as to obtain the maximum possible satisfaction from present and future consumption. He would know the exact returns available from investment and the timing of these returns, as well as future income from noninvestment sources. Investment would be merely a means of balancing present against future consumption.[2]

Return on Investment

Not knowing what lies ahead, the investor is unable to plan his lifetime consumption pattern with certainty. Because the returns from investment and the timing of those returns are uncertain, he compensates for the lack of certainty by requiring an expected return sufficiently high to offset it. But what constitutes the return on a common stock? For a one-year holding period, the benefits associated with ownership include the cash dividends paid during the year together with any appreciation in market price, or capital gain, realized at the end of the year. More formally, the one-period return is

$$r = \frac{\text{Dividends} + (\text{Ending price} - \text{Beginning price})}{\text{Beginning price}} \qquad (2\text{-}14)$$

where the term in parentheses in the numerator is the capital gain or loss during the holding period.

Suppose an individual were to purchase a share of stock of a corporation for $50. The company is expected to pay a $2 dividend at the end of the year, and its market price after the payment of the dividend is expected to be $53 a share. Thus the expected return would be

$$r = \frac{2.00 + (53.00 - 50.00)}{50.00} = 0.10$$

[2]See Irving Fisher, *The Theory of Interest* (New York: Augustus M. Kelley, 1965), Chaps. 10–13.

where r is the expected return. Another way to solve for r is

$$50.00 = \frac{2.00}{(1 + r)} + \frac{53.00}{(1 + r)}$$

When we solve for the rate of discount that equates the present value of the dividend and terminal value at the end of one year with the purchase price of the stock at time 0, we find it to be 10 percent. Thus the investor expects a 10 percent return on his investment.

Now suppose that instead of holding the security one year, he intends to hold it two years and sell it at the end of that time. Moreover, suppose he expects the company to pay a \$2.20 dividend at the end of year 2 and the market price of the stock to be \$56.10 after the dividend is paid. His expected return can be found by solving the following equation for r:

$$50.00 = \frac{2.00}{(1 + r)} + \frac{2.20}{(1 + r)^2} + \frac{56.10}{(1 + r)^2}$$

When we solve for r by the method described earlier, we find it to be 10 percent also. For general purposes, the formula can be expressed as

$$P_0 = \sum_{t=1}^{2} \frac{D_t}{(1 + r)^t} + \frac{P_2}{(1 + r)^2} \tag{2-15}$$

where P_0 is the market price at time 0, D_t is the expected dividend at the end of period t, the capital Greek sigma denotes the sum of discounted dividends at the end of periods 1 and 2, and P_2 is the expected terminal value at the end of period 2.

If an investor's holding period were ten years, the expected rate of return would be determined by solving the following equation for r:

$$P_0 = \sum_{t=1}^{10} \frac{D_t}{(1 + r)^t} + \frac{P_{10}}{(1 + r)^{10}} \tag{2-16}$$

Now, suppose that the investor were a perpetual trust fund and that the trustee expected to hold the stock forever. In this case, the expected return would consist entirely of cash dividends and perhaps a liquidating dividend. Thus the expected rate of return would be determined by solving the following equation for r:

$$P_0 = \sum_{t=1}^{\infty} \frac{D_t}{(1 + r)^t} \tag{2-17}$$

where ∞ is the sign for infinity.[3] What we are saying here is that the formula takes account of all possible future dividends that might be paid. For practical purposes, this needs to be fifty years or so, but beyond this horizon the present-value ramifications are slight.

It is clear that the intended holding period of different investors will vary greatly. Some will hold a stock only a few days, while others might expect to hold it forever. Investors with holding periods shorter than infinity expect to be able to sell the stock in the future at a price higher than they paid for it. This assumes, of course, that at that time there will be investors willing to buy it. In turn, these investors will base their judgments as to what the stock is worth on expectations of future dividends and future terminal value beyond that point. That terminal value, however, will depend upon other investors at that time being willing to buy the stock. The price they are willing to pay will depend upon their expectations of dividends and terminal value. And so the process goes through successive investors. Note that the total cash return to all successive investors in a stock is the sum of the dividends paid, including any liquidating dividend. Thus, cash dividends are all that stockholders as a whole receive from their investment; they are all the company pays out. Consequently, the foundation for the valuation of common stocks must be dividends.

The logical question to be raised is, Why do the stocks of companies that pay no dividends have positive, and often quite high, values? The answer is that investors expect to be able to sell the stock in the future at a price higher than they paid for it. Instead of dividend income plus terminal value, they rely only upon the terminal value. In turn, terminal value will depend upon the expectations of the marketplace at the end of the horizon period. The ultimate expectation is that the firm eventually will pay dividends, either regular or liquidating ones, and that future investors will receive a cash return on their investment. In the interim, however, investors are content with the expectation that they will be able to sell the stock at a subsequent time because there will be a market for it. In the meantime, the company is reinvesting earnings and, hopefully, enhancing its future earning power and ultimate dividends.

Growth Models

We saw in Eq. (2-17) that the return on investment is the rate of discount that equates the present value of the stream of expected future divi-

---

[3]For longer holding periods, portfolio theorists usually work with continuously compounded rates of return. The assumption is that the portfolio's return follows a log normal distribution. While the expression of returns on a continuously compounded basis is preferred, such an expression is difficult for the reader to follow in a basic finance course. For ease of understanding, we work with returns based on discrete time periods. The interested reader is referred to the last section of Chapter 4, where continuously compounded returns are employed in connection with option valuation.

dends with the current market price of the stock. If dividends of a company are expected to grow at a constant rate, g, in keeping, say, with a growth in earnings, Eq. (2-17) becomes

$$P_0 = \frac{D_0(1 + g)}{(1 + r)} + \frac{D_0(1 + g)^2}{(1 + r)^2} + \cdots + \frac{D_0(1 + g)^\infty}{(1 + r)^\infty} \qquad (2\text{-}18)$$

where D_0 is the dividend per share at time 0. Thus the dividend expected in period n is equal to the most recent dividend times the compound growth factor, $(1 + g)^n$.

Assuming r is greater than g, Eq. (2-18) can be expressed as[4]

$$P_0 = \frac{D_1}{r - g} \qquad (2\text{-}19)$$

Rearranging, the expected return becomes

$$r = \frac{D_1}{P_0} + g \qquad (2\text{-}20)$$

The critical assumption in this valuation model is that dividends per share are expected to grow perpetually at a compound rate of g. For some companies, this assumption may be a fair approximation of reality. To illustrate the use of Eq. (2-20), suppose that A & G Company's dividend per share at

---

[4]If we multiply both sides of Eq. (2-18) by $(1 + r)/(1 + g)$ and subtract Eq. (2-18) from the product, we obtain

$$\frac{P_0(1 + r)}{(1 + g)} - P_0 = D_0 - \frac{D_0(1 + g)^\infty}{(1 + r)^\infty}$$

Because r is greater than g, the second term on the right side will be zero. Consequently,

$$P_0 \left[\frac{1 + r}{1 + g} - 1 \right] = D_0$$

$$P_0 \left[\frac{(1 + r) - (1 + g)}{1 + g} \right] = D_0$$

$$P_0[r - g] = D_0(1 + g)$$

$$P_0 = \frac{D_1}{r - g}$$

If r were less than g, it is easy to determine that the market price of the stock would be infinite. See David Durand, "Growth Stocks and the Petersburg Paradox," *Journal of Finance,* 12 (September 1957), 348–63.

$t = 1$ was expected to be \$3, to grow at a 4 percent rate forever, and that the current market price was \$60 a share. The expected return would be

$$r = \frac{\$3}{\$60} + .04 = 9 \text{ percent}$$

When the pattern of expected growth is such that a perpetual growth model is not appropriate, modifications of Eq. (2-18) can be used. A number of valuation models are based upon the premise that the growth rate will taper off eventually. For example, the transition might be from a present above-normal growth rate to one that is considered normal. If dividends per share were expected to grow at an 8 percent compound rate for ten years and then grow at a 4 percent rate, Eq. (2-18) would become

$$P_0 = \sum_{t=1}^{10} \frac{D_0(1.08)^t}{(1 + r)^t} + \sum_{t=11}^{\infty} \frac{D_{10}(1.04)^{t-10}}{(1 + r)^t} \tag{2-21}$$

The transition from an above-normal to a normal rate of growth could be specified as more gradual than the rate above. For example, we might expect dividends to grow at an 8 percent rate for five years, followed by a 6 percent rate for the next five years, and a 4 percent growth rate thereafter. The more growth segments that are added, the more closely the growth in dividends will approach a curvilinear function.

It seems clear that a company will not grow at an above-normal rate forever. Typically, companies tend to grow at a very high rate initially, after which their growth opportunities slow down to a rate that is normal for companies in general. For any growth model, Eq. (2-18) can be modified so that it portrays the expected stream of future dividends.

MEASURING RISK—THE STANDARD DEVIATION

So far we have worked only with the expected return from holding a security. In a world of uncertainty, of course, this return may not be realized. Risk can be thought of as the possibility that the actual return from holding a security will deviate from the expected return. The greater the magnitude of deviation and the greater the probability of its occurrence, the greater the risk of the security. Figure 2-2 shows the probability distributions of possible returns for two securities. Because the actual return of security B has a greater likelihood of deviating from its expected return than that of security A, we would say that it had greater risk. While the investor is principally concerned with downside risk, or the possibility of a negative return, a more useful measure of risk takes into account all divergence of the actual return from that which was expected.

figure 2-2
Illustration of risk

a.

b.

To illustrate this measure, suppose an investor believed that the possible one-year returns from investing in a particular common stock were those shown in Table 2-3. This probability distribution can be summarized in terms of two parameters—the *expected value* of return and the *standard deviation*. The expected value of return is

$$\bar{R} = \sum_{i=1}^{n} R_i P_i \qquad (2\text{-}22)$$

where R_i is the return for the ith possibility, P_i is the probability of occurrence of that return, and n is the total number of possibilities. The standard deviation is

$$\sigma = \sqrt{\sum_{i=1}^{n} (R_i - \bar{R})^2 P_i} \qquad (2\text{-}23)$$

The square of the standard deviation, σ^2, is known as the variance of the distribution.

table 2-3
Probability distribution of possible returns
for a one-year holding period

Probability of occurrence	.05	.10	.20	.30	.20	.10	.05
Possible return	−.10	−.02	.04	.09	.14	.20	.28

To illustrate these measures, consider again the distribution of possible returns shown in Table 2-3. The expected value of return is

$$\overline{R} = -.10(0.05) - .02(0.10) + .04(0.20) + .09(0.30) + .14(0.20)$$
$$+ .20(0.10) + .28(0.05)$$
$$= 9 \text{ percent}$$

The standard deviation is

$$\sigma = [(-.10 - .09)^2 0.05 + (-.02 - .09)^2 0.10 + (.04 - .09)^2 0.20$$
$$+ (.09 - .09)^2 0.30 + (.14 - .09)^2 0.20 + (.20 - .09)^2 0.10$$
$$+ (.28 - .09)^2 0.05]^{1/2}$$
$$= [.00703]^{1/2}$$
$$= 8.38 \text{ percent}$$

Use of Standard Deviation Information

For the normal, bell-shaped probability distribution, approximately 0.68 of the distribution falls within one standard deviation of the expected value, 0.95 falls within two standard deviations, and 0.997 within three standard deviations. By expressing differences from the expected value in terms of standard deviations, we are able to determine the probability that the actual return will be greater or less than such and such an amount. To illustrate, suppose we wished to determine the probability that the actual return in our example would be less than zero. Standardizing the deviation from the expected value, we have 9 percent/8.38 percent = 1.07 standard deviations. Turning to the normal probability distribution table in Appendix B at the end of the book, we find that there is approximately a 14 percent probability that the actual return will be more than 1.07 standard deviations from the mean of the distribution. Therefore there is a 14 percent likelihood that the actual return on investment will be zero or less.

Thus the dispersion, or wideness, of the probability distribution of possible returns reflects the degree of investor uncertainty. A distribution with a small standard deviation relative to its expected value indicates little dispersion and a high degree of confidence in the outcome. A distribution with a large standard deviation relative to its expected value indicates a high degree of uncertainty about the possible return on investment. In the immediate discussion, we assume that probability distributions can be summarized in terms of two parameters—the expected value and the standard deviation.

Having considered the probability distribution of possible returns from holding a security, the question becomes, How do investors use this information in making investment choices? In turn, this depends on their utility preferences with respect to expected return and risk. In the remainder of this chapter, we consider the derivation of such preferences. The foundation provided in this chapter will then be used in the next chapter when we take up the actual valuation of a security.

INVESTOR UTILITY PREFERENCES

In this section, we examine investor utility preferences as they specifically relate to security investments. The expected utility model presented is widely used in the literature on decision making under uncertainty. We employ it as a means for describing how individual investment decisions are made. In so doing, we hope to come to a better understanding of security risk and investor behavior with respect to such risk.

We assume that the objective of investors, as well as of other individuals, is to maximize their utility. In turn, utility is derived from present and prospective future consumption. We can think of the investor as deciding at various discrete intervals during his lifetime what portion of his wealth will be consumed and what portion invested. That portion invested is expected to increase future wealth, which, in turn, will be allocated between consumption and investment. Determination of an optimal consumption-investment sequence is complicated by the fact that we live in an uncertain world where future wealth levels associated with various investment decisions are not known with certainty.[5]

Therefore we assume that individuals maximize expected utility, which is a function of both expected return and uncertainty. Assuming that the individual makes rational and consistent choices,[6] it is possible to derive a utility of wealth function for him. The index derived portrays the individual's preferences with respect to risky investments, which in turn are expressed as probability distributions of possible outcomes. In the subsequent section, we show how a utility of wealth function might be derived. This is followed by the application of the function to the problem of choosing among investment alternatives on the basis of the one that maximizes expected utility. Finally, we take up various utility functions in the context of our example. Hopefully, this decision will give us a basic understanding of investor decision making under uncertainty.

Derivation of Utility of Wealth Function

To determine an individual's utility of wealth function, we might pose to him the opportunity to invest his initial wealth in a group of lotteries

[5]See Eugene F. Fama and Merton H. Miller, *The Theory of Finance* (New York: Holt, Rinehart & Winston, 1972), Chap. 5.

[6]The utility approach considered in this section has its origin in the classic work of John von Neumann and Oskar Morgenstern, *Theory of Games and Economic Behavior*, rev. ed. (Princeton, N.J.: Princeton University Press, 1955). For an excellent discussion of the axioms as they pertain to investments, see Fama and Miller, *Theory of Finance*, pp. 192–96; J. Hirshleifer, *Investment, Interest, and Capital* (Englewood Cliffs, N.J.: Prentice-Hall, 1970), Chap. 8; and Harry M. Markowitz, *Portfolio Selection* (New York: John Wiley, 1959), Chap. 10.

or gambles. By so doing, we are able to derive a utility index for money. We measure utility in units, which we call "utiles." Arbitrarily, we initially assign utile values of 0 and 1 to a pair of dollar amounts that represent extreme prospects—say zero dollars of wealth and $100,000 of wealth, respectively.

Suppose now that we pose a risk situation to the individual by offering him an instantaneous lottery with a 0.5 chance of receiving no money, and a 0.5 chance of receiving $100,000. We then ask him how much he would be willing to pay for the lottery. If his answer is $33,000, we would attach a utile value of 0.5 to $33,000. Thus we have determined the certainty equivalent at which the individual is indifferent between that sum and the lottery. Next, we have him consider a lottery providing a 0.4 probability of receiving $33,000 and a 0.6 probability of receiving $100,000. Suppose he were willing to buy this lottery for $63,000. The utile value of $63,000 is then

$$U(\$63,000) = 0.4U(\$33,000) + 0.6U(\$100,000)$$
$$= 0.4(0.5) + 0.6(1.0) = 0.80 \qquad (2\text{-}24)$$

We now offer him a lottery providing a 0.3 probability of receiving zero dollars and a 0.7 probability of receiving $33,000. Suppose he were willing to pay $21,000 for this lottery. The utile value of $21,000 can then be calculated as

$$U(\$21,000) = 0.3U(\$0) + 0.7U(\$33,000)$$
$$= 0.3(0) + 0.7(0.5)$$
$$= 0.35 \qquad (2\text{-}25)$$

Similarly, we can pose other lotteries to him until we have enough observations to construct his utility of wealth function. This utility function can be graphed by drawing a line through the points. It may look like that shown in Figure 2-3; in the figure, dollars are plotted along the horizontal

figure 2-3
Utility of wealth function for a risk averter

axis, while utile values are plotted on the vertical. Note that the individual's utility for wealth increases at a decreasing rate. This utility function is consistent with diminishing marginal utility and risk aversion throughout. Each additional dollar gives the individual less utility or satisfaction than does the previous one. Thus the individual is willing to take fair gambles only if the price is less than the expected value of these gambles. For example, the expected value of the first lottery is 0.5($0) + 0.5($100,000) = $50,000, yet he is willing to pay only $33,000 for it. Thus the individual is averse to risk; in essence, he pays an insurance premium to avoid it.

Risk Seeking and Risk Neutrality   In addition to risk aversion, there are two other types of utility of wealth functions. A utility function for a risk seeker is shown in Figure 2-4a. This function implies that marginal utility is an increasing function of wealth. In this case, the individual prefers risk and is willing to pay more than the expected monetary value for a fair gamble. Stated differently, the certainty equivalent of a risky investment is more than its expected monetary value. The individual is a risk seeker and is unlikely to diversify his security holdings. Indeed such an individual frequently "plunges" by investing everything in a single investment opportunity.

Finally, Figure 2-4b describes a linear utility function in which marginal utility bears a constant relationship to wealth. The individual described by this function is said to be risk-indifferent or risk-neutral; he is willing to pay the expected value of a fair gamble. Although certain individuals may display combinations of risk aversion, risk preference, and risk neutrality at various levels of wealth, we assume that an individual's utility function is consistent throughout all levels of wealth. Moreover, we would expect most investors to be risk-averse. One can better appreciate this assertion if one considers a toss of a coin. While many of us would be willing to wager a few dollars on the toss of a coin at even odds, few people are willing to stake their entire wealth on such a toss. This behavior, of course, is consistent with risk aversion. Accordingly, the major emphasis in this book will be on risk-averse investment behavior.

figure 2-4
Utility of wealth functions for a risk seeker and for risk neutrality

a.

b.

Expected Utility of an Investment

Once an individual's utility function is specified, we are able to calculate the expected utility of an investment. This calculation involves multiplying the utile value of a particular outcome times the probability of its occurrence and adding together the products for all probabilities. To illustrate, consider two investments that provide the following probability distributions of instantaneous outcomes with respect to increments of wealth:

Investment A		Investment B	
Outcome	Probability	Outcome	Probability
$ 0	0.4	$33,000	0.4
33,000	0.1	63,000	0.6
100,000	0.5		

The expected monetary value of investment A is 0.4(0) + 0.1($33,000) + 0.5($100,000) = $53,300, while that for investment B is 0.4 ($33,000) + 0.6($63,000) = $51,000. Suppose that the individual's utility function is described by the risk aversion situation used in our illustration. The expected utility of investment A would be

$$U_A = 0.4U(\$0) + 0.1U(\$33,000) + 0.5U(\$100,000)$$
$$= 0.4(0) + 0.1(0.5) + 0.5(1.0) = 0.55 \tag{2-26}$$

while that of investment B is

$$U_B = 0.4U(\$33,000) + 0.6U(\$63,000)$$
$$= 0.4(0.5) + 0.6(0.8) = 0.68 \tag{2-27}$$

Thus investment B provides the higher expected utility and is the preferred alternative from the standpoint of the individual examined. This preference occurs in spite of the higher expected monetary value of investment A. The possibility of a $0 outcome for investment detracts considerably from its utility value for the risk averter.

Mean-Variance

As stated earlier, Figure 2-3 portrays the utility function for a risk-averse investor. It suggests that utility increases at a decreasing rate with successive increments in wealth. Therefore the greater the variance, or standard deviation, of the probability distribution of possible returns for an investment, the less the expected utility of that investment.

By way of illustration, suppose an investor's utility of wealth function can be expressed by the following equation:[7]

$$U = 2X - 0.05X^2$$

where U is the number of utiles and X is the increments of wealth in units of $1,000. Two investments are being considered: investment A has a 50 percent probability of providing a $10,000 increment in wealth and a 50 percent probability of a $20,000 increment, while investment B has a 50 percent probability of providing a $12,000 increment in wealth and a 50 percent probability of an $18,000 increment. We note that both investments have the same expected monetary value, $15,000, but that investment A has a higher variance. The expected utilities of the two investments are

$$U_A = [2(10) - 0.05(10)^2]0.5 + [2(20) - 0.05(20)^2]0.5 = 17.5$$
$$U_B = [2(12) - 0.05(12)^2]0.5 + [2(18) - 0.05(18)^2]0.5 = 18.3$$

Thus investment A, which has the greater variance of possible outcomes, has a lower expected utility. For the risk averter, the certainty equivalent of a risky investment is always less than its expected monetary value. These illustrations show why the variance of a distribution is an appropriate measure of risk.

In the chapter that follows, we assume that investors select stocks according to the principle of maximizing expected utility. Expected utility is determined on the basis of the probability distribution of possible returns from an investment. We assume that an individual is able to summarize his beliefs about the probability distribution of possible returns from an investment or portfolio of investments in terms of two parameters of the distribution.[8] These parameters are the expected value and the standard deviation; both measures were illustrated earlier. Thus, expected utility is expressed as a function of two parameters as opposed to the entire distribution of possible outcomes:

$$E(U) = f(\overline{R}, \sigma) \tag{2-28}$$

On the basis of expected return and standard deviation, then, investors are described as determining the expected utility to be derived from an investment. In the next chapter, we follow up on these ideas in showing how the utility preferences of investors can be applied to the selection of portfolios of securities.

[7]Eventually the quadratic equation shown will result in decreases in utility for subsequent increases in wealth. As is customary, we ignore this segment and define the relevant range as that where the first derivative is positive.

[8]For an analysis of the conditions under which this is possible, see David P. Baron, "On the Utility Theoretic Foundation of Mean-Variance Analysis," *Journal of Finance*, 32 (December 1977), 1683–98.

In this book, we examine the impact of investment, financing, and dividend decisions on the value of the firm's common stock. A key concept underlying this valuation is the time value of money. In considering this topic, the determination of both terminal values and present values was illustrated. Both formulas may be modified for compounding more than once a year. Using present-value techniques, we are able to isolate differences in the timing of cash flows for various investments.

In purchasing a common stock, the investor gives up present consumption with the expectation of increasing future consumption. The expected return is the rate of discount that equates the present market value of the stock with the present value of the stream of expected future dividends. Because cash dividends are all that investors as a whole receive from their investment, these dividends are the foundation for valuation. A dividend-valuation model is consistent with the fact that many investors expect to sell their stock in the future and realize a capital gain. Given the basic valuation model, we saw how it could be modified to solve for different expectations as to future growth.

In investing, individuals attempt to maximize their expected utility, which is a function of expected return and risk. Depending on one's utility of wealth function, an investor will be risk-averse, risk-neutral, or risk-seeking. Once an individual's utility function is defined, it is possible to calculate the expected utility of an investment. In order to simplify the problem, however, we assume that individuals are able to summarize their beliefs about the probability distribution of possible returns from an investment in terms of two parameters of the distribution—the expected value and the standard deviation. In the subsequent chapter, we show how these concepts are applied to the selection of a portfolio of securities and the implications of such selection for the required rate of return and valuation of the individual firm.

APPENDIX
Mathematics of Bond Yields

The yield to maturity on a bond is the rate of discount that equates the present value of all future interest and principal payments with the market price of the bond. If interest payments are made at the end of each year, and the face value of the bond is $1,000, we solve the following equation for r, the yield to maturity:

$$P = \frac{I}{(1 + r)} + \frac{I}{(1 + r)^2} + \cdots + \frac{I}{(1 + r)^n} + \frac{1,000}{(1 + r)^n} \tag{2A-1}$$

where P is the present market price, I is the annual interest payment as given by the coupon rate, and n is the number of years to final maturity. To illustrate, suppose that the 8% bonds of Bailey Corporation have ten years to final maturity and that the current market price is $950 a bond. Therefore

$$950 = \frac{80}{(1+r)} + \frac{80}{(1+r)^2} + \cdots + \frac{80}{(1+r)^{10}} + \frac{1,000}{(1+r)^{10}} \qquad \text{(2A-2)}$$

Solving for r in the manner described in the chapter, we find the yield to maturity to be 8.77 percent.

Suppose now that we reverse the example somewhat and that we wish to determine the market price necessary for an 8% ten-year bond to yield 7 percent to maturity. The equation becomes

$$P = \frac{80}{(1.07)} + \frac{80}{(1.07)^2} + \cdots + \frac{80}{(1.07)^{10}} + \frac{1,000}{(1.07)^{10}} \qquad \text{(2A-3)}$$

YEARS AND MONTHS **5%**

Mat. Yield	18-9	18-10	18-11	19-0	19-1	19-2	19-3	19-4
3.95	113.81	113.85	113.90	113.94	113.98	114.02	114.06	114.10
4.00	113.10	113.14	113.18	113.22	113.26	113.29	113.33	113.37
4.05	112.39	112.43	112.47	112.51	112.54	112.57	112.61	112.65
4.10	111.69	111.72	111.76	111.80	111.83	111.86	111.90	111.93
4.15	110.99	111.03	111.06	111.10	111.13	111.16	111.19	111.22
4.20	110.30	110.33	110.37	110.40	110.43	110.45	110.48	110.51
4.25	109.62	109.65	109.68	109.71	109.73	109.76	109.79	109.81
4.30	108.94	108.97	109.00	109.03	109.05	109.07	109.10	109.12
4.35	108.27	108.29	108.32	108.35	108.37	108.39	108.41	108.43
4.40	107.60	107.62	107.65	107.67	107.69	107.71	107.73	107.75
4.45	106.94	106.96	106.98	107.00	107.02	107.04	107.06	107.08
4.50	106.28	106.30	106.32	106.34	106.35	106.37	106.39	106.40
4.55	105.63	105.65	105.66	105.68	105.70	105.71	105.72	105.74
4.60	104.98	105.00	105.01	105.03	105.04	105.05	105.07	105.08
4.65	104.34	104.35	104.37	104.38	104.39	104.40	104.41	104.43
4.70	103.70	103.72	103.73	103.74	103.75	103.76	103.77	103.78
4.75	103.07	103.08	103.09	103.11	103.11	103.12	103.12	103.13
4.80	102.45	102.45	102.46	102.47	102.48	102.48	102.49	102.49
4.85	101.83	101.83	101.84	101.85	101.85	101.85	101.86	101.86
4.90	101.21	101.21	101.22	101.23	101.23	101.23	101.23	101.23
4.95	100.60	100.60	100.61	100.61	100.61	100.61	100.61	100.61
5.00	99.99	99.99	100.00	100.00	100.00	99.99	99.99	99.99
5.05	99.39	99.39	99.39	99.39	99.39	99.38	99.38	99.38
5.10	98.79	98.79	98.79	98.79	98.78	98.78	98.78	98.77
5.15	98.20	98.20	98.20	98.20	98.19	98.18	98.17	98.17
5.20	97.61	97.61	97.61	97.60	97.59	97.58	97.58	97.57
5.25	97.03	97.03	97.02	97.02	97.00	96.99	96.99	96.98
5.30	96.45	96.45	96.44	96.43	96.42	96.41	96.40	96.39
5.35	95.88	95.87	95.86	95.86	95.84	95.83	95.82	95.81
5.40	95.31	95.30	95.29	95.28	95.27	95.25	95.24	95.23
5.45	94.75	94.73	94.72	94.72	94.70	94.68	94.67	94.66
5.50	94.19	94.17	94.16	94.15	94.13	94.11	94.10	94.09
5.60	93.08	93.06	93.05	93.04	93.02	93.00	92.98	92.96
5.70	91.99	91.97	91.96	91.94	91.92	91.89	91.87	91.85
5.75	91.45	91.43	91.42	91.40	91.37	91.35	91.33	91.31
5.80	90.92	90.90	90.88	90.86	90.83	90.81	90.79	90.77
5.90	89.86	89.84	89.82	89.80	89.77	89.74	89.72	89.69
6.00	88.83	88.80	88.78	88.75	88.72	88.69	88.67	88.64
6.10	87.80	87.77	87.75	87.72	87.69	87.66	87.63	87.60
6.20	86.80	86.77	86.74	86.71	86.68	86.64	86.61	86.58
6.25	86.30	86.27	86.24	86.21	86.17	86.14	86.11	86.08
6.30	85.80	85.77	85.74	85.72	85.68	85.64	85.61	85.58
6.40	84.83	84.79	84.76	84.73	84.69	84.66	84.62	84.59
6.50	83.87	83.83	83.80	83.77	83.73	83.69	83.65	83.61
6.60	82.92	82.88	82.85	82.82	82.77	82.73	82.69	82.66
6.70	81.99	81.95	81.92	81.88	81.84	81.79	81.75	81.71
6.75	81.53	81.49	81.45	81.42	81.37	81.33	81.29	81.25
7.00	79.28	79.24	79.20	79.16	79.11	79.06	79.02	78.97
7.25	77.12	77.07	77.03	76.99	76.93	76.88	76.83	76.79
7.50	75.04	74.99	74.94	74.90	74.84	74.78	74.73	74.69
8.00	71.10	71.05	71.00	70.95	70.89	70.83	70.77	70.72

1207

figure 2-5
Bond-yield table
monthly bond values

Referring to Table A-2 in Appendix A at the back of the book, the present value of $80 per year for ten years, discounted at 7 percent, is $561.89, and the present value of $1,000 received at the end of the tenth year is $508.35 (from Table A-1). The market price, P, is simply the sum of the present values of these two components, or $1,070.24.

If interest is paid more than once a year, Eq. (2A-1) needs to be modified somewhat. In keeping with the discussion in the preceding section, if interest is paid semiannually, the yield to maturity can be found by solving the following equation for r:

$$P = \frac{I/2}{\left(1 + \frac{r}{2}\right)} + \frac{I/2}{\left(1 + \frac{r}{2}\right)^2} + \frac{I/2}{\left(1 + \frac{r}{2}\right)^3} + \cdots$$
$$+ \frac{I/2}{\left(1 + \frac{r}{2}\right)^{2n}} + \frac{1,000}{\left(1 + \frac{r}{2}\right)^{2n}} \tag{2A-4}$$

If the 7% bonds of IBK Corporation had ten years to final maturity, and the current market price were $1,040 per bond, Eq. (2A-4) becomes

$$1,040 = \frac{35}{\left(1 + \frac{r}{2}\right)} + \frac{35}{\left(1 + \frac{r}{2}\right)^2} + \frac{35}{\left(1 + \frac{r}{2}\right)^3} + \cdots$$
$$+ \frac{35}{\left(1 + \frac{r}{2}\right)^{20}} + \frac{1,000}{\left(1 + \frac{r}{2}\right)^{20}} \tag{2A-5}$$

Solving the equation for r, we find the yield to maturity to be 6.64 percent. Similarly, the equation for calculating bond yields where interest is compounded m times a year is

$$P = \frac{I/m}{\left(1 + \frac{r}{m}\right)} + \frac{I/m}{\left(1 + \frac{r}{m}\right)^2} + \frac{I/m}{\left(1 + \frac{r}{m}\right)^3} + \cdots$$
$$+ \frac{I/m}{\left(1 + \frac{r}{m}\right)^{mn}} + \frac{1,000}{\left(1 + \frac{r}{m}\right)^{mn}} \tag{2A-6}$$

Given any three of the four factors discussed above (coupon rate, final maturity, market price, and yield to maturity), we are able to solve for the fourth. Fortunately, elaborate bond value tables are available, so we need not go through the calculations. These tables are constructed in exactly the same manner as the present-value tables discussed previously. The only difference is that they take account of the coupon rate and of the fact that the face value of the bond will be paid at the final maturity date. An example of a bond-yield table for a 5 percent coupon rate, and semiannual interest payments, is shown in Figure 2-5. In the figure, the time to maturity is represented by the columns and the yield to maturity by the rows. The figures inside represent the prices, or present values, based upon a face value of

$100. For example, the market price of a 5% bond with nineteen years to final maturity yielding 5.25 percent is $97.02. By consulting a bond-yield table, we are able to determine easily the yield to maturity of a bond—given its market price, coupon rate, and maturity date—or the market price for a particular yield—given the coupon rate and maturity date.

Perpetuities

It is conceivable that we might be confronted with an investment opportunity that, for all practical purposes, is a perpetuity. With a perpetuity, a fixed cash inflow is expected at equal intervals forever. A case in point is the British Consol, which is a bond with no maturity date; it carries the obligation of the British government to pay a fixed coupon perpetually. If the investment required an initial cash outflow at time 0 of A_0 and were expected to pay A^* at the end of each year forever, its yield is the discount rate, r, that equates the present value of all future cash inflows with the present value of the initial cash outflow

$$A_0 = \frac{A^*}{(1 + r)} + \frac{A^*}{(1 + r)^2} + \cdots + \frac{A^*}{(1 + r)^n} \qquad (2A\text{-}7)$$

In the case of a bond, A_0 is the market price of the bond and A^* the fixed annual interest payment. When we multiply both sides of Eq. (2A-7) by $(1 + r)$, we obtain

$$A_0(1 + r) = A^* + \frac{A^*}{(1 + r)} + \frac{A^*}{(1 + r)^2} + \cdots + \frac{A^*}{(1 + r)^{n-1}} \qquad (2A\text{-}8)$$

Subtracting Eq. (2A-7) from Eq. (2A-8):

$$A_0(1 + r) - A_0 = A^* - \frac{A^*}{(1 + r)^n} \qquad (2A\text{-}9)$$

As n approaches infinity, $A^*/(1 + r)^n$ approaches 0. Thus

$$A_0 r = A^* \qquad (2A\text{-}10)$$

and

$$r = \frac{A^*}{A_0} \qquad (2A\text{-}11)$$

Here r is the yield on a perpetual investment costing A_0 at time 0 and paying A^* at the end of each year forever. Suppose that we had the opportunity to buy for $1,000 a security that was expected to pay $70 a year forever. The yield, or internal rate of return, of the security would be

$$r = \frac{\$70}{\$1,000} = 7 \text{ percent} \qquad (2A\text{-}12)$$

PROBLEMS

1. Do the following exercises on terminal values:

   (a) $100 initial deposit is worth how much at the end of three years?

      (1) Assuming an annual interest rate of 10 percent
      (2) Assuming an annual interest rate of 100 percent
      (3) Assuming an annual interest rate of 0 percent

   (b) $100 initial deposit is worth how much at the end of three years?

      (1) Assuming an interest rate of 10 percent compounded quarterly
      (2) Assuming an interest rate of 100 percent compounded quarterly

   (c) Why does your answer to (b) differ from that to (a)?

   (d) $100 initial deposit is worth how much at the end of ten years?

      (1) Assuming an interest rate of 10 percent compounded annually
      (2) Assuming an interest rate of 10 percent compounded semiannually
      (3) Assuming an interest rate of 10 percent compounded quarterly
      (4) Assuming an interest rate of 10 percent compounded continuously

2. Do the following exercises on present values.

   (a) $100 at the end of three years is worth how much today?

      (1) Assuming a discount rate of 10 percent
      (2) Assuming a discount rate of 100 percent
      (3) Assuming a discount rate of 0 percent

   (b) What is the aggregate present value of $500 received at the end of each of the next three years?

      (1) Assuming a discount rate of 4 percent
      (2) Assuming a discount rate of 25 percent

   (c) $100 is received at the end of one year, $500 at the end of two years, and $1,000 at the end of three years. What is the aggregate present value of these receipts?

      (1) Assuming a discount rate of 4 percent

      (2) Assuming a discount rate of 25 percent

   (d) $1,000 is to be received at the end of one year, $500 at the end of two years, and $100 at the end of three years. What is the aggregate present value of these receipts?

      (1) Assuming a discount rate of 4 percent
      (2) Assuming a discount rate of 25 percent

   (e) Compare your solutions in 1(c) with those in 1(d) and explain the reason for the differences.

3. Do the following exercises on internal rates of return.

   (a) An investment of $1,000 today will return $2,000 at the end of ten years. What is its *IRR*?

   (b) An investment of $1,000 today will return $500 at the end of each of the next three years. What is its *IRR*?

   (c) An investment of $1,000 today will return $1,000 at the end of one year, $500 at the end of two years, and $100 at the end of three years. What is its *IRR*?

   (d) An investment of $1,000 will return $60 per year forever. What is its *IRR*?

4. Graph the present value of $1 per year for 5, 10, 15, 20, and 25 years at 0, 10, 20, 30, and 40 percent rates of discount. Explain the difference in the slopes of the curves.

5. The stock of the Health Corporation is currently selling for $20 and is expected to pay a $1 dividend at the end of the year. If an investor bought the stock now and sold it for $23 after receiving the dividend, what rate of return would he earn?

6. James Farnsworth Tuttle, founder and holder of the controlling interest in Tuttle, Inc., has vowed that his firm will never pay a dividend as long as he lives. His current life expectancy is twenty-five years. After that time it is estimated that Tuttle, Inc., could pay dividends of $50 per year per share forever. At present the firm could afford to pay $10 per share forever. The marginal Tuttle shareholder requires a 20 percent return.

   (a) What is the current value of Tuttle stock?
   (b) What is the cost to each shareholder of James Farnsworth Tuttle's policies?

7. Delphi Products Corporation currently pays a dividend of $2 per share and this dividend is expected to grow at a 15 percent annual rate for three years, then at a 10 percent rate for the next three years, after which it is expected to grow at a 5 percent rate forever.

   (a) What value would you place on the stock if a 9 percent rate of return were required?
   (b) Would your valuation change if you expected to hold the stock only three years?

8. You have been asked to graph Mr. Barclay's utility of wealth function. You feel that three observations are sufficient for this purpose and know that Mr. Barclay is quite wealthy. You begin by asking him what he would pay for a lottery with a .5 chance of receiving 0 and a .5 chance of receiving $1 million. He responds that he would pay $400,000. You then pose the following lotteries to him and his responses are:

Lottery	Price Mr. Barclay Will Pay
.5 chance to win $400,000 and .5 chance to win $1 million	$660,000
.6 chance to receive 0 and .4 chance to win $400,000	$120,000

   (a) Determine the utile values of these observations and plot Mr. Barclay's utility of wealth function.
   (b) What type of function is it? What does it tell you? What would a risk-neutral utility function look like?

9. Suppose an investor's utility of wealth function can be expressed as

$$U = 1.5x - 0.1x^2$$

where U is utility as denoted by utiles and x is increments of wealth, in units of $1,000. The investor is considering two possible investments which can be described by the following probability distributions:

Investment A		Investment B	
Prob.	x	Prob.	x
0.1	−4	0.3	1
0.3	0	0.4	2
0.4	4	0.3	3
0.2	8		

(a) Compute the utile values associated with each of these investments. Which investment provides the greater utility?

(b) Compute the expected value of wealth increment, x. Which investment provides the greater expected value of increment?

(c) If there is a difference between the preferred investment depending on the method employed? Explain the reason for it.

10. Wally Whittier is considering investing in a security that has the following distribution of possible returns:

Probability	.10	.20	.30	.30	.10
Return	−.10	.00	.10	.20	.30

(a) What is the expected value of return and standard deviation associated with the investment?

(b) Is there much downside risk? How can you tell?

11. North Great Timber Company will pay a dividend of $1.50 next year. After this, earnings and dividends are expected to grow at a 5 percent annual rate indefinitely. Investors now require a rate of return of 9 percent. The company is considering several business strategies and wishes to determine the effect of these strategies on the market price per share of its stock.

(a) Continuing the present strategy will result in the expected growth rate and required rate of return shown above.

(b) Expanding timber holdings and sales will increase the expected dividend growth rate to 7 percent but will increase the risk of the company. As a result, the rate of return required by investors will increase to 12 percent.

(c) Integrating into retail stores will increase the dividend growth rate to 6 percent and increase the required rate of return to 10 percent.

From the standpoint of market price per share, which strategy is best?

SELECTED REFERENCES

ALEXANDER, GORDON J., A Reevaluation of Alternative Portfolio Selection Models Applied to Common Stock," *Journal of Financial and Quantitative Analysis*, 13 (March 1978), 71–78.

ARROW, KENNETH J., *Essays in Risk Bearing*. Amsterdam: North Holland Press, 1970.

BARON, DAVID P., "On the Utility Theoretic Foundation of Mean-Variance Analysis," *Journal of Finance*, 32 (December 1977), 1683–98.

BAUMAN, W. SCOTT, "Investment Returns and Present Values," *Financial Analysts Journal,* 25 (November-December 1969), 107–18.

BLUME, MARSHALL E., "On the Assessment of Risk," *Journal of Finance,* 26 (March 1971), 1–10.

BRIGHAM, EUGENE F., AND JAMES L. PAPPAS. "Duration of Growth, Changes in Growth Rates, and Corporate Share Prices," *Financial Analysts Journal,* 22 (May-June 1966), 157–62.

FAMA, EUGENE F., "Components of Investment Performance," *Journal of Finance,* 27 (June 1972), 551–67.

———, "Multiperiod Consumption—Investment Decisions," *American Economic Review,* 60 (March 1970), 163–74.

FAMA, EUGENE F., AND MERTON H., MILLER, *The Theory of Finance,* New York: Holt, Rinehart & Winston, 1972.

GORDON, MYRON, *The Investment, Financing, and Valuation of the Corporation.* Homewood, Ill.: Richard D. Irwin, 1962.

HIRSHLEIFER, J., *Investment, Interest and Capital.* Englewood Cliffs, N.J.: Prentice-Hall, 1970.

HOLT, CHARLES C., "The Influence of Growth Duration on Share Price," *Journal of Finance,* 17 (September 1962), 465–75.

IBBOTSON, ROGER G., AND REX A. SINQUEFIELD, "Stocks, Bonds, Bills and Inflation: Year-by-Year Historical Returns (1926–74)," *Journal of Business,* 49 (January 1976), 11–47.

LORIE, JAMES H., AND MARY T. HAMILTON, *The Stock Market.* Homewood, Ill.: Richard D. Irwin, 1973.

MALKIEL, BURTON G., "Equity Yields, Growth, and the Structure of Share Prices," *American Economic Review,* 53 (December 1963), 467–94.

MODIGLIANI, FRANCO, AND GERALD A. POGUE, "An Introduction to Risk and Return," *Financial Analysts Journal,* 30 (March-April 1974), 68–80, and (May-June 1974), 69–86.

MOSSIN, JAN, *Theory of Financial Markets.* Englewood Cliffs. N.J.: Prentice-Hall, 1973.

OFER, AHARON R., "Investors' Expectations of Earnings Growth, Their Accuracy and Effects on the Structure of Realized Rates of Return," *Journal of Finance,* 30 (May 1975), 509–23.

POGUE, GERALD A., AND KISHORE LALL, "Corporate Finance: An Overview," *Sloan Management Review,* 15 (Spring 1974), 19–38.

ROBICHEK, ALEXANDER A., AND STEWART C. MYERS, *Optimal Financing Decisions,* Chaps. 4–6. Englewood Cliffs, N.J.: Prentice-Hall, 1965.

SHARPE, WILLIAM F., *Investments.* Englewood Cliffs, N.J.: Prentice-Hall, 1978.

VAN HORNE, JAMES C., *Financial Market Rates and Flows.* Englewood Cliffs, N.J.: Prentice-Hall, 1978.

VAN HORNE, JAMES C., AND WILLIAM F. GLASSMIRE, JR., "The Impact of Unanticipated Changes in Inflation on the Value of Common Stocks," *Journal of Finance,* 27 (December 1972), 1081–92.

WARREN, JAMES M., "A Note on the Algebraic Equivalence of the Holt and Malkiel Models of Share Valuation," *Journal of Finance,* 29 (June 1974), 1007–10.

3

valuation
of a firm's stock

In this chapter, we continue our examination of valuation. Our ultimate goal is to come to an understanding of how a firm is valued in the market. Most investors are not concerned with a single investment opportunity, but rather with a portfolio of investments. We therefore concentrate on how investors select portfolios of securities. We then move on to consider how market equilibrium is achieved and how the individual firm is valued under the assumption that investors overall are diversified in the portfolios of common stocks they hold.

The notion of market efficiency underlies the development of this chapter. This notion simply states that the market price of a security represents the market's consensus estimate of the value of that security. Those investors who choose to hold the security must think that it is worth at least the current market price, while those who do not purchase it must think that it is worth less. An efficient financial market exists when security prices reflect all available public information about the economy, about financial markets, and about the specific company involved. Implied is that market prices of individual securities adjust very rapidly to new information. As a result, security prices are said to fluctuate randomly about their "intrinsic" values. To be sure, new information can result in a change in the "intrinsic" value of a security, but subsequent security price movements will follow what is known as a *random walk*.[1]

On balance, the evidence indicates that the market for stocks, particularly those listed on the New York Stock Exchange, is efficient. Security prices appear to reasonably reflect available information, and market prices adjust quickly to new information. Market participants seem to be ready to seize on any recurring price pattern so as to drive price changes about a security's "intrinsic" value to a random walk.

MEASUREMENT OF PORTFOLIO RISK

Before proceeding to the question of portfolio analysis and selection by investors and the valuation of the firm, we must spend some time on the measurement of portfolio risk. In the preceding chapter, we were concerned only with measuring risk for a single investment. When multiple securities are involved and one is concerned with their combined risk, the measurement procedure differs from that for a single security. The risk of a portfolio depends not only on the riskiness of the securities constituting the portfolio but also on the relationship between those securities.

By selecting securities that have little relationship with each other, an investor is able to reduce relative risk. The idea is illustrated in Figure 3-1. Here the returns over time for security *A* are cyclical in that they move with the economy in general. However, the returns for security *B* are mildly countercyclical. By investing equal amounts in both securities, we see that the dispersion of the return on investment is reduced over what occurs for either security individually. The combination of securities in such a way as to reduce relative risk is known as *diversification*.

figure 3-1
Effect of diversification

[1]For a formalized presentation of this condition, see Eugene F. Fama, "Efficient Capital Markets: A Review of Theory and Empirical Work," *Journal of Finance*, 25 (May 1970), 384–87.

To illustrate with another example involving less than counter-cyclical behavior, consider two securities whose one-period returns under three possible states of nature are the following:

State	Probability of State Occurring	Return on Security A	Return on Security B
Boom	0.25	24%	6%
Normal	0.50	11	9
Recession	0.25	−6	6

The expected return and standard deviation of the probability distribution of possible returns for the two securities are:[2]

	Security A	Security B
Expected return	10.0%	7.5%
Standard deviation	10.7	1.5

$$\bar{R} = \varepsilon\, R_i\, P_i$$

$$\sigma = \sqrt{\varepsilon\,(R_i - \bar{R})^2 P_i}$$

If equal amounts of money are invested in the two securities, the expected return of the portfolio is 10%(.5) + 7.5%(.5) = 8.75 percent. The weighted average of the individual standard deviations is simply 10.7%(.5) + 1.5%(.5) = 6.1 percent.

However, this is not the standard deviation of the overall portfolio. The returns for a portfolio consisting of equal investments in both securities are:

State	Probability of State Occurring	Return on Portfolio
Boom	0.25	15%
Normal	0.50	10
Recession	0.25	0

where the return on the portfolio is simply the weighted average of the returns on the individual securities. The expected return for the portfolio is 15%(.25) + 10%(.50) + 0(.25) = 8.75 percent, the same as before. However, the standard deviation of the portfolio is

$$[(.15 - .0875)^2\, 0.25 + (.10 - .0875)^2\, 0.50 + (0 - .0875)^2\, 0.25]^{1/2} = 5.4 \text{ percent}$$

[2]The expected return and standard deviation are determined by using Eq. (2-22) and Eq. (2-23) in Chapter 2.

which is less than the weighted average of the individual standard deviations, 6.1 percent. The missing ingredient in the latter calculation is the relationship or covariance between the returns on the two securities.

Covariance of Returns

Therefore a simple weighted average of the individual standard deviations will not do. Instead, the standard deviation of a probability distribution of possible portfolio returns is

A = weight, percentage

$$\sigma_p = \sqrt{\sum_{j=1}^{m} \sum_{k=1}^{m} A_j A_k \sigma_{jk}} \qquad (3\text{-}1)$$

where m is the total number of securities in the portfolio, A_j is the proportion of the total funds invested in security j, A_k is the proportion invested in security k, and σ_{jk} is the covariance between possible returns for securities j and k. (The covariance term will be illustrated shortly.)

The two capital Greek sigmas mean that we consider the covariances for all possible pairwise combinations of securities in the portfolio. For example, suppose that m were four. The matrix of covariances for possible pairwise combinations would be:

$$
\begin{array}{cccc}
\sigma_{1,1} & \sigma_{1,2} & \sigma_{1,3} & \sigma_{1,4} \\
\sigma_{2,1} & \sigma_{2,2} & \sigma_{2,3} & \sigma_{2,4} \\
\sigma_{3,1} & \sigma_{3,2} & \sigma_{3,3} & \sigma_{3,4} \\
\sigma_{4,1} & \sigma_{4,2} & \sigma_{4,3} & \sigma_{4,4}
\end{array}
$$

The combination in the upper left-hand corner is 1,1, which means that $j = k$ and that our concern is with the variance of security #1. That is, $\sigma_1 \sigma_1 = \sigma_1^2$ in Eq. (3-1), or the standard deviation squared. As we trace down the diagonal, there are four situations in all where $j = k$, and we would be concerned with the variances in all four. The second combination in row 1 is $\sigma_{1,2}$, which signifies the covariance between possible returns for securities #1 and #2. Note, however, that the first combination in row 2 is $\sigma_{2,1}$, which signifies the covariance between projects #2 and #1. In other words, we count the covariance between projects #1 and #2 twice. Similarly, we count the covariances between all other combinations not on the diagonal twice. The double summation signs in Eq. (3-1) simply mean that we sum all variances and covariances in the matrix of possible pairwise combinations. In our matrix above, it is sixteen, represented by four variances and six covariances counted twice.

The covariance term in Eq. (3-1) is

$$\sigma_{jk} = r_{jk} \sigma_j \sigma_k \qquad (3\text{-}2)$$

where r_{jk} is the expected correlation between possible returns for securities

j and k, σ_j is the standard deviation for security j, and σ_k is the standard deviation for security k. The standard deviations of the probability distributions of possible returns for securities j and k are determined by the methods taken up in the preceding chapter. When $j = k$ in Eq. (3-2), the correlation coefficient is 1.0, and $\sigma_j\sigma_k$ becomes σ_j^2. That is, we are concerned only with the variance of securities along the diagonal of the matrix.

The correlation between returns may be positive, negative, or zero, depending upon the nature of the association. A correlation coefficient of 1.00 indicates that variations in the return for one security are associated with proportional changes in the return for the other security; a correlation coefficient of -1.00 indicates that they vary inversely in the same proportions; and a zero coefficient indicates an absence of correlation.

Illustration of Calculations

To illustrate the determination of the standard deviation for a portfolio using Eq. (3-1), consider an investor who holds a stock whose expected value of annual return is 10 percent, with a standard deviation of 15 percent. Suppose further that he is considering another stock with an expected value of annual return of 8 percent, a standard deviation of 12 percent, and that the expected correlation between the two stocks is 0.40. By investing equal portions in each of the stocks, the expected value of return for the portfolio would be

$$R_p = (0.5)0.10 + (0.5)0.08 = 9 \text{ percent} \tag{3-3}$$

This contrasts with a 10 percent return when the portfolio is comprised entirely of the first stock. However, the standard deviation for the probability distribution of possible returns for the new portfolio is

$$\sigma_p = [(0.5)^2(1.00)(0.15)^2 + (2)(0.5)(0.5)(0.4)(0.15)(0.12) + (0.5)^2(1.00)(0.12)^2]^{1/2}$$
$$= 11.3 \text{ percent} \tag{3-4}$$

From Eq. (3-1) we know that the covariance between the two stocks must be counted twice. Therefore we multiply the covariance by two. When $j = 1$ and $k = 1$ for stock 1, the proportion invested (0.5) must be squared, as must the standard deviation (0.15). The correlation coefficient, of course, is 1.00. The same thing applies for stock 2 when $j = 2$ and $k = 2$. The important principle to grasp is that as long as the correlation coefficient between two securities is less than 1.00, the standard deviation of the portfolio will be less than the weighted average of the two individual standard deviations.

The example suggests that by diversifying one's holdings to include securities with less than perfect positive correlation among themselves, the risk-averse investor is able to reduce the dispersion of the probability distribution of possible returns relative to the expected value of return for that distribution. In so doing, he reduces the risk of holding securities. Whereas the standard deviations for two securities were 15 and 12 percent, respectively, the standard deviation for the portfolio is only 11.3 percent. We will have considerably more to say about diversification later in the chapter; it is important now to present the rudiments of portfolio analysis and selection before getting into certain refinements.

PORTFOLIO ANALYSIS AND SELECTION

The best combination of expected value of return and standard deviation depends upon the investor's utility function. This function is derived in the manner described in the preceding chapter. If an investor is risk-averse and associates risk with divergence from expected value of return, his utility function might be that depicted graphically by Figure 3-2. The expected value of return is plotted on the vertical axis, while the standard deviation is along the horizontal. The curves are known as *indifference curves;* the investor is indifferent between any combination of expected value of return and standard deviation on a particular curve. In other words, a curve is defined by those combinations of expected return and standard deviation that result in a fixed level of expected utility.[3]

From our discussion of expected utility theory in the preceding chapter, we know that all points on a specific indifference curve have the

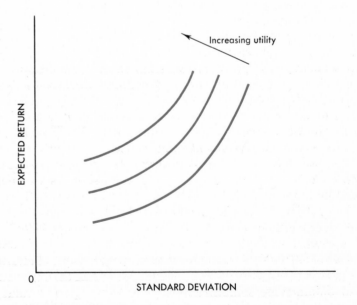

figure 3-2
Hypothetical
indifference
curves

[3]For further duscussion and proof that indifference curves for a risk-averse investor are concave, see Eugene F. Fama and Merton H. Miller, *The Theory of Finance* (New York: Holt, Rinehart & Winston, 1972), pp. 226–28.

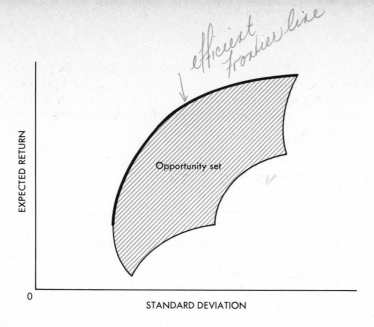

efficient frontier line

EXPECTED RETURN

Opportunity set

0

STANDARD DEVIATION

figure 3-3
Hypothetical
opportunity set

same certainty equivalent. The greater the slope of the indifference curves, the more averse the investor is to risk. As we move to the left in Figure 3-2, each successive curve represents a higher level of expected utility. It is important to note that the exact shape of the indifference curves will be different for different investors. While the curves for all risk-averse investors will be upward sloping, a variety of shapes are possible depending on the risk preferences of the individual.

The individual investor will want to hold that portfolio of securities that places him on the highest indifference curve, choosing it from the opportunity set of available portfolios. An example of an opportunity set, based upon the subjective probability beliefs of an individual investor, is shown in Figure 3-3. This opportunity set reflects all possible portfolios of securities as envisioned by the investor. In other words, every point in the shaded area represents a portfolio that is attainable by the investor. The dark line at the top of the set is the line of efficient combinations, or the efficient frontier. It depicts the tradeoff between risk and expected value of return. According to the Markowitz mean-variance maxim, an investor should seek a portfolio of securities that lies on the efficient frontier.[4] A portfolio is not efficient if there is another portfolio with a higher expected value of return and a lower standard deviation, a higher expected value and the same standard deviation, or the same expected value but a lower standard deviation. If an investor's portfolio is not efficient, he can increase the expected value of return without increasing the risk, decrease the risk without decreasing the expected value of return, or obtain some combination of increased expected value and decreased risk by switching to a portfolio on the efficient frontier.

[4]Harry M. Markowitz, *Portfolio Selection: Efficient Diversification of Investments* (New York: John Wiley, 1959), Chaps. 7 and 8.

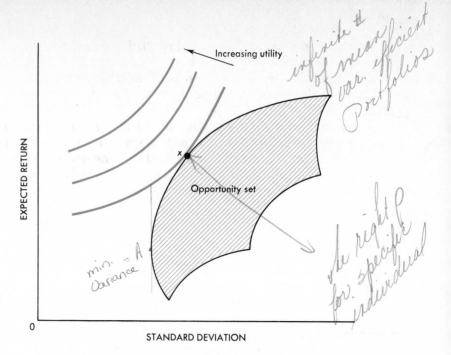

Increasing utility

EXPECTED RETURN

x

Opportunity set

min. = A Variance

infinite # of mean var. efficient portfolios

the right p for specific individual

0

STANDARD DEVIATION

figure 3-4
Selection of optimal portfolio

As can be seen, the efficient frontier is determined on the basis of dominance. Portfolios of securities tend to dominate individual securities because of the reduction in risk obtainable through diversification. As discussed before, this reduction is evident when one explores the implications of Eqs. (3-1) and (3-2). The objective of the investor is to choose the best portfolio from those that lie on the efficient frontier. The portfolio with the maximum utility is the one at the point of tangency of the opportunity set with the highest indifference curve. This tangency is illustrated in Figure 3-4, and the portfolio represented by the point of tangency is the optimal one for an investor with those expectations and utility function.[5]

Presence of Risk-Free Security

If a risk-free security exists that yields a certain future return, the portfolio selection process described above must be modified. This security might be a U.S. Treasury security that is held to maturity. Although the expected return may be low relative to other securities, there is complete certainty as to return. Suppose for now that the investor is able not only to lend at the risk-free rate but to borrow at it as well. (We relax this assumption later on.) To determine the optimal portfolio under these conditions, we first draw a line from the risk-free rate, i, through its point of tangency with the

[5]For a more sophisticated and mathematical discussion of the point of tangency, see Fama and Miller, *Theory of Finance*, pp. 223–26 and 243–50. For ease of understanding, we purposely have kept the presentation graphical.

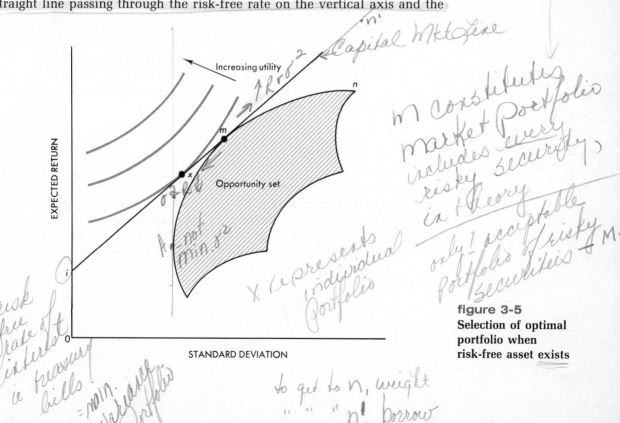

opportunity set of portfolio returns, as illustrated in Figure 3-5. This line then becomes the new efficient frontier. Note that only one portfolio of risky securities—namely, m—would be considered. In other words, this portfolio now dominates all others, including those on the efficient frontier of the opportunity set.

Any point on the straight line tells us the proportion of the risky portfolio, m, and the proportion of loans or borrowings at the risk-free rate. To the left of point m, the investor would hold both the risk-free security and portfolio m. To the right, he would hold only portfolio m and would borrow funds, in addition to his initial investment funds, in order to invest further in it. The farther to the right in the figure, the greater borrowings will be. The optimal investment policy is determined by the point of tangency between the straight line in Figure 3-5 and the highest indifference curve. As shown in the figure, this point is portfolio x and it consists of an investment in both the risk-free security and the risky security portfolio, m. If borrowing were prohibited, the efficient frontier would no longer be a straight line throughout but would consist of line i-m-n. The optimal portfolio would be determined in the same manner as before—namely, the tangency of the efficient frontier with the highest indifference curve.

Capital Market Line

Assuming both borrowing and lending at the risk-free rate, the straight line passing through the risk-free rate on the vertical axis and the

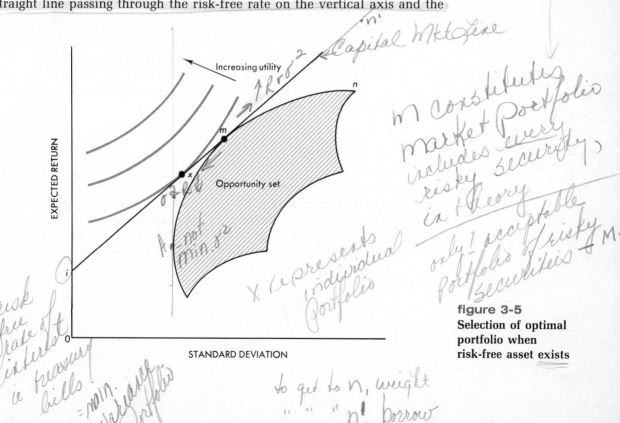

Increasing utility

Capital Mkt Line

EXPECTED RETURN

Opportunity set

STANDARD DEVIATION

figure 3-5
Selection of optimal
portfolio when
risk-free asset exists

expected return–standard deviation point for the market portfolio is known as the *capital market line.* It is shown in Figure 3-5, but we illustrate it separately in Figure 3-6. This line describes the tradeoff between expected return and risk for various holdings of the risk-free security and the market portfolio. Thus two things are involved—the price of time and the price of risk. The former is depicted by the intercept of the capital market line and the vertical axis. The risk-free rate, then, can be thought of as the reward for waiting. The slope of the capital market line represents the market price of risk. It tells us the amount of additional expected return that is required for an increment in standard deviation. Thus the capital market line depicts the *ex ante* equilibrium relationship between return and risk.

Separation Theorem   Note that in the construct of the capital market line, the utility preferences of the individual affect only the amount that is borrowed or loaned. They do not affect the optimal portfolio of risky assets. Turning to Figure 3-5, the investor would select portfolio *m* of risky assets no matter what the nature of his indifference curves. The reason is that when a risk-free security exists, and borrowing and lending are possible at that rate, the market portfolio dominates all others. Thus the individual's utility preferences are independent or separate from the optimal portfolio of risky assets. This condition is known as the *separation theorem.*[6] Put another way, it states that the determination of an optimal portfolio of risky assets is independent of the individual's risk preferences. Such a determination

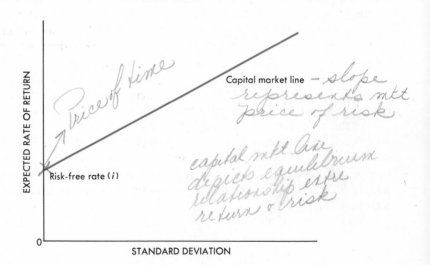

figure 3-6
The capital
market line

[6]This theorem was originally stated by J. Tobin, "Liquidity Preference as Behavior towards Risk," *Review of Economic Studies,* 25 (February 1958), 65–86.

depends only on the expected returns and standard deviations for the various possible portfolios of risky assets. In essence, the individual's approach to investing is two phased. First he determines an optimal portfolio of risky assets, and then he determines the most desirable combination of the risk-free security and this portfolio. Only the second phase depends on his utility preferences.

CAPITAL-ASSET PRICING MODEL

Based on these considerations of behavior by the risk-averse investor, there is implied an equilibrium relationship between risk and expected return for each security. In market equilibrium, a security will be expected to provide a return commensurate with its *unavoidable* risk. This is simply the risk that cannot be avoided by diversification. The greater the unavoidable risk of a security, the greater the return that investors will expect from the security. The relationship between expected return and unavoidable risk and the valuation of securities in this context is the essence of the capital-asset pricing model. This model was developed by Sharpe and Lintner in the 1960s, and it has had important implications for finance ever since.[7]

As with any model, there are assumptions to be made. First, we assume that capital markets are highly efficient where investors are well informed, transaction costs are zero, there are negligible restrictions on investment, and no investor is large enough to affect the market price of the stock. We assume also that investors are in general agreement about the likely performance and risk of individual securities and that their expectations are based on a common holding period, say one year.

There are two types of investment opportunities with which we will be concerned. The first is a risk-free security whose return over the holding period is known with certainty. Frequently, the rate on Treasury bills is used as surrogate for the risk-free rate. The second investment opportunity with which we are concerned is the market portfolio of common stocks. It is represented by all available stocks, weighted according to their market values outstanding. As the market portfolio is a somewhat unwieldy thing with which to work, most people use a surrogate such as Standard & Poor's 500-stock index.

---

[7]See William F. Sharpe, "Capital Asset Prices: A Theory of Market Equilibrium under Conditions of Risk," *Journal of Finance,* 19 (September 1964), 425–42; John Lintner, "The Valuation of Risk Assets and the Selection of Risky Investments in Stock Portfolios and Capital Budgets," *Review of Economics and Statistics,* 47 (February 1965), 13–37; and Eugene F. Fama, "Risk, Return, and Equilibrium—Some Clarifying Comments," *Journal of Finance,* 23 (March 1968), 29–40.

We now are in a position to compare the expected return for an individual stock with the expected return for the market portfolio.[8] In our comparison, it is useful to deal with returns in excess of the risk-free rate. The *excess return* is simply the expected return less the risk-free return. If the expected relationship is based upon past experience, excess returns would be calculated using historical data. Suppose, for example, that we felt that monthly returns over the last five years were a good proxy for the future. For each of the last sixty months, we then would compute excess returns for the particular stock involved and for the market portfolio, as represented by Standard & Poor's 500-stock index.

Having calculated historical excess returns for the stock and for the market portfolio, these returns are plotted. Figure 3-7 compares the expected excess returns for a stock with those for the market portfolio.[9] The dots represent the monthly plots of the excess returns, sixty in all. The dark line fitted to the dots describes the historical relationship between excess returns for the stock and excess returns for the market portfolio. This line is known as the *characteristic line,* and it is used as a proxy for the expected relationship between the two sets of excess returns.

One notes in the graph that the greater the expected excess return for the market, the greater the expected excess return for the stock. Three measures are important. The first is known as the *alpha,* and it is simply the intercept of the characteristic line on the vertical axis. If the excess return for the market portfolio were expected to be zero, the alpha would be the expected excess return for the stock. In theory, the alpha for an individual stock should be zero.[10] Using past data to approximate the characteristic line, however, alphas that differ from zero might be observed if the market were in disequilibrium, if there were market imperfections, or if there were statistical problems. We assume for now, however, that the alpha for a particular stock is zero.

[8]The immediate subsequent development draws on William F. Sharpe, "Efficient Capital Markets with Risk," Research Paper No. 71 (Stanford Graduate School of Business, 1972). There are problems in using any index as a proxy for the overall market portfolio. The "true" market portfolio consists of all assets—stocks, bonds, real estate, and human capital. For a discussion of the problems involved in using a proxy like Standard & Poor's 500-stock index, see Richard Roll, "A Critique of the Asset Pricing Theory Tests, Part 1: On Past and Potential Testability of the Theory," *Journal of Financial Economics,* 4 (March 1977), 129–76.

[9]For a more detailed, and actual, example, see Franco Modigliani and Gerald A. Pogue, "An Introduction to Risk and Return," *Financial Analysts Journal,* 30 (May-June 1974), 73–77.

[10]The alpha for the market portfolio is simply a weighted average of the alphas for the individual stocks making up the portfolio. As efficient markets and the resulting arbitrage will assure that no alpha for an individual stock will be negative, every alpha must be zero for the weighted average to be zero. See Sharpe, "Efficient Capital Markets with Risk." It should be pointed out that some empirical tests have shown positive alphas for low beta stocks and negative alphas for high beta stocks. Various reasons have been advanced for this occurrence.

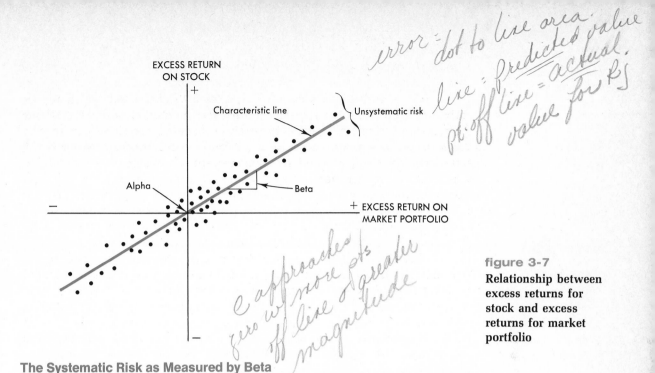

(handwritten annotations:) error = dot to line area. line = predicted value. pt. off line = actual value for Rj

(handwritten annotation:) e approaches zero w/ more pts off line of greater magnitude

figure 3-7

Relationship between excess returns for stock and excess returns for market portfolio

The Systematic Risk as Measured by Beta

The second measure with which we are concerned, and the most important, is the *beta*. The beta is simply the slope of the characteristic line. It depicts the sensitivity of the security's excess return to that of the market portfolio. If the slope is one, it means that excess returns for the stock vary proportionally with excess returns for the market portfolio. In other words, the stock has the same unavoidable or systematic risk as the market as a whole. A slope steeper than one means that the stock's excess return varies more than proportionally with the excess return of the market portfolio. Put another way, it has more systematic risk than the market as a whole. This type of stock is often called an "aggressive" investment. A slope less than one means that the stock has less unavoidable or systematic risk than the market as a whole. This type of stock is often called a "defensive" investment.

The greater the slope of the characteristic line for a stock, as depicted by its beta, the greater its systematic risk. This means that for both upward and downward movements in market excess returns, movements in excess returns for the individual stock are greater or less depending on its beta. For example, if the beta for a particular stock were 1.70 and the market excess return for a specific month were −2.00 percent, this would imply an expected excess return for the stock of −3.40 percent. Thus the beta represents the systematic risk of a stock due to underlying movements in security prices. This risk cannot be diversified away by investing in more stocks, as it depends on such things as changes in the economy and in the political atmosphere which affect all stocks.

Empirical work on the stability of historical beta information over time suggests that past betas are useful in predicting future betas. However,

(handwritten annotations:)
$\beta = 1$
$\beta > 1$: aggressive
$\beta < 1$: defensive

the ability to predict seems to vary with the size of the portfolio. The larger the number of securities in a portfolio, the greater the stability of the beta for that portfolio over time.[11] However, even for the individual stock, past beta information has been found to have reasonable predictive value. Put another way, measured betas show stability over time even at the individual security level. In addition to portfolio size, betas tend to show greater stability over time the longer the time intervals being studied.

Several organizations compute and publish betas for actively traded stocks on an ongoing basis. The typical analysis involves monthly returns on the stock and on the market index for three to five years in the past. In certain cases, weekly instead of monthly returns are employed. The better-known services include those of Merrill Lynch, Pierce, Fenner and Smith; Wells Fargo Bank; and Value Line. By looking up beta as well as other information, one is saved the task of computing this information on one's own. An example of betas for a sample of companies is shown in Table 3-1. The betas of most stocks range from 0.7 to 1.4, though some are lower and some are higher, as shown in the table. If one feels the past systematic risk of a stock is likely to prevail in the future, the historical beta can be used as a proxy for the expected beta coefficient.

Unsystematic Risk

The last of the three measures with which we are concerned is the unsystematic risk of a stock. This risk is described by the dispersion of the estimates involved in predicting a stock's characteristic line. In Figure 3-7, it is represented by the relative distance of the dots from the solid line. The greater the dispersion, the greater the unsystematic risk of a stock. By

---

[11]For such tests, see Marshall E. Blume, "On the Assessment of Risk," *Journal of Finance,* 26 (March 1971), 1–10; Robert A. Levy, "On the Short Term Stationarity of Beta Coefficients," *Financial Analysts Journal,* 27 (November-December 1971), 55–62; Jerome B. Baesel, "On the Assessment of Risk: Some Further Considerations," *Journal of Finance,* 29 (December 1974), 1491–94; Robert C. Klemkosky and John D. Martin, "The Adjustment of Beta Forecasts," *Journal of Finance,* 30 (September 1975), 1123–28; William F. Sharpe and Guy M. Cooper, "Risk-Return Classes of New York Stock Exchange Common Stocks," *Financial Analysts Journal,* 28 (March-April 1972), 46–54; Menachem Brenner and Seymour Smidt, "A Simple Model of Non-Stationarity of Systematic Risk," *Journal of Finance,* 32 (September 1977), 1081–92; and Frank J. Fabozzi and Jack Clark Francis, "Stability Tests for Alpha and Betas over Bull and Bear Market Conditions," *Journal of Finance,* 32 (September 1977), 1093–99.

However, there does appear to be a tendency for the measured betas of individual securities and of portfolios of securities to revert over time toward the beta of the market portfolio, which of course is 1.0. See Marshall E. Blume, "Betas and Their Regression Tendencies," *Journal of Finance,* 30 (June 1975), 783–96. This tendency may be due to economic factors affecting the operations and financing of the firm as well as perhaps to statistical factors. In order to adjust for this tendency, some people calculate an adjusted beta which is a weighted average of the measured beta based on past observations and 1.0. If the measured beta were 1.5 and a 0.70 weight were attached to it and 0.30 to 1.0, the adjusted beta would be 1.5(0.70) + 1.0(0.30) = 1.35.

table 3-1
Betas for selected stocks

Stock	Beta
American Can Company	0.70
American Hospital Supply	1.20
Bankamerica Corporation	1.05
Beatrice Foods	0.90
Eastman Kodak	1.15
General Electric	1.10
General Motors	1.05
Homestake Mining (gold)	0.45
International Business Machines (IBM)	1.00
Iowa-Illinois Gas & Electric	0.65
Mohawk Data Sciences	1.60
Northwest Airlines	1.55
Pillsbury Company	0.95
Reynolds Metals	1.30
Standard Oil of Indiana	0.90
Wrigley (chewing gum)	0.70

(September 1978)

diversification of stocks in one's portfolio, however, a person is able to reduce unsystematic risk.

Thus the total risk involved in holding a stock is comprised of two parts:

$$\text{Total risk} = \text{Systematic risk} + \text{Unsystematic risk}$$
$$\begin{array}{cc} \text{(nondiversifiable} & \text{(diversifiable} \\ \text{or unavoidable)} & \text{or avoidable)} \end{array} \tag{3-5}$$

The first part is due to the overall market risk and it cannot be diversified away. Examples here include changes in the overall economy, tax reform by the Congress, and a change in the world energy situation. These risks affect securities overall and, consequently, cannot be diversified away. In other words, even the investor who holds a well-diversified portfolio will be exposed to these types of risk. The second risk component, however, is unique to the particular company, being independent of economic, political, and other factors that affect securities in a systematic manner. Examples here include a wildcat strike affecting only the company, a new competitor who begins to produce essentially the same product, and a technological breakthrough that makes an existing product obsolete. By diversification, this kind of risk can be reduced and even eliminated if diversification is efficient. Therefore not all of the risk involved in holding a stock is relevant; part of it can be diversified away.

It has been shown that unsystematic risk is reduced at a decreasing rate toward zero as more randomly selected securities are added to the portfolio. Various studies suggest that fifteen to twenty stocks selected randomly are sufficient to eliminate most of the unsystematic risk of a portfolio. Thus a substantial reduction in unsystematic risk can be achieved with a relatively moderate amount of diversification. Conceptually, diversification can be viewed in the manner portrayed in Figure 3-8. As the number of randomly selected securities held in the portfolio is increased, the total risk of the portfolio is reduced in keeping with the reduction in unsystematic risk. However, such a reduction is at a decreasing rate. Efficient diversification reduces the total risk of the portfolio to the point where only systematic risk remains. Implied then in the capital-asset pricing model is that all risk other than systematic risk has been diversified away. Stated differently, if capital markets are efficient and investors at the margin are well diversified, the important risk of a stock is its unavoidable or systematic risk.

EXPECTED RETURN FOR INDIVIDUAL SECURITY

For the individual security, then, the relevant risk is not the standard deviation of the security itself (total risk), but the marginal effect the security has on the standard deviation of an efficiently diversified portfolio (systematic risk). As a result, a security's expected return should be related to its degree of systematic risk, not to its degree of total risk. The former is the risk that

figure 3-8
Total, unsystematic,
and systematic risk

matters to an investor holding a well-diversified portfolio. If we assume that unsystematic risk is diversified away, the expected rate of return for stock j is

$$\overline{R}_j = i + (\overline{R}_m - i)\beta_j \qquad (3\text{-}6)$$

[handwritten annotation: → CAPM!]

[handwritten annotation: $\overline{R}_j = i + (R_p - i)\beta_j$]

where again i is the risk-free rate, $\overline{R}_m$ is the expected value of return for the market portfolio, and β_j is the beta coefficient for security j as defined earlier. As can be seen, the greater the beta of a security, the greater the risk and the greater the expected return that is required. By the same token, the lower the beta, the lower the risk, the more valuable it becomes, and the lower the expected return that is required.

Put another way, the expected rate of return for a stock is equal to the return required by the market for a riskless investment plus a risk premium. In turn, the risk premium is a function of (1) the expected market return less the risk-free rate, which represents the risk premium required for the typical stock in the market; and (2) the beta coefficient. Suppose that the expected return on short-term Treasury securities were 7 percent, the expected return on the market portfolio were 13 percent, and the beta of Pro-Fli Corporation were 1.3. The last indicates that Pro-Fli has more systematic risk than the typical stock. Given this information and using Eq. (3-6), the expected return on Pro-Fli's stock would be

$$\overline{R}_j = .07 + (.13 - .07)1.3 = 14.8 \text{ percent}$$

What this tells us is that on average the market expects Pro-Fli to show a 15 percent annual return. Because Pro-Fli has more systematic risk than the typical stock in the marketplace, its expected return is higher. Suppose now that we are interested in a defensive stock whose beta coefficient is only 0.7. Its expected return is

$$\overline{R}_j = .07 + (.13 - .07)0.7 = 11.2 \text{ percent}$$

Because this stock has less systematic risk than the typical stock in the market, its expected return is less. Therefore, different stocks will have different expected returns depending on their betas.

Expected Return Expressed Differently

Equation (3-6) can be expressed in a different way.[12] If we go back to our discussion of the calculation of covariance, we know that the beta of a security is a measure of the responsiveness of its excess returns to those of the market portfolio. Mathematically, this responsiveness is nothing more

---

[12]This section can be passed over without loss of continuity by those not interested in a mathematical representation of expected return.

than the covariance between possible returns for security j and the market portfolio divided by the variance of the probability distribution of possible returns for the market portfolio. Therefore the beta of security j can be expressed as

$$\beta_j = (r_{jm}\sigma_j\sigma_m)/\sigma_m^2 \tag{3-7}$$

where $(r_{jm}\sigma_j\sigma_m)$ is the covariance of returns for security j with those of the market. In turn, it embodies r_{jm}, which is the expected correlation between possible returns for security j and the market portfolio, σ_j, which is the standard deviation of the probability distribution of possible returns for security j, and σ_m, which is the standard deviation of the probability distribution of possible returns for the market portfolio. Therefore, σ_m^2 is the variance of the market portfolio.

Substituting Eq. (3-7) into Eq. (3-6), we obtain

$$\overline{R}_j = i + \frac{\overline{R}_m - i}{\sigma_m^2} (r_{jm}\sigma_j\sigma_m) \tag{3-8}$$

The expression of the expected return for a security in this format is useful for the development of the topic later on in the book. For the diversified investor $r_{jm}\sigma_j$ in the last term in parentheses represents the portion of the total standard deviation of security j that is undiversifiable. In other words, the investor cannot avoid this risk through diversification. The term $(\overline{R}_m - i)/\sigma_m^2$ represents the market equilibrium relationship between systematic risk and returns in excess of the risk-free rate. To this measure of market-risk aversion we now turn.

The Security Market Line

In market equilibrium, the relationship between an individual security's expected rate of return and its systematic risk, as measured by beta, will be linear. The relationship is known as the *security market line,* and it is illustrated in Figure 3-9. Under the assumptions of the capital-asset pricing model, all securities lie along this line. The figure shows that the expected return on a risky security is a combination of the risk-free rate plus a premium for risk. This risk premium is necessary in order to induce risk-averse investors to invest in a risky security. We see that the expected return for the market portfolio is $\overline{R}_m$, consisting of the risk-free rate, i, plus the risk premium, $\overline{R}_m - i$. Inasmuch as the unsystematic risk of a security can be eliminated by the well-diversified investor, investors overall are not compensated for bearing such risk according to the capital-asset pricing model. While the investor in only a single security will be exposed to both systematic and unsystematic risk, he will be rewarded only for the systematic risk that is borne.

In fact, it is possible for a security with a great deal of total risk to actually have lower systematic risk than a security with only a moderate

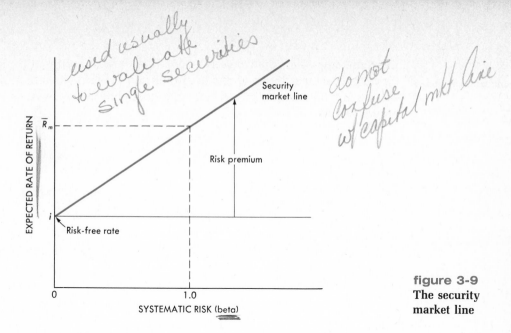

figure 3-9
The security
market line

[handwritten annotations: "used usually to evaluate single securities" and "do not confuse w/ capital mkt line"]

amount of total risk. Take, for example, the case of a new mining company that is endeavoring to discover new veins of gold and silver in the Rocky Mountains. While the total risk of the company is considerable, the finding of gold and silver deposits is almost a chance event. As a result, the security's return bears little relation to the market overall. In a well-diversified portfolio, its unsystematic risk is unimportant. Only its systematic risk matters and this by definition is low, say a beta of 0.2. On the other hand, the return from a stock of a large manufacturing company such as IBM or a large retailer such as Sears, Roebuck and Company is closely tied to the overall economy. Such stocks have only moderate unsystematic risk, so that their total risk may be less than that of the new mining company. However, their systematic risk is approximately that of the market as a whole, say a beta of 1.0.

As an individual security, the mining company may be considerably more risky than IBM or Sears, Roebuck and Company. However, as part of a well-diversified portfolio, it is much less risky. As a result, its expected or required return in the market will be less. This counterintuitive example points to the importance of differentiating systematic risk from total risk. Although there is a tendency for stocks with large systematic risk to have large unsystematic risk as well,[13] there can be exceptions to this generalization.

Thus, in market equilibrium the capital-asset pricing model implies an expected return-risk relationship for all individual securities (the security market line). The risk an investor associates with realizing a stream of expected future dividends depends upon the correlation of that stream with expected dividend streams available from other securities in the market. The risk of an individual security to him is the marginal effect it has on

---

[13]See Robert C. Klemkosky and John D. Martin, "The Effect of Market Risk on Portfolio Diversification," *Journal of Finance,* 30 (March 1975), 147–54.

the dispersion of the distribution of possible portfolio returns. Although the model is framed in terms of certain simplifying assumptions, this basic conclusion and the concept of market equilibrium hold when such assumptions are relaxed.

IMPLICATIONS FOR THE VALUATION OF THE FIRM

Our purpose in this chapter has been to explore some of the foundations of valuation in a market context. No claim is made that the treatment is complete. However, the concepts discussed give us the background necessary to explore more fully the valuation implications of decisions by the individual firm. As we have seen, value depends not only upon the security, or firm, itself but upon other securities available for investment. By analyzing decisions in relation to their likely effect on expected return and systematic risk, one is able to judge their effect on valuation. According to the presentation so far, unsystematic or risk unique to the firm is not important because it can be diversified away. More will be said about this shortly.

In keeping with the capital-asset pricing model and the separation theorem which follows, we are able to make certain generalizations about the valuation of a firm without having to determine directly the risk preferences of investors. If we assume that management wishes to act in the best interests of the owners of the firm, it will attempt to maximize the market value of the stock. Recall from Chapter 2 that the market value per share can be expressed as the present value of the stream of expected future dividends:

$$P_0 = \sum_{t=1}^{\infty} \frac{D_t}{(1 + k)^t} \tag{3-9}$$

where P_0 is the market price per share at time 0, D_t is the expected dividend at the end of period t, and k is the required rate of return. The capital-asset pricing model approach allows us to determine the appropriate discount rate to employ in discounting expected dividends to their present value. The rate used will be the risk-free rate plus a premium sufficient to compensate for the systematic risk associated with the expected dividend stream. The greater the systematic risk, of course, the greater the risk premium and the return required, and the lower the value of the stock, all other things the same. Thus the discussion in this chapter has been pointed toward determining required rates of return for individual securities.

Seemingly, all decisions of the firm should be judged in a market context using the capital-asset pricing model. Recall, however, that the model presented has a number of simplifying assumptions. Some of these do not hold in the real world. To the extent that they do not, unique or unsystematic risk may become a factor affecting valuation. Indeed, a good portion of our discussion in Parts II and III is devoted to exploring market imperfections that make unique risk a factor of importance.

Nonetheless, the capital-asset pricing model serves as a useful framework for evaluating financial decisions. The basic tenets of the model hold even when assumptions are relaxed to reflect real-world conditions. Given that investors tend to be risk-averse, a positive tradeoff exists between risk and expected return for efficient portfolios. Moreover, expected returns for individual securities should bear a positive relationship to their marginal contributions of risk to the market portfolio (i.e., systematic risk). In the ensuing chapters, we will make frequent reference to the capital-asset pricing model. Let us turn now to modifying some of the assumptions, which will also occupy our attention in later chapters.

Relaxing Assumptions in the Model

In this section, we briefly examine the effect of relaxing some of the earlier assumptions of the capital-asset pricing model. The first is that the investor can both borrow and lend at the risk-free rate. Obviously, the investor can lend at this rate. If the borrowing rate is higher, however, an imperfection is introduced, and the capital market line is no longer linear throughout. As shown in Figure 3-10, it is straight through market portfolio M_l. This segment represents combinations of the risk-free asset and the market portfolio M_l. Because the borrowing rate is higher, another tangency point is introduced, namely M_b. The relevant portion of this line is from point M_b to the right; it represents borrowing to invest in the market portfolio M_b. The segment of the capital market line between M_l and M_b is curved and is

figure 3-10
Effect of differing borrowing and lending rates

simply a portion of the efficient frontier of the opportunity set of risky securities. As is evident from the figure, the greater the spread between the borrowing and the lending rates, the greater the curved segment in the capital market line.[14] Different borrowing rates for different investors complicates the picture even more because the equilibration process involves an interaction among investors.

Relaxation of another major assumption, homogeneous expectations, complicates the problem in a different way. With heterogeneous expectations, a complex blending of expectations, wealth, and utility preferences across individual investors emerges in the equilibrating process. In essence, each investor has his own capital market line. This complex equilibrating process has been examined by the author elsewhere and will not be presented here.[15] The principal implication is that precise generalizations are not possible; the overall capital market line becomes fuzzy. With only moderate heterogeneity in expectations, however, the basic tenets of the capital-asset pricing model still hold and rough estimates of the expected return-risk tradeoffs for portfolios and individual securities are possible. Still, the lack of precise description must be recognized.[16]

Transaction costs also affect market equilibrium. The greater these costs, the less investors will undertake transactions to make their portfolios truly efficient. Rather than all portfolios being on the efficient frontier or capital market line, some may be on one side or the other because transaction costs more than offset the advantages of being right on the line. In other words, there may be bands on either side of the capital market line within which portfolios would lie. The greater the transaction costs, the wider the bands might be. Similarly, when securities are not infinitely divisible, as is the case in the real world, investors are able to achieve an efficient portfolio only up to the nearest share of stock or the nearest bond.

Another capital market imperfection is the differential tax on dividends and capital gains. This imperfection makes dividend-paying stocks less attractive than "capital gains" stocks, which pay little or no dividends, all other things the same. We will have much more to say about this imperfection in Chapter 11 when we discuss dividend policy. The last imperfection we

---

[14]Even with different borrowing and lending rates, essentially the same risk-return conclusions are possible as with the capital-asset pricing model if investors are able to engage in unrestricted short sales. Using a zero beta portfolio in place of a risk-free asset, Fischer Black, "Capital Market Equilibrium with Restricted Borrowing," *Journal of Business,* 45 (July 1972), 444–54, provides a model for the equilibrium risk-return relationship for risky securities when borrowing at the risk-free rate is not possible.

[15]James C. Van Horne, *Financial Market Rates and Flows* (Englewood Cliffs, N.J.: Prentice-Hall, 1978), Chap. 3.

[16]Another assumption is that the probability distributions of possible returns on all portfolios are normal. As long as the distributions are close to symmetric, however, this condition is met in a practical sense.

consider is imperfections in information to investors.[17] Recall that an assumption of perfect capital markets is that all information about a firm is instantaneously available to all investors without cost. To the extent that there are delays in and costs to information, there will be differing expectations among investors for this reason alone. The effect here is the same as that for heterogeneous expectations, which we discussed earlier.

In summary, the introduction of capital market imperfections and the relaxation of other assumptions complicate the generalizations possible with the capital-asset pricing model.[18] A number of authors have expanded the model by relaxing the major assumptions and have found the theory to be fairly robust even with such relaxation.[19] However, while the basic relationship between expected return and risk for individual securities holds, this relationship is not as clear or as exact as described previously. In general, the greater the imperfections, the more important the unique, or unsystematic, risk of the firm. Recall that the capital-asset pricing model assumes that this risk can be diversified away. If it cannot, certain implications of the model do not entirely hold. In the chapters that follow, we will analyze these imperfections further to see how they affect the valuation of the firm as well as influence the decisions of the financial manager.

SUMMARY

Capital markets are said to be efficient when security prices fully reflect all available information. In such a market, security prices adjust very rapidly to new information. The risk of a portfolio of securities depends not only on the standard deviations of the individual securities comprising the portfolio but also on the correlation of possible returns. The calculation of the standard deviation for a portfolio of securities was presented and illustrated.

By diversifying one's holdings to include securities that are not perfectly correlated with each other, an investor can reduce risk relative to expected return. The investor will wish to hold that portfolio which results in the greatest utility. It is determined by the point of tangency between

[17]For an analysis of the effect of short-sale restrictions and other imperfections, see Stephen A. Ross, "The Capital Asset Pricing Model (CAPM), Short-Sale Restrictions and Related Issues," *Journal of Finance*, 32 (March 1977), 177–83.

[18]For an excellent overview of the capital-asset pricing model and its limitations, see Stephen A. Ross, "The Current Status of the Capital Asset Pricing Model (CAPM)," *Journal of Finance*, 33 (June 1978), 885–901.

[19]For a review of these studies, see Michael C. Jensen, "Capital Markets: Theory and Evidence," *Bell Journal of Economics and Management Science*, 3 (Autumn 1972), 371–91; and Richard J. Rogalski and Seha M. Tinic, "Risk-Premium Curve vs. Capital Market Line: A Reexamination," *Financial Management*, 7 (Spring 1978), 73–84.

the opportunity set of portfolios of securities and the highest indifference curve. If a risk-free security exists, portfolio selection involves not only a portfolio of risky securities but also the risk-free asset.

The capital-asset pricing model allows us to draw certain implications about the expected return of a specific security. The key assumptions in the model are that perfect capital markets exist and that investors have homogeneous expectations. In this context, the relevant risk of a security is its undiversifiable risk. This risk is described by the slope of the characteristic line, where security returns in excess of the risk-free rate are related to excess returns for the market portfolio. Known also as beta, it is used as a measure of the systematic risk of a security. The total risk of a security can be broken down into systematic and unsystematic components. Systematic risk is that risk which cannot be diversified away, for it affects all securities in the market. Unsystematic risk is unique to the particular security and can be eliminated with efficient diversification.

In market equilibrium, the capital-asset pricing model tells us that the expected return on a security is the risk-free rate plus a premium for systematic risk, as measured by beta. The greater the systematic risk of a security, the greater the expected return that is required by the market. The market-determined relationship between systematic risk and expected return is known as the security market line. The capital-asset pricing model has important implications for the valuation of the firm, and some of these implications were explored. However, certain market imperfections complicate the generalizations possible with the model. In subsequent chapters of the book, we explore additional implications of the capital-asset pricing model under real-world conditions.

PROBLEMS

1. Securities D, E, and F have the following characteristics with respect to expected return, standard deviation, and correlation between them:

			Correlation Coefficients		
	R	σ	D–E	D–F	E–F
Company D	.08	.02	.4	.6	
Company E	.15	.16	.4		.8
Company F	.12	.08		.6	.8

What is the expected value of return and standard deviation of a portfolio comprised of equal investments in each?

2. The securities of Companies A and B have the expected return and standard deviations given below; the expected correlation between the two stocks is 0.20.

	R	σ
Company A	.16	.20
Company B	.08	.03

(a) Compute the risk and return for the following portfolios:

   (1) 100 percent A
   (2) 100 percent B
   (3) 80 percent A–20 percent B
   (4) 80 percent B–20 percent A
   (5) 60 percent A–40 percent B
   (6) 60 percent B–40 percent A
   (7) 50 percent A–50 percent B

(b) Graph your results.
(c) Which of these portfolios is optimal? Why?
(d) Suppose that the investor could borrow or lend at 6 percent. How would this affect your graph?

3. The following portfolios are available in the market:

Portfolio	A	B	C	D	E
Expected return	.13	.05	.11	.15	.09
Standard deviation	.11	.02	.08	.15	.05

(a) Assume that you can invest in only one of these portfolios; that is, it is not possible to mix portfolios. Plot the risk-return tradeoff. Which portfolio do you prefer?
(b) Assume now that you are able to borrow and lend at a risk-free rate of 4 percent. Which portfolio is preferred? Would you borrow or lend at the risk-free rate to achieve a desired position? What is the effect of borrowing and lending on the expected value of return and upon the standard deviation?

4. On the basis of an analysis of past returns and of inflationary expectations, Marta Gomez feels that the expected return on stocks in general is 13 percent. The risk-free rate on short-term Treasury securities is now 7 percent. Ms. Gomez is particularly interested in the return prospects for Kessler Electronics Corporation. Based upon monthly data for the past five years, she has fitted a characteristic line to the responsiveness of excess returns of the stock to excess returns of Standard and Poor's 500-stock index and has found the slope of the line to be 1.67. If financial markets are believed to be efficient, what return can she expect from investing in Kessler Electronics Corporation?

5. For the past two years, Natchez Steamboat Company and Standard & Poor's 500-stock index have had the following excess monthly returns:

	Natchez Steamboat	Standard & Poor's 500-Stock Index
January, 19–1	−4%	−2%
February	−5	−6
March	2	−1
April	1	3
May	7	5
June	−1	2
July	−1	−3
August	8	4
September	3	1
October	−10	−5
November	2	1
December	4	4
January, 19–2	3	2
February	−3	−4
March	1	1
April	5	3
May	8	7
June	0	−1
July	−1	−2
August	−7	−4
September	2	3
October	−2	1
November	−5	−5
December	−3	−1

(a) Plot these observations on graph paper and fit a characteristic line to them by eye.
(b) What is the approximate beta for Natchez Steamboat Company?
(c) Does the stock have much unsystematic risk? How can you tell?

6. In the context of the capital-asset pricing model, what is the expected return of security j if it has the following characteristics and if the following information holds for the market portfolio?

Standard deviation, security j	.20
Standard deviation, market portfolio	.15
Expected return, market portfolio	.10
Correlation between possible returns for security j and the market portfolio	.80
Risk-free rate	.04

(a) What would happen to the required return if the standard deviation of security j were higher?
(b) What would happen if the correlation coefficient were less?
(c) What is the functional relationship between the required return for a security and market risk?

7. At present, the risk-free rate is 5 percent and the expected return on the market portfolio is 10 percent. The expected returns for four stocks are listed below, together with their expected betas:

Stock	Expected Return	Expected Beta
1. Stillman Zinc Corporation	12.0%	1.3
2. Union Paint Company	9.5	0.8
3. National Automobile Company	10.5	1.1
4. Parker Electronics, Inc.	13.0	1.7

(a) On the basis of these expectations, which stocks are overvalued? Which are undervalued?

(b) If the risk-free rate were to rise to 7 percent and the expected return on the market portfolio rose to 11 percent, which stocks would be overvalued? Which would be undervalued? (Assume the expected returns and the betas stay the same.)

8. What are the critical assumptions in the capital-asset pricing model? What are the implications of relaxing these assumptions?

SELECTED REFERENCES

BAESEL, JEROME B., "On the Assessment of Risk: Some Further Considerations," *Journal of Finance,* 29 (December 1974), 1491–94.

BLACK, FISCHER, "Capital Market Equilibrium with Restricted Borrowing," *Journal of Business,* 45 (July 1972), 444–54.

BLUME, MARSHALL E., "Betas and Their Regression Tendencies," *Journal of Finance,* 30 (June 1975), 785–96.

———, "On the Assessment of Risk," *Journal of Finance,* 26 (March 1971), 1–10.

BLUME, MARSHALL, AND IRWIN FRIEND, "A New Look at the Capital-Asset Pricing Model," *Journal of Finance,* 28 (March 1973), 19–34.

BRENNAN, M. J., "The Optimal Number of Securities in a Risky Asset Portfolio When There Are Fixed Costs of Transacting: Theory and Some Empirical Results," *Journal of Financial and Quantitative Analysis,"* 10 (September 1975), 483–96.

BRENNER, MENACHEM AND SEYMOUR SMIDT, "A Simple Model for Non-Stationarity of Systematic Risk," *Journal of Finance,* 32 (September 1977), 1801–92.

ELTON, EDWIN, AND MARTIN J. GRUBER, "Estimating the Dependence Structure of Share Prices— Implications for Portfolio Selection," *Journal of Finance,* 28 (December 1973), 1203–32.

EVANS, JACK, AND STEPHEN H. ARCHER, "Diversification and the Reduction of Dispersion: An Empirical Analysis," *Journal of Finance,* 23 (December 1968), 761–67.

FAMA, EUGENE F., "Components of Investment Performance," *Journal of Finance,* 27 (June 1972), 551–67.

———, "Efficient Capital Markets: A Review of Theory and Empirical Work," *Journal of Finance,* 25 (May 1970), 383–417.

———, "Multiperiod Consumption–Investment Decisions," *American Economic Review,* 60 (March 1970), 163–74.

FAMA, EUGENE F., *Foundations of Finance.* New York: Basic Books, Inc., 1976.

FAMA, EUGENE F., AND MERTON H. MILLER, *The Theory of Finance,* New York: Holt, Rinehart & Winston, 1972.

FINNERTY, JOSEPH E., "Insiders and Market Efficiency," *Journal of Finance,* 31 (September 1976), 1141–48.

FOSTER, GEORGE, "Asset Pricing Models: Further Tests," *Journal of Financial and Quantitative Analysis,* 13 (March 1978), 39–54.

FOSTER, GEORGE, *Financial Statement Analysis.* Englewood Cliffs, N.J.: Prentice-Hall, Inc., 1978, Part III.

FRANCIS, JACK CLARK, "Intertemporal Differences in Systematic Stock Price Movements," *Journal of Financial and Quantitative Analysis,* 10 (June 1975), 205–20.

HAKANSSON, NILS H., "Capital Growth and the Mean-Variance Approach to Portfolio Selection," *Journal of Financial and Quantitative Analysis,* 6 (January 1971), 517–58.

HAMADA, ROBERT S., "Portfolio Analysis, Market Equilibrium and Corporation Finance," *Journal of Finance,* 24 (March 1969), 13–32.

HIRSHLEIFER, JACK, *Investment, Interest and Capital.* Englewood Cliffs, N.J.: Prentice-Hall, 1970.

JAFFE, JEFFREY J., "Special Information and Insider Trading," *Journal of Business,* 47 (July 1974), 410–28.

JENSEN, MICHAEL C., "Capital Markets: Theory and Practice," *Bell Journal of Economics and Management Science,* 3 (Autumn 1972), 357–98.

————, "Risk, the Pricing of Capital Assets, and the Evaluation of Investment Portfolios," *Journal of Business,* 42 (April 1969), 167–247.

————, *Studies in the Theory of Capital Markets.* New York: Praeger, 1972.

JOHNSON, K. H., AND D. S. SHANNON, "A Note on Diversification and the Reduction of Dispersion," *Journal of Financial Economics,* 1 (December 1974), 365–72.

KLEMKOSKY, ROBERT C., AND JOHN D. MARTIN, "The Adjustment of Beta Forecasts," *Journal of Finance,* 30 (September 1975), 1123–28.

LEVY, ROBERT A., "On the Short Term Stationarity of Beta Coefficients," *Financial Analysts Journal,* 27 (November–December 1971), 55–62.

LINTNER, JOHN, "Security Prices, Risk and Maximal Gains from Diversification," *Journal of Finance,* 20 (December 1965), 587–616.

————, "The Market Price of Risk, Size of Market and Investor's Risk-Aversion," *Review of Economics and Statistics,* 52 (February 1970), 87–99.

LORIE, JAMES H., AND MARY T. HAMILTON, *The Stock Market.* Homewood, Ill.: Richard D. Irwin, 1973.

MAYERS, DAVID, "Nonmarketable Assets and the Determination of Capital Asset Prices in the Absence of a Riskless Asset," *Journal of Business,* 46 (April 1973), 258–67.

MERTON, ROBERT C., "Theory of Finance from the Perspective of Continuous Time," *Journal of Financial and Quantitative Analysis,* 10 (November 1975), 659–74.

MODIGLIANI, FRANCO, AND GERALD A. POGUE, "An Introduction to Risk and Return," *Financial Analysts Journal,* 30 (March–April 1974), 68–80, and (May–June 1974), 69–86.

MOSSIN, JAN., *Theory of Financial Markets.* Englewood Cliffs, N.J.: Prentice-Hall, 1973.

MYERS, STEWART C., "A Time-State Preference Model of Security Valuation," *Journal of Financial and Quantitative Analysis,* 3 (March 1968), 1–34.

PETTIT, R. RICHARDSON, AND RANDOLPH WESTERFIELD, "Using the Capital Asset Pricing Model and the Market Model to Predict Security Returns," *Journal of Financial and Quantitative Analysis,* 9 (September 1974), 579–606.

POGUE, GERALD A., AND KISHORE LALL, "Corporate Finance: An Overview," *Sloan Management Review,* 15 (Spring 1974), 19–38.

RABINOVITCH, RAMON, AND JOEL OWEN, "Non-Homogeneous Expectations and Information in the Capital Asset Market," *Journal of Finance,* 33 (May 1978), 575–88.

ROGALSKI, RICHARD J. AND SEHA M. TINIC, "Risk-Premium Curve vs. Capital Market Line: A Re-examination," *Financial Management,* 7 (Spring 1978), 73–84.

ROLL, RICHARD, "A Critique of the Asset Pricing Theory Tests, Part I: On Past and Potential Testability of the Theory," *Journal of Financial Economics,* 4 (March 1977), 129–76.

ROSS, STEPHEN A., "The Capital Asset Pricing Model (CAPM), Short Sale Restrictions and Related Issues," *Journal of Finance,* 32 (March 1977), 177–83.

———, "The Current Status of the Capital Asset Pricing Model (CAPM)," *Journal of Finance,* 33 (June 1978), 885–901.

RUBINSTEIN, MARK, "Securities Market Efficiency in an Arrow-Debreu Economy," *American Economic Review,* 65 (December 1975), 812–24.

SHARPE, WILLIAM F., "A Simplified Model for Portfolio Analysis," *Management Science,* 10 (January 1963), 277–93.

———, "Capital Asset Prices: A Theory of Market Equilibrium under Conditions of Risk," *Journal of Finance,* 19 (September 1964), 425–42.

———, *Investments,* Englewood Cliffs, N.J.: Prentice-Hall, Inc., 1978.

TOBIN, JAMES, "Liquidity Preference as Behavior Towards Risk," *Review of Economic Studies,* 25 (February 1958), 65–86.

TURNBULL, STUART M., "Market Value and Systematic Risk," *Journal of Finance,* 32 (September 1977), 1125–42.

VAN HORNE, JAMES C., *Financial Market Rates and Flows.* Englewood Cliffs, N.J.: Prentice-Hall, Inc., 1978, Chapter 3.

WAGNER, W. H., AND S. C. LAU, "The Effect of Diversification on Risk," *Financial Analysts Journal,* (November-December 1971), 48–53.

4

valuation from a relative standpoint

In Chapters 2 and 3, our concern was with the valuation of a firm's common stock. Valuation was in an absolute sense of trying to determine a specific value for a stock based on its expected stream of dividends and on its risk to investors, who were presumed to hold diversified portfolios. In this chapter, our focus is different. We are concerned with the valuation of contracts which give the holder the right to buy or sell the common stock of a company at some specified price. Known as options, these financial instruments are valued in relation to the common stock of the company involved. Hence we have valuation in a relative sense.

There are a variety of option contracts. The most prevalent is the *call option,* which gives the holder the right to buy a share of stock at a specified price, known as the *exercise price.* For example, we might have a call option to buy one share of ABC Corporation's common stock at $10 through December 31 of the current year. Thus the option has an exercise price of $10 through December 31, which is the expiration date. In contrast, a *put option* gives the holder the right to sell a share of stock at a specified price up to the expiration date. As can be seen, it is the mirror image of a call option. In addition to these two types of options, various options can be formed which are combinations of the call and put options. Finally, convertible securities and warrants, which are analyzed later in the book, are forms of options. Many options are traded in the market. In recent years, active option markets have developed, the first and largest of which is the Chicago Board Options Exchange.

In this chapter, our concern is only with call options. We restrict our focus because other options are not relevant to our discussion in later chapters. Our purpose in this chapter is to acquire a basic understanding of option valuation. The concepts involved have a number of applications to financial theory and to the valuation of certain financial instruments. The number of applications has grown tremendously in recent years, so a study of financial management without reference to option valuation is incomplete.

EXPIRATION DATE VALUE OF AN OPTION

We begin our study of options by analyzing the *European option*, which can be exercised only at its expiration date. This type of option differs from an *American option*, which can be exercised any time up to and including the expiration date. We assume also that the associated stock does not pay a dividend. (Both of these assumptions are later relaxed.)

The value of the call option at its expiration date is simply

$$V_o = \text{Max. } (V_s - E, O) \tag{4-1}$$

where V_s is the market price of one share of stock, E is the exercise price of the option, and Max. means the maximum value of $V_s - E$ or zero, whichever is greater. To illustrate the formula, suppose one share of Selby Corporation's stock were $25 at the expiration date and that the exercise price of a call option were $15. Therefore the value of the option would be $25 − $15 = $10. Note that the value of the option is determined solely by the value of the stock, less the exercise price. However, the option cannot have a negative value. When the exercise price exceeds the value of the stock, the value of the option becomes zero. For example, if the stock value in the example above were $12, the value of the option would not be $12 − $15 = −$3, but rather it would be zero.

The expiration value of an option can be visualized graphically in Figure 4-1. Here the value of the stock is on the horizontal axis, and the value of the option is on the vertical axis. We see that when the value of the stock exceeds the exercise price, the option has a positive value and increases in a linear one-to-one manner with increases in the value of the stock. When the value of the stock equals or is less than the exercise price, the option has a value of zero.

To determine whether the investor in the option gains or loses, we must take account of the price, or premium, paid for the option. The in-

figure 4-1
Value of option at
expiration

vestor's gain or loss is simply the value of the option at the expiration date less the price paid for it. In order to break even, the value of the stock must exceed the exercise price by an amount equal to the premium paid for the option. This is illustrated in the top panel of Figure 4-2. Here we see that the investor suffers a loss until the stock rises in price to the point where it equals the exercise price of the option plus the premium, and that further increases in the price of the stock result in gains to the investor in the option.

For the writer, or seller, of the option, the opposite picture emerges. This is illustrated in the lower panel of the figure. Here the writer receives the premium and realizes a gain as long as the value of the stock at the expiration date is less than the exercise price plus the premium. If it is more, a loss is experienced which increases with increases in the value of the stock. In options, then, the expiration date gain or loss to the investor and to the writer of the option are mirror images of one another. It is a "zero-sum" game where one can gain only at the expense of the other.

VALUATION WITH ONE PERIOD TO EXPIRATION: A GENERAL CONSIDERATION

Consider now the option with one period to expiration. Again we assume a European option, which can be exercised only at the expiration date. While we do not know the value of the stock at the expiration date, we assume that we are able to formulate probabilistic beliefs about its value one period hence.

In Figure 4-3, we illustrate the theoretical relationship between the beginning-of-period price of a share of common stock and the price of an option to buy that stock. The 45-degree line represents the theoretical value of the option. It is simply the current stock price less the exercise price of the option. When the price of the stock is less than the exercise price of the

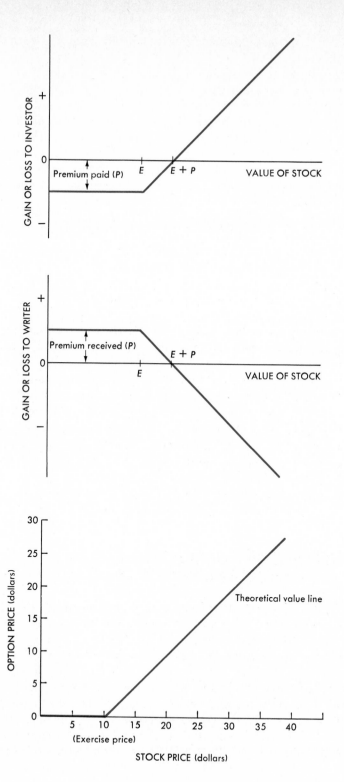

figure 4-2
Gain or loss of option to the investor and to the writer

figure 4-3
Theoretical value of an option for ABC Corporation stock

option, the option has a zero theoretical value; when more, it has a theoretical value on the line.

As long as there is some time to expiration, it is possible for the market value of an option to be greater than its theoretical value. The reason for this is the very nature of the contract—namely, it is an option that affords the holder flexibility with respect to the purchase of stock. To illustrate, suppose the current market price of ABC Corporation's stock were $10, which is equal to the exercise price. Theoretically, the option would have no value. However, if there is some probability that the price of the stock will exceed $10 before expiration, the option should have a positive value inasmuch as it *may* permit the holder to exercise it advantageously. To illustrate, suppose further that the option has thirty days to expiration and that there is a 0.3 probability that the stock will have a market price of $5 per share at the end of the thirty days, 0.4 that it will be $10, and 0.3 that it will be $15. The expected value of the option at the end of thirty days is thus

$$0(0.3) + 0(0.4) + (\$15 - \$10)(0.3) = \$1.50$$

Therefore it is possible for an option whose associated stock value is less or equal to the exercise price to have a positive value. Because the option cannot go below zero in value, even when the stock price less the exercise price is negative, the option is frequently worth more than its theoretical value. How much more depends in part upon the time to expiration. Figure 4-4 illustrates the general relationship between stock prices and option prices for various terms to expiration.[1]

figure 4-4
Relation between stock price and option price for various expiration dates

[1]Perhaps the first to draw attention to this type of presentation was Paul A. Samuelson, "A Rational Theory of Warrant Pricing," *Industrial Management Review,* 6 (Spring 1965).

The Boundaries for Option Valuation

The highest value the option can take is the value of the stock, represented by the 45-degree line X. This would presumably occur only if the option had a very long time to expiration, perhaps forever, and if the option was not expected to be exercised until far into the future. Under these circumstances, the present value of the exercise price to be paid in the future would approach zero. As a result, the value of the option would approach the value of the associated stock. The lowest value the option can take, of course, is its theoretical value, represented in the figure by zero up to the exercise price and by line Y for values of the stock greater than the exercise price. One might think of the theoretical value line as representing the values of an option with only a moment to expiration. Thus lines X and Y constitute the boundaries for the value of an option in relation to the value of the associated stock.

For most options, however, the relationship lies between these two boundaries. In general, it can be described by a convex relationship where the value of the option commands the greatest premium over its theoretical value at the exercise price and where the premium declines with increases in the value of the stock beyond that point. Because of the lesser investment required, an option will change in value by a greater percentage than will the stock. The percentage change in option price tends to be a decreasing function of the stock price.

In general, the longer the expiration date, the greater the value of the option relative to its theoretical value. One reason is that there is more time in which the option may have value. Moreover, the greater the time to expiration, the lower the present value of the exercise price to be paid in the future, and this too enhances the value of the option, all other things the same. As the expiration date of an option approaches, however, the relationship between the option value and the stock value becomes more convex. In Figure 4-4, line 1 represents an option with a shorter time to expiration than that for line 2; and line 2, an option with a shorter time to expiration than that for line 3.

The Volatility of the Stock

Usually the most important factor in the valuation of options is the price volatility of the associated stock. More specifically, the greater the possibility of extreme outcomes, the greater the value of the option to the holder, all other things the same. To illustrate with a simple example, suppose that at the beginning of a period we were considering options on the two stocks shown in Table 4-1. The expected value of stock price at the end of the period is the same for both stocks, namely $40. However, we see that for stock B, there is a much larger dispersion of possible outcomes. Suppose that the exercise prices of options to purchase stock A and stock B at the end of the period are also the same, say $38. Thus the two stocks have the same expected values at the end of the period and the options have the same exercise price.

table 4-1

Probability distributions of
two stocks at the end
of the period

Probability of Occurrence	Price of Stock A	Price of Stock B
0.10	$30	$20
0.25	36	30
0.30	40	40
0.25	44	50
0.10	50	60

However, the expected value of the option for stock A at the end of the period is

$$\text{Option } A = 0(0.10) + 0(0.25) + (\$40 - \$38)(0.30) + (\$44 - \$38)(0.25)$$
$$+ (\$50 - \$38)(0.10)$$
$$= \$3.30,$$

whereas that for stock B is

$$\text{Option } B = 0(0.10) + 0(0.25) + (\$40 - \$38)(0.30) + (\$50 - \$38)(0.25)$$
$$+ (\$60 - \$38)(0.10)$$
$$= \$5.80.$$

Thus the greater dispersion of possible outcomes for stock B leads to a greater expected value of option price on the expiration date. In turn, this is due to the fact that negative values for the option cannot occur. As a result, the greater the dispersion, the greater the magnitude of favorable outcomes as measured by the stock price minus the exercise price. Therefore, increases in the volatility of the stock increase the magnitude of favorable outcomes for the option buyer and, hence, increase the value of the option.

We will see later in the chapter that the value of an option does not depend on the expected value of the stock price. It is the variance, or volatility, of the stock price that is important. This is a fundamental proposition of option valuation, and it will permeate our application of this concept to various problems in financial management throughout the book. We emphasize again that our example has been kept purposely simple in looking at the value of the option at the end of the period. The determination of value at the beginning of the period involves the present value of outcomes at the end of the period and is more complicated. We shall explore this determination in the sections that follow. However, the fundamental importance of the volatility of stock price in the valuation of options continues to hold as in our example.

THE USE OF A HEDGED POSITION AND MARKET EQUILIBRIUM

The fact that we have two financial assets—a stock and the option on that stock—that are related to each other permits us to set up a risk-free hedged position. In this way price movements in one of the financial assets will be offset by opposite price movements in the other. To illustrate this situation, consider again a European option with one period to expiration where the stock pays no dividend. Moreover, assume that there are no transaction costs involved in buying and selling stock nor in buying or writing options. In addition to the return on the option and the return on the stock, the opportunity cost of funds is important when it comes to establishing a hedged position. We assume this cost is the risk-free rate, denoted by r; and it might be thought of as rate of return on Treasury bills.

An Illustration of Hedging

Consider now a time-branching process where at the end of the period there are two possible values for the common stock. One is a higher value than the current value of the stock and it is denoted by uV_s and the other is a lower value, denoted by dV_s. Because V_s represents the current value of the stock, u represents one plus the percentage increase in value of the stock from the beginning of the period to the end and d represents one minus the percentage decrease in the value of the stock.[2] Associated with the upward movement of the stock is a probability of q; and with the downward movement, a probability of $1 - q$.

To give some numbers and probabilities to these symbols, consider the example shown in the upper panel of Figure 4-5. We see that there is a two-thirds probability that the stock will increase in value by 20 percent and a one-third probability that it will decrease in value by 10 percent. The expected value of stock price at the end of the period is $55, which, on the basis of a $50 investment, represents a return of 10 percent. Assume now that the risk-free rate, r, is 5 percent for the period and that the exercise price of the option is $50. With this information, we see in the lower panel of Figure 4-5 that the value of the option at the end of the period is either $10 or 0, depending on whether the stock rises or falls in value.

In this situation a hedged position can be established by buying the stock (holding it long) and by writing options. In our example, the idea is

---

[2]In order that pure arbitrage opportunities not exist, u must exceed and d must be less than one plus the risk-free rate. This example is based in part on John Cox, "A Discrete Time, Discrete State Option Pricing Model" (unpublished teaching note, Graduate School of Business, Stanford University, 1977). It also draws upon William F. Sharpe, *Investments* (Englewood Cliffs, N.J.: Prentice-Hall, 1978), pp. 364–70.

(a) Stock Value at End of Period

Current Stock Price	Probability of Occurrence	Stock Price at End of Period
$V_s = \$50$	2/3	1.20 ($50) = $60
	1/3	0.90 ($50) = $45

Expected Value of Stock Price at the End
of the Period = (2/3) ($60) + (1/3) ($45) = $55.

(b) Option Value at End of Period

Stock Price at End of Period	Probability of Occurrence	Option Value at End of Period
$60	2/3	Max. ($60 − $50, 0) = $10
$45	1/3	Max. ($45 − $50, 0) = 0

**figure 4-5
Hedged position
example**

Expected Value of Option Value at End
of the Period = (2/3) ($10) + (1/3)(0) = $6.667

to establish a riskless hedged position. The appropriate hedge ratio of stock to options can be determined by

$$\text{Hedge Ratio} = \frac{uV_o - dV_o}{uV_s - dV_s} = \frac{\$10 - 0}{\$60 - \$45} = 2/3$$

where uV_o is the end-of-period value of the option when the stock price, uV_s, is $60 at the end of the period, and dV_o is the value of the option when the stock price, dV_s, is $45 at the end of the period. This hedge ratio means that the individual who wishes to hedge should purchase two shares of stock (the long position) and write three options (the short position).

By undertaking such transactions, the end-of-period values for the two future states will be:[3]

Stock Price at End of Period	Value of Long Position in Stock	Value of Short Position in Option	Value of Combined Hedged Position
$60	2($60) = $120	−3($10) = −$30	$90
45	2($45) = $ 90	−3(0) = 0	$90

[3]Again we have assumed the absence of transaction costs.

We see that when the stock price at the end of the period is $60, the value
of two shares of stock is $120. However, we must subtract from this value
the negative value of our short position in options of $30 to get the overall
value of our hedged position. When the stock price is $45, two shares are
worth $90, and in this case, there is no loss on the short position. There-
fore the overall position is perfectly hedged in the sense of providing the
same value at the end of the period regardless of the stock-price outcome
that occurs.

Determining the Value of the Option

The return on this hedged position depends on the value of the
option, or the premium, at the beginning of the period. Since the hedged
position is riskless, in efficient financial markets we would expect the return
on this position to equal the risk-free rate, or 5 percent. We know that the
ending value of the hedged position is $90 and that the investment in the
two shares of stock at the beginning of the period is $100. The overall invest-
ment in the hedged position at the beginning of the period is $100 less the
price received on the three options that are written. In other words, the short
position results in a cash inflow, whereas the long position results in a cash
outflow. Our concern is with the net position.

The value of the option at the beginning of the period which must
prevail if the overall return is to be 5 percent can be determined by solving
the following equation for V_{oB}:

$$[\$100 - 3(V_{oB})]1.05 = \$90$$
$$3.15 V_{oB} = \$105 - 90$$
$$V_{oB} = \frac{\$15}{3.15}$$
$$V_{oB} = \$4.762$$

Thus the overall investment in the hedged position at the beginning of the
period is $100 - 3($4.762) = $85.714. The return on this hedged position
is ($90 - $85.714)/$85.714 = 5 percent, or the risk-free rate. In other words,
the return on the hedged position is the same as that which could be realized
by investing $85.714 in Treasury bills. As both investments are risk free, they
should promise the same rate of return.

The expected return from the stock for the period is

$$\frac{(\$55 - \$50)}{\$50} = 10 \text{ percent}$$

where $55 is the expected value of stock price at the end of the period, as
shown in Figure 4-5. The expected return for the option is

$$\frac{(\$6.667 - \$4.762)}{\$4.762} = 40 \text{ percent}$$

where $6.667 is the expected value of option value at the end of the period, again as shown in Figure 4-5. Thus the option has a considerably higher expected return than does the stock, which is in accord with its greater risk. The important thing is that the option be priced correctly so that when it is combined with the stock in a hedged position, the overall return is the risk-free rate.

The Tendency toward Correct Pricing

What would happen if the market price of the option at the beginning of the period were something other than $4.762? The opportunity then would exist for earning returns in excess of the risk-free rate on a riskless investment. If the option were overpriced—for example, say at $5—the rational investor would borrow at the risk-free rate of 5 percent and invest in the hedged position. His return on the hedged position would be

$$\frac{\$90 - [\$100 - 3(\$5)]}{\$100 - 3(\$5)} = 5.88\%$$

Thus the return on a riskless investment exceeds the cost of borrowing. Obviously the individual would want to borrow as much as possible in order to make a sure profit. This action together with that of others will exert selling pressure on the option and drive its price down. In equilibrium, of course, the price will be that required to provide a 5 percent return on the hedged position, or $4.762.

On the other hand, if the option were underpriced, say at $4.50, the rational investor would buy the options, sell the stock short, and invest the proceeds of the short sale at the risk-free rate. His position at the beginning of the period would be:

Three options long	$13.50
Two shares of stock short	−100.00
Treasury bills long	100.00
	$13.50

At the end of the period, the following would prevail for the two states:

Stock Price at End of Period	Value of Long Position in Options	Value of Short Position in Stock	Value of Treasury Bills	Value of Combined Hedged Position
$60	$30	−$120	$105	$15
45	0	− 90	105	15

Thus the position is perfectly hedged in providing the same value at the end of the period regardless of the stock-price outcome. Note also that the value of the Treasury bills increases by 5 percent from the beginning to the end of the period. The return on the riskless investment of $13.50 at the beginning of the period is

$$\frac{(\$15 - \$13.50)}{\$13.50} = 11.11\%$$

As this return exceeds the risk-free rate, we would expect a number of investors to engage in this strategy. Their action will drive up the price of the option until the opportunity for returns in excess of the risk-free rate no longer exists.

In summary, the option should be priced so that when it is combined with the stock in a hedged position the return on the position equals the risk-free rate. To the extent that excess returns are available on a fully hedged position, individuals will have an incentive to take such positions. The impact of their transactions in order to establish hedged positions will affect the relative prices in such a way as to drive out any excess returns that might be earned. As a result, prices will adjust until the return on the hedged position is the risk-free rate and the option is neither overvalued nor undervalued.[4]

So far we have worked with simple examples in order to provide a basic understanding of option pricing. A number of restrictive assumptions were imposed, and the derivation of the option's value was relevant only to the example presented. In the next section, we consider a more exacting option valuation framework.

THE BLACK–SCHOLES OPTION MODEL

In a seminal paper, Fischer Black and Myron Scholes developed a precise model for determining the equilibrium value of an option.[5] They then went on to observe that the option pricing concepts can be used to value other contingent claims. In particular, the model provides rich insight into the valuation of debt relative to equity. This application as well as others are taken up later in the book once we have the foundations provided in this chapter. The

[4]For a much more rigorous presentation of the arbitrage conditions, see Robert C. Merton, "A Rational Theory of Option Pricing," *Bell Journal of Economics,* 4 (Spring 1973), 141–83.

[5]"The Pricing of Options and Corporate Liabilities," *Journal of Political Economy,* 81 (May-June 1973), 637–54.

Black-Scholes model has been extended and refined in major ways,[6] and new applications are continually unfolding. The model has both theoretical importance for valuing contingent claims and practical importance for identifying overvalued and undervalued options in the market.[7]

The Model in General

A number of assumptions are in order before we can discuss the model:

1. Only "European" options are considered; that is, options that can be exercised only at maturity.
2. There are no transaction costs; options and stocks are infinitely divisible; and information is available to all without cost.
3. No imperfections exist in selling an option or a stock short.
4. The short-term interest rate is known and constant throughout the duration of the option contract. Market participants can both borrow and lend at this rate.
5. The stock pays no dividend.
6. Stock prices behave in a manner consistent with a random walk in continuous time. The variance of the return is constant over the life of the option contract and is known to market participants.

Given these assumptions, the equilibrium value of an option can be determined. Should the actual price of the option differ from that given by the model, a person would be able to establish a riskless hedged position and earn a return in excess of the short-term interest rate in the manner illustrated in the previous section. As arbitragers entered the scene, the excess return would eventually be driven out and the price of the option would equal that value given by the model.

To illustrate a hedged position, suppose that the appropriate relationship between the option and the stock of XYZ Corporation were that shown in Figure 4-6. Suppose further that the current market price of the

---

[6]See Robert C. Merton, "A Rational Theory of Option Pricing," *Bell Journal of Economics,* 4 (Spring 1973), 141–83; John C. Cox and Stephen A. Ross, "The Valuation of Options for Alternative Stochastic Processes," *Journal of Financial Economics,* 3 (January-March 1976), 145–79; Mark E. Rubinstein, "The Valuation of Uncertain Income Streams and the Pricing of Options," *Bell Journal of Economics,* 7 (Autumn 1976), 407–25; and Eduardo S. Schwartz, "The Valuation of Warrants: Implementing a New Approach," *Journal of Financial Economics,* 4 (January 1977), 79–93.

[7]For an excellent review of the area, see Clifford W. Smith, Jr., "Option Pricing: A Review," *Journal of Financial Economics,* 3 (January-March 1976), 3–51. See also Mark Rubinstein with the assistance of John C. Cox, *Options Markets* (Englewood Cliffs, N.J.: Prentice-Hall, 1979).

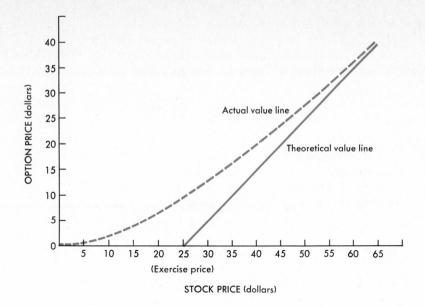

figure 4-6
Relation between the
option price and the
stock price for XYZ
Corporation

stock were $20 and the price of the option $7. At $20 a share, the slope of the line in Figure 4-6 is one-half. A hedged position could be undertaken by buying a share of stock for $20 and writing two options at $7 each. The "net money" invested in this position is $20 − 2($7) = $6.

This combination of holding one share of stock long and two options short leaves the individual essentially hedged with respect to risk. If the stock drops slightly in value, the value of the short position goes up by approximately an equal amount. We say *approximately* because with changes in the price of the common and with changes in time, the ideal hedge ratio changes. With a stock price increase, for example, the slope of the line in Figure 4-6 increases. Therefore, fewer options would need to be written. If the stock price declines, the slope decreases and more options would need to be written to maintain a hedge. In addition, the line itself will shift downward as time goes on and the expiration date approaches. This was illustrated in Figure 4-4 earlier in the chapter. The downward shift due to the passage of time causes the line to be more concave and, therefore, its slope to be affected.

Thus it is necessary to continually adjust one's short position in options for changes in the stock price and for changes in time if a riskless hedged position is to be maintained. Given the assumptions of the model, this of course is possible. In the real world with transaction costs, it is not possible to continuously adjust one's short position. Even here, however, the risk that will appear as a result of moderate changes in stock price or of the passage of time will be small. Moreover, it can be diversified away. For practical purposes, then, it is possible to maintain a hedged position that is approximately risk-free. Arbitrage will ensure that the return on this position is approximately the short-term, risk-free rate.

The Specific Model

In this context, the equilibrium value of an option that entitles the holder to buy one share of stock is shown by Black and Scholes to be

$$V_o = V_s N(d_1) - \frac{E}{e^{rt}} N(d_2)$$

(4-2)

where V_s = the current price of the stock

E = the exercise price of the option

e = 2.71828

r = the short-term interest rate continuously compounded

t = the length of time in years to the expiration of the option

$N(d)$ = the value of the cumulative normal density function

$$d_1 = \frac{ln(V_s/E) + (r + 1/2\sigma^2)t}{\sigma\sqrt{t}}$$

$$d_2 = \frac{ln(V_s/E) + (r - 1/2\sigma^2)t}{\sigma\sqrt{t}}$$

ln = the natural logarithm

σ = the standard deviation of the annual rate of return on the stock continuously compounded

The important implication of this formula is that the value of the option is a function of the short-term interest rate, of the time to expiration, and of the variance rate of return on the stock, but it is not a function of the expected return on the stock. As either or all of the terms for duration to expiration of the option, t, for the variance rate, σ^2, and for the short-term interest rate, r, increase, the value of the option in Eq. (4-2) increases. The reasons for these relationships were discussed earlier in the chapter. Of the three factors affecting the value of the option, however, the short-term interest rate generally has the least impact. With increases in t, r, and σ^2 in Eq. (4-2), the value of the option approaches the value of a share of stock as a limit.[8]

Given the valuation equation for options, Black and Scholes derive the ratio of shares of stock to options necessary to maintain a fully hedged position. It is shown to be $N(d_1)$, which was defined earlier. Thus the Black-Scholes model permits the quantification of the various factors that affect the value of an option.[9]

---

[8]Black and Scholes, "Pricing of Options and Corporate Liabilities," p. 644.

[9]The option pricing model can be integrated with the capital-asset pricing model. From Chapter 3, we know that the expected excess return for a stock is $R_s - i = \beta_s(R_m - i)$, where R_s is the expected return on the stock, i is the risk-free rate, R_m is the expected return on the market portfolio, and β_s is the beta of the stock. If we assume that the short-term interest

Solving the Formula

With respect to solving the formula, we know four of the five variables: the current stock price, the time to expiration of the option, the exercise price, and the short-term interest rate. The key unknown, then, is the standard deviation of the stock price. Black and Scholes assume that the stock's continuously compounded rate of return is normally distributed with constant variance.[10] The usual approach to the problem is to use the recent past volatility of the stock as a proxy for its volatility during the life of the option. For example, we might use weekly observations of stock prices over the last year and derive the annualized standard deviation of the natural logarithm of price relatives.[11] This standard deviation then would be used in the formula. Where the historic volatility of the stock's price is not thought to be a good proxy for the future, a subjective estimate of the standard deviation will be necessary. However, the usual procedure is to compute the standard deviation on the basis of past stock-price behavior.

To illustrate the use of the Black-Scholes option pricing formula, suppose that on the basis of an analysis of past volatility, we found the standard deviation of the stock's continuously compounded return to be

---

rate in the option pricing model is the same as i, the expected excess return for an option on the stock can be expressed as

$$R_0 - i = \left(\frac{V_s}{V_0}\frac{\partial V_0}{\partial V_s}\right)(R_s - i)$$

where R_0 is the expected return on the option, V_s is the value of the stock, and V_0 is the value of the option. Combining these two equations, we have

$$R_0 - i = \left(\frac{V_s}{V_0}\frac{\partial V_0}{\partial V_s}\right)\beta_s(R_m - i)$$

Therefore the beta of the option is

$$\left(\frac{V_s}{V_0}\frac{\partial V_0}{\partial V_s}\right)\beta_s$$

As the stock price changes, so too does the beta of the option.

[10]While this assumption is open to question, solving the problem without a stationarity assumption is exceedingly complex. The valuation formula is very sensitive to the standard deviation employed as an estimate of the volatility of the stock.

[11]A *price relative* is simply the stock price this week divided by the stock price last week. For example, if the stock price this week were $33 and the price last week $31.50, the price relative would be $33/$31.50 = 1.04762. The natural logarithm of this number is .04652, and it can be found in a natural log table or on a calculator equipped with this function. Given a listing of 52 price relatives and their natural logarithms, the standard deviation can be easily derived. To annualize this weekly standard deviation, it must be multiplied by the square root of 52. For an illustration of such a derivation as well as the use of the Black-Scholes formula, see Mark Rubinstein, *Option Markets* (Englewood Cliffs, N.J.: Prentice-Hall, 1979), Chapter 6.

0.40. By referring to a financial newspaper, we are able to look up the other four terms necessary to solve the option pricing formula. Suppose that they were the following:

Stock price:	$V_s = \$30$
Exercise price of option:	$E = \$28$
Short-term rate of interest continuously compounded:	$r = .05$
Time to expiration:	$t = .50$ (one-half year)

Solving first for d_1 and d_2 we obtain:

$$d_1 = \frac{ln(30/28) + [.05 + 1/2(.40)^2].50}{.40\sqrt{.50}} = \frac{.133993}{.282843} = .474$$

$$d_2 = \frac{ln(30/28) + [.05 - 1/2(.40)^2].50}{.40\sqrt{.50}} = \frac{.053993}{.282843} = .191$$

The expression $ln(30/28)$ can be solved either by using a calculator having such a function or by looking it up in a natural log table. In our example, $ln(30/28) = .068993$.

In Eq. (4-2), $N(d_1)$ and $N(d_2)$ are the probabilities that a random variable with a standardized normal distribution will take on values less than d_1 and less than d_2. With the bell-shaped normal distribution, slightly over two-thirds of the distribution falls within one standard deviation on either side of the mean, 95 percent within two standard deviations, and 99.7 percent within three standard deviations. In Appendix B at the end of the book, an abbreviated table for the normal distribution appears which tells us the area of the distribution that is so many standard deviations to the left or to the right of the mean. For a d_1 of .474, we see that it lies between standard deviations of .45 and .50 shown in the table. Interpolating, we come up with

$$.3264 - \left(\frac{.24}{.50}\right)(.3264 - .3085) = .318$$

This represents the area of a normal distribution that is .474 or more standard deviations greater than the mean. To determine the area of the normal distribution that is less than .474 standard deviations, we merely subtract .318 from one.[12] Therefore

$$N(d_1) = N(.474) = 1 - .318 = .682$$

---

[12]If the value of d_1 were negative, we would be concerned with the area of the distribution that was to the left of the standard deviation. As a result, we would not subtract it from one. It is only with positive values that we subtract the area of the normal distribution from one.

For the d_2 of .191, we see that it lies between the standard deviations of .15 and .20 in Appendix B. Interpolating here, we obtain:

$$.4404 - \left(\frac{.41}{.50}\right)(.4404 - .4207) = .424$$

Therefore

$$N(d_2) = N(.191) = 1 - .424 = .576$$

Given $N(d_1)$ and $N(d_2)$ together with the information on the stock price, the exercise price, the interest rate, and the length of time to expiration of the option, we are able to compute the equilibrium value of the option using Eq. (4-2). For our example problem,[13]

$$V_o = \$30(.682) - \frac{\$28}{e^{(.05)(.50)}}(.576) = \$4.73$$

Thus the Black-Scholes option pricing model suggests that an option to buy one share of stock having the characteristics specified is worth $4.73.

Moreover, the value of $N(d_1)$ tells us the appropriate hedge ratio to employ. In our example, the ratio is .682. This means that a movement in the stock price will be accompanied by a 0.682 movement in the option price. In order to hedge, the individual should purchase .682 shares of stock for each option that is written. With these proportions, price movements of the two financial assets will be offsetting. The equation above also tells us that if the actual market price is more than or less than $4.73, it is over or under valued. However, caution is necessary in interpreting the results because our estimate of the stock's future volatility is based upon its past volatility. This may or may not be an accurate proxy for the future. As the formula is quite sensitive to the standard deviation employed, caution is necessary in judging whether an option is over or under valued.

EFFECT OF CHANGES IN ASSUMPTIONS

In the preceding section, we assumed a European option on a stock paying no dividends and then proceeded to value it given a hypothetical example with respect to the stock's volatility, its price, the exercise price of the option, the length of time to expiration, and the short-term interest rate. It is obvious that the higher the stock price and the lower the exercise price, the greater the value of the option. Also, we discovered that the greater the volatility of the

---

[13]In the equation, $e = 2.71828$, as stated earlier. Many calculators have this function, which allows for easy solution to the problem. When this is not the case, resort must be made to a table of natural logarithms.

stock, the greater the value of the option, all other things the same. In most cases, this is the most important factor affecting option values. Finally, the greater the length of time to expiration of the option and the greater the interest rate, the greater the value of the option, all other things the same. We now need to determine the effect on the value of an option when we drop the assumptions of a European option and of no dividends.

American Options

With an American option, the option can be exercised by the holder anytime up to the expiration date. As the American option provides all the rights of a European option plus the ability to exercise it before the expiration date, its value must be at least that of an identical European option. In certain cases, it will be worth more. However, it has been demonstrated that an American option on a non-dividend-paying stock should not be exercised before the expiration date.[14] Hence the American and European options will be priced the same if they are alike in all other respects. It is only with options on dividend-paying stocks that the distinction between the European and the American option becomes important. To this issue we now turn.

The Effect of Dividends

When the common stock on which an option is written pays a cash dividend, this tends to lower the value of the option the greater the dividend, all other things the same. In essence, a cash dividend represents the partial liquidation of a company to which the stockholders, but not the option holders, are entitled. With a complete liquidating dividend, the price of the stock will go to zero, as will the price of the option. When a stock goes ex-dividend,[15] the market price of the stock should drop by the amount of the dividend in the absence of taxes. The greater the present value of cash dividends that are likely to be paid prior to the expiration of the option, the lower its value, all other things the same.[16] This relationship is illustrated in Figure 4-7. The curved lines represent actual option values for different levels of dividend. The greater the dividend, as represented by a higher number, the lower the value of the option relative to its theoretical value, all other things the same.

---

[14]Merton, "Rational Theory of Option Pricing," pp. 142–45. See also Smith, "Option Pricing: A Review," pp. 8–11. With a non-dividend-paying stock, the value of a perpetual option will equal the value of the underlying stock.

[15]In declaring a dividend, the board of directors specifies an ex-dividend date. At that date, the stock trades ex-dividend in that investors who purchase it are not entitled to the declared dividend.

[16]For stock splits and stock dividends, the option usually is protected in that adjustments are made in its terms to offset the adverse effect of the stock split or stock dividend. For a discussion of stock splits and stock dividends, see Chapter 12.

figure 4-7
Relation between
stock price and option
price for different
levels of dividend

With an American option, the presence of a cash dividend may affect the timing of when the option is exercised.[17] There is an incentive to exercise the option just before an ex-dividend date. The obvious advantage to the option holder is the receipt of the dividend on the stock. The disadvantage associated with the early exercise of the option is the opportunity cost of the interest that would have been earned on the exercise price. As a result, the optimal time to exercise involves a tradeoff between these factors.[18] One way to adjust for the presence of dividends in the Black-Scholes option pricing model is to treat all expected future dividends up to the expiration date as though they had been paid. The present value of these dividends is subtracted from the current price of the stock. The option pricing formula then is based on this adjusted as opposed to the actual price of the stock.[19]

While the presence of cash dividends complicates the picture, the basic tenets of the Black-Scholes option pricing model continue to hold. For many options, the expiration date is relatively near and the quarterly dividends which are likely to be paid on the stock before the option's expiration are not material. In situations of this sort, it may not be worthwhile to

[17]For a numerical method for valuing options on dividend-paying stocks, see Eduardo S. Schwartz, "The Valuation of Warrants: Implementing a New Approach," *Journal of Financial Economics,* 4 (January 1977), 79-93.

[18]See Rubinstein, *Options Markets,* Appendix B to Chapter 4. For an optimal strategy of when to exercise the option using numerical procedures, see Schwartz, "Valuation of Warrants: Implementing a New Approach."

[19]See William F. Sharpe, *Investments* (Englewood Cliffs, N.J.: Prentice-Hall, 1978), pp. 382-83. For the adjustment of the option pricing model when the dividend yield on the underlying stock is stochastic, see Robert Geske, "The Pricing of Options with Stochastic Dividend Yield," *Journal of Finance,* 33 (May 1978), 617-25.

make a dividend adjustment, particularly if the next ex-dividend date is some time away. For applications of the model later in this book, no dividend adjustments will be made because our focus will be on the conceptual insights provided by the model.

SUMMARY

A call option gives the holder the right to buy a share of stock at a specified price, known as the exercise price. A European option can be exercised only at the expiration date, whereas an American option can be exercised anytime through the expiration date. The value of the option at the expiration date is the greater of the value of the stock minus the exercise price, or zero. The most important factor affecting the value of the option is the price volatility of the stock; the greater the volatility, the more valuable the option, all other things the same. In addition, however, the longer the time to the expiration date and the higher the interest rate, the greater the value of the option, all other things the same.

With a stock and an option on the stock, it is possible to establish a riskless hedged position by buying the stock and by writing options or selling them short. The hedge ratio determines the portion of stock held long in relation to the options in the short position. (A riskless hedge also could be established by buying options and selling the stock short.) With a discrete time example, we showed how the value of the hedged position was the same regardless of the stock-price outcome. In efficient financial markets, the rate of return on a perfectly hedged position would be the risk-free rate. If this is the case, it is possible to determine the appropriate value of the option at the beginning of the period. If the actual value is above or below this value, arbitrage should drive the price of the option toward the correct price.

The Black-Scholes option pricing model provides an exact formula for determining the value of an option based on the volatility of the stock, the price of the stock, the exercise price of the option, the time to expiration of the option, and the short-term interest rate. With an example we showed how this formula could be used, and we discussed some of the problems. The model is based on the notion that investors are able to maintain reasonably hedged positions over time and that arbitrage will drive the return on such positions to the risk-free rate. As a result, the option price will bear a precise relationship to the stock price. The Black-Scholes model provides considerable insight into the valuation of contingent claims.

Finally, we modified our discussion to consider the impact of American options and of stocks that pay dividends. The combination of these factors may result in the option's having a lower value than would be the case if it were a European option where the associated stock paid no dividend.

1. Given the following data, determine the value of the call options at their expiration dates:

Option	Market Price per Share at the Expiration Date	Exercise Price of the Option
A	$10	$12
B	25	21
C	48	52
D	7	5

2. Two companies, X-Gamma Company and X-Theta Company, each have actively traded options on their stocks with the same exercise price, $30. Moreover, the current market prices of the two stocks are the same, $27 per share. Yet the current market price of the X-Gamma option is $2.25 while that of the X-Theta option is $3.90. How can this difference in option prices occur?

3. Julia Malone is considering writing a 30-day option on Video Sonics Corporation, which is currently trading at $60 per share. The exercise price will also be $60 per share, and the premium received on the option will be $3.75. At what common stock prices will she make money, at what price will she begin to lose money, and at what prices will she lose $5 and $10 on each option that is written?

4. The stocks of Carson Can Company and Tahoe Forest Products Company are expected to have the following probability distributions with respect to market price per share six months hence:

Probability of Occurrence	Carson Can	Tahoe Forest Products
0.15	$34	$22
0.20	38	28
0.30	40	36
0.20	42	44
0.15	46	50

Options exist for each of these stocks, and both have an exercise price of $38 and an expiration date six months from now.

(a) What is the expected value of market price per share six months hence for the two companies?
(b) What is the expected value of option price for the two options at expiration, assuming the options are held to this time?
(c) Reconcile your answers to (a) and (b).

5. Shinto Carbon Steel Company's stock price at the beginning of the period is $40

per share. At the end of the period, there is a 50 percent chance that the stock will increase in value to $50 and a 50 percent chance that it will fall in value to $38 per share. An option exists on the stock which can be exercised only at the end of the period and at an exercise price of $41. The risk-free rate is now 5 percent per period.

(a) How would you establish a perfectly hedged position using the stock and the option?

(b) Show how the value of your position will be the same regardless of the stock-price outcome.

6. In problem 5, what will be the market price of the option at the beginning of the period if financial markets are efficient and rational? What would happen if the actual market price of the option were in excess of the price you compute? What would happen if it were less?

7. Baloff Marine Company has a call option on its stock which enables the holder to acquire one share of stock at $45 a share for each option held. The option has six months until its expiration. The market price of the stock is currently $40 a share and the expected standard deviation of its continuously compounded return over the near future is 0.30. The short-term interest rate is 5 percent.

(a) On the basis of this information, what is the proper value of the option using the Black-Scholes option pricing model? (The calculations can be made with a reasonably sophisticated calculator or with an ordinary calculator and various tables.)

(b) What is the appropriate hedge ratio and how does it work?

8. Zilcon Laboratories, Inc., is a high-technology new company whose common stock sells for $23 per share. A call option exists on this stock with three months to expiration. It has an exercise price of $18 and sells for $5.30. You have made a careful study of the stock's volatility and conclude that a standard deviation of .50 is appropriate for the next three months. Currently the rate on short-term Treasury bills is 6 percent.

(a) Using the Black-Scholes option pricing model, is the option overvalued, undervalued, or priced just right? (These calculations are possible with a reasonably sophisticated calculator or with a plain calculator and various tables.)

(b) If you believe in these numbers, what should you do?

9. For Zilcon Laboratories, Inc., in problem 8, determine the value of the option with the following changes, holding all else constant, and explain why the change in the value of the option occurs.

(a) The length of time to expiration is one year instead of three months.

(b) The short-term interest rate is 8 percent instead of 6 percent.

(c) The standard deviation is .10 instead of .50.

SELECTED REFERENCES

BLACK, FISCHER, "Fact and Fantasy in the Use of Options," *Financial Analysts Journal*, 31 (July-August 1975), 36–72.

BLACK, FISCHER, AND MYRON SCHOLES, "The Pricing of Options and Corporate Liabilities," *Journal of Political Economy*, 81 (May-June 1973), 637–54.

———, "The Valuation of Option Contracts and a Test of Market Efficiency," *Journal of Finance*, 27 (May 1972), 399–417.

BRENNAN, MICHAEL, J., AND EDUARDO S. SCHWARTZ, "Finite Difference Methods and Jump Processes Arising in the Pricing of Contingent Claims: A Synthesis," *Journal of Financial and Quantitative Analysis*, 13 (September 1978), 461–74.

COX, JOHN C., AND STEPHEN A. ROSS, "A Survey of Some New Results in Financial Option Pricing Policy," *Journal of Finance*, 31 (May 1976), 383–402.

———, "The Valuation of Options for Alternative Stochastic Processes," *Journal of Financial Economics*, 3 (January-March 1976), 145–79.

FINNERTY, JOSEPH E., "The Chicago Board Options Exchange and Market Efficiency," *Journal of Financial and Quantitative Analysis*, 13 (March 1978), 29–38.

GALAI, DAN, "On the Boness and Black-Scholes Models for Valuation of Call Options," *Journal of Financial and Quantitative Analysis*, 13 (March, 1978), 15–28.

GESKE, ROBERT, "The Pricing of Options with Stochastic Dividend Yield," *Journal of Finance*, 33 (May 1978), 617–25.

LATANE, HENRY A., AND RICHARD J. RENDLEMEN, JR., "Standard Deviations of Stock Price Ratios Implied in Option Prices," *Journal of Finance*, 31 (May 1976), 369–82.

MERTON, ROBERT C., "The Impact on Option Pricing of Specification Error in Underlying Stock Price Returns," *Journal of Finance*, 31 (May 1976), 333–50.

———, "A Rational Theory of Option Pricing," *Bell Journal of Economics*, 4 (Spring 1973), 141–82.

REBACK, ROBERT, "Risk and Return in Option Trading," *Financial Analysts Journal*, 31 (July-August 1975), 42–52.

RENDLEMAN, RICHARD J., JR., "The Effects of Default Risk on the Firm's Investment and Financing Decisions," *Financial Management*, 7 (Spring 1978), 45–53.

ROLL, RICHARD, "An Analytic Valuation Formula for Unprotected American Call Options with Known Dividends," *Journal of Financial Economics*, 5 (November 1977), 251–58.

RUBINSTEIN, MARK E., with the assistance of John C. Cox, *Options Markets*. Englewood Cliffs, N.J.: Prentice-Hall, 1979.

RUBINSTEIN, MARK E., "The Valuation of Uncertain Income Streams and the Pricing of Options," *Bell Journal of Economics*, 7 (Autumn 1976), 407–25.

SCHMALENSEE, RICHARD, AND ROBERT R. TRIPPI, "Common Stock Volatility Expectations Implied by Option Premia," *Journal of Finance*, 33 (March 1978), 129–47.

SCHOLES, MYRON, "Taxes and the Pricing of Options," *Journal of Finance*, 31 (May 1976), 319–30.

SCHWARTZ, EDUARDO S., "The Valuation of Warrants: Implementing a New Approach," *Journal of Financial Economics*, 4 (January 1977), 79–93.

SHARPE, WILLIAM F., *Investments*, Chap. 14. Englewood Cliffs, N.J.: Prentice-Hall, 1978.

SMITH, CLIFFORD W., JR., "Option Pricing: A Review," *Journal of Financial Economics*, 3 (January-March 1976), 3–51.

investments in assets and required returns

5

principles of capital investment

CAPITAL FORMATION

The capital expenditure decisions of corporations exert considerable influence on the overall growth of the economy. A society's productive resources, such as land, machines, buildings, natural resources, and workers, are limited. These resources may all be devoted to producing goods and services for current consumption; or a part of them may go toward things that will enhance the nation's ability to produce, and hence consume, in the future. This process might involve the production of machinery, the exploration for iron ore, or the training of workers in new technology. *Capital formation* can be defined as any investment that increases the productive capacity of society. If resources are fully employed, the only way to make such investments is to refrain from current consumption. If resources are less than fully employed, however, it is possible to have capital formation without necessarily foregoing current consumption.

Corporate capital expenditures for new plant and equipment have ranged from 7.0 to 8.5 percent of the Gross National Product in recent years.

At the end of an economic downturn, the percentage tends to be in the lower part of this range; in periods of economic prosperity, it tends to be in the upper part of the range. The pattern of growth in capital expenditures is shown in Figure 5-1. In the last several years, much of the growth in expenditures was attributed to inflation as opposed to a growth in real outlays.

What is a capital investment by a firm? A capital investment involves a current cash outlay in the anticipation of benefits to be realized in the future. In keeping with our discussion in Chapters 2 and 3, an investment proposal should be judged in relation to whether it provides a return equal to or greater than that required by investors. Thus the required return is the link by which we relate the effect of an investment decision to share price. Much of our analysis of how investment projects affect share price draws heavily upon the valuation concepts presented in Chapters 2 and 3. Although our objective in the subsequent four chapters is to come to grips with this issue, we first must take up certain fundamental concepts and that is the purpose of this chapter. To simplify the presentation of these basics, we assume for now that the required rate of return on investment projects is given and is the same for all projects. This assumption necessitates our holding constant the financing and dividend decisions of the firm. Moreover, it implies that the selection of any investment project or combination of projects does not alter the business-risk complexion of the firm as perceived by suppliers of capital.

In the next chapter, we relax this assumption and allow for the fact that different projects have different degrees of business risk. Consequently,

figure 5-1
New plant
and equipment
expenditures by
business, 1961–78

Source: *Economic Report of the President, 1978.*

the selection of an investment project may affect the business-risk complexion of the firm, which, in turn, may affect the required rate of return of suppliers of capital and share price. In the same chapter, we consider ways to take account of risk for individual projects and external acquisitions. In addition, we take up the question of the divestiture of a portion of the enterprise within a capital-budgeting framework. In Chapters 7 and 8, we focus on the required rate of return for a project, for a division of a company, for the company as a whole, and for an acquisition. In these latter chapters, we tie together the valuation concepts discussed earlier with the cash-flow information discussed in this and the next chapter. It is important to stress, then, that certain facilitating assumptions imposed in this chapter subsequently will be relaxed once we have an understanding of the rudiments of capital budgeting.

THE ADMINISTRATIVE FRAMEWORK

The successful administration of capital investments by a company involves a number of facets: the generation of investment proposals; the estimate of cash flows for the proposals; the evaluation of cash flows; the selection of projects based upon an acceptance criterion; and, finally, the continual reevaluation of investment projects after their acceptance. The first four are examined in this chapter, although the fourth is analyzed in much greater depth in Chapters 7 and 8. The last aspect, the continual reevaluation of existing projects, is taken up in Chapter 6 when we consider the question of divestiture.

Depending upon the firm involved, investment proposals can emanate from various sources. For purposes of analysis, projects may be classified into one of five categories:

1. New products or expansion of existing products
2. Replacement of equipment or buildings
3. Research and development
4. Exploration
5. Others

The last category comprises miscellaneous items such as the expenditure of funds to comply with certain health standards or the acquisition of a pollution-control device. In the case of a new product, the proposal usually originates in the marketing department. On the other hand, a proposal to replace a piece of equipment with a more sophisticated model usually emanates from the production area of the firm. In each case, it is important to have efficient administrative procedures for channeling investment requests.

Most firms screen proposals at multiple levels of authority. For a proposal originating in the production area, the hierarchy of authority might run from section chiefs to (1) plant managers to (2) the vice-president for operations to (3) a capital-expenditures committee under the financial manager to (4) the president to (5) the board of directors. How high a proposal must go before it is finally approved usually depends upon its size. The greater the capital outlay, the greater the number of screens usually required. Plant managers, for example, may be able to approve moderate-sized projects on their own; but final approval for larger projects is received only at higher levels of authority. Because the administrative procedures for screening investment proposals vary greatly from firm to firm, it is not possible to generalize. The best procedure will depend upon the circumstances. It is clear, however, that companies are becoming increasingly sophisticated in their approach to capital budgeting.[1]

Estimating Cash Flows

One of the most important tasks in capital budgeting is estimating future cash flows for a project. The final results we obtain are really only as good as the accuracy of our estimates. The reason we express the benefits expected to be derived from a project in terms of cash flows rather than in terms of income is that cash is what is central to all decisions of the firm. The firm invests cash now in the hope of receiving cash returns in a greater amount in the future. Only cash receipts can be reinvested in the firm or paid to stockholders in the form of dividends. Thus cash, not income, is what is important in capital budgeting.

For each investment proposal, we need to provide information on expected future cash flows on an after-tax basis. In addition, the information must be provided on an *incremental* basis so that we analyze only the difference between the cash flows of the firm with and without the project. For example, if a firm contemplates a new product that is likely to compete with existing products, it is not appropriate to express cash flows in terms of the estimated sales of the new product. We must take into account that there

---

[1]For surveys of the administrative practices of companies with respect to capital budgeting as well as of the evaluation techniques being used, see J. William Petty, David F. Scott, Jr., and Monroe M. Bird, "The Capital Expenditure Decision-Making Process of Large Corporations," *Engineering Economist,* 20 (Spring 1975), 159–72; Thomas Klammer, "Empirical Evidence of the Adoption of Sophisticated Capital Budgeting Techniques," *Journal of Business,* 45 (July 1972), 387–97; Lawrence D. Schall, Gary L. Sundem, and William R. Geijsbeek, Jr., "Survey and Analysis of Capital Budgeting Methods," *Journal of Finance,* 33 (March 1978), 281–87; Lawrence J. Gitman and John R. Forrester, Jr., "Forecasting and Evaluation Practices and Performance: A Survey of Capital Budgeting Techniques Used by Major U.S. Firms," *Financial Management,* 6 (Fall 1977), 66–71; and J. William Petty and Oswald D. Bowlin, "The Financial Manager and Quantitative Decision Models," *Financial Management,* 4 (Winter 1976), 32–41.

See also James B. Weaver, "Organizing and Maintaining a Capital Expenditure Program," *Engineering Economist,* 20 (Fall 1974), 1–36; and E. Eugene Carter, "Designing the Capital Budgeting Process, *TIMS Studies in the Management Sciences,* 5 (1977), 25–42, for a discussion of administrative procedures. Finally, for a discussion of the importance of a postcompletion audit as well as of its form, see James S. Schnell and Roy S. Nicolosi, "Capital Expenditure Feedback: Project Reappraisal," *Engineering Economist,* 19 (Summer 1974), 253–61.

probably will be some "cannibalization" of existing products and make our cash-flow estimates on the basis of incremental sales. The key is to analyze the situation with and without the new investment. Only *incremental* cash flows matter.

To illustrate the information needed for a capital-budgeting decision, consider the following situation. Suppose a firm is considering the introduction of a new product. In order to launch the product, it will need to spend $150,000 for special equipment and the initial advertising campaign. The marketing department envisions the product life to be six years and expects incremental sales revenue to be:

Year 1	Year 2	Year 3	Year 4	Year 5	Year 6
$60,000	$120,000	$160,000	$180,000	$110,000	$50,000

Cash outflows include labor and maintenance costs, material costs, and various other expenses associated with the product. As with sales, these costs must be estimated on an incremental basis. In addition to these outflows, the firm will need to pay higher taxes if the new product generates higher profits; and this incremental outlay must be included. Cash outflows *should not* include interest costs on debt employed to finance the project. Such costs are embodied in the required rate of return to be discussed in Chapters 7 and 8. To deduct interest charges from net cash flows would result in double counting.

Suppose that on the basis of these considerations the firm estimates total incremental cash outflows to be:

Year 1	Year 2	Year 3	Year 4	Year 5	Year 6
$40,000	$70,000	$100,000	$100,000	$70,000	$40,000

Because depreciation is a noncash expense, it is not included in these outflows. The expected net cash flows from the project are:

	Initial Cost	Year 1	Year 2	Year 3	Year 4	Year 5	Year 6
Cash inflows		$60,000	$120,000	$160,000	$180,000	$110,000	$50,000
Cash outflows	$150,000	40,000	70,000	100,000	100,000	70,000	40,000
Net cash flows	−$150,000	$20,000	$ 50,000	$ 60,000	$ 80,000	$ 40,000	$10,000

Thus, for an initial cash outflow of $150,000, the firm expects to generate net cash flows of $20,000, $50,000, $60,000, $80,000, $40,000 and $10,000 over the next six years. These cash flows represent the relevant information we need in order to judge the attractiveness of the project.

To go to a somewhat more complicated replacement-decision example, suppose that we are considering the purchase of a new lathe to replace an old one and that we need to obtain cash-flow information in order to evaluate the attractiveness of this project. The purchase price of the new machine is $18,500; and it will require an additional $1,500 to install, bringing the total cost to $20,000. The old machine can be sold for its depreciated book value of $2,000. The initial net cash outflow for the investment project, therefore, is $18,000. The new machine is expected to cut labor and maintenance costs and effect other cash savings totaling $7,600 a year before taxes for the next five years, after which it is not expected to provide any savings, nor is it expected to have a salvage value. These savings represent the net savings to the firm if it replaces the old machine with the new. In other words, we are concerned with the difference between the cash flows resulting from the two alternatives—continuing with the old machine or replacing it with a new one.

Because machines of this sort have useful lives in excess of one year, their cost cannot be charged against income for tax purposes but must be depreciated over the depreciable life of the asset. Depreciation then is deducted from income in order to compute taxable income. If the firm employs straight-line depreciation, the annual depreciation charge is 20 percent of the total depreciable cost of $20,000, or $4,000 a year. Assume additionally that the corporate income tax rate is 50 percent. Moreover, assume that the old machine has a remaining depreciable life of five years, that there is no expected salvage value at the end of this time, and that the machine also is subject to straight-line depreciation. Thus, the annual depreciation charge on the old machine is 20 percent of its depreciated book value of $2,000, or $400 a year. Because we are interested in the incremental impact of the project, we must subtract depreciation charges on the old machine from depreciation charges on the new one to obtain the incremental depreciation charges associated with the project. Given the information cited, we now are able to calculate the expected net cash flow (after taxes) resulting from the acceptance of the project.

	Book Account	Cash-Flow Account
Annual cash savings	$7,600	$7,600
Depreciation on new machine	4,000	
Less depreciation on old machine	400	
Additional depreciation charge	$3,600	
Additional income before taxes	4,000	
Income tax (50%)	2,000	2,000
Additional income after taxes	$2,000	
Annual net cash flow		$5,600

In figuring the net cash flow, we simply deduct the additional cash outlay for federal income taxes from the annual cash savings. The expected annual net cash inflow for this replacement proposal is $5,600 for each of the next five years; this figure compares with additional income after taxes of $2,000 a year. The cash flow and net profit figures differ by the amount of additional depreciation. As our concern is not with income, as such, but with cash flows, we are interested in the right-hand column. For an initial cash outlay of $18,000, then, we are able to replace an old lathe with a new one that is expected to result in net cash savings of $5,600 a year over the next five years. As in the previous example, the relevant cash-flow information for capital-budgeting purposes is expressed on an incremental, after-tax basis.

Efficient procedures must be set up to collect the information necessary for the capital-budgeting decision. This information must be standardized as much as possible for all investment proposals; otherwise, proposals cannot be compared objectively. We recognize the difficulty in quantifying expected cash flows for certain investment proposals. The returns on all investments, other than the U.S. Treasury securities held to maturity, are subject to varying degrees of uncertainty. In addition, projects proposed for safety or environmental reasons are difficult to quantify, often representing a constraint of what *must* be done as opposed to what *might* be done. Despite these problems, in most cases management must make some estimate of the probable outcome if it is to consider an investment proposal. These estimates can be subject to probability distributions; indeed, using probability distributions is desirable, as we shall see in the next chapter. In this chapter, however, we work with the expected values of these estimates.

METHODS FOR EVALUATING EXPECTED PROFITABILITY

Once we have collected the necessary information, we are able to evaluate the attractiveness of the various investment proposals under consideration. Because our purpose in this chapter is to examine the basic concepts of capital budgeting, we assume that the risk or quality of all investment proposals under consideration does not differ from the risk of existing investment projects of the firm and that the acceptance of any proposal or group of investment proposals does not change the relative business risk of the firm. The investment decision will be either to accept or to reject the proposal. In this section, we evaluate four approaches to capital budgeting: the average-rate-of-return method; the payback method; the internal-rate-of-return method; and the net-present-value method. The first two represent approximate methods for assessing the economic worth of a project. For simplicity, we assume throughout that the expected cash flows are realized at the end of each year.

Average Rate of Return

The average rate of return is an accounting method and represents the ratio of the average annual profits after taxes to the average investment in the project. In our first example, the average annual book earnings for the five-year period are $2,000; and the average net investment in the project, assuming straight-line depreciation, is $18,000/2, or $9,000. Therefore

$$\text{Average rate of return} = \frac{\$2,000}{\$9,000} = 22.22 \text{ percent} \tag{5-1}$$

The average-rate-of-return method is sometimes based upon the original investment rather than upon the average investment. In the above example, the average rate of return would be $2,000/$18,000 = 11.11 percent under this version of the average-rate-of-return method.

The principal virtue of the average rate of return is its simplicity; it makes use of readily available accounting information. Once the average rate of return for a proposal has been calculated, it may be compared with a required, or cutoff, rate of return to determine if a particular proposal should be accepted or rejected. The principal shortcomings of the method are that it is based upon accounting income rather than upon cash flows and that it fails to take account of the timing of cash inflows and outflows. The time value of money is ignored; benefits in the last year are valued the same as benefits in the first year.

Suppose that we have three investment proposals, each costing $9,000 and each having an economic and depreciable life of three years. Assume that these proposals are expected to provide the following book profits and cash flows over the next three years:

	Project A		Project B		Project C	
Period	Book Profit	Net Cash Flow	Book Profit	Net Cash Flow	Book Profit	Net Cash Flow
1	$3,000	$6,000	$2,000	$5,000	$1,000	$4,000
2	2,000	5,000	2,000	5,000	2,000	5,000
3	1,000	4,000	2,000	5,000	3,000	6,000

If straight-line depreciation is employed, each proposal will have the same average rate of return—$2,000/4,500, or 44.44 percent. However, few, if any, firms would regard the three projects as equally favorable. Most would prefer Project A, which provides a larger portion of total cash benefits in the first year. For this reason, the average rate of return leaves much to be desired as a method for project selection.

Payback Method

The payback period of an investment project tells us the number of years required to recover our initial cash investment. It is the ratio of the initial fixed investment over the annual cash inflows for the recovery period. For our example,

$$\text{Payback period} = \frac{\$18,000}{\$5,600} = 3.2 \text{ years} \qquad \frac{To}{annual\ cash\ inflows} \quad (5\text{-}2)$$

If the annual cash inflows are not equal, the job of calculation is somewhat more difficult. Suppose that annual cash inflows are $4,000 in the first year, $6,000 in the second and third years, and $4,000 in the fourth and fifth years. In the first three years, $16,000 of the original investment will be recovered, followed by $4,000 in the fourth year. With an initial cash investment of $18,000, the payback period is: 3 years + ($2,000/$4,000), or $3\frac{1}{2}$ years.

If the payback period calculated is less than some maximum acceptable payback period, the proposal is accepted; if not, it is rejected. For example, if the required payback period is four years, the project in our example would be accepted. The major shortcoming of the payback method is that it fails to consider cash flows after the payback period; consequently, it cannot be regarded as a measure of profitability. Two proposals costing $10,000 each would have the same payback period if they both had annual net cash inflows of $5,000 in the first two years. However, one project might be expected to provide no cash flows after two years, while the other might be expected to provide cash flows of $5,000 in each of the next three years. Thus the payback method can be very deceptive as a yardstick of profitability. In addition to this shortcoming, the method does not take account of the magnitude or timing of cash flows during the payback period; it considers only the recovery period as a whole.

Nevertheless, the payback method continues in use, frequently as a supplement to other, more sophisticated, methods. It does afford management limited insight into the risk and liquidity of a project. The shorter the payback period, supposedly, the less risky the project, and the greater its liquidity. The company that is cash poor may find the method to be very useful in gauging the early recovery of funds invested. There is some merit to its use in this regard, but the method does not take into account the dispersion of possible outcomes—only the magnitude and timing of the expected value of these outcomes relative to the original investment. Therefore it cannot be considered an adequate indicator of risk. When the payback method is used, it is more appropriately treated as a constraint to be satisfied than as a profitability measure to be maximized.[2]

[2]See H. Martin Weingartner, "Some New Views on the Payback Period and Capital Budgeting Decisions," *Management Science*, 15 (August 1969), 594–607. For a detailed analysis of the payback method and the accounting-rate-of-return method as approximations of the internal rate of return, see Marshall Sarnat and Haim Levy, "The Relationship of Rules of Thumb to the Internal Rate of Return: A Restatement and Generalization," *Journal of Finance*, 24 (June 1969), 479–89.

Internal-Rate-of-Return Method

Because of the various shortcomings in the average-rate-of-return and payback methods described above, it generally is felt that discounted cash-flow methods provide a more objective basis for evaluating and selecting investment projects. These methods take account of both the magnitude and the timing of expected cash flows in each period of a project's life. The two discounted cash-flow methods are the internal-rate-of-return and the present-value methods; the mechanics of these methods were described in Chapter 2. Recall that the internal rate of return for an investment proposal is the discount rate that equates the present value of the expected cash outflows with the present value of the expected inflows. It is represented by that rate, r, such that

$$\sum_{t=0}^{n} \left[\frac{A_t}{(1 + r)^t} \right] = 0 \tag{5-3}$$

where A_t is the cash flow for period t, whether it be a net cash outflow or inflow, and n is the last period in which a cash flow is expected. If the initial cash outlay or cost occurs at time 0, Eq. (5-3) can be expressed as

$$A_0 = \frac{A_1}{(1 + r)} + \frac{A_2}{(1 + r)^2} + \cdots + \frac{A_n}{(1 + r)^n} \tag{5-4}$$

Thus r is the rate that discounts the stream of future cash flows—A_1 through A_n—to equal the initial outlay at time 0—A_0. For our example, the problem can be expressed as

$$18{,}000 = \frac{5{,}600}{(1 + r)} + \frac{5{,}600}{(1 + r)^2} + \frac{5{,}600}{(1 + r)^3} + \frac{5{,}600}{(1 + r)^4} + \frac{5{,}600}{(1 + r)^5} \tag{5-5}$$

Solving for r either by means of a computer or by the manual method described in Chapter 2, we find the internal rate of return for the project to be 16.8 percent. When solving for r, it is important to recognize the possibility that there may be more than one internal rate of return that equates the present value of cash inflows with the present value of cash outflows. This can occur when there are net cash outflows in more than one period and the outflows are separated by one or more periods of net cash inflows. We examine the problem in Appendix A at the end of this chapter but should point out at this time that the existence of multiple internal rates of return is unusual. For the typical capital budgeting project, a unique internal rate of return exists.

Acceptance Criterion   The acceptance criterion generally employed with the internal-rate-of-return method is to compare the internal rate of return with a required rate of return, known also as the cutoff, or hurdle, rate. If the internal rate of return exceeds the required rate, the project is accepted;

if not, it is rejected. For example, if the required rate of return were 10 percent and this criterion is used, the investment proposal considered above would be accepted. If the required rate of return is the return investors expect the firm to earn on the project, accepting a project with an internal rate of return in excess of the required rate of return should result in an increase in the market price of the stock, because the firm accepts a project with a return greater than that required to maintain the present market price per share. Much more will be said in Chapters 7 and 8 about relating the investment decision to the objective of the firm. We assume for now that the required rate of return is given.

Present-Value Method

Like the internal-rate-of-return method, the present-value method is a discounted cash-flow approach to capital budgeting. With the present-value method, all cash flows are discounted to present value using the required rate of return. The net-present value of an investment proposal is

$$NPV = \sum_{t=0}^{n} \frac{A_t}{(1 + k)^t}$$

(5-6)

where k is the required rate of return. If the sum of these discounted cash flows is equal to, or greater than, 0, the proposal is accepted; if not, it is rejected. Another way to express the acceptance criterion is to say that the project will be accepted if the present value of cash inflows exceeds the present value of cash outflows. The rationale behind the acceptance criterion is the same as that behind the internal-rate-of-return method. If the required rate of return is the return investors expect the firm to earn on the investment proposal, and the firm accepts a proposal with a net-present value greater than zero, the market price of the stock should rise. Again, the firm is taking on a project with a return greater than that necessary to leave the market price of the stock unchanged.

If we assume a required rate of return of 10 percent after taxes, the net-present value of our example problem is

$$NPV = -18,000 + \frac{5,600}{(1.10)} + \frac{5,600}{(1.10)^2} + \frac{5,600}{(1.10)^3} + \frac{5,600}{(1.10)^4} + \frac{5,600}{(1.10)^5}$$
$$= -18,000 + 21,228.48$$
$$= 3,228.48$$

(5-7)

An easier way to solve this problem, of course, is by direct reference to Table A-2 in Appendix A at the end of the book, where we find the appropriate discount factor—3.7908—and multiply $5,600 by it to obtain $21,228.48. Subtracting the initial outlay of $18,000, we obtain $3,228.48. Inasmuch as the net-present value of this proposal is greater than 0, the proposal should be accepted, using the present-value method.

With the internal-rate-of-return method, we are given the cash flows and solve for the rate of discount that equates the present value of the cash inflows with the present value of the outflows. The internal rate of return is then compared with the required rate of return to determine whether the proposal should be accepted. With the present-value method, we are given the cash flows and the required rate of return and solve for the net-present value. The acceptability of the proposal is determined by whether the net-present value is equal to, or greater than, 0.

Mutual Exclusion and Dependency

In evaluating a group of investment proposals, it is important to determine whether the proposals are independent of each other. A proposal is said to be mutually exclusive if the acceptance of it precludes the acceptance of one or more other proposals. For example, if the firm is considering investment in one of two temperature-control systems, acceptance of one system will rule out acceptance of the other. Two mutually exclusive proposals cannot both be accepted.

A *contingent* or *dependent* proposal is one whose acceptance depends upon the acceptance of one or more other proposals. An example of a contingent proposal might be an investment in a large machine, which depends upon the construction of an addition to a plant. A combination of investment proposals containing a contingent proposal must contain the proposal(s) upon which it is dependent. When an investment proposal is not independent of all other proposals, this occurrence must be recognized and investment decisions made accordingly.

Profitability Index

The profitability index, or benefit-cost ratio, of a project is the present value of future net cash flows over the initial cash outlay. It can be expressed as

$$PI = \frac{\sum_{t=1}^{n} \frac{A_t}{(1+k)^t}}{A_0} \qquad (5\text{-}8)$$

For our example,

$$PI = \frac{\$21,228.48}{\$18,000.00} = 1.18 \qquad (5\text{-}9)$$

As long as the profitability index is equal to or greater than 1.00, the investment proposal is acceptable. In calculating the profitability index, we compute the net rather than the aggregate index. The aggregate index is simply the present value of cash inflows over the present value of cash outflows. The reason we use the net index is that we wish to differentiate the initial cash outlay from subsequent cash outlays. The initial outlay is discretionary in the sense that the firm can choose to either commit funds to the project or employ them elsewhere. Subsequent cash outflows are not discretionary in this sense; they are embodied in the system. The aggregate index does not differentiate between the cash outlay the firm has to put up initially and subsequent cash outlays.[3] For this reason, the net profitability index is a more rational measure of profitability than is the aggregate index.

For any given project, the net-present-value method and the profitability index give the same accept-reject signals. If we must choose between mutually exclusive projects, however, the net-present-value measure is preferred because it expresses in absolute terms the expected economic contribution of the project. In contrast, the profitability index expresses only the relative profitability. To illustrate, consider the following mutually exclusive projects:

	Project A	Project B
Present value of net cash flows	$20,000	$8,000
Initial cash outlay	$15,000	$5,000
Net-present value	$ 5,000	$3,000
Profitability index	1.33	1.60

Scale effects

According to the net-present-value method, Project *A* would be preferred; whereas according to the profitability indexes, Project *B* would be preferred. Because the net-present value represents the expected economic contribution of a project, we should prefer *A* to *B*. Thus the net-present-value method is the better of the two methods when we must choose between mutually exclusive projects that involve different initial cash outlays.

PRESENT-VALUE METHOD VERSUS INTERNAL-RATE-OF-RETURN METHOD

In general, the present-value and internal-rate-of-return methods lead to the same acceptance or rejection decision. In Figure 5-2, we illustrate graphically the two methods applied to a typical investment project. The figure shows the relationship between the net-present value of a project and the discount rate employed. When the discount rate is 0, net-present value is, simply, the total cash inflows less the total cash outflows of the project. Assuming that total inflows exceed total outflows and that outflows are followed by inflows, the typical project will have the highest net-present value when the discount rate

[3]See Bernhard Schwab and Peter Lusztig, "A Comparative Analysis of the Net Present Value and the Benefit-Cost Ratio as Measures of the Economic Desirability of Investments," *Journal of Finance*, 24 (June 1969), 507–11.

is 0. As the discount rate increases, the present value of future cash inflows decreases relative to the present value of cash outflows.[4]

If the required rate of return is less than the internal rate of return, we would accept the project using either method. Suppose that the required rate were 10 percent. As seen in Figure 5-2, the net-present value of the project then would be Y. Inasmuch as Y is greater than 0, we would accept the project using the present-value method. Similarly, we would accept the project using the internal-rate-of-return method because the internal rate of 15 percent exceeds the required rate. For required rates greater than the internal rate of return, we would reject the project under either method. Thus we see that the internal-rate-of-return and present-value methods give us identical answers with respect to the acceptance or rejection of an investment project.

Differences between Methods

However, important differences exist between the methods, and they must be recognized. When two investment proposals are mutually exclusive,

**figure 5-2
Relation between
discount rate and net-
present value**

[4]Again, we must recognize the possibility of multiple internal rates of return. See Appendix A at the end of this chapter.

so that we can select only one, the two methods may give contradictory results. To illustrate the nature of the problem, suppose a firm had two mutually exclusive investment proposals that were expected to generate the following cash flows:

Cash Flows					
Year	0	1	2	3	4
Proposal A	−$23,616	$10,000	$10,000	$10,000	$10,000
Proposal B	−23,616	0	5,000	10,000	32,675

Internal rates of return for proposals A and B are 25 percent and 22 percent, respectively. If the required rate of return is 10 percent, however, and we use this figure as our discount rate, the net-present values of proposals A and B are $8,083 and $10,347, respectively. Thus proposal A is preferred if we use the internal-rate-of-return method, whereas proposal B is preferred if we use the present-value method. If we can choose but one of these proposals, we obviously have a conflict.

Compounding Rate The conflict between these two methods is due to differences in the implicit compounding of interest. The IRR method implies that funds are compounded at the internal rate of return. For proposal A, the assumption is that $23,616 invested at 25 percent will compound in such a way as to release $10,000 at the end of each of the next four years. The present-value method implies compounding at the required rate of return used as the discount rate. For proposal A, the assumption is that $8,083 plus $23,616 or $31,699 invested at 10 percent will compound in such a way as to release $10,000 at the end of each of the next four years. Since the proposal cost $23,616, its worth or present value is $31,699 minus this amount, or $8,083.

To illustrate further the nature of the problem, consider two additional mutually exclusive proposals with the following cash flows:

Cash Flows				
Time	0	1	2	3
Proposal C	−$155.22	100.00	0	100.00
Proposal D	−155.22	0	0	221.00

The net-present value of each of these proposals is $10.82 if we assume a required rate of return of 10 percent. However, we would be indifferent between the two proposals only if the firm had opportunities for reinvestment at a rate of 10 percent. More specifically, it must be able to realize a reinvestment rate of 10 percent through time 3 on the $100 cash inflow for proposal C at time 1. This concept is illustrated in Figure 5-3, where the functional relationship between net-present value and the discount rate is

figure 5-3
Relation between discount rate and net-present values, proposals C and D

graphed for the two proposals. The intercepts on the 0 horizontal line represent the internal rates of return of the two proposals that equate their net-present values to 0. For proposal *C,* the internal rate of return is 14 percent; for proposal *D,* it is 12.5 percent. The intercepts on the vertical axis represent total cash inflows less total cash outflows for the two proposals, because the discount rate is 0. We see that proposal *D* ranks higher than proposal *C* if the required rate of return is below 10 percent and lower if it is above 10 percent. At the point of intersection, 10 percent, the proposals have identical net-present values. Given a marginal reinvestment rate of 10 percent, then, the two proposals would have equal ranking. For reinvestment rates other than this percentage, we would prefer one proposal to the other. In a similar manner, other mutually exclusive investment proposals can be evaluated according to the intersections.[5]

[5]Under certain circumstances, it is possible to have multiple intersections. Because these circumstances tend to be unusual, we will not go into an analysis of them. For further discussion, see J. Hirshleifer, "On the Theory of Optimal Investment Decision," *Journal of Political Economy,* 66 (August 1958), 95–103.

Scale of Investment   In addition to the problem of different implicit compounding rates, a problem arises if the initial cash outlays are different for two mutually exclusive investment proposals. Because the results of the internal-rate-of-return method are expressed as a percentage, the scale of investment is ignored. Without allowance for this factor, a 50 percent return on a $100 investment would always be preferred to a 25 percent return on a $500 investment. In contrast, the results of the present-value method are expressed in absolute terms. If the investment proposals above were each for one year, we would have the following, assuming a required rate of return of 10 percent:

Cash Flows				
	Year 0	Year 1	IRR	NPV(10%)
Proposal X	$100	$150	50%	$36.36
Proposal Y	500	625	25	68.18

With respect to absolute returns, the second proposal is superior despite the fact that its internal rate of return is less. The reason is that the scale of investment is greater, which affords a greater net-present value.

Which Method Provides Better Results

The question to be answered is, which method—the internal-rate-of-return method or the present-value method—is better for purposes of evaluating investment proposals? The question hinges upon what is the appropriate rate of reinvestment for the intermediate cash flows and upon the scale of investment. The internal-rate-of-return method implies a reinvestment rate equal to the internal rate of return, whereas the present-value method implies a reinvestment rate equal to the required rate of return used as the discount factor. In addition, the former method does not factor into consideration the scale of investment. Again, these differences become an issue only when it comes to mutually exclusive investment proposals; otherwise the methods provide the same accept or reject decisions.

If a choice must be made, the present-value method generally is considered to be superior theoretically. With the internal-rate-of-return method, the implied reinvestment rate will differ depending upon the cash-flow stream for each investment proposal under consideration. For proposals with a high internal rate of return, a high reinvestment rate is assumed; for proposals with a low internal rate of return, a low reinvestment rate is assumed. Only rarely will the internal rate of return calculated represent the relevant rate for reinvestment of intermediate cash flows. With the present-value method, however, the implied reinvestment rate—namely, the required rate of return—is the same for each proposal. In essence, this reinvestment rate represents the minimum return on opportunities available to the firm, given our assumptions. To the extent that we can regard the required rate of return, *k,* as an approximate measure of the opportunity rate for reinvestment, the present-value method is preferred over the internal-rate-of-return method. In addition, the present-value method takes account of differences in the scale of investment and for this reason it also is preferred.

However, the internal-rate-of-return method can be modified so that it involves an incremental type of analysis. When one is faced with two mutually exclusive investment proposals, both of whose internal rates of return exceed the required rate of return, the following additional steps could be undertaken:[6]

1. Calculate the differential cash flows between the two proposals.
2. If the internal rate of return on the differential cash flows exceeds the required rate of return, the project with the greater nondiscounted net cash flows should be selected.

To illustrate, consider again proposals *A* and *B* and the differential cash flows:

| | Cash Flows | | | | |
	0	1	2	3	4
Proposal A	−$23,616	$10,000	$10,000	$10,000	$10,000
Proposal B	−23,616	0	5,000	10,000	32,675
B less A	0	−$10,000	−5,000	0	22,675

The internal rate of return that equates outflows of $10,000 and $5,000 at the end of years 1 and 2, respectively, with an inflow of $22,675 at the end of year 4 is 16.65 percent. Because this rate exceeds the required rate of return of 10 percent, proposal *B* should be selected, despite the fact that its internal rate of return is 22 percent compared with 25 percent for proposal *A*. In addition, the method allows for differences in the scale of investment, as can be visualized if *B* less *A* for year 0 were either positive or negative.

Thus the internal-rate-of-return method can be modified to deal with the special case of mutually exclusive investment proposals. Given such a modification, it provides a decision identical to that given by the net-present-value method. Many financial managers feel that the internal rate of return is easier to visualize and to interpret than is the net-present-value measure. In addition, one does not have to specify a required rate of return in the calculations. To the extent that the required rate of return is but a rough estimate, the use of the internal-rate-of-return method may permit a more

[6]See H. Martin Weingartner, "The Excess Present Value Index—A Theoretical Basis and Critique," *Journal of Accounting Research,* 1 (Autumn 1963), 213–24.

realistic comparison of projects. The principal shortcoming of the method is the possibility of multiple internal rates of return, a subject that we discuss in Appendix A at the end of this chapter.

SOME REFINEMENTS IN CASH-FLOW INFORMATION

In our machine replacement example, we assumed straight-line depreciation, no investment tax credit, no salvage value, and no working capital requirement. Our purpose was to keep the example simple so that we could analyze the methods for evaluating expected profitability. We shall now digress for a while in order to examine the effect of the above considerations on the magnitude and timing of cash flows.

Accelerated Depreciation

In our earlier example, recall that the replacement of the old machine with a new one was expected to result in annual cash savings of $7,600 a year over the next five years. Straight-line depreciation charges on the new machine were $4,000 a year; and when we subtracted $400 annual depreciation charges on the old machine, we obtained incremental depreciation charges of $3,600 a year. Thus the additional income before taxes was $4,000, resulting in additional taxes of $2,000 a year, assuming a 50 percent tax rate. When this $2,000 outlay was subtracted from the $7,600 cash savings, the net cash inflow became $5,600 a year. Consider now the modification of the example occasioned by accelerated depreciation.

Accelerated depreciation can be either the double-declining-balance method or the sum-of-the-years'-digits method. The formula for the double-declining-balance method is $2(1/n)$, or 2 divided by the depreciable life of the asset. In the case of a five-year depreciable life, the annual depreciation charge would be $2(1/5)$, or 40 percent of the depreciated book value balance at the beginning of the year. If the depreciable value were $10,000 initially, depreciation charges would be $4,000 in the first year, $2,400 in the second (40 percent of $10,000—4,000), and so on. A second method of accelerated depreciation is the sum-of-the-years'-digits method. Here, we add up each year of the depreciable life of the asset to obtain the denominator. In our case, the denominator is $1 + 2 + 3 + 4 + 5 = 15$. The numerator is the depreciable life for the first year, the depreciable life minus 1 for the second year, and so on. Thus the first-year depreciation charge on an asset having a five-year depreciable life would be 5/15, followed by 4/15, 3/15, 2/15, and 1/15 for the remaining years.

Given a depreciable value of $20,000 in our example and a five-year depreciable life, the annual depreciation charges for these accelerated methods are:

Year	Double-Declining Balance (40%)	Sum-of-the Years' Digits
1	$ 8,000.00	$ 6,666,67
2	4,800.00	5,333.33
3	2,880.00	4,000.00
4	1,728.00	2,666.67
5	2,592.00	1,333.33
	$20,000.00	$20,000.00

Note that for the first method, the firm is able to claim the full remaining depreciable value of the asset in the last year, rather than only 40 percent of it.

If the old machine were still depreciated on a straight-line basis of $400 a year, the additional depreciation charge and annual net cash flow for these two methods over the five-year period would be:

	Double-Declining Balance (40%)		Sum-of-the Years' Digits	
Year	Additional Depreciation	Net Cash Flow	Additional Depreciation	Net Cash Flow
1	$7,600.00	$7,600.00	$6,266.67	$6,933.33
2	4,400.00	6,000.00	4,933.33	6,266.67
3	2,480.00	5,040.00	3,600.00	5,600.00
4	1,328.00	4,464.00	2,266.67	4,933.33
5	2,192.00	4,896.00	933.33	4,266.67

We see that the use of accelerated depreciation increases the depreciation charge in the early years of the project's life over what it would be if straight-line depreciation were used, resulting in lower taxes and higher cash flows in these years. The use of accelerated depreciation changes the timing of cash flows from what they would be if straight-line depreciation were used.

If money does have a time value, accelerated depreciation is advantageous to the firm. For example, the internal rate of return using the double-declining-balance method is 18.7 percent, compared with 16.8 percent when the straight-line method of depreciation is employed. The net-present value, assuming a required rate of return of 10 percent, is $3,743.33 under the double-declining-balance method, compared with $3,228.48 under the straight-line method. For the sum-of-the-years'-digits method, the internal rate of return is 18.5 percent and the net-present value, $3,708.30. Thus the method of depreciation affects the timing of cash flows and the resulting attractiveness of the investment project. The total amount of taxes is not reduced with accelerated depreciation; taxes simply are paid at a date later than would be the case with straight-line depreciation.

Investment Tax Credit

The investment tax credit is available to companies and individuals who invest in capital assets. The maximum credit of 10 percent of full value is available on qualified property with a useful life of seven or more years. (The useful life of an asset can be the same as that used for computing depreciation.) However, if the useful life of the asset is less than seven years, the tax credit is less than 10 percent. If the useful life is at least five but less than seven years, only two-thirds of the total investment qualifies. If the useful life is at least three years but less than five years, only one-third of the investment would qualify. Property with a useful life of less than three years is not eligible for the investment tax credit. The tax credit itself is available only at the time the property is placed in service.

In our example, the new machine has a useful life of five years and the total cost of purchase and installation is $20,000. Therefore two-thirds, or $13,333.33, is eligible for the investment tax credit. This means that the company receives a tax credit of $1,333.33 when the machine is placed in service at time 0. Assuming the company has sufficient taxable income to utilize the full tax credit, this means that it receives a cash inflow of $1,333.33 at time 0. Effectively, this reduces the net cash outflow at time 0 from $18,000 to $16,666.67.[7] This obviously enhances the profitability of the project. The net-present value becomes $3,228.48 + $1,333.33 = $4,561.81, compared with $3,228.48 with previous calculations (straight-line depreciation assumed). The internal rate of return becomes 20.2 percent compared with 16.8 percent before.

Salvage Value and Taxes

The cash-flow pattern also will differ from that shown in the example if the new machine is expected to have a salvage, or scrap, value at the end of the five-year period. When there is a salvage value, it may affect depreciation charges as well as the cash flow in the last year. Assume that the salvage value of the new machine is expected to be $2,000 at the end of the fifth year. The total depreciable value becomes $18,000 instead of $20,000; and, assuming straight-line depreciation, annual depreciation charges for the new machine become $3,600 instead of $4,000. If we follow through with the previous calculations, we find that the annual net cash flow for years 1 through 4 is $5,400 instead of $5,600. The net cash flow in the fifth year is $5,400, plus the salvage value of $2,000, or $7,400.

In addition to the salvage value, there are other tax considerations. If the machine can be sold for more than its depreciated book value, the

---

[7]The investment tax credit does not alter the basis for depreciation; it remains at $20,000.

difference is subject to income taxes if the sales price is less than the machine's original cost. For example, if the machine could be sold for $4,000 instead of $2,000, there would be a gain of $2,000. If the corporate tax rate were 50 percent, the total cash proceeds realized from the sale would be $4,000 − .50 ($2,000) = $3,000. As long as the gain is less than the total depreciation claimed, it is reported as fully taxable income. In our example, the machine cost $20,000 and $18,000 in depreciation is claimed through year 5. As the $2,000 gain is less than the total depreciation claimed, it is taxed at the ordinary corporate tax rate.

If the machine could be sold for $23,000, however, $18,000 of the total gain of $21,000 would be reported as fully taxable income, while $3,000 would be subject to the capital gains tax treatment, which usually is more favorable.[8] If the effective capital gains tax rate for the firm were 28 percent, there would be an $840 tax on the capital gain and a $9,000 tax on the $18,000 in ordinary income. In this case, the total cash proceeds realized from the sale of the machine would be $23,000 − $840 − $9,000 = $13,260. There are many other variations that we could illustrate, but these examples are enough to show that tax considerations are very important in calculating the cash flow.

Working-Capital Requirement

In addition to the investment in a fixed asset, in our example a machine, it is sometimes necessary to carry additional cash, receivables, or inventories. This investment in working capital is treated as a cash outflow at the time it occurs. For example, if $1,000 of additional inventory were required in connection with the new machine and the investment occurred at the outset, there would be an additional cash outflow of $1,000 at time 0, bringing the total outflow to $19,000. At the end of the project's life, the working-capital investment presumably is recaptured. Therefore there would be a $1,000 additional cash inflow in year 5. As a result, the cash inflow in that year would be $6,600 instead of $5,600.

If we solve for the net-present value using a 10 percent discount rate, it is

$$NPV = -19,000 + \frac{5,600}{(1.10)} + \frac{5,600}{(1.10)^2} + \frac{5,600}{(1.10)^3} + \frac{5,600}{(1.10)^4} + \frac{6,600}{(1.10)^5}$$

$$= \$2,849.34 \tag{5-10}$$

This compares with $3,228.48 before. The internal rate of return is 15.6 percent compared with 16.8 percent before. While the presence of a working-capital requirement does not affect the total cash flows, inasmuch as it is subtracted at the beginning and added at the end, it does affect the timing of cash flows and, hence, the net-present value and the internal rate of return.

---

[8]See *Federal Tax Course* (Englewood Cliffs, N.J.: Prentice-Hall, 1979), Chaps. 6 and 22.

Capital rationing occurs anytime there is a budget ceiling, or constraint, on the amount of funds that can be invested during a specific period of time, such as a year. Such constraints are prevalent in a number of firms, particularly in those that have a policy of financing all capital expenditures internally. Another example of capital rationing is when a division of a large company is allowed to make capital expenditures only up to a specified budget ceiling, over which the division usually has no control. With a capital-rationing constraint, the firm attempts to select the combination of investment proposals that will provide the greatest profitability.

To illustrate, suppose a firm had the following investment opportunities, ranked in descending order of profitability indexes (the ratio of the present value of future net cash flows over the initial cash outlay):

Proposal	4	7	2	3	6	5	1
Profitability index	1.25	1.19	1.16	1.14	1.09	1.05	0.97
Initial outlay	$400,000	$100,000	$175,000	$125,000	$200,000	$100,000	$150,000

If the budget ceiling for initial outlays during the present period were $1 million, and the proposals were independent of each other, we would select proposals in descending order of profitability until the budget was exhausted. With capital rationing, we would accept the first five proposals, totaling $1 million in initial outlays. In other words, we do not necessarily invest in all proposals that increase the net-present value of the firm; we invest in an acceptable proposal only if the budget constraint allows such an investment. In the above example, we do not invest in proposal 5, even though the profitability index in excess of 1.00 would suggest its acceptance. The critical aspect of the capital-rationing constraint illustrated is that capital expenditures during a period are strictly limited by the budget ceiling, regardless of the number of attractive investment opportunities.

Size of Initial Outlay
and Multiperiod Problems

Under capital rationing, the objective is to select the combination of investment proposals that provides the highest net-present value, subject to the budget constraint for the period. If this constraint is strictly enforced, it may be better to accept several smaller, less profitable proposals that allow full utilization of the budget than to accept one large proposal that results in part of the budget's being unused. Suppose that we had the following investment opportunities:

Proposal	3	1	2	4
Profitability index	1.15	1.13	1.11	1.08
Initial outlay	$200,000	$125,000	$175,000	$150,000

If the budget constraint were $300,000 for the period, we should accept proposals 1 and 2 rather than proposal 3, despite the fact that the profitability indexes are lower for the first two proposals. The total net-present value of proposals 1 and 2 is

$$
\begin{array}{lll}
\text{Proposal 1} & \$125,000(1.13 - 1) = & \$16,250 \\
\text{Proposal 2} & \$175,000(1.11 - 1) = & \underline{\$19,250} \\
& & \$35,500
\end{array}
$$

whereas the net-present value of proposal 3 is

$$
\text{Proposal 3} \quad \$200,000(1.15 - 1) = \$30,000
$$

The total net-present value of proposals 1 and 2 is higher than that of proposal 3 because we are able to use more of the available budget. Thus the "lumpiness" of the initial outlays makes full utilization of the budget an important consideration for the firm that rations capital. Implied in the evaluation above is that uninvested capital has a net-present value of 0; that is, it corresponds to an investment yielding the required rate of return. If the net-present value of uninvested capital is less, the full utilization of the budget becomes a more important consideration.

A fixed one-period constraint is highly artificial. Seldom will a budget be set so rigidly that it does not provide for some flexibility. In addition, the cost of certain investment projects may be spread over several years. Consequently, we must consider more than just a one-period constraint. With a multiperiod analysis, the postponement of investment proposals is possible. If there is an abundance of acceptable investment proposals this year, the least profitable may be postponed until a subsequent period when the budget will permit investment.

Moreover, a one-period analysis does not take account of intermediate cash flows generated by a project. Some projects provide relatively high net cash flows in the early years; these cash flows serve to reduce the budget constraints in the early years because they may be used to finance other investment projects. A project with net cash flows expected to occur entirely in the first several years may be more valuable to the firm than a project with an identical initial outlay and profitability index, but which is expected to produce net cash flows over a longer span of time. For the reason discussed above, we should consider more than one period in the allocation of limited capital to investment projects.

Opportunity Costs and Objections
to Capital Rationing

The cost to the firm of a budget ceiling might be regarded as the opportunity forgone on the next most profitable investment after the cutoff. In our first example, the opportunity forgone by the $1 million budget ceiling is proposal 5, which has a profitability index of 1.05. Though all cash flows are discounted at the required rate of return, we do not necessarily accept proposals that provide positive net-present values. Acceptance is determined by the budget constraint, which tells us which proposals can be accepted before the budget is exhausted. To be sure, the required rate of return sets a lower limit; we would not accept proposals yielding less than this required rate even if the budget were not exhausted.[9] However, we may reject projects that provide positive net-present values, as was shown with proposal 5. Under capital rationing, the required rate of return is not the acceptance criterion. Should it then be used as the discount rate in present-value calculations, or should the opportunity cost be used? The implied discount rate in any budget period is the yield foregone on the most profitable investment opportunity rejected, or the required rate of return, whichever is the higher.[10]

Capital rationing usually results in an investment policy that is less than optimal. In some periods, the firm accepts projects down to its required rate of return; in others, it may reject projects that would provide returns substantially in excess of the required rate. If the required rate of return corresponds to the project's cost of capital, and the firm actually can raise capital at that approximate real cost, should it not invest in all projects yielding more than the required rate of return? If it rations capital and does not invest in all projects yielding more than the required rate, is it not foregoing opportunities that would enhance the market price of its stock?

In the final analysis, the firm should accept all proposals yielding more than their required rate of return. By so doing, it should increase the market price per share because projects are accepted that will provide a return higher than that necessary to maintain the present market price per share. Certainly, there are circumstances that complicate the use of this rule. However, in general, this policy should tend to maximize the market price of the stock over the long run. If capital is rationed, and projects are rejected that would yield more than their real cost of capital, the firm's investment policy,

[9]The exception is contingent projects, as illustrated earlier.

[10]In a mathematical-programming approach, the opportunity rate for investment corresponds to the dual variable. Thus the discount rate depends upon the optimal solution which in turn depends upon the discount rate employed. For an analysis of this problem of mutual dependence and a review and analysis of the extensive literature dealing with the problem, see H. Martin Weingartner, "Capital Rationing: n Authors in Search of a Plot," *Journal of Finance*, 32 (December 1977), 1403–31. See also Stephen P. Bradley and Sherwood C. Frey, Jr., "Equivalent Mathematical Programming Models of Pure Capital Rationing," *Journal of Financial and Quantitative Analysis*, 13 (June 1978), 345–61.

by definition, is less than optimal. Management could increase the value of the firm to the shareholders by accepting these projects.

In situations of capital rationing, capital-budgeting decisions can be undertaken within a mathematical-programming framework. The principles of this approach are explored in Appendix B to this chapter.

INFLATION AND CAPITAL BUDGETING

In general, the presence of inflation in the economy distorts capital-budgeting decisions. The principal reason is that depreciation charges are based on original rather than replacement costs. As income grows with inflation, an increasing portion is taxed, with the result that real cash flows do not keep up with inflation. To illustrate, consider an investment proposal costing $24,000 under the assumption that no inflation is expected, that depreciation is straight line, and that the tax rate is 50 percent. The following cash flows are expected to occur:

Year	Cash Savings	Depreciation	Taxes	Cash Flow after Taxes
1	$10,000	$6,000	$2,000	$8,000
2	10,000	6,000	2,000	8,000
3	10,000	6,000	2,000	8,000
4	10,000	6,000	2,000	8,000

Depreciation is deducted from cash savings to obtain taxable income, on which taxes of 50 percent are based.[11] Without inflation, depreciation charges represent the "cost" of replacing the investment as it wears out. Because nominal income on which taxes are paid represents real income, the last column represents real cash flows after taxes. The internal rate of return which equates the present value of the cash inflows with the cost of the project is 12.6 percent.

Consider now a situation where inflation is at a rate of 7 percent per annum and cash savings are expected to grow at this overall rate of inflation. The after-tax cash flows become:

Year	Cash Savings	Depreciation	Taxes	Cash Flow after Taxes
1	$10,700	$6,000	$2,350	$8,350
2	11,449	6,000	2,725	8,724
3	12,250	6,000	3,125	9,125
4	13,108	6,000	3,554	9,554

[11]This example is similar to one in John A. Tatom and James E. Turley, "Inflation and Taxes: Disincentives for Capital Formation," *Review of the Federal Reserve Bank of St. Louis,* 60 (January 1978), 2–8.

While these cash flows are larger than before, they must be deflated by the inflation rate if one is concerned with the real as opposed to the nominal rate of return. Therefore the last column becomes:

	Year			
	1	2	3	4
Real after-Tax Cash Flow	$7,804	$7,620	$7,449	$7,289

As we see, the real after-tax cash flows are less than before and decline steadily over time. The reason is that depreciation charges do not change in keeping with inflation, so that an increasing portion of the tax savings is subject to taxation. As taxes increase at a rate faster than inflation, real after-tax cash flows must decline. The internal rate of return based on real after-tax cash flows is 9.9 percent compared with 12.6 percent without inflation.

Therefore the presence of inflation results in lower real rates of return.[12] Consequently, there is less incentive for companies to undertake capital investments. While the cash-flow situation is improved with accelerated depreciation, the same unfavorable comparisons hold. There simply is a disincentive for companies to undertake capital expenditures, with the result that the amount invested typically is less than it would be in the absence of inflation. It follows also that there will be an incentive to seek investments with faster paybacks (shorter economic lives) and that industry will become less capital intensive.[13]

The Bias in Cash-Flow Estimates

In estimating cash flows, it is important that the individual company take anticipated inflation into account. Often there is a tendency to assume that price levels remain unchanged throughout the life of the project. Frequently, this assumption is imposed unknowingly; future cash flows simply are estimated on the basis of existing prices. However, a bias arises in the selection process in that the required rate of return for the project is usually based on current capital costs, which in turn embody a premium for anticipated inflation.[14]

---

[12]In testing for the tax effect, Hai Hong, "Inflation and the Market Value of the Firm: Theory and Tests," *Journal of Finance,* 32 (September 1977), 1031–48, found that inflation affected stock prices through the additional tax burden on the firm. Therefore, there was a wealth transfer from corporations to the government.

[13]For an analysis of these points, see Charles R. Nelson, "Inflation and Capital Budgeting," *Journal of Finance,* 31 (June 1976), 923–31.

[14]This section is based on James C. Van Horne, "A Note on Biases in Capital Budgeting Introduced by Inflation," *Journal of Financial and Quantitative Analysis,* 6 (January 1971), 653–58.

Assume a situation where the hurdle rate for a project is its required rate of return as perceived by investors and creditors. (The ways by which it is measured are taken up in Chapter 7.) There is general agreement that security prices depend on anticipated changes in prices. In fact, over eighty years ago Irving Fisher expressed the nominal rate of interest on a financial instrument as the sum of the real rate and the rate of price change expected over the life of the instrument.[15] This observed phenomenon has come to be known as the *Fisher effect*.[16] Implied is that the required rate of return for a project is

$$R_j = R_j^* + \rho \qquad (5\text{-}11)$$

where R_j is the required rate of return in nominal terms, R_j^* is the required rate in real terms, and ρ is the weighted average anticipated rate of inflation over the life of the project.

If anticipated inflation is embodied in the acceptance criterion, it is important that it be reflected in the estimated cash flows for the project as well. The expected cash flows of a project are affected by anticipated inflation in several ways. If cash inflows ultimately arise from the sale of a product, these inflows are affected by expected future prices. As for cash outflows, inflation affects both expected future wages and material costs. Note that future inflation does not affect depreciation charges on existing assets. Once the asset is acquired, these charges are known with certainty. The effect of anticipated inflation on cash inflows and cash outflows will vary with the nature of the project. In some cases, cash inflows, through price increases, will rise faster than cash outflows; while in other cases the opposite will hold. No matter what the relationship, it is important that it be embodied in the cash-flow estimates. Otherwise, a bias of the type described before arises.

Illustration of Inflation Bias

To illustrate this bias, assume that a project that cost $100,000 at time 0 was under consideration and was expected to provide cash-flow benefits over the next five years. Assume further straight-line depreciation of $20,000 a year and corporate tax rate of 50 percent. Suppose that cash flows were estimated on the basis of price levels at time 0, with no consideration to the effect of future inflation upon them, and that these estimates were:

---

[15]*Appreciation and Interest* (New York: Macmillan, 1896).

[16]Strictly speaking, $1 + R_j = (1 + R_j^*)(1 + \rho)$, so $R_j = R_j^* + \rho + R_j^*\rho$. Inasmuch as the cross-product term usually is small, it is conventional to drop it from consideration. In the appendix to Chapter 9, we explore the Fisher effect in more detail. Our purpose now is just to point out the biases possible from lack of consideration of inflation in the cash-flow estimates.

	Period				
	1	2	3	4	5
Expected cash inflow, I_t	$30,000	$40,000	$50,000	$50,000	$30,000
Expected cash outflow, O_t	10,000	10,000	10,000	10,000	10,000
	$20,000	$30,000	$40,000	$40,000	$20,000
Times (1 − tax rate)	.50	.50	.50	.50	.50
	$10,000	$15,000	$20,000	$20,000	$10,000
Depreciation times tax rate	10,000	10,000	10,000	10,000	10,000
Net cash flow	$20,000	$25,000	$30,000	$30,000	$20,000

If the project's required rate of return were 10 percent, the net-present value of the project would be −$5,709. As this figure is negative, the project would be rejected.

However, the results are biased in the sense that the discount rate embodies an element attributable to anticipated future inflation, whereas the cash-flow estimates do not. Suppose that the existing rate of inflation, as measured by changes in the price-level index, were 5 percent, and that this rate was expected to prevail over the next five years. If both cash inflows and cash outflows were expected to increase at this rate, the net-present value of the project would be

$$NPV = \sum_{t=1}^{5} \frac{[I_t(1.05)^t - O_t(1.05)^t][.5] + 20,000_t[.5]}{(1.10)^t} - 100,000$$

(5-12)

$$= \$3,044$$

where I_t is the cash inflow in year t, O_t is the cash outflow in year t, and $20,000 is the annual depreciation in year t which is multiplied by the tax rate to give the tax-shield cash savings. Because the net-present value is positive, the project would be acceptable now, whereas before it was not. To reject it under the previous method of estimating cash flows would result in an opportunity loss to stockholders, for the project provides a return in excess of that required by investors.

The example serves to illustrate the importance of taking anticipated inflation into account explicitly when estimating future cash flows. Too often, there is a tendency not to consider its effect in these estimates. Because anticipated inflation is embodied in the required rate of return, not to take account of it in the cash-flow estimates will result in a biased appraisal of the project and, in turn, the possibility of a less than optimal allocation of capital.

A More Exacting Adjustment Method

It is possible, of course, that cash inflows and cash outflows will increase by more or less than the rate of inflation. If this is the case, one needs to employ a more complicated inflation adjustment formula than that illustrated in Eq. (5-12). One approach might be the following:

$$NPV = \sum_{t=1}^{n} \frac{[I_t(1 + \alpha\rho)^t - O_t(1 + \beta\rho)^t][1 - T] + F_t T}{(1 + k)^t} - C_o \tag{5-13}$$

where:

NPV = the expected value of net-present value of the project at time 0

n = final period in which cash flows are expected

I_t = expected value of cash inflow in period t in the absence of future inflation

ρ = anticipated rate of inflation as denoted by expected annual rate of change in the price index

α = portion of ρ applicable to cash inflows

O_t = expected value of cash outflows in period t in the absence of future inflation

β = portion of ρ applicable to cash outflows

T = corporate tax rate

F_t = depreciation charges on the asset in period t, which are known with certainty

C_o = cost of project at time 0, which is assumed to be known with certainty

The values α and β represent the expected sensitivity of cash inflows and outflows to inflation, assuming this sensitivity is invariant with respect to t. If the latter assumption does not hold, α and β can be made to vary with t. Added sophistication (in Eq. (5-13)) can be achieved by breaking down the cash inflows and cash outflows into individual components. For example, we might subdivide cash outflows into wages and material costs and calculate the sensitivity of each to ρ. If the project is expected to have a salvage value, the effect of inflation on this value must be recognized explicitly.

If a project has a net-present value greater than zero, as depicted by Eq. (5-13), it provides an inflation-adjusted return greater than that required by suppliers of capital. As a result, its acceptance should result in a higher market price per share. In the Appendix to Chapter 9, we will consider further the impact of inflation on the cost of financing. Our purpose in this chapter is to illustrate the problem from the standpoint of project selection and to propose an adjustment procedure.

SUMMARY

Capital budgeting involves the outlay of current funds in anticipation of cash-flow benefits to be realized in the future. Capital-budgeting decisions by corporations have a major impact on capital formation and on the economic growth of a country. An important topic taken up initially was the collection of cash-flow information essential for the evaluation of investment proposals. The key is to measure incremental cash flows with and without the investment proposal being analyzed. Later in the chapter the effects of accelerated depreciation, the investment tax credit, salvage value, and a working capital requirement on the pattern of cash flows were examined.

Capital-budgeting methods, including the average-rate-of-return and payback methods, were evaluated under the assumption that the acceptance of any investment proposal does not change the business-risk complexion of the firm as perceived by suppliers of capital. It was shown that the two discounted cash-flow methods—internal rate of return and net-present value—were the only appropriate means by which to judge the economic contribution of an investment proposal. The important distinction between the internal-rate-of-return method and the present-value method is the implied compounding rate and the scale of investment. Depending upon the situation, contrary answers can be given with respect to the acceptance of mutually exclusive investment proposals. On theoretical grounds, a case can be made for the superiority of the present-value method.

The problem of capital rationing was examined, and we concluded that such a policy is likely to result in investment decisions that are less than optimal. Inflation creates a disincentive for capital investment. The reason is that depreciation charges do not reflect replacement costs, with the result that a firm's taxes grow at a faster rate than inflation. In estimating cash flows, it is important to take account of anticipated inflation. Otherwise a bias arises and there is a tendency to reject some projects that should be accepted. This bias was illustrated and an adjustment formula was proposed.

Although the capital-budgeting methods discussed in this chapter appear to be very exact, it should be pointed out that we are able only to approximate the true value of an investment proposal to the firm. The meaningfulness of the values we calculate is only as good as our cash-flow estimates and the required rate of return employed. In the next chapter, we consider the cash-flow estimates in greater detail; in Chapters 7 and 8, we evaluate the required rate of return. Together, these chapters provide the basis for making sound investment decisions in keeping with the objective of maximizing the market price of the company's stock. In subsequent chapters, the link between investment in capital projects and the objective of the firm will become clearer.

APPENDIX A
Multiple Internal Rates of Return

In a well-known article, Lorie and Savage pointed out that certain streams of cash flows may have more than one internal rate of return.[17] To illustrate the problem, suppose that we had the following stream of cash flows corresponding to the "pump" proposal of Lorie and Savage:

---

[17]See James H. Lorie and Leonard J. Savage, "Three Problems in Rationing Capital," *Journal of Business,* 28 (October 1955), 229–39.

Year	0	1	2
Cash flow	−$1,600	$10,000	−$10,000

In this example, a new, more effective pump is substituted for an existing pump. On an incremental basis, there is an initial outlay followed by net cash inflows resulting from the increased efficiency of the new pump. If the quantity of oil, for example, is fixed, the new pump will exhaust this supply more quickly than the old pump would. Beyond this point of exhaustion, the new pump alternative would result in an incremental outflow, because the old pump would still be productive.

When we solve for the internal rate of return for the above cash-flow stream, we find that it is not one rate, but two: 25 percent and 400 percent. This unusual situation is illustrated in Figure 5-4, where the discount rate is plotted along the horizontal axis and net-present value along the vertical axis. At a 0 rate of discount, the net-present value of the project is simply the sum of all the cash flows. It is −$1,600 because total cash outflows exceed total cash inflows. As the discount rate increases, the present value of the second-year outflow diminishes with respect to the first-year inflow; and the present value of the proposal becomes positive when the discount rate exceeds 25 percent. As the discount rate increases beyond 100 percent, the present value of all future cash flows (years 1 and 2) diminishes relative to the initial outflow of −$1,600. At 400 percent, the present value of all cash flows again becomes 0.

This type of proposal differs from the usual case, shown in Figure 5-2 in this chapter, in which net-present value is a decreasing function of the discount rate, and in which there is but one internal rate of return that equates the present value of all inflows with the present value of all outflows.

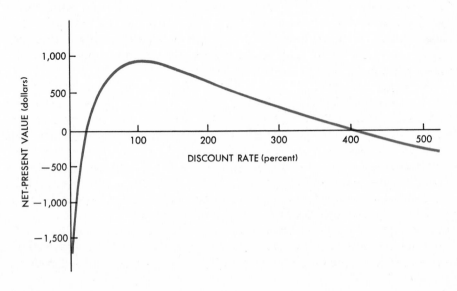

figure 5-4
Dual rates of return

An investment proposal may have any number of internal rates of return,

depending upon the cash-flow pattern. Consider the following series of cash flows:

Year	0	1	2	3
Cash flow	−$1,000	$6,000	−$11,000	$6,000

In this example, discount rates of 0, 100 percent, and 200 percent result in the net-present value of all cash flows equaling 0.

The number of internal rates of return is limited to the number of reversals of sign in the cash-flow stream. In the above example, we have three reversals and three internal rates of return. Although a multiple reversal in signs is a necessary condition for multiple internal rates of return, it is not sufficient for such an occurrence. The occurrence of multiple internal rates of return also depends upon the magnitude of cash flows. For the following series of cash flows, there is but one internal rate of return (32.5 percent), despite two reversals of sign:

Year	0	1	2
Cash flow	−$1,000	$1,400	−$100

We note that the equation for solving for the internal rate of return, Eq. (5-3), is an nth degree polynomial, having n years in which cash flows occur. Therefore the formula has n roots. For conventional investment proposals, only one of these roots is a real number and $n-1$ roots are imaginary. As a result, the proposal is said to have a *unique* internal rate of return. In other words, the net-present value line in Figure 5-3 crosses the zero line only once. With a nonconventional investment proposal, such as those illustrated, more than one of the roots is a real number, and the present-value line crosses the zero line more than once. For dual rates of return, for example, two of the roots are real numbers and $n-2$ roots are imaginary.

When confronted with a proposal having multiple rates of return, how does one decide which is the correct rate? In our dual-rate example, is the correct rate 25 percent or 400 percent? Actually, neither rate is correct, because neither is a measure of investment worth. In essence, the firm has "borrowed" $10,000 from the project at the end of year 1 and will pay it back at the end of year 2. The relevant question is, What is it worth to the firm now to have the use of $10,000 for one year beginning at the end of year 1? This question, in turn, depends upon the investment opportunities available to the firm for that period of time. If the firm could earn $2,000 on the use of these funds and realize these earnings at the end of the period, the value of this opportunity would be $2,000, to be received at the end of year 2. This amount would then be compared with the initial outlay of $1,600 to determine whether the project is worthwhile. Similarly, other proposals can be evaluated in this manner to determine whether they are worthwhile.[18]

APPENDIX B
Mathematical Programming of Capital Budgeting

Mathematical programming can be used to allocate capital under conditions of capital rationing.[19] A comprehensive treatment of the problem appears in Weingartner.[20] His basic model, which uses the Lorie-Savage problem as a point of departure, may be expressed as

Maximize $$\sum_{j=1}^{n} b_j x_j$$

Subject to $$\sum_{j=1}^{n} c_{tj} x_j \leq C_t \qquad \text{(5B-1)}$$

$$0 \leq x_j \leq 1$$

where b_j is net-present value of investment proposal j, x_j is an amount between 0 and 1, c_{tj} is the net cash outlay required for proposal j in period t, and C_t is the budget constraint in period t. In words, the model maximizes the net-present value from currently available investment proposals, given the budget constraint in each period.

To illustrate, consider the Lorie-Savage example, which involves budget constraints for two periods.[21] This example was employed by Weingartner, and it is shown in Table 5-1. The present values of the two budget constraints are $50 in period 1 and $20 in period 2. If the projects under consideration are independent, Eq. (5B-1) can be expressed as

Maximize

$$14x_1 + 17x_2 + 17x_3 + 15x_4 + 40x_5 + 12x_6 + 14x_7 + 10x_8 + 12x_9 \qquad \text{(5B-2)}$$

[18]For a rigorous analysis of the problem of multiple rates of return, see Daniel Teichroew, Alexander A. Robichek, and Michael Montalbano, "An Analysis of Criteria for Investment and Financing Decisions under Certainty," *Management Science*, 12 (November 1965), 151–79.

[19]This appendix supposes a familiarity with mathematical programming. It should be omitted if the reader does not have such familiarity.

[20]H. Martin Weingartner, *Mathematical Programming and the Analysis of Capital Budgeting Problems.* Copyright © H. Martin Weingartner, 1963.

[21]Lorie and Savage, "Three Problems in Rationing Capital," pp. 229–39.

table 5-1

Investment proposals available

Investment Project	Present Value of Outlay, Period 1	Present Value of Outlay, Period 2	Present Value of Investment
1	$12	$ 3	$14
2	54	7	17
3	6	6	17
4	6	2	15
5	30	35	40
6	6	6	12
7	48	4	14
8	36	3	10
9	18	3	12

Source: Lorie and Savage, "Three Problems in Rationing Capital."

Subject to

$$12x_1 + 54x_2 + 6x_3 + 6x_4 + 30x_5 + 6x_6 + 48x_7 + 36x_8 + 18x_9 \leq 50$$
$$3x_1 + 7x_2 + 6x_3 + 2x_4 + 35x_5 + 6x_6 + 4x_7 + 3x_8 + 3x_9 \leq 20$$
$$0 \leq x_j \leq 1, (x_j = 1, \ldots, 9)$$

The solution of this problem is shown in Table 5-2. From the table we see that, under the direct-problem variables, we should invest to the extent of 100 percent in projects 1, 3, 4, and 9; 97 percent in project 6; and 4.5 percent in project 7. Substituting these values into the objective function of Eq. (5B-2), the increase in present value from this optimal solution is found to be $70.27.

Weingartner analyzes the dual variables as the opportunity costs, or "shadow prices," of the budget constraints for the various future periods. These variables tell us the present value that can be gained if a budget constraint is relaxed by $1. For example, the dual variable of 0.136 for period 1 indicates that present value can be increased by $0.136 if the budget in period 1 is increased from $50 to $51; while the dual variable of 1.864 for period 2 indicates that present value can be increased by $1.864 if the budget is increased from $20 to $21. Dual variables are valuable in deciding whether to shift funds from one period to another and in evaluating the desirability and timing of external financing.

table 5-2

Optimal values for example problem

Direct	$X_1 = 1.0$	$X_2 = 0$	$X_3 = 1.0$	$X_4 = 1.0$	$X_5 = 0$	$X_6 = 0.97$	$X_7 = 0.045$	$X_8 = 0$	$X_9 = 1.0$
Dual*	$W_1 = 0.136$	$W_2 = 1.864$							

*W_1 and W_2 are the dual variables for the budget constraints in periods 1 and 2. The dual variables for the constraints, $0 \leq x_j \leq 1$, are not shown.

We note in this example problem that the investment projects are divisible in the sense that a partial undertaking of an investment proposal is possible. In the optimal program, both projects 6 and 7 were fractional. However, most investment projects are not divisible; they are either accepted, whereupon an absolute amount is invested, or rejected, in which case investment is 0. To deal with this problem, Weingartner develops an integer programming model by requiring the x_j to be an integer of either 0 or 1. Thus, fractional investment in a proposal is precluded by virtue of the fact that the x_j is an "either/or" variable. For the example problem, the optimal solution using integer programming calls for accepting projects 1, 3, 4, 6, and 9. When compared with Table 5-2, we see that the solutions are quite similar.

The model can also be modified to take account of mutually exclusive and contingent projects. If investment projects 1, 4, and 5 were mutually exclusive, for example, we could simply add the constraint $x_1 + x_4 + x_5 \leq 1$. With integer programming and this constraint, we are assured that only one of these projects will appear in the final solution. If project 2 is contingent upon the acceptance of project 3, the constraint $x_2 \leq x_3$ would assure that this contingency was recognized in the solution.

In addition, the model can be extended to handle manpower and other constraints of this type. For a labor constraint

$$\sum_{j=1}^{n} d_{jt} x_j \leq L_t \qquad (5B\text{-}3)$$

where d_{jt} is the number of man-hours of a certain type labor input required for project j in period t; and L_t is the number of such hours available in that period. Restrictions for other scarce resources also can be formulated in this manner. Moreover, the model can be expanded to allow for liquidity requirements in various periods and for the reinvestment of intermediate cash flows from one investment project into other projects. The model also can be adapted to situations of borrowing funds in the external market, subject to certain constraints. For the deterministic case, then, the integer programming technique can be realistically adapted to many "real-world" constraints.

The principal difficulty of mathematical programming approaches to capital budgeting, however, is that they are based upon the assumption that all future investment opportunities are known. In reality, the generation of investment opportunities is an unfolding process. Consequently, the budget constraints for other than the earliest years are not likely to be binding. There simply are not enough known investment opportunities. Only as new investment proposals are generated are these budgets likely to be fully utilized. Therefore the selection process must be revised continually. As new proposals are generated, they should be evaluated on a consistent basis.

Most programming approaches for capital budgeting do not allow for uncertainty in the cash-flow estimates. Attempts have been made to introduce probabilistic concepts through chance constraint programming. With chance constraints, lower levels of cash flows must be satisfied with some minimum probability. It is possible also to specify chance constraints for the net-present value of a combination of investment projects. Overall, the treatment of uncertainty in this manner has not been particularly satisfactory, primarily because of the lack of realism. More encompassing results with respect to the full range of possible outcomes can be achieved with simulation. Another problem is the assumption of capital rationing and the resulting issue of investment decisions that are less than optimal. This issue was discussed earlier in the chapter. Despite these limitations, however, mathematical programming provides a systematic and comprehensive means for screening investment projects.

PROBLEMS

1. The Symington Corporation is considering investing in one of two mutually exclusive projects. Each requires an immediate cash outlay of $1,000. Project A has a life of four years; project B, five years. Both projects will be depreciated on a straight-line basis (no salvage). The firm's tax rate is 50 percent, and its required return is 10 percent. Net cash flows before taxes generated by each investment have been projected as follows:

Years	1	2	3	4	5
A	$300	$300	$400	$400	0
B	$300	$300	$200	$200	$200

   (a) Compute the payback for each investment.
   (b) Compute the average rate of return for each investment.
   (c) Compute the profitability index for each investment.
   (d) Which alternative would you select? Why?

2. What criticisms may be offered against the average-rate-of-return method as a capital-budgeting technique? What criticisms may be offered against the payback method?

3. A company can make either of two investments at period p_0. Assuming a required rate of return of 10 percent, determine for each project: (a) the payback period, (b) the profitability index, (c) the internal rate of return. You may assume straight-line depreciation.

	A	B
Investment	$20,000	$28,000
Expected life		
(no salvage)	5 yrs.	5 yrs.
Projected net income after taxes		
Year 1	$ 5,000	$ 8,000
Year 2	5,000	8,000
Year 3	6,000	8,000
Year 4	6,000	8,000
Year 5	6,000	8,000

4. Two mutually exclusive projects have projected cash flows as follows:

Period	0	1	2	3	4
A	−$10,000	$5,000	$5,000	$5,000	$5,000
B	−$10,000	0	0	0	$30,000

(a) Determine the internal rate of return for each project.
(b) Assuming a required rate of return of 10 percent, determine the present value for each project.
(c) Which project would you select? Why? What assumptions are inherent in your decision?

5. The Homes Corporation is faced with two mutually exclusive investment proposals. One would cost $100,000 and provide net cash benefits of $30,000 per year for five years. The other would cost $50,000 and provide net cash benefits of $16,000 for five years. Homes has a 10 percent after-tax opportunity cost of funds. Compute the net-present value and profitability index of each project. Which should be accepted?

6. Rework problem 5, assuming a 17 percent opportunity cost of funds. How would this change your answer?

7. Hi Grade Tool Company is faced with the prospect of having to replace a large stamping machine. Two machines currently being marketed will do the job satisfactorily. The Superior Stamping machine costs $50,000 and will require cash operating expenses of $20,000 per year. The Peerless machine costs $75,000, but operating expenses are only $15,000 per year. Both machines have a ten-year useful life with no salvage value and would be depreciated on a straight-line basis. An investment tax credit is available at the time either machine is purchased and placed in service.

(a) If the company pays taxes at a 50 percent rate and has a 12 percent after-tax required rate of return, which machine should be purchased?
(b) Would your answer be different if the required return were 8 percent?

8. Rework problem 7, assuming that the Peerless machine has a $10,000 salvage value at the end of year 10 and that the Superior machine has a $5,000 salvage value. Do your answers change? (In both cases, salvage value represents the book value of the machine after ten years.)

9. The city of San Jose must replace a number of its concrete mixer trucks with new trucks. It has received several bids and has closely evaluated the performance characteristics of the various trucks. Each Patterbilt truck costs $74,000, but it is "top-of-the-line" equipment. The truck has a life of eight years, assuming that the engine is rebuilt in the fifth year. Maintenance costs of $2,000 a year are expected in the first four years, followed by total maintenance and rebuilding costs of $13,000 in the fifth year. During the last three years, maintenance costs are expected to be $4,000 a year. At the end of eight years, the truck will have an estimated scrap value of $9,000.

A bid from Bulldog Trucks, Inc., is for $59,000 a truck. However, maintenance costs for this truck will be higher. In the first year, they are expected to be $3,000 and this amount is expected to increase by $1,500 a year through the eighth year. In year 4, the engine will need to be rebuilt and this will cost the company $15,000 in addition to maintenance costs in that year. At the end of eight years, the Bulldog truck will have an estimated scrap value of $5,000.

The last bidder, Best Tractor and Trailer Company, has agreed to sell Lawton Transit trucks at $44,000 each. Maintenance costs in the first four years are expected to be $4,000 the first year and to increase by $1,000 a year. For Lawton Transit Company's purposes, the truck has a life of only four years. At that time, it can be traded in for a new Best truck which is expected to cost $52,000. The likely trade-in value of the old truck is $15,000. During years 5 through 8, the second truck is expected to have maintenance costs of $5,000 in year 5 and these are expected to increase by $1,000 each year. At the end of eight years, the second truck is expected to have a resale or salvage value of $18,000.

(a) If the city of San Jose's cost of funds is 8 percent, which bid should it accept? Ignore any tax considerations, as the city pays no taxes.

(b) If its opportunity cost were 15 percent, would your answer change?

10. Los Morale Corporation is considering a small business computer costing $70,000. The presence of this machine is expected to save one full-time clerical worker and one part-time worker at an annual savings of $20,000. The computer has a useful life of seven years, and a 10 percent investment tax credit is available at the time the computer is placed in service. The company's marginal tax rate is 40 percent, and the after-tax required rate of return on the project is 13 percent.

(a) Using straight-line depreciation, what is the project's net-present value?

(b) If sum-of-the-years'-digits depreciation were used, what would be its net-present value? Why does your answer to (b) differ from that to (a)?

(c) If a working-capital investment of $5,000 were required in addition to the cost of the computer and this additional requirement were needed over the life of the project, what is the effect on net-present value? (Assume straight-line depreciation.)

11. The Platte River Perfect Cooker Company is evaluating three investment situations: (1) produce a new line of aluminum skillets; (2) expand its existing cooker line to include several new sizes; and (3) develop a new higher-quality line of cookers. The amounts of investment required, after taking all investment tax credits, and the expected present values, if only the project in question is undertaken, are:

Project	Investment Required	Present Value of Future Cash Flows
1	$200,000	$290,000
2	115,000	185,000
3	270,000	400,000

If projects 1 and 2 are jointly undertaken, there will be no economies; the investment required and present values will simply be the sum of the parts. With projects 1 and 3, economies are possible in investment because one of the machines acquired can be used in both production processes. The total investment required for projects 1 and 3 combined is $440,000. If projects 2 and 3 are undertaken, there are economies to be achieved in marketing and producing the products but not in investment. The expected present value of future cash flows for projects 2 and 3 is $620,000. If all three projects are undertaken simultaneously, the economies noted above will still hold. However, a $125,000 extension on the plant will be necessary, as space is not available for all three projects. Which project or projects should be chosen?

12. The Lake Tahoe Ski Resort is considering a half dozen capital improvement projects. It has allocated $1 million for capital-budgeting purposes. The following proposals and associated profitability indexes have been determined. The projects themselves are independent of one another.

Project	Amount	Profitability Index
1. Extend ski lift #3	$500,000	1.22
2. Build a new sports shop	150,000	0.95
3. Extend ski lift #4	350,000	1.20
4. Build a new restaurant	450,000	1.18
5. Addition to housing complex	200,000	1.20
6. Build an indoor skating rink	400,000	1.05

(a) With strict capital rationing, which of the above investments should be undertaken?
(b) Is this an optimal strategy?

13. Rioka Corporation is considering investing in a project that costs $100,000 and has a useful life of five years. The expected cash flows from the project are:

		Year		
1	2	3	4	5
$20,000	$40,000	$40,000	$30,000	$20,000

The company's tax rate is 50 percent, and its cost of capital based on present conditions in the financial markets is 12 percent. The company uses straight-line depreciation.

(a) Compute the net-present value of the project without the consideration of inflation.
(b) If inflation of 7 percent per annum is expected over the life of the project and cash flows are adjusted upward, what is the project's net-present value?

14. An investment has an outlay of $800 today, an inflow of $5,000 at the end of one year, and an outflow of $5,000 at the end of two years. What is its internal rate of return? If the initial outlay were $1,250, what would be its IRR? (*Hint:* This case is an exception rather than the rule.)

15. An investment has an inflow of $200 today, an outflow of $300 at the end of one year, and an inflow of $400 at the end of two years. What is its internal rate of return?

BACON, PETER W., "The Evaluation of Mutually Exclusive Investments," *Financial Management,* 6 (Summer 1977), 55–58.

BEEDLES, WILLIAM L., "A Note on Evaluating Non-Simple Investments," *Journal of Financial and Quantitative Analysis,* 13 (March 1978), 173–76.

BERNHARD, RICHARD H., "Mathematical Programming Models for Capital Budgeting—A Survey, Generalization, and Critique," *Journal of Financial and Quantitative Analysis,* 4 (June 1969), 111–58.

BIERMAN, HAROLD, JR., AND SEYMOUR SMIDT, *The Capital Budgeting Decision,* 4th ed. New York: Macmillan, 1975.

BRADLEY, STEPHEN P., AND SHERWOOD C. FREY, JR., "Equivalent Mathematical Programming Models of Pure Capital Rationing," *Journal of Financial and Quantitative Analysis,* 13 (June 1978), 345–61.

CARTER, E. EUGENE, "Designing the Capital Budgeting Process, *TIMS Studies in the Management Sciences,* 5 (1977), 25–42.

ELTON, EDWIN J., "Capital Rationing and External Discount Rates," *Journal of Finance,* 25 (June 1970), 573–84.

FOGLER, H. RUSSELL, "Ranking Techniques and Capital Rationing," *Accounting Review,* 47 (January 1972), 134–43.

GITMAN, LAWRENCE J., AND JOHN R. FORRESTER, JR., "Forecasting and Evaluation Practices and Performance: A Survey of Capital Budgeting," *Financial Management,* 6 (Fall 1977), 66–71.

HERBST, ANTHONY, "The Unique, Real Internal Rate of Return: Caveat Emptor!" *Journal of Financial and Quantitative Analysis,* 13 (June 1978), 363–70.

HONG, HAI, "Inflation and the Market Value of the Firm: Theory and Tests," *Journal of Finance,* 32 (September 1977), 1031–48.

KLAMMER, THOMAS, "Empirical Evidence of the Adoption of Sophisticated Capital Budgeting Techniques," *Journal of Business,* 45 (July 1972), 387–97.

LEVY, HAIM, AND MARSHALL SARNAT, *Capital Investment and Financial Decisions.* Englewood Cliffs, N.J.: Prentice-Hall International, 1978.

LORIE, JAMES H., AND LEONARD J. SAVAGE, "Three Problems in Rationing Capital," *Journal of Business,* 28 (October 1955), 227–39.

NELSON, CHARLES R., "Inflation and Capital Budgeting," *Journal of Finance,* 31 (June 1976), 923–31.

PETTY, J. WILLIAM, AND OSWALD D. BOWLIN, "The Financial Manager and Quantitative Decision Models," *Financial Management,* 4 (Winter 1976), 32–41.

PETTY, J. WILLIAM, DAVID F. SCOTT, JR., AND MONROE M. BIRD, "The Capital Expenditure Decision-Making Process of Large Corporations," *Engineering Economist,* 20 (Spring 1975), 159–72.

SARNAT, MARSHALL, AND HAIM LEVY, "The Relationship of Rules of Thumb to the Internal Rate of Return: A Restatement and Generalization," *Journal of Finance,* 24 (June 1969), 479–89.

SCHALL, LAWRENCE D., GARY L. SUNDEM, AND WILLIAM R. GEIJSBEEK, JR., "Survey and Analysis of Capital Budgeting Methods," *Journal of Finance,* 33 (March 1978), 281–87.

SCHNELL, JAMES S., AND ROY S. NICOLOSI, "Capital Expenditure Feedback: Project Reappraisal," *Engineering Economist,* 19 (Summer 1974), 253–61.

SCHWAB, BERNHARD, AND PETER LUSZTIG, "A Comparative Analysis of the Net Present Value and the Benefit-Cost Ratios as Measures of the Economic Desirability of Investments," *Journal of Finance,* 24 (June 1969), 507–16.

SOLOMON, EZRA, "The Arithmetic of Capital-Budgeting Decisions," *Journal of Business,* 29 (April 1956), 124–29.

————, *The Theory of Financial Management.* New York: Columbia University Press, 1963.

TATOM, JOHN A., AND JAMES E. TURLEY, "Inflation and Taxes: Disincentives for Capital Formation," *Review of the Federal Reserve Bank of St. Louis,* 60 (January 1978), 2–8.

TEICHROEW, DANIEL, ALEXANDER A. ROBICHEK, AND MICHAEL MONTALBANO, "An Analysis of Criteria for Investment and Financing Decisions under Certainty," *Management Science,* 12 (November 1965), 151–79.

VAN HORNE, JAMES C., "Capital Budgeting under Conditions of Uncertainty as to Project Life," *Engineering Economist,* 17 (Spring 1972), 189–99.

————, "A Note on Biases in Capital Budgeting Introduced by Inflation," *Journal of Financial and Quantitative Analysis,* 6 (March 1971).

————, "The Variation of Project Life as a Means for Adjusting for Risk," *Engineering Economist,* 21 (Spring 1976), 151–58.

WEAVER, JAMES B., "Organizing and Maintaining a Capital Expenditure Program," *Engineering Economist,* 20 (Fall 1974), 1–36.

WEINGARTNER, H. MARTIN, "Capital Budgeting of Interrelated Projects: Survey and Synthesis," *Management Science,* 12 (March 1966), 485–516.

————, "Capital Rationing: n Authors in Search of a Plot," *Journal of Finance,* 32 (December 1977), 1403–31.

————, *Mathematical Programming and the Analysis of Capital Budgeting Problems.* Copyright © H. Martin Weingartner, 1963.

————, "Some New Views on the Payback Period and Capital Budgeting Decisions," *Management Science,* 15 (August 1969), 594–607.

WHISLER, WILLIAM D., "Sensitivity Analysis of Rates of Return," *Journal of Finance,* 31 (March 1976), 63–70.

6

risk analysis in capital budgeting

In the preceding chapter, we assumed that acceptance of any investment proposal or group of proposals did not alter the business-risk complexion of the firm as perceived by suppliers of capital. This assumption allowed us to work with the expected values of projected cash flows, thereby facilitating greatly the introduction of capital budgeting. We know, however, that different investment proposals have different degrees of risk. If the acceptance of an investment proposal or group of proposals alters the business-risk complexion of the firm, investors and creditors are likely to view the company differently before and after the acceptance of the proposal(s). Consequently, the total valuation of the company may change. In evaluating investment proposals, a firm should take into account the effect that their acceptance will have on its perceived risk, as envisioned by investors and creditors.

Chapters 6 through 8 constitute a package when it comes to the impact of risky investments on the valuation of the firm. In this chapter, we take up the kinds of information necessary to evaluate risky investment opportunities. In Chapters 7 and 8, we discuss the use of this information in reaching capital investment decisions. It is important to stress that this chapter is concerned with ways of quantifying risk for the project, for groups of projects, and for potential acquisitions. It does not enable one to make accept/reject decisions. This comes in the two subsequent chapters where we link the risk information provided in this chapter with the rates of return required by suppliers of capital. First we need information about the risk involved in a particular investment proposal or proposals, and then we must reach a decision with respect to its (their) desirability. This chapter is concerned with the first part. It is only when Chapters 6 through 8 are viewed collectively that statements as to the worth of an investment can be made.

INTRODUCTION

The riskiness of an investment proposal is defined in this book as the variability of its possible returns. Decision situations may be broken down into three types: certainty, risk, and uncertainty. The distinction between risk and uncertainty is that risk involves situations in which the probabilities of a particular event occurring are known; whereas with uncertainty, these probabilities are not known.[1] The problems we analyze in this chapter involve risk situations, although frequently the terms *risk* and *uncertainty* are used interchangeably. A wide range of factors gives rise to risk in capital investments. The economy in general, economic factors peculiar to investment, competition, technological development, consumer preferences, and labor conditions, as well as other factors, make it impossible to foretell the future. Consequently, the revenues, costs, and economic life of a particular investment are less than certain.

With the introduction of risk, a firm no longer may be indifferent between two investment proposals having the same net-present values or internal rates of return as was the case in Chapter 5. These measures of profitability are based only upon the expected values of the possible cash flows in various future periods. Suppose that we had two investments proposals, each costing $8,000 at time 0 and having expected cash inflows of $4,000 in each of the next three years, after which no cash flows or salvage values were expected. According to the discussion in previous chapters, the firm would rank these two proposals equally. However, suppose the probability distributions of the annual cash flows were those shown in Figure 6-1.

Can we conclude that the value of each of these investment opportunities is the same when the dispersion of the probability distribution of possible cash flows for proposal *A* is greater than that for proposal *B*? If risk is associated with the deviation of actual outcome from that which was expected, proposal *A* is the riskier investment. It is clear that risk is important and must be incorporated into out analysis.

[1]See R. Duncan Luce and Howard Raiffa, *Games and Decisions* (New York: John Wiley, 1957), p. 13.

figure 6-1
Comparison
of probability
distributions

Standard Deviation and Expected Value

What is needed is a measure of risk that gives information about the dispersion or tightness of the probability distribution. We know from Chapter 2 that the conventional measure of dispersion is the standard deviation, which, for a single period's possible outcome, is

$$\sigma = \sqrt{\sum_{x=1}^{n} (A_{xt} - \overline{A}_t)^2 P_{xt}} \qquad (6\text{-}1)$$

where A_{xt} is a cash flow for the xth possibility in period t, P_{xt} is the probability of occurrence of that cash flow, and $\overline{A}_t$ is the expected value of cash flows in period t. The square of the standard deviation, σ^2, is the variance. The expected value is calculated by

$$\overline{A}_t = \sum_{x=1}^{n} A_{xt} P_{xt} \qquad (6\text{-}2)$$

To illustrate these concepts, suppose two investment proposals, call them C and D, have the following discrete probability distribution of expected cash flows in each of the next three years:

Proposal C		Proposal D	
Probability	Cash Flow	Probability	Cash Flow
0.10	$3,000	0.10	$2,000
0.20	3,500	0.25	3,000
0.40	4,000	0.30	4,000
0.20	4,500	0.25	5,000
0.10	5,000	0.10	6,000

The expected value of cash flows in each of the next three years for proposal C is

$$\overline{A} = 0.10(3{,}000) + 0.20(3{,}500) + 0.40(4{,}000) + 0.20(4{,}500) + 0.10(5{,}000)$$
$$= \$4{,}000$$

which is the same as that for proposal D:

$$\overline{A} = 0.10(2{,}000) + 0.25(3{,}000) + 0.30(4{,}000) + 0.25(5{,}000) + 0.10(6{,}000)$$
$$= \$4{,}000$$

However, the standard deviation for proposal C is

$$\sigma = [0.10(3{,}000 - 4{,}000)^2 + 0.20(3{,}500 - 4{,}000)^2 + 0.40(4{,}000 - 4{,}000)^2$$
$$+ 0.20(4{,}500 - 4{,}000)^2 + 0.10(5{,}000 - 4{,}000)^2]^{1/2}$$
$$= [300{,}000]^{1/2}$$
$$= \$548$$

while that for proposal D is

$$\sigma = [0.10(2{,}000 - 4{,}000)^2 + 0.25(3{,}000 - 4{,}000)^2 + 0.30(4{,}000 - 4{,}000)^2$$
$$+ 0.25(5{,}000 - 4{,}000)^2 + 0.10(6{,}000 - 4{,}000)^2]^{1/2}$$
$$= [1{,}300{,}000]^{1/2}$$
$$= \$1{,}140$$

Thus proposal D has a significantly higher standard deviation, indicating a greater dispersion of possible outcomes.

A measure of relative dispersion is the *coefficient of variation*, which simply is the standard deviation of the probability distribution over its expected value. This coefficient serves as a relative measure of the degree of business risk. Because the coefficient of variation for proposal D, 0.29, is greater than that for proposal C, 0.14, we would say that proposal D had the greater degree of risk. Resort to a relative measure of risk is necessary if a comparison between projects involves considerably different absolute magnitudes of expected value and standard deviation. Frequent reference will be made to these concepts in the remainder of this chapter.

MEASURING RISK: CORRELATION OF CASH FLOWS OVER TIME

The preceding discussion points to the importance of risk in capital budgeting. In the remainder of this chapter, we consider ways to measure it under varying assumptions as to cash-flow behavior. The idea is to develop pertinent information about the expected value and dispersion of the probability distribution of possible returns. We begin by considering a single project where the cash flows are independent from period to period. Our concern

is with measuring the overall riskiness of an investment proposal when
the probability distributions of cash-flow outcomes for different periods
are not necessarily the same. Figure 6-2 illustrates this idea. As can be seen,
both the expected value of cash flow and the dispersion of the probability
distributions change over time. Once we have presented the basic method
of analysis under the assumption of independent probability distributions,
we will move on to consider varying degrees of correlation of cash flows
over time in the remainder of the chapter.

Assumption of Independence

With independence of cash flows over time, the outcome in period t
does not depend upon what happened in period $t - 1$. Stated differently,
there is no causative relationship between cash flows from period to period.[2]
The expected value of the probability distribution of possible net-present
values for a proposal is

$$NPV = \sum_{t=0}^{n} \frac{\overline{A}_t}{(1 + i)^t}$$

(6-3)

where $\overline{A}_t$ is the expected value of net cash flow in period t, i is the risk-free
rate, and n is the number of periods over which cash flows are expected.

The risk-free rate is used at this time as the discount rate because we
attempt to isolate the time value of money. To include a premium for risk

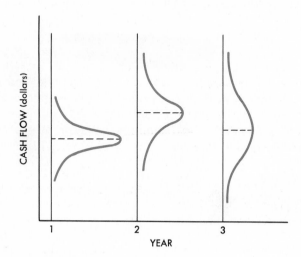

figure 6-2
**Illustration of
changing risk over
time**

[2]For a discussion of this assumption as well as those for perfect correlation and partial
dependency, see Lynn E. Bussey and G. T. Stevens, Jr., "Formulating Correlated Cash Flow
Streams," *Engineering Economist*, 18 (Fall 1972), 10–14.

in the discount rate would result in double counting with respect to our analysis. The required rate of return for a project embodies a premium for risk. If this rate is used as the discount rate, we would be adjusting for risk in the discounting process itself. (The greater the discount rate, the greater the risk adjustment, assuming a constant risk-free rate.) We then would use the probability distribution of net-present values to judge the risk of the proposal. However, the probability distribution is obtained using a risk-adjusted discount rate. In essence we would adjust for risk a second time in our analysis of the dispersion of the probability distribution of possible net-present values. Because of the problems inherent in double counting for risk, we take account only of the time value of money in the discounting process.[3]

Given the assumption of serial independence of cash flows for various future periods, the standard deviation of the probability distribution of net-present values is

$$\sigma = \sqrt{\sum_{t=0}^{n} \frac{\sigma_t^2}{(1+i)^{2t}}} \tag{6-4}$$

where σ_t is the standard deviation of the probability distribution of possible net cash flows in period t. To illustrate the calculations involved with Eq. (6-3) and Eq. (6-4), suppose that we had an investment proposal costing $10,000 at time 0 that was expected to generate net cash flows during the first three periods with the probabilities shown in Table 6-1. The expected values of net cash flows for periods 1, 2, and 3 are $5,000, $4,000, and $3,000, respectively. The standard deviation of possible cash flows for period t, σ_t, is computed by

$$\sigma_t = \sqrt{\sum_{x=1}^{5} (A_{xt} - \overline{A}_t)^2 P_{xt}} \tag{6-5}$$

where A_{xt} is the xth possible net cash flow, $\overline{A}_t$ is the expected value of net cash flow for period t, and P_{xt} is the probability of occurrence of A_{xt}.

In the above example, the standard deviation of possible net cash flows for period 1 is

$$\begin{aligned} \sigma_1 &= [0.10(3{,}000 - 5{,}000)^2 + 0.25(4{,}000 - 5{,}000)^2 + 0.30(5{,}000 - 5{,}000)^2 \\ &\quad + 0.25(6{,}000 - 5{,}000)^2 + 0.10(7{,}000 - 5{,}000)^2]^{1/2} \\ &= \$1{,}140 \end{aligned} \tag{6-6}$$

---

[3]This is not to say that for purposes of reaching an accept or reject decision the expected values of cash flows should be discounted at the risk-free rate. Indeed, in Chapter 7, we show that the appropriate discount rate is the required rate of return, which embodies a premium for the project's risk. For discounting the dispersion of the distribution, however, we use the risk-free rate for the above-mentioned reasons.

table 6-1
Expected cash flows for example problem

Period 1		Period 2		Period 3	
Probability	Net Cash Flow	Probability	Net Cash Flow	Probability	Net Cash Flow
0.10	$3,000	0.10	$2,000	0.10	$1,000
0.25	4,000	0.25	3,000	0.25	2,000
0.30	5,000	0.30	4,000	0.30	3,000
0.25	6,000	0.25	5,000	0.25	4,000
0.10	7,000	0.10	6,000	0.10	5,000

Because the probability distributions for periods 2 and 3 have the same dispersion about their expected values as that for period 1, σ_2 and σ_3 are $1,140 also. Given this information, we are able to calculate the expected value of net-present value for the proposal as well as the standard deviation about this expected value. If we assume a risk-free rate of 4 percent, the expected value of net-present value for the proposal is

$$NPV = -10,000 + \frac{5,000}{(1.04)} + \frac{4,000}{(1.04)^2} + \frac{3,000}{(1.04)^3} = \$1,173 \tag{6-7}$$

Using Eq. (6-4), under the assumption of mutual independence of cash flows over time, the standard deviation about the expected value is

$$\sigma = \sqrt{\frac{1,140^2}{(1.04)^2} + \frac{1,140^2}{(1.04)^4} + \frac{1,140^2}{(1.04)^6}} = \$1,827 \tag{6-8}$$

how to calculate?

Standardizing the Dispersion

The expected value and the standard deviation of the probability distribution of possible net-present values give us a considerable amount of information by which to evaluate the risk of the investment proposal. If the probability distribution is approximately normal, we are able to calculate the probability of a proposal's providing a net-present value of less or more than a specified amount. The probability is found by determining the area under the curve to the left or to the right of a particular point of interest. Suppose that we had the normal probability distribution shown in Figure 6-3, where the expected value is 10. If we were concerned with the probability that the actual outcome would be less than 5, it is represented by the shaded area under the curve to the left of 5. On the other hand, if our concern is with the probability that the actual outcome will be greater than 20, it is represented by the shaded area to the right of 20.

To go to our previous, more specific illustration, suppose we wish to determine the probability that the net-present value will be zero or less. To

figure 6-3
Area under the curve
for a normal
distribution

determine this probability, we first calculate the difference between zero and the expected value of net-present value for the project. In our example, this difference is −$1,173. We then standardize this difference by dividing it by the standard deviation of possible net-present values. The formula is

$$S = \frac{X - NPV}{\sigma}$$

(6-9)

where X is the outcome in which we are interested, NPV is the expected value, and σ the standard deviation of the probability distribution. In our case,

$$S = \frac{0 - 1,173}{1,827} = -0.642$$

This figure tells us that a net-present value of 0 lies 0.642 standard deviations to the left of the expected value of the probability distribution of possible net-present values.

To determine the probability that the net-present value of the project will be zero or less, we consult a normal probability distribution table found in Appendix B at the end of this book. (More detailed tables are found in most statistics texts.) With respect to the problem at hand, we find that there is a 0.26 probability that an observation will be less than −0.642 standard deviations from the expected value of that distribution. Thus there is a 0.26 probability that the net-present value of the proposal will be zero or less. Put another way, there is a 0.26 probability that the internal rate of return of the project will be less than the risk-free rate. If we assume a continuous distribution, the probability density function of our example problem can be shown in Figure 6-4.

The mean of the probability distribution of possible net-present values is $1,173. One standard deviation on either side of the mean gives us net-present values of −$654 and $3,000. With a normal distribution, 0.683 of the distribution or area under the curve falls within one standard deviation

figure 6-4
Probability density
function, example
problem

on either side of the mean or expected value.[4] Thus we know that there is approximately a two-thirds probability that the net-present value of the proposal examined will be between −$654 and $3,000. We know also that there is a 0.26 probability that the net-present value will be less than 0 and a 0.74 probability that it will be greater than 0. By expressing differences from the expected value in terms of standard deviations, we are able to determine the probability that the net-present value for an investment proposal will be greater or less than a particular amount.

Knowledge of these probabilities is fundamental for a realistic assessment of risk. For example, suppose that the firm is considering another investment project, proposal Y. The probability density function for this proposal is shown in Figure 6-5, as is that for our example problem, proposal X. We see that the expected value of net-present value for proposal Y, $2,200, is higher than that for proposal X, $1,173; but there is also greater dispersion of the probability distribution about the expected value. If risk is directly

figure 6-5
Probability
distributions of net-
present values for
proposals X and Y

[4]Approximately 0.954 of a normal distribution falls within two standard deviations on either side of the mean, and 0.997 within three standard deviations.

related to dispersion, proposal Y has both a higher expected profitability and a greater risk than does proposal X.

Information Generated

The approach outlined above can be adapted to internal rates of return. What is involved is expression of the distribution in terms of possible internal rates of return as opposed to net-present values. By varying the discount rate, *i,* in Eq. (6-4), one obtains standard deviations for different discount rates. For each standard deviation, the probability that net-present value will be zero or less can be computed. These probabilities then are plotted with the discount rate along the horizontal axis in ascending order and with the corresponding probabilities on the vertical axis. A probability distribution of possible internal rates of return emerges from which the expected value and standard deviation can be computed. Using the standard deviation together with the expected value of possible internal rates of return, one is able to perform the same type of analysis as before. Whether net-present values or internal rates of return are used, the approach provides management with important information from which it is able to judge the risk of a project. This information was missing in the conventional evaluation of capital-budgeting projects in Chapter 5, where only the expected values of future cash flows were used.

In the above examples, we have assumed normal probability distributions. Although this property is very desirable for purposes of calculation, it is not a necessary condition for the use of the above approach. Even when the distribution is not normal, we usually are able to make reasonably strong probability statements by using Tchebycheff's inequality. This approach is based upon the fact that regardless of the form of the distribution, there is a close relationship between the magnitude of deviations from the expected value of the distribution and probability.[5] Again, we are interested in the area under the curve, or probability density function, that is to the left or right of a particular net-present value or internal rate of return. By computing this area, we are able to determine the probability that the index will be greater or less than a particular amount and judge the risk of the project accordingly.

Estimating Future Cash Flows

Instead of expressing estimates of future cash flows in terms of a discrete probability distribution, we might specify them only in terms of the expected value and standard deviation of the probability distribution. For

---

[5]For an extensive discussion and application of this technique, see Stephen L. Buzby, "Extending the Applicability of Probabilistic Management and Control Models," *Accounting Review,* 49 (January 1974), 42–49.

example, we might ask management for estimates of the most likely cash flow and the maximum possible deviation on either side. This type of estimating procedure corresponds to the PERT method, whereby, most likely, optimistic and pessimistic estimates are made. If we assume a normal distribution of net cash flows for various future periods, we are able to use the maximum possible deviation to determine the standard deviation.

With a normal distribution, we know that the probabilities that the actual value will fall within 1, 2, or 3 standard deviations on either side of the most likely value are 0.683, 0.954, and 0.997, respectively. If management felt that there were a 5 percent probability that the maximum possible deviation would be positive and an equal probability that it would be negative, we would consult a normal probability distribution table and find that this probability corresponds to approximately 1.65 standard deviations on either side of the most likely value. In other words, 90 percent of a normal probability distribution falls within 1.65 standard deviations on either side of the most likely value—the mean. By dividing the maximum deviation by 1.65, we obtain the standard deviation for the probability distribution. Thus, if the most likely value of net cash flow for period t were $5,000 and the minimum and maximum cash flows were $3,000 and $7,000, respectively, the standard deviation would be $2,000/1.65 = $1,212.

This relatively simple approach enables us to obtain the probability information necessary to determine the expected value of net-present value for an investment proposal and the standard deviation about this expected value. The approach differs somewhat in mechanics but not in concept from the discrete probability-distribution approach described earlier. To use the approach, however, it is important that the probability estimates be approximately normal.

DEPENDENCE OF CASH FLOWS OVER TIME

In the preceding section, we assumed serial independence of cash flows from one future period to another. For most investment proposals, however, the cash flow in one future period depends in part upon the cash flows in previous periods. If an investment proposal turns bad in the early years, the probability is high that cash flows in later years also will be lower than originally expected. To assume that an extremely unfavorable or favorable outcome in the early life of an investment proposal does not affect the later outcome is unrealistic in most investment situations. The consequence of cash flows being correlated over time is that the standard deviation of the probability distribution of possible net-present values or possible internal rates of return is larger than it would be if we assumed independence. The greater the degree of correlation, the greater the dispersion of the probability distribution. The expected value of net-present value, however, is the same, regardless of the degree of correlation over time. In this section, we explore varying degrees of dependence of cash flows over time.

Perfect Correlation

Cash flows are perfectly correlated over time if the deviation of an actual cash flow for a period from the mean of the probability distribution of expected cash flows for the period implies that cash flows in all other periods deviate in exactly the same relative manner. In other words, the cash flow in period t depends entirely upon what happened in previous periods. If the actual cash flow in period t is X standard deviations to the right of the expected value of the probability distribution of possible cash flows for that period, actual cash flows in all other periods will be X standard deviations to the right of the expected values of their respective probability distributions. Stated differently, the cash flow in any period is a linear function of the cash flows in all other periods. The formula for the standard deviation of a perfectly correlated stream of cash flows over time is[6]

$$\sigma = \sum_{t=0}^{\infty} \frac{\sigma_t}{(1 + i)^t} \qquad (6\text{-}10)$$

To illustrate its use, consider the same example as before. The standard deviation about the expected value of net-present value for the proposal, using Eq. (6-10), is

$$\sigma = \frac{1,140}{(1.04)} + \frac{1,140}{(1.04)^2} + \frac{1,140}{(1.04)^3} = \$3,164$$

$$\sigma_t$$

$$1140 \cdot 2.7751$$

This compares with a standard deviation of $1,827 when we used Eq. (6-4) under the assumption of serial independence over time. Thus the standard deviation for a perfectly correlated stream of cash flows is significantly greater than the standard deviation for the same stream under the assumption of mutual independence. The standard deviation for a less than perfectly correlated stream of cash flows will be somewhere between these two values.[7] The probabilistic analysis of a project with a perfectly correlated stream of cash flows over time is the same as that illustrated previously for a project with an uncorrelated stream.

---

[6]The standard deviation of the probability distribution of possible internal rates of return can be determined in the same manner as described before. The discount rate is varied in Eq. (6-10) to obtain different standard deviations, the probability of net-present value being less than zero is determined for each discount rate, these probabilities are arranged to form a probability distribution of IRRs, and the standard deviation of the distribution is calculated.

[7]Frederick S. Hillier, "The Derivation of Probabilistic Information for the Evaluation of Risky Investments," *Management Science*, 9 (April 1963), 443–57, combines the assumptions of mutual independence and perfect correlation of cash flows in developing a model to deal with mixed situations. Essentially, the overall cash flows of the firm are broken down and classified as either independent or perfectly correlated over time. A formula is derived for calculating the standard deviation.

Moderate Correlation

Where the cash flows of the firm are neither approximately independent nor perfectly correlated over time, the classification of the cash-flow stream as one or the other is not appropriate. One method for dealing with the problem of moderate correlation is with a series of conditional probability distributions. To illustrate, suppose that the investment in a project costing $10,000 at time 0 were expected to generate net cash flows in periods 1, 2, and 3 with the probabilities in Table 6-2. As seen in the table, there are 27 possible cash-flow series. The last column depicts the joint

table 6-2

Illustration of conditional probability distribution approach

Period 1		Period 2		Period 3			
Initial Probability P(1)	Net Cash Flow	Conditional Probability P(2|1)	Net Cash Flow	Conditional Probability P(3|2,1)	Net Cash Flow	Cash Flow Series	Joint Probability P(1,2,3)
		.30	−$2,000	.25	$5,000	1	.01875
				.50	7,000	2	.03750
				.25	9,000	3	.01875
.25	−$6,000	.40	1,000	.25	7,000	4	.02500
				.50	9,000	5	.05000
				.25	11,000	6	.02500
		.30	4,000	.25	9,000	7	.01875
				.50	11,000	8	.03750
				.25	13,000	9	.01875
		.25	3,000	.30	10,000	10	.03750
				.40	12,000	11	.05000
				.30	14,000	12	.03750
.50	−4,000	.50	6,000	.30	12,000	13	.07500
				.40	14,000	14	.10000
				.30	16,000	15	.07500
		.25	9,000	.30	14,000	16	.03750
				.40	16,000	17	.05000
				.30	18,000	18	.03750
		.30	8,000	.25	15,000	19	.01875
				.50	17,000	20	.03750
				.25	19,000	21	.01875
.25	−2,000	.40	11,000	.25	17,000	22	.02500
				.50	19,000	23	.05000
				.25	21,000	24	.02500
		.30	14,000	.25	19,000	25	.01875
				.50	21,000	26	.03750
				.25	23,000	27	.01875

probability of occurrence of a particular cash-flow series. For series 1, the joint probability of a $-\$6,000$ cash flow in period 1 being followed by cash flows of $-\$2,000$ and $\$5,000$ in periods 2 and 3, respectively, is $.25 \times .30 \times .25 = .01875$. Similarly, joint probabilities for the other cash-flow series can be determined in this manner.[8]

The use of conditional probability distributions enables us to take account of the correlation of cash flows over time. In the above example, the cash flow in period 3 depends upon what happened in periods 1 and 2. However, the correlation of cash flows over time is not perfect. Given a cash flow in period 1, the cash flow in period 2 can vary within a range. Similarly, the cash flow in period 3 can vary within a range, given the outcomes in periods 1 and 2.

The calculation of the expected value of net-present value using this approach is the same as before (Eq. (6-3)). The standard deviation may be determined mathematically for the simple case by

$$NPV = \frac{\sum A_t}{(1+i)^t}$$

$$\sigma = \sqrt{\sum_{x=1}^{l} (NPV_x - \overline{NPV})^2 P_x} \qquad (6\text{-}11)$$

where NPV_x is the net-present value for series x of net cash flows, covering all periods. $\overline{NPV}$ is the expected value of net-present value of the proposal, and P_x is the probability of occurrence of that series. For the above example, there are 27 possible series of cash flows, so that $l = 27$. The first series is represented by a net cash flow of $-\$10,000$ at time 0, $-\$6,000$ at time 1, $-\$2,000$ at time 2, and $\$5,000$ at time 3. The probability of occurrence of that series is .01875. For the internal-rate-of-return approach, the standard deviation is

$$\sigma = \sqrt{\sum_{x=1}^{l} (IRR_x - \overline{IRR})^2 P_x} \qquad (6\text{-}12)$$

where IRR_x is the internal rate of return for series x of net cash flows, and $\overline{IRR}$ is the expected value of internal rate of return.

Unfortunately, for complex situations, the mathematical calculation of the standard deviation is unfeasible. For these situations, we can *approximate* the standard deviation by means of simulation. With simulation, the net-present values or internal rates of return for randomly selected series of cash flows are calculated. These net-present values or internal rates of return then are ordered according to their probability of occurrence, and a probability distribution of possible net-present values or internal rates of return is formed. The expected value and standard deviation of the

---

[8]For another illustration of this type, using various scenarios of events to determine the dependence of cash flows over time, see Charles P. Bonini, "Comment on Formulating Correlated Cash Flow Streams," *Engineering Economist,* 20 (Spring 1975), 210–14.

probability distribution can then be calculated and this information analyzed

in the same manner as before.[9]

We have seen that our assumption as to the degree of correlation of cash flows over time is an important one. The risk of a project will be considerably greater if the cash flows are highly correlated over time than if they are mutually independent, all other things being the same. Although independence often is assumed for ease of calculation, this assumption greatly underestimates project risk if in fact the cash flows are highly correlated over time. Thus it is important that careful consideration be given to the likely degree of dependence of cash flows over time. Otherwise, the assessment of risk may well be distorted. Of the approaches for dealing with the problem, the use of conditional probabilities is the most accurate, although the most difficult to implement.

A SIMULATION APPROACH

In an important contribution to evaluating risky investments, David B. Hertz proposed the use of a simulation model to obtain the expected return and dispersion about this expected return for an investment proposal.[10] Hertz considers the following factors in evaluating an investment proposal:

Market Analysis
    1. Market size
    2. Selling price
    3. Market growth rate
    4. Share of market (which results in physical sales volume)
Investment Cost Analysis
    5. Investment required
    6. Residual value of investment
Operating and Fixed Costs
    7. Operating costs
    8. Fixed costs
    9. Useful life of facilities

[9]It should be noted that the distribution of simulated internal rates of return for a project generally will not have the same "profile" as the distribution of net-present values. Simulated internal rates of return for cash flows above the mean of the distribution of cash flows are closer to the mean of the distribution of simulated internal rates of return than are simulated internal rates of return for cash flows below the mean of the distribution of cash flows. As a result, there is a bias toward skewness to the left in the distribution of simulated internal rates of return. Therefore the mean of the distribution of simulated internal rates of return generally will be less than the mean of the distribution of internal rates of return. Elaboration on this point is contained in Alexander A. Robichek, "Interpreting the Results of Risk Analysis," *Journal of Finance,* 30 (December 1975), 1384–86.

[10]David B. Hertz, "Risk Analysis in Capital Investment," *Harvard Business Review,* 42 (January-February 1964), 95–106; and Hertz, "Investment Policies That Pay Off," *Harvard Business Review,* 46 (January-February 1968), 96–108.

Probability distributions are assigned to each of these factors, based upon management's assessment of the probable outcomes. Thus the possible outcomes are charted for each factor according to their probability of occurrence.

Once the probability distributions are determined, the next step is to determine the average rate of return that will result from a random combination of the nine factors listed above. To illustrate the simulation process, assume that the market-size factor had the following probability distribution:

Market size (in thousand units)	450	500	550	600	650	700	750
Probability	0.05	0.10	0.20	0.30	0.20	0.10	0.05

Now suppose that we have a roulette wheel with 100 numbers, on which numbers 1 to 5 represent a market size of 450,000 units, 6 to 15 represent a market size of 500,000, 16 to 35 a market size of 550,000 units, and so on through 100. As in roulette, we spin the wheel, and the ball falls in one of the 100 slots—number 26. For this trial, then, we simulate a market size of 550,000 units. Fortunately, we do not have to have a roulette wheel to undertake a simulation; the same type of operation can be carried out on a computer in a much more efficient manner.

Simulation trials are undertaken for each of the other eight factors. The first four factors (market analysis) give us the annual sales per year, while factors 7 and 8 give us the operating costs and fixed costs per year. Together, these six factors enable us to calculate the annual earnings per year. When trial values for these six factors are combined with trial values for the required investment, the useful life, and the residual value of the project, we have sufficient information to calculate the return on investment for that trial run. Thus the computer simulates trial values for each of the nine factors and then calculates the return on investment based upon the values simulated. The process is repeated a number of times; each time we obtain a combination of values for the nine factors and the return on investment for that combination. When the trial is repeated often enough, the rates of return obtained can be plotted in a frequency distribution.

From this frequency distribution, we are able to evaluate the expected return and the dispersion about this expected return, or risk, in the same manner as before—in other words, we can determine the probability that an investment will provide a return greater or less than a certain amount. By comparing the probability distribution of rates of return for one proposal with the probability distribution of rates of return for another, management is able to evaluate the respective merits of different risky investments. Hertz's simulation method has been used widely and applied to a wide variety of investment projects. In one interesting application, Lawrence Kryzanowski, Peter Lusztig, and Bernhard Schwab present an algorithm for implementing the technique in the case of an actual proposed plant expansion by a major natural resource firm.[11]

Before closing, two points should be made about the simulation method. Although the simulation model computes the average rate of return on investment, the method could easily be modified to calculate the internal rate of return, the net-present value, or the profitability index.[12] In addition, although Hertz allows for dependency among the nine factors,[13] the model presented treats the factors as though they were independent. To the extent that dependency exists among factors, it must be taken into account in determining the probability distributions. For example, there is likely to be significant correlation between the market size and the selling price. These interrelationships add considerable complexity to the estimating procedure. Notwithstanding the added complexity of estimating and specifying the relationships between factors, it must be done if the model is to provide realistic results. These estimates may be based upon empirical testing when such testing is feasible. Once the relationships are incorporated in the model, those factors that are correlated would be simulated jointly. Rates of return for the simulated trials would be calculated and a frequency distribution of simulated trials formed in the same manner as before.

MEASURING RISK: MULTIPLE INVESTMENT PROJECTS

Heretofore, our concern has been with measuring risk for a single investment project. When multiple investment projects are involved, the measurement of risk may differ from that for a single project owing to the properties of diversification. Diversification of securities was illustrated in Chapter 3, and this concept applies also to capital assets. However, it is important to recognize that investment in capital assets differs somewhat from that in securities. For one thing, capital assets typically are not divisible, whereas securities are. Moreover, it usually is much more costly, and sometimes impossible, to divest oneself of a capital asset, whereas selling a marketable security is relatively easy. Finally, there is the problem of mutual exclusion and contingency that does not occur with securities.[14] All of these factors make diversification with respect to capital assets more "lumpy" than diversification with securities. Whether diversification of capital assets is a thing of value for the firm is

[11]"Monte Carlo Simulation and Capital Expenditure Decisions—A Case Study," *Engineering Economist,* 18 (Fall 1972), 31–48.

[12]Again there is the problem discussed in footnote 9 in working with simulated internal rates of return.

[13]Hertz, "Risk Analysis in Capital Investment," p. 101.

[14]See Haim Levy and Marshall Sarnat, "The Portfolio Analysis of Multiperiod Capital Investments under Conditions of Risk," *Engineering Economist,* 16 (Fall 1970), 8.

a subject of considerable controversy, and this controversy will be analyzed in the next two chapters. Our purpose here is only to show how to measure risk for combinations of risky investments, given the fact that such a measure is desired.

As was true earlier, the two pieces of information we seek are the expected value and standard deviation of the probability distribution of possible net-present values for the combination of projects being analyzed. The expected value usually is simply a weighted average of the expected values of the projects making up the combination. From Chapter 3, we know that the total variance, or risk, of a combination of risky investments depends to a large extent upon the degree of correlation between the investments.[15] The standard deviation of the probability distribution of possible net-present values for a portfolio of capital investments can be expressed as

$$\sigma = \sqrt{\sum_{j=1}^{m} \sum_{k=1}^{m} r_{jk} \sigma_j \sigma_k} \qquad (6\text{-}13)$$

Where m is the total number of assets in the portfolio, r_{jk} is the expected correlation between the net-present values for investments j and k, σ_j is the standard deviation about the expected value of net-present value for investment j, and σ_k is the standard deviation for investment k.

Equation (6-13) indicates that the standard deviation, or risk, of a portfolio of projects depends upon (1) the degree of correlation between various projects and (2) the standard deviation of possible net-present values for each project. We note that the higher the degree of positive correlation, the greater the standard deviation of the portfolio of projects, all other things remaining constant. Moreover, the greater the standard deviations of the individual projects, the greater the standard deviation of the portfolio, if the correlation is positive. The standard deviations of the individual investment projects, necessary for the calculation of Eq. (6-13), are obtained through the methods presented earlier in the chapter.

Correlation between Projects

As was the case with a portfolio of securities discussed in Chapter 3, the correlation between expected net-present values of two projects may be positive, negative, or zero, depending upon the nature of the association. A correlation coefficient of 1.00 indicates that the net-present values of two investment proposals vary directly in the same proportional manner; a correlation coefficient of -1.00 indicates that they vary inversely in the same proportional manner; and a zero correlation coefficient usually indicates that they are independent.

---

[15]The development of this section assumes that the reader has covered portfolio selection in Chapter 3.

For most pairs of investment projects, the correlation coefficient lies between 0 and 1.00. The lack of negatively correlated projects is due to most investments being correlated positively with the economy. Still it is possible to find projects having low or moderate degrees of correlation. For example, management might have reason to expect only slight correlation between an investment project involving an electronics product and one involving a new consumer product. It might, however, expect high positive correlation between investments in a milling machine and a turret lathe if both machines are to be used in the production of industrial lift trucks. Projects in the same general line of business tend to be highly correlated with each other, while projects in essentially unrelated lines of business tend to have low degrees of correlation.

Estimates of correlation coefficients must be carefully made if the standard deviation obtained in Eq. (6-13) is to be realistic. When investment projects are like projects with which the firm has had experience, it may be feasible to compute the correlation coefficients using historical data. For other investments, however, estimates of correlation coefficients must be based solely on an assessment of the future. It is not unreasonable to suppose that management is able to make fairly accurate estimates of the correlation between investment projects. To the extent that actual correlation differs from that expected, future correlation estimates on existing projects should be revised in keeping with the learning process. The learning process also applies to future estimates of correlation between investments similar to existing investments.[16]

Feasible Combinations and Dominance

With the above procedures, one can determine the total expected value and the standard deviation of the probability distribution of possible net-present values for a combination of investments. A combination includes all existing investment projects and one or more proposals under consideration. We assume that a firm has existing investment projects generating expected future cash flows and that disinvestment with respect to these projects is not possible. Existing projects comprise a subset that is included in all combinations. Proposals under consideration are assumed to represent all future proposals on the investment horizon.

The next step involves analyzing feasible combinations of existing projects and proposals under consideration according to their expected

[16]For simulation approaches to determining the functional relationship between project cash flows, see Kalman J. Cohen and Edwin J. Elton, "Inter-Temporal Portfolio Analysis Based upon Simulation of Joint Returns," *Management Science,* 14 (September 1967), 5–11; Rudolfo C. Salazar and Subrata K. Sen, "A Simulation Model of Capital Budgeting under Uncertainty," *Management Science,* 15 (December 1968), 161–79; and R. K. Harvey and A. V. Cabot, "A Decision Theory Approach to Capital Budgeting under Risk," *Engineering Economist,* 20 (Fall 1974), 37–49.

figure 6-6
Opportunity set of
project portfolios

values of net-present value and standard deviations to see which combinations dominate. Figure 6-6 is an example of a scatter diagram; here the expected value of net-present value is along the horizontal axis, and the standard deviation is on the vertical axis. Each dot represents a feasible combination of proposals under consideration and existing investment projects for the firm.

Collectively, the dots represent the total set of feasible combinations of investment opportunities available to the firm. This set corresponds to the opportunity set of security portfolios discussed in Chapter 3, the major difference being that combinations of investment projects are not as divisible as portfolios of securities. Certain dots in Figure 6-6 dominate others in the sense that they represent a higher expected value of net-present value and the same standard deviation, a lower standard deviation and the same expected value of net-present value, or both a higher expected value and a lower standard deviation. The dots that dominate others are those that are farthest to the right in Figure 6-6, and they correspond to the efficient frontier for an opportunity set of security portfolios.

If E represents the existing portfolio of investment projects, we see that it is dominated by combinations H, L, and P with respect to expected value of net-present value and by combination B with respect to both expected value of net-present value and standard deviation. Other dots dominate E, but these are not on the frontier. With the type of information in Figure 6-6, most combinations of investment proposals can be eliminated simply because they are dominated by other combinations. In Chapter 8, we take up the evaluation of this information and the acceptance criterion. Our purpose in this chapter is only to present the measurement of portfolio risk.

It is important to recognize that the combination of projects ultimately chosen determines the new investment proposal or proposals that will be accepted. An exception occurs only when the portfolio selected is comprised of existing projects. In this situation, no investment proposals under consideration would be accepted. In our case, the portfolio of existing projects is represented by dot E in Figure 6-6. Therefore the selection of any of the four outlying portfolios would imply the acceptance of one or more new investment proposals. Those investment proposals under consideration that were not in the portfolio finally selected would be rejected, of course. The incremental expected value of net-present value and standard deviation can be determined by measuring on the horizontal and vertical axes the distance from dot E to the dot representing the combination finally selected. Instead of working with net-present values, the framework described can be expressed in terms of internal rates of return. The reader should easily be able to visualize this change, for the principles are the same.

INFORMATION NEEDED TO ANALYZE AN ACQUISITION

Investment proposals under consideration are not necessarily confined to proposals generated internally. A proposal can consist of the acquisition of a company, or a portion thereof. The topic of acquisitions is treated in Chapter 23; in the present chapter and in Chapter 8, we consider the capital-budgeting aspects of the problem. In principle, the prospective acquisition is much the same as any investment proposal; there is an initial outlay of cash or stock, followed by expected future benefits. The major difference is that with an acquisition, the initial cost may not be established; indeed, it frequently is subject to bargaining. The framework for analyzing the expected return and risk involved with an acquisition is similar to that discussed above. The critical thing is the accurate measurement of incremental cash flows, a topic to which we now turn.

Measuring Cash Flows

In order to consider an acquisition in a capital-budgeting framework, expected future cash flows must be expressed on a basis consistent with those for investment proposals generated internally. In evaluating the prospective acquisition, the buying company should first estimate the future cash income the acquisition is expected to add. Because we are interested in the marginal impact of the acquisition, these estimates should embody any expected economies, known as synergism, which are involved in the merger.

In an acquisition, there are the usual problems with respect to estimating future cash flows. However, the process may be somewhat easier than for a capital-budgeting proposal, because the company being acquired is a going concern. The acquiring company buys more than assets; it buys experience, an organization, and proven performance. The estimates of sales and costs are based upon past results; consequently, they are likely to be more accurate than the estimates for a new investment proposal.

In making the various estimates, it is important to isolate from consideration the capital structure that results from the merger. The reason is that once the merger is consummated, the buying company can modify the capital structure that results from the merger. Therefore, prospective incremental cash income from the acquisition should be estimated before interest charges. In other words, we attempt to measure the expected incremental earning power of the acquisition, apart from considerations of financing.

Expected incremental cash income should be adjusted for taxes. As was the case in Chapter 5, we deduct expected depreciation charges from cash income and compute the amount of taxes to be paid on the residual. By subtracting expected taxes from expected incremental cash income, we obtain cash income after taxes for each future period. From this expected cash income after taxes, we must subtract any new investments the acquiring firm believes it will have to make in order to generate the expected stream of earnings. The residual represents the expected cash flow after taxes for the period. It is extremely important that we take account of these investments; otherwise, incremental cash-flow estimates will be biased upward.

An error frequently made is to treat as cash flows expected future earnings after taxes of the firm being considered for acquisition. The problem is that an earnings estimate for a future period usually is predicated upon reinvesting a portion of earnings from previous periods.[17] To use expected earnings in evaluating an acquisition results in double counting, as does the use of expected future earnings per share in a dividend valuation model. In summation, the appropriate measure of incremental cash flow is expected earnings after taxes plus depreciation in each future period, less any investment required in that period.

To illustrate the information needed, suppose the incremental cash flows shown in Table 6-3 were expected from an acquisition. In the case of an

table 6-3
Illustration of incremental cash flows from
an acquisition

	Average for Years (in thousands)				
	1–5	6–10	11–15	16–20	21–∞
Expected cash income from acquisition before taxes	$1,500	$2,000	$2,500	$3,000	$3,200
Taxes	− 500	− 700	− 1,000	− 1,200	− 1,300
Expected cash income after taxes	$1,000	$1,300	$1,500	$1,800	$1,900
Investment required	− 800	− 900	− 800	− 700	− 600
Net cash flow	$ 200	$ 400	$ 700	$1,100	$1,300

[17]It is also assumed that funds generated through depreciation allowances are reinvested to maintain the company's existing level of earnings.

acquisition investment, the life of the project is indefinite. In many cases, analysts assume some horizon such as twenty-five years, beyond which incremental cash flows are not estimated. While the present-value effect of these distant cash flows usually is not material, we choose to show cash flows into perpetuity, denoted by ∞, so that the valuation of a merger is consistent with the valuation of a common stock. In addition to expected cash flows, the acquiring firm should specify other possible net cash-flow series, with a probability attached to each. In other words, it needs to obtain a probability tree of possible net cash flows. The method for obtaining this probability tree was illustrated earlier; therefore we do not discuss it here.

If the acquisition is evaluated with respect to its marginal impact on the risk of the firm as a whole, we need additional information. More specifically, we need to estimate correlation coefficients for the relationships between the acquisition's present value and the present values for existing projects as well as investment proposals under consideration. The acquisition then becomes one more investment proposal in a portfolio of projects to be considered. Note, however, that we have calculated only the present value of the acquisition. If the price to be paid is known, it should be subtracted from the expected value of present value to obtain the expected value of *net*-present value. With this information, one is able to evaluate the acquisition as part of a portfolio of projects in the same manner as described earlier. In most cases, however, the price to be paid is not set and must be negotiated.

In Chapter 8, we will investigate the question of whether an acquisition should be evaluated in isolation or as one of many companies whose stocks are publicly traded. Our concern in this chapter has been only with the information needed for the various types of evaluation possible. We leave to later the valuation principles inherent in the problem.

SUMMARY

In this chapter, we recognize that investment proposals have differing degrees of business risk. In addition to the expected profitability of a proposal, we must analyze possible deviations in profitability from that which is expected. Risk is expressed in terms of the dispersion of the probability distribution of possible net-present values or possible internal rates of return and is measured by the standard deviation. Our focus in this chapter was on measuring the standard deviation under a variety of assumptions and to use it in relation to the expected value of the distribution in order to determine the probability of certain events occurring.

We first explored the measurement of risk under the assumption of serial independence of cash flows over time. We then considered its measurement when cash flows from one period to the next are dependent over time. Here we looked at perfect correlation and at the use of conditional probability distributions for dealing with situations of moderate correlation of cash flows over time. We saw also that simulation techniques show promise for the analysis of risk.

A portfolio approach was presented for measuring the marginal risk of a project in relation to existing investment projects and proposals under consideration. As indicated, this approach has merit only under certain circumstances. Finally, we considered the types of information necessary to evaluate an acquisition. In general, an acquisiton can be evaluated in much the same manner as an investment proposal generated internally. Of crucial importance, however, is the expression of expected cash flows in a manner consistent with internal projects; a specific method was presented for accomplishing such expression.

In the next two chapters, we consider the evaluation of investments given information about risk and expected return developed in this chapter. We will investigate the acceptance or rejection of risky investments in relation to the objective of maximizing share price. Our discussion will involve us in the valuation of the firm and in the considerable theoretical controversy that surrounds the question of risky investments and acquisitions. Again, we point out that Chapters 6 through 8 must be treated as a package; the measurement of risk in this chapter is valuable only in relation to the ultimate evaluation of the proposal(s).

APPENDIX A
Decision-Tree Approach for Sequential Decisions

In capital budgeting, some investment opportunities involve a sequence of decisions over time. Heretofore, we have considered only a single accept-reject decision at the outset of the project. An analytical technique used in sequential decisions is the decision tree, where various decision points are studied in relation to subsequent chance events. This technique enables one to choose among alternatives in an objective and consistent manner.

Illustrating the Method

To illustrate the method, let us suppose that a firm is considering the introduction of a new product. Initially, it must decide whether to distribute the product in the Midwest or nationally. Regional distribution will require an expenditure of $1 million for a new plant and for the initial marketing effort. Depending upon demand during the first two years, the firm then would decide whether or not to expand to national distribution. If it goes from regional to national distribution, it will need to spend an additional $3 million for expansion of the existing plant and to make an additional marketing effort. Of course, the firm can distribute nationally from the very outset. If it does, it will cost $3 million to construct a plant and to launch the marketing of the product. Thus we see that there are economies associated

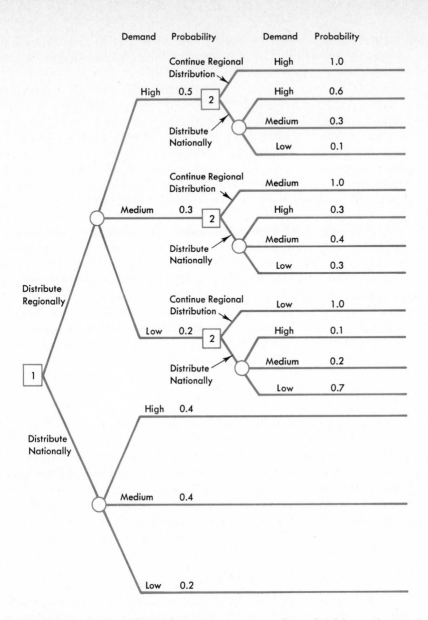

Demand	Probability		Demand	Probability
		Continue Regional Distribution	High	1.0
High	0.5	2		
		Distribute Nationally	High	0.6
			Medium	0.3
			Low	0.1
		Continue Regional Distribution	Medium	1.0
Medium	0.3	2		
		Distribute Nationally	High	0.3
			Medium	0.4
			Low	0.3
		Continue Regional Distribution	Low	1.0
Low	0.2	2		
		Distribute Nationally	High	0.1
			Medium	0.2
			Low	0.7

Distribute Regionally

1

Distribute Nationally

High	0.4
Medium	0.4
Low	0.2

figure 6-7
Decision tree-national versus regional distribution

with distributing nationally at the outset. For one thing, building a large plant is less expensive than building a small one and having to enlarge it later. Moreover, there are economies in marketing.

The decision process is illustrated graphically by the decision tree shown in Figure 6-7. The squares represent decision points. For example, the first decision is whether to distribute regionally or nationally. The circles represent chance event nodes. If the firm decides to distribute nationally at the outset, there is 0.4 probability that demand will prove to be high, 0.4 that demand will turn out to be medium, and 0.2 that it will be low. On the other hand, if the firm distributes regionally, there is 0.5 probability that demand will be high, 0.3 probability that it will be medium, and 0.2 probability that it will be low. At the end of year 2, the firm must decide whether to continue to distribute regionally, in which case demand will continue to be high, low, or medium, or whether it should distribute nationally, in which case the national demand is shown by the subsequent chance event in the figure.

In all cases, the product is expected to have a life of eight years. Moreover, we assume for simplicity's sake that at the end of the eighth year, the plant has no more useful life and no salvage value. The expected cash flows over the eight years are shown in Table 6-4 for the various outcomes. We note in the table that if the firm switches from regional to national distribution at the end of year 2, there is a cash expenditure of $3 million at the end of the year. When this expenditure is combined with the cash flow generated from regional demand for the year, we obtain the net cash flow for year 2. In general, the lower the combination of regional and national demand, the lower the cash-flow sequence. Assuming a risk-free rate of 4 percent after taxes, the net-present values of the various combinations are shown in the last column of the table. We need now to incorporate these net-present values into our decision tree. In Figure 6-8, they are shown at the branch tips, indicating the expected net-present values associated with the sequence of decisions and chance events comprising the branch.

Optimal Set of Decisions

The optimal sequence of decisions is determined by "rolling back" the tree from the right-hand side. In other words, we appraise first the most distant decision—namely, the choice of whether or not to switch from regional to national distribution. To do so we must determine the expected value of net-present value for national distribution, given that demand for the regional distribution proves to be high, medium, or low. The expected value of net-present value is simply the net-present values at the branch tips times the probabilities of occurrence. For high regional demand, the expected value of net-present value for subsequent national distribution is

$$NPV = 0.6(4,096.9) + 0.3(1,573.1) + 0.1(-704.1)$$
$$= \$2,859.6 \qquad\qquad (6A\text{-}1)$$

This amount appears at the chance event node for national distribution, given high regional demand.

In a similar fashion, the expected values of net-present value for national distribution, given medium and low regional demands, are computed and shown at the appropriate chance event nodes. We note that the expected value of net-present value for national distribution, given low regional demand, is −$1,363,800. This figure compares with an expected net-present value of −$637,100 if the firm continues with regional distribution. Thus, if regional demand is low, the firm should not distribute nationally but should continue to distribute regionally. On the other hand, if regional

table 6-4

Expected cash flows for various branches of decision tree (000 omitted)

	Time									NPV
	0	1	2	3	4	5	6	7	8	
Regional distribution throughout:										
High demand	−$1,000	$100	$300	$400	$500	$400	$300	$200	$100	$947.4
Medium demand	−1,000	0	150	250	350	250	200	100	50	136.2
Low demand	−1,000	−100	0	100	200	100	100	50	0	−637.1
Regional distribution followed by national distribution:										
High regional–high national demand	−1,000	100	−2,700	1,200	1,800	2,400	1,800	1,200	800	4,096.9
High regional–medium national demand	−1,000	100	−2,700	700	1,200	1,800	1,200	700	500	1,573.1
High regional–low national demand	−1,000	100	−2,700	200	700	1,300	700	200	200	−704.1
Medium regional–high national demand	−1,000	0	−2,850	1,100	1,700	2,300	1,700	1,100	700	3,377.4
Medium regional–medium national demand	−1,000	0	−2,850	600	1,100	1,700	1,200	600	400	932.6
Medium regional–low national demand	−1,000	0	−2,850	100	600	1,100	700	100	100	−1,426.8
Low regional–high national demand	−1,000	−100	−3,000	1,000	1,500	2,100	1,500	1,000	600	2,411.2
Low regional–medium national demand	−1,000	−100	−3,000	500	1,000	1,500	1,000	500	300	51.9
Low regional–low national demand	−1,000	−100	−3,000	0	500	900	500	0	0	−2,307.5
National distribution throughout:										
High demand	−3,000	300	1,000	1,500	2,000	1,500	1,000	700	300	4,030.5
Medium demand	−3,000	0	500	1,000	1,500	1,000	500	100	100	1,151.6
Low demand	−3,000	−300	0	500	1,000	500	0	−100	−100	−1,727.3

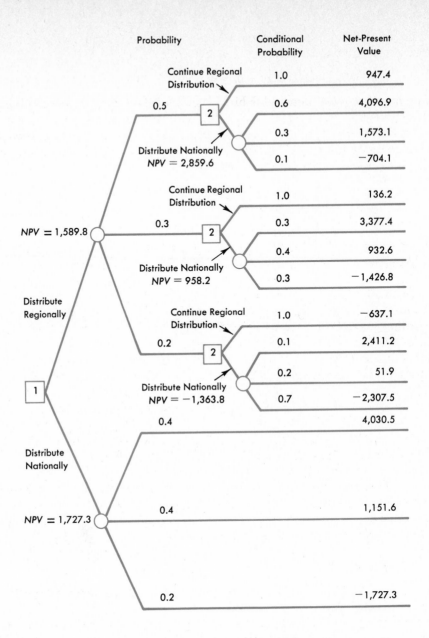

	Probability	Conditional Probability	Net-Present Value
Continue Regional Distribution	1.0		947.4
	0.5	0.6	4,096.9
		0.3	1,573.1
Distribute Nationally NPV = 2,859.6		0.1	−704.1
Continue Regional Distribution	1.0		136.2
	0.3	0.3	3,377.4
		0.4	932.6
Distribute Nationally NPV = 958.2		0.3	−1,426.8
Continue Regional Distribution	1.0		−637.1
	0.2	0.1	2,411.2
		0.2	51.9
Distribute Nationally NPV = −1,363.8		0.7	−2,307.5
	0.4		4,030.5
	0.4		1,151.6
	0.2		−1,727.3

NPV = 1,589.8

Distribute Regionally

Distribute Nationally

NPV = 1,727.3

figure 6-8
Decision tree-net-present values of branches

demand turns out to be either high or medium, the firm should go to national distribution, for the expected value of net-present value is higher than it is if the firm continues with regional distribution. By backward induction, then, we are able to determine the optimal decision at the most distant decision point.

The next step is to determine the optimal decision at the first decision point—that is, to decide whether to distribute nationally or regionally at the outset. The expected value of net-present value for regional distribution, given optimal decisions at decision point 2, is

$$NPV = 0.5(2,859.6) + 0.3(958.2) + 0.2(-637.1) = \$1,589.8 \qquad (6A\text{-}2)$$

Note that if regional demand is high or medium, we use the expected value of net-present value associated with subsequent national distribution. If regional demand is low, we use the expected net-present value associated with continuing regional distribution. The expected value of net-present value for initial national distribution is

$$NPV = 0.4(4,030.5) + 0.4(1,151.6) + 0.2(-1,727.3)$$
$$= \$1,727.3 \qquad (6A\text{-}3)$$

Thus the expected value of net-present value for initial national distribution exceeds that for initial regional distribution. When we compute the standard deviations of the probability distributions of possible net-present values, we find them to be \$2,073,400 for initial regional distribution and \$2,154,400 for initial national distribution. Therefore initial national distribution has a higher expected return but also a somewhat higher standard deviation. The economies associated with building the plant and initiating the marketing effort all at once as opposed to piecemeal give rise to the higher expected return, but the lesser flexibility, when compared with initial regional distribution, results in greater risk. Whether management will prefer initial national distribution will depend on its risk preferences. Given the fact that the coefficient of variation is higher for initial national distribution, $\$1,727.3/\$2,154.4 = 0.802$, versus that for initial regional distribution, $\$1,589.8/\$2,073.4 = 0.767$, it will probably prefer the former unless risk aversion is high. However, the decision itself will be based upon considerations discussed in the next two chapters.

We have seen that a decision-tree approach allows us to handle sequential investment decisions. By backward induction, we are able to determine optimal decisions at various decision points. Alternative branches are eliminated on the basis of dominance.[18]

APPENDIX B
Abandonment Value and Capital Budgeting

At times it may be desirable to abandon a project, even though its economic life is not over. Recognition of this possibility may enhance the project's expected return as well as lower its risk over what would be the case if abandonment value were ignored. The economic rationale for abandonment

---

[18]For additional discussion of the decision-tree approach to capital investment, see John F. Magee, "Decision Trees for Decision Making," *Harvard Business Review*, 42 (July-August 1964), 126–38; Magee, "How to Use Decision Trees in Capital Investment," *Harvard Business Review*, 42 (September-October 1964), 79–96; and Richard F. Hespos and Paul A. Strassmann, "Stochastic Decision Trees for the Analysis of Investment Decisions," *Management Science, 9* (August 1966), 244–59.

is the same as that for capital budgeting. Funds should be removed from a project, or disinvested, whenever the project does not economically justify use of these funds.

For ease of understanding, we assume initially that disinvestment does not alter the business-risk complexion of the firm as a whole or the covariance of its stock with other stocks in the market. Under such circumstances, the opportunity cost of funds tied up in a project is the firm's cost of capital. In general, an investment project should be abandoned when its abandonment value exceeds the present value of the project's subsequent expected future cash flows, discounted at the cost-of-capital rate. In certain cases, this rule must be modified so that abandoning the project at a later time can be considered. The abandonment value of a project is assumed to represent its disposal value, which would become available to the firm either in cash or in cash savings. An asset does not actually have to be sold to be abandoned; it may simply be employed in another area of the enterprise. In either case, an abandonment value can be estimated.

The abandonment rule posed can be expressed more formally as[19]

1. Compute the present value of the sum of cash flows expected to be generated from the project and the expected abandonment value at the end of the holding period. If there were n years remaining in the life of the project, we would have the following formula:

$$PV_{\tau \cdot a} = \sum_{t=\tau+1}^{a} \frac{A_t}{(1 + k)^{(t-\tau)}} + \frac{AV_a}{(1 + k)^{(a-\tau)}} \qquad \text{(6B-1)}$$

where

$PV_{\tau \cdot a}$ = present value at time τ of expected future net cash flows through period a, plus the present value of the expected abandonment value at the end of period a

a = period in which the project is abandoned

A_t = expected net cash flow of the project in period t

k = cost-of-capital rate

AV_a = expected abandonment value at the end of period a

2. For $a = n$, compute $PV_{\tau \cdot a}$. If $PV_{\tau \cdot n}$ is greater than the current abandonment value, AV_τ, we continue to hold the project and evaluate it at time $\tau + 1$, based on our expectations at that time.

3. If $PV_{\tau \cdot n}$ is less than or equal to AV_τ, we compute $PV_{\tau \cdot a}$ for $a = n - 1$. If $PV_{\tau \cdot n-1}$ is greater than AV_τ, we continue to hold the project as in (2) above. If $PV_{\tau \cdot n-1} \le AV_\tau$, we compute $PV_{\tau \cdot a}$ for $a = n - 2$ and com-

[19]See Alexander A. Robichek and James C. Van Horne, "Abandonment Value and Capital Budgeting," *Journal of Finance*, 22 (December 1967), 557–89; Edward A. Dyl and Hugh W. Long, "Comment," *Journal of Finance*, 24 (March 1969), 88–95; and Robichek and Van Horne, "Reply," ibid., 96–97.

pare it with AV_τ. This procedure is continued until either a decision to
hold the project is reached or $a = \tau + 1$.

4. If $PV_{\tau \cdot a} \leq AV_\tau$ for all $\tau + 1 \leq a \leq n$, then we would abandon the project
    at time τ.

In other words, these steps would have us abandon a project only if
the present value of possible future benefits is less than the current abandonment value and if it does not appear that abandoning the project in the
future would be more favorable than doing so currently. To continue with
a project that the above rules suggest should be given up means that capital
is being less than optimally employed. From an economic standpoint, the
project simply is not earning its keep; therefore, it should be abandoned.
In the discussion that follows, we assume that projects are abandoned
according to the rules given above.

Effect upon Project Selection

The recognition of abandonment value may have a significant effect
upon project selection. Implied in most capital-budgeting decisions is the
notion that funds will be committed to an investment proposal over its entire
estimated life.[20] Proposals are evaluated as though all outlays were sunk.
However, many projects have significant abandonment values. Too often,
this value is ignored, despite the fact that it can affect a project's expected
profitability and risk. In this section, we propose another decision-tree approach for incorporating abandonment value into the analysis for capital
budgeting. As some readers will appreciate, an abandonment problem can be
formulated in a dynamic programming context.[21] For complex problems
involving a number of branches and periods, this approach should be used.
For purposes of illustration, however, we do not do so.

Consider an investment proposal that costs $3,000 at time zero and is
expected to generate net cash flows over the next two years. These cash flows
and their probabilities of occurrence are shown as a series of conditional
probabilities in Table 6-5. For simplicity of illustration, we assume that after
the second year, the proposal is not expected to provide any cash flow or
residual value. We also assume an expected abandonment value of $1,500 at
the end of the first period. There are nine possible series of cash flows over
the two-year period, the first series representing a cash flow of $1,000 in
period 1, followed by a cash flow of 0 in period 2. The joint probability of
each series of cash flows is shown in the last column of the table; for the first
series, it is $0.25 \times 0.25 = 0.0625$.

[20]This section is adapted from Robichek and Van Horne, "Abandonment Value and
Capital Budgeting."

[21]Charles P. Bonini, "Capital Investment under Uncertainty with Abandonment Options," *Journal of Financial and Quantitative Analysis*, 12 (March 1977), 39–54.

table 6-5
Conditional probability distribution series for abandonment example

Period 1		Period 2		
Cash Flow	Initial Probability P(1)	Cash Flow	Conditional Probability P(2|1)	Joint Probability P(1, 2)
$1,000	0.25	$ 0	0.25	0.0625
		1,000	0.50	0.1250
		2,000	0.25	0.0625
2,000	0.50	1,000	0.25	0.1250
		2,000	0.50	0.2500
		3,000	0.25	0.1250
3,000	0.25	2,000	0.25	0.0625
		3,000	0.50	0.1250
		3,500	0.25	0.0625
Abandonment value $1,500		$0		

If we assume a required rate of return of 10 percent and use this rate as our discount factor, we are able to determine the expected value of net-present value of the proposal without abandonment by (1) computing the net-present value for each cash-flow series; (2) obtaining the expected net-present value for each series by multiplying the computed net-present value by the probability of occurrence of that series; and (3) adding the expected net-present values of all sequences. The standard deviation about the expected value of net-present value can be found using Eq. (6-11). When we carry out these computations, we find the expected value of net-present value and the standard deviation to be $444 and $1,313, respectively, under the assumption of no abandonment.

When we allow for the possibility of abandonment, however, the results change dramatically. Following the decision rules specified earlier, we would divest ourselves of the project if its abandonment value at the end of period 1 exceeds the expected cash flows for the subsequent period, discounted at 10 percent.[22] Because cash flows are only expected for two periods, the possibility of abandoning the project beyond period 1 does not exist. Consequently, a number of the computational steps involved in the abandonment decision rules discussed are not applicable in this case. Referring again to Table 6-5, we find that we should abandon the project at the end of the first period if the cash flow in that period turns out to be $1,000. The

---

[22]For purposes of illustration, we assume that the abandonment value is known with certainty. The approach could be modified to include a probability distribution of abandonment values. As pointed out by James L. Pappas, "The Role of Abandonment Value in Capital Asset Management," *Engineering Economist,* 22 (Fall 1976), 60, the use of a risk-adjusted cost of capital as the discount factor is not consistent with an abandonment value that is known with certainty.

reason is that the expected value of present value of possible cash flows in period 2, discounted to period 1, $909, is less than the abandonment value at the end of the period, $1,500. If the cash flow in period 1 turns out to be either $2,000 or $3,000, however, abandonment would not be worthwhile because the expected value of present value of period 2 cash flows discounted to period 1 exceeds $1,500.

When we allow for abandonment, the expected cash flows in Table 6-5 must be revised; these revisions are shown in Table 6-6. For the first branch in Table 6-5, the cash flow for period 1 becomes $2,500, the sum of the $1,000 cash flow during the period plus the abandonment value of $1,500. Because the proposal is abandoned at the end of period 1, there is no cash flow for this branch in period 2. Recalculating the expected value of net-present value deviation for the proposal based upon the information, we find them to be $578 and $1,110, respectively. Note the significant improvement in net-present value and the lower risk when the possibility of abandonment is considered. A portion of the downside risk for the proposal is eliminated if it is abandoned when events turn unfavorable. For example, with abandonment, there is no probability that net-present value will be less than $228; without abandonment, there is an 18.75 percent probability that net-present value will be less than that amount.

Implications

Although our example has purposely been kept simple, it does illustrate the importance of considering abandonment value when evaluating investment proposals.[23] Not to do so will result in an incomplete appraisal of

table 6-6
Conditional probability distribution series
for revised case

Period 1		Period 2		
Cash Flow	Initial Probability P(1)	Cash Flow	Conditional Probability P(2|1)	Joint Probability P(1, 2)
$2,500	0.25	$ 0		0.2500
2,000	0.50	1,000	0.25	0.1250
		2,000	0.50	0.2500
		3,000	0.25	0.1250
3,000	0.25	2,000	0.25	0.0625
		3,000	0.50	0.1250
		3,500	0.25	0.0625

[23]In Robichek and Van Horne, "Abandonment Value and Capital Budgeting," a simulation method is developed to serve as a "practical" substitute for the conditional probability approach illustrated in Tables 6-5 and 6-6. The latter approach is unfeasible when the possible number of cash-flow series is large.

the economic worth of an investment opportunity. The funds committed to certain proposals are relatively flexible; whereas those committed to others are not. For example, an investment in a multipurpose plant in a large city differs considerably from an investment in a special-purpose metal extraction complex in the wilderness of Canada. The former is reasonably marketable and may have a fairly high abandonment value; the latter represents a sunk cost that may never be recovered.[24] If the two projects had the same expected values of net-present values and standard deviations about these expected values, we would much prefer the former investment. A conventional analysis in capital budgeting, however, would not consider the important difference in abandonment values. If capital is to be allocated optimally, we must take into account possible differences in the future mobility of funds when evaluating investment proposals.[25]

In addition to evaluating new investment proposals, the procedure outlined above can be used to continually evaluate existing investment projects. The decision here is simply one of whether it is better to continue with the project or to abandon it and employ the funds elsewhere. Even though the project is profitable, it may make sense to abandon it if the abandonment value is sufficiently high. In other words, the optimal time to abandon is the point where the combination of expected future cash flows and future abandonment value has the highest present value. Through the continual assessment of projects, a company is able to weed out those that no longer are economically viable.

PROBLEMS

1. The Rettig Company can invest in one of two mutually exclusive projects. The two proposals have the following discrete probability distributions of net cash flows for period p:

A		B	
Probability	Cash Flow	Probability	Cash Flow
0.20	$1,000	0.10	$1,000
0.30	2,000	0.40	2,000
0.30	3,000	0.40	3,000
0.20	4,000	0.10	4,000

[24]As mentioned before, an investment project does not have to be sold externally to have abandonment value. Abandonment value can be depicted by the economic use of the asset in fields of endeavor within the firm other than those in which it is currently being used.

[25]For extensions and clarifications of this approach, see Pappas, "Role of Abandonment Value in Capital Asset Management," pp. 53–61; O. Maurice Joy, "Abandonment Values and Abandonment Decisions: A Clarification," *Journal of Finance*, 31 (December 1976), 1225–28; and Anthony F. Herbst, "An Algorithm for Systematic Economic Analysis of Abandonment Value in Capital Budgeting," *Engineering Economist*, 22 (Fall 1976), 63–71.

(a) Without calculating a mean and a coefficient of variation, can you select
the better proposal, assuming a risk-averse management?
(b) Verify your intuitive determination.

2. The probability distribution of possible net-present values for project x has an
expected value of $20,000 and a standard deviation of $10,000. Assuming a
normal distribution, calculate the probability that the net-present value will be
zero or less; that it will be greater than $30,000; and that it will be less than
$5,000.

3. The Dewitt Corporation has determined the following discrete probability distributions for net cash flows generated by a contemplated project:

Period 1		Period 2		Period 3	
Prob.	Cash Flow	Prob.	Cash Flow	Prob.	Cash Flow
0.10	$1,000	0.20	$1,000	0.30	$1,000
0.20	2,000	0.30	2,000	0.40	2,000
0.30	3,000	0.40	3,000	0.20	3,000
0.40	4,000	0.10	4,000	0.10	4,000

(a) Assume the probability distributions of cash flows for future periods are
independent. Also, assume that the after-tax risk-free rate is 4 percent. If the
proposal will require an initial outlay of $5,000, determine the expected value
of the net-present value.
(b) Determine the standard deviation about the expected value.
(c) If the total distribution is approximately normal and assumed continuous,
what is the probability of the net-present value being zero or less?
(d) What is the probability that the net-present value will be greater than zero?
(e) What is the probability that the profitability index will be 1.00 or less?
(f) What is the probability that the profitability index will be greater than 2?

4. Gomez Drug Products Company is considering investing in a new drug project
with an estimated life of three years. If demand for the new drug in the first period
is favorable, it is almost certain that it will be favorable in periods 2 and 3. By the
same token, if demand is low in the first period, it will be low in the two subsequent periods as well. Owing to this likely demand relationship, the company
feels that an assumption of perfect correlation of cash flows over time is appropriate. The cost of the project is $1 million, and possible cash flows for the three
periods are:

Period 1		Period 2		Period 3	
Prob.	Cash Flow	Prob.	Cash Flow	Prob.	Cash Flow
0.10	$ 0	0.15	$ 100,000	0.15	$ 0
0.20	200,000	0.20	400,000	0.20	150,000
0.40	400,000	0.30	700,000	0.30	300,000
0.20	600,000	0.20	1,000,000	0.20	450,000
0.10	800,000	0.15	1,300,000	0.15	600,000

Assuming the risk-free rate is 4 percent and it is used as the discount rate, calculate the expected value and standard deviation of the probability distribution of possible net-present values. Assuming a normal distribution, what is the probability of the project providing a net-present value of zero or less, of $300,000 or more, of $1,000,000 or more? Is the standard deviation calculated larger or smaller than it would be under an assumption of independence of cash flows over time?

5. The Dewitt Corporation (problem 3) has determined that its cash-flow distributions are not independent. Further, the company has estimated that the period 1 results will affect the period 2 flows as follows:

If P_1 = $1,000, the distribution for P_2 is:

.50	$1,000
.40	2,000
.10	3,000

If P_1 = $2,000, the distribution for P_2 is:

.20	$1,000
.50	2,000
.30	3,000

If P_1 = $3,000, the distribution for P_2 is:

.10	$1,000
.20	2,000
.50	3,000
.20	4,000

If P_1 = $4,000, the distribution for P_2 is:

.10	$2,000
.30	3,000
.50	4,000
.10	5,000

(a) What is the probability that the cash flow for P_2 will be $3,000?
(b) What is the probability that the cash flow for P_2 will be $5,000?
(c) What is the probability that the cash flow for P_2 will be $6,000?
(d) If P_1 = $3,000, what is the probability P_2 = $3,000?
(e) What is the probability that P_1 = $1,000 and P_2 = $1,000?
(f) What is the probability that P_2 will be greater than $3,000?
(g) What is the probability that P_2 will be greater than $3,000, given the fact that P_1 is greater than $3,000?

6. The Hume Corporation is faced with several possible investment projects. For each, the total cash outflow required will occur in the initial period. The cash outflows, expected net-present values, and standard deviations are as follows. (All projects have been discounted at a risk-free rate of 5 percent, and it is assumed that the distributions of their possible net-present values are normal.)

Project	Cost	Net-Present Value	σ
A	$100,000	$10,000	$20,000
B	50,000	10,000	30,000
C	200,000	25,000	10,000
D	10,000	5,000	10,000
E	500,000	75,000	75,000

(a) Construct a risk profile for each of these projects in terms of the profitability index.

(b) Ignoring size problems, are some projects clearly dominated by others?

(c) May size problems be ignored?

(d) What is the probability that each of the projects will have a net-present value ≥ 0?

(e) What decision rule would you suggest for adoption of projects within this context? Which (if any) of the above projects would be adopted under your rule?

7. Xonics Graphics, Inc., is evaluating a new technology for its reproduction equipment. The technology will have a three-year life and will cost $1,000, and its impact on cash flows is subject to risk. Management estimates that there is a fifty-fifty chance that the technology will either save the company $1,000 in the first year or save it nothing at all. If nothing at all, savings in the last two years would be zero as well. However, even here there is some possibility that in the second year an additional outlay of $300 will be required to convert back to the original process, for the new technology may result in a decrease in efficiency. Management attaches a 40 percent probability to this occurrence, given the fact that the new technology "bombs out" in the first year. If the technology proves itself, it is felt that second-year cash flows will be either $1,800, $1,400, or $1,000, with probabilities of 0.20, 0.60, and 0.20, respectively. In the third year, cash inflows are expected to be $200 greater or $200 less than the cash flow in period 2, with an equal chance of occurrence. (Again, these cash flows depend on the cash flow in period 1 being $1,000.)

(a) Set up a probability tree to depict the above cash-flow possibilities.

(b) Calculate a net-present value for each three-year possibility using a risk-free rate of 5 percent.

(c) What is the risk of the project?

8. The Bertz Company uses a simulation approach to judge investment projects. Three factors are employed: market demand, in units; price per unit minus cost per unit; and investment required at time 0. These factors are felt to be independent of one another. In analyzing a new consumer product, Bertz estimates the following probability distributions:

| | | **Price Minus** | | | |
| **Annual Demand** | | **Cost per Unit** | | **Investment Required** | |
Prob.	Units	Prob.	Dollars	Prob.	Dollars
0.05	10,000	0.10	$3.00	0.30	$1,800,000
0.10	20,000	0.20	4.50	0.40	2,000,000
0.20	30,000	0.40	6.00	0.30	2,300,000
0.30	45,000	0.20	7.00		
0.20	60,000	0.10	8.00		
0.10	75,000				
0.05	90,000				

(a) Using a random number table or some other random process, simulate twenty or more trials for these three factors and compute the return on investment for each trial. (Note: return = profit/investment.)

(b) Approximately what is the most likely return? How risky is the project?

9. The Windrop Company is considering investment in two of three possible proposals, the cash flows of which are normally distributed. The expected net-present value (discounted at a risk-free rate of 6 percent) and the standard deviation for each proposal are given as follows:

	1	2	3
Expected net-present value	$10,000	$8,000	$6,000
Standard deviation	4,000	3,000	4,000

Assuming the following correlation coefficients for each possible combination, which two proposals dominate?

Proposals	1	2	3	1 and 2	1 and 3	2 and 3
Correlation coefficients	1.00	1.00	1.00	.60	.40	.70

10. Zello Ice Cream Company is considering investing in a new product line—puddings. The expected value and standard deviation of the probability distribution of possible net-present values for the product line are $12,000 and $9,000, respectively. The company's existing lines are ice cream, cottage cheese, and yogurts. The expected values of net-present value and standard deviation for these product lines are:

	Net-Present Value	σ
Ice cream	$16,000	$8,000
Cottage cheese	20,000	7,000
Yogurts	10,000	4,000

184

The correlation coefficients between products are:

	Ice Cream	Cottage Cheese	Yogurts	Puddings
Ice cream	1.00			
Cottage cheese	0.90	1.00		
Yogurts	0.80	0.84	1.00	
Puddings	0.40	0.20	0.30	1.00

(a) Compute the expected value and the standard deviation of the probability distribution of possible net-present values for a combination consisting of existing products.

(b) Compute the expected value and standard deviation for a combination consisting of existing products plus puddings. Compare your results in (a) and (b). What can you say about the pudding line?

11. The Plaza Corporation is confronted with several combinations of risky investments:

Old Portfolios:	Net-Present Value	σ
A	$100,000	$200,000
B	20,000	80,000
C	75,000	100,000
D	60,000	150,000
E	50,000	20,000
F	40,000	60,000

New Portfolios:	Net-Present Value	σ
G	$120,000	$170,000
H	90,000	70,000
I	50,000	100,000
J	75,000	30,000

(a) Plot the above portfolios.

(b) Which portfolios dominate?

12. The R. Z. Frank Company is considering the acquisition of Aziz Car Leasing Company. Frank estimates that Aziz will provide incremental net income after taxes of $2 million in the first year, $3 million the second, $4 million the third, $5 million in each of the years 4 through 6, and $6 million annually thereafter. Due to the need to replenish the fleet, heavier than usual investments are required in the first two years. Capital investments and depreciation charges are expected to be:

Year	1	2	3	4	5	6	7 on
Capital investment (in millions)	$5	$5	$4	$4	$4	$4	$4
Depreciation (in millions)	$3	$4	$4	$4	$4	$4	$4

The risk-free rate is 6 percent and Aziz has $40 million in debt. Compute the adjusted present value of the acquisition based on these expectations. If you had a range of possible outcomes, how would you obtain the information necessary to analyze the acquisition?

APPENDIX A
Problem

1. The Kazin Corporation is considering introducing a new product, which it can distribute initially either in the state of Georgia or in the entire Southeast. If it distributes in Georgia alone, plant and marketing will cost $5 million, and Kazin can reevaluate the project at the end of three years to decide whether to go regional. To go regional at the end of three years would cost another $10 million. To distribute regionally from the outset would cost $12 million. The risk-free after-tax cost of funds to the firm is 4 percent. In either case, the product will have a life of six years, after which the plant will be worthless. Given the following data, what policy should Kazin adopt?

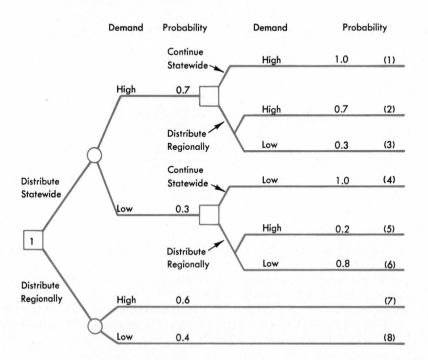

Decision tree—regional versus statewide distribution

Expected cash flows (in thousands)

Branch	0	1	2	3	4	5	6
				Years			
1	−$ 5,000	$1,000	$ 3,000	$ 5,000	$ 7,000	$ 4,000	$2,000
2	− 5,000	1,000	3,000	− 7,000	10,000	20,000	8,000
3	− 5,000	1,000	3,000	− 7,000	8,000	6,000	4,000
4	− 5,000	200	400	1,000	2,000	1,000	200
5	− 5,000	200	400	− 11,000	8,000	15,000	5,000
6	− 5,000	200	400	− 11,000	3,000	4,000	4,000
7	− 12,000	3,000	10,000	15,000	20,000	12,000	5,000
8	− 12,000	1,000	2,000	3,000	4,000	3,000	1,000

Problem

1. ABC Corporation is considering investing in a special-purpose piece of machinery costing $9,000 with a life of two years, after which there is no expected
salvage value. The possible incremental net cash flows are:

Year 1		Year 2	
Cash Flow	Probability	Cash Flow	Conditional Probability
$6,000	.3	$2,000	.3
		3,000	.5
		4,000	.2
7,000	.4	4,000	.3
		5,000	.4
		6,000	.3
8,000	.3	6,000	.2
		7,000	.5
		8,000	.3

The company's cost of capital is 8 percent.

(a) Calculate the expected value and standard deviation of the probability
distribution of possible net-present values.

(b) Suppose now that the possibility of abandonment exists and that the abandonment value of the project at the end of year 1 is $4,500. Calculate the new
expected value and standard deviation assuming the company abandons
the project if it is worthwhile to do so. Compare your calculations with those
in (a). What are the implications?

SELECTED REFERENCES

BAUM, SANFORD, ROBERT C. CARLSON, AND JAMES V. JUCKER, "Some Problems in Applying the Continuous Portfolio Selection Model to the Discrete Capital Budgeting Problem," *Journal of Financial and Quantitative Analysis*, 13 (June 1978), 333–44.

BIERMAN, HAROLD, JR., AND WARREN H. HAUSMAN, "The Resolution of Investment Uncertainty through Time," *Management Science*, 18 (August 1972), 654–62.

BIERMAN, HAROLD, JR., AND SEYMOUR SMIDT, *The Capital Budgeting Decision.* New York: Macmillan, 1975.

BOGUE, MARCUS C., AND RICHARD ROLL, "Capital Budgeting of Risky Projects with 'Imperfect' Markets for Physical Capital," *Journal of Finance*, 29 (May 1974), 601–13.

BONINI, CHARLES P., "Capital Investment under Uncertainty with Abandonment Options," *Journal of Financial and Quantitative Analysis*, 12 (March 1977), 39–54.

———, "Comment on Formulating Correlated Cash Flow Streams," *Engineering Economist*, 20 (Spring 1975), 209–14.

BOUDREAUX, KENNETH J., "Divestiture and Share Price," *Journal of Financial and Quantitative Analysis*, 10 (November 1975), 619–26.

BRUMELLE, SHELBY L., AND BERNHARD SCHWAB, "Capital Budgeting with Uncertain Future Opportunities: A Markovian Approach," *Journal of Financial and Quantitative Analysis*, 7 (January 1973), 111–22.

BUSSEY, LYNN E., AND G. T. STEVENS, JR., "Formulating Correlated Cash Flow Streams," *Engineering Economist*, 18 (Fall 1972), 1–30.

BUZBY, STEPHEN L., "Extending the Applicability of Probabilistic Management Planning and Control Models," *Accounting Review*, 49 (January 1974), 42–49.

CARTER, E. EUGENE, *Portfolio Aspects of Corporate Capital Budgeting.* Lexington, Mass.: Heath, 1974.

COHEN, KALMAN J., AND EDWIN J. ELTON, "Inter-Temporal Portfolio Analysis Based upon Simulation of Joint Returns," *Management Science*, 14 (September 1967), 5–18.

GREER, WILLIS R., JR., "Theory versus Practice in Risk Analysis: An Empirical Study," *Accounting Review*, 49 (July 1974), 496–505.

HARVEY, R. K., AND A. V. CABOT, "A Decision Theory Approach to Capital Budgeting under Risk," *Engineering Economist*, 20 (Fall 1974), 37–49.

HAYES, ROBERT H., "Incorporating Risk Aversion into Risk Analysis," *Engineering Economist*, 20 (Winter 1975), 99–121.

HERBST, ANTHONY F., "An Algorithm for Systematic Economic Analysis of Abandonment Value in Capital Budgeting," *Engineering Economist*, 22 (Fall 1976), 63–71.

HERTZ, DAVID B., "Investment Policies That Pay Off," *Harvard Business Review*, 46 (January-February 1968), 96–108.

———, "Risk Analysis in Capital Investment," *Harvard Business Review*, 42 (January-February 1964), 95–106.

HESPOS, RICHARD F., AND PAUL A. STRASSMANN, "Stochastic Decision Trees for the Analysis of Investment Decisions," *Management Science*, 11 (August 1965), 244–59.

HILLIER, FREDERICK S., "The Derivation of Probabilistic Information for the Evaluation of Risky Investments," *Management Science*, 9 (April 1963), 443–57.

———, "A Basic Model for Capital Budgeting of Risky Interrelated Projects," *Engineering Economist*, 20 (Fall 1974), 37–49.

JARRETT, JEFFREY E., "An Abandonment Decision Model," *Engineering Economist*, 19 (Fall 1973), 35–46.

JOY, O. MAURICE, "Abandonment Values and Abandonment Decisions: A Clarification," *Journal of Finance*, 31 (December 1976), 1225–28.

KEELEY, ROBERT, AND RANDOLPH WESTERFIELD, "A Problem in Probability Distribution Techniques for Capital Budgeting," *Journal of Finance,* 27 (June 1972), 703–9.

KRYZANOWSKI, LAWRENCE, PETER LUSZTIG, AND BERNHARD SCHWAB, "Monte Carlo Simulation and Capital Expenditure Decisions—A Case Study," *Engineering Economist,* 18 (Fall 1972), 31–48.

LEVY, HAIM, AND MARSHALL SARNAT, *Capital Investment and Financial Decisions.* Englewood Cliffs, N.J.: Prentice-Hall, 1978.

——,"The Portfolio Analysis of Multiperiod Capital Investment under Conditions of Risk," *Engineering Economist,* 16 (Fall 1970), 1–19.

LEWELLEN, WILBUR G., AND MICHAEL S. LONG, "Simulation versus Single-Value Estimates in Capital Expenditure Analysis," *Decision Sciences,* 3 (1973), 19–33.

LOCKETT, A. GEOFFREY, AND ANTHONY E. GEAR, "Multistage Capital Budgeting under Uncertainty," *Journal of Financial and Quantitative Analysis,* 10 (March 1975), 21–36.

MAGEE, J. F., "How to Use Decision Trees in Capital Investment," *Harvard Business Review,* 42 (September-October 1964), 79–96.

PAPPAS, JAMES L., "The Role of Abandonment Value in Capital Asset Management," *Engineering Economist,* 22 (Fall 1976), 53–61.

PORTER, R. BURR, ROGER P. BEY, AND DAVID C. LEWIS, "The Development of a Mean-Semivariance Approach to Capital Investment," *Journal of Financial and Quantitative Analysis,* 10 (November 1975), 639–49.

ROBICHEK, ALEXANDER A., "Interpreting the Results of Risk Analysis," *Journal of Finance,* 30 (December 1975), 1384–86.

ROBICHEK, ALEXANDER A., AND STEWART C. MYERS, "Conceptual Problems in the Use of Risk-Adjusted Discount Rates," *Journal of Finance,* 21 (December 1966), 727–30.

ROBICHEK, ALEXANDER A., AND JAMES C. VAN HORNE, "Abandonment Value and Capital Budgeting," *Journal of Finance,* 22 (December 1967), 577–89; EDWARD A. DYL AND HUGH W. LONG, "Comment," *Journal of Finance,* 24 (March 1969), 88–95; and ROBUCHEK AND VAN HORNE, "Reply," ibid., 96–97.

SALAZAR, RUDOLFO C., AND SUBRATA K. SEN, "A Simulation Model of Capital Budgeting under Uncertainty," *Management Science,* 15 (December 1968), 161–79.

SUNDEM, GARY L., "Evaluating Capital Budgeting Models in Simulated Environments," *Journal of Finance,* 30 (September 1975), 977–92.

VAN HORNE, JAMES C., "The Analysis of Uncertainty Resolution in Capital Budgeting for New Products," *Management Science,* 15 (April 1969), 376–86.

——, "Capital-Budgeting Decisions Involving Combinations of Risky Investments," *Management Science,* 13 (October 1966), 84–92.

——, "Capital Budgeting under Conditions of Uncertainty as to Project Life," *Engineering Economist,* 17 (Spring 1972), 189–99.

——, "The Variation of Project Life as a Means for Adjusting for Risk," *Engineering Economist,* 21 (Spring 1976), 151–58.

7

evaluation of risky investments: required rates of return for projects

A BRIEF CHARTING OF OUR COURSE

Having examined the measurement of risk for the individual investment proposal and combinations of proposals in Chapter 6, we turn now to the way this information might be evaluated in order to reach investment decisions consistent with a goal of maximizing the value of the firm to its stockholders. Both this chapter and the next are devoted to this endeavor. In this chapter, we take up the evaluation of individual investment projects. In Chapter 8, we consider the acceptance criterion for the company as a whole or for a division under restricted assumptions as to the homogeneity of project risk. We explore also in that chapter the evaluation of acquisitions.

The first part of this chapter discusses the implications the capital-asset pricing model has for decisions involving risky investments. This model was presented in Chapter 3 and involved such assumptions as efficient and perfect capital markets, well-diversified investors, and homogeneous expectations on their part. Given these assumptions, we will see that the required rate of return for a project depends only on that project's sys-

191

evaluation of risky
investments: required
rates of return
for projects

tematic risk. Recall that this is the risk associated with underlying movements in security prices and cannot be diversified away. The implication of this approach is that diversification of assets by the firm is not a thing of value. Accordingly, management should ignore the impact the project has on the firm's total variability of returns. The only thing that is important is the project's systematic risk, and this risk is completely divorced from the present risk complexion of the firm. On the surface, this may seem rather implausible. However, it will be shown that this implication follows from the assumptions implicit in the capital-asset pricing model. As a result, the diversification attributes of a project would not be considered in the investment decision.

If some of the underlying assumptions do not hold, however, the effect of a project on the overall risk of the firm may be a factor of importance. Bankruptcy costs, in particular, may affect things in this way. In the second part of this chapter, we explore the evaluation of risky investments when the impact of their acceptance on the total risk of the firm is a factor of importance. Under such circumstances, a project's diversification properties with respect to the total risk of the firm are a relevant consideration. Consequently, the firm would want to consider the "portfolio" effect of the project on its existing asset portfolio.

Having covered market-risk and firm-risk approaches to evaluating risky investments, we then attempt to reconcile the two approaches. Whether a person supplements the capital-asset pricing model approach with an analysis of the project's impact on the overall risk of the firm depends on the strength of one's convictions regarding the assumptions underlying the former approach. Bankruptcy costs and other underlying assumptions are examined. In the end, it will be seen that we advocate a combined approach to the problem. It is important to recognize that the topic of risky capital investments has undergone a considerable change in thinking in recent years. We hope to capture some of the controversy involved, but in the process the reader may become somewhat frustrated with the unsettled nature of the issue.

This leads us to the last part of the chapter. While conceptually a case can be made for a combined approach, using the capital-asset pricing model and a total variability analysis, we recognize that in practice many companies do not evaluate risky investments in this manner. Decision making is more subjective in nature. Even here, however, the expected return and risk of a project can be quantified and such information provided to management. Management, in turn, is able to make informed investment decisions based on this information. In the last section, we explore this approach. As we shall see, the critical factor is how accurately management is able to link risk-return information for an investment project with share price. The linkage tends to be subjective, thus detracting from the merit of this approach.

Having briefly charted the somewhat murky and unsettled waters that lie ahead, we are ready to begin. It is important that the reader keep this overview in mind as he or she sorts out some of the conflicting approaches to the problem. Depending on one's judgment of the importance of certain capital market imperfections, one approach or the other will seem more important.

EVALUATING PROJECTS IN A CAPITAL-ASSET PRICING MODEL CONTEXT

We turn now to the evaluation of investment proposals in a market equilibrium context.[1] Essentially, we will study the risk-return impact of a proposal on investors' portfolios of stocks rather than on the firm's portfolio of assets. In this regard, our concern is with systematic rather than with total risk. Assume initially that the firm has an all-equity capital structure. This facilitating assumption will be relaxed later in the section. Recall from Chapter 3 that according to the capital-asset pricing model, the expected rate of return on security j is

$$R_j = i + \frac{\overline{R}_m - i}{\sigma_m^2}(r_{jm}\sigma_j\sigma_m)$$

(7-1)

where i = risk-free rate

$\overline{R}_m$ = expected rate of return on the market portfolio of risky assets

σ_j = standard deviation of the probability distribution of possible returns for security j

σ_m = standard deviation of the probability distribution of possible returns for the market portfolio

r_{jm} = correlation between rates of return for security j and the market portfolio

The term $(r_{jm}\sigma_j\sigma_m)$ is the covariance of returns for security j with those of the market portfolio. For the diversified investor, $r_{jm}\sigma_j$ represents the portion of the total standard deviation of security j that is systematic. In other words, the investor cannot avoid this risk through diversification, because it arises from general movements in the market. The difference between total risk for security j, as measured by its standard deviation σ_j, and systematic risk is the risk that can be eliminated through efficient diversification. The term $(\overline{R}_m - i)/\sigma_m^2$ represents the market equilibrium relationship between risk and returns in excess of the risk-free rate. From Chapter 3, we know that it represents a measure of market-risk aversion and, when depicted graphically, the relationship is known as the security market line. (See Figure 3-9 in Chapter 3.) Implied is that in market equilibrium, security prices will be such that there is a linear tradeoff between the required rate of return and risk. The slope of the line indicates the degree of systematic risk for security j.

[1]This section assumes the reader has covered Chapters 2 and 3.

Application to Capital Budgeting

This framework has been applied to capital-budgeting projects.[2] It implies that projects should be judged in relation to their systematic risk. Thus the appropriate discount rate for project k is

$$R_k = i + \frac{\overline{R}_m - i}{\sigma_m^2}(r_{km}\sigma_k\sigma_m) \qquad (7\text{-}2)$$

where R_k = required rate of return for capital-budgeting proposal k

σ_k = standard deviation of the probability distribution of possible returns for proposal k

r_{km} = correlation between rates of return for proposal k and the market portfolio

We know from Chapter 3 that the beta of an asset is $\beta_k = (r_{km}\sigma_k\sigma_m)/\sigma_m^2$, so Eq. (7-2) can be expressed in terms of the more familiar

$$R_k = i + (\overline{R}_m - i)\beta_k \qquad (7\text{-}3)$$

where β_k is the slope of the characteristic line which describes the relationship between expected excess market rates of return for the project and expected excess returns for the market portfolio.[3] Later in this section we

---

[2]See Donald L. Tuttle and Robert H. Litzenberger, "Leverage, Diversification and Capital Market Effects on a Risk-Adjusted Capital Budgeting Framework," *Journal of Finance*, 23 (June 1968), 427–43; John Lintner, "The Valuation of Risk Assets and the Selection of Risky Investments in Stock Portfolios and Capital Budgets," *Review of Economics and Statistics*, 47 (February 1965), 13–27; Jan Mossin, "Equilibrium in a Capital Asset Model," *Econometrica*, 34 (October 1966), 768–75; Robert S. Hamada, "Portfolio Analysis, Market Equilibrium and Corporation Finance," *Journal of Finance*, 24 (March 1969), 13–31; Mark E. Rubinstein, "A Mean-Variance Synthesis of Corporate Financial Theory," *Journal of Finance*, 28 (March 1973), 167–82; Lawrence D. Schall, "Asset Valuation, Firm Investment, and Firm Diversification," *Journal of Business*, 45 (January 1972), 11–28; and Harold Bierman, Jr., and Jerome E. Hass, "Capital Budgeting under Uncertainty: A Reformulation," *Journal of Finance*, 28 (March 1973), 119–29. For support of the valuation of investment projects as securities using a state-preference framework, see Avraham Beja and Hayne E. Leland, "Direct Valuation and Corporate Financial Theory" (Working paper, Institute of Business and Economic Research, University of California, Berkeley, August 1977).

[3]The capital-asset pricing model is single period in time frame. For the extension of its application to capital-budgeting decisions involving multiperiod investments, see Richard Roll and Marcus C. Bogue, "Capital Budgeting of Risky Projects with Imperfect Markets for Physical Capital" *Journal of Finance*, 29 (May 1974), 606–12; Michael J. Brennan, "An Approach to the Valuation of Uncertain Income Streams," *Journal of Finance*, 28 (June 1973), 661–74; Stewart C. Myers and Stuart M. Turnbull, "Capital Budgeting and the Capital Asset Pricing Model: Good News and Bad News," *Journal of Finance*, 32 (May 1977), 321–32; and Eugene F. Fama, "Risk-Adjusted Discount Rates and Capital Budgeting under Uncertainty," *Journal of Financial Economics*, 5 (1977), 3–24.

In the last article, Fama investigates multiperiod cash flows in the context of the capital-asset pricing model. In particular, he analyzes the pattern of risk-adjusted discount rates

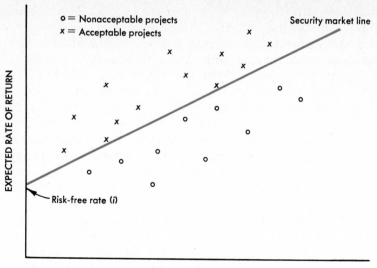

figure 7-1
Relationship between expected return and systematic risk

will show how the beta for a project can be determined and discuss the problems inherent in its determination. Now, however, we want to continue to concentrate on the general implications of the capital-asset pricing model approach to evaluating risky investments.

The acceptance criterion using this approach is to invest in a project if its expected return exceeds the required return, R_k, as determined with Eq. (7-3). The process can be viewed graphically in Figure 7-1. The line in the figure represents the security market line, and, as we know, it describes the market-determined relationship between systematic risk and required rate of return. All projects with expected internal rates of return lying on or above the line should be accepted, for they provide excess returns. These projects are depicted by the x's. All projects lying below the line, shown by the o's, would be rejected. The acceptance of projects lying above the line should result in an increase in share price.[4] With a higher risk-adjusted return than the market requires, investors will bid up the price of the stock until once again equilibrium is reached. At that point, all projects of the firm will lie on the security market line.

---

up to the time a cash flow is realized. Due to uncertainties about reassessments through time of the cash flow to be realized and its covariance with the cash flows of other firms in the market portfolio, the discount rates for different periods need not be the same. Fama demonstrates that implicit in the capital-asset pricing model is the fact that discount rates either are constant or follow a deterministic path over time. In general, the article describes the restrictions under which the capital-asset pricing model will work in a multiperiod setting. In our presentation above, we assume for simplicity a constant risk-adjusted discount rate through time. The reader interested in the problem should refer to the above articles.

[4]For proof that if a project's expected return exceeds the required rate under the assumptions above, market value share will rise, see Bierman and Hass, "Capital Budgeting under Uncertainty: A Reformulation," pp. 122–25.

195

evaluation of risky
investments: required
rates of return
for projects

The goal of the firm in this context is to search for investment opportunities lying above the line. This merely suggests that because security portfolios are available in the external financial markets that lie along the security market line, it makes little sense for the firm to invest in internally generated investment proposals unless they lie above the line. However, if product markets were perfect, one could not expect to find such opportunities. Investment opportunities would lie along or below the line, and the firm could expect to earn no more than the required rate of return. Thus the combination of perfect product markets along with perfect capital markets would rule out the ability of firms to earn excess returns for their stockholders. Put another way, firms could expect to earn no more on a project than the return required by the market on the basis of the systematic risk involved.

If product markets are less than perfect owing to such things as lags in adjustment, constraints on resource allocation, monopolistic powers, barriers to entry, and so forth, it is possible to find projects with expected returns above the security market line. While competition among firms will tend to drive expected returns toward the line, there may be sufficient lags so as to allow excess returns to be temporarily earned. The mark of a successful company is one that is able to continually identify and exploit such opportunities. In what follows, we assume that product markets are less than perfect.

Implications and Support of Position

One implication of the capital-asset pricing model approach to evaluating risky investments is that the required rate of return for the project does not depend on the company undertaking the investment. Given the project's systematic risk, the market expects a single return. Therefore the required rate of return on the project is the same for any firm that might invest in it. Stated differently, the systematic risk of a project is the same for all firms; therefore, the project's required return is the same. This is not to say that the project is equally valuable to all firms. Some firms will be able to derive greater incremental cash flows from it than others. Because of differences in expertise, management efficiency, synergism, and so forth, the expected return can vary among firms. Consequently, the project will be more valuable to some firms than to others. However, the acceptance standard will be the same for all firms considering the project.

Because the capital-asset pricing model assumes that all risk other than systematic risk is diversified away by investors in their portfolios of stocks, diversification by the firm in its portfolio of capital assets is not a thing of value. In other words, the model implies that the firm is unable to do something for investors that they cannot do for themselves.[5] Given the as-

---

[5]For an evaluation of this concept in a state-preference mold, see Stewart C. Myers, "Procedures for Capital Budgeting under Uncertainty," *Industrial Management Review,* 9 (Spring 1968), 1–15.

sumptions of the model, investors are able to achieve the same diversification as the firm is able to do for them. One could argue that while investors are able to diversify across companies whose stocks are publicly traded, they cannot diversify across capital assets held by these companies. In other words, they purchase shares in the income stream of the company as a whole, not in the income streams of the individual assets of the company.

However, investors do not need to acquire direct claims on capital assets in order to accomplish such diversification. As long as there is information available about the actual returns on individual assets, investors are able to effectively diversify across capital assets of individual companies. In essence, an investor can replicate the return stream of the individual capital asset held by a firm.[6] For example, suppose a firm holds three productive assets—A, B, and C—and that complete information exists about the actual ex-post returns on these assets. In order to "invest" in asset A, but not in assets B and C, the investor could buy x percent of the stock of the company. He then would sell claims against himself based on promises to pay x percent of the future income streams associated with assets B and C. That is, in a particular year if asset B were to provide a $100 return and asset C a $200 return, he would pay $100 x and $200 x to the holders of the claims. In this way, the investor is able to effectively replicate the income stream of a single capital asset of a firm, that of asset A in our example.

It is in this sense that investors are able to diversify effectively across capital assets of individual firms. As a result, the firm is said not to be able to do something for investors through diversification of capital assets that they cannot do for themselves. Therefore investment projects should be evaluated only on the basis of their systematic risk, not on the basis of their total risk or the incremental risk they contribute to the firm as a whole.

We have tried to present the implications of the capital-asset pricing model for capital investment in their purest form. From Chapter 3, we know that there are many assumptions implicit in the model. When these assumptions are relaxed, certain implications arising from the use of the model must be modified. Later in this chapter we explore such modifications. First, however, we need to show how the required rate of return for a project can be measured, using the capital-asset pricing model approach.

Measuring the Required Return

To measure the required rate of return for an investment proposal using the capital-asset pricing model approach, one needs to estimate the relationship between its cash flows and the returns available on the market

---

[6]See Schall, "Asset Valuation, Firm Investment, and Firm Diversification," pp. 13–21, for amplification on this point as well as proof of the irrelevancy of diversification decisions by the firm.

portfolio. Using the index model method described in Chapter 3, the required rate of return on project k can be expressed as

$$R_k = i + \beta_k[R_m - i] \qquad (7\text{-}4)$$

where β_k is a measure of the responsiveness of the excess return for the project (over the risk-free rate, i) to the excess return on the market portfolio, $R_m - i$. Though this expression of a project's required rate of return is simple enough in concept, its measurement is complicated by the fact that the usual measures of return for a stock and for a project are not directly comparable. As pointed out in Chapters 2 and 3, the return for a stock or for a portfolio of stocks is expressed as the return on investment for a month, a quarter, or a year, depending on the time frame used. Thus the return on investment is

$$R = \frac{P_t - P_{t-1} + D_t}{P_{t-1}} \qquad (7\text{-}5)$$

where P_t = price of stock or market index at time t
D_t = dividend paid during period t

Using historical data, the excess return for the stock is regressed against the excess return for the market index to obtain the beta, or regression coefficient. This coefficient indicates the responsiveness of excess returns for a stock to excess returns for the market index. Because one-period returns are measured in the same way for both series, the procedure is appropriate.

With investment projects, however, profitability usually is expressed in terms of the internal rate of return or the net-present value. Both involve multiperiod as opposed to single-period time frames. Therefore, the return for the market index, a single-period measure, and the return for a capital investment project, a multiperiod measure, are not directly comparable.[7] Moreover, there is a problem in the way the two measures are calculated. The return on investment for the market index involves the change in its capitalized value from the start of a period to the end. The cash-flow measures of profitability for an investment project do not take account of changes in capitalized value from period to period. Thus there is a basic problem of incompatibility between the two measures of return.

Surrogate Market Information

One way to come to grips with the problem is to try to express the profitability of an investment project in terms of its cash flow during the period and its change in value from the beginning of the period to the end.

---

[7]For further discussion of this problem, see Donald R. Lessard and Richard S. Bower, "An Operational Approach to Risk Screening," *Journal of Finance,* 28 (May 1973), 321–38.

In this way, the two return measures would be compatible. The one-period return for an investment project would be

$$R_t = \frac{V_t + A_t - V_{t-1}}{V_{t-1}}$$

(7-6)

where V_t = the market value of the project at the end of period t

A_t = net cash flow received at the end of period t

The difficulty, of course, is in estimating the value of the project at the end of a period. One approach is to use externally determined market values for the asset. In the case of certain investment projects, the market value is fairly well established. For machine tools, for example, a secondary market of sorts exists where prices are established for used machines of various ages. Other assets have similar markets where prices can be determined. Later in this section, we will illustrate the derivation of the required rate of return using this method. First, however, we wish to explore other surrogates.

In many cases, the project is sufficiently similar to a company whose stock is publicly held so that one is able to use that company's beta in deriving the required rate of return for the project. In the case of large projects, such as new products, one frequently can identify publicly traded stocks that are engaged entirely, or almost entirely, in this type of operation. The important thing is to identify a company or companies with systematic risk characteristics similar to the project in question.

Suppose, for example, that a steel company was considering the formation of a real estate subsidiary. As there are a number of real estate companies with publicly traded stocks, one simply could determine the beta for one of those companies or a group of them and use it in Eq. (7-4) to derive the required rate of return for the project. Note that the relevant required rate of return is not that for the steel company, but that for other real estate firms. Stated differently, the real estate venture of the steel company is viewed by the market in the same way as are other firms engaged solely in real estate. By concentrating on companies in the same line of business as that which the firm desires to enter, surrogates of this sort often can be found which approximate the systematic risk of the project. While an exact duplication of the project's risk is unlikely, reasonable approximations are possible.[8]

[8]Another approach to the problem is to develop betas for a company, or part thereof, based on accounting data. Here an accounting measure of return for a company or division, such as the return on assets, is related to an economy-wide index of returns, such as the average return on assets for nonfinancial corporations. Regressing the former on the latter, a beta or regression coefficient is determined which is said to depict the systematic risk of returns for the company or division. The procedure for determining and evaluating accounting betas is analogous to that used for market betas previously illustrated. The appeal of this approach is that it does not require data on market returns for the project. Such data often are difficult, if not impossible, to obtain. In contrast, data on accounting returns are readily available.

Recognizing the advantages of data availability, then, the question becomes whether accounting betas are good surrogates for market betas. While various empirical studies show a

199

evaluation of risky
investments: required
rates of return
for projects

To illustrate, suppose that the average beta for a sample of real estate companies whose stocks were publicly traded and whose basic businesses were similar to the venture contemplated by the steel company were 1.6. We then could use this beta as a surrogate for the beta of the project. If we expected the average return on the market portfolio of stocks to be 12 percent and the risk-free rate to be 6 percent, the required rate of return for the project would be $R_k = .06 + (.12 - .06)1.6 = 15.6$ percent. Therefore, 15.6 percent would be used as the required rate of return for the project. If the real estate venture were expected to provide an internal rate of return in excess of, or equal to, this rate, the project would be accepted. If not, it would be rejected.

For publicly held stocks, one does not have to calculate the betas oneself. Instead, a number of services provide historical beta information on stocks. These betas are computed on the basis of weekly, monthly, or quarterly data for three to ten years in the past. Services providing beta information include Merrill Lynch, Pierce, Fenner and Smith; Wells Fargo Bank; and the Value Line Investment Survey. These services allow one to obtain betas for a particular company with relative ease. Thus, when a prospective investment project is similar to a company whose stock is publicly traded, one should definitely use such beta information.

Illustration of Derivation of Required Rate of Return

In this section, we illustrate the derivation of the required rate of return for a project when the beta surrogate of a publicly traded company is not available. The example has been simplified to work with annual as opposed to quarterly, monthly, or weekly data. Also for the sake of simplicity

---

significant statistical association between accounting and market betas for companies, the explanatory power is only moderate. For the individual company, the ability to predict market betas on the basis of accounting betas is too low to make the approach anything but a crude approximation. Therefore we concentrate on developing market return information.

For development of the accounting-market beta issue as well as empirical tests in this regard, see William Beaver, Paul Kettler, and Myron Scholes, "The Association between Market Determined and Accounting Determined Risk Measures," *Accounting Review,* 45 (October 1970), 654–82; William Beaver and James Manegold, "The Association between Market-Determined and Accounting-Determined Measures of Systematic Risk: Some Further Evidence," *Journal of Financial and Quantitative Analysis,* 10 (June 1975) 231–84; H. Richardson Pettit and Randolph Westerfield, "A Model of Capital Asset Risk," *Journal of Financial and Quantitative Analysis,* 7 (March 1972), 1649–68; Myron J. Gordon and Paul J. Halpern, "Cost of Capital for a Division of a Firm," *Journal of Finance,* 29 (September 1974), 1153–63; Nicholas J. Gonedes, "A Note on Accounting-Based and Market-Based Estimates of Systematic Risk," *Journal of Financial and Quantitative Analysis,* 10 (June 1975), 355–65; John S. Bildersee, "The Association between a Market-Determined Measure of Risk and Alternative Measures of Risk," *Accounting Review,* 50 (January 1975), 81–98; and Paul A. Griffin, "The Association between Relative Risk and Risk Estimates Derived from Quarterly Earnings and Dividends," *Accounting Review,* 51 (July 1976), 499–515. Many of these studies are summarized in George Foster, *Financial Statement Analysis* (Englewood Cliffs, N.J.: Prentice-Hall, 1978), Chap. 9.

we assume an all-equity company. A careful study of this example will show how beta information can be derived in practice and how such information can be used to approximate the required rate of return for a project.

Suppose Albar Dairy Products Company is considering investing in a multiple-purpose machine costing $130,000 to use in the production of cottage cheese. The company has had experience with similar machines in the past and feels it is appropriate to use past behavior as a proxy for the future. Suppose that the history of a comparable machine was that shown in Table 7–1. In this table, the external market price of the asset is an estimate of the price prevailing in the market for used machines. This value is set by the forces of supply and demand. The return computed in column (4) is simply the external value at the end of the year less the beginning value plus the net cash flow that occurred, all over the beginning value.

Now that the project cash flows are expressed in terms of market-based annual returns, we are able to compute the beta. Our procedure is to determine the slope of the "least squares" linear regression line, where the excess return of the project is regressed against the excess return of the market index.[9] For purposes of illustration, this slope, or regression coefficient, is computed by hand. The "least squares" method is described in most statistics texts and the reader should have little difficulty in following the example. Thankfully, computer routines exist to compute the relevant statistics associated with a regression analysis. Still, it is instructive to go through the calculations and that is one of the purposes of this illustration.

Suppose that Standard and Poor's 500-stock index showed the one-year returns reported in column (1) of Table 7-2. These returns are computed

table 7-1
History of machine used by Albar Dairy Products Company

Year-End	(1) Purchase Price	(2) External Market Value	(3) Actual Net Cash Flow (after tax)	(4) Annual Return $\frac{(2)_t + (3)_t - (2)_{t-1}}{(2)_{t-1}}$
Start	$110,000	$110,000		
19–0		$100,000	$20,000	.091
19–1		84,000	27,000	.110
19–2		64,000	22,000	.024
19–3		53,000	26,000	.234
19–4		40,000	20,000	.132
19–5		33,000	18,000	.275
19–6		24,000	13,000	.121
19–7		19,000	12,000	.292
19–8		13,000	8,000	.105
19–9	(Salvage value)	9,000	5,000	.077

[9]The least squares method fits a regression line to the observations so that the sum of the squares of the deviations from that line are as small as possible.

table 7-2
Computation of excess returns for market index and project, and cross product

Year	(1) Market Return R_{mt}	(2) Risk-Free Rate i	(3) Excess Market Return (M) (1) − (2)	(4) Excess Market Return Squared $(M)^2$ (3)²	(5) Project Return R_{kt}	(6) Excess Return Project (K) (5) − (2)	(7) Cross Product Excess Returns (MK) (3) × (6)
19—0	.09	.03	.06	.0036	.091	.061	.0037
19—1	.15	.05	.10	.0100	.110	.060	.0060
19—2	(.04)	.04	(.08)	.0064	.024	(.016)	.0013
19—3	.23	.06	.17	.0289	.234	.174	.0296
19—4	.16	.04	.12	.0144	.132	.092	.0110
19—5	.26	.05	.21	.0441	.275	.225	.0473
19—6	(.10)	.05	(.15)	.0225	.121	.071	(.0107)
19—7	.25	.07	.18	.0324	.292	.222	.0400
19—8	.12	.05	.07	.0049	.105	.055	.0039
19—9	(.02)	.06	(.08)	.0064	.077	.017	(.0014)
Total	1.10	.50	.60	.1736	1.461	.961	.1307
Average return	.11	.05	.06		.146	.096	

with Eq. (7-5) and constitute capital gains or losses, together with dividends received. The risk-free rate, shown in column (2), might simply be the yield available on relative short-term government securities. In column (3) of the table, the excess return for the market index is determined simply by subtracting the risk-free rate from the market return. In the next column, this excess return is squared and the sum appears at the bottom. The return on the project (shown in the last column of Table 7-1) is reported in column (5) of Table 7-2. In column (6), the excess return on the project is determined. In the last column, the cross product is calculated by multiplying the excess return for the market by the excess return for the project. At the bottom of the columns, the sums of the numbers of the columns are determined and, in the next row, the average is computed for the five return columns. The average is simply the total divided by the number of years, which is ten.

The beta, or slope of the regression line, is determined by the following formula:

$$\text{Beta} = \frac{\Sigma MK - n\overline{M}\overline{K}}{\Sigma M^2 - n\overline{M}^2} \tag{7-7}$$

where ΣMK is the sum of the cross products, n is the number of years, $\overline{M}$ is the average excess market return, $\overline{K}$ is the average excess project return, and $\Sigma \overline{M}^2$ is the sum of the squares of excess market returns. For our example in Table 7-2, the beta is

$$\text{Beta} = \frac{.1307 - (10)(.06)(.096)}{.1736 - (10)(.06)^2} = \frac{.0731}{.1376} = 0.53 \tag{7-8}$$

Again it is important to stress that computer routines can easily solve for the slope of a linear regression line, which is the beta as defined. A beta of 0.53 suggests that the project has only moderate systematic risk. Recall from Chapter 3 that any beta less than 1.00 is said to characterize a defensive investment. Given the beta, we have the most important piece of information necessary to calculate the project's required rate of return.

However, there are two additional pieces of information necessary before we can make such a computation—the expected risk-free rate and the market rate of return. As with the beta, one is interested in likely *future* outcomes. If the past seems like a reasonable proxy for the future, however, one might use average historical rates of return. For example, suppose one felt that the arithmetic means of the risk-free rates and market returns that prevailed over the ten-year period in our example were reasonable proxies for the future. From Table 7-2, these averages are seen to be 5 percent and 11 percent, respectively. With this additional information, we now are able to estimate the required rate of return for the project. Using Eq. (7-3), it is

$$R_k = \bar{i} + (\overline{R}_m - \bar{i})\beta_k = .05 + (.11 - .05).53 = .082 \tag{7-9}$$

where $\bar{I}$ and $\bar{R}_m$ are the arithmetic means of risk-free rates and actual S & P 500-stock index returns, respectively. Thus the required rate of return, or cost of capital, for the project is 8.2 percent. The reason the required return is less than the average return for the market index, 11 percent, is that the project has a relatively low covariance with the market index.

The critical assumption is that past experience is a good proxy for the future. That is, the association between project returns and market returns is likely to be the same in the future as it has been in the past. In addition, future returns on a riskless investment and on the market portfolio must be expected to be approximately the same as their returns in the past. If these assumptions hold, R_k can be used as an approximation of the project's required rate of return. Expected net cash flows for the new, but similar, project would be discounted at this rate. If the net-present value were positive, the project would be accepted; if not, it would be rejected. To illustrate the acceptance criterion, suppose the expected net cash flows for the project under consideration were:

Time	0	1	2	3	4	5	6	7	8	9	10
Expected net cash flow after tax (in thousands)	$(130)	$35	$32	$28	$25	$22	$18	$15	$12	$10	$8

When we discount this cash-flow stream at the proposed required rate of return of 8.2 percent, we find the net-present value to be $19,663. Because this figure is positive, the proposal should be accepted according to the method employed.

Qualifications as to Measuring Valuation Changes

As can be visualized, the procedure is crude in that we use the past as a proxy for the future. Nevertheless, all required-rate-of-return calculations are similarly plagued. The real problem is when the project being evaluated is unlike past projects with which the firm or outside specialists have had experience. Here estimates of the responsiveness of project returns to market returns must be estimated subjectively, and they are subject to considerable error.

If the project is relatively self-contained, such as a new division, it should be compared with another firm or subsidiary of a firm. If the firm or subsidiary has publicly traded stock, it is an easy matter to use such returns to compute the beta and the required rate of return for the project. As suggested earlier in our example of a steel company investing in a real estate venture, this proxy is likely to be quite accurate. Whenever possible, then, comparisons of a project with publicly held companies should be used.

The important thing is that the project return estimates be rooted in market data either directly or indirectly. Estimates of beta will vary in quality with the capability of the project with assets whose capitalized value can be determined from period to period. For many investment projects, reasonable market-based estimates are possible. However, certain projects are sufficiently unique to make the estimation of beta nothing more than a guess. This operational shortcoming of the capital-asset pricing model approach must be recognized.

In addition to the beta, it is important that the numbers used for the market return and for the risk-free rate be the best estimates of the future that are possible. The past may or may not be a good proxy. For example, if the past were represented by a period of relative economic stability but in the future considerable inflation were expected, averages of past market returns and past risk-free rates would be biased and low estimates of the future. In this case, it would be a mistake to use historical average returns in the calculation of the required return for a project. In another situation, realized market returns in the recent past might be very high and not expected to continue. As a result, the use of the historical past would result in too high an estimate of the future market return.

In situations of this sort, direct estimates of the market return and of the risk-free rate must be made. These estimates might be consensus estimates of security analysts, economists, and others who regularly predict such returns. In recent years, consensus estimates of the expected market return have ranged between 9 and 14 percent, and estimates of the short-term risk-free rate between 4 and 8 percent. In periods of high anticipated inflation, estimates tend to be in the upper part of these ranges. The important thing is that the market return and the risk-free rate employed in Eq. (7–4) be the current market consensus of the expected return on common stocks and the expected return on short-term Treasury securities. Many of the problems raised in this section will be discussed later when we attempt to reconcile market and nonmarket approaches to capital budgeting for risky investments.

EVALUATING PROJECTS IN TERMS OF THE TOTAL RISK OF THE FIRM

We stated in the introduction to this chapter that if some of the assumptions of the capital-asset pricing model do not hold, the effect of a project on the total risk of the firm may be important. Leaving aside for the moment whether or not these assumptions hold, we want to explore here the evaluation of risky investments if they do not. That is, we assume that the *only* thing that is important is the risk and return of the individual firm, and that projects are evaluated with respect to their marginal impact on these two factors. In the subsequent section, we examine the critical assumptions of the capital-asset pricing model and attempt to reconcile the capital-asset pricing model approach with the total variability approach presented in this section. Our attention now, however, is directed to the evaluation of risky investments solely in relation to their impact on the total risk and return of the firm.

205

evaluation of risky
investments: required
rates of return
for projects

Evaluation of Combinations
of Risky Investments

From Chapter 6 we know that the marginal risk of an individual proposal to the firm as a whole depends upon its correlation with existing projects as well as its correlation with proposals under consideration that might be accepted. We suggested that the appropriate information was the standard deviation and expected value of the probability distribution of possible net-present values for all feasible combinations of existing projects and investment proposals under consideration. We consider now the selection of the most desirable combination, deferring until later in the chapter the fundamental question of whether a portfolio approach should be used at all. We assume that management is interested only in the marginal impact of an investment proposal on the risk complexion of the firm as a whole.

The selection of the most desirable combination of investments will depend upon its utility preferences with respect to net-present value and variance, or standard deviation. If management is averse to risk and associates risk with the variance of net-present value, its utility function may be similar to that shown in Figure 7-2.[10] As discussed in Chapter 3, the curves in the figure are indifference curves; management is indifferent to any combination of expected value of net-present value and standard deviation on a

figure 7-2
**Selection of the
best portfolio**

[10]See Chapter 2 for a discussion of one way to map a decision maker's utility preferences.

particular curve. Thus a specific curve portrays the tradeoff between the two parameters for a particular company. The indifference curves in Figure 7–2 suggest that management's utility function is a monotonic increasing concave one, indicating decreasing marginal rates of substitution between standard deviation and net-present value. As the dispersion of possible net-present values of the firm increases, it takes increasing amounts of net-present value for management to accept additional increments of risk.

As we move to the right in Figure 7–2, each successive curve represents a higher level of utility. Thus management would choose the combination of investments that lies on the highest indifference curve, the one farthest to the right, because this curve represents the greatest utility. This combination is determined by the intersection of a dot in the figure—point L—with the highest indifference curve. Point L represents the portfolio of existing projects and proposals under consideration that possesses the most desirable combination of expected value of net-present value and risk. One should recognize that the presentation above is mainly conceptual in that it assumes a utility function for management can be graphed. In fact, a group utility function can be derived only under very restricted conditions.[11]

Project Combination Dominance

However, the framework for evaluating combinations of risky investments developed above is quite useful even if management's utility function is not defined. For example, we might present management with the information shown by the dots in Figure 7–2. With this, management can eliminate most combinations simply because they are dominated by other combinations. Unless management is quite averse to risk, it probably would consider only four portfolios of risky investments, B, H, L, and P. From these management would choose the one that it felt offered the best combination of expected return and risk.

This selection determines the new investment proposal or proposals that will be accepted. An exception would occur only when the portfolio selected was comprised of existing projects. In this situation, no investment proposals under consideration would be accepted. If the portfolio of existing projects were represented by portfolio E in Figure 7-2, however, the selection of any of the four portfolios would imply the acceptance of one or more new investment proposals. Those investment proposals under consideration that were not in the portfolio finally selected would be rejected, of course.

If management's indifference curves were approximately linear, the evaluation procedure described above would be reduced to a simple comparison of reward-to-variability ratios with and without the investment

---

[11]See Robert Wilson, "The Theory of Syndicates," *Econometrica*, 36 (January 1968), 119–32.

proposal(s) under consideration. In the case of only one proposal being considered, it should be accepted if

207

evaluation of risky
investments: required
rates of return
for projects

$$\frac{\overline{NPV}_{k+e}}{\sigma_{k+e}} > \frac{\overline{NPV}_e}{\sigma_e} \tag{7-10}$$

where $\overline{NPV}_{k+e}$ = expected value of the probability distribution of possible net-present values for all existing assets, e, and the proposal under consideration, k

σ_{k+e} = standard deviation of this probability distribution

$\overline{NPV}_e$ = expected value of the probability distribution of possible net-present values for all existing assets

σ_e = standard deviation of this probability distribution

The approach can be expanded to include multiple investment proposals under consideration in obvious ways.

In summary, management is able to determine which investment proposals under consideration offer the best marginal contribution of expected value of net-present value and standard deviation to the firm as a whole. In determining the standard deviation for a portfolio, consideration is given to the correlation of an investment proposal with existing investment projects, as well as with other new investment proposals. Implied in this evaluation is that the total risk of the firm is what is important; therefore, investment decisions should be made in light of their marginal impact on total risk. The evaluation is firm-risk oriented in the sense that management does not consider explicitly the impact of the project on investors' portfolios, only upon the portfolio of assets of the firm.[12]

RECONCILIATION OF THE TWO APPROACHES

We have examined two ways to evaluate risky investments. One involves evaluating a project in relation to its systematic risk; the other involves analyzing the incremental impact of the project on the business-risk complexion of the firm as a whole. The obvious question is, Which is correct? Perhaps the best insight into this question can be gained if we examine in more detail the assumptions of the capital-asset pricing model. Recall that the risk or total variability of an individual stock is comprised of non-diversifiable, or systematic, risk as well as residual risk. The assumptions of the capital-asset pricing model imply that the latter risk can be diversified away by efficient investors and, consequently, is not a factor affecting value.

[12]For an empirical study that finds a high degree of correlation between total risk and systematic risk and which argues for the evaluation of investment projects in a total firm-risk context, see M. Chapman Findlay III, Arthur E. Gooding, and Wallace Q. Weaver, Jr., "On the Relevant Risk for Determining Capital Expenditure Hurdle Rates," *Financial Management*, 5 (Winter 1976), 9–16.

If the assumptions of the capital-asset pricing model do not entirely hold under real-world conditions, residual risk may be a factor that, in some measure, affects the value of the firm. In this case, the impact of a project on the firm's total variability of returns would be of some importance.

Critical Assumptions in the Capital-Asset Pricing Model

One assumption in the capital-asset pricing model is particularly crucial, and that is that the cost of insolvency or bankruptcy is zero. If a firm fails, assets presumably can be sold for their economic values without selling or legal costs. After creditors have been paid, the residual proceeds are distributed to stockholders. As long as assets can be sold at their economic values in a frictionless world, investors are able to effectively diversify their risk. Under real-world conditions, however, assets often have to be sold in bankruptcy at distress prices. Moreover, there are selling costs, legal fees, and other out-of-pocket costs involved. Finally, and probably most important, there are a number of delays and inefficiencies involved in the process of going through a bankruptcy. As bankruptcy is approached, there are losses of supplies, of employees, and of sales, which make operations inefficient to say the least. Due to a cumbersome legal process, delays occur in a creditor takeover during which asset values deteriorate. All of these factors represent a "drain on the system" to suppliers of capital and work either directly or indirectly to the detriment of stockholders, the residual owners of the firm.

It is important to recognize that the probability of a firm's becoming insolvent depends on its *total* risk, not just on its *systematic* risk. Therefore a case can be made for choosing projects in light of their effect on both the systematic and the total (systematic plus residual) risk of the firm. Put another way, when insolvency and/or bankruptcy costs are significant, investors may well be served by the firm's paying attention to the total risk of the firm in capital budgeting for risky investments and not just to its systematic risk. If management exercises a degree of risk aversion greater than that which would maximize shareholder wealth, it will place an even greater emphasis upon residual risk.

Other market imperfections also make residual risk important. Recall that the capital-asset pricing model assumes borrowing and lending by investors is possible at the same rate, that there are no transaction costs, and that information is available without cost to all market participants. In the real world, the borrowing rate typically exceeds the lending rate, there are transactions costs, and investors incur costs in obtaining information. All of these factors limit the effectiveness with which investors are able to diversify away unsystematic, or residual, risk. As a result, residual risk becomes a factor of at least some importance in valuation. Although these imperfections probably are not as important as the cost of insolvency and/or bankruptcy, nonetheless they contribute to the importance of residual risk.

Where does this leave us? It suggests that one should consider the impact of a project on both the systematic risk and the total risk of the firm.[13] If both the capital-asset pricing model approach and the total variability approach for evaluating a project give clear accept or reject signals, those signals should be followed. The obvious problem is when one approach gives an accept signal and the other a reject one. When this occurs, management needs to assess which approach is more applicable. If the stock of the company involved is publicly held, if the possibility of insolvency is remote, and if the firm is able to realistically express expected project returns in terms of changes in market-based capitalized values on a one-period basis, a strong case can be made for using the signal given by the capital-asset pricing model. However, if the stock is traded in a market with high transaction and information costs, if the possibility of insolvency and/or bankruptcy is significant, and if the expression of project returns in terms of market-based returns is crude, greater reliance should be placed on the total variability approach. Even here, however, one should recognize that a portion of the residual risk can be diversified away.

It should be obvious that the methods proposed are not operationally perfect. Still, they represent a means for judging risky investments. In the years to come, we can expect the state of the art to be improved. It is clear that the impact of a project on risk is important and must be considered if the firm is to make investment decisions that maximize shareholder wealth. It also is clear that management must consider the effect of a project not only upon the risk complexion of the firm but upon the systematic risk of investors. The latter is a relatively new consideration that is only beginning to have operational feasibility. Although the approach has many difficulties, we can expect to see improvements in the future. The idea that the market for common stocks is relatively efficient forces a firm in this direction if its objective is truly one of maximizing shareholder wealth.

EVALUATING A SINGLE PROJECT IN A RISK CONTEXT

Although we have advocated the combined approach described above for evaluating risky investments, we must recognize that other approaches are used. In fact, most firms use neither of the two approaches examined in their evaluation of risky investments. The risk and return of individual projects

---

[13]This posture is taken also by Lessard and Bower, "An Operational Approach to Risk Screening," pp. 321–38.

often is quantified, and management makes a decision whether to accept or reject the project on the basis of this information. In so doing, it assesses neither the systematic risk of the project nor its likely effect on the variability of cash flows and earnings of the firm as a whole.

We have purposely postponed consideration of this approach until last. It is not that we do not recognize the practical reasons for its use, but we wanted to present the sounder conceptual approach first. Lest one feel that this was for nought, it should be remembered that actual practices with respect to the evaluation of risky investments have changed dramtically over time. Whereas a short time back risk was seldom quantified and investment projects were evaluated on the basis of their expected accounting rates of return, many companies now quantify risk in a sophisticated manner and most use discounted cash-flow types of analyses. It is not unreasonable to expect that the approach suggested earlier in this chapter will find increasing acceptance. Indeed, certain corporations are already using variations of it. With this in mind, let us consider the evaluation of individual projects in a firm-risk context.

Expected Value–Standard Deviation Judgments

From Chapter 6 we saw that information about the expected return and risk of the probability distribution of possible returns can be determined for the individual investment proposal. Given this information, the question becomes whether the project should be accepted or rejected. For purposes of illustration, we will work only with the expected value and standard deviation of the probability distribution of possible net-present values. Because the concepts presented are for the internal-rate-of-return method, it is not necessary to illustrate them twice. Recall from Chapter 6 that the information generated for an investment proposal was the probability distribution of possible net-present values using the risk-free rate as the discount factor. From this distribution, one is able to derive the probability that the net-present value of the project will be zero or less. This probability corresponds to the probability that the project's internal rate of return will be less than the risk-free rate.

In the evaluation of a single proposal, it is unlikely that management would accept an investment proposal having an expected value of net-present value of zero unless the probability distribution had no dispersion. In this special case, the proposal, by definition, would be riskless. For risky investments, the net-present value would have to exceed zero. How much it would have to exceed zero before acceptance were warranted depends upon the amount of dispersion of the probability distribution and the utility preferences of management with respect to risk.

figure 7-3
**Probability
distribution of
profitability indexes
—proposal** X

Use of Risk Profiles

In order to facilitate selection as well as to make it consistent over time, management may wish to formulate maximum risk profiles. To express the probability distributions in relative instead of absolute terms, we can convert the net-present value probability distribution into a distribution of possible profitability indexes. For proposal X, our example problem in Chapter 6, the initial cash outflow was $10,000 and the expected value of the probability distribution of net-present values was $1,173. Thus the profitability index is ($1,173 + $10,000)/$10,000 = 1.12. The profitability index for zero net-present value is (0 + $10,000)/$10,000 = 1.00. Similarly, we can convert the entire probability distribution to a probability distribution of possible profitability indexes. The converted probability distribution for the example problem is seen in Figure 7-3.

If management has specified maximum risk profiles for various expected values of profitability indexes, one would simply compare proposal X with the maximum risk profile for an expected value of profitability index of 1.12. If the dispersion of the proposal is less than that for the risk profile, the proposal would be accepted. If not, it would be rejected. The maximum level of dispersion permitted, as depicted by the risk profile, will increase with the expected value of profitability index. For a profitability index of 1.02, the dispersion of the maximum risk profile will be narrower than that for a profitability index of 1.10. An illustration of some hypothetical risk profiles is shown in Figure 7-4. We note that the greater the expected value of profitability index, the greater the dispersion that is tolerable to management.

Once maximum risk profiles are specified, project selection becomes automatic. For a given expected value of profitability index, the dispersion of the probability distribution for the proposal must be less than or equal to that for the maximum risk profile in order for the proposal to be accepted. Management's specification of these risk profiles will depend upon its toler-

figure 7-4
Risk profiles

ances. While one would expect the allowable dispersion to increase with increases in the expected value of profitability index, as shown in Figure 7-4, there is still the question of whether the profiles overall are too conservative or too liberal.

The real problem, of course, is that the link to share price is not direct. Management is presented with information about the expected return and risk of a project and on the basis of this information reaches a decision. However, there is no direct link to the likely reaction of well-diversified investors. This link depends entirely upon the perceptiveness of management in judging investors' tradeoff between profitability and risk. Moreover, there is no analysis of the impact of the project on the total risk of the firm; as we know, this factor becomes important if capital markets are less than perfect. In essence, the project is evaluated in isolation of investors and of existing investment projects. For these reasons, the approach leaves much to be desired. Still, we must recognize that in practice most investment decisions are made by management in this way. By providing management with information about the dispersion of possible outcomes, more informed decisions are possible than in the conventional capital-budgeting analysis where only the expected values of cash flows are considered.

213

evaluation of risky
investments: required
rates of return
for projects

SUMMARY

In this chapter, we considered the evaluation of risky investments, given information developed in the preceding chapter about the expected value and the standard deviation of the probability distribution of possible returns. The first approach was the application of the capital-asset pricing model to capital investments. This approach relates the acceptance of a project to the undiversifiable risk of investors. Thus projects are evaluated in a market context, and the cost of capital, or required rate of return, is computed for each project. The method was illustrated with an example. We saw that there is a problem of incompatibility between the usual measures of return for stocks and for capital investment projects. This problem can be resolved by expressing project returns on a one-period basis and in terms of changes in capitalized value. The principle implication of the approach is that investors are able to diversify away all residual risk on their own. Therefore diversification by the firm of capital investment projects is not a thing of value. Investors are able to accomplish the same thing on their own.

The second approach examined was the evaluation of projects with respect to their incremental impact on the total return and risk of the firm. Here one is concerned with various combinations of existing investment projects and investment proposals under consideration. A portfolio framework was presented for analyzing the tradeoff between risk and expected value of net-present value for different combinations of investments. Management can then choose the best combination of risk and return for the firm as a whole. This approach has particular value in the case of a privately held company. It also has merit if the assumptions of the capital-asset pricing model do not entirely hold in practice.

In the next section, we attempted to reconcile the two approaches under real-world conditions. We saw that the capital-asset pricing model depends on several assumptions, one of which is perfect markets. When we allow for the cost of bankruptcy as well as other market imperfections, residual risk becomes a factor of importance. In such cases, a dual system for evaluating risky investments can be used where both the capital-asset pricing model and the total variability approaches are employed.

Finally, we presented the evaluation of single investment projects without reference to either systematic risk considerations or considerations of the impact of the project on the total risk of the firm. Here management makes a decision to accept or reject a project on the basis of the expected value and standard deviation of the distribution of possible returns. Because of the reasons cited, the link to share price is far from direct and the approach accordingly suffers. Still, it is widely used and represents a step toward increasing sophistication in the evaluation of risky investments. In the next chapter, "Required Rates of Return for Companies, Divisions, and Acquisitions," we continue our investigation of the evaluation of risky investments.

PROBLEMS

1. The capital-asset pricing model suggests that the required rate of return on a project is

$$R_k = i + \frac{\overline{R}_m - i}{\sigma_m^2}(r_{km}\sigma_k\sigma_m),$$

where the symbols are identified under Eq. (7-2). If a regression model is used, how is the beta, the responsiveness coefficient, defined in terms of the above equation? Substituting beta into the above equation, what does it become?

2. Acosta Sugar Company has estimated that the overall return for Standard & Poor's 500-stock index will be 14 percent over the next ten years. The company also feels that the interest rate on Treasury bills will average 7 percent over this interval. The company is considering expanding into a new product line, almonds. It has had no experience in this line but has been able to obtain information on various companies involved in producing and processing nuts. While no company examined is entirely in almonds, Acosta's management feels that the beta for such a company would be 1.10 once the almond operation was ongoing. However, there is some uncertainty as to the beta that will actually prevail. Management has attached the following probabilities to possible outcomes:

Probability	0.2	0.3	0.2	0.2	0.1
Beta	1.00	1.10	1.20	1.30	1.40

(a) What is the required rate of return for the project using the mode beta of 1.10?

(b) What is the range of required rates of return?

(c) What is the expected value of required rate of return?

3. The North Bend Bait Company is contemplating an investment to get it into the **215**

evaluation of risky
investments: required
rates of return
for projects
production and sale of spinning rods and reels. Heretofore, it has produced only
artificial baits. The financial manager of the company, Mr. Bruno Litzenberger,
feels that the only way to analyze the merit of the project is with a capital-asset
pricing model approach. Fortunately, there is a publicly held company that is in
the business of producing only spinning fishing equipment—Super Splash
Spinning Corporation. Mr. Litzenberger feels it appropriate to use this company
as a benchmark for measuring risk.

The actual returns to investors in Super Splash Spinning Corp. over the last
ten years were those shown in the following table. Also shown are one-year
returns for Standard & Poor's 500-stock index and the risk-free rate.

Year-End	Annual Return Super Splash Spinning Corporation	Annual Return Market Index	Risk-Free Rate
19–0	.12	.09	.03
19–1	.19	.15	.05
19–2	(.08)	(.04)	.04
19–3	.28	.23	.06
19–4	.22	.16	.04
19–5	.32	.26	.05
19–6	(.14)	(.10)	.05
19–7	.30	.25	.07
19–8	.17	.12	.05
19–9	(.12)	(.02)	.06
Average return	.126	.11	.05

Mr. Litzenberger believes that the average annual return for the market index and
the average annual return for the risk-free rate over the ten-year period are
reasonable proxies for what are likely to prevail in the future.

(a) Compute the beta for Super Splash Spinning Corporation.
(b) What is the required return for the project? What assumptions are critical?

4. The spinning rod and reel project in problem 3 costs $600,000 and is expected to
provide the following incremental net cash flows:

Year	1	2	3	4	5	6	7	8	9	10
Net cash flow (in thousands)	$50	$100	$125	$125	$150	$150	$150	$100	$75	$50

No cash flows are predicted beyond ten years, as North Bend Bait Company has
found that the product life for profitable operations is about ten years. North
Bend has an all-equity capital structure. Should the company undertake the
spinning equipment project?

5. Rich Diggings Gold Mining Company is considering the purchase of a new
dredge. During the last ten years it has used an old dredge which is about worn
out. A viable secondary market exists for dredges, as with proper conversion

they can be used for purposes other than gold mining. The external market values, as well as the actual incremental cash flows generated as a result of having the old dredge, were as follows:

	Purchase Price	External Market Value	Actual Net Cash Flow
Start	$400,000	$400,000	$ —
19–1	—	360,000	100,000
19–2	—	300,000	75,000
19–3	—	250,000	60,000
19–4	—	220,000	80,000
19–5	—	180,000	70,000
19–6	—	150,000	66,000
19–7	—	120,000	30,000
19–8	—	80,000	70,000
19–9	—	50,000	21,000
19–0	—	40,000	17,000

(a) Compute the annual returns, using external market values as the base.

(b) If the information on annual returns for the market index and for the risk-free rate is the same as that shown in problem 3, compute the required return for the project, assuming past relationships are a reasonable proxy for the future.

(c) Suppose the new dredge costs $600,000 and the expected cash flows are exactly the same as in problem 4 for the spinning equipment project. Should the new dredge be purchased? If your answer differs from that in problem 4, explain the reason why.

6. The Empire Mining Company's existing portfolio of assets has an expected value of net-present value of $30 million and a standard deviation of $20 million. The company is considering four new explorations. The sixteen possible portfolios have the following characteristics.

Possible Portfolio	Expected Net-Present Value (in millions)	Standard Deviation (in millions)
1. Existing assets (EA) only	$30	$20
2. EA plus #1	33	23
3. EA plus #2	32	21
4. EA plus #3	35	24
5. EA plus #4	34	25
6. EA plus 1 and 2	35	23
7. EA plus 1 and 3	38	25
8. EA plus 1 and 4	37	26
9. EA plus 2 and 3	37	24
10. EA plus 2 and 4	36	25
11. EA plus 3 and 4	39	28
12. EA plus 1, 2, and 3	40	26
13. EA plus 1, 2, and 4	39	27
14. EA plus 1, 3, and 4	42	30
15. EA plus 2, 3, and 4	41	28
16. EA plus 1, 2, 3, and 4	44	31

(a) Plot these various portfolio possibilities on graph paper.
(b) With a firm-risk approach to evaluating risky investment, which portfolio do you prefer?
(c) If you had a risk-neutral utility function, which portfolio would you choose?

17
evaluation of risky
investments: required
rates of return
for projects

7. Two investment proposals are under consideration that are mutually exclusive. The following information is relevant:

	Expected Value of Net-Present Value	Standard Deviation
Proposal A	$10,000	$ 5,000
Proposal B	12,000	10,000

What is the probability that the actual net-present value will be zero or less? Which proposal would you accept?

8. After making a careful study of the risk preferences of its management, the Henken Aviation Company has determined certain risk profiles for investment projects. These risk profiles depict the maximum standard deviation of profitability index that is tolerable for a particular expected value of profitability index. (The profitability index is the present value of future cash flows of a project divided by the initial cash outlay.) The risk profiles for various profitability indexes are as follows:

Expected Profitability Index	Maximum Standard Deviation
1.00	0
1.05	0.04
1.10	0.10
1.15	0.15
1.20	0.21
1.25	0.26

The company is considering two new investment proposals which are expected to have the following characteristics:

Proposal X Cost = $2 million		Proposal Y Cost = $5 million	
Net-Present Value	Probability of Occurrence	Net-Present Value	Probability of Occurrence
−$0.5 million	0.10	−$0.4 million	0.10
0	0.20	0.1 million	0.15
0.5 million	0.40	0.5 million	0.50
1.0 million	0.20	0.9 million	0.15
1.5 million	0.10	1.4 million	0.10

Given the risk profiles of the company, should either or both of the two proposals be accepted?

SELECTED REFERENCES

BEAVER, WILLIAM, PAUL KETTLER, AND MYRON SCHOLES, "The Association between Market Determined and Accounting Determined Risk Measures," *Accounting Review*, 45 (October 1970), 654–82.

BEAVER, WILLIAM, AND JAMES MANEGOLD, "The Association between Market Determined and Accounting Determined Measures of Systematic Risk: Some Further Evidence," *Journal of Financial and Quantitative Analysis*, 10 (June 1975).

BEN-SHAHAR, HAIM, AND FRANK M. WERNER, "Multiperiod Capital Budgeting under Uncertainty: A Suggested Application," *Journal of Financial and Quantitative Analysis*, 12 (December 1977), 859–78.

BIERMAN, HAROLD, JR., AND JEROME E. HASS, "Capital Budgeting under Uncertainty: A Reformulation," *Journal of Finance*, 28 (March 1973), 119–30.

BILDERSEE, JOHN S., "The Association between a Market-Determined Measure of Risk and Alternative Measures of Risk," *Accounting Review*, 50 (January 1975), 81–98.

BRENNAN, MICHAEL J., "An Approach to the Valuation of Uncertain Income Streams," *Journal of Finance*, 28 (June 1973), 661–74.

CHEN, A. H., AND A. J. BONESS, "Effects of Uncertain Inflation on the Investment and Financing Decisions of a Firm," *Journal of Finance*, 30 (May 1975), 469–84.

FAIRLEY, WILLIAM B., AND HENRY D. JACOBY, "Investment Analysis Using the Probability Distribution of the Internal Rate of Return," *Management Science*, 21 (August 1975), 1428–37.

FAMA, EUGENE F., "Risk-Adjusted Discount Rates and Capital Budgeting under Uncertainty," *Journal of Financial Economics*, 5 (1977), 3–24.

FAMA, EUGENE F., AND MERTON H. MILLER, *The Theory of Finance*, Chap. 7. New York: Holt, Rinehart & Winston, 1972.

FINDLAY, M. CHAPMAN, III, ARTHUR E. GOODING, AND WALLACE Q. WEAVER, JR., "On the Relevant Risk for Determining Capital Expenditure Hurdle Rates," *Financial Management*, 5 (Winter 1976), 9–16.

FOSTER, GEORGE, *Financial Statement Analysis*, Chap. 9. Englewood Cliffs, N.J.: Prentice-Hall, 1978.

GONEDES, NICHOLAS J., "A Note on Accounting-Based and Market-Based Estimates of Systematic Risk," *Journal of Financial and Quantitative Analysis*, 10 (June 1975), 355–65.

HAMADA, ROBERT S., "Portfolio Analysis, Market Equilibrium and Corporation Finance," *Journal of Finance*, 24 (March 1969), 13–31.

HAYES, ROBERT H., "Incorporating Risk Aversion into Risk Analysis," *Engineering Economist*, 20 (Winter 1975), 99–121.

HILLIER, FREDERICK S., "A Basic Model for Capital Budgeting of Risky Interrelated Projects," *Engineering Economist*, 17 (Fall 1971), 1–30.

LESSARD, DONALD R., AND RICHARD S. BOWER, "An Operational Approach to Risk Screening," *Journal of Finance*, 28 (May 1973), 321–38.

LINTNER, JOHN, "The Evaluation of Risk Assets and the Selection of Risky Investments in Stock Portfolios and Capital Budgets," *Review of Economics and Statistics*, 47 (February 1965), 13–37.

MYERS, STEWART C., "Procedures for Capital Budgeting under Uncertainty," *Industrial Management Review,* 9 (Spring 1968), 1–15.

MYERS, STEWART C., AND STUART M. TURNBULL, "Capital Budgeting and the Capital Asset Pricing Model: Good News and Bad News," *Journal of Finance,* 32 (May 1977), 321–32.

PETTIT, H. RICHARDSON, AND RANDOLPH WESTERFIELD, "A Model of Capital Asset Risk," *Journal of Financial and Quantitative Analysis,* 7 (March 1972), 1649–68.

ROLL, RICHARD, AND MARCUS C. BOGUE, "Capital Budgeting of Risky Projects with Imperfect Markets for Physical Capital," *Journal of Finance,* 29 (May 1974), 606–12.

RUBINSTEIN, MARK E., "A Mean-Variance Synthesis of Corporate Financial Theory," *Journal of Finance,* 28 (March 1973), 167–82.

SCHALL, LAWRENCE D., "Asset Valuation, Firm Investment, and Firm Diversification," *Journal of Business,* 45 (January 1972), 11–28.

————, "Firm Financial Structure and Investment," *Journal of Financial and Quantitative Analysis,* 6 (June 1971), 925–42.

STAPLETON, RICHARD C., "Portfolio Analysis, Stock Valuation and Capital Budgeting Rules for Risky Projects," *Journal of Finance,* 26 (March 1971), 95–118.

THOMPSON, HOWARD E., "Mathematical Programming, the Capital Asset Pricing Model and Capital Budgeting of Interrelated Projects," *Journal of Finance,* 31 (March 1976), 125–31.

TURNBULL, STUART M., "Market Value and Systematic Risk," *Journal of Finance,* 32 (September 1977), 1125–42.

TUTTLE, DONALD L., AND ROBERT H. LITZENBERGER, "Leverage, Diversification and Capital Market Effects on a Risk-Adjusted Capital Budgeting Framework," *Journal of Finance,* 23 (June 1968), 427–43.

VAN HORNE, JAMES C., "The Analysis of Uncertainty Resolution in Capital Budgeting for New Products," *Management Science,* 15 (April 1969), 376–86.

————, "Capital-Budgeting Decisions Involving Combinations of Risky Investments," *Management Science,* 13 (October 1966), 84–92.

————, "Optimal Initiation of Bankruptcy Proceedings by Debt Holders," *Journal of Finance,* 31 (June 1976), 897–910.

WESTON, J. FRED, "Investment Decisions Using the Capital Asset Pricing Model," *Financial Management,* 2 (Spring 1973), 25–33.

219

evaluation of risky
investments: required
rates of return
for projects

8
required rates of return for companies, divisions, and acquisitions

In this chapter, we extend our evaluation of risky investments to the company as a whole, to divisions of a company, and to prospective acquisitions. Our focus is on determining the required rate of return for each. In the case of a company or subunit thereof, there is an aggregation of assets. As we shall see, the use of an aggregate required rate of return is appropriate only when those assets are homogeneous with respect to risk, and investment proposals under consideration are of the same character. If investment projects are widely variant with respect to risk, an aggregate required rate of return is not appropriate as an acceptance criterion.

The advantage to using an aggregate required rate is its simplicity. Once it is computed, projects can be evaluated using a single rate which does not change unless underlying conditions change. This avoids the problems involved in computing individual required rates of return for each investment proposal, as was taken up in the last chapter. However, it is important that if an aggregate required rate of return is used, projects correspond to the above conditions.

The development of this chapter will parallel to some extent that of

Chapter 7. First we consider the required rate of return under the assumptions of the capital-asset pricing model and then move on to consider other means for measuring it. The degree to which the former approach needs modification depends on the strength of one's convictions regarding the assumptions inherent in the model. We begin with the cost of capital of a company and then consider the required rate of return for a division. Most of the concepts applicable to the company apply also to the division. Therefore, in discussing the latter, we concentrate on the distinguishing features as well as the implications involved in the use of a divisional cost of capital. Finally, we consider the evaluation of a potential acquisition and the appropriate acceptance criterion for that decision.

COST OF CAPITAL OF THE FIRM

The overall cost of capital of a firm is comprised of the costs of the various components of financing. The most difficult of these costs to measure is the cost of equity capital, and this topic will occupy most of our attention. However, we also consider the costs of debt and preferred stock. To the extent that the historical cost of a source of funds parallels closely the present cost, historical costs may give us some insight. However, our concern is with the *marginal* cost of a specific source of financing. Only if the past is a good surrogate for the future are historical costs of use to us. After covering the various individual costs, we will show how they can be combined into an overall cost of capital for the company.

Cost of Equity Capital in a Market Context

In theory, *cost of equity capital* can be defined as the minimum rate of return that a company must earn on the equity-financed portion of its investments in order to leave unchanged the market price of its stock. From the preceding chapter and Chapter 3, we know that the capital-asset pricing model implies that the required return on a stock is

$$R_j = i + \left(\frac{R_m - i}{\sigma_m^2} \right) (r_{jm} \sigma_j \sigma_m)$$

(8-1)

where i = the risk-free rate

R_m = the expected value of return for the market portfolio

σ_m = standard deviation of the probability distribution of possible market returns

σ_j = standard deviation of the probability distribution of possible returns for security j

r_{jm} = correlation coefficient between returns for security j and the market portfolio

The last term, $(r_{jm}\sigma_j\sigma_m)$, represents the covariance of returns for security j with those of the market. We know that the greater the covariance, the greater the return that will be required for security j. The key consideration is that investors cannot diversify away this risk. Therefore the greater the covariance, the greater the systematic risk and the greater the required return. This required return represents the cost of equity capital of the firm in a market context.

Measuring the Cost of Equity Capital   If the historical relationship between security returns and those for the market portfolio is believed to be a reasonable proxy for the future, one can use past returns to generate the information necessary to compute the required rates of return. Recall from Chapters 3 and 7 that Eq. (8-1) can be expressed as

$$R_j = i + (R_m - i)\beta_j \tag{8-2}$$

where beta is the measure of the responsiveness of the excess return for the security to the excess return for the market portfolio. If a broad-based market index, such as Standard & Poor's 500-stock index, is used as a surrogate for the market portfolio, the actual return on security j, less the risk-free rate, in each period would be regressed against the return for the market index, less the risk-free rate. The return for a particular period is simply the ending price less the beginning price plus dividends received during the period, all over the beginning price.

The regression equation is

$$R_{jt} - i_t = \beta_j(R_{mt} - i_t) \tag{8-3}$$

where R_{jt} is the return for security j in period t, i_t is the risk-free rate in period t, β_j is the regression coefficient, and R_{mt} is the return for the market index in period t. Using a reasonable number of past observations, a regression study is run and the regression coefficient, β_j, generated.

As mentioned in the preceding chapter, several services provide beta information on stocks that are actively traded. These betas are computed on the basis of weekly, monthly, and quarterly data for anywhere from three to ten years in the past. Among the larger "beta providers" are Merrill Lynch, Pierce, Fenner and Smith; Wells Fargo Bank; and the Value Line Investment Survey. Through these services one can readily obtain the beta for a company, thereby facilitating the calculation of the cost of equity capital for that company.

An Example   To illustrate the calculation of beta and the cost of equity capital by hand, however, we turn to a simple example. Instead of using monthly data, on which most beta calculations are based, we use annual data for ease of illustration. Suppose that during the last ten years, the one-year returns for Standard & Poor's 500-stock index were those shown in column (1) of Table 8-1, and that returns for security j were those shown in

table 8-1

Computation of excess returns for market index and security j, and cross product

Year	(1) Market Return R_{mt}	(2) Risk-Free Rate i	(3) Excess Market Return (M) (1)–(2)	(4) Excess Market Return Squared $(M)^2$ (3)^2	(5) Stock Return R_{jt}	(6) Excess Return Stock (J) (5)–(2)	(7) Cross Product Excess Returns (MJ) (3)×(6)
19–0	.09	.03	.06	.0036	.05	.02	.0012
19–1	.15	.05	.10	.0100	.31	.26	.0260
19–2	(.04)	.04	(.08)	.0064	(.06)	(.10)	.0080
19–3	.23	.06	.17	.0289	.18	.12	.0204
19–4	.16	.04	.12	.0144	.25	.21	.0252
19–5	.26	.05	.21	.0441	.12	.07	.0147
19–6	(.10)	.05	(.15)	.0225	(.07)	(.12)	.0180
19–7	.25	.07	.18	.0324	.09	.02	.0036
19–8	.12	.05	.07	.0049	.22	.17	.0119
19–9	(.02)	.06	(.08)	.0064	(.12)	(.18)	.0144
Total	1.10	.50	.60	.1736	.97	.47	.1434
Average return	.11	.05	.06		.097	.047	

column (5). The arithmetic means of the returns are shown at the bottom of the two columns. In the second column, the risk-free rate as depicted by the yield on short-term government securities is shown, with the arithmetic mean computed at the bottom.

We know from Chapter 7 that with this information we can compute the beta, which is simply the slope of the regression line when the stock's excess return is regressed against the market excess return. The problem can be solved by hand or with a regression program. In any real-world situation involving a number of observations, one would want to use a regression routine. However, we will illustrate the calculations by hand, as we did in the preceding chapter. In the third and sixth columns of Table 8-1, the excess returns (above the risk-free rate) for the market index and for stock j are computed. In column (4), the market excess return is squared; and in column (7), the cross product of the two excess returns is computed. At the bottom of the table, the totals of the columns are shown, as are the average returns.

With this information, we are able to compute the beta, or slope of the regression line, with the following formula:

$$\text{Beta} = \frac{\Sigma MJ - n\overline{M}\overline{J}}{\Sigma M^2 - n\overline{M}^2} \tag{8-4}$$

where ΣMJ is the sum of the cross products, n is the number of years, $\overline{M}$ is the average excess market return, and $\overline{J}$ is the average excess return for security j. For our example,

$$\text{Beta} = \frac{.1434 - (10)(.06)(.047)}{.1736 - (10)(.06)^2} = \frac{.1152}{.1376} = 0.837 \tag{8-5}$$

This result suggests that returns of security j fluctuate somewhat less than those of the market. (A beta of 1.00 would indicate an exact correspondence.) Therefore the security is somewhat less risky than the market as a whole. If the expected risk-free rate is an average of the risk-free rates that prevailed over the ten-year period and the expected market return is an average of market returns over that period, the required return for security j is

$$R_j = .05 + (.11 - .05)0.837 = .1002$$

Thus the required rate of return or cost of equity capital is approximately 10 percent for security j. In a manner similar to our example, we can approximate the cost of equity capital for other securities using the capital-asset pricing model approach. The critical assumption is that the past relationship between a security's return and the market return will hold in the future. In addition, it is important that the market return and the risk-free rate represent expected future returns. When past returns are believed not to be good proxies for the future, it may be better to estimate these returns directly. As mentioned in Chapter 7, in recent years consensus estimates of the expected market return have ranged between 9 and 14 percent and estimates of the risk-free rate between 4 and 8 percent. These estimates tend to be in the upper part of the range in periods of high anticipated inflation and in the lower part of the range when inflation is moderate.

Once the required rate of return for security j has been determined, it is used as the cost of equity capital. In essence, we are saying that this is the rate that investors expect the firm to earn on its equity. This cost then is employed in a weighted-average cost of capital for the firm. Determination of the latter will be taken up shortly, once we have explored further the cost of equity capital as well as the costs of other sources of financing.

Some Qualifications

As discussed in the preceding chapter, the capital-asset pricing model assumes the presence of perfect capital markets. Under this as well as other assumptions, the required rate of return on equity is determined by the company's systematic risk. When these assumptions are relaxed to take account of real-world conditions, the residual risk of a stock may take on a degree of importance. Recall that the total risk of a security is comprised of its systematic risk as well as its residual risk. The assumption of the capital-asset pricing model is that the latter can be completely diversified away, which leaves us only with the former risk.

However, we showed in Chapter 7 that the costs of bankruptcy work to the detriment of stockholders. In essence, these costs represent external drains on the system. As they cannot be diversified away by investors, the total risk of the firm becomes a factor of concern. Stated differently, the probability of a firm going bankrupt depends on the total variability of its cash flows. If there were no costs associated with a creditor takeover, investors would concern themselves only with the systematic risk of a security. As long as the assets of the bankrupt firm could be sold or traded at their economic values, no penalty would be involved. The fact that an individual firm might go bankrupt would be embraced in the overall systematic risk the investor was willing to tolerate in his portfolio.

With bankruptcy costs, however, there is a penalty to the investor. The greater the cost of bankruptcy and the greater the probability of its occurrence, the more concerned the investor will be with the total risk of the firm. Thus the greater the residual risk of a company, the greater the expected bankruptcy costs to be incurred, holding systematic risk constant. As a result, investors will demand a higher required return for the company than that dictated by its systematic risk alone. Therefore the required rate of return given by the capital-asset pricing model needs to be adjusted upward if this factor is to be taken into account. Stipulating the exact adjustment is difficult in practice, though in theory it can be rigorously specified.[1] However, we

225

required rates of return
for companies, divisions,
and acquisitions

---

[1]For a state-preference approach to the measurement of bankruptcy costs, see James C. Van Horne, "Optimal Initiation of Bankruptcy Proceedings by Debt Holders," *Journal of Finance,* 31 (June 1976), 897–910.

know that the greater the probability of bankruptcy occurring, the greater the upward adjustment necessary. Fragmentary evidence suggests that administrative expenses in a business bankruptcy are approximately 20 percent of the value of the estate. By multiplying the probability of occurrence of bankruptcy times the asset value of the firm under distress conditions times 20 percent, one obtains a very crude picture of the expected bankruptcy costs that might be involved. The required rate of return would be adjusted upward accordingly.

In addition to bankruptcy costs, other relaxations in the assumptions of the capital-asset pricing model will result in residual risk being a factor of importance. In effect, imperfections in the capital markets impede investment behavior consistent with efficient diversification. Therefore the greater the imperfections, the greater the allowance that must be made for residual risk, and the greater the upward adjustment necessary in the required rate of return.

Another Way to Measure the Cost of Equity Capital

In measuring the cost of equity capital, one is concerned with approximating the rate of return required by investors. The capital-asset pricing model approach, with appropriate adjustments, is one means by which this can be done. Another way we might approach the problem of determining the required rate of return is to estimate the stream of expected future dividends per share, as perceived by investors at the margin, and then solve for the rate of discount that equates this stream with the current market price of the stock.

Briefly reviewing from Chapter 2, the value of a share of stock to investors can be viewed as the present value of the expected future stream of income paid to them. Because dividends are all that stockholders as a whole receive from their investment, this stream of income is the cash dividends paid in future periods and, perhaps, a final liquidating dividend. At time 0, the value of a share of stock is

$$P_0 = \frac{D_1}{(1 + k_e)} + \frac{D_2}{(1 + k_e)^2} + \cdots + \frac{D_\infty}{(1 + k_e)^\infty}$$

$$P_0 = \sum_{t=1}^{\infty} \frac{D_t}{(1 + k_e)^t} \tag{8-6}$$

where P_0 is the value of a share of stock at time 0, D_t is the dividend per share expected to be paid in period t, and k_e is the appropriate rate of discount. We suggested in Chapter 2 that investors formulate subjective probability distributions of dividends per share expected to be paid in various future periods. For the individual investor, the D_t in Eq. (8-6) are the expected values, or means, of these probability distributions. For the market as a whole, the D_t represent the expected values for investors at the margin, and k_e is the market discount factor appropriate for the risk involved. The

cost of equity capital is defined as the market rate of discount, k_e, that equates the present value of all expected future dividends per share with the current market price of the stock. This cost is found by solving Eq. (8-6) for k_e.

If dividends per share are expected to grow at a constant rate, g, and k_e is greater than g, we discovered in Chapter 2 that

$$P_0 = \frac{D_1}{k_e - g} \tag{8-7}$$

where D_1 is the dividend per share expected to be paid at the end of period 1. Thus the cost of equity capital would be

$$k_e = \frac{D_1}{P_0} + g \tag{8-8}$$

The critical assumption, of course, is that dividends per share are expected to grow at a compound rate of g forever. In certain situations, this assumption may be a fair approximation of investor expectations. For example, if ABC Company's expected dividend per share at the end of period 1 is $2, the current market price is $40, and earnings and dividends per share are expected to grow about 6 percent per annum, the company's cost of equity capital is

$$k_e = \frac{2}{40} + .06 = 11 \text{ percent}$$

For the k_e to be realistic, expectations in the marketplace must be such that dividends per share are believed to grow in fact at a rate of g. The important factor, then, is measuring the growth in dividends per share as perceived by investors at the margin.

To the extent that the past trend in earnings per share is felt to be meaningful for predicting this expected future growth, it may be used as the growth variable. For example, suppose a company had the following history of earnings per share:

	Earnings per Share		Earnings per Share
1971	$1.50	1976	$2.19
1972	1.68	1977	2.38
1973	1.78	1978	2.49
1974	1.92	1979	2.45
1975	2.07	1980	2.70

If one averaged the figures for the first three years and the last three years, he would find that the compound annual growth rate between these two averages is 6.4 percent. If it is felt that this growth rate is the best approximation of expected future growth perceived by investors at the margin and that a perpetual-growth model is an appropriate valuation model, Eq. (8-8) might be used in determining the cost of equity capital.

When the expected growth in dividends per share is other than perpetual, a modification of Eq. (8-6) can be used. As brought out in Chapter 2, a number of valuation models assume that the growth rate will eventually taper off. Frequently, the transition is from an above-normal growth rate to one that is considered normal. For example, if dividends were expected to grow at a 15 percent compound rate for five years, at a 10 percent rate for the next five years, and then grow at a 5 percent rate, we would have

$$P_0 = \sum_{t=1}^{5} \frac{D_0(1.15)^t}{(1 + k_e)^t} + \sum_{t=6}^{10} \frac{D_5(1.10)^{t-5}}{(1 + k_e)^t} + \sum_{t=11}^{\infty} \frac{D_{10}(1.05)^{t-10}}{(1 + k_e)^t} \tag{8-9}$$

We see that the current dividend, D_0, is the base on which the expected growth in future dividends is built. By solving for k_e, we obtain the cost of equity capital as defined. For example, if the current dividend, D_0, were $2 a share and market price per share, P_0, were $75, k_e in Eq. (8-9) would be 9.5 percent. For other patterns of expected future growth, the equation can be easily modified to deal with the situation. The more growth segments we specify, of course, the more the growth pattern will approximate a curvilinear relationship.

For all growth situations, the important thing is to solve for the k_e that equates the expected future dividends perceived by investors at the margin with the current market price of the stock. Because the expected growth in dividends is not directly observable, it must be estimated. Herein lies the major difficulty involved in estimating the cost of equity capital. For reasonably stable patterns of past growth, one might project this trend into the future.[2] However, we must temper the projection to take account of current market sentiment. Insight into such sentiment can come from reviewing various analyses of the industry and company by investment advisers as well as from articles about the company in financial newspapers and magazines.

On the basis of the long-range plans of the company, the financial manager can make internal estimates of expected future growth in earnings per share and dividends per share. These estimates should take account of economic and other factors that bear on the firm's future operating performance. Because the financial manager has access to a great deal of relevant

[2]For an analysis of the accuracy of earnings-per-share forecasts produced by various mechanical forecasting techniques using past data, see Edwin J. Elton and Martin J. Gruber, "Earnings Estimates and the Accuracy of Expectational Data," *Management Science,* 18 (April 1972), 409–24. The article also serves as a presentation of these techniques. For yet another method for estimating expected growth, see Aharon R. Ofer, "Investors' Expectations of Earnings Growth, Their Accuracy and Effects on the Structure of Realized Rates of Return," *Journal of Finance,* 30 (May 1975), 509–23.

information, his estimates of future earnings may be the most accurate of all. However, it is important that investors also expect these earnings. There is an obvious bias if the financial manager uses his estimate of growth to solve for k_e and his estimate differs significantly from that of the market. The important question to ask is, What growth in dividends do investors at the margin expect that leads them to pay x dollars for a share of stock? Every effort should be made to get as accurate a handle as possible on this expected growth pattern. Once it is obtained, it is an easy matter to solve for the cost of equity capital as defined.

If measurement were exact and certain assumptions held, the discount rate determined by this method would be the same as the required rate of return determined by the capital-asset pricing model approach. When the assumptions underlying the capital-asset pricing model do not seem appropriate to the situation involved, the second approach serves as a useful benchmark for adjusting the required rate of return. By now it should be apparent that measuring the cost of equity capital of a company is an inexact science. We can only hope to approximate it as carefully as possible.

We believe that the methods suggested above enable such an approximation. However, we will be more or less accurate depending on the situation. Usually we are able to place far more confidence in estimates for a large company whose stock is actively traded on the New York Stock Exchange and whose systematic risk is close to that of the market as a whole than we are in estimates for a moderate-sized machine tool company whose stock is inactively traded in the over-the-counter-market and whose systematic risk is very large. We must live with the inexactness involved in the measurement process and try to do as good a job as possible. We turn now to measuring the costs of other types of financing. These types pose far fewer problems than the cost of equity capital, as the brevity of their treatment will attest.

Cost of Debt

The explicit cost of debt can be derived by solving for that discount rate, k, that equates the net proceeds of the debt issue with the present value of interest plus principal payments, and then adjusting the explicit cost obtained for the tax effect. If we denote the after-tax cost of debt by k_i, it can be approximated by

$$k_i = k(1 - t) \tag{8-10}$$

where k is the internal rate of return or yield, and t is the marginal tax rate.[3]

[3]Fred D. Arditti and Haim Levy, "The Weighted Average Cost of Capital as a Cutoff Rate: A Critical Analysis of the Classical Textbook Weighted Average," *Financial Management*, 6 (Fall 1977), 24–34, argue that the cost of debt should not be adjusted for taxes. Their contention is that the tax advantage of debt already is reflected in the cost of equity capital because dividends are higher than would otherwise be the case.

Because interest charges are tax deductible, the after-tax cost of debt is substantially less than the before-tax cost. If a company were able to sell a new issue of twenty-year bonds with a 9 percent coupon rate and realize net proceeds (after underwriting expenses) of $1,000 for each $1,000 face value bond, k would be 9 percent.[4] If the income tax rate were 50 percent,

$$k_i = 9.00(1 - 0.50) = 4.50 \text{ percent}$$

We note that the 4.50 percent after-tax cost in our example represents the marginal, or incremental, cost of additional debt. It does not represent the cost of debt already employed.

If a firm has the policy of maintaining a given proportion of debt in its capital structure, debt is never really paid. Individual debt instruments are paid, of course, but they are replaced by new debt. Thus debt can be regarded as a permanent part of the financing mix. Under these circumstances, the appropriate formula for calculating the explicit cost of debt is the formula for a perpetuity:

$$k_i = \frac{C_t}{I_0}(1 - t)$$

(8-11)

where C_t is the fixed interest cost in all periods, and I_0 is the net proceeds of the issue.

It is important to point out that the adjustment of the cost of debt for taxes holds only if the company has now and will have in the future a marginal tax rate of t. An unprofitable company that pays no taxes would have a cost of debt equal to the before-tax cost, k. Therefore if interest payments on debt are to be entirely and immediately deductible for tax purposes, reported earnings must be zero or positive. If not, the loss may be carried back three years and applied to taxes previously paid.[5] If reported

---

[4]When the price paid for a bond differs from its face value, the premium or discount is amortized for federal income tax purposes. If the premium or discount is significant, the after-tax cost of debt should take it into account. The approximate cost of a bond sold at a discount or a premium is

$$k_i = \frac{(1 - t)\left[C_t + \frac{1}{n}(P - I_0)\right]}{\frac{1}{2}(P + I_0)}$$

where P is the face value of the bond (usually $1,000), I_0 is the price at which the bond is sold, n is the number of years to maturity, and C_t is the fixed interest cost in all periods. $1/n(P - I_0)$ represents the amortization of the discount or premium over the life of the bond, and the denominator represents the average amount outstanding. If sinking-fund payments are made, the formula must be revised. The formula above is but an approximation of the explicit cost because it does not take account of annual compounding.

[5]The loss must be first applied to the earliest preceding year and if not entirely consumed to the next earliest year and then to the preceding year.

earnings are sufficient in those years, the firm receives a tax refund, and the cash-flow effect is nearly the same as that which occurs if operations in the current year are profitable. However, if reported earnings in the prior three years do not offset the current-year loss, the residual is carried forward to be applied to reported profits during the subsequent five years. In this case, part or all of the interest tax subsidy is postponed. If reported earnings during the five years are insufficient to offset the current-year loss, part or all of the interest tax subsidy is forgone. Therefore, if reported earnings are negative and the firm is unable to entirely qualify for a carry-back tax refund, the interest tax subsidy is either postponed or forgone. In addition to the uncertainty regarding reported income, there is some uncertainty regarding the corporate tax rate itself. This rate can be changed by Congress, and while the band within which a change may occur is narrow, there still remains a degree of uncertainty.

The import of all of this is that in most cases the tax deductibility of interest payments on a firm's debt contracts is not certain. There may be some possibility that because of adverse operations, the firm will be unable to utilize its interest payments as a tax-deductible item. As a result, the full cash-flow burden of these payments is felt by the firm. Consequently, it may be inappropriate to treat the cost of debt as the interest rate times one minus the tax rate. Assuming there are time-states during the life of the instrument in which the tax shield is not entirely applicable, this computation understates the cost of debt financing. The greater the number of time-states in which the tax shield cannot be used, the more important it becomes to explicitly consider this factor in cost-of-debt analyses. In general, the greater the business risk of a firm and the closer it approaches marginal profitability, the more important it becomes to allow for the possibility of losing the tax shield advantage traditionally associated with the employment of debt funds.

Cost of Preferred Stock

The cost of preferred stock is a function of its stated dividend. As we discuss in Chapter 21, this dividend is not a contractual obligation on the part of the firm but is payable at the discretion of the board of directors. Consequently, unlike debt, there is no risk of legal bankruptcy. However, from the standpoint of common stockholders, preferred stock represents a security senior to their interests. Because most corporations that issue preferred stock intend to pay the stated dividend, the dividend on the preferred stock represents a prior claim on income.[6] As preferred stock has no maturity date, its cost may be represented as

$$k_p = \frac{D}{I_0}$$

(8-12)

---

[6]The consequences of not paying the dividend are examined in Chapter 21.

where D is the stated annual dividend and I_0 represents the net proceeds of the preferred stock issue. If a company were able to sell a 7½ percent preferred stock issue ($100 par value) and realize net proceeds of $98½ a share, the cost of the preferred stock would be 7½/98½ = 7.61 percent. Note that this cost is not adjusted for taxes, because the preferred stock dividend is paid after taxes. Thus the explicit cost of preferred stock usually is substantially greater than that for debt.

Other Types of Financing

Although equity, debt, and preferred stock are the major sources, there are other types of financing. These include leasing, convertible securities, warrants, and other options. Because determining the costs of these types of financing involves some special and rather complex valuation issues, we postpone their treatment until Chapters 19 and 22. For our purposes in this chapter, knowing the costs of equity, debt, and preferred stock financing is sufficient for illustrating the overall cost of capital of a firm. When costs are later determined for other types of financing, they can be inserted in the weighting scheme to be discussed now.

Weighted-Average Cost of Capital

Once the costs of the individual components of the capital structure have been computed, these costs may be weighted according to some standard and a weighted-average cost of capital calculated. As an illustration of *the mechanics* of the calculations, suppose that a firm had the following capital structure at the latest statement date, where the amounts shown represent market values:

	Amount	Proportion
Debt	$30 million	30%
Preferred stock	10 million	10
Common-stock equity	60 million	60
	$100 million	100%

Common stock equity includes both common stock issues and retained earnings. In calculating proportions, it is important that market value as opposed to book-value weights be used.[7] Because our concern is with max-

[7]For an analysis of the weighting system and the question of book value versus market value weights, see William Beranek, "The Weighted Average Cost of Capital and Shareholder Wealth Maximization," *Journal of Financial and Quantitative Analysis*, 12 (March, 1977), 17–32; Michael J. Brennan, "A New Look at the Weighted Average Cost of Capital," *Journal of Business Finance*, 5, No. 1 (1973), 24–30; and Timothy J. Nantell and C. Robert Carlson, "The Cost of Capital as a Weighted Average," *Journal of Finance*, 30 (December 1975), 1343–55.

imizing the value of the firm to its shareholders, only market-value weights are consistent with this objective. Market values are used in the calculation of the costs of the various components of financing, so market value weights should be used in determining the weighted average cost of capital.

To continue with our illustration, suppose that the firm computed the following after-tax costs for the component methods of financing.

	Cost
Debt	4.5%
Preferred stock	8.0
Common-stock equity	12.0

Therefore the weighted-average cost of capital for this example problem is:

	(1) Proportion	(2) Cost	(3) Weighted Cost (1) × (2)
Debt	30%	4.5%	1.35%
Preferred stock	10	8.0	0.80
Common-stock equity	60	12.0	7.20
			9.35%

Thus, given the assumptions of this example, 9.35 percent represents the weighted average cost of the component methods of financing where each component is weighted according to market value proportions.

With the calculation of a weighted-average cost of capital, the critical question is whether the figure represents the firm's "true" cost of capital. The answer to this question depends upon how accurately we have measured the individual marginal costs, upon the weighting system, and upon certain other assumptions. Assume for now that we are able to measure accurately the marginal costs of the individual sources of financing; let us examine the importance of the weighting system.

Marginal Weights The critical assumption in any weighting system is that the firm will in fact raise capital in the proportions specified. Because the firm raises capital *marginally* to make a *marginal* investment in new projects, we need to work with the marginal cost of capital to the firm as a whole. This rate depends upon the package of funds employed to finance investment projects. In other words, our concern is with new or incremental capital, not with capital raised in the past. In order for the weighted-average cost of capital to represent a marginal cost, the weights employed must be marginal; that is, the weights must correspond to the proportions of financing inputs the firm intends to employ. If they do not, capital is raised on a marginal basis in proportions other than those used to calculate this cost. As a result, the "true" weighted-average cost of capital will differ from that calculated and used for capital-investment decisions. An obvious bias results. If the "true" cost is greater than that which is measured, certain investment projects will be accepted that will leave investors worse off than before. On the other hand, if the "true" cost is less than the measured cost, projects will be rejected that could increase shareholder wealth. Therefore the 9.35 percent weighted-average cost of capital computed in our example is realistic only if the firm intends to finance in the future in the same proportions as its existing capital structure.

It is recognized that the raising of capital is "lumpy," and strict proportions cannot be maintained. For example, a firm would have difficulty in financing each project undertaken with 30 percent debt, 10 percent preferred stock, and 60 percent common-stock equity. In practice, it may finance with debt in one instance and with preferred stock or common-stock equity in another. Over time, most firms are able to finance in roughly a proportional manner. It is in this sense that we try to measure the marginal cost of capital for the package of financing employed. In other words, temporary deviations from a target capital structure should be ignored in weighted-average cost-of-capital calculations.

Change in Capital Structure   A problem occurs whenever the firm wishes to change its capital structure. The costs of the component methods of financing usually are based upon the existing capital structure, and these costs may differ from those that rule once the firm has achieved its desired capital structure. Because the firm cannot measure its costs directly at the desired capital structure, these costs must be estimated. During the period of transition from the present capital structure to one that is desired, the firm usually will rely upon one type of financing. For example, it might finance with debt until the desired capital structure is achieved. Although there may be some discrepancy, it is best to use the estimated weighted-average cost of capital based upon the financing mix to be employed once the target capital structure is reached. There would be no transitional problem if the firm undertook an immediate change in its capital structure by issuing debt and repurchasing stock. However, most firms are reluctant to do this; consequently, the transition period will usually be gradual.

Flotation Costs   Flotation costs involved in the sale of common stock, preferred stock, or a debt instrument affect the profitability of a firm's investments. In many cases, the new issue must be priced below the market price of existing financing; in addition, there are out-of-pocket flotation costs.[8] Due to flotation costs, the amount of funds the firm receives is less than the price at which the issue is sold. The presence of flotation costs in financing requires that an adjustment be made in the evaluation of investment proposals.

The adjustment necessary is the addition of the flotation costs involved in financing to the project's initial cash outlay. For example, suppose

---

[8]See Chapter 20 for a discussion of these costs.

that an investment proposal costs $100,000 and that to finance the project the company must raise $60,000 externally. Both debt and common stock are involved, and flotation costs come to $4,000. Therefore $4,000 should be added to $100,000, bringing the total initial outlay to $104,000. In this way, the proposal is properly "penalized" for the flotation costs associated with its financing. The expected future cash flows associated with the project are discounted at the weighted-average cost of capital. If the project were expected to provide annual cash inflows of $12,000 forever and the weighted-average cost of capital were 10 percent, the project's net-present value would be

$$NPV = \frac{\$12,000}{0.10} - \$104,000 = \$16,000$$

This amount contrasts with a net-present value of $20,000 if no adjustment is made for flotation costs.

Thus the adjustment for flotation costs is made in the project's cash flows and not in the cost of capital.[9] To adjust the cost of capital results in an excessive "penalty" whenever the net-present value of the project is positive. To illustrate with out previous example, $4,000 in flotation costs represents 4 percent of the $100,000 investment, so the "adjusted" cost of capital would be 10 percent/$(1 - .04)$ = 10.42 percent. Therefore the net-present value of the project would be

$$NPV = \frac{\$12,000}{0.1042} - \$100,000 = \$15,163$$

As we see, the use of an adjusted cost of capital results in a biased and low estimate of the net-present value of a project whenever this value is positive. On the other hand, the estimate is biased and high whenever the net-present value is negative. In summary, the adjustment of the cost of capital for flotation costs results in biased net-present value calculations. The appropriate procedure is to adjust the project's initial cash outlay and to use the weighted-average "unadjusted" cost of capital as the discount rate.

Flotation costs represent a capital market imperfection. The greater the portion of external financing, the greater the adjustment that must be made for flotation costs, all other things the same. Because flotation costs for new issues of common stock exceed those for debt, the greater the portion of financing with new equity, the greater the adjustment, all other things the same. If the issue involved is a rights offering to existing stockholders, theoretically the amount of underpricing does not matter. Therefore the adjustment would involve only out-of-pocket flotation costs. (We will discuss the question of a rights offering versus a public offering in Chapter 20.)

[9]For a defense of the procedure, see Simon E. Keane, "The Investment Discount Rate—In Defence of the Market Rate on Interest," *Accounting and Business Research* (Summer 1976), 234; and John R. Ezzell and R. Burr Porter, "Flotation Costs and the Weighted Average Cost of Capital," *Journal of Financial and Quantitative Analysis*, 11 (September 1976), 403–13.

The rationale behind the use of a weighted-average cost of capital is that by financing in the proportions specified and accepting projects yielding more than the weighted-average cost, the firm is able to increase the market price of its stock. This increase occurs because the investment projects accepted are expected to yield more on their equity-financed portions than the cost of equity capital, k_e. Once these expectations are apparent to the marketplace, the market price of the stock should rise, all other things remaining the same. The firm has accepted projects that are expected to provide a return greater than that required by investors at the margin, based on the risk involved.

Using Eq. (8–6) as our valuation model and holding constant the dividend policy of the firm, we see that the acceptance of the projects raises expected future dividends per share, D_t, in the numerator of the equation. If the equity-financed portion of the new investment projects consists of a common-stock offering, market price per share will rise with an upward shift in expectations of future dividends per share. Embodied in these expectations is the dilution that necessarily will occur with the common-stock offering. In other words, the rise in expected future earnings must be sufficient to raise expected future *dividends per share,* not just expected future dividends.

If the equity-financed portion of the new investment projects consists of retained earnings, no dilution will occur. Here the rise in expected future dividends per share must be sufficient so that when the incremental increases are discounted by the market discount rate, k_e, their present value exceeds the equity capital employed in the projects. One can visualize the process as the firm's employing investors' capital at time 0 to invest in a project whose cash-flow benefits are expected to give rise to higher future dividends. In order for the project to be worthwhile, the present value of the incremental dividends must equal or exceed the equity capital employed in it. If the present value exceeds the equity capital employed in the project, the market price of the stock, P_0, will rise. If the present value is just equal to the amount of equity capital employed, P_0 will remain unchanged.[10]

A Pool of Financing   The weighted-average cost-of-capital approach implies that investment projects are financed out of a pool of funds as opposed to

---

[10]As an aside, market price per share will rise over time if the firm invests in projects whose return on the equity-financed portion just equals the cost of equity capital. This type of situation is known as expansion. In essence, dividends per share would rise over time because of the increase in earnings occasioned by the reinvestment of retained earnings. As a result, the present value of expected future dividends also would rise over time. For example, if a perpetual-growth model were applicable,

$$P_0 = \frac{D_1}{k_e - g}$$

237

required rates of return
for companies, divisions,
and acquisitions

being individually financed out of debt, preferred stock, common stock, or what have you. To illustrate in the context of the capital-asset pricing model, refer to Figure 8-1. Here we have the familiar security market line with the required returns on debt, preferred stock, and common stock being specified for a particular company. The cost of capital of the company is a weighted average of the required rates of return of the various components. If projects are accepted with a systematic risk of X and an expected return of k_o, the expected return will be just sufficient to compensate the various security holders at their required rates of return—k_i, k_p and k_e. As a result, the investment will leave share price unchanged. If the expected return from the project is higher than k_o, with systematic risk the same, then this return will be more than sufficient to compensate debtholders, preferred stockholders and common stockholders. As the maximum claims of debtholders and preferred stockholders are fixed, most of the benefit will accrue to the common stockholders. In other words, their expected return will be in excess of that required, k_e. As a result, share price will increase as investors bid up the price of the stock until equilibrium is restored.

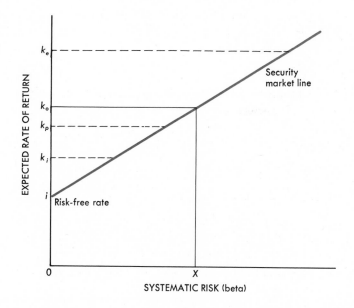

figure 8-1
Required rates of
return for debt (k_i),
preferred stock (k_p),
common-stock equity
(k_e), and the overall
cost of capital (k_o) for
an individual company

If expectations and the market rate of discount remained unchanged, the market price at time 1 would be

$$P_1 = \frac{D_2}{k_e - g}$$

Because D_2 is greater than D_1, P_1 will be greater than P_0. Similarly, it can be shown that $P_t > P_{t-1}$ for all t under our assumptions.

Qualifications to the Use of a Weighted-Average Cost The use of a weighted-average cost-of-capital figure must be qualified for the points raised earlier. It assumes that the investment proposals being considered do not differ in systematic risk from that of the firm as a whole and that the residual risk of the proposals does not provide any diversification benefits to the firm, if indeed residual risk is a factor of importance. Only under these circumstances is the cost-of-capital figure obtained appropriate as an acceptance criterion. These assumptions are extremely binding. They imply that the projects of a firm are completely homogeneous with respect to risk and that only projects of exactly the same risk will be considered.

In practice, of course, the issue is one of degree. If the conditions above are approximately met, the company's weighted-average cost of capital may be used as the acceptance criterion. For example, if a firm produced only one product and all proposals considered were in conjunction with the marketing and production of that product, the use of the firm's overall cost of capital as the acceptance criterion might be appropriate. (Even here, however, there may be significant enough differences in risk among investment proposals to warrant separate consideration.) For a multiproduct firm with investment proposals of varying risk, the use of an overall required rate of return is inappropriate. Here the required rate of return for the specific proposal should be used, as determined with the methods proposed in the preceding chapter. The key, then, is the homogeneity of existing investment projects and investment proposals under consideration with respect to risk. While this condition may be met for certain companies, we would expect it to be met more often for subunits of companies, such as divisions.

DIVISIONAL COSTS OF CAPITAL

Where the use of a company-wide cost of capital is inappropriate as an acceptance criterion, the use of a divisional cost of capital may be valid. By *division,* we mean some subunit of a company that carries on a set of activities that can be differentiated from the other activities of the firm. Usually these activities are differentiated along product or service lines as well as along management lines. Henceforth, we will refer to these subunits as divisions, whether they be called subsidiaries, divisions, units, or whatever.

Each division employs in it assets which must be financed. The question is, What is an appropriate acceptance criterion? Again the key is the homogeneity of activities. If the products or services involved are homogeneous with respect to risk, and new investment proposals are of the same sort, a case can be made for a divisional cost of capital as the acceptance criterion. It represents the transfer price of capital from the company to the division. Stated differently, it is the rate of return the company expects the division to earn on its capital investments. The question is, What is the proper rate of return for a division, assuming the activities of that division are homogeneous with respect to risk?

Determining a Division's Required Rate of Return

The concepts taken up in the preceding chapter and earlier in this one can be applied here. As we have gone through the mechanics of measurement several times before, we assume the reader is able to undertake the necessary calculations. Therefore our presentation will be mainly verbal, with an emphasis on implications.

As with individual investment projects and the company as a whole, the capital-asset pricing model can be used to determine a required rate of return on equity for a division. What one would do is try to identify companies with publicly traded stocks which were engaged solely in the line of business of the division. This would involve a careful comparison of the products and/or services involved. For an electrical products division, for example, one would concentrate on companies engaged solely in the manufacture and sale of electrical products. Sometimes the matching can only be approximate. The important thing is to try to find a publicly traded company or companies that have nearly the same degree of systematic risk as the division.

Once the company is identified, its beta can be computed and the required rate of return on equity determined according to the procedures illustrated in our previous examples. Having determined the required rate of return on equity for the company, it is used as a proxy for the required rate of return on equity for the division. In other words, the beta information for a company whose stock is publicly traded is substituted for that of the division. The implication is that the systematic risk of the company is the same as that for the division. To the extent that multiple companies can be identified, some sort of average of their required rates of return can be used as a proxy for the division's required rate of return.

In situations where it is difficult to identify companies that closely parallel the division in question, one can resort to the methods taken up in the last chapter where we measured the beta for a project based on the market value of the specific asset. However, the much preferred and more accurate way is to find a company whose stock is publicly traded. Typically, this is much easier for a division than it is for an individual investment project. There usually exist companies that carry on activities similar to those of the division. The principal exception would be an industry comprised entirely of multidivision companies. Once the cost of equity capital for the division is determined, it is combined with the cost of debt and other sources of financing to obtain a weighted-average cost of capital for the division.

Nonequity Financing   The amount of nonequity financing that is assigned to a division is an important consideration. Conceptually, it should approximate the same relative amount as that used by the proxy company. In other words, the proportion of nonequity financing allocated to a division cannot be significantly out of line with that of the external company being used.

Otherwise, one will not get a reasonable proxy for the systematic risk of the division. Where the proportions are not nearly the same, the proxy company's beta should be adjusted before it is used as the cost of equity capital for the division. A procedure for adjusting the beta is presented in the Appendix to this chapter. Using this procedure, one can approximate the beta for the proxy company assuming it had the same relative proportion of nonequity financing as that contemplated for the division. The cost of equity capital for the division can then be determined in the same manner as before. For the cost of debt for a division, most people prefer to use the company's overall borrowing cost. However, even here adjustments can, and probably should, be made if a division has significantly more risk or less risk than the company as a whole.

Once the cost of equity capital and the costs of nonequity financing are determined, a weighted-average required rate of return for the division is derived. The weighting process and the calculation of the weighted-average required rate of return are the same as in the previous section. What we end up with is a required rate of return for investment proposals undertaken by that division. This is the return demanded by investors for projects having the same proportional systematic risk as the division now possesses.

Implications for Project Selection

Once divisional costs of capital are computed for each division, capital is allocated, or transferred, throughout the firm on a risk-adjusted return basis. The higher the systematic risk of a division, the higher the required rate of return. This approach provides a consistent framework for allocating capital among divisions with greatly different risks. Too often in a multidivision firm, a single cutoff rate is used for project selection. An edict comes from above stating that "no project shall be undertaken unless it provides a return of 15 percent"! The problem is that certain "safe" projects with little systematic risk are rejected because they do not provide a return above the company's stated goal. However, some of these projects may provide expected returns greater than the "true" cost of capital for the division. In contrast, divisions characterized by large systematic risk may accept projects with expected returns higher than the company-wide norm, but lower than they should earn given the systematic risk involved.

This problem is illustrated in Figure 8-2. The horizontal dashed line is the company's overall cost of capital, and the bars represent the costs of capital for the various divisions of the company, based on their systematic risk. The x's and o's represent investment projects of the type described: namely, those with expected returns below the company's overall cost of capital, but above the division's cost of capital; and those with expected returns above the company's cost of capital, but below the division's cost of capital. The rejection of the former projects and acceptance of the latter is

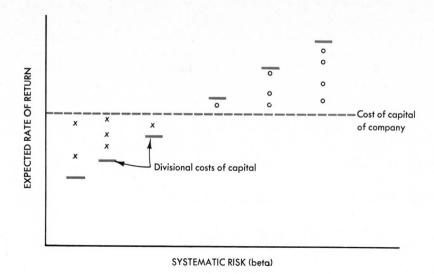

figure 8-2
Comparison of company-wide cost of capital and divisional costs of capital

suboptimal.[11] The former provide expected returns in excess of the return required by the market for the systematic risk involved, while the latter provide expected returns lower than that required. While the problem may seem obvious, this very thing happens either directly or indirectly in many a multidivision company.

The incentives in such a company are such that divisions with low systematic risk often are too conservative in project generation and selection, while divisions with large systematic risk are too aggressive. Too often there is a tendency for a company to put its money in those divisions providing the greatest growth opportunities, and to ration capital to other divisions so that they will accept only projects consistent with the overall growth objectives. Frequently, the high-growth divisions have a "license" to do most anything they want, as long as the expected returns on the projects selected are above the company's overall required return. However, some of the projects selected provide too low an expected return for the systematic risk involved. As a result, the company may become riskier over time without commensurate increases in expected return.

The incentive scheme is skewed in the direction of growth and the acceptance of risky projects. "Safe" divisions may be starved for capital, even

[11]Stuart M. Turnbull, "Market Value and Systematic Risk," *Journal of Finance,* 32 (September 1977), 1125–42, demonstrates under restricted assumptions that a firm's systematic risk depends upon the maturity and growth rate of its cash flows. He argues that if the firm's overall capitalization rate is used as the hurdle rate for project selection, the projects must in general have the same maturity and growth rates as those of the firm. He concludes that for most companies, the use of an overall capitalization rate as the hurdle rate will lead to nonoptimal decisions. Turnbull also shows that under those assumptions, systematic risk does not increase with the rate of growth of cash flows.

though they are able to generate investment proposals that are expected to
provide returns in excess of those required for the systematic risk involved.
The problem is a mistaken belief that growth in itself is the panacea for all
problems. The value of a firm rests on two foundations—expected return and
risk. Growth in the former is good, but growth in the latter is bad. Whether
the overall result is good or bad depends on the combined effect of these
two factors.

What is needed is a system for allocating capital to divisions on a
risk-adjusted return basis. The approach presented provides such a means.
As long as investment proposals emanating from the division are homogeneous with respect to systematic risk, the approach will result in consistent
investment decisions being made among the divisions of a company. When
investment proposals are not homogeneous, they should be evaluated on a
proposal-by-proposal basis, using the methods taken up in the preceding
chapter.

Residual Risk Considerations

In our discusssion of the required rate of return for a division, we
have considered only the systematic risk of that division. Implied is that the
market evaluates the parts of a company, in our case its divisions, separately
according to their systematic risk. (The reasoning behind this assumption was
taken up in the preceding chapter, so we will not repeat it here.) As in all of
our previous discussions, the question becomes, What happens if residual
risk is important? As we know from before, the greater the imperfections in
the capital markets, generally the greater the importance of residual risk.
However, it is not the residual risk of the division that is important, but the
residual risk of the firm as a whole. Take the imperfection of bankruptcy
costs, for example. A particular division might experience difficulties and go
into bankruptcy on its own, but the company as a whole would not because of
the offsetting performance of other divisions which are not experiencing such
adversities. It is only if the firm as a whole goes bankrupt that bankruptcy
costs are incurred.

Following the methods outlined in the preceding chapter, one can
determine the impact of a division on the total risk of the firm (that is, its
systematic and residual risk). In that chapter, a dual approach for evaluating
risky investments was presented. Recall that this consisted of evaluating
investment proposals according to the capital-asset pricing model and then
according to their incremental impact on the total risk of the firm. Accept or
reject decisions are reached for both approaches. Where these decisions are
the same, there is no problem. When conflicting decisions are reached, however, the final decision depends on the perceived importance of imperfections in the capital markets. On the basis of this, one would favor one approach or the other and would make a decision.

The same dual approach can be applied to the evaluation of the
divisions of a company. Such an approach results in one's using the capital-

asset pricing model to determine the "underlying" required rate of return for the division commensurate with the systematic risk involved. Analysis of the impact of the various divisions on the total risk of the firm allows consideration of the diversification properties of those divisions. This consideration is important only if imperfections exist in the capital markets which make the residual risk of a firm a significant factor to investors. Thus we are able to take account of residual risk in the same manner as we did for individual investment projects.

THE EVALUATION OF ACQUISITIONS

The last topic in this chapter is the evaluation of acquisitions. We saw in Chapter 6 that an acquisition can be analyzed according to its expected return and risk in the same manner as any capital investment. In what should by now be a familiar procedure, we examine the issue under the assumptions of the capital-asset pricing model and then under conditions where residual risk might be a factor of at least some importance.

Evaluation under the Assumptions of the Capital-Asset Pricing Model

Given the assumptions of the model, it is clear that investors are able to achieve the same diversification as the firm is able to do for them. This point is particularly apparent in the case of the acquisition of a company whose stock is publicly held. In fact, the investor has an advantage in that he is able to diversify by buying only a few shares of stock, whereas the acquisition for the buying company is much more "lumpy." Thus the acquiring firm is unable to do something for investors that they are not able to do for themselves at least as efficiently. Therefore, pure diversification by the firm through acquisitions is not a thing of value.[12] The whole will simply equal the sum of the parts.

This is not to say that an acquisition will not enhance the value of the firm to its shareholders. Indeed, economies may be involved that benefit the acquiring firm and its stockholders. The prospect of synergism may make a prospective acquisition more attractive to one company than to another.

---

[12]For further discussion and demonstration of this point, see Corry Azzi, "Conglomerate Mergers, Default Risk, and Homemade Mutual Funds," *American Economic Review,* 68 (March 1978), 161–72; Stewart C. Myers, "Procedures for Capital Budgeting under Uncertainty," *Industrial Management Review,* 9 (Spring 1968), 1–15; Jan Mossin, "Equilibrium in a Capital Asset Model," *Econometrica,* 34 (October 1966), 768–75; Haim Levy and Marshall Sarnat, "Diversification, Portfolio Analysis, and the Uneasy Case for Conglomerate Mergers," *Journal of Finance,* 25 (September 1970), 795–802; and Michael Gort, "An Economic Disturbance Theory of Mergers," *Quarterly Journal of Economics,* 83 (November 1969), 624–42. For a comprehensive review of the literature on mergers, see Dennis C. Mueller, "The Effects of Conglomerate Mergers," *Journal of Banking and Finance,* 1 (December 1977), 315–47.

However, diversification itself would not be beneficial. In particular, conglomerate mergers where the sole purpose is diversification would be suspect: they would not enhance shareholder wealth. If an acquisition is to be worthwhile, there must be the prospect of synergism. In other words, the acquiring company must be able to effect operating economies, distribution economies, or other things of this sort if the acquisition is to be a thing of value.

It is an easy matter to measure the required rate of return for the acquisition of a company whose stock is publicly traded. Direct beta information is available, so one simply calculates the required rate using the procedures illustrated earlier. No proxy is necessary. The expected incremental cash flows arising from the acquisition[13] are then discounted at the required rate of return. If the present value of these cash flows exceeds the purchase price, the acquisition is worthwhile; if not, it should be rejected.

The important thing to remember is that under the assumptions of the capital-asset pricing model, the present value of cash flows will exceed the purchase price *only* if there is synergism. Stated differently, in the absence of synergism, the expected return arising from the acquisition will be no more than the required return. This suggests that the analysis of a prospective acquisition should focus on the likelihood of synergism. For the acquiring company, this usually means doing those things that it does well. Acquiring a company in an unrelated line of business where management has no expertise is unlikely to produce synergism. There are too many cases of this having been done under the mistaken belief that it is the only way to achieve growth. Too often the result is that inefficiencies develop, and the acquiring company earns an incremental return less than that required by the market for the systematic risk involved. As a result, the market price of the stock suffers relative to what would have occurred if the acquisition had not been made.

If the stock of the prospective acquisition is priced efficiently in the market, the acquiring company will pay at least what the company is worth as an independent entity. If a premium is paid, and it usually must be paid, then the acquiring company pays more than the acquisition is worth as an independent operation. Only if synergism is possible can the premium be offset and the acquisition provide an incremental expected return equal to or greater than that required by the market, given the systematic risk involved. In evaluating an acquisition, then, one should concentrate on the prospect of synergism. Only this will make the acquisition a thing of value, given our assumptions.

The Diversification Effect

If residual risk is felt to be important or if management is concerned only with the impact of an acquisition on the expected risk and return of the firm as a whole, the evaluation process needs to be altered. One can evaluate

---

[13]The development of this information was taken up in Chapter 6.

245

required rates of return
for companies, divisions,
and acquisitions

an acquisition from the standpoint of the "portfolio" effect on the firm. This was illustrated for investment proposals in Chapter 7, and the procedures are the same for an acquisition. To briefly reiterate them in this context, however, recall from Chapter 6 our discussion of how to derive the probability distribution of possible incremental present values arising from an acquisition. If the price to be paid has been established, it should be subtracted from the expected value of present value to obtain the expected value of net-present value. The next step is to estimate the correlation coefficients for the relationship between the net-present value for the prospective acquisition and the net-present values for existing projects and investment proposals under consideration.

The acquisition then becomes one more investment proposal in a portfolio of projects to be considered. The methods of analysis and selection are the same as those employed in the preceding chapter. Management chooses the best combination of expected value of net-present value and risk. If the portfolio of projects represented by this combination includes the prospective acquisition, the firm should acquire the company involved. In this way, an acquisition is evaluated in the same manner as any internally generated investment proposal. A decision is made with attention to the marginal impact of the acquisition on the total risk of the firm.

Whether the capital-asset pricing model approach is altered depends upon the importance of the diversification effect. In turn, its importance depends upon imperfections in the capital market. If significant imperfections exist, such as bankruptcy costs, a case can be made for the diversification properties of an investment being important.[14] As with individual assets or divisions, the acquisition then would be evaluated according to the systematic risk involved as well as according to its incremental impact on the total risk of the firm.

Debtholders versus Equityholders Even in the absence of bankruptcy costs, Wilbur G. Lewellen argues that mergers result in "financial synergism," beneficial to investors.[15] By merging, he contends that the debt capacity of the combined entity will be greater than the sum of the individual debt capacities of the two companies involved. If, in a world of taxes, debt funds are "cheaper" than equity funds,[16] borrowing more will increase the value of the

---

[14]For an analysis of the conditions under which an acquisition benefits stockholders, see Robert C. Higgins and Lawrence D. Schall, "Corporate Bankruptcy and Conglomerate Merger," *Journal of Finance*, 30 (March 1975), 106–11; and James H. Scott, Jr., "On the Theory of Conglomerate Mergers," *Journal of Finance*, 32 (September 1977), 1235–50. In their article, Higgins and Schall consider the covariance of bankruptcy costs with the market return, a consideration that we do not explore. The greater the covariance, the less important bankruptcy costs become, and vice versa.

[15]"A Pure Financial Rationale for the Conglomerate Merger," *Journal of Finance*, 26 (May 1971), 521–37. A similar argument is made in A. Melnik and M. A. Pollatschek, "Debt Capacity, Diversification and Conglomerate Mergers," *Journal of Finance*, 28 (December 1973), 1263–74. For further amplification, see Li Way Lee, "Co-insurance and Conglomerate Merger," *Journal of Finance*, 32 (December 1977), 1527–37.

[16]This issue is analyzed in Chapter 9.

equity. The reason debt capacity supposedly increases is that the variance about the mean of two streams of cash flows can be reduced by combining them.[17] By reducing the dispersion of the probability distribution of possible cash flows relative to the mean of the distribution, the probability that principal and interest payments on the debt will not be met is reduced.

As a result, lenders are willing to lend more to the combined entity than they are willing to lend to the two companies separately. (The reduction in relative dispersion of cash flows affords them a greater degree of protection.) One might be tempted to argue that a lender can achieve this diversification on his own. Though it is true that a lender can diversify loans, he is unable to reduce the probability that independent companies will default because he cannot merge their cash flows. Only through an actual merger are these cash flows fused and *relative* dispersion reduced. For reasons of "financial synergism," then, Lewellen argues that mergers, and particularly conglomerate mergers, enhance shareholder wealth.

Higgins and Schall take issue with this conclusion.[18] They agree that a merger between two firms reduces the bankruptcy risk to creditors by providing a form of coinsurance in the sense that the premerger cash flows of the two firms are fused. However, they argue that under perfect capital market assumptions, this benefits only the debtholders. The market price of the debt instruments rises and, because the total value of the company remains the same under the assumption of perfect capital markets, equity values fall.[19]

Perhaps the situation can be better visualized in the option pricing model context of Chapter 4. The equityholders can be thought of as holding an option on the total value of the firm. At the maturity of the debt,[20] they can exercise their option by paying off the debt, thereby realizing this total value less the exercise price of the option. The latter is simply the face value of the debt. If the total value of the firm is less than the face value of the debt, equityholders will elect not to exercise their option, and the value of their stock will be zero. Debtholders will own the firm, but its total value will be less than the debt's face value. With an option, of course, an increase in the volatility of the underlying asset results in an increase in the value of the option, whereas a decrease in volatility results in a lower value of the option, all other things the same. In this case, the underlying asset is the total value of the firm, so a reduction in its variance will result in a lower value of the

---

[17]This statement assumes that less than perfect correlation exists between the two streams.

[18]Higgins and Schall, "Corporate Bankruptcy and Conglomerate Merger," pp. 93–106.

[19]With taxes, increased leverage in keeping with the increased debt capacity occasioned by the merger works to the advantage of equityholders. This advantage must be balanced against the disadvantage mentioned above, according to Higgins and Schall.

[20]The assumption is that the debt is represented by discount bonds which are payable entirely at maturity.

option, as represented by the value of the stock.[21] On the other hand, reduced volatility, as may occur with a merger, works to the advantage of the writer of the option, so the value of the debt should increase.

247

required rates of return
for companies, divisions,
and acquisitions

Thus Higgins and Schall suggest that equity values usually decrease with mergers, whereas debt values increase. They go on to suggest that this can be prevented if the premerger debt is retired at its premerger market value.[22] In this case, equityholders would not suffer any loss in value with a merger, as debt would later be reissued at a higher postmerger value. Essentially, equityholders protect themselves against an erosion in the value of their claim by imposing restrictions on the company. These restrictions frequently are called "me first" rules; their purpose is to protect debtholders and equityholders against financial policy changes that work to the detriment of their respective wealth positions.

In a similar vein, Scott looks for ways in which the market value of a firm's debt may be insulated from changes in policies as determined by management.[23] One way is that suggested by Higgins and Schall: give the firm the ability to repurchase or call its debt at its premerger market value. Another way is to provide debtholders "perfect protection" through various protective covenants so that management cannot make decisions that decrease the market value of the debt. With these restrictions imposed, the value of the debt will be insulated from changes in firm policies. In turn, management, in behalf of stockholders, will have an incentive to maximize the total value of the firm.

Diversification in the Presence of Market Imperfections   When we leave the "zero-sum" game between debtholders and stockholders posed above and allow for bankruptcy costs and taxes, it is possible to increase the value of the firm through merging, apart from any synergistic effects. By diversifying through a merger, the probability of bankruptcy can be reduced. As a result, there will be a reduction in the expected costs of bankruptcy, assuming these costs are positive and significant. As we demonstrated earlier, this reduction

[21]See Dan Galai and Ronald W. Masulis, "The Option Pricing Model and the Risk Factor of Stock," *Journal of Financial Economics,* 3 (January-March 1976), 66–69.

[22]E. Han Kim and John J. McConnell, "Corporate Merger and the Co-insurance of Corporate Debt," *Journal of Finance,* forthcoming, suggest that the same thing can be accomplished by the firm's increasing its financial leverage to the point where the increase in the postmerger default risk of the previously outstanding debt just cancels any wealth transfer that might occur from stockholders to debtholders. Kim and McConnell go on to test empirically for any indication of wealth transfer using a paired sample of bonds for merging and nonmerging companies, In addition, a two-index (stocks and bonds) market model is used to determine abnormal performance for the bonds of the merging companies. Testing monthly data from two years before to two years after the merger, the authors found no evidence of significantly positive excess returns to the debtholders of the merging companies. However, they observe that postmerger financial leverage increased for the sample and interpret this finding as consistent with any wealth transfers from stockholders to debtholders being negated by increases in leverage. Kim and McConnell conclude that the evidence does not support the notion of a wealth transfer.

[23]"On the Theory of Conglomerate Mergers," 1239–42.

will increase the value of the firm, all other things the same. In a world of corporate income taxes and the deductibility of interest, a merger may reduce expected total future tax payments if there are future states in which one company would go bankrupt while the other would not.[24] In this situation, a merger may permit the losses of the one firm to be applied against the profits of the other. As a result, the future taxes paid may be less for the merged company than they are for the two firms separately.[25] This occurrence would result in the merged company's having a greater value than the sum of the parts, all other things the same.

Both of these factors (bankruptcy costs and taxes) are defined as market imperfections. While we would not imagine these imperfections to have a large impact on the value of the acquiring firm, they nonetheless may be important enough to make the diversification effect of a merger a significant factor. In most cases, however, the really important thing to evaluate in a prospective acquisition is the prospect for synergism. This is particularly true if a premium in stock value must be offered in order to acquire the company.

SUMMARY

The use of the cost of capital for a company or division as an acceptance criterion is predicated on its activities being homogeneous with respect to risk, and investment proposals under consideration being of the same sort. A company has available to it an assortment of financing methods, each with a cost. By far the most difficult to measure is the cost of equity capital. One way to measure it is with a capital-asset pricing model approach. With this approach, we are able to determine the return investors require the company to earn on equity, given the systematic risk involved. To the extent that imperfections exist in the capital markets and they are felt to be important, this required rate of return may have to be adjusted upward to reflect the significance of residual risk. Another way to measure the cost of equity capital is to solve for the rate of discount that equates the stream of expected future dividends, as perceived by investors at the margin, with the current market price of the stock.

---

[24]We ignore at this time the tax loss carry-forward, which can be an important consideration in some mergers. For a discussion of this effect, see John Lintner, "Expectations, Mergers and Equilibrium in Purely Competitive Securities Markets," *American Economic Review,* 61 (May 1971), 101–11.

[25]Ibid., pp. 1244–45. Scott also advances the argument that when noncontractual creditors exist, a merger will reduce the total value of the firm to contractual debtholders and to stockholders if there are future states where one firm would go bankrupt while the other would not. With a merger, Scott contends that there is a wealth transfer from stockholders to noncontractual creditors. This is due to the fact that in the absence of such a merger, the noncontractual creditors of the bankrupt firm would not be paid in full.

249

required rates of return
for companies, divisions,
and acquisitions

Once the costs of the individual methods of financing are determined, a weighted-average cost of capital for the firm can be computed. The market-value weights employed should correspond to the proportions with which the firm intends to finance. Once computed, the weighted-average cost is used as the basis for accepting or rejecting investment projects. The rationale for its use was explored in some detail. Again, a key condition is the homogeneity of existing investment projects and investment proposals under consideration with respect to risk. When this condition does not hold, the overall company cost of capital should not be used as an acceptance criterion.

Often the condition above is met for divisions of a company but is not met for the company as a whole. Again using the capital-asset pricing model approach, one can determine the required return on equity for that division. The important thing is to identify a publicly traded company whose line of business and systematic risk closely parallels that of the division. This company then is used as a proxy for developing beta information. Once the cost of equity is determined, it is combined with other costs in a weighted-average cost of capital for the division. The implications of its use in project selection were discussed, and it was concluded that the approach has considerable merit for allocating capital among the divisions of a company on a consistent risk-adjusted return basis. We then extended our discussion to allow for residual risk being a factor of importance and analyzed it along the lines proposed in the preceding chapter. Where the condition of homogeneity of projects with respect to risk is not met, investment proposals emanating from a division should be evaluated using the required rate of return for the project and not for the division.

In the final section, we took up the evaluation of acquisitions. If most of the assumptions of the capital-asset pricing model hold, it is clear that investors are able to achieve the same diversification on their own as the acquiring company is able to do for them. Therefore, diversification by the firm in acquisitions would not be a thing of value. This argues that a company should focus its analysis on the likelihood of synergism when studying prospective acquisitions. Only synergism will result in incremental value being gained. We then examined the conditions under which the diversification effect in mergers might be a factor of importance.

APPENDIX
Adjusting the Beta for Leverage

The systematic risk of a stock is due to both the business and the financial risk of the company. In the calculation of a division's cost of equity capital, the external company used as a proxy for the business risk of the division will sometimes have a significantly different proportion of debt than that used by the division. As a result, it may be desirable to adjust the beta of the proxy company for this difference in relative debt. In what follows, we present a procedure for making such an adjustment under the assumptions of the capital-asset pricing model. In the end, we will qualify the results for the considerations to be taken up in Chapter 9.

With corporate income taxes, interest payments are deductible for tax purposes. Under these circumstances, Hamada, as well as others, has demonstrated that the required rate of return for a stock is[26]

$$R_j = i + \left(\frac{R_m - i}{\sigma_m^2}\right)(r_{ju,m}\sigma_{ju}\sigma_m)\left[1 + \frac{B}{S}(1 - T)\right] \tag{8A-1}$$

where i = risk-free rate

R_m = the expected return on the market portfolio

σ_m = standard deviation of the probability distribution of possible market returns

σ_{ju} = standard deviation of the probability distribution of possible returns for security j *in the absence of leverage*

$r_{ju,m}$ = correlation coefficient between returns for security j *in the absence of leverage* and the market portfolio

B/S = the debt-to-equity ratio in market value terms

T = corporate tax rate

The important thing to note is that the covariance between returns, which is the second bracketed term in the equation, is as if the company had an all-equity capital structure.

Equation (8A-1) can be expressed in terms of the more familiar beta:

$$R_j = i + (R_m - i)\beta_{ju}\left[1 + \frac{B}{S}(1 - T)\right] \tag{8A-2}$$

where β_{ju} is the beta measuring the responsiveness of the excess return for the security *in the absence of leverage* to the excess return for the market portfolio. Thus the overall required rate of return is comprised of the risk-free rate, i, plus a premium for business risk, $(R_m - i)\beta_{ju}$, and a premium for financial risk,

$$(R_m - i)\beta_{ju}\left[\frac{B}{S}(1 - T)\right]$$

The measured beta for the stock, β_j, embodies both risks and it is simply

$$\beta_j = \beta_{ju}\left[1 + \frac{B}{S}(1 - T)\right] \tag{8A-3}$$

---

[26]Robert S. Hamada, "Portfolio Analysis, Market Equilibrium and Corporation Finance," *Journal of Finance,* 24 (March 1969), 19–30.

Rearranging, the beta for the stock *in the absence of leverage* is

251

required rates of return
for companies, divisions,
and acquisitions

$$\beta_{ju} = \frac{\beta_j}{\left[1 + \dfrac{B}{S}(1 - T)\right]}$$

(8A-4)

Given these expressions, we are able to derive the beta *in the absence of leverage* for a particular stock. To illustrate, suppose the measured beta, β_j, for security j were 1.4; the debt-to-equity ratio, B/S, were 0.6; and the tax rate were 50 percent. Therefore the beta *in the absence of leverage* would be

$$\beta_{ju} + \frac{1.4}{[1 + 0.6(0.5)]} = 1.08$$

If we now wished to determine the beta for a different amount of leverage, we would use Eq. (8A-3). Suppose that we were interested in using security j as a proxy for the systematic risk of one of our divisions. However, the debt-to-equity ratio employed in this division is 0.3 as opposed to the 0.6 for security j. Therefore the adjusted beta would be

$$\text{Adjusted } \beta_j = 1.08[1 + 0.3(0.5)] = 1.24$$

This beta contrasts with 1.08 for security j *in the absence of leverage,* and with 1.40 for security j with a debt-to-equity ratio of 0.6.

In summary, we are able to derive an adjusted beta for a security under the assumption of a different proportion of debt than what occurs. We first estimate the beta for the stock *in the absence of leverage* and then adjust this figure for the proportion of leverage we wish to employ. The final result is an approximation of the beta that would prevail if the external company were to employ the desired proportion of debt.

It is important to recognize that the adjustment procedure assumes that all the tenets of the capital-asset pricing model hold. One of these is that in the absence of taxes, changes in the capital structure of a firm do not affect its valuation. With taxes, value increases in a linear manner with leverage. Chapter 9, which follows, analyzes this proposition in depth. While the adjustment procedure presented provides an approximate beta when the proportion of debt is varied, it is but an approximation.

PROBLEMS

1. On March 10, International Copy Machines (ICOM), one of the "favorites" of the stock market, was priced at $300 per share. This price was based on an expected annual growth rate of at least 20 percent for quite some time in the future. In July, economic indicators turned down, and investors revised downward to 15 percent

their estimate for future growth of ICOM. What should happen to the price of the stock? Assume the following:

(a) A perpetual-growth valuation model is a reasonable representation of the way the market values ICOM.

(b) The measured cost of equity capital to the firm is the true cost.

(c) The firm does not change its dividend, the risk complexion of its assets, or its degree of financial leverage.

(d) The dividend next year will be $3 per share.

2. K-Far Stores has launched an expansion program that should result in the saturation of the Bay Area marketing region of California in six years. As a result, the company is predicting a growth in earnings of 12 percent for three years, 6 percent for years four through six, after which it expects constant earnings for the foreseeable future. The company expects to increase its dividend per share, now $2, in keeping with this growth pattern. Currently, the market price of the stock is $25 per share. Estimate the company's cost of equity capital.

3. During the last six years, excess returns above the risk-free rate were the following for the market index and for the common stock of Rayfil Manufacturing Company:

Year	1	2	3	4	5	6
Excess return market	.08	(.02)	.14	.18	(.06)	.04
Excess return Rayfil	.02	.06	.22	.17	(.02)	(.03)

Over this same period, the risk-free rate averaged 6 percent. On the basis of these limited observations and using the past as a proxy for the future, compute the cost of equity capital of the firm in the context of the capital-asset pricing model.

4. Over the same period of time as in problem 3, Kay Wyman Stores, Inc., had the following excess returns:

Year	1	2	3	4	5	6
Excess return Kay Wyman Stores	.12	(.07)	.26	.28	(.12)	.07

What is the cost of equity capital? Why does it differ from that of Rayfil Manufacturing Company in problem 3?

5. Assuming the firm has a tax rate of 50 percent, compute the after-tax cost of the following:

(a) A bond, sold at par, with a 9¼ percent coupon.

(b) A twenty-year-, 8½ percent, $1,000 par bond sold at $855. (Use an approximation method.)

(c) A preferred stock sold at $100 with a 7 percent coupon and a call price of $110 if the company plans to call the issue in five years. (Use an approximation method.)

(d) A common stock selling at $20 and paying a $2 dividend, which is expected to be continued indefinitely.

(e) The same common stock if dividends are expected to grow at the rate of 5 percent per year and the expected dividend in year 1 is $2.

6. The Kalog Precision Tool Company was recently formed to manufacture a new product. The company has the following capital structure:

10% debentures of 1999	$6,000,000
8% preferred stock	2,000,000
Common stock (320,000 shares)	8,000,000
	$16,000,000

The common stock sells for $25 a share and the company has a marginal tax rate of 50 percent. A study of publicly held companies in this line of business suggests that the required return on equity is about 14 percent for a company of this sort. (A capital-asset pricing model approach was used to determine the required rate of return.)

(a) Compute the firm's present weighted-average cost of capital.
(b) Is the figure computed an appropriate acceptance criterion for evaluating investment proposals?
(c) Would it be appropriate for a division of the company?

7. The Tumble Down D Ranch in Montana is considering investing in a new mechanized barn which will cost $600,000. The new barn is expected to save $90,000 in annual labor costs indefinitely (for practical purposes of computation, forever). The ranch, which is incorporated and has a public market for its stock, has a weighted-average cost of capital of 14.5 percent. For this project, Howard Kelsey, the president, intends to use $200,000 in retained earnings and to finance the balance half with debt and half with a new issue of common stock.

Flotation costs on the debt issue amount to 2 percent of the total debt raised, whereas flotation costs on the new common-stock issue come to 15 percent of the issue. What is the net-present value of the project after allowance for flotation costs? Should the ranch invest in the new barn?

8. Ponza International Inc. has three divisions engaged in leisure wear, in graphics, and in household paint. The company has identified proxy companies in these lines of business whose stocks are publicly traded. On the basis of analyzing these stocks in relation to the market index, Ponza has estimated that the systematic risks of its three divisions are as follows:

Division	Beta
Leisure	1.16
Graphics	1.64
Paint	0.70

The expected return on the market index is 13 percent in the foreseeable future and the risk-free rate is currently 7 percent. The divisions are evaluating a number of projects, which have the following expected returns:

Project	Division	Expected Return
#1	Graphics	18%
#2	Paint	12
#3	Paint	10
#4	Leisure	26
#5	Leisure	13
#6	Graphics	21
#7	Paint	14
#8	Graphics	16

(a) Which projects should be accepted and which rejected?
(b) What are the assumptions involved in your acceptance criterion?

9. The Williams Warbler Company is contemplating acquiring the Acme Brass Company. Incremental cash flows arising from the acquisition are expected to be the following:

	Average of Years (in thousands)		
	1–5	6–10	11–∞
Cash flow after taxes	$100	$150	$200
Investment required	50	60	70
Net cash flow	$ 50	$ 90	$130

Acme has an all-equity capital structure. Its beta is 1.60, based on the past sixty months of data relating its excess return to that of the market. The expected risk-free rate is 5 percent, and the expected return on the market portfolio is 10 percent.

(a) What is the maximum price that Williams Warbler Company might pay for Acme?
(b) On what assumptions does a price that high depend?

10. Cougar Pipe Company is considering the cash acquisition of Red Wilson Rod, Inc., for $750,000. The acquisition is expected to result in incremental cash flows of $125,000 in the first year, and this amount is expected to grow at a 6 percent compound rate. In the absence of the acquisition, Cougar expects net cash flows of $600,000 this year (after capital expenditures), and these are expected to grow at a 6 percent compound rate forever. At present, investors and creditors require a 14 percent overall rate of return for Cougar Pipe Company. However, Red Wilson Rod is much more risky, and the acquisition of it will raise the company's overall required return to 15 percent.

(a) Should Cougar Pipe Company acquire Red Wilson Rod, Inc.?

(b) Would your answer be the same if the overall required rate of return stayed the same?

(c) Would your answer be the same if the acquisition increased the surviving company's growth rate to 8 percent forever?

SELECTED REFERENCES

ALBERTS, W. W., AND S. H. ARCHER, "Some Evidence on the Effect of Company Size on the Cost of Equity Capital," *Journal of Financial and Quantitative Analysis*, 8 (March 1973), 229–45.

ALVAZIAN, VAROUJ, AND JEFFREY L. CALLEN, "Investment, Market Structure, and the Cost of Capital," *Journal of Finance*, 34 (March 1979), 85–92.

ARDITTI, FRED D., AND HAIM LEVY, "The Weighted Average Cost of Capital as a Cutoff Rate: A Critical Analysis of the Classical Textbook Weighted Average," *Financial Management*, 6 (Fall 1977), 24–34.

AZZI, CORRY, "Conglomerate Mergers, Default Risk and Homemade Mutual Funds," *American Economic Review*, 68 (March 1978), 161–72.

BERANEK, WILLIAM, "Some New Capital Budgeting Theorems," *Journal of Financial and Quantitative Analysis*, 13 (December 1978), 809–24.

———, "The Weighted Average Cost of Capital and Shareholder Wealth Maximization," *Journal of Financial and Quantitative Analysis*, 12 (March 1977), 17–32.

BOWER, RICHARD S., AND JEFFREY M. JENKS, "Divisional Screening Rates," *Financial Management* 4 (Autumn 1975), 42–49.

BRENNAN, MICHAEL J., "A New Look at the Weighted Average Cost of Capital," *Journal of Business Finance*, 5, No. 1 (1973), 24–30.

BRICK, JOHN R., AND HOWARD E. THOMPSON, "The Economic Life of an Investment and the Appropriate Discount Rate," *Journal of Financial and Quantitative Analysis*, 13 (December 1978), 831–46.

ELTON, EDWIN J. AND MARTIN J. GRUBEN, "Earnings Estimates and the Accuracy of Expectational Data," *Management Science*, 18 (April 1972), 409–24.

EZZELL, JOHN R., AND R. BURR PORTER, "Flotation Costs and the Weighted Average Cost of Capital," *Journal of Financial and Quantitative Analysis*, 11 (September 1976), 403–13.

FAMA, EUGENE F., AND MERTON H. MILLER, *The Theory of Finance*, Chap. 7. New York: Holt, Rinehart & Winston, 1972.

FRANKS, J. R., J. E. BROYLES, AND M. J. HECHT, "An Industry Study of the Profitability of Mergers in the United Kingdom," *Journal of Finance*, 32 (December 1977), 1513–25.

GORDON, MYRON J., AND PAUL J. HALPERN, "Cost of Capital for a Division of a Firm," *Journal of Finance*, 29 (September 1974), 1153–63.

GORDON, M. J., AND L. I. GOULD, "The Cost of Equity Capital: A Reconsideration," *Journal of Finance*, 33 (June 1978), 849–61.

HALEY, CHARLES W., AND LAWRENCE D. SCHALL, "Problems with the Concept of the Cost of Capital," *Journal of Financial and Quantitative Analysis*, 13 (December 1978), 847–70.

HAMADA, ROBERT S., "Portfolio Analysis, Market Equilibrium and Corporation Finance," *Journal of Finance*, 24 (March 1969), 13–31.

HAUGEN, ROBERT A., AND TERENCE C. LANGETIEG, "An Empirical Test for Synergism in Merger," *Journal of Finance*, 30 (September 1975), 1003–14.

HIGGINS, ROBERT C., AND LAWRENCE D. SCHALL, "Corporate Bankruptcy and Conglomerate Merger," *Journal of Finance*, 30 (March 1975), 93–114.

JOEHNK, MICHAEL D., AND JAMES F. NIELSEN, "The Effects of Conglomerate Merger Activity on Systematic Risk," *Journal of Financial and Quantitative Analysis,* 9 (March 1974), 215–26.

KEANE, SIMON E., "The Investment Discount Rate—In Defence of the Market Rate of Interest," *Accounting and Business Research* (Summer 1976), 228–36.

KIM, E. HAN, AND JOHN J. McCONNELL, "Corporate Merger and the Co-insurance of Corporate Debt," *Journal of Finance,* 33, forthcoming.

LEE, LI WAY, "Co-insurance and Conglomerate Merger," *Journal of Finance,* 32 (December 1977), 1527–37.

LEVY, HAIM, AND MARSHALL SARNAT, "Diversification, Portfolio Analysis and the Uneasy Case for Conglomerate Mergers," *Journal of Finance,* 25 (September 1970), 795–802.

LEWELLEN, WILBUR G., "A Pure Financial Rationale for the Conglomerate Merger," *Journal of Finance,* 26 (May 1971), 521–37.

LINKE, CHARLES M., AND MOON K. KIM, "More on the Weighted Average Cost of Capital: A Comment and Analysis," *Journal of Financial and Quantitative Analysis,* 9 (December 1974), 1069–81.

LITZENBERGER, ROBERT H., AND O. MAURICE JOY, "Decentralized Capital Budgeting Decisions and Shareholder Wealth Maximization," *Journal of Finance,* 30 (September 1975), 993–1002.

MANDELKER, GERSHON, "Risk and Return: The Case of Merging Firms," *Journal of Financial Economics,* 1 (December 1974), 303–35.

MERVILLE, L. J., AND L. A. TAVIS, "Financial Planning in a Decentralized Firm under Conditions of Competitive Capital Markets," *Financial Management,* 6 (Fall 1977). 17–23.

MOSSIN, JAN, *Theory of Financial Markets,* Chaps. 7–8. Englewood Cliffs, N.J.: Prentice-Hall, 1973.

MUELLER, DENNIS C., "The Effects of Conglomerate Mergers," *Journal of Banking and Finance,* 1 (December 1977), 315–47.

MYERS, STEWART C., "The Application of Finance Theory to Public Utility Rate Cases," *Bell Journal of Economics and Management Science,* 3 (Spring 1972), 58–97.

NANTELL, TIMOTHY J., AND C. ROBERT CARLSON, "The Cost of Capital as a Weighted Average," *Journal of Finance,* 30 (December 1975), 1343–55.

OFER, AHARON R., "Investors' Expectations of Earnings Growth, Their Accuracy and Effects on the Structure of Realized Rates of Return," *Journal of Finance,* 30 (May 1975), 509–23.

REILLY, RAYMOND R., AND WILLIAM E. WECKER, "On the Weighted Average Cost of Capital," *Journal of Financial and Quantitative Analysis,* 8 (January 1973), 123–26.

RUBINSTEIN, MARK E., "A Mean-Variance Synthesis of Corporate Financial Theory," *Journal of Finance,* 28 (March 1972), 167–82.

SCHALL, LAWRENCE D., "Asset Valuation, Firm Investment, and Firm Diversification," *Journal of Business,* 45 (January 1972), 11–28.

——, "Firm Financial Structure and Investment," *Journal of Financial and Quantitative Analysis,* 6 (June 1971), 925–42.

SCOTT, JAMES H., JR., "On the Theory of Conglomerate Mergers," *Journal of Finance,* 32 (September 1977), 1235–50.

SENBET, LEMMA W., AND HOWARD E. THOMPSON, "The Equivalence of Alternative Mean-Variance Capital Budgeting Models," *Journal of Finance,* 33 (May 1978), 395–402.

STAPLETON, RICHARD C., "Portfolio Analysis, Stock Valuation and Capital Budgeting Rules for Risky Projects," *Journal of Finance,* 26 (March 1971), 95–118.

TURNBULL, STUART, "Market Value and Systematic Risk," *Journal of Finance,* 32 (September 1977), 1125–42.

Tuttle, Donald L., and Robert H. Litzenberger, "Leverage, Diversification and Capital Market Effects on a Risk-Adjusted Capital Budgeting Framework," *Journal of Finance*, 23 (June 1968), 427–43.

Van Horne, James C., "Optimal Initiation of Bankruptcy Proceedings by Debt Holders," *Journal of Finance*, 31 (June 1976), 897–910.

financing and dividend policies

9

theory of capital structure

In Part II, we were concerned with how capital might be allocated to investment proposals, given a certain financing mix. In this chapter and the next, we are concerned with whether the way in which investment proposals are financed matters; and, if it does matter, what is the optimal capital structure? If we finance with one mix of securities rather than another, is the market price of the stock affected? If the firm can affect the market price of its stock by its financing decision, it will want to undertake a financing policy that will maximize market price. For simplicity, we examine the question of capital structure in terms of the proportion of debt to equity. However, the principles taken up in this chapter can be easily expanded to include consideration of the specific type of security being issued.

First we explore the theory with respect to the valuation of the firm. From previous discussion of the capital-asset pricing model, one's intuition should be that if the assumptions of the model hold, variations in the proportion of debt in the capital structure do not affect the firm's total valuation. That is, in the absence of taxes, bankruptcy costs, and other imperfections of this sort, the value of the firm is independent of its capital structure. If firms are valued only according to their systematic risk in a no-tax world, the degree of leverage should not matter. Unlike the development of the last two chapters, however, we do not begin with an analysis of the issue in the context of the capital-asset pricing model. While the subject could be developed in this manner, for ease of understanding we take a different tack.

Our examination involves a partial equilibrium analysis where we hold constant the investment and dividend decisions of the firm and try to determine the effect of a change in financing mix on share price. In this regard, we focus on the arbitrage process as the means by which equilibrium is achieved. Upon completion of this presentation, we then show how the problem ties into the capital-asset pricing model. Hopefully, this treatment will provide not only an easier understanding of the problem but also a much richer insight. Following this, we relax the initial assumptions and study the impact of various capital-market imperfections on the way capital structure decisions affect the valuation of the firm. In the end, we hope to make some generalizations about the implications of the theory presented for financing decisions. In the subsequent chapter, we consider how a firm in practice can determine a capital structure suitable for its particular situation.

INTRODUCTION TO THE THEORY

Even a casual review of the literature brings one quickly to the key question of whether or not capital structure matters. Can the firm affect its total valuation and its cost of capital by changing its financing mix? In this section, our attention is directed to the question of what happens to the total valuation of the firm and to its cost of capital when the ratio of debt to equity, or degree of leverage, is varied. In this regard, we use a capital market equilibrium approach. The advantage of this approach is that it allows us to abstract from factors other than leverage which affect valuation.

Assumptions and Definitions

So that the analysis that follows can be presented as simply as possible, we make the following facilitating assumptions:

1. We assume that there are no income taxes. This assumption is removed later.
2. The ratio of debt to equity for a firm is changed by issuing debt to repurchase stock or issuing stock to pay off debt. In other words, a change in capital structure is effected immediately. In this regard, we assume no transaction costs.
3. The firm has a policy of paying 100 percent of its earnings in dividends. Thus we abstract from the dividend decision.

4. The expected values of the subjective probability distributions of expected future operating earnings for each company are the same for all investors in the market.

5. The operating earnings of the firm are not expected to grow. The expected values of the probability distributions of expected operating earnings for all future periods are the same as present operating earnings.

Given these assumptions, we are concerned with the following three rates[1]

$$k_i = \frac{F}{B} = \frac{\text{Annual interest charges}}{\text{Market value of debt outstanding}} \qquad (9\text{-}1)$$

In this equation, k_i is the yield on the company's debt, assuming this debt to be perpetual.

$$k_e = \frac{E}{S} = \frac{\text{Earnings available to common stockholders}}{\text{Market value of stock outstanding}} \qquad (9\text{-}2)$$

The required rate of return for investors in a firm whose earnings are not expected to grow and that has a 100 percent dividend-payout ratio is the earnings/price ratio. Given our restrictive assumptions, then, the earnings/price ratio represents the market rate of discount that equates the present value of the stream of expected future dividends with the current market price of the stock. This is not to say that it should be used as a general rule to depict the cost of equity capital (see Chapter 8). We use it only because of its simplicity in illustrating the theory of capital structure. The final rate we consider is

$$k_o = \frac{O}{V} = \frac{\text{Net operating earnings}}{\text{Total market value of the firm}} \qquad (9\text{-}3)$$

where $V = B + S$. Here, k_o is an overall capitalization rate for the firm. It is defined as the weighted-average cost of capital and may also be expressed as

$$k_o = k_i\left(\frac{B}{B+S}\right) + k_e\left(\frac{S}{B+S}\right) \qquad (9\text{-}4)$$

Our concern will be with what happens to k_i, k_e, and k_o when the degree of leverage, as denoted by the ratio B/S, increases.

[1]Ezra Solomon, *The Theory of Financial Management* (New York: Columbia University Press, 1963), Chaps. 7–9. For an analysis of the use of these rates in calculating a weighted average cost, see Timothy J. Nantell and C. Robert Carlson, "The Cost of Capital as a Weighted Average," *Journal of Finance*, 30 (December 1975), 1343–55.

Net Income Approach

Durand has proposed two approaches to the valuation of the earnings of a company: the net income approach (NI) and the net operating income approach (NOI).[2] These approaches represent the extremes in valuing the firm with respect to the degree of leverage. Because they give us a basis for additional discussion, we consider them in turn. To illustrate the net income approach, assume that a firm has $3,000 in debt at 5 percent interest, that the expected value of annual net operating earnings is $1,000, and that the equity-capitalization rate, k_e, is 10 percent. Given this information, the value of the firm may be calculated as

O	Net operating earnings	$ 1,000
F	Interest	150
E	Earnings available to common stockholders	$ 850
k_e	Equity-capitalization rate	0.10
S	Market value of stock	$ 8,500
B	Market value of debt	3,000
V	Total value of firm	$11,500

With the net income approach, earnings available to common stockholders are capitalized at a constant rate, k_e. The implied overall capitalization rate in the above example is

$$K_o = \frac{O}{V} = \frac{\$1,000}{\$11,500} = 8.7 \text{ percent}$$

Assume now that the firm increases its debt from $3,000 to $6,000 and uses the proceeds of the debt issue to repurchase stock. Also, suppose that the interest rate on debt remains unchanged at 5 percent. The value of the firm then is

O	Net operating earnings	$ 1,000
F	Interest	300
E	Earnings available to common stockholders	$ 700
k_e	Equity-capitalization rate	0.10
S	Market value of stock	$ 7,000
B	Market value of debt	6,000
V	Total value of firm	$13,000

[2]David Durand, "The Cost of Debt and Equity Funds for Business," in *The Management of Corporate Capital*, ed. Ezra Solomon (New York: Free Press, 1959), pp. 91–116.

The implied overall capitalization rate now is

$$k_o = \frac{O}{V} = \frac{\$1,000}{\$13,000} = 7.7 \text{ percent}$$

According to the net income approach, the firm is able to increase its total valuation, V, and lower its cost of capital, k_o, as it increases the degree of leverage. As a result, the market price per share increases. To illustrate, assume in our example that the firm with \$3,000 in debt has 850 shares of common stock outstanding. Thus the market price per share is \$10 a share (\$8,500/850). The firm issues \$3,000 in additional debt and, at the same time, repurchases \$3,000 of stock at \$10 a share, or 300 shares in total. It then has 550 shares outstanding. We saw in the example that the total market value of the firm's stock after the change in capital structure is \$7,000. Therefore the market price per share is \$7,000/550 = \$12.73, where before it was \$10.

Graphically, the approach is illustrated in Figure 9-1. The degree of leverage, B/S, is plotted along the horizontal axis, while the percentage rates for k_i, k_e, and k_o are on the vertical axis. This graph can be constructed based upon the hypothetical examples we have shown. As can be seen, the critical assumptions of the net income approach are that k_i and, more particularly, k_e remain unchanged as the degree of leverage increases. As the proportion of cheaper debt funds in the capital structure is increased, the weighted-average cost of capital, k_o, decreases and approaches the cost of debt, k_i. The optimal capital structure would be the one at which the total value of the firm is greatest and the cost of capital the lowest. At that structure, the market price per share of stock is maximized. Using the net income approach, the optimal capital structure is the one farthest to the right in Figure 9-1. The significance of this approach is that a firm can lower its cost of capital continually and increase its total valuation by the use of debt funds. Again, the critical assumption is that the firm does not become increasingly more risky in the minds of investors and creditors as the degree of leverage is increased.

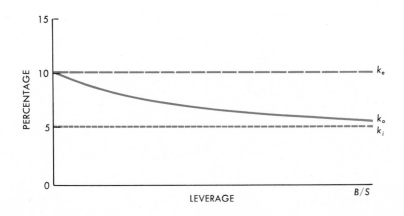

figure 9-1
**Capital costs: net
income approach**

Net Operating Income Approach

We turn now to the net operating income approach. The assumption here is that the overall capitalization rate of the firm, k_o, is constant for all degrees of leverage. Assume the same example as before but with k_o equal to 10 percent. For $3,000 in debt, we have

O	Net operating income	$ 1,000
k_o	Overall capitalization rate	0.10
V	Total value of firm	$10,000
B	Market value of debt	3,000
S	Market value of stock	$ 7,000

The implied equity-capitalization rate in this case is[3]

$$k_e = \frac{E}{S} = \frac{\$850}{\$7,000} = 12.1 \text{ percent}$$

With this approach, net operating income is capitalized at an overall capitalization rate to obtain the total market value of the firm. The market value of the debt then is deducted from the total market value to obtain the market value of the stock.

Suppose, as before, that the firm increases the amount of debt from $3,000 to $6,000 and uses the proceeds of the debt issue to repurchase stock. The valuation of the firm then is

O	Net operating income	$ 1,000
k_o	Overall capitalization rate	0.10
V	Total value of firm	$10,000
B	Market value of debt	6,000
S	Market value of stock	$ 4,000

The implied equity-capitalization rate is

$$k_e = \frac{E}{S} = \frac{\$700}{\$4,000} = 17.5 \text{ percent}$$

We see that the equity-capitalization rate, k_e, rises with the degree of leverage. This approach implies that the total valuation of the firm is unaffected

[3] k_e also can be calculated as

$$k_e = k_o + (k_o - k_i)\frac{B}{S}$$

figure 9-2
Capital costs: net
operating income
approach

by its capital structure. Graphically, the approach is shown in Figure 9-2.

The critical assumption with this approach is that k_o is constant regardless of the degree of leverage. The market capitalizes the value of the firm as a whole; as a result, the breakdown between debt and equity is unimportant. An increase in the use of supposedly "cheaper" debt funds is offset exactly by the increase in the equity-capitalization rate, k_e. Thus the weighted average of k_e and k_i remains unchanged for all degrees of leverage. As the firm increases its degree of leverage, it becomes increasingly more risky; and investors penalize the stock by raising the equity-capitalization rate (lowering the P/E ratio) directly in keeping with the increase in the debt-to-equity ratio. As long as k_i remains constant, k_e is a constant linear function of the debt-to-equity ratio.

According to the net operating income approach, the real cost of debt and the real cost of equity are the same—namely, k_o. The cost of debt has two parts: the explicit cost represented by the rate of interest, and the implicit cost, or "hidden" cost, which is represented by the increase in the equity-capitalization rate that accompanies an increase in the proportion of debt to equity. Because the cost of capital of the firm cannot be altered through leverage, this approach implies that there is no one optimal capital structure. All capital structures are optimal, for market price per share does not change with leverage. To illustrate, assume again that our example firm with $3,000 in debt has 850 shares of common stock outstanding. The market price per share in this case is $7,000/850 = $8.23. With the $3,000 in additional debt, the firm repurchases $3,000 of stock at $8.23 a share, or 364 shares in total. Therefore the market price per share after the change in capital structure is $4,000/(850 − 364) = $8.23, the same as before. Thus capital structure would be a matter of indifference to the investor.

So far, our discussion of the net operating income approach has been purely definitional; it lacks behavioral significance. However, Modigliani and Miller, in their famous 1958 article, offered behavioral support for the independence of the total valuation and the cost of capital of the firm from its capital structure.[4] Before taking up the implications of their position, however, we examine the traditional approach to valuation.

Traditional Approach

The traditional approach to valuation and leverage assumes that there is an optimal capital structure and that the firm can increase the total value of the firm through the judicious use of leverage. Actually, this approach encompasses all the ground between the net income approach and the net operating income approach. To illustrate one variation of the approach, assume that our hypothetical firm has $3,000 in debt at 5 percent interest. Assume, however, that the equity-capitalization rate is 11 percent, rather than the 10 percent or 12.1 percent assumed with the net income or net operating income approaches illustrated previously. The valuation of the firm then is

O	Net operating income	$ 1,000
F	Interest on debt	150
E	Earnings available to common stockholders	$ 850
k_e	Equity-capitalization rate	0.11
S	Market value of stock	$ 7,727
B	Market value of debt	3,000
V	Total value of firm	$10,727

The implied overall capitalization rate is

$$k_o = \frac{O}{V} = \frac{\$1,000}{\$10,727} = 9.3 \text{ percent}$$

This example suggests that the firm can lower its cost of capital and increase the total value of the firm and share price by leverage. With no leverage, $B/S = 0$; and the overall capitalization rate, k_o, is 10 percent. Although investors raise the equity-capitalization rate, k_e, as the firm becomes more financially risky with leverage, the increase in k_e does not offset entirely the benefit of using cheaper debt funds. As a result, total valuation and share price increase, and the cost of capital decreases. With $3,000 in debt and 850

[4]Franco Modigliani and Merton H. Miller, "The Cost of Capital, Corporation Finance and the Theory of Investment," *American Economic Review*, 48 (June 1958), 261–77.

shares outstanding, the market price per share is $7,727/850 = $9.09. This
contrasts with $8.23 under the assumption of a net operating income ap-
proach to valuation.

The traditional approach implies that beyond some point, k_e rises at
an increasing rate with leverage. Moreover, k_i also may rise beyond some
point. To illustrate, suppose now that the firm increases its debt from $3,000 to
$6,000 and uses the proceeds of the debt issue to repurchase stock. Assume
also that the average rate of interest on all debt rises to 6 percent and that the
equity-capitalization rate, k_e, at that degree of leverage is 14 percent. The
valuation of the firm then is

O	Net operating income	$ 1,000
F	Interest on debt	360
E	Earnings available to common stockholders	$ 640
k_e	Equity-capitalization rate	0.14
S	Market value of stock	$ 4,571
B	Market value of debt	6,000
V	Total value of firm	$10,571

The implied overall capitalization rate is

$$k_o = \frac{O}{V} = \frac{\$1,000}{\$10,571} = 9.5 \text{ percent}$$

Thus the total valuation of the firm is lower and its cost of capital slightly
higher than when the amount of debt was $3,000. This result is due to the
increase in k_e and, to a lesser extent, the increase in k_i. From these two
observations, we know that the optimal capital structure in this example
occurs before a debt-to-equity ratio of 6,000/4,571, or 1.31.

Graphically, one variation of the traditional approach is shown in
Figure 9-3. As can be seen in the figure, k_e is assumed to rise at an increasing
rate with leverage, whereas k_i is assumed to rise only after significant leverage has occurred. At first, the weighted-average cost of capital declines with
leverage because the rise in k_e does not offset entirely the use of cheaper debt
funds. As a result, the weighted-average cost of capital, k_o, declines with
moderate use of leverage. After a point, however, the increase in k_e more than
offsets the use of cheaper debt funds in the capital structure, and k_o begins to
rise. The rise in k_o is supported further once k_i begins to rise. The optimal
capital structure is the point at which k_o bottoms out; in the figure, this
optimal capital structure is point X.

Thus the traditional position implies that the cost of capital is not
independent of the capital structure of the firm and that there is an optimal
capital structure. At that optimal structure, the marginal real cost of debt

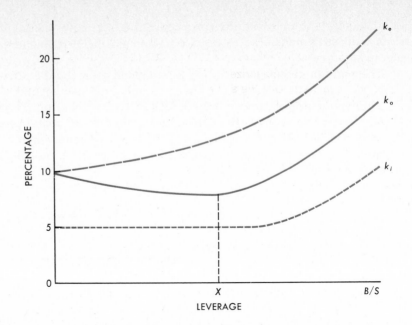

figure 9-3
Traditional approach

(explicit and implicit) is the same as the marginal real cost of equity in equilibrium. For degrees of leverage before that point, the marginal real cost of debt is less than that of equity; beyond that point, the marginal real cost of debt exceeds that of equity. It is important to mention again that there are wide variations in the traditional approach with all falling somewhere between the extremes, the net income and the net operating income approaches. Having taken up all three approaches, we now are able to consider in more detail the question of whether capital structure matters.

MODIGLIANI-MILLER POSITION

As mentioned previously, Modigliani and Miller (MM) advocate that the relationship between leverage and the cost of capital is explained by the net operating income approach. They make a formidable attack on the traditional position by offering behavioral justification for having the cost of capital, k_o, remain constant throughout all degrees of leverage. As their assumptions are extremely important, it is necessary to spell them out.

1. Capital markets are perfect. Information is costless and readily available to all investors; there are no transaction costs; and all securities are infinitely divisible. Investors are assumed to be rational, and to behave accordingly.
2. The average expected future operating earnings of a firm are represented by a subjective random variable. It is assumed that the expected values of the probability distributions of all investors are the same.

Implied in the MM illustration is that the expected values of the probability distributions of expected operating earnings for all future periods are the same as present operating earnings.

3. Firms can be categorized into "equivalent return" classes. All firms within a class have the same degree of business risk. As we shall see later, this assumption is not essential for their proof.

4. The absence of corporate income taxes is assumed. MM remove this assumption later.

In taking the net operating income approach, MM draw essentially the same conclusions as described when we discussed that approach. Their three basic propositions are[5]

1. The total market value of the firm and its cost of capital are independent of its capital structure. The total market value of a firm is given by capitalizing the expected stream of operating earnings at a discount rate appropriate for its risk class.

2. The expected yield of a share of stock, k_e, is equal to the capitalization rate of a pure equity stream, plus a premium for financial risk equal to the difference between the pure equity-capitalization rate and k_i, times the ratio B/S. In other words, k_e increases in a manner to exactly offset the use of cheaper debt funds.

3. The cutoff rate for investment purposes is completely independent of the way in which an investment is financed. This proposition along with the first implies a complete separation of the investment and financing decisions of the firm.

Arbitrage Support of Propositions

MM argue that the total risk for all security holders of a firm is not altered by changes in its capital structure. Therefore the total value of the firm must be the same regardless of its financing mix. The crucial support for this hypothesis is the presence of arbitrage in the capital markets. Arbitrage precludes perfect substitutes from selling at different prices in the same market. In their case, the perfect substitutes are two or more firms in the same homogeneous risk class that differ only with respect to capital structure. MM contend that the total value of these firms has to be the same; otherwise, arbitragers will enter and drive the values of the two firms together. The essence of their argument is that arbitragers are able to substitute personal leverage for corporate leverage.[6]

Consider two firms that comprise a single risk class. These firms are identical in every respect except that Company A is not levered and Com-

[5]Modigliani and Miller, "Cost of Capital, Corporation Finance and the Theory of Investment."

[6]Ibid., pp. 270–72.

pany B has $30,000 of 5% bonds outstanding. According to the traditional position, Company B may have a higher total value and lower average cost of capital than Company A. The valuation of the two firms is assumed to be the following:

		Company A	Company B
O	Net operating income	$ 10,000	$ 10,000
F	Interest on debt		1,500
E	Earnings available to common stockholders	$ 10,000	$ 8,500
k_e	Equity-capitalization rate	0.10	0.11
S	Market value of stock	$100,000	$ 77,272
B	Market value of debt		30,000
V	Total value of firm	$100,000	$107,272
k_o	Implied overall capitalization rate	10%	9.3%
B/S	Debt-to-equity ratio	0	38.8%

MM maintain that this situation cannot continue, for arbitrage will drive the total values of the two firms together. Company B cannot command a higher total value simply because it has a different financing mix than Company A. MM argue that investors in Company B are able to obtain the same dollar return with no increase in financial risk by investing in Company A. Moreover, they are able to do so with a smaller investment outlay.[7] Because investors would be better off with the investment requiring the lesser outlay, they would sell their shares in Company B and buy shares in Company A. These arbitrage transactions would continue until Company B's shares declined in price and Company A's shares increased in price enough so that the total value of the two firms was identical.

To illustrate, suppose that a rational investor owned 1 percent of Company B, the levered firm, worth $772.72 (market value). Given this situation, he should

1. Sell his stock in Company B for $772.72.
2. Borrow $300 at 5 percent interest. This personal debt is equal to 1 percent of the debt of Company B—his previous proportional ownership of the company.
3. Buy 1 percent of the shares of Company A, the unlevered firm, for $1,000.

Prior to this series of transactions, the investor's expected return on investment in Company B was 11 percent on a $772.72 investment, or $85. His

[7]This arbitrage proof appears in Franco Modigliani and Merton H. Miller, "Reply to Heins and Sprenkle," *American Economic Review*, 59 (September 1969), 592–95.

expected return on investment in Company A is 10 percent, or $100 on an
investment of $1,000. From this return, he must deduct the interest charges on
his personal borrowings. Thus his net dollar return is

Return on investment in Company A	$100
Less interest (300 × 0.05)	15
Net return	$ 85

We see then that his net dollar return, $85, is the same as it was for his
investment in Company B. However, his cash outlay of $700 ($1,000 less
personal borrowings of $300) is less than the $772.72 investment in Company
B, the levered firm. Because of the lower investment, the investor would
prefer to invest in Company A under the conditions described. In essence, the
investor is able to "lever" the stock of the unlevered firm by taking on
personal debt.

    The action of a number of rational investors undertaking similar
arbitrage transactions will tend to drive up the price of Company A shares,
and lower its k_e, and drive down the price of Company B, increasing its k_e.
This arbitrage process will continue until there is no further opportunity for
reducing one's investment outlay and achieving the same dollar return. At
this equilibrium, the total value of the two firms must be the same. As a result,
their average costs of capital, k_o, also must be the same.

    If for some reason the value of the unlevered firm, Company A, were
to exceed that of the levered firm, Company B, arbitrage would work in the
opposite direction. Suppose that Company A in our example had an equity
capitalization rate of 8 percent, giving it a total market value of $125,000.
Here, the investor owning 1 percent of Company A's shares would sell his
holdings for $1,250. He then would buy 1 percent of the stock of Company B
for $772.72 as well as buy 1 percent of the debt of that company for $300. His
total expected dollar return in Company B would be

Return on investment in Company B stock	$ 85
Return on investment in Company B debt	15
Net return	$100

This return is the same as his expected return in Company A's stock. Thus his
total return is the same as before; and he needs to invest only $1,072.72,
compared with $1,250.00 previously. As a result, he would prefer investing in
Company B. Again, the action of a number of investors behaving in this
manner will tend to drive the total values of the two firms together. The
principle involved is simply that investors are able to reconstitute their
former positions by offsetting changes in corporate leverage with changes in
personal leverage. As a result, the investment opportunities available to them
are not altered by changes in the capital structure of the firm.

It is important to realize that proof of the proposition that leverage is irrelevant does not depend on the two firms' belonging to the same risk class. This assumption was invoked in order that we might more easily illustrate the arbitrage process. However, equilibrium occurs across securities of different risk companies on the basis of expected return and risk. In the Appendix to this chapter, we show under MM assumptions that the required rate of return on equity is a linear function of its debt-to-equity ratio in the context of the capital-asset pricing model. (This linear function corresponds to proposition 2 of MM.) Therefore the arbitrage proof of MM is not dependent upon the existence of homogeneous risk classes. This risk-class notion was introduced by MM to simplify the illustration of the equilibrium process; none of their basic propositions depend upon it. All of the propositions can be illustrated in the context of the capital-asset pricing model without companies belonging to risk classes.

THE EFFECT OF MARKET IMPERFECTIONS

Given the assumptions inherent in perfect capital markets, the market equilibrating process assures the validity of MM's thesis that the cost of capital and total valuation of a firm are independent of its capital structure. To dispute this stand, one needs to look for capital market imperfections that impede the equilibration of security prices according to their expected returns and systematic risk. Under these circumstances, leverage may have an effect on the value of the firm and its cost of capital. However, the imperfections not only must be material, but they must be one-directional. For example, we know that transaction costs restrict the arbitrage process described earlier. That is, arbitrage will take place only up to the limits imposed by transaction costs. However, the net effect of this imperfection is not predictable as to direction if in fact there is a net effect at all.[8]

In what follows, we examine certain imperfections that may have a predictable effect on the question of whether capital structure decisions matter. We defer until last the most important imperfection, corporate income taxes, because there is general agreement on its impact. After we have presented the various imperfections, we will attempt to reconcile the more important of them with respect to the question of determining an optimal capital structure.

---

[8]The presence of transaction costs may result in incomplete markets in that distinct marketable securities do not correspond to every contingency in the world. Under these circumstances, it may be possible for a company to tailor a security issue to a particular class of investors to take advantage of the situation. However, the effect here is not systematic as to direction. See J. Hirshleifer, *Investment, Interest, and Capital* (Englewood Cliffs, N.J.: Prentice-Hall, 1970), pp. 264–75.

Bankruptcy Costs

If there is a possibility of bankruptcy, and if administrative and other costs associated with bankruptcy are significant, the levered firm may be less attractive to investors than the unlevered one.[9] With perfect capital markets, zero bankruptcy costs are assumed. If the firm goes bankrupt, assets presumably can be sold at their economic values with no liquidating or legal costs involved. Proceeds from the sale are distributed according to the claim on assets described in Chapter 24. If capital markets are less than perfect, however, there may be bankruptcy costs, and assets may have to be liquidated at less than their economic values. These costs and the "shortfall" in liquidating value from economic value represent a drain in the system from the standpoint of debt and equity holders.

In the event of bankruptcy, security holders as a whole receive less than they would in the absence of bankruptcy costs. To the extent that the levered firm has a greater possibility of bankruptcy than the unlevered one, it would be a less attractive investment, all other things the same. The possibility of bankruptcy usually is not a linear function of the debt/equity ratio, but it increases at an increasing rate beyond some threshold.[10] As a result, the expected cost of bankruptcy increases in this manner and would be expected to have a corresponding negative effect upon the value of the firm and upon its cost of capital.[11] While the ex-post cost of bankruptcy is borne by creditors, in perfect capital markets creditors would be expected to pass on the ex-ante cost to stockholders in the form of higher interest rates.[12] Hence the

---

[9]Joseph E. Stiglitz, "Some Aspects of the Pure Theory of Corporate Finance: Bankruptcies and Takeovers," *Bell Journal of Economics and Management Science,* 3 (Autumn 1972), 458–82, suggests that bankruptcy affects the cost of capital even in the absence of bankruptcy costs. He contends that because of a divergence in expectations as to the chance of bankruptcy between the lender and the borrower, the interest rate is an increasing function of the debt/equity ratio. With bankruptcy penalties, the scale of the firm becomes important and the firm's investment and financing decisions are no longer independent.

[10]Using a state-preference approach in a world of taxes and bankruptcy penalties, Alan Kraus and Robert H. Litzenberger, in "A State-Preference Model of Optimal Financial Leverage," *Journal of Finance,* 28 (September 1973), 911–22, show that with discrete states of nature the relationship between the value of the firm and the amount of debt is jagged. Value is increased with leverage up to the point where a further debt increase causes a change in state from a state in which the firm would be solvent to one in which it would be insolvent. At that point the market value drops due to bankruptcy penalties. It increases with subsequent leverage (because of the tax advantage of debt) only to fall when another change in state occurs.

[11]See James C. Van Horne, "Optimal Initiation of Bankruptcy Proceedings by Debt Holders," *Journal of Finance,* 31 (June 1976), 897–910.

[12]Robert A. Haugen and Lemma W. Senbet, "The Irrelevance of Bankruptcy Costs to the Theory of Optimal Capital Structure," *Journal of Finance,* 33 (June 1978), 383–94, argue that bankruptcy costs are not a factor of importance. They assume that rationality prevails on the part of customers, suppliers, employees, and creditors so that when bankruptcy approaches, the company simply reorganizes by selling stock and repurchasing debt. They reason that all parties

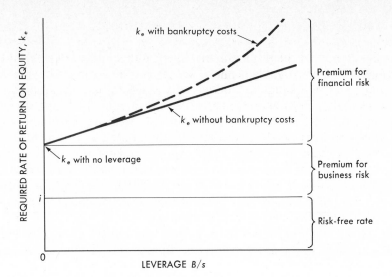

figure 9-4
Required rate of return for equity capital when bankruptcy costs exist

latter would bear the burden of ex-ante bankruptcy costs and the lower valuation of the firm which follows. Because bankruptcy costs represent a "dead weight" loss, investors are unable to diversify away these costs even though the market equilibration process is assumed to be efficient.

As a result, investors are likely to penalize the price of the stock as leverage increases. The nature of the penalty is illustrated in Figure 9-4. Here the required rate of return for investors, k_e, is broken down into its component parts. There is the risk-free rate, i, plus a premium for business risk. This premium is depicted on the vertical axis by the difference between the required rate of return for an all-equity capital structure and the risk-free rate. As debt is added, the required rate of return rises and this increment represents a financial risk premium. In the absence of bankruptcy costs, the required return would rise in a linear manner according to Modigliani-Miller, and this relationship is shown. However, with bankruptcy costs and an increasing probability of bankruptcy with leverage, the required rate of return would be expected to rise at an increasing rate beyond some point. At first there might be a negligible probability of bankruptcy, so there would be little or no penalty. As increasing leverage occurs, however, an increasing penalty is found. For extreme leverage, the penalty becomes very substantial indeed.

---

have an incentive to avoid the costs of a formal reorganization and will seek an informal reorganization instead where the costs are lower. The authors distinguish between a bankruptcy, where debtholders take over the company, and a liquidation. The latter is said to be a rational abandonment decision on the part of the firm (see the Appendix to Chapter 6) and is independent of the event of bankruptcy. The argument that bankruptcy costs are insignificant depends on complete rationality by all parties in a distress situation, no restrictions on arbitrage, and no imperfections when it comes to selling stock and repurchasing debt. While it is an empirical question, based on fragmentary evidence the contention in this book is that imperfections exist and that bankruptcy costs are positive and significant.

As the bankruptcy imperfection has been considered at length in previous chapters, we do not discuss it further. However, the brevity of treatment is not meant to convey any lack of importance to the leverage question. In fact, it probably is one of the two most important imperfections, particularly when it comes to extreme leverage, and we shall incorporate it into an overall analysis shortly.

Corporate and Homemade Leverage Not Being Perfect Substitutes

The perceived risks of personal leverage and corporate leverage may differ. Implied in the MM analysis is that personal and corporate leverage are perfect substitutes. However, there are various reasons for suspecting that this may not be the case. For one thing, if the investor borrows personally and pledges his stock as collateral, he is subject to possible margin calls. Many investors view this possibility with alarm. Moreover, personal leverage involves a certain amount of inconvenience on the part of the investor, which he does not experience with corporate leverage. In addition, the stockholder has limited liability with a stock investment, whereas his liability with a personal loan is unlimited. If the levered company goes bankrupt, the investor's loss is limited to his investment in the stock. He is not liable for the debts of the company. However, if he borrows personally and defaults, lenders can claim assets in addition to the stock. For these reasons, personal leverage may not be a perfect substitute for corporate leverage in the minds of many investors.

However, arbitrage need not occur in terms of the individual actually borrowing in the market. The same thing may be accomplished by changing his holdings of bonds. Moreover, the arbitrage process is not confined to individuals. If opportunities for profit exist, financial intermediaries may enter the scene and replicate the financial claims of either the levered or the unlevered company and buy the stock of the other. The free entry of financial intermediaries without cost will assure the efficient functioning of the arbitrage process, which in turn will result in the irrelevance of corporate leverage.[13] Therefore we are inclined to discount the importance of this argument.[14]

[13]See Stiglitz, "Reexamination of the Modigliani-Miller Theorem," pp. 786–88; and Stiglitz, "On the Irrelevance of Corporate Financial Policy," *American Economic Review,* 64 (December 1974), 864–65.

[14]Another consideration under this heading might be the impact of margin requirements. The Federal Reserve regulates the percentage of advance under a margin loan. This precludes a person from borrowing the full value of the stock pledged as collateral. Thus the requirement restricts the ability of arbitragers to substitute "homemade" leverage for corporate leverage. One means for circumventing this requirement is to purchase the stock of a company with debt as opposed to purchasing the stock of a company without debt and then borrowing personally. The margin requirement is said to encourage the use of debt financing by companies. See Peter R. Lloyd-Davies, "Optimal Financial Policies in Imperfect Markets," *Journal of Financial and Quantitative Analysis,* 10 (September 1975), 467–69.

Differing Costs of Borrowing

Due to capital market imperfections, the effective cost of borrowing may be higher for the individual than for the corporation. The corporation is larger and is likely to be able to borrow at a lower rate of interest than the rate on a personal loan. As a result, investors may prefer that the corporation do the borrowing rather than having to do it themselves. If so, the levered company could have a somewhat higher total value than the unlevered company for this reason alone.[15] Again it should be pointed out that the individual can engage in arbitrage by varying his holdings of bonds. In addition, some institutional investors are able to borrow on a basis as favorable as that of the corporation. Therefore, differing borrowing costs may not be as important as they seem at first.

Institutional Restrictions

Restrictions on investment behavior may retard the arbitrage process. Many institutional investors, such as pension funds and life insurance companies, are not allowed to engage in the "homemade" leverage that was described. In addition, stock and bond investments often are restricted by regulatory bodies to a list of companies meeting certain quality standards. One of these standards is that the company involved have only a "safe" amount of leverage. If a company breaches that amount, it may be removed from the acceptable list, thereby precluding certain institutions from investing in it. This reduction in investor demand can have an adverse effect on the market value of the company's financial instruments.

David W. Glenn argues that the combination of restrictions on the investment behavior of financial institutions, together with restrictions on short sales, results in there being an optimal capital structure for the firm.[16] By way of definition, a *short sale* is the borrowing of a security and selling it with the obligation to deliver the borrowed security back to the lender some time in the future. One hopes to buy the security back at a lower price than the price at which it was sold, thereby realizing a profit from the two transactions. The presence of restrictions on the investment behavior of institutions will result in those securities approved for investment selling at higher prices than otherwise would be the case. If unrestricted investors (those investors who are not legally restricted in their investment behavior) could freely engage in short selling, they would eliminate the higher relative prices for these securities. Unrestricted investors would sell short the approved securities and use the proceeds of the short sale to buy other securities that

---

[15]For further discussion of this point, see David P. Baron, "Default Risk, Homemade Leverage, and the Modigliani-Miller Theorem," *American Economic Review,* 64 (March 1974), 176–82.

[16]"Super Premium Security Prices and Optimal Corporate Financing Decisions," *Journal of Finance,* 31 (May 1976), 507–24.

were more favorably priced in the market, given their expected return and systematic risk.

The action of a number of unrestricted investors behaving in this manner would drive down the prices of approved securities and up the prices of other securities until equilibrium was achieved. However, this process depends on there being no restrictions on short sales. In practice, the proceeds of a short sale are not available to the party selling the security short, but rather are held in escrow. Moreover, there is a margin requirement. These impediments to short selling result in unrestricted investors not being able to eliminate the premiums in prices for securities that are approved investments for restricted institutional investors. Under these circumstances, an optimal capital structure exists, according to Glenn. For most firms, it would involve issuing the maximum amount of debt consistent with obtaining a preferential investment grade rating suitable for institutional investors.

Income Taxes

When we allow for corporate income taxes, we must reexamine the earlier arguments for irrelevance. Because the payment of interest is deductible for tax purposes, leverage lowers the weighted-average after-tax cost of capital found with the MM position. To illustrate, suppose that the expected value of annual net operating income for two firms is $2,000 before taxes, the corporate income tax rate is 50 percent, the after-tax capitalization rate is 10 percent for both companies, and Company A has no debt, whereas Company B has $8,000 in 7% bonds. According to the MM position, the total values of the two companies would be:

	Company A	Company B
1. Net operating income	$ 2,000	$ 2,000
2. Taxes	1,000	1,000
3. Profit before interest, but after taxes	$ 1,000	$ 1,000
4. After-tax capitalization rate for debt-free company	.10	.10
5. Capitalized value of (3)	$10,000	$10,000
6. Interest on debt	0	560
7. (1 − Tax rate) (6)	0	280
8. Tax savings on interest	0	$ 280
9. Interest rate		.07
10. Capitalized value of (8)	0	4,000
11. Total value of firm (5) + (10)	$10,000	$14,000

We see that while Companies A and B have the same operating income, Company B pays lower taxes owing to the deductibility of interest as an expense. As a result, there is more money available to suppliers of capital.

Because stockholders are the residual owners of the company, the tax shield benefit goes directly to them. If we assume that the tax shield remains unchanged in all future years, its present value using the perpetuity formula is

$$\text{Present value of tax shield} = \frac{t_c r B}{r} = t_c B \qquad (9\text{-}5)$$

where t_c is the corporate tax rate, r is the interest rate on the debt, and B is the market value of the debt. Therefore in row 10 of the example we capitalize the $280 tax savings arising from interest payments by 7 percent to obtain a present value of $4,000.

With taxes then, the value of the firm is

$$V = \frac{O(1 - t_c)}{\rho_k} + t_c B \qquad (9\text{-}6)$$

where ρ_k is the after-tax capitalization rate for a company with no debt in a given risk class, and O is the expected net operating income. As before, a 100 percent dividend-payout ratio is assumed. The first expression on the right is the value of the firm if it were unlevered. However, its actual value exceeds this unlevered value by the present value of the tax shield. Therefore, in our example for Company B we add the present value of the tax shield, $4,000, to the value of the firm if it were unlevered, $10,000, to obtain its total value of $14,000.

In essence, the federal government pays a subsidy to the levered company for the use of debt financing. The greater the amount of debt employed, the greater the subsidy and the greater the value of the firm, all other things the same. Similarly, the greater the debt, the lower the cost of capital, which, with corporate taxes, can be expressed as

$$k_o = \rho_k(1 - t_c L) \qquad (9\text{-}7)$$

where L is the "target proportion of debt."[17] As L increases, we see that the cost of capital steadily declines. If this were all there were, the optimal strategy would be to take on the maximum amount of leverage possible. As we shall see later in the chapter, however, various market imperfections come into play which make the optimal capital structure one that has less than 99.9 percent debt. First, however, we need to explore the tax effect in more depth.

As discussed in the preceding chapter, the tax savings associated with the use of debt are not certain. If reported income is consistently low or negative, the tax shield on debt, as denoted by $t_c B$ in Eq. (9-5), is reduced or

[17]Miller and Modigliani, "Some Estimates of the Cost of Capital to the Electric Utility Industry," p. 342. See also Modigliani and Miller, "Corporate Income Taxes and the Cost of Capital: A Correction," *American Economic Review*, 53 (June 1963), 433–42.

even eliminated.[18] As a result, the near full or full cash-flow burden of interest payments would be felt by the firm. If the firm should go bankrupt, of course, the potential future tax savings associated with debt will stop altogether.[19] We must recognize also that Congress can change the corporate tax rate, though the band within which changes are likely to occur is relatively narrow. All of these things make the tax shield associated with debt financing less than certain.

Taxes on Personal Income   The presence of taxes on personal income may reduce the tax advantage associated with debt financing. If the return on debt to the investor is taxed at a higher rate than his return on common stock, then the overall tax advantage associated with corporate debt is reduced.[20] Within the MM tax framework for market equilibrium, the tax advantage of leverage can be expressed as[21]

$$A = \left[1 - \frac{(1 - t_c)(1 - t_{ps})}{1 - t_{pd}} \right] B \tag{9-8}$$

where t_{ps} is the personal income tax rate applicable to common-stock income to the investor, t_{pd} is the personal tax rate applicable to income from the company's debt, and B is the market value of the firm's debt. We see that as long as t_{pd} is greater than t_{ps}, the tax advantage of debt is less than $t_c B$, which we determined to be the advantage in a world of corporate but not personal taxes.

However, if the income from holding a common stock consists only of dividends and if dividends and interest both are taxed as ordinary income, t_{ps} would equal t_{pd}. As a result, the tax advantage in Eq. (9-8) would reduce to $t_c B$, which is the same as appears in Eq. (9-6) for the valuation of a levered firm with corporate income taxes but no personal income taxes. Suppose, however, that part of the income from holding a stock consists of capital gains. Under our assumptions, this would occur if the company repurchased a

---

[18]The reader is referred to Chapter 8 for a detailed discussion of the conditions under which the tax shield is forgone.

[19]M. J. Brennan and E. S. Schwartz, "Corporate Income Taxes, Valuation, and the Problem of Optimal Capital Structure," *Journal of Business,* 51 (January 1978), 103–15, analyze the tradeoff between the incremental tax savings that additional debt affords if the firm survives and the increased probability of bankruptcy and loss of tax savings. The authors show that an optimal capital structure may exist as a result of these two factors alone. See E. Han Kim, "A Mean-Variance Theory of Optimal Capital Structure and Corporate Debt Capacity," *Journal of Finance,* 33 (March 1978), 45–64, who also analyzes this issue.

[20]For an analysis of this question, see Donald E. Farrar and Lee L. Selwyn, "Taxes, Corporate Financial Policies and Returns to Investors," *National Tax Journal,* 20 (December 1967), 444–54; and M. J. Brennan, "Taxes, Market Valuation and Corporate Financial Policy," *National Tax Journal,* 23 (December 1970), 417–27.

[21]Merton H. Miller, "Debt and Taxes," *Journal of Finance,* 32 (May 1977), 266–68.

portion of its stock.[22] Assuming the tax rate on capital gains is less than that on ordinary income, t_{pd} would be greater than t_{ps}. As a result, the tax advantage associated with leverage would be less than t_cB. In other words, investors overall must hold both a company's common stock and its debt instruments. If the tax on debt income is greater than that on common-stock income, increases in a company's debt ratio result in an increase in the personal income taxes that must be paid. Therefore the existence of personal income taxes, differential tax rates on ordinary income and capital gains, and share repurchase will reduce but probably not eliminate the corporate income tax advantage associated with leverage.[23]

Implications of Taxes and Bankruptcy Costs

Where does this leave us with respect to the proportion of debt to employ? It should be apparent from the controversy presented that no universally accepted answer exists. It depends upon one's views of the strengths of the various arguments presented. If one believes that capital markets are perfect, that investors are rational, and that there are a sufficient number of arbitragers with funds to drive out any advantage between stocks differing only in the degree of leverage, then one must basically accept the MM position. In a world of taxes, this implies that an optimal capital structure will have in it a very high proportion of debt.

If one allows for bankruptcy costs, and if the probability of bankruptcy increases at an increasing rate with the degree of leverage, extreme leverage is likely to be penalized by investors. (As discussed earlier, bankruptcy costs represent a drain in the system to security holders.) In a world of both taxes and bankruptcy costs, there would likely be an optimal capital structure even if all of the other behavioral tenets of the MM position held. The cost of capital of a firm would decline as leverage was first employed because of the tax advantage of debt. Gradually, however, the prospect of bankruptcy would become increasingly important, causing the cost of capital to decrease at a decreasing rate as leverage increased. As leverage became extreme, the bankruptcy effect might more than offset the tax effect, causing the cost of capital of the firm to rise. By definition, this would be the point at which the capital structure of the firm was optimal. The joint effect of

---

[22]For an analysis of this situation in a capital-asset pricing model context, see Brennan, "Taxes, Market Valuation and Corporate Financial Policy."

[23]Miller, "Debt and Taxes," 261–75, argues that the tax advantage of corporate debt is eliminated in market equilibrium. If this were the case, the value of the firm and its cost of capital would be independent of its capital structure even with taxes. Essentially his argument is based on corporations adjusting the supply of corporate debt to take advantage of clienteles of investors with different tax brackets. In market equilibrium, Miller claims that $(1 - t_c)(1 - t_{ps}) = (1 - t_{pd})$, so that the term in brackets in Eq. (9-8) is zero. However, Robert H. Litzenberger and James C. Van Horne, "Elimination of the Double Taxation of Dividends and Corporate Financial Policy," *Journal of Finance*, 33 (June 1978), footnote 10, demonstrate that this relationship is inconsistent with market clearing and that the tax advantage of debt remains.

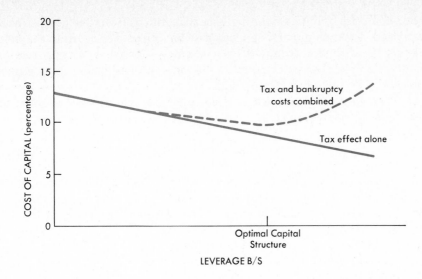

figure 9-5
Cost of capital with
taxes and
bankruptcy costs

taxes and bankruptcy is illustrated in Figure 9-5 for a hypothetical firm.[24]

If one feels other imperfections and/or behavioral factors dilute the MM position further, the point at which the cost-of-capital line turns up would be earlier than that depicted in the figure. Recall that these imperfections include higher costs of borrowing for individuals than for corporations as a rule, institutional restrictions, and imperfections in information. The greater the importance one attaches to these factors, the less effective the arbitrage process becomes, and the greater the case that can be made for an optimal capital structure.

DEBT VERSUS EQUITY IN AN OPTION PRICING MODEL FRAMEWORK

Another way to look at the capital structure issue is in the option pricing model framework presented in Chapter 4.[25] The equity of a firm can be viewed as a call option on the firm's total value, the latter being the associated or underlying asset of the option. The writers of the option are the debtholders. For simplicity, assume that debt is represented by discount

[24]For determining the optimal capital structure of a firm in the face of positive taxes and bankruptcy costs, see E. Han Kim, "A Mean-Variance Theory of Optimal Structure and Corporate Debt Capacity," *Journal of Finance*, 33 (March 1978), 45–64; James H. Scott, Jr., "A Theory of Optimal Capital Structure," 7 (Spring 1976), 33–54; Wayne Y. Lee and Henry H. Barker, "Bankruptcy Costs and the Firm's Optimal Debt Capacity," *Southern Economic Journal*, 43 (April 1977), 1453–65; and David P. Baron, "Default Risk, Homemade Leverage, and the Modigliani-Miller Theorem," *American Economic Review*, 64 (March 1974), 176–82. For an excellent review of the tradeoff, see Andrew Chen, "Recent Developments in the Cost of Debt Capital," *Journal of Finance*, 33 (June 1978), 863–77.

[25]This section assumes the reader has covered Chapter 4. If not, it should be passed over.

bonds where the only payment made is at maturity.[26] Under these circumstances, the stockholders can be viewed as having sold the firm to the debtholders with an option to buy it back at a specified price. In this case the option has an exercise price equal to the face value of debt and its expiration date is the maturity of the debt.[27]

The value of the option at the expiration date, which by definition is the value of the stock, is

$$V_o = \text{Max. } (V_f - D, O) \tag{9-9}$$

where V_f is the value of the firm at the expiration date, D is the face value of the debt which is the exercise price of the option, and Max. means the maximum value of $V_f - D$ or zero, whichever is greater. The value of the debt at the expiration date is simply

$$V_o = \text{Min. } (V_f, D) \tag{9-10}$$

where Min. means V_f or D, whichever is less. In other words, if V_f is greater than D, the debtholders are entitled only to the face value of the debt and the stockholders exercise their option. If V_f is less than D, the debtholders as owners of the firm are entitled to its value. The stockholders receive nothing. Note that the value of their option at expiration cannot be negative, because they have limited liability. Therefore the debtholder-stockholder relationship can be pictured in an option pricing framework.

The Effect of Variance and the Riskiness of Assets

We know from Chapter 4 that the greater the variance or volatility in value of the underlying asset, the greater the value of the option, all other things the same. Therefore it is in the interest of the option holders, in this case the stockholders, to increase the variance of the firm. With a given exercise price of D, an increase in the dispersion of the probability distribution of possible firm values increases the value of their option. Thus, by increasing the riskiness of the assets of the firm, stockholders can increase the value of their option. This works to the disadvantage of the debtholders because there will be a corresponding decrease in the market value of their investment.

To illustrate, we use the Black-Scholes option pricing model which was illustrated in Chapter 4. In this regard, the same assumptions are made

---

[26]The interest rate is embodied in the discount. For example, if the bond had a face value of $1,000, a maturity of one year, and a discount of $70, the interest rate would be $70/$930 = 7.53 percent.

[27]See Fischer Black and Myron Scholes, "The Pricing of Options and Corporate Liabilities," *Journal of Political Economy*, 81 (May-June 1973), 649–51.

as before.[28] Suppose that the total value of Belgrazia Tube Company is $4

million and that it has just issued debt with a face value of $3 million payable entirely at the end of five years. At present the standard deviation of the continuously compounded rate of return on the overall value of the company is 0.12. Also, the short-term, risk-free rate is 6 percent. Given this information, we first solve for d_1 and d_2 in the Black-Scholes option pricing formula.[29]

$$d_1 = \frac{ln(\$4/\$3) + [.06 + 1/2(.12)^2]5}{.12\sqrt{5}} = \frac{.623682}{.268328} = 2.32 \qquad \text{(9-11)}$$

In the equation, ln refers to the natural log and 5 to the length of time to the expiration of the option. For d_2, we have

$$d_2 = \frac{ln(\$4/\$3) + [.06 - 1/2(.12)^2]5}{.12\sqrt{5}} = \frac{.551682}{.268328} = 2.06 \qquad \text{(9-12)}$$

In Appendix B at the end of the book, we see that the area of a normal distribution to the right of 2.30 standard deviations is .0107 and to the right of 2.35 standard deviations, .0094. Interpolating, 2.32 standard deviations is found to correspond to .0102. Therefore the area of the distribution less than 2.32 standard deviations to the right of the mean is $1 - .0102 = .9898$. For the area 2.06 standard deviations to the right of the mean, we find by interpolating that this standard deviation corresponds to .0197. The area of the distribution less than 2.06 standard deviations is $1 - .0197 = .9803$. Therefore, $N(d_1) = .9898$, and $N(d_2) = .9803$. Solving for the option pricing formula, Eq. (4-2) in Chapter 4, we obtain

$$V_o = \$4 \text{ million } (.9898) - \frac{\$3 \text{ million}}{e^{(.06)(5)}} (.9803) = \$1,780,526 \qquad \text{(9-13)}$$

where $e = 2.71828$ and the exponent is the interest rate times the length of time to expiration. Thus the value of the stock is $1,780,526, and the value of the debt is $4,000,000 - \$1,780,526 = \$2,219,474$.

Suppose now that Belgrazia Tube Company dramatically increases the riskiness of its business so that the standard deviation of its continuously compounded rate of return becomes 0.36 in contrast to 0.12 before. As a result, we have the following for d_1 and d_2:

---

[28]These include no transaction costs, no taxes, no financial market imperfections, no restrictions on short sales, no dividends on the stock, a known and constant short-term interest rate at which parties can both lend and borrow, and the value of the firm following a random walk in continuous time with a constant variance rate over time.

[29]For an extended discussion of how to solve the formula, see Eq. (4-2) in Chapter 4 and the illustration.

$$d_1 = \frac{ln(\$4/\$3) + [.06 + 1/2(.36)^2]5}{.36 \sqrt{5}} = \frac{.911682}{.804984} = 1.13 \tag{9-14}$$

$$d_2 = \frac{ln(\$4/\$3) + [.06 - 1/2(.36)^2]5}{.36 \sqrt{5}} = \frac{.263682}{.804984} = 0.33 \tag{9-15}$$

We find in Appendix B at the end of the book that these standard deviations correspond to areas to the right of the mean of .1293 and .3708, respectively. Thus the areas of the distribution less than these standard deviations are $1 - .1293 = .8707$, and $1 - .3708 = .6292$. Therefore the value of the stock is

$$V_o = \$4 \text{ million } (.8707) - \frac{\$3 \text{ million}}{e^{(.06)(5)}} (.6292) = \$2,084,431 \tag{9-16}$$

In this case the value of the stock is $2,084,431 in contrast to $1,780,526 before, and the value of the debt is $4,000,000 − $2,084,431 = $1,915,569 in contrast to $2,219,474 before.

Therefore, by increasing the riskiness of the company, stockholders are able to increase the value of their stock at the direct expense of the debtholders. The reason for this occurrence is that stockholders have an option on the total value of the firm. As with any option, increased variance of the underlying asset increases the option's value.

However, debtholders should be aware of the effect of variance on the writer of an option. They can protect themselves at the time of the loan by imposing constraints on the company. Known as protective covenants, these covenants may be used to restrict the stockholders' ability to increase the riskiness of the company. In Chapter 18, we discuss protective covenants and how they may be used in an option pricing model context. For now, it is sufficient to say that debtholders are able to protect themselves, and if rationality prevails in the market for loans, they will protect themselves. More will be said about this after we have considered changes in the capital structure.

Changing the Proportion of Debt

Given the perfect market assumptions of the option pricing model, changing the proportion of debt in the capital structure will not affect the total value of the firm. In other words, the Modigliani-Miller irrelevance proposition holds. However, such a change will affect the relative valuations of the debt and of the equity. We know that the option pricing formula can be used to determine the value of the common stock, and that by deducting this value from the value of the total firm we can determine the value of the debt. By comparing values for different proportions of debt, we are able to determine the relationship between the proportion of debt and valuation.

To illustrate, we use our last example but assume that the face value of the debt is $1 million instead of $3 million. For d_1 and d_2 in the Black-

Scholes formula, we have

$$d_1 = \frac{ln(\$4/\$1) + [.06 + 1/2(.36)^2]5}{.36 \sqrt{5}} = \frac{2.010295}{.804984} = 2.50 \qquad (9\text{-}17)$$

$$d_2 = \frac{ln(\$4/\$1) + [.06 - 1/2(.36)^2]5}{.36 \sqrt{5}} = \frac{1.362295}{.804984} = 1.69 \qquad (9\text{-}18)$$

In Appendix B at the end of the book, we see that 2.50 standard deviations to the right of the mean corresponds to an area of .0062, and 1.69 standard deviations to an area of .0436. Therefore $N(d_1) = 1 - .0062 = .9938$, and $N(d_2) = 1 - .0436 = .9564$. Therefore the value of the stock is

$$V_o = \$4 \text{ million } (.9938) - \frac{\$1 \text{ million}}{e^{(.06)(5)}}(.9564) = \$3,266,681 \qquad (9\text{-}19)$$

The value of the debt is $\$4,000,000 - \$3,266,681 = \$733,319$.

When the face value of debt is increased from $1 million to $3 million, we obtained from our earlier example a value of stock of $2,084,431 and a value of debt of $1,915,569. The percentage increases for the debt are:

			Percentage Change
Face value of debt	$1,000,000	$3,000,000	200%
Value of debt	733,319	1,915,569	161

Thus the increase in the face value of the debt is accompanied by a smaller percentage increase in the value of the debt, holding constant the total value of the firm.[30] The reason is that the probability of default has increased, and with the greater default risk the value of the debt (per dollar of face value) is reduced.

In the context of the option pricing model, issuing debt and retiring stock, thereby increasing the proportion of debt in the capital structure, will result in a decline in the price of the existing debt (per dollar of face value) and an increase in share price. For example, if the face value of each bond were $1,000 there would be 1,000 bonds outstanding at $1 million in debt and 3,000 bonds outstanding at $3 million in debt. The value per bond at the lower level of debt is $733,319/1,000 = $733.32 per bond. At the higher level it is $1,915,569/3,000 = $638.52. In essence, the stockholders have expropriated some of the wealth of the existing debtholders. The new debtholders are not hurt, because they lend money on the basis of the default risk associated with the new capital structure. In our example, they would

[30]See Black and Scholes, "Pricing of Options and Corporate Liabilities," 650.

lend $638.52 for each $1,000 face value bond. It is only the old debtholders who suffer. Similar to the previous discussion of a change in the overall risk of the firm, there is a wealth transfer from the old debtholders to the stockholders.[31]

Again, however, debtholders can protect themselves against such expropriation by imposing protective covenants. In this case, the restriction would be on the firm issuing new debt without compensation to the old debtholders. One way is to require that any new debt be subordinated to the old debt with respect to the claim on assets and on income. In this way, the debtholders can assure themselves that the value of their claim will not decline with increases in the proportion of debt. Existing debtholders should also be concerned with the dividends paid to stockholders. In the extreme case, the firm could declare a liquidating dividend and steal the company away from the debtholders. For this reason, debtholders will want a restriction on the dividends the firm can pay to its stockholders.

The Modigliani-Miller argument for the irrelevance of capital structure requires that security holders protect themselves against capital structure changes that work to erode their position. Known as "me first" rules, these rules ensure that one party cannot gain at the expense of the other.[32] While usually the party that gains is the stockholders and the party that loses is the old debtholders, it is possible for the reverse to occur. With certain protective covenants, debtholders might obtain a claim on future retained earnings at the expense of stockholders. Therefore stockholders also must assure themselves that their positon will not be eroded without compensation.

In order, then, for the Modigliani-Miller position to have validity, it is essential that suppliers of capital protect themselves against expropriations of the sort described above. Otherwise capital structure decisions will not be a matter of indifference to debtholders and to stockholders. Even though the total value of the firm would not change, the relative wealth positions of the two parties could change. Presumably with perfect capital markets, suppliers of capital would protect themselves. The expression of the capital-structure problem in an option pricing model context points out

[31]For an analysis of this transfer from a theoretical standpoint as well as an empirical investigation of it as it relates to newly formed captive finance companies, see E. Han Kim, John J. McConnell, and Irwin H. Silberman, "Capital Structure Rearrangements and Me-First Rules in an Efficient Capital Market," *Journal of Finance,* 32 (June 1977), 789–810.

[32]For further discussion of this point, see Fama and Miller, *The Theory of Finance* (New York: Holt, Rinehart & Winston, 1972), pp. 151–53. In a subsequent paper, Eugene F. Fama, "The Effects of a Firm's Investment and Financing Decisions on the Welfare of Its Security Holders," *American Economic Review,* 68 (June 1978), 272–84, shows that if there are truly perfect capital markets, "me-first" rules are not necessary to ensure the irrelevance of leverage. In general equilibrium, prices of debt securities will reflect whether or not they are protected from expropriation. In such a world, investors are able to insulate themselves from the effects of financing decisions by firms.

the importance of such behavior. However, exact protection is difficult to achieve. As taken up in Chapter 18, where we examine protective covenants in depth, some of these covenants are rather crude constraints. To the extent that "me first" rules are not effective, capital structure decisions may be relevant even in the absence of taxes and bankrupty costs.

THE PRESENCE OF AGENCY COSTS

Protective covenants can be thought of as a way for creditors to monitor the actions of stockholders so as to preclude the erosion in value of their claim. However, resources must be spent in order to monitor, and the costs involved are one form of *agency costs*. As discussed in Chapter 1, Michael C. Jensen and William H. Meckling have expounded a sophisticated theory of agency costs.[33] Among other things, the authors show that regardless of who makes the monitoring expenditures, they ultimately are borne by the stockholders as a wealth reduction. This is due to debtholders taking account of potential monitoring costs in the interest rate charged. The greater the likely monitoring costs by debtholders, the higher the interest rate, and the lower the value of the firm to its shareholders, all other things the same.

Complete protection would require the specification of extremely detailed protective covenants and extraordinary enforcement costs. Virtually every decision of the firm would need to be monitored. Not only would there be substantial legal and enforcement costs, but the firm would operate inefficiently. All of these agency costs go to reduce the overall value of the firm. As residual owners of the firm, stockholders have an incentive to see that such monitoring costs are minimized. However, there is a tradeoff involved. In the absence of any protective covenants, debtholders may charge very high interest rates, and these rates may cost stockholders more than the agency costs associated with reasonable protective covenants.

It is not that monitoring costs are bad *per se* for the owners of a company, it is that monitoring needs to be efficient. As more and more safeguards and enforcement procedures are imposed, debtholders' protection rises, but at a decreasing rate. Beyond a point, the reduction in interest rate is more than offset by escalating agency costs, which ultimately are borne by the stockholders. Therefore an optimal balance needs to be struck between monitoring costs and the interest rate charged on a debt instrument at the time it is sold. Some activities of the firm are relatively inexpensive to monitor, whereas others are expensive. For example, dividend and financing decisions can be monitored with only moderate cost, whereas the production

[33]"Theory of the Firm: Managerial Behavior, Agency Costs and Ownership Structure," *Journal of Financial Economics,* 3 (October 1976), 305–60. For a somewhat different approach, see Stewart C. Myers, "Determinants of Corporate Borrowing," *Journal of Financial Economics,* 5 (November 1977), 147–75.

and investment decisions of the firm are much more costly to monitor.[34] The relative costs of monitoring need to be taken into account in determining the protective covenants that should be used.

In addition, the firm should endeavor to see that efficient monitoring occurs. To the extent that management together with an outside auditor or appraiser can produce information at a lower cost than the lender, it should undertake the production of such information. (This assumes that the "quality" of the information is the same.) The important thing to realize is that ultimately the costs of monitoring are borne by the stockholders. Therefore it is always in their interest to see that monitoring is efficiently administered, regardless of the level that occurs.

The presence of monitoring costs acts as a disincentive to the issuance of debt. If capital markets were perfect with the exception of these costs and we lived in a no-tax world, the firm would not want to issue any debt. However, we know that the corporate income tax makes the issuance of debt attractive. Like bankruptcy costs, however, monitoring costs may limit the amount of debt that it is optimal for a firm to issue. It is likely that the amount of monitoring required by debtholders increases with the amount of debt oustanding. When there is little or no debt, lenders may engage in only limited monitoring, whereas with a great deal of debt outstanding they may insist upon extensive monitoring. In turn, this monitoring may involve considerable costs. As a result, the situation illustrated in Figure 9-5, where the tradeoff between taxes and bankruptcy costs on the cost of capital is shown, would need to be modified. Monitoring costs would act as a further factor increasing the cost of capital for extreme leverage. The situation is illustrated in Figure 9-6. As seen in the figure, the optimal capital structure occurs at

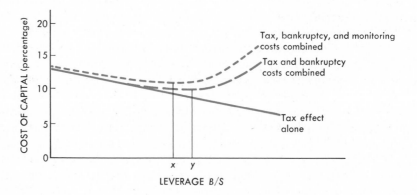

figure 9-6
Cost of capital with taxes, bankruptcy costs, and monitoring costs

[34]Clifford W. Smith, Jr., and Jerold B. Warner, in "On Financial Contracts and Optimal Capital Structure: An Analysis of Bond Covenants" (unpublished research paper, University of Rochester, May 1978), explore specific protective covenants in the context of maximizing shareholder wealth.

point X, somewhat before that which occurs with taxes and bankruptcy costs alone, point Y.[35]

In conclusion, there are a number of reasons for believing that an optimal capital structure exists. One of these is the presence of monitoring costs with any debt contract. Depending upon one's view as to the strengths of the various capital market and behavioral imperfections, the expected optimal capital structure may occur earlier or later along the scale of possible leverage.

SUMMARY

A great deal of controversy has developed over whether the capital structure of a firm, as determined by its financing decision, affects its cost of capital. Traditionalists argue that the firm can lower its cost of capital and increase market value per share by the judicious use of leverage. However, as the company levers itself and becomes increasingly risky financially, lenders begin to charge higher interest rates on loans. Moreover, investors require an increasingly higher return, all other things the same. Beyond a point, the cost of capital begins to rise. According to the traditional position, that point denotes the optimal capital structure. Modigliani and Miller, on the other hand, argue that in the absence of corporate income taxes, the cost of capital is independent of the capital structure of the firm. They contend that the cost of capital and the total market value of the firm are the same for all degrees of leverage.

We saw that the behavioral support for their position was based upon the arbitrage process. Arguments for the relevance of capital structure decisions must be rooted in capital markets being less than perfect. In this regard, we examined several imperfections, including bankruptcy costs, differences between corporate and "homemade" leverage, institutional restrictions on investors, and corporate taxes. With the introduction of corporate income taxes, debt has a tax advantage and serves to lower the cost of capital, even in the MM case. This effect is reduced if there are personal income taxes and if the personal tax on debt income is higher than that on common-stock income. Unfortunately, empirical testing has been little more than suggestive with respect to the true relationship between leverage and the cost of capital. We know, however, that the combination of corporate income taxes and bankruptcy costs may result in an optimal capital structure.

One can analyze the capital structure problem in an option pricing model framework where the stockholders have an option to buy back the

---

[35]Jensen and Meckling, in "Theory of the Firm: Managerial Behavior, Agency Cost and Ownership Structure," consider not only the question of debt versus equity but the optimal fraction of stock owned by the manager as well. An important part of their analysis pertains to the agency cost to the owners in monitoring the behavior of the manager.

firm at the maturity of the debt. As with any option, an increase in the variance of the associated asset—in this case the value of the firm—will increase the value of the option. It is to the stockholders' advantage to increase variance, either by increasing the riskiness of the assets of the firm or by increasing the proportion of debt. Debtholders can protect themselves against this occurrence by imposing protective covenants. To a lesser extent, stockholders also need to protect therselves against the erosion of their position. The Modigliani-Miller thesis depends upon suppliers of capital protecting themselves against expropriation of value without compensation. However, this protection involves monitoring costs, which are a form of agency costs. As these costs ultimately are borne by the stockholders, they have an incentive to see that monitoring is efficient. Beyond some threshold, monitoring costs are likely to increase at an increasing rate with leverage. Like bankruptcy costs, monitoring costs may limit the amount of debt in an optimal capital structure. In the next chapter, we examine ways by which a firm can analyze which capital structure is appropriate.

APPENDIX
The Irrelevance of Capital Structure in the Context of the Capital-Asset Pricing Model

In this chapter, we illustrated the irrelevance of capital structure under the assumption of perfect capital markets using an arbitrage example. The example was based on two firms belonging to the same risk class. However, the presence of risk classes is not necessary for the Modigliani-Miller (MM) irrelevance argument to be valid. Market equilibrium occurs across stocks of companies having varying degrees of business risk. If the assumptions of the capital-asset pricing model discussed in Chapters 3, 7, and 8 hold, only the systematic risk of a stock is important. It follows, then, that leverage does not matter in the context of the capital-asset pricing model.

From our earlier discussion of the model, we know that the equilibrium expected return for a stock can be expressed as

$$k_e = i + \frac{R_m - i}{\sigma_m^2}(r_{em}\sigma_e\sigma_m) \tag{9A-1}$$

where i = the risk-free rate

R_m = expected return on the market portfolio

r_{em} = the correlation coefficient between k_e and R_m

σ_e = standard deviation of the probability distribution of possible k_e's

σ_m = standard deviation of the probability distribution of possible R_m's

The term in parentheses is the expected covariance between returns on the stock and returns on the market portfolio. Thus the expected return on a stock is determined by its correlation with the market portfolio and by its standard deviation, a measure of risk. Similarly, the expected return on the company's debt can be expressed as follows, assuming it is priced according to the capital-asset pricing model:

$$k_{\text{debt}} = i + \frac{R_m - i}{\sigma_m^2}(r_{\text{debt},m}\sigma_{\text{debt}}\sigma_m) \tag{9A-2}$$

where $r_{\text{debt},m}$ is the correlation coefficient between returns on the company's debt and returns on the market portfolio, which is comprised of both debt and equity instruments, and σ_{debt} is the standard deviation of the probability distribution of possible returns for the company's debt.

The covariance between returns on the stock of a levered company and returns on the market portfolio can be expressed as[36]

$$r_{em}\sigma_e\sigma_m = \left(\frac{B+S}{S}\right)(r_{em}\sigma_e\sigma_m)^* + \left(1 - \frac{B+S}{S}\right)(r_{\text{debt},m}\sigma_{\text{debt}}\sigma_m) \tag{9A-3}$$

where $(r_{em}\sigma_e\sigma_m)^*$ is the expected covariance between returns on the stock *in the absence of leverage* and returns on the market portfolio, and B and S are the market values of the company's debt and equity, respectively. In other words, the starred term is the expected covariance if the company had an all-equity capital structure. Substituting Eq. (9A-3) into Eq. (9A-1) and rearranging, we obtain

$$\begin{aligned}
k_e &= i + \left[\frac{R_m - i}{\sigma_m^2}\right]\left[\frac{B+S}{S}(r_{em}\sigma_e\sigma_m)^* - \frac{B}{S}(r_{\text{debt},m}\sigma_{\text{debt}}\sigma_m)\right] \\
&= i + \left[\frac{R_m - i}{\sigma_m}\right]\left[\frac{B+S}{S}(r_{em}\sigma_e)^* - \frac{B}{S}(r_{\text{debt},m}\sigma_{\text{debt}})\right]
\end{aligned} \tag{9A-4}$$

As $(B + S)/S$ is the same as $1 + B/S$, we can express Eq. (9-A4) as

$$\begin{aligned}
k_e = i + \left(\frac{R_m - i}{\sigma_m}\right)(r_{em}\sigma_e)^* + \frac{B}{S}\left[\left(\frac{R_m - i}{\sigma_m}\right)(r_{em}\sigma_e)^* \right.\\
\left. - \left(\frac{R_m - i}{\sigma_m}\right)(r_{\text{debt},m}\sigma_{\text{debt}})\right]
\end{aligned} \tag{9A-5}$$

Finally, this becomes

$$k_e = k_e^* + \frac{B}{S}(k_e^* - k_{\text{debt}}) \tag{9A-6}$$

[36]This development is based on Robert A. Haugen and James L. Pappas, "Equilibrium in the Pricing of Capital Assets, Risk-Bearing Debt Instruments and the Question of Optimal Capital Structure," *Journal of Financial and Quantitative Analysis*, 6 (June 1971), 943-54. See also Yutaka Imai and Mark E. Rubinstein, "Comment," and Haugen and Pappas, "Reply," *Journal of Financial and Quantitative Analysis*, 7 (September 1972), 1995–2004. Essentially the same point was made earlier by Robert S. Hamada, "Portfolio Analysis, Market Equilibrium and Corporation Finance," *Journal of Finance*, 24 (March 1969), 13–19. In addition, see Jack Becker, "General Proof of Modigliani-Miller Propositions I and II using Parameter-Preference Theory," *Journal of Financial and Quantitative Analysis*, 13 (March 1978), 65–69.

where k_e is the expected or required rate of return on a levered stock, k_e^* is the required return if the company were not levered, and k_{debt} is the required return on the company's debt.

Thus the required rate of return on equity is a linear function of the firm's debt-to-equity ratio in the context of the capital-asset pricing model. This of course is the same as proposition II of MM, which states that k_e is a linear function of leverage. Therefore the arbitrage proof of MM is not dependent upon the existence of homogeneous risk classes. In fact, there need not be any two firms in the market with exactly the same risk characteristics. All of the MM propositions can be illustrated in the context of the capital-asset pricing model, though with more difficulty.

PROBLEMS

1. The Malock Company has net operating earnings of $10 million and $20 million of debt with a 7 percent interest charge. In all cases, assume no taxes.

   (a) Using the net income method and an equity-capitalization rate of 12 1/2 percent, compute the total value of the firm and the implied overall capitalization rate.

   (b) Next, assume that the firm issues an additional $10 million in debt and uses the proceeds to retire stock; the interest rate and equity-capitalization rate remain the same. Compute the new total value of the firm and overall capitalization rate.

   (c) Using the net operating income concept and an overall capitalization rate of 11 percent, compute the total market value, the stock-market value, and the implied equity-capitalization rate for the Malock Company prior to the sale of additional debt.

   (d) Determine the answers to (c) if the company were to sell the additional $10 million in debt.

2. The Blalock Corporation has a $1 million capital structure and will always maintain this book value amount. Blalock currently earns $250,000 per year before taxes of 50 percent, has an all-equity capital structure of 100,000 shares, and pays all earnings in dividends. The company is considering issuing some debt in order to retire some stock. The cost of the debt and the price of the stock at various levels of debt are given below. It is assumed that the new capital structure would be reached all at once by purchasing stock at the current price. In other words, the following table is a schedule at a point in time.

Amount of Debt	Average Cost of Debt	Price of Stock Per Share
—	—	$10.00
$100,000	6.0%	10.50
200,000	6.0	10.80
300,000	6.5	11.00
400,000	7.0	11.15
500,000	8.0	10.50
600,000	10.0	9.50

(a) By observation, what do you think is the optimal capital structure?

(b) Construct a graph in terms of k_e, k_i, and k_o based upon the above data.

(c) Are your conclusions in (a) confirmed?

3. The Veblen Company and the Knight Company constitute a single risk class. These firms are identical in every respect except that the Veblen Company is not levered, while the Knight Company has $1 million in 6% bonds outstanding. The valuation of the two firms is assumed to be the following:

		Veblen	Knight
O	Net operating income	$ 300,000	$ 300,000
F	Interest on debt	—	60,000
E	Earnings to common	$ 300,000	$ 240,000
k_e	Equity-capitalization rate	.125	.140
S	Market value of stock	$2,400,000	$1,714,000
B	Market value of debt	—	1,000,000
V	Total value of firm	$2,400,000	$2,714,000
k_o	Implied overall capitalization rate	12.5%	11.0%
B/S	Debt/equity ratio	0	58.34%

(a) An investor owns $10,000 worth of Knight stock. Show the process and the amount by which he could reduce his outlay through the use of arbitrage.

(b) According to Modigliani and Miller, when will this arbitrage process cease?

(c) What arguments can be raised against this hypothesis?

4. Sam Peltz is planning to form a corporation. He has determined that $10 million will be required as an initial capital investment. Several financial backers have indicated that they would be willing to buy the bonds of the new corporation or personally lend Sam the capital he needs. Sam has delineated these alternative financing plans:

(1) Form the corporation with 1 million shares of $10 par stock, borrowing the entire $10 million from his associates on a personal basis (paying 6 percent interest on his note).

(2) Form the corporation with 500,000 shares of $10 par stock, borrowing the $5 million from his associates on a personal basis (6 percent note). Sell $5 million worth of 6% bonds to his associates.

(3) Form the corporation with 250,000 shares of $10 par stock, borrowing $2.5 million from his associates on a personal basis (6 percent note). Sell $7.5 million worth of 6 percent bonds to his associates.

(a) Assuming no corporate or personal taxes, which of the three alternatives should Sam select if the firm is expected to earn $1 million per year before the payment of interest? Assume that all of net earnings are paid out in dividends.

(b) Assuming a 50 percent corporate income tax and a personal income tax rate for Sam of 40 percent, which of the three alternatives should Sam select if the firm were expected to earn the same amount as in (a)? Assume all earnings are paid out in dividends.

5. Bakor Baking Company has an all-equity capital structure, net operating income before taxes of $400,000, and an after-tax capitalization rate of 10 percent. The corporate tax rate is 50 percent.

(a) Assuming perfect capital markets, graph the cost of capital of the firm for various levels of debt. (Assume that the firm issues debt to repurchase stock, thereby effecting an immediate change in its capital structure.) What happens to the cost of capital with leverage?

(b) Assume now that bankruptcy costs exist. What happens to the cost of capital in the above example as leverage increases?

6. Loveless Electrical Products Company has $4 million in debt outstanding. The corporate income tax rate is 50 percent. In an extensive study of investors, G. Rosenberg and Associates, an outside consulting firm, has estimated that the marginal personal tax rate on common-stock income for investors overall is 30 percent. Included in this income are both dividends and capital gains. The firm also has estimated that the marginal personal tax rate on debt income is 40 percent.

(a) Determine the tax advantage to Loveless Electrical Products Company for the use of debt under the assumption of corporate income taxes but no personal income taxes. (Assume the debt is perpetual and that the tax shield will be the same throughout.)

(b) Determine the tax advantage with both corporate and personal income taxes. Why does your answer to (b) differ from that to (a)?

(c) What would be the tax advantage if the personal tax rate on common-stock income were 40 percent? If it were 20 percent? (Assume all else stays the same.)

7. Acme-Menderhall Corporation is trying to determine an appropriate capital structure. It knows that as its leverage increases, its cost of borrowing will eventually increase, as will the required rate of return on its common stock. The company has made the following estimates for various leverage ratios:

| | | Required Rate of Return on Equity | |
| | | Without | With |
Debt/(Debt + Equity)	Interest Rate on Borrowings	Bankruptcy and Agency Costs	Bankruptcy and Agency Costs
0	—	10 %	10 %
.10	8 %	10½	10½
.20	8	11	11¼
.30	8½	11½	12
.40	9	12¼	13
.50	10	13¼	14½
.60	11	14½	16¼
.70	12½	16	18½
.80	15	18	21

(a) Assuming a tax rate of 50 percent, what is the weighted-average cost of capital of the company at various leverage ratios in the absence of bankruptcy and agency costs? What is the optimal capital structure?

(b) With bankruptcy and agency costs, what is the optimal capital structure?

8. Mohave Sand and Transit Company currently has an overall value of $8 million. The debt has a face value of $4 million and is represented by discount bonds that mature in three years. The standard deviation of the continuously compounded rate of return on overall value is 20 percent. The short-term risk-free rate is currently 6 percent.

(a) Treating the stock as an option and using the Black-Scholes option model, Eq. (4-2) in Chapter 4, determine the value of the equity and the value of debt.

(b) If the company were to increase the riskiness of its business so that the standard deviation became 50 percent, what would happen to the value of the stock and to the value of the debt?

(c) Does one party gain at the expense of the other? If this is the case, how can the other party protect itself?

9. Suppose in problem 8 that Mohave Sand and Transit Company decided to issue $2 million in additional debt (face value) with a three-year maturity and repurchase $2 million in stock.

(a) What is the effect on the value of the stock and on the value of the debt if the standard deviation is 50 percent?

(b) Does the value of the debt increase proportionally with the increase in its face value? Why or why not?

SELECTED REFERENCES

ARDITTI, FRED D., AND JOHN M. PINKERTON, "The Valuation and Cost of Capital of the Levered Firm with Growth Opportunities," *Journal of Finance,* 33 (March 1978), 65–73.

BARON, DAVID P., "Default Risk and the Modigliani-Miller Theorem: A Synthesis," *American Economic Review,* 66 (March 1976), 204–12.

———, "Default Risk, Homemade Leverage, and the Modigliani-Miller Theorem," *American Economic Review,* 64 (March 1974), 176–82.

———, "Firm Valuation, Corporate Taxes, and Default Risk," *Journal of Finance,* 30 (December 1975), 1251–64.

BAXTER, NEVINS D., "Leverage, Risk of Ruin, and the Cost of Capital," *Journal of Finance,* 22 (September 1967), 395–404.

BECKER, JACK, "General Proof of Modigliani-Miller Propositions I and II Using Parameter-Preference Theory," *Journal of Financial and Quantitative Analysis,* 13 (March 1978), 65–69.

BLACK, FISCHER, AND JOHN C. COX, "Valuing Corporate Securities: Some Effects on Bond Indenture Provisions," *Journal of Finance,* 31 (May 1976), 351–68.

BLACK, FISCHER, AND MYRON SCHOLES, "The Pricing of Options and Corporate Liabilities," *Journal of Political Economy,* 81 (May-June 1973), 637–54.

BRENNAN, M. J., "Taxes, Market Valuation and Corporate Financial Policy," *National Tax Journal,* 23 (December 1970), 417–27.

BRENNAN, M. J., AND E. S. SCHWARTZ, "Corporate Income Taxes, Valuation and the Problem of Optimal Capital Structure," *Journal of Business,* 51 (January 1978), 103–15.

CHEN, ANDREW, "Recent Developments in the Cost of Debt Capital," *Journal of Finance,* 33 (June 1978), 863–877.

DURAND, DAVID, "Costs of Debt and Equity Funds for Business: Trends and Problems of Measurement," reprinted in *The Management of Corporate Capital,* ed. Ezra Solomon, pp. 91–116. New York: Free Press, 1959.

FAMA, EUGENE F., "The Effects of a Firm's Investment and Financing Decisions on the Welfare of Its Security Holders," *American Economic Review,* 68 (June 1978), 272–84.

FAMA, EUGENE F., AND MERTON H. MILLER, *The Theory of Finance,* Chap. 4. New York: Holt, Rinehart & Winston, 1972.

GALAI, DAN, AND RONALD W. MASULIS, "The Option Pricing Model and the Risk Factor of Stock," *Journal of Financial Economics,* 3 (January-March 1976), 53–81.

GLENN, DAVID W., "Super Premium Security Prices and Optimal Corporate Financing Decisions," *Journal of Finance,* 31 (May 1976).

HALEY, CHARLES W., AND LAWRENCE D. SCHALL, "Problems with the Concept of the Cost of Capital," *Journal of Financial and Quantitative Analysis,* 13 (December 1978), 847–70.

HAMADA, ROBERT S., "The Effect of the Firm's Capital Structure on the Systematic Risk of Common Stocks," *Journal of Finance,* 27 (May 1972), 435–52.

——, "Portfolio Analysis, Market Equilibrium, and Corporation Finance," *Journal of Finance,* 24 (March 1969), 13–31.

HAUGEN, ROBERT A., AND JAMES L. PAPPAS, "Equilibrium in the Pricing of Capital Assets, Risk-Bearing Debt Instruments, and the Question of Optimal Capital Structure," *Journal of Financial and Quantitative Analysis,* 6 (June 1971), 943–53. See also Yutaka Imai and Mark Rubinstein, "Comment," *Journal of Financial and Quantitative Analysis,* 7 (September 1972), 2001–3; and Haugen and Pappas, "Reply," ibid., 2005–8.

HAUGEN, ROBERT A., AND LEMMA W. SENBET, "The Irrelevance of Bankruptcy Costs to the Theory of Optimal Capital Structure," *Journal of Finance,* 33 (June 1978), 383–94.

HEINS, A. JAMES, AND CASE M. SPRENKLE, "A Comment on the Modigliani-Miller Cost of Capital Thesis," *American Economic Review,* 59 (September 1969), 590–92.

HITE, GAILEN L., "Leverage, Output Effects, and the M-M Theorems," *Journal of Financial Economics,* 4 (March 1977), 177–202.

JENSEN, MICHAEL C., AND WILLIAM E. MECKLING, "Theory of the Firm: Managerial Behavior, Agency Costs and Ownership Structure," *Journal of Financial Economics,* 3 (October 1976), 305–60.

KEANE, SIMON M., "Some Aspects of the Cost of Debt," *Accounting and Business Research* (Autumn 1975), 298–304.

KIM, E. HAN, "A Mean-Variance Theory of Optimal Structure and Corporate Debt Capacity," *Journal of Finance,* 33 (March 1978), 45–64.

KIM, E. HAN, JOHN J. MCCONNELL, AND IRWIN SILBERMAN, "Capital Structure Rearrangements and Me-First Rules in an Efficient Capital Market," *Journal of Finance,* 32 (June 1977), 789–810.

KRAUS, ALAN, AND ROBERT H. LITZENBERGER, "A State-Preference Model of Optimal Financial Leverage," *Journal of Finance,* 28 (September 1973), 911–22.

KUMAR, PREM, "Growth Stocks and Corporate Capital Structure Theory," *Journal of Finance,* 30 (May 1975), 533–47.

LEE, WAYNE Y., AND HENRY H. BARKER, "Bankruptcy Costs and the Firm's Optimal Debt Capacity," *Southern Economic Journal,* 43 (April 1977), 1453–65.

LITZENBERGER, ROBERT H., AND JAMES C. VAN HORNE, "Elimination of the Double Taxation of Dividends and Corporate Financial Policy," *Journal of Finance,* 33 (June 1978), 737–49.

LLOYD-DAVIES, PETER R., "Optimal Financial Policy in Imperfect Markets," *Journal of Financial and Quantitative Analysis,* 10 (September 1975), 457–82.

MERTON, ROBERT C., "On the Pricing of Contingent Claims and the Modigliani-Miller Theorem," *Journal of Financial Economics,* 5 (November 1977), 241–49.

MILLER, MERTON H., "Debt and Taxes," *Journal of Finance*, 32 (May 1977), 266–68.

MILLER, M. H., AND FRANCO MODIGLIANI, "Cost of Capital to Electric Utility Industry," *American Economic Review*, 56 (June 1966), 333–91.

MILNE, F., "Choice over Asset Economics: Default Risk and Corporate Leverage," *Journal of Financial Economics*, 2 (June 1975), 165–85.

MODIGLIANI, FRANCO, AND M. H. MILLER, "The Cost of Capital, Corporation Finance and the Theory of Investment," *American Economic Review*, 48 (June 1958), 261–97.

———, "The Cost of Capital, Corporation Finance and the Theory of Investment: Reply," *American Economic Review*, 48 (September 1958), 655–69; "Taxes and the Cost of Capital: A Correction," ibid., 53 (June 1963), 433–43; "Reply," ibid., 55 (June 1965), 524–27; "Reply to Heins and Sprenkle," ibid., 59 (September 1969), 592–95.

MOSSIN, JAN, "Security Pricing and Investment Criteria in Competitive Markets," *American Economic Review*, 59 (December 1969), 749–56.

MYERS, STEWART C., "Determinants of Corporate Borrowing," *Journal of Financial Economics*, 5 (November 1977), 147–75.

RENDLEMAN, RICHARD J., "The Effects of Default Risk on the Firm's Investment and Financing Decisions," *Financial Management*, 7 (Spring 1978), 45–53.

ROSS, STEPHEN A., "The Determination of Financial Structure: The Incentive-Signalling Approach," *Bell Journal of Economics*, 8 (Spring 1977), 23–40.

RUBINSTEIN, MARK E., "Corporate Financial Policy in Segmented Securities Markets," *Journal of Financial and Quantitative Analysis*, 8 (December 1973), 749–62.

———, "A Mean-Variance Synthesis of Corporate Financial Theory," *Journal of Finance*, 28 (March 1973), 167–82.

SCHALL, LAWRENCE D., "Firm Financial Structure and Investment," *Journal of Financial and Quantitative Analysis*, 6 (June 1971), 925–42.

SCOTT, JAMES H., JR., "Bankruptcy, Secured Debt, and Optimal Capital Structure," *Journal of Finance*, 32 (March 1977), 1–20.

———, "A Theory of Optimal Capital Structure," *Bell Journal of Economics*, 7 (Spring 1976), 33–54.

SMITH, CLIFFORD W., JR., "Option Pricing: A Review," *Journal of Financial Economics*, 3 (January–March 1976), 3–51.

SMITH, CLIFFORD W., JR., AND JEROLD B. WARNER, "On Financial Contracts and Optimal Capital Structure: An Analysis of Bond Covenants." Unpublished research paper, University of Rochester, May 1978.

STIGLITZ, JOSEPH E., "On the Irrelevance of Corporate Financial Policy," *American Economic Review*, 64 (December 1974), 851–66.

———, "A Reexamination of the Modigliani-Miller Theorem," *American Economic Review*, 59 (December 1969), 784–93.

VAN HORNE, JAMES C., "Optimal Initiation of Bankruptcy Proceedings by Debt Holders," *Journal of Finance*, 31 (June 1976), 897–910.

10
making capital-structure decisions in practice

In theory, the optimal capital structure is one in which the marginal real cost of each available method of financing is the same. By *real cost*, we mean the sum of both the explicit and the implicit costs. Up to now, our discussion has been theoretical. We now wish to consider how the financial manager might determine in practice an appropriate capital structure for his particular firm. In this regard, we examine various methods of analysis that can be used in practice. None of the methods considered is completely satisfactory in itself. Taken collectively, however, they provide the financial manager with sufficient information for making a rational decision. One should hold no illusions that the financial manager will be able to identify the precise percentage of debt that will maximize share price. Rather, he should try to determine the approximate proportion of debt to employ in keeping with an objective of maximizing share price. In the last part of the chapter, we explore briefly the questions of timing and flexibility of a single security issue.

One widely used means of examining the effect of leverage is to analyze the relationship between earnings before interest and taxes (EBIT) and earnings per share (EPS). Essentially, the method involves the comparison of alternative methods of financing under various assumptions as to EBIT.[1] To illustrate, suppose that a firm wished to compare the impact on earnings per share of financing a $10 million expansion program either with common stock at $50 a share or with 8% bonds. The tax rate is 50 percent, and the firm currently has an all-equity capital structure consisting of 800,000 shares of common stock. At $50 a share, the firm will need to sell 200,000 additional shares in order to raise $10 million. If we choose a hypothetical EBIT level of $8 million, earnings per share for the two alternatives would be:

	Common-Stock Financing	Debt Financing
EBIT	$8,000,000	$8,000,000
Interest	$ 0	$ 800,000
Earnings before taxes	$8,000,000	$7,200,000
Taxes	$4,000,000	$3,600,000
Earnings after taxes	$4,000,000	$3,600,000
Shares outstanding	1,000,000	800,000
Earnings per share	$4.00	$4.50

In order for the firm to show zero earnings per share under the debt alternative, it is clear that it will need to have EBIT of $800,000.

With this information, we are able to construct an EBIT–EPS chart, and it is shown in Figure 10-1. The intercepts on the horizontal axis represent the amount of before-tax charges. For equity, the intercept is zero; for debt, it is $800,000. We then plot earnings per share for both alternatives under the assumption of an EBIT of $8 million. When we connect the intercepts with the appropriate EPS points at an EBIT level of $8 million, we obtain the straight lines shown. They tell us the earnings per share for the two financing alternatives that will occur under varying levels of EBIT.

Analysis of Intersection

Because the debt line has a steeper slope, it intersects the common-stock line at an EBIT level of $4 million. At all levels of EBIT above $4 million, there is an earnings-per-share advantage to the use of debt. At levels of EBIT below $4 million, the advantage is in favor of common-stock financing.

[1]For detailed discussion of the calculations involved in this type of analysis, see Chapter 27. Our concern in the present chapter is with how the method might be used.

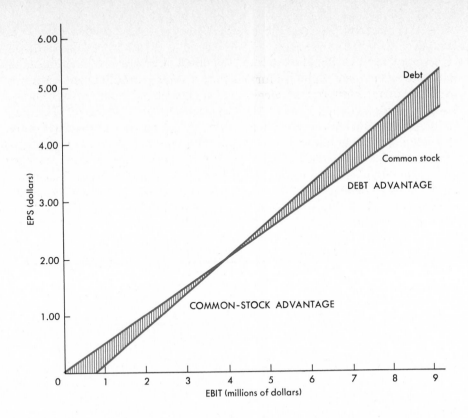

figure 10-1
EBIT-EPS
chart

Constructing an EBIT–EPS chart gives the financial manager infor-mation about the differential impact on earnings per share of alternative methods of financing. We note that as long as the firm is able to earn more than 8 percent before taxes on its investment, debt financing will show an EPS advantage. But the method does not consider directly the implicit costs associated with debt. In an analysis of financial risk, however, an EBIT–EPS chart can be useful to the financial manager. He can compare the point of intersection with the most likely level of EBIT; he can also determine the probability that EBIT will fall below that point.

For example, suppose that actual EBIT in our example is now $7 million and that the company is considering the debt alternative. Given the business risk of the company and the possible fluctuations in EBIT, the financial manager should assess the probability of EBIT's falling below $4 million. If the probability is negligible, the use of the debt alternative would be supported. On the other hand, if EBIT is now only slightly above the indifference point and the probability of EBIT's falling below this point is high, the financial manager may conclude that the debt alternative is too risky. In summary, the greater the level of EBIT and the lower the probability of downside fluctuation, the stronger the case that can be made for the use of debt.

To further illustrate the effect of leverage, suppose the firm were considering financing the $10 million expansion program not only with all common stock or all debt but also with half common stock at $50 a share and half debt at 8 percent. Suppose further that if the economy is normal, EBIT is expected to be $6 million. If a recession occurs, however, EBIT is expected to be $2 million; whereas if boom conditions occur, it is expected to be $10 million. The effect of these conditions on earnings per share under the various financing alternatives is shown in Table 10-1. We see that in the case of a recession, all common-stock financing has the most favorable impact on earnings per share, while under normal and boom economic conditions, all debt financing is the most favorable alternative. The table gives further insight into how leverage accelerates the impact of changes in EBIT on earnings per share.

Although an EBIT–EPS chart does not focus on the implicit costs of senior securities, the financial manager is able to obtain insight into these implicit costs through proper analysis. Although crude, the method is a useful supplement to other methods of analysis.

CASH-FLOW ABILITY TO SERVICE DEBT

When considering the appropriate capital structure, it is extremely important to analyze the cash-flow ability of the firm to service fixed charges. The greater the dollar amount of senior securities the firm issues and the shorter their maturity, the greater the fixed charges of the firm. These charges include principal and interest payments on debt, lease payments, and preferred stock dividends. Before assuming additional fixed charges, the firm should analyze its expected future cash flows, for fixed charges must be met with cash. The inability to meet these charges, with the exception of preferred stock dividends, may result in financial insolvency. The greater and more stable the expected future cash flows of the firm, the greater the debt capacity of the company.

Coverage Ratios

Among the ways we can gain insight into the debt capacity of a firm is through the use of coverage ratios. In the computation of these ratios, one typically uses earnings before interest and taxes as a rough measure of the cash flow available to cover debt-servicing obligations. Perhaps the most widely used coverage ratio is times interest earned, which is simply:

$$\text{Times interest earned} = \frac{\text{EBIT}}{\text{Interest on debt}} \qquad (10\text{-}1)$$

Suppose that the most recent annual earnings before interest and taxes for a company were $6 million, and that interest payments on all debt obligations

table 10-1

Effect of economic conditions on earnings per share under the various financing alternatives (in millions of dollars)

	Common-Stock Financing			Common-Stock and Debt Financing			Debt Financing		
	Recession	Normal	Boom	Recession	Normal	Boom	Recession	Normal	Boom
EBIT	$2.0	$6.0	$10.0	$2.0	$6.0	$10.0	$2.0	$6.0	$10.0
Interest	$0	$0	$ 0	$0.4	$0.4	$ 0.4	$0.8	$0.8	$ 0.8
Earnings before taxes	$2.0	$6.0	$10.0	$1.6	$5.6	$ 9.6	$1.2	$5.2	$ 9.2
Taxes	$1.0	$3.0	$5.0	$0.8	$2.8	$ 4.8	$0.6	$2.6	$ 4.6
Earnings after taxes	$1.0	$3.0	$ 5.0	$0.8	$2.8	$ 4.0	$0.6	$2.6	$ 4.6
Shares outstanding	1.0	1.0	1.0	0.9	0.9	0.9	0.8	0.8	0.8
Earnings per share	$1.00	$3.00	$ 5.00	$0.89	$3.11	$ 5.33	$0.75	$3.25	$ 5.75

were $1.5 million. Therefore, times interest earned would be four times. This tells us that EBIT can drop by as much as 75 percent and the firm still will be able to cover its interest payments out of earnings.

However, a coverage ratio of only one indicates that earnings are *just* sufficient to satisfy the interest burden. While generalizations as to what is an appropriate interest coverage ratio are difficult, one usually is concerned when the ratio gets much below 3:1. However, circumstances differ. In a highly stable industry, a relatively low times-interest-earned ratio may be appropriate, whereas it is not appropriate in a highly cyclical industry.

It is important to note that the times-interest-earned ratio tells us nothing about the ability of the firm to meet principal payments or its debt. The inability to meet a principal payment constitutes the same legal default as failure to meet an interest payment. Therefore it is useful to compute the coverage ratio for the full debt-service burden. This ratio is

$$\text{Debt-service coverage} = \frac{\text{EBIT}}{\text{Interest} + \dfrac{\text{Principal payments}}{1 - \text{Tax rate}}} \qquad (10\text{-}2)$$

Here principal payments are adjusted upward for the tax effect. The reason is that EBIT represents earnings before taxes. Because principal payments are not deductible for tax purposes, they must be paid out of after-tax earnings. Therefore we must adjust principal payments so that they are consistent with EBIT. If principal payments in our previous example were $1 million per annum and the tax rate were 40 percent, the debt-service coverage ratio would be

$$\text{Debt-service coverage} = \frac{\$4 \text{ million}}{\$1.5 \text{ million} + \dfrac{\$1 \text{ million}}{1 - .4}} = 1.26$$

A coverage ratio of 1.26 means that EBIT can fall by only 21 percent before earnings coverage is insufficient to service the debt.[2] Obviously the closer the ratio is to 1.0, the worse things are, all other things the same. However, even with the coverage ratio of less than one, a company may still meet its obligations if it can renew some of its debt when it comes due.

The financial risk associated with leverage should be analyzed on the basis of the firm's ability to service total fixed charges. While lease financing is not debt *per se*, its impact on cash flows is exactly the same as the payment of interest and principal on a debt obligation. (See Chapter 19 for an analysis of lease financing.) Therefore annual lease payments should be added to the denominator of Eq. (10-2) in order to properly reflect the total cash-flow burden associated with financing.

[2]The percentage is determined by $1 - (1/1.26) = .21$.

figure 10-2
Possible EBIT in
relation to debt-
service burden

Like the times-interest-earned ratio, there are no exact rules of thumb for what constitutes a good or bad debt-service ratio. It varies according to the business risk of the firm. This is illustrated in Figure 10-2, where the probability distributions of EBIT for two hypothetical companies are shown. The expected value of EBIT is the same for both companies, as is the debt-service burden as described by the denominator in Eq. (10-2). Therefore the debt-service coverage ratios also are the same, $100/$60 = $1.67. However, Company A has much more business risk. The probability that EBIT will fall below the debt-service burden is depicted by the shaded areas in the figure. We see that this probability is much greater for Company A than it is for Company B. While a debt-service coverage ratio of 1.67 may be appropriate for Company B, it may not be appropriate for Company A. Simply put, a company with stable cash flows is able to take on relatively more fixed charges. This explains why electric utility companies have low coverage ratios when compared with manufacturing companies.

As we discuss in Chapter 25 on financial ratios, two types of comparison should be undertaken with a coverage ratio. First, it should be compared with past and expected future ratios of the same company. Called trend analysis, the idea is to determine if there has been an improvement or a deterioration in coverage over time. The second type of comparison is with similar companies, perhaps in the same industry. The idea here is to try to isolate business risk as nearly as possible by comparing like companies. As the sources of data and types of analysis possible are described in Chapter 25, we do not dwell on them here.

Ultimately, one wants to make generalizations about the appropriate amount of debt (and leases) for a firm to have in its capital structure. It is clear that over the long run the wherewithal to service debt for the going concern is earnings. Therefore coverage ratios are an important tool of analysis. However, they are but one tool by which a person is able to reach conclusions with respect to the appropriate capital structure for the firm. Coverage ratios are subject to certain limitations and, consequently, cannot be used as a sole means for determining a capital structure. For one thing, the fact that EBIT falls below the debt-service burden does not spell immediate doom for the company. Often alternative sources of funds, including renewal of the loan, are available, and these sources must be considered. To this topic we now turn.

Probability of Cash Insolvency

The important question for the firm is not so much whether a coverage ratio will fall below one, but the chances for insolvency occurring. In turn this depends on whether all sources of payment—EBIT, cash, a new financing arrangement, or the sale of assets—are collectively deficient. A coverage ratio tells only part of the story. In order to address the broader question of cash insolvency, we must obtain information on the possible deviation of actual cash flows from those that are expected. As we discuss in Chapter 26, cash budgets can be prepared for a range of possible outcomes, with a probability attached to each. This information is extremely valuable to the financial manager in evaluating the ability of the firm to meet fixed obligations. Not only are expected earnings taken into account in determining this ability but other factors as well—the purchase or sale of assets, the liquidity of the firm, dividends, seasonal patterns, and any other factors impacting on cash flows. Given the probabilities of particular cash-flow sequences, the financial manager is able to determine the amount of fixed charges and debt the company can undertake while still remaining within the insolvency limits tolerable to management.

Suppose management feels that a 5 percent probability of being out of cash is the maximum that can be tolerated, and that this probability corresponds to a cash budget prepared under pessimistic assumptions. In this case, debt might be undertaken up to the point where the cash balance under the pessimistic cash budget is just sufficient to cover the fixed charges associated with the debt. In other words, debt would be increased to the point at which the additional cash drain would cause the probability of cash insolvency to equal the risk tolerance specified by management. It is not necessary that debt be increased to this point, of course. Note that the method of analysis simply provides a means for assessing the effect of increases in debt on the risk of cash insolvency. On the basis of this information, management would determine the most appropriate level of debt.

Donaldson has proposed a similar type of analysis.[3] He suggests that the ultimate concern of a company is whether cash balances during some future period will be involuntarily reduced below zero. Therefore he advocates examining the cash flows of the company under the most adverse circumstances—that is, in his definition, under recession conditions. These conditions may or may not be the most adverse; however, in keeping with the

---

[3]Gordon Donaldson, *Corporate Debt Capacity* (Boston: Division of Research, Harvard Business School, 1961). See also Donaldson, "Strategy for Financial Emergencies," *Harvard Business Review,* 47 (November-December 1969), 67–79.

spirit of his proposal, the firm should evaluate its cash flows under adverse circumstances. Donaldson defines the net cash balance in a recession as

$$CB_r = CB_o + NCF_r \tag{10-3}$$

where CB_o = cash balance at start of recession
NCF_r = net cash flows during recession

Donaldson then analyzes the cash-flow behavior of a firm during a recession by calculating a probability distribution of expected net cash flows.[4] By combining the beginning cash balances, CB_o, with the probability distribution of recession cash flows, NCF_r, he prepares a probability distribution of cash balances in the recession—CB_r.

To ascertain its debt capacity, a firm first would calculate the fixed charges associated with additional increments of debt. For each addition, the firm then would determine the probability of being out of cash, based upon the probability distribution of cash balances during the recession. As before, management could set tolerance limits on the probability of being out of cash. For example, suppose the firm were considering issuing $20 million in additional debt and that the annual fixed charges were $3 million. By subtracting $3 million from the expected cash balances shown for the probability distribution of CB_r, we obtain the probability distribution of CB_r with the addition of $20 million in debt. If the probability of being out of cash with this increment of debt is negligible, Donaldson would contend that the company has unused debt capacity. Therefore it would be possible to increase the amount of debt until the probability of being out of cash equaled the risk tolerance of management.

Inventory of Resources Donaldson extends his analysis to calculate the probability of *cash inadequacy*. Our discussion before was in terms of *cash insolvency,* which is defined as lack of cash after all nonessential expenditures have been cut. Cash inadequacy is said to occur if the firm is out of cash after making certain desired expenditures such as dividends, R & D expenditures, and capital expenditures. Thus, cash insolvency is the extreme form of cash inadequacy. In all cases, the firm should take stock of the resources it has at its disposal to meet an unexpected cash drain.[5] Typically, a number of alternatives are available, ranging from the use of surplus cash to the sale of fixed assets at distress prices.

Donaldson categorizes these resources into uncommitted reserves, the reduction of outflows, and the liquidation of assets. These categories and their various subsets are shown in Table 10-2. The first category of resource

---

[4]The determinants of net cash flows with which he works are sales collections, other cash receipts, payroll expenditures, raw-material expenditures, and nondiscretionary cash expenditures. By analyzing each of these determinants, he determines the range and probability of recession net cash flows.

[5]Donaldson, "Strategy for Financial Emergencies."

table 10-2
Inventory of resources to meet possible cash drains

Resources	Available for Use Within:		
	One Quarter	One Year	Three Years
I. Uncommitted reserves			
Instant reserves			
Surplus cash	$		
Unused line of credit	$		
Negotiable reserves			
Additional bank loans			
Unsecured	$		
Secured	$		
Additional long-term debt		$	
Issue of new equity		$	
II. Reduction of planned outflows			
Volume-related			
Change in production schedule	$		
Scale-related			
Marketing program		$	
R & D budget		$	
Administrative overhead		$	
Capital expenditures		$	
Value-related			
Dividend payments		$	
III. Liquidation of assets			
Shutdown		$	
Sale of unit			$
	$ —→	$	
		$ —→	$
Total resources			$

Source: Donaldson, "Strategy for Financial Emergencies," p. 72.

represents contingency reserves held by the firm as insurance against adverse outcomes. While these reserves are not expected to be used if everything goes according to plan, they nonetheless are there in case things do not go according to plan. For the most part these reserves can be tapped in a short period of time. The second category represents operating cuts and cuts in dividends. Cash is realized from these cuts only over time. Usually changes in operations are at the expense of long-term profitability. In other words, future profitability is sacrificed in order to release cash to meet current obligations. The final category is the most draconian of all. By liquidating assets, management cuts into the very "bone" of the company.

      Once an inventory of resources has been compiled, the adequacy of these resources should be judged in relation to potential cash drains. Embodied in this analysis should be the fixed charges associated with various levels of debt. Thus the liquidity of the firm should be analyzed in relation to its debt capacity.

Cash-Flow Analysis and Debt-to-Equity Ratios

A probabilistic approach to analyzing the ability of a firm to service fixed charges is extremely useful. In this regard, simulation can be employed to determine the outcome under changing conditions. The analysis of the cash-flow ability of the firm to service fixed charges is perhaps the best way to analyze financial risk, but there is some question as to whether the external market analyzes a company in this manner. Sophisticated lenders and institutional investors certainly analyze the amount of fixed charges and evaluate financial risk in keeping with the ability of the firm to service these charges. However, individual investors may look more to the book value proportions of debt to equity in judging financial risk.

There may or may not be a reasonable correspondence between the ratio of debt to equity and the amount of fixed charges relative to the firm's cash-flow .ability to service these charges. Some firms may have relatively high ratios of debt to equity but substantial cash-flow ability to service debt. Consequently, the analysis of debt-to-equity ratios alone can be deceiving, and an analysis of the magnitude and stability of cash flows relative to fixed charges is extremely important in determining the appropriate capital structure for the firm. To the extent that creditors and investors analyze a firm's cash-flow ability to service debt, and management's risk preferences correspond to those of investors, capital structure decisions made on this basis should tend to maximize share price.

OTHER METHODS OF ANALYSIS

Comparison of Capital Structure Ratios

Another method of analyzing the appropriate capital structure for a company is to evaluate the capital structure of other companies having similar business risk. Companies used in this comparison may be those in the same industry. If the firm is contemplating a capital structure significantly out of line with that of similar companies, it is conspicuous to the marketplace. This is not to say, however, that the firm is wrong; other companies in the industry may be too conservative with respect to the use of debt. The optimal capital structure for all companies in the industry might call for a higher proportion of debt to equity than the industry average. As a result, the firm may well be able to justify more debt than the industry average. Because investment analysts and creditors tend to evaluate companies by industry, however, the firm should be able to justify its position if its capital structure is noticeably out of line in either direction.

Regression Studies and Simulation

Certain companies undertake regression studies in an effort to determine the effect of capital structure on stock valuation. Most of the empirical testing has involved regression studies in which either the "measured" average cost of capital or the required return on equity is used as the dependent variable and either leverage or leverage plus additional explanatory variables are used as the independent variable(s). When independent variables additional to leverage are employed, the analysis is known as a multiple-regression study. The purpose of a multiple-regression study is to hold constant statistically other factors that affect valuation in order to obtain an unbiased estimate of the effect of leverage on valuation. More sophisticated studies have incorporated a stock's systematic risk as depicted by its beta into the analysis. (See Chapter 3.) Most of the regression studies undertaken have been based upon cross-sectional samples of companies in particular industries.

In general, the results of empirical testing of the relationship between leverage and cost of capital have been tenuous. The major difficulty is in holding constant all other factors that affect valuation. Frequently, the range of leverage for a sample of companies in the same industry is narrow. Without extreme values of leverage, a regression study is unlikely to denote a very strong relationship between leverage and valuation. If all firms in a sample are at an optimal capital structure, an unbiased regression study would fail to show any relationship between leverage and valuation. In summary, there are a number of limitations to the empirical testing of the relationship between leverage and valuation. Consequently, evidence of this relationship is only suggestive. Nevertheless, regression studies based upon a sample of similar companies may give the firm some insight into the impact of leverage on the market price of its stock.

In addition to regression analysis, simulation sometimes is employed as a means of providing management with valuation information about the expected consequences of a particular investment, financing, or dividend decision. For example, management might be considering a large increase in the proportion of debt to equity because the firm needs to buy out certain minority interests. Before actually making the decision, management may wish to simulate the expected effect of this action on the market price of the stock. By observing the range of simulated outcomes, management has better information on which to base its decision. Most simulation problems in finance are stochastic and involve the use of probabilistic models. These models make use of the Monte Carlo technique described in Chapter 6. If the probability distributions are accurate and the interrelationship of variables properly specified, simulation can be a valuable aid in formulating financial decisions.

However, the results achieved are no better than the probability information used and the realism of the interrelationship of variables specified. Probabilistic information usually is based upon empirical testing of valuation models, the results of which have been far from precise or consistent. An equally thorny problem is the specification of the relationship between variables. Again, empirical studies have been less than satisfactory in sorting out the interrelationships in a consistent manner. We do not wish to undervalue the importance of regression analysis and simulation techniques in providing valuation information to the financial manager, but it is important to point out the practical limitations of the models.

The firm may profit by talking with investment analysts, institutional investors, and investment houses to obtain their views on the appropriate amount of leverage. These analysts examine many companies and are in the business of recommending stocks. Therefore they have an influence upon the market, and their judgments with respect to how the market evaluates leverage may be worthwhile. Similarly, a firm may wish to interview lenders to see how much debt it can undertake before the cost of borrowing is likely to rise. Finally, the management of a company may develop a "feel" for what has happened in the past to the market price of the stock when they have issued debt. As suggested in Chapter 8, the financial manager must think the way investors think if he is to evaluate the impact of a financial decision on share price.

The methods described above for analyzing the appropriate amount of leverage do not give an exact answer. Nevertheless, by undertaking a variety of analyses, the financial manager should be able to determine, within some range, the appropriate capital structure for his firm. By necessity, the final decision has to be somewhat subjective. However, it can be based upon the best information available. In this way, the firm is able to obtain the capital structure most appropriate for its situation—the one that will, it is hoped, tend to maximize the market price of the stock, all other factors held constant.

TIMING AND FLEXIBILITY

Once a firm has determined an appropriate capital structure, it still has the problem of timing security issues. When external financing is required, a company is often faced with the question of how to time an issue appropriately and whether to use debt or common stock. Because financing is "lumpy," it is difficult for a firm to maintain strict proportions in its capital structure. Frequently, it must decide whether to finance now with a stock issue and later with a debt issue, or vice versa. Consequently, it is forced to evaluate the alternative methods of financing in light of general market conditions and expectations for the company itself.

If the future were certain, it would be an easy matter to determine today an optional financing sequence for many years to come. The sequence would be timed to take advantage of known future changes in the stock market and in the market for fixed-income securities. Unfortunately, the future is not known. Prices in financial markets, particularly in the equity market, are unstable. Instead of making decisions based on a sure thing, decisions must be based on management's best estimate of the future. For example, if management believes interest rates now are high and expects them to fall, it may wish to postpone a debt issue and go with common-stock financing now. On the other hand, if the market for the company's stock is depressed but is expected to improve as better earnings are realized, management may prefer to postpone the equity issue until a later date and issue debt now.

If it chooses this alternative, however, it may sacrifice a certain amount of flexibility. By *flexibility*, we simply mean that future financing options may be closed by virtue of a financing decision today. It must be remembered that a company cannot issue debt continually without building its equity base. It is neither desirable, given our discussion in the preceding chapter, nor possible once default risk becomes too great. Therefore the equity base must be increased over time, and this is where flexibility becomes important. If a company undertakes a substantial debt issue and things take a turn for the worse, the firm may be forced to issue stock on unfavorable terms in the future. In order to preserve its flexibility in tapping the capital markets, it may be better for a firm to issue stock now so as to have unused debt capacity for future needs. The preservation of unused debt capacity can be an important consideration for the company whose funds requirements are sudden and unpredictable. It gives the company financial maneuverability by virtue of leaving the options open. This flexibility, of course, could also be achieved simply by maintaining excess liquidity. However, there is an opportunity cost that might be avoided by maintaining flexibility in the raising of funds.

For a growth company, however, preservation of financial maneuverability has a drawback. By issuing stock now so as to have unused debt capacity, the company will probably have to issue more shares than it would if it postponed the stock issue. Consequently, there is more dilution to existing shareholders over time. The tradeoff is between preserving financial flexibility and dilution in earnings per share. If the price of the stock is high, however, and expected to fall, the firm can achieve both flexibility and minimum dilution by issuing stock now.

Although the benefits of good timing usually are limited for debt financing, they can be substantial for equity financing. Depending upon the stock market in general and expectations for the firm in particular, the price of the stock can vary significantly. Management has an implied responsibility to existing stockholders to try to sell a stock issue at as favorable a price as possible. By the same token, it has a responsibility to try to place debt at as favorable an interest rate as possible. While the timing of a stock issue is probably the more important of the two, they both have a significant influence upon earnings per share.

However, we must bear in mind that if the financial markets are efficient, all available information is reflected in the price of the security. Under these circumstances, the market price of the security is the market's best estimate of the value of that security. If management is no better at forecasting future market prices than the average investor, efforts by a company to time security offerings will be for naught. In other words, management will be wrong about as much of the time as it is right. In order that timing be a thing of value, management's expectations must be more correct than those of the market. In Part VI, we examine specific methods of long-term financing. Included in this analysis is a discussion of the timing of a specific security issue and the flexibility afforded by the instrument.

SUMMARY

In deciding upon an appropriate capital structure, the financial manager should consider a number of factors. He can obtain considerable insight from an analysis of the cash-flow ability of the firm to service fixed charges associated with senior securities and leasing. One way to determine this ability is through the analysis of coverage ratios. However, coverage ratios consider only the earnings of a company as a means to service debt. A more inclusive analysis involves the probability of cash insolvency where account is taken of all resources available to service debt. Using this type of analysis, the financial manager is better able to estimate the debt capacity of the firm.

Another method for gaining insight into the question of the appropriate capital structure involves analyzing the relationship between earnings before interest and taxes (EBIT) and earnings per share for alternative methods of financing. When this analysis is expanded to consider likely fluctuations in EBIT, light is shed on the question of financial risk.

In addition, the financial manager can learn much from a comparison of capital structure ratios for similar companies, through regression studies and simulations, and through discussions with investment analysts, investment bankers, and other lenders. Collectively, the methods of analysis taken up in this chapter should provide sufficient information on which to base a capital structure decision. Once an appropriate capital structure has been determined, the firm should finance investment proposals in roughly those proportions.

Finally, we examined the problem of timing a debt or equity issue. Where sequential financing is involved, the choice of debt or equity has an important influence on the future financial flexibility of the firm.

APPENDIX
Inflation and Debt

It is generally agreed that the nominal rate of interest on a bond embodies a premium for inflation. As discussed in Chapter 5, the impact of inflation on nominal yields has come to be known as the *Fisher effect*. Many years ago Irving Fisher expressed the nominal rate of interest on a bond as the sum of the real rate and the rate of price change expected to occur over the life of the instrument.[6] Fisher obtained an estimate of the latter by regressing the nominal rate on a geometrical declining weighted average of past rates of price change. The distributed lag technique for estimating future inflation has been used by a number of subsequent investigators. These studies have

---

[6]*Appreciation and Interest* (New York: Macmillan, 1896). Actually, Fisher expressed the nominal rate as $R + \alpha + R\alpha$, where R is the real rate, α is the expected rate of inflation, and $R\alpha$ is the product of the two. Like others, we ignore the product term, as it has not been found to be important.

shown that prior to the mid-1960s there were long lags in the formation of
price expectations. That is, bond yields adjusted very slowly to past changes
in prices, taking a number of years before a change in inflation was fully
reflected.[7]

Studies using the distributed lag type of analysis with data obtained
since the mid-1960s have shown a marked acceleration in the formulation of
price expectations.[8] With the sharp increase in the rate of inflation since that
time, bond yields have been found to adjust relatively quickly to these
changes in prices. Price expectations, as reflected in bond yields, appear to
adjust more rapidly to large observed changes in prices, such as those that
have occurred since the mid- to late-1960s, than they do to small changes. All
in all, then, the evidence, particularly in recent years, supports the notion of a
Fisher effect, where nominal rates of interest embody an element attributable
to expected future inflation.[9] While the relationship usually is not found to be
one-for-one, it is nonetheless quite important.

[7]See, for example, William E. Gibson, "Price Expectations Effects on Interest Rates,"
Journal of Finance, 25 (March 1970), 19–34; Roman L. Weil, "Realized Interest Rates and Bondholders' Returns," *American Economic Review,* 60 (June 1970), 502–11; and Martin Feldstein
and Otto Eckstein, "The Fundamental Determinants of the Interest Rate," *Review of Economics
& Statistics,* 52 (November 1970), 363–75.

[8]See Patric H. Hendershott and James C. Van Horne, "Expected Inflation Implied by
Capital Market Rates," *Journal of Finance,* 28 (May 1973), 301–14; William P. Yohe and Dennis P.
Karnosky, "Interest Rates and Price Level Changes, 1952–69," *Review of the Federal Reserve
Bank of St. Louis,* 52 (December 1969), 18–38; and Thomas F. Cargill and Robert A. Meyer, "Inter-
est Rates and Prices since 1950," *International Economic Review,* 15 (June 1974), 458–71.

[9]In perhaps the most extensive study of actual nominal and real returns over time,
Roger G. Ibbotson and Rex A. Sinquefield, "Stocks, Bonds, Bills and Inflation: Year-by-Year
Historical Returns (1926–74), *Journal of Business,* 49 (January 1976), 11–47, analyzed Treasury
bills, long-term Treasury bonds, long-term corporate bonds, and common stocks over the 1926–74
period. The authors found that over the entire period Treasury bills provided a zero real return.
In other words, on average the nominal return matched inflation. For Treasury bonds, the
average annual real return was about 1 percent; and for corporate bonds, 1.4 percent. Finally, the
real rate of return on common stocks averaged 6.1 percent per annum. It is important to recognize
that year-to-year differences in real returns occurred. The fluctuations were smallest for Treasury bills, whereas they were quite substantial for common stocks.

In another comprehensive empirical test, Eugene F. Fama and G. William Schwert,
"Asset Returns and Inflation," *Journal of Financial Economics,* 5 (November 1977), 115–46,
estimated the extent to which Treasury bills, Treasury bonds, common stocks, private residential
real estate, and labor income provided hedges against expected inflation and unexpected
inflation for the 1953–71 period. The authors found real estate was a complete hedge against both
expected and unexpected inflation. Treasury bills and bonds were found to be complete hedges
against expected inflation, but not against unexpected inflation. While labor income was found
to be a partial hedge against both kinds of inflation, there were a number of estimation problems
which made generalizations difficult. Finally, stock returns were found to be negatively related
to expected inflation and also, though less consistently, to unexpected inflation. Therefore stocks
could not be regarded as an inflation hedge for the sample period, as commonly supposed.

Benjamin M. Friedman, "Who Puts the Inflation Premium into Nominal Interest
Rates?" *Journal of Finance,* 33 (June 1978), 833–45, expresses the inflation premium in terms of
supply and demand in the corporate bond market and looks at shifts that occur with changes in
inflation. Testing with data over the 1960–73 period, he finds the adjustment on bond yield to be
approximately 0.64 percent in response to a 1 percent increase in expected inflation.

Debtor-Creditor Position

Given the fact that bond yields embody expectations of future inflation, what are the implications for the firm? One important implication is the redistributional effects of inflation on debtors and creditors. Simply phrased, the question here is whether debtors or creditors gain during periods of inflation. This in turn depends on whether the inflation is anticipated. If anticipated, it will be incorporated into the rate of interest and firms will repay debt obligations in keeping with anticipated inflation.[10] In other words, the terms of the loan will reflect anticipated inflation. If inflation occurs over the life of the debt instrument in exactly the manner that was anticipated at the time the terms were set, the borrower will neither gain nor lose with respect to the inflation that actually occurs.

It is only if there is an *unanticipated increase* in inflation that the borrower tends to gain. This gain occurs in an opportunity sense because the borrower previously has "locked in" financing at a lower cost than currently prevails. Put another way, the firm is able to pay off the obligation with "cheaper" money than was originally believed. The opposite occurs for the financial assets of a firm. With an unanticipated increase in inflation, a creditor suffers in that his real rate of return is less than that anticipated at the time the contract was made. In the case of an unanticipated decrease in inflation, a debtor tends to suffer and a creditor gain. This occurs because the real rate of return is higher than that originally anticipated. Thus the important thing is not inflation *per se*, but the unanticipated change in inflation.[11] This can be either positive or negative.

Unanticipated increases in inflation result in a transfer of real wealth from net creditors to net debtors, whereas the opposite occurs with unanticipated decreases. A *net creditor* is defined as one whose financial assets exceed his financial liabilities, whereas for the *net debtor* the opposite holds. Whether a given company gains or loses with respect to inflation depends on whether there is an unanticipated increase or decrease in inflation and whether the firm is a net debtor or a net creditor. In the aggregate, nonfinancial corporations have been consistent net debtors while households have been consistent net creditors. However, individual companies can be net debtors or net creditors, and this can vary over time.[12] Over the post-

[10]For a theoretical analysis of this point, see James C. Van Horne and William F. Glassmire, Jr., "The Impact of Unanticipated Inflation on the Value of Common Stocks," *Journal of Finance*, 27 (December 1972), 1081–92.

[11]For an illustration of the effect of changing inflation expectations on the value of a firm's debt and equity, see Robert S. Kaplan, "Purchasing Power Gains on Debt: The Effect of Expected and Unexpected Inflation," *Accounting Review*, 52 (April 1977), 369–78.

[12]For a discussion of this question and of empirical tests, see Jerome B. Baesel and Steven Globerman, "Unanticipated Inflation and Wealth Redistribution among Business Firms: Additional Evidence," *Journal of Economics and Business*, 30 (Winter 1978), 82–88; and Louis De Alessi, "Do Business Firms Gain from Inflation? Reprise," *Journal of Business*, 48 (April 1975), 264–66. A major earlier work on the subject was by Reuben A. Kessel, "Inflation-Caused Wealth Redistribution: A Test of a Hypothesis," *American Economic Review*, 46 (March 1956), 43–66.

World War II period, substantial inflation has occurred. G. L. Bach and James B. Stephenson estimate that the total dollar value of creditors' claims in the United States which were wiped out by inflation over the 1946–71 period amounted to $1.2 trillion.[13] This figure does not allow for the fact that part of the inflation was anticipated and, therefore, offset by increased interest payments to creditors. However, if inflation was partially unanticipated over the period, and most believe that a good deal was unanticipated, the redistribution effects of real wealth transfer from net creditors to net debtors were large.

At the present high levels of inflation, however, there is little reason to believe that future unanticipated changes in inflation will always be positive. Whether a firm can predict inflation better than can the market for debt instruments is problematical. If it cannot, it should simply accept the rate of inflation embodied in interest rates as the best estimate of future inflation. Thus it is extremely important to differentiate anticipated from unanticipated inflation, and to concentrate on the latter in judging whether it is better to move in the direction of being a net creditor or a net debtor.

Inflation and Taxes

As discussed in Chapter 5, however, taxes come into play. With taxes, the nominal rate of interest must rise by a greater percentage than the increase in inflation in order for debtholders to be as well off in real terms.[14] To illustrate, the after-tax real return to a lender whose loan is specified in nominal dollars is

$$R^* = i - it - \alpha \tag{10A-1}$$

where R^* = the real rate of interest

i = the nominal rate of interest

t = the marginal tax rate

α = the expected rate of inflation

all of which are expressed in terms of the length of the loan.

Rearranging Eq. (10A-1), the nominal rate of interest is

$$i = \frac{(R^* + \alpha)}{(1 - t)} \tag{10A-2}$$

[13]"Inflation and the Redistribution of Wealth," *Review of Economics and Statistics,* 56 (February 1974), 1–13. However, in a study of stock prices during the 1954–68 period, Hai Hong, "Inflation and the Market Value of the Firm: Theory and Tests," *Journal of Finance,* 32 (September 1977), 1031–48, could not find support for transfers in wealth between creditors and debtors.

[14]See Michael, R. Darby, "The Financial Effects of Monetary Policy on Interest Rates," *Economic Inquiry,* 13 (June 1975), 266–76. See also John A. Tatom and James E. Turley, "Inflation and Taxes: Disincentives for Capital Formation," *Federal Reserve Bank of St. Louis Review,* 60 (January 1978), 2–8; and Martin Feldstein, Jerry Green, and Eytan Sheshinski, "Inflation and Taxes in a Growing Economy with Debt and Equity Finance," *Journal of Political Economy,* 86 (April 1978), S53–S70.

Suppose now that expected inflation increases from α to α', but that the marginal tax rate remains unchanged as does the after-tax real return that is required. From Eq. (10A-2) it is seen that the nominal rate must rise by

$$\Delta i = \frac{\alpha' - \alpha}{(1 - t)} \qquad\qquad \text{(10A-3)}$$

If the tax rate is positive, the nominal rate needs to increase by more than the increase in anticipated inflation. This is needed simply to pay the additional taxes. The higher the tax rate, the greater the nominal rate increase that is required. With taxes, then, increasing inflation tends to increase the nominal interest cost on a company's new borrowings by more than the change in inflation—a double whammy. While the after-tax real return to the lender is assumed to remain unchanged in our illustration above, the before-tax real return must rise in order for this to happen. As the before-tax real return (to the lender) is what the company must pay in order to borrow, it experiences an increase in the real cost of debt financing.

Though somewhat more difficult to visualize, in general the same thing occurs for equity financing whether it be a common-stock issue or retained earnings.[15] In this case, income to the investor is represented by dividends and capital gains, both of which are in nominal terms. Taxes are paid on this nominal income, not on real income. Therefore, with taxes and inflation the nominal return on equity required by investors must rise by more than the increase in inflation. In other words, investors require compensation not only for inflation but for the additional tax burden as well. This is the same principle as in the case of debt financing.

Therefore, with taxes, increasing inflation causes an increase in the real costs of debt and equity capital. With a higher real cost of capital, some investment projects will no longer be attractive even though the cash flows are adjusted for expected inflation.[16] In the aggregate, corporations will tend to undertake fewer capital investments, all other things the same. When the inflation-tax effect on capital costs is combined with that on project cash flows (discussed in Chapter 5), the attractiveness of capital investments is even less. Therefore capital formation in real terms will tend to decline in a period of rising inflation.

[15]See Feldstein, Green, and Sheshinski, "Inflation and Taxes in a Growing Economy with Debt and Equity Finance." Martin Feldstein and Joel Slemrod, "Inflation and the Excess Taxation of Capital Gains on Corporate Stock" (Working paper, National Bureau of Economic Research, February 1978), test for the effect of inflation as it pertains to the capital gains taxes that are paid. They find that substantial taxes are paid on nominal capital gains which often are capital losses in real terms.

[16]See Chapter 5 for the adjustment of project cash flows for anticipated inflation.

1. Hi Grade Regulator Company currently has 100,000 shares of common stock outstanding with a market price of $60 per share. It also has $2 million in 6 percent bonds. The company is considering a $3 million expansion program that it can finance with either (1) all common stock at $60 a share; (2) straight bonds at 8 percent interest; (3) preferred stock at 7 percent; or (4) half common stock at $60 per share and half 8 percent bonds.

   (a) For a hypothetical EBIT level of $1 million, calculate the earnings per share for each of the alternative methods of financing. Assume a corporate tax rate of 50 percent.

   (b) Construct an EBIT–EPS chart. What are the indifference points between alternatives? What is your interpretation of them?

2. Hi Grade Regulator Company (see problem 1) expects the EBIT level after the expansion program to be $1 million, with a two-thirds probability that it will be between $600,000 and $1,400,000.

   (a) Which financing alternative do your prefer? Why?

   (b) Suppose that the expected EBIT level were $1.5 million and that there were a two-thirds probability that it would be between $1.3 million and $1.7 million. Which financing alternative do you prefer now? Why?

3. The Power Corporation currently has 2 million shares outstanding at a price of $20 each and needs to raise an additional $5 million. These funds could be raised with stock or 10 percent debentures. Expected EBIT after the new funds are raised will be normally distributed with a mean of $4 million per year forever and a standard deviation of $2 million. Power Corporation has a 50 percent tax rate. What is the probability that the debt alternative is superior with respect to earnings per share?

4. Cornwell Real Estate Speculators, Inc., and the Northern California Electric Utility Company have the following EBIT and debt-servicing burden:

	Cornwell	Northern California
Expected EBIT	$5,000,000	$100,000,000
Annual interest	1,600,000	45,000,000
Annual principal payments on debt	2,000,000	35,000,000

   The tax rate for Cornwell is 40 percent, while that for Northern California Electric Utility is 50 percent. Compute the times-interest-earned ratio and the debt-service coverage ratio for the two companies. With which company would you feel more comfortable if you were a lender? Why?

5. Gamma Tube Company plans to undertake a $12 million capital improvement program and is considering how much debt to use. It feels that it could obtain debt financing at the following interest rates (assume that this debt is perpetual):

Amounts	First $4 million	Next $3 million	Next $3 million	Next $2 million
Interest cost	7 percent	8 percent	9 percent	10 percent

The company has made projections of its net cash flows (exclusive of new financing) during a period of adversity such as a recession. In a recession, it expects a net-cash flow of $3 million with a standard deviation of $2 million (assume a normal distribution). Its beginning cash balance is $1 million. If the company is willing to tolerate only a 5 percent probability of running out of cash during a recession, what is the maximum proportion of the $12 million capital improvement program that can be financed with debt? (Ignore any tax considerations.)

6. The Great Northwest Oil Corporation has decided that it must raise $100 million within the next six months to finance an expansion program. The firm believes it now has an optimal capital structure. Nevertheless, GNOC realizes that this "ideal" structure may be temporarily sacrificed unless the needed funds are secured on a proportionate basis to the current structure. It has been determined that the "normalized" price of the firm's common stock is $100 per share, though the current price is only $80 because of a general stock-market decline. The Company's bonds currently yield 8 percent to maturity. The prime rate available to the firm for a one-year bank loan is 8½ percent. What alternative financing (and timing) plans are open to the firm? Outline the separate assumptions that must be made in order to justify each alternative.

GNOC Capital Structure	
Bonds	$250,000,000
Common stock	200,000,000
Retained earnings	300,000,000
	$750,000,000

7. Tahoe Power and Light Company currently has the following long-term capitalization:

	Amount	Average before-Tax Cost
Debt	$80 million	9.50%
Preferred stock	10	8.00
Common stock (1 million shares)	5	
Retained earnings	65 million	
	$160 million	

Earnings before interest and taxes (EBIT) are now $16 million. As a utility servicing a recreational area, however, it's revenues are more volatile than those of most public utilities.

The company needs to undertake a $20 million plant expansion program in order to keep up with growing demand. Management estimates the following EBIT possibilities for the near future if the expansion program is undertaken:

EBIT	Probability of Occurrence
$17 million	5%
18	5
19	10
20	20
21	25
22	20
23	10
24	5

The bonds of the company currently are rated A by Moody's and the tax rate is 50 percent. To finance the expansion program, stock could be sold at a price that would result in net proceeds to the company of $33⅓ per share. If debt financing were used, the company's bond rating would be lowered to Baa and the interest rate would be 10½% on the new debt.

(a) What are present earnings per share?

(b) What are earnings per share for the various possible levels of EBIT if common stock is used to finance the expansion program?

(c) What are earnings per share if debt is used?

(d) Which method of financing would you recommend? Is there adequate information? Does the use of debt affect the value of existing debt and equity?

8. *Research Project* Compile a list of business firms operating in your area. On the basis of information available to you, group these firms into roughly equivalent risk classes.

Next, obtain a recent balance sheet for each firm. Does each firm in a given risk class have a similar capital structure? Could any divergence reflect the risk preferences of management?

Finally, compute the average capital structure of the firms in a given risk class. Place these averages on a continuum running from the average of the class of least risk to that of the greatest. Can a trend be noted? Are there significant deviations from this trend?

SELECTED REFERENCES

ANG, JAMES S., "The Intertemporal Behavior Policy," *Journal of Financial and Quantitative Analysis,* 9 (November 1976), 555–66.

BACH, G. L., AND JAMES B. STEPHENSON, "Inflation and the Redistribution of Wealth," *Review of Economics and Statistics,* 56 (February 1974), 1–13.

BIERMAN, HAROLD, JR., "Risk and the Addition of Debt to the Capital Structure," *Journal of Financial and Quantitative Analysis,* 3 (December 1968), 415–23.

DONALDSON, GORDON, *Corporate Debt Capacity.* Boston: Division of Research, Harvard Business School, 1961.

———, "New Framework for Corporate Debt Capacity," *Harvard Business Review,* 40 (March-April 1962), 117–31.

———, "Strategy for Financial Emergencies," *Harvard Business Review,* 47 (November-December 1969), 67–79.

FAMA, EUGENE F., AND G. WILLIAM SCHWERT, "Asset Returns and Inflation," *Journal of Financial Economics,* 5 (November 1977), 115–46.

FELDSTEIN, MARTIN, JERRY GREEN, AND EYTAN SHESHINSKI, "Inflation and Taxes in a Growing Economy with Debt and Equity Finance," *Journal of Political Economy,* 86 (April 1978), 553–70.

FRIEDMAN, BENJAMIN M., "Who Puts the Inflation Premium into Nominal Interest Rates?" *Journal of Finance,* 33 (June 1978), 833–45.

HANDORF, WILLIAM C., "Flexible Debt Financing," *Financial Management,* 3 (Summer 1974), 17–23.

HENDERSHOTT, PATRIC H., AND JAMES C. VAN HORNE, "Expected Inflation Implied by Capital Market Rates." *Journal of Finance,* 28 (May 1973), 301–14.

HONG, HAI, AND ALFRED RAPPAPORT, "Debt Capacity, Optimal Capital Structure, and Capital Budgeting," *Financial Management,* 7 (Autumn 1978), 7–11.

IBBOTSON, ROGER G., AND REX A. SINQUEFIELD, "Stocks, Bonds, Bills and Inflation: Year-by-Year Historical Returns (1926–74), *Journal of Business,* 49 (January 1976), 11–47.

LINTNER, JOHN, "Inflation and Security Returns," *Journal of Finance,* 30 (May 1975), 259–80.

MELNYK, Z. LEW, "Cost of Capital as a Function of Financial Leverage," *Decision Sciences,* 1 (July-October 1970), 372–86.

SCHWARTZ, ELI, AND J. RICHARD ARONSON, "Some Surrogate Evidence in Support of the Concept of Optimal Capital Structure," *Journal of Finance,* 22 (March 1967), 10–18.

SCOTT, DAVID F., JR., AND JOHN D. MARTIN, "Industry Influence on Financial Structure," *Financial Management,* 4 (Spring 1975), 67–73.

VAN HORNE, JAMES C., *Financial Market Rates and Flows.* Englewood Cliffs, N.J.: Prentice-Hall, 1978.

VAN HORNE, JAMES C., AND WILLIAM F. GLASSMIRE, JR., "The Impact of Unanticipated Inflation on the Value of Common Stocks," *Journal of Finance,* 27 (December 1972), 1081–92.

WEIL, ROMAN L., "Realized Interest Rates and Bondholders' Returns," *American Economic Review,* 60 (June 1970), 502–11.

11
dividends and valuation

The third major decision of the firm is its dividend policy. In this chapter, we investigate only one aspect of dividend policy—the percentage of earnings paid to stockholders in cash. In the next chapter, we take up other aspects of dividend policy. The dividend-payout ratio, of course, determines the amount of earnings retained in the firm and affects the total amount of internal financing. Consequently, it must be analyzed in relation to the overall financing decision. In this chapter, we evaluate dividend policy in light of the objective of the firm—namely, to maximize the value of the firm to its shareholders. Shareholder wealth includes not only the market price of the stock but also current dividends. Again, we assume that business risk is held constant; that is, the acceptance of any investment proposal does not affect the business-risk complexion of the firm as perceived by suppliers of capital.

The dividend-payout ratio of a firm obviously depends upon the way earnings are measured. For ease of theoretical exposition, we use accounting net earnings but assume that these earnings conform to the true economic earnings of the firm. In practice, net earnings may not so conform; as a result, they may not be an appropriate measure of the ability of the firm to pay dividends. Certain writers argue that cash flow, the sum of earnings and depreciation, is a better measure of the capacity of a firm to pay dividends. John A. Brittain, for example, suggests that the liberalization of depreciation allowances in the post-World War II period renders net earnings an invalid measure of the ability of corporations to pay dividends.[1] Although the argument that cash flow best approximates the "true" earnings of a firm is persuasive, we shall continue to use net earnings in the theoretical development that follows.

DIVIDEND POLICY AS A RESIDUAL DECISION

In order to evaluate properly the question of whether dividend policy affects shareholder wealth, it is necessary to examine first the firm's policy solely as a financing decision involving the retention of earnings. Consider the situation in which the use of funds from earnings, and the dividend policy that results, is strictly a financing decision. As long as the firm has investment projects whose returns exceed those that are required, it will use retained earnings, and the amount of senior securities the increase in equity base will support, to finance these projects. If the firm has retained earnings left over after financing all acceptable investment opportunities, these earnings would then be distributed to stockholders in the form of cash dividends. If not, there would be no dividends. If the number of acceptable investment opportunities involved a total dollar amount that exceeded the amount of retained earnings plus the senior securities these retained earnings will support, the firm would finance the excess with a combination of a new equity issue and senior securities.

When we treat dividend policy as strictly a financing decision, the payment of cash dividends is a passive residual. The amount of dividend payout will fluctuate from period to period in keeping with fluctuations in the amount of acceptable investment opportunities available to the firm. If these opportunities abound, the percentage of dividend payout is likely to be zero. On the other hand, if the firm is unable to find profitable investment opportunities, dividend payout will be 100 percent. For situations between these two extremes, the payout will be a fraction between 0 and 1.

The treatment of dividend policy as a passive residual determined strictly by the availability of acceptable investment proposals implies that dividends are irrelevant; the investor is indifferent between dividends and capital gains. If investment opportunities promise a return greater than their required return, the investor is happy to have the company retain earnings. Contrarily, if the return is less than the required return, he prefers dividends.

[1]John A. Brittain, *Corporate Dividend Policy* (Washington, D.C.: Brookings Institution, 1966), Chap. 3.

Supposedly, if the firm can earn more on projects than the required return, then investors are perfectly happy to let the firm retain as much in earnings as it needs to finance the investments.

A residual theory of dividend policy does not necessarily mean that dividends need fluctuate from period to period in keeping with fluctuations in investment opportunities. A firm may smooth out actual payments by saving some funds in surplus years in anticipation of deficit ones.[2] If forecasting is relatively accurate, the firm can establish its dividend payment at a level at which the cumulative distribution over time corresponds to cumulative residual funds over the same period. The fact that dividends do not correspond to residual funds period by period does not negate the residual theory of dividends.

The critical question is whether dividends are more than just a means of distributing unused funds. Should dividend policy be an active decision variable as opposed to a passive one? To answer these questions, we must examine more thoroughly the argument that dividends are irrelevant so that changes in the payout ratio (holding investment opportunities constant) do not affect shareholder wealth.

IRRELEVANCE OF DIVIDENDS

The most comprehensive argument for the irrelevance of dividends is found in Modigliani and Miller's 1961 article.[3] They assert that, given the investment decision of the firm, the dividend-payout ratio is a mere detail. It does not affect the wealth of shareholders. MM argue that the value of the firm is determined solely by the earning power on the firm's assets or its investment policy and that the manner in which the earnings stream is split between dividends and retained earnings does not affect this value. The critical assumptions of MM are

1. Perfect capital markets in which all investors are rational. Information is available to all at no cost; transactions are instantaneous and without cost; securities are infinitely divisible; and no investor is large enough to affect the market price of a security.
2. An absence of flotation costs on securities issued by the firm.
3. A world of no taxes.
4. A given investment policy for the firm, not subject to change.
5. Perfect certainty by every investor as to future investments and profits of the firm. MM drop this assumption later.

---

[2]See Robert C. Higgins, "The Corporate Dividend-Saving Decision," *Journal of Financial and Quantitative Analysis*, 7 (March 1972), 1531–38, who finds some empirical support for the notion that single-period dividends are a function of a longer-term trend.

[3]Merton H. Miller and Franco Modigliani, "Dividend Policy, Growth, and the Valuation of Shares," *Journal of Business*, 34 (October 1961), 411–33.

Dividends Versus Terminal Value

The crux of MM's position is that the effect of dividend payments on shareholder wealth is offset exactly by other means of financing. Consider first selling additional stock in lieu of retaining earnings. When the firm has made its investment decision, it must decide whether to retain earnings or to pay dividends and sell new stock in the amount of these dividends in order to finance the investments. MM suggest that the sum of the discounted value per share after financing and dividends paid is equal to the market value per share before the payment of dividends. In other words, the stock's decline in market price because of external financing offsets exactly the payment of the dividend. Thus the stockholder is said to be indifferent between dividends and the retention of earnings and subsequent capital gains.

The market price of a share of stock at the beginning of a period is defined as equal to the present value of the dividend paid at the end of the period plus the market price at the end of the period. Thus

$$P_0 = \frac{1}{1 + \rho}(D_1 + P_1) \tag{11-1}$$

where P_0 = market price per share at time 0

ρ = capitalization rate for firm in that risk class (this rate is assumed to be constant throughout time)

D_1 = dividend per share at time 1

P_1 = market price per share at time 1

Assume that n is the number of shares of record at time 0 and that m is the number of new shares sold at time 1 at a price of P_1. Eq. (11-1) then can be rewritten as

$$nP_0 = \frac{1}{(1 + \rho)}[nD_1 + (n + m)P_1 - mP_1] \tag{11-2}$$

In words, the total value of all shares outstanding at time 0 is the present value of total dividends paid at time 1 on those shares plus the total value of all stock outstanding at time 1, less the total value of the new stock issued. The total amount of new stock issued is

$$mP_1 = I - (X - nD_1) \tag{11-3}$$

where I = total new investments during period 1

X = total net profit of firm for the period

Eq. (11-3) merely states that the total sources of funds must equal total uses. That is, net profit plus new stock sales must equal new investments plus dividends.

The total amount of financing by the sale of new stock is determined by the amount of investments in period 1 not financed by retained earnings. By substituting Eq. (11-3) into Eq. (11-2), MM find that the nD_1 term cancels out and

$$nP_0 = \frac{1}{(1 + \rho)}[(n + m)P_1 - I + X] \tag{11-4}$$

Because D_1 does not appear directly in the expression and because X, I, $(n + m)P_1$, and ρ are assumed to be independent of D_1, MM conclude that the current value of the firm is independent of its current dividend decision.[4] What is gained by the stockholder in increased dividends is offset exactly by the decline in the terminal value of his stock. MM go on to show that nP_0 is unaffected not only by current dividend decisions but by future dividend decisions as well. Under the assumption of perfect certainty by all investors, the price of the stock at time 1, time 2, and time n is determined solely by Eq. (11-4). Thus, stockholders are indifferent between retention and the payment of dividends (and concurrent stock financing) in all future periods. As a result, shareholder wealth is unaffected by current and future dividend decisions; it depends entirely upon the expected future earnings stream of the firm.

Given MM's assumptions of perfect certainty as well as their other assumptions, the irrelevance of dividends follows. As with our example for corporate leverage, arbitrage assures that the sum of market value plus current dividends of two firms identical in all respects other than dividend-payout ratios will be the same. The individual investor can retain and invest his own earnings, and do this as well as the corporation can for him.[5]

One point needs clarification, however. In our example, we have assumed that external financing involves the sale of new stock and that the effect of this sale on the market price of the stock offsets exactly the payment of dividends. What if the external financing involved debt? MM's position then rests upon their previous indifference thesis with respect to leverage: the real cost of debt is the same as the real cost of equity financing. Therefore, according to MM, the means of external financing used to offset the payment of dividends does not affect their hypothesis that dividends are irrelevant. Thus we see the interdependency of MM's two positions. Dividend policy does not affect their thesis regarding leverage; in their position on dividends, the means of external financing is not a factor.

If dividends are irrelevant, a firm's cost of capital would be independent of its dividend-payout ratio. If both leverage and dividends are ir-

---

[4]Ibid., p. 416.

[5]For illustrations of the arbitrage process for the dividend decision, see Wilbur G. Lewellen, *The Cost of Capital* (Belmont, Calif.: Wadsworth, 1969), pp. 54–57; and James E. Walter, *Dividend Policy and Enterprise Valuation* (Belmont, Calif.: Wadsworth, 1967), pp. 106–10.

relevant, the firm would be indifferent as to whether investment opportunities were financed with debt, retained earnings, or a common-stock issue. One method of financing would be as satisfactory as the next. Now one might ask, How does this correspond to our earlier chapters when we said that dividends are the foundation for the valuation of common stocks? While it is true that the market value of a share of stock is the present value of all expected future dividends, the timing of the dividends can vary. The irrelevance position simply argues that the present value of future dividends remains unchanged even though dividend policy changes their timing. It does not argue that dividends, including liquidating dividends, are never paid, only that their postponement is a matter of indifference when it comes to market price per share.

Dividends under Uncertainty

MM drop their assumption of complete certainty and consider the case of uncertainty. Despite their admission that D_1 and P_1 in Eq. (11-1) are subject to uncertainty, they conclude that dividend policy continues to be irrelevant. Their conclusion is based upon the familiar arbitrage argument. Given two firms of identical business risk and the same prospective future earnings and investment policies, the market prices of the two firms must be the same if there is "symmetric market rationality."[6] Symmetric market rationality occurs when every market participant behaves rationally in preferring more wealth to less, and believes that other market participants behave in the same manner. According to MM, differences in current and future dividend policies cannot affect the market value of these two firms, for the present value of prospective dividends plus terminal value are the same. Even under uncertainty, then, MM continue to maintain that dividend policy is irrelevant, given the investment policy of the firm. Attacks upon the irrelevance doctrine have been centered on the case of uncertainty and imperfections in the markets.

ARGUMENTS FOR RELEVANCE

A number of arguments have been advanced in support of the contrary position—namely, that dividends are relevant under conditions of uncertainty. In other words, the investor is not indifferent as to whether he receives his return on investment in dividend income or stock-price appreciation. We shall examine these arguments under conditions of uncertainty but will keep intact MM's other assumptions—no transaction or flotation costs, the absence of taxes, and a given fixed investment policy of the firm. Later, all but the last

---

[6]Miller and Modigliani, "Dividend Policy," pp. 425–28.

of these assumptions will be removed when we investigate dividend policy under real-world conditions.

Resolution of Uncertainty

It has been argued that the payment of current dividends resolves uncertainty in the minds of investors, and therefore an investor is not indifferent between dividends and capital gains. He prefers dividends. Gordon, for example, contends that uncertainty on the part of investors increases at an increasing rate with the distance in the future of prospective cash payments.[7] As a result, the discount rate, ρ_t, is said to rise with the distance in the future, t. When a company cuts its dividend to finance investments, its near dividend is reduced, while distant dividends are increased. If the discount rate rises with the length of time in the future, the reduction in the near dividend is said to lead to a lower share price, all other things the same.

According to Gordon, investors are not indifferent between current dividends and the retention of earnings with the prospect of future dividends, capital gains, or both. They prefer the early resolution of uncertainty and are willing to pay a higher price for the stock that offers the greater current dividend, all other things held constant. This is not to say that the basic business risk of a firm's investments is affected by its dividend payout. Rather, it is contended that investors' *perception* of such riskiness may be affected.[8]

A number of authors have taken issue with Gordon.[9] Even if current dividends are perceived as less risky than future ones, it is argued that stockholders are able to sell a portion of their shares to obtain the desired cash distribution.[10] In essence, investors are able to manufacture "homemade dividends" in the same way as they are "homemade leverage" in the case of the capital structure decision. Because "homemade" dividends supposedly are perfect substitutes for corporate dividends, the Gordon argument is said not to hold. The company is said not to be able to do something for investors that they cannot do for themselves; therefore dividend policy is not a thing of value.

[7]Myron J. Gordon, "Optimal Investment and Financing Policy," and "The Savings Investment and Valuation of a Corporation," *Review of Economics and Statistics*, 44 (February 1962), 37–51.

[8]For amplification of this point, see Simon M. Keane, "Dividends and the Resolution of Uncertainty," *Journal of Business Finance & Accounting*, 1 (Autumn 1974), 389–93.

[9]See Michael Brennan, "A Note on Dividend Irrelevance and the Gordon Valuation Model," *Journal of Finance*, 26 (December 1971), 1115–21; Robert C. Higgins, "Dividend Policy and Increasing Discount Rates: A Clarification," *Journal of Financial and Quantitative Analysis*, 7 (June 1972), 1757–62; and Robert E. Krainer, "A Pedagogic Note on Dividend Policy," *Journal of Financial and Quantitative Analysis*, 6 (September 1971), 1147–54.

[10]Higgins, "Dividend Policy and Increasing Discount Rates."

The argument above is allied closely to the "informational content of dividends" argument. The latter argument implies that dividends have an impact on share price because they communicate information to investors about the firm's profitability. When a firm has a target payout ratio that is stable over time, and it changes this ratio, investors may believe that management is announcing a change in the expected future profitability of the firm. Accordingly, the price of the stock may react to this change in dividends. The idea here is that the reported accounting earnings of a company may not be a proper reflection of its economic earnings. To the extent that dividends provide information on economic earnings not provided by reported earnings, share price will respond. Empirical tests have been conflicting with respect to the importance of dividend announcements on share price. Some conclude that there is a substantial information effect, whereas others conclude that the effect, if any, is small.[11]

A somewhat different interpretation of the information effect is advanced by Simon M. Keane.[12] He suggests that the disclosure requirements by regulatory bodies, such as the Securities and Exchange Commission, are much greater for a company involved in a new issue of stock than they are for a company that finances with retained earnings. Because the company that pays a dividend and then issues stock must disclose more information about itself, the payment of dividends and resulting new equity issues result in less uncertainty in the minds of investors. This argument, then, is tied in with the previous one on the resolution of uncertainty.

MM do not deny the possibility of a dividend-announcement information effect, but they continue to maintain that present and expected future earnings are what determine value. They assert that dividends are merely a reflection of these factors and do not in themselves determine value; therefore the irrelevance proposition holds.[13] Thus dividends are said to be used by investors as predictors of the firm's future performance; they convey management's expectation of the future. If subsequent observed behavior is consistent with the information conveyed previously, investors will come to rely upon dividends as predictors of what is to come. However, the basic factor affecting value is not dividends but expectations of future performance.

[11]For an example of the former, see R. Richardson Pettit, "Dividend Announcements, Security Performance, and Capital Market Efficiency," *Journal of Finance,* 27 (December 1972), 993–1007; and Pettit, "The Impact of Dividend and Earnings Announcements: A Reconciliation," *Journal of Business,* 49 (January 1976), 86–96. For the latter view, see Ross Watts, "The Information Content of Dividends," *Journal of Business,* 46 (April 1973), 191–211; and Watts, "Comments," *Journal of Business,* 49 (January 1976), 97–106. See also Eugene Fama, Lawrence Fisher, Michael C. Jensen, and Richard Roll, "The Adjustment of Stock Prices to New Information," *International Economic Review,* 10 (February 1969), 1–26.

[12]"Dividends and the Resolution of Uncertainty," p. 392.

[13]Miller and Modigliani, "Dividend Policy," p. 428.

Another aspect of the uncertainty question involves investors who have a preference for current income. Under the irrelevance proposition, MM would argue that these investors can sell stock on a periodic basis to obtain income. With perfect markets, the investor could always sell part of his holdings or reinvest the dividends to satisfy his desire for consumption. Over the long run, the investor should be able to obtain the same income as he would with regular dividends. However, with uncertainty, stock prices fluctuate. Certain investors may regard as unsatisfactory the alternative of selling a portion of their stock for income at fluctuating prices. As a result, they may have a definite preference for current dividends. In addition to the uncertainty of the selling price, the inconvenience of selling a small portion of stock periodically for income may be a factor. For this reason alone, certain investors might prefer current dividends to capital gains.

The Clientele Effect The critical question is whether the "quality" of a dividend payment is greater than the "quality" of a capital gain. Proponents of the irrelevance proposition argue that there is no difference and, as a result, there is no systematic preference in the market as a whole for current dividends. Whereas certain investors may prefer dividends, others prefer capital gains. At the margin, the market is said to behave in a manner consistent with the irrelevance proposition. MM suggest:

> *If, for example, the frequency distribution of corporate-payout ratios happened to correspond exactly with the distribution of investor preferences for payout ratios, then the existence of these preferences would clearly lead ultimately to a situation whose implications were different in no fundamental respect from the perfect market case. Each corporation would tend to attract to itself a "clientele" consisting of those preferring its particular payout ratio, but one clientele would be entirely as good as another in terms of the valuation it would imply for the firm.*[14]

Essentially, the "clientele" argument is that if groups of investors have dividend preferences, corporations will adjust their dividend policies to take advantage of the situation. Suppose that one-third of all investors prefer a zero dividend payout, one-third prefer a 30 percent payout ratio, and the remaining one-third prefer a 60 percent payout ratio. If most companies pay out 30 percent of their earnings as dividends, there would be excess demand for the shares of companies paying zero dividends and for the shares of companies whose dividend payout ratio is 60 percent. A number of companies supposedly would recognize this excess demand and adjust their payout ratios in order to increase share price. The action of these companies would eventually eliminate the excess demand. In equilibrium, the dividend policies

[14]Ibid., p. 429.

of corporations would match the dividend desires of investor groups. At this point, no company would be able to affect its share price by altering its dividend policy.[15]

Thus proponents of the irrelevance of dividends argue that the mere existence of dividend preferences by various investor clienteles does not negate their position. As long as the "supply" of dividends by companies matches the demand for them by investor groups, their argument will hold. However, this argument depends on corporations' having full knowledge of the demands of investors for dividends. It also depends on there being no capital market imperfections that impede the adjustment of corporate dividend payouts when the market is not in equilibrium. (For example, flotation costs on new stock issues, which we consider shortly, represent such an impediment.) Because of these factors, the case for the exact correspondence of the distribution of demand for dividends with that of supply is tenuous.

Sale of Stock at a Lower Price

The irrelevance doctrine also rests upon the assumption that the sale of stock by the firm to replace the dividend will be at the current price. In order to sell the stock, however, the firm must appeal to new investors or to existing stockholders to increase their holdings. With divergent investor expectations, Lintner contends that the equilibrium price of a share of stock will decline as the firm sells additional stock to replace dividends.[16] In other words, there is a downward-sloping demand curve for the stock. Those investors holding the stock believe that its value is at least as great as the prevailing price. However, investors who do not hold the stock believe that the value is less than this price. In order to entice them into buying a new issue of stock, the issuing price must be lower than the prevailing price.

Thus "the payment of an added cash dividend ... requires that ownership . . . be transferred to others whose expectations justify *their* holding (buying) the stock only at a lower price, so that *this* shift in finance-mix and current dividend *reduces* the (conditional) expected *aggregate* market value of the company's equity *ceteris paribus.*"[17] With underpricing, the firm

[15]See Fischer Black and Myron Scholes, "The Effects of Dividend Yield and Dividend Policy on Common Stock Prices and Returns," *Journal of Financial Economics*, 1 (May 1974), 1–5. In testing a modification of the capital-asset pricing model to include a variable to measure the deviation of a stock's dividend yield from that of the market portfolio, they find the coefficient of the variable to be insignificant. Stocks with high payout ratios did not provide returns significantly different from those with low payout ratios. The authors interpret this finding as being consistent with the idea that dividend policy does not matter. However, other authors have made a case for the relevance of dividend policy based on empirical tests using the capital-asset pricing model. See, for example, Sasson Bar-Yosef and Richard Kolodny, "Dividend Policy and Capital Market Theory," *Review of Economics and Statistics*, 58 (May 1976), 181–90.

[16]John Lintner, "Dividends, Earnings, Leverage, Stock Prices and the Supply of Capital to Corporations," *Review of Economics and Statistics*, 44 (August 1962), 256–59.

[17]Ibid., p. 258.

will need to sell more shares to replace the dividend. This dilution is said to cause a lower discounted value per share after financing than was true in the case of our irrelevance example. Thus a downward-sloping demand curve for new issues of stock implies a preference toward retention, as opposed to paying higher dividends.

Market Imperfections

We now consider other factors that were assumed away by MM. Any attack on MM, however, must be based upon factors other than the ones we take up now. Nevertheless, the market imperfections we discuss are important in evaluating the effect of dividends upon valuation in the real world.

Tax Effect When we allow for taxes, there is a variety of effects. The most important is due to capital gains being taxed at a lower rate than dividends. Moreover, the capital gains tax is deferred until the investor actually sells his stock. Thus there is a strong bias in favor of capital gains as opposed to dividends, and this bias favors the retention of earnings.[18] Suppose a corporation pays a substantial dividend and expands by selling stock on a privileged-subscription basis to existing stockholders. These stockholders receive dividends, which are taxed at the ordinary income tax rate, and then purchase more stock. If the corporation had retained the earnings, the tax would have been avoided. The stockholder could realize value on his investment by selling some of his shares and paying only a capital gains tax. The effect of the tax differential must be qualified to take account of the growing number of tax-free institutional investors. For these investors, the tax effect does not influence their preference for dividends or capital gains.

Other tax laws favor current dividends over capital gains. Individuals are able to exclude the first $100 of dividend income; such income is not taxed. Presumably, this tax provision creates a preference for current dividends on the part of small investors. For corporate investors, intercompany dividends are taxed at a rate below that applicable to capital gains. For example, if Laurel Corporation owns one hundred shares of Hardy Corporation which pays a $1-per-share dividend, 85 percent of the dividend income is tax exempt. In other words, Laurel Corporation would pay taxes on $15 of

[18]In testing the price behavior of stocks when they go ex-dividend in relation to the magnitude of dividend for a large sample of companies, Edwin J. Elton, and Martin J. Gruber, "Marginal Stockholder Tax Rates and the Clientele Effect," *Review of Economics and Statistics,* 52 (February 1970), 68–74, found an inverse relationship between the dividend payout ratio and the implied tax bracket of marginal investors. They interpret this result as consistent with a clientele effect where investors in high tax brackets show a preference for capital gains over dividends, and vice versa. The day a stock goes ex-dividend, the investor no longer receives the declared dividend. As a result, the stock price should decline. The question Elton and Gruber address is whether it declines by the amount of the dividend or by less. An investor can buy the stock either before or after the ex-dividend date. If before, he receives dividend income; if after, he receives additional capital gains. As capital gains are taxed at a lower rate than dividend income, the stock should decline by less than the amount of the dividend. In fact, the authors found that on average the stock declined by 0.78 of the dividend on the ex-dividend date.

dividend income at the corporate tax rate. The overall tax effect will be less than if Hardy Corporation had share appreciation of $100, and all of this were taxed at the capital gains rate. Accordingly, there would be a preference for current dividends on the part of corporate investors. However, the two effects described here are overshadowed by the differential tax on dividends and capital gains, which, as stated earlier, creates a preference for capital gains.[19]

Flotation Costs The irrelevance proposition is based upon the idea that, given the investment policy of the firm, funds paid out by the firm must be replaced by funds acquired through external financing. The introduction of flotation costs favors the retention of earnings in the firm. For each dollar paid out in dividends, the firm nets less than a dollar after flotation costs per dollar of external financing. Moreover, the smaller the size of the issue, the greater in general the flotation costs as a percentage of the total amount of funds raised. In addition, stock financing is "lumpy" in the sense that small issues are difficult to sell even with high flotation costs. The fact that in practice common-stock financing is less than perfectly divisible favors the retention of earnings.

Transaction Costs and Divisibility of Securities Transaction costs involved in the sale of securities tend to restrict the arbitrage process in the same manner as that described for debt. The stockholder who desires current income must pay a brokerage fee on the sale of a portion of his stock if the dividend paid is not sufficient to satisfy his current desire for income. This fee varies inversely, per dollar of stock sold, with the size of the sale. For a small sale, the brokerage fee can be rather significant percentagewise. Because of this fee, stockholders with consumption desires in excess of current dividends will prefer that the company pay additional dividends. Perfect capital markets also assume that securities are infinitely divisible. The fact that the smallest integer is one share may result in "lumpiness" with respect to selling shares for current income. This too acts as a deterrent to the sale of stock in lieu of dividends. On the other hand, the stockholder not desiring dividends for current consumption purposes will need to reinvest his dividends. Here again transaction costs and divisibility problems work to the disadvantage of the stockholder, although in the opposite direction.

---

[19]Merton H. Miller and Myron S. Scholes, "Dividends and Taxes" (Working paper, University of Chicago, 1978), argue that even with taxes dividend policy is irrelevant. The paper is an extension of Miller's tax proposition with respect to leverage (see footnote 24 in Chapter 9). Essentially, the authors maintain that a change in dividends by a corporation will leave an investor's overall tax liability unchanged. Therefore the presence of taxes is said not to affect the dividend question. While the position is complicated, it hinges on investors altering their personal leverage used to buy stock in keeping with a change in dividends. Because interest paid on debt is deductible as an expense for tax purposes, the change in dividend income to the individual can be offset by the change in his interest expense. The expected increase in the value of the stock bought through personal leverage is a capital gain, and not ordinary income. In this way, the authors contend that dividends can be transformed into capital gains by the individual investor. Finally, the authors argue that the effective tax rate on capital gains is close to zero because of the many ways to defer such taxes. Therefore the transformation of dividends to capital gains does not result in a change of taxes for the individual, and dividend policy is said to be irrelevant.

Thus transaction costs and divisibility problems cut both ways. However, there is reason to believe that in recent years the net impact of these factors has created a slight bias on the side of a preference for current dividends. Many companies now have automatic dividend reinvestment plans. These plans allow the stockholder to specify a reduction in the amount of dividends he is to receive. This reduction is then used to purchase additional shares of stock in the company.[20] The reinvestment is administered by a bank in behalf of the company and is automatic. Transaction costs are lower than what a stockholder could do on his own, and there is virtually no inconvenience involved. Because of the increasing use of automatic dividend reinvestment programs, the scales may be tipped slightly in favor of the stockholder who desires to reinvest dividends as opposed to the one who desires greater current income. As a result, transaction costs overall may result in a net preference in the market for current dividends, all other things the same.

Other Legal Impediments   Certain institutional investors are restricted by law as to the types of common stock in which they can invest. The prescribed list of eligible securities is determined in part by the duration over which dividends have been paid. If a company does not pay a dividend or has not paid dividends over a sufficiently long period of time, certain institutional investors are not able to invest in the stock.

Universities, on the other hand, sometimes have restrictions on the expenditure of capital gains from their endowment. Also, a number of trusts have a prohibition against the liquidation of principal. In the case of common stocks, the beneficiary is entitled to the dividend income, but not to the proceeds from the sale of stock. As a result of this stipulation, the trustee who manages the investments may feel constrained to pay particular attention to dividend yield and seek stocks paying reasonable dividends. Though the two influences described above are small in aggregate, they work in the direction of a preference for current income as opposed to capital gains.

Of the market imperfections taken up in this section, the differential tax effect on dividends and capital gains is the strongest. As mentioned previously, this imperfection creates a preference for the retention of earnings in the firm.

OPTIMAL DIVIDEND POLICY

A company should endeavor to establish a dividend policy that will maximize shareholder wealth. In theory, the optimal dividend payout should be determined in keeping with the firm's investment opportunities and any preference that investors have for dividends as opposed to capital gains.

---

[20]For a survey of the use of these plans, see Richard H. Pettway and R. Phil Malone, "Automatic Dividend Reinvestment Plans for Nonfinancial Corporations," *Financial Management*, 2 (Winter 1973), 11–18.

Insight into such a preference can be gained through an empirical study of the relationship between share price and dividend payout for a sample of similar companies. The following key arguments support the notion that investors overall have a systematic preference for current dividends over capital gains: the desire for current income in the form of dividends; the net impact of transaction and inconvenience costs; and legal and other restrictions on institutional investors, universities, and trusts which constrain their investment into stocks with reasonable and consistent dividends. Even without the last two factors, many investors are likely to view the receipt of current income from the sale of stock as unsatisfactory, owing to the uncertainty associated with the selling price.

Offsetting these factors is the more favorable tax treatment of capital gains relative to that of dividends. This factor, of course, creates a preference for capital gains as opposed to current dividends. Whether there is a net preference on the part of investors for dividends as opposed to capital gains or vice versa is determined to a large extent by the combined influence of the desire for current income, transaction costs, restrictions on investors, and differential tax rates.

If there exists a net preference among investors for capital gains as opposed to dividends, the firm's dividend policy would be strictly a residual decision determined by the profitability of its investment opportunities. Only if the firm had earnings remaining after financing all "acceptable" investment opportunities would it distribute dividends to stockholders. Justification for paying a dividend in excess of unused earnings requires a net preference among investors for current dividends as opposed to capital gains, and that this net preference be sufficiently strong to offset the difference in "cost" between retained earnings and new equity financing. Flotation costs and underpricing, of course, make the sale of common stock a more "expensive" form of financing than the retention of earnings. Therefore, both a net preference of investors for current dividends as opposed to capital gains as well as a sufficient magnitude of net preference are required.

Illustration of Dividend Policy and Investment Opportunities

To illustrate this concept, suppose a firm had a capital structure consisting entirely of equity and had enough acceptable investment opportunities to just exhaust its earnings plus depreciation.[21] Suppose further that, on the basis of an empirical test, it determined that investors had a net preference for current dividends and that share price initially could be raised

---

[21]In reality, the acceptance criterion may be affected by the dividend policy employed. However, we assume for simplicity that the last acceptable project provides a return significantly in excess of the required rate of return, while the next most profitable project provides a return significantly below the required return.

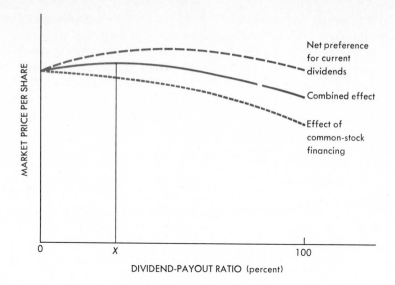

figure 11-1
Hypothetical
relationship between
share price and
dividend payout

by increasing the payout ratio, all other things remaining the same. This phenomenon is illustrated by the upper curve in Figure 11-1. We see that share price increases at a decreasing rate with dividend payout until eventually it turns down. This pattern is consistent with the preference for current dividends being quite important to investors when dividends are first declared. However, as more dividends are paid, it becomes less important vis-à-vis the tax disadvantage of dividends relative to capital gains. Eventually, the tax disadvantage causes the net preference line to turn down.

Any net preference for current dividends must be balanced against the difference in "cost" between financing with common stock and with retained earnings. Recall that the difference is attributable to underpricing and flotation costs. Given our assumptions, if a dividend is paid, it must be financed with common stock. If either there is a net preference for capital gains as opposed to current dividends, or there is a net preference for current dividends but this net preference does not offset the difference in "cost" between common-stock financing and financing with retained earnings, the firm in our example should pay no dividends. Suppose that, on the basis of a study, the firm determined that the relationship between share price and the payout ratio, attributable to the difference in cost between common-stock and retained earnings financing, could be depicted by the lower curve in Figure 11-1. The greater the payout ratio, of course, the greater the common-stock financing that is necessary. The line would be expected to decline because of flotation costs and underpricing, both of which cause increased dilution relative to that which would occur if stock could be sold at the current price with no flotation costs. If the amount of underpricing increases with the amount of financing, the line might decline at an increasing rate, as illustrated in the figure.

The combined influence of these two factors determines the relationship between the share price and the payout ratio, holding other things constant. The optimal dividend payout would be the one that maximized share price, point X in the figure. Thus the optimal dividend-payout ratio is determined by balancing any net preferences of investors for current dividends as opposed to capital gains with the flotation cost and underpricing disadvantage of common-stock financing. Recall that in our example we assumed the firm had acceptable investments exactly equal to its earnings. In other words, there were no residual funds and the dividend paid came from the sale of common stock.

If the firm does not have enough attractive investment projects to utilize its entire earnings, the optimal payout ratio is affected by this factor as well. Under such circumstances, the firm should determine the portion of earnings that cannot be employed profitably in investment projects. These earnings should be earmarked for payment to stockholders in the form of dividends. The firm should then analyze, on the basis of the considerations discussed above, whether it should pay an even higher dividend than that dictated by the amount of funds left over after investment. When this has been decided, the amount of dividend and the dividend-payout ratio can be determined. In other words, the dividend paid may come from both residual earnings and the sale of common stock.

A Final Perspective

In conclusion, if dividend policy is not relevant, a firm should choose its dividend policy solely in keeping with its long-run investment opportunities. At the point at which the return on investment is less than the cost of capital, the firm should stop investing and should pay the unused funds out as dividends. The growth company that expands faster than its growth in earnings would pay no dividends; whereas a firm in a shrinking industry might have a 100 percent dividend payout or even a liquidating dividend. The firm need not pay out the exact unused portion of earnings every period. Some years, the payout may be more; other years, it may be less. Indeed, the firm may want to stabilize the absolute amount of dividends paid from period to period but in such a manner that over the long run the total earnings retained, plus the senior securities the increasing equity base will support, correspond to the amount of profitable investment opportunities available. Dividend policy would still be a passive decision variable determined by the amount of investment opportunities.

For the firm to be justified in paying a dividend larger than that dictated by the amount of profitable investment opportunities, there must be a net preference of investors for current dividends as opposed to capital gains. Moreover, this net preference must more than offset the fact that owing to flotation costs and underpricing, common stock is a more expensive form of financing than is the retention of earnings. Although empirical evidence concerning the effect of dividends on the market price of a stock is far from

clear in this regard, many companies appear to behave as if dividends are relevant. For example, a number of growth companies that expand at a rate faster than their growth in earnings pay small dividends. If these companies believed dividends were irrelevant, they would retain all their earnings. A number of other companies that pay significant dividends go to the capital markets for additional equity capital rather than retain a greater portion of earnings. Examples include public utilities and airlines. Whereas these actions do not support the idea that dividends are relevant, they do indicate that many companies behave as though they were. The dividend-payout ratio that these firms believe is optimal is greater than that dictated by investment opportunities alone.

SUMMARY

The critical question in dividend policy is whether dividends have an influence upon the value of the firm, given its investment decision. If dividends are irrelevant, as Modigliani and Miller believe, the firm should retain earnings only in keeping with its investment opportunities. If there are not sufficient investment opportunities to provide expected returns in excess of the required return, the unused funds should be paid out as dividends.

The key issue is whether dividends are more than just a means of distributing unused funds. If they do affect the value of the common stock, dividend policy becomes more than a passive variable determined solely by the investment opportunities available. The firm could affect shareholder wealth by varying its dividend-payout ratio; as a result there would be an optimal dividend policy.

In this chapter, we have examined the various arguments for and against the importance of dividends. Arguments in the former camp include a preference of investors for current dividends, the possible effect of the resolution of uncertainty, the $100 dividend tax exclusion, the 85 percent tax exemption to corporate investors in stock, and restrictions on certain investors in favor of dividend-paying stocks. Arguments against the payment of dividends include the differential tax rate on dividend income and capital gains, and flotation costs and underpricing associated with the sale of stock. While transaction costs and security divisibility problems impede the arbitrage process, the direction of the effect is hard to predict.

If dividends are relevant, the net preference of investors for current dividends as opposed to capital gains must be balanced against the difference in cost between the sale of stock and the retention of earnings in determining the optimal dividend-payout ratio. Unfortunately, empirical evidence on the relevance of dividends has been little more than suggestive. Nevertheless, we know that many companies behave as if dividends do matter and can affect shareholder wealth. In the next chapter, we extend our analysis of the dividend payout and examine other aspects of dividend policy.

APPENDIX
The Double Taxation of Dividends

Dividends paid by corporations are taxed twice in the sense that earnings are taxed at the corporate level and then dividends paid out of after-tax earnings are taxed at the personal level to the stockholder. In recent years, there has been a great deal of discussion in Congress and elsewhere about eliminating the double taxation of dividends. Many people feel that such a tax reform would be a stimulant to corporations raising capital and to capital formation. In some measure the debate is kept alive by the conspicuousness of the United States in being one of the few advanced industrial countries in the world to tax dividends twice. Called the integration of corporate and personal income taxes, proposals to eliminate the double taxation of dividends fall into two categories.

Under the *dividend deduction method,* the corporation is allowed a tax deduction for dividends in the same way that it is allowed an interest deduction for its debt. Thus the tax saving is received by the corporation, and stockholders continue to pay taxes on the earnings that are distributed. Under the *stockholder credit method,* the corporation does not receive a tax deduction for dividends, but the stockholder gets a credit. However, he must "gross up" his dividends by the amount of corporate income taxes attributable to these dividends. To illustrate, suppose a stockholder receives $108 in dividends during a year and the corporation is taxed at the 46 percent rate. The amount of corporate taxes attributable to these dividends is $108/(1−.46) − $108 = $92; the stockholder would receive a tax credit of $92 and would "gross up" his dividends by $92 to $200 and report this amount as ordinary income. Thus the stockholder in effect receives a taxable income distribution of $200. The tax saving would be received directly by shareholders, and the corporation would continue to pay taxes on total earnings to equity. It is possible, of course, to combine the dividend deduction method with the stockholder credit method so that the direct tax saving would be shared between the two parties.

If one of these two methods for eliminating the double taxation of dividends were to come to pass, it would have important implications for dividend, capital structure, and liquidity decisions by companies. For one thing, there would be an incentive for companies to pay out a greater portion of their earnings in the form of dividends. Under the present tax system, there is a systematic tax bias (which was discussed in this chapter) that favors the retention of earnings over the payment of dividends. With the elimination of the double taxation of dividends, a dollar of retained earnings is equivalent to a dollar of dividends forgone when it comes to the after-tax effect. As a result, there would likely be a pronounced increase in the amount of dividends paid by corporations in the aggregate and a corresponding reduction in the amount of retained earnings.[22]

However, the amount of equity capital employed by corporations would not necessarily decline. In fact, it would probably increase because the financing decision also is affected by the elimination of the double taxation of dividends. With the dividend deduction method, for example, dividends would be deductible as an expense for tax purposes in the same manner that interest on debt is deductible. As a result, the relative tax advantage associated with debt, which was discussed in Chapter 9, would disappear. With the elimination of the systematic tax bias which favors debt over equity financing, we would expect to see substantially less debt financing by corporations, all other things the same. In other words, debt and equity would be on the same footing with respect to the tax consequences of financing. Economically the dividend deduction method and the shareholder credit method have virtually the same effect with respect to dividend and capital structure decisions, and this sameness of effect can be demonstrated theoretically.[23]

If bankruptcy costs and agency costs exist, as discussed in Chapter 9, there would be a definite disadvantage to the issuance of debt, particularly beyond some point. Gone would be the major advantage associated with debt financing, the tax advantage. This does not mean that debt financing would disappear. With incomplete financial markets,[24] corporations would try to tailor the types of securities issued to the preferences of different investors. Certainly debt would be used, but instruments with features similar to debt would increase in importance. In particular, the use of preferred stock and income bonds would likely increase.[25] With the elimination of the double taxation of dividends, these instruments would be on the same footing as debt from a tax standpoint. Their advantage to the corporation is that they do not trigger bankruptcy if the preferred dividend or the income bond interest is not paid. Therefore debt financing would be expected to decline relative not only to common-stock financing but also to preferred-stock and, perhaps, income-bond financing.

In addition to these effects, eliminating the double taxation of dividends is likely to affect the liquidity holdings of corporations. Under the

[22]For a general discussion of this effect as well as others on net savings, see Martin Feldstein and Daniel Frisch, "Corporate Tax Integration: The Estimated Effects on Capital Accumulation and Tax Distribution of Two Integration Proposals," *National Tax Journal*, 30 (March 1977), 37–52.

[23]For such a demonstration in a state-preference framework, see Robert H. Litzenberger and James C. Van Horne, "Elimination of the Double Taxation of Dividends and Corporate Financial Policy," *Journal of Finance*, 33 (June 1978), 737–49.

[24]Complete capital markets exist when every contingency in the world corresponds to a distinct marketable security. In incomplete capital markets, the number of future contingencies exceeds the number of linearly independent marketable securities.

[25]See Chapter 21 for a description of preferred stock and income bonds.

present tax system, there is a disincentive to holding liquidity because the interest earned on marketable securities is taxed at the corporate level and again at the individual level if paid out as dividends.[26] With the double taxation of dividends eliminated, the tax disincentive for holding marketable securities would be greatly reduced. The combined effect of greater liquidity and lower debt ratios would be expected to reduce the occurrence of bankruptcy. As the cost of bankruptcy is largely a dead weight loss in society, the reduction in bankruptcies would be beneficial, all other things the same.

In this Appendix, we have explored the likely effects that would occur if the double taxation of dividends were eliminated. Whether this elimination will occur is problematical. While it would be expected to have a positive effect on capital formation, there would be a substantial revenue loss to the federal government, in excess of $25 billion. If this loss were made up by other taxes, there would be a redistribution of the tax burden. Whether corporations and their shareholders would be better off or worse off would depend on the nature of the new taxes. Without new taxes, federal expenditure programs would have to be forgone or the federal deficit increased to offset the revenue loss associated with the elimination of the double taxation of dividends. Here again it is not possible to know the effect on corporations and shareholders without knowing the specifics. Therefore one must take account of the second-order effects associated with the revenue loss to the federal government before being able to state whether a corporation and its shareholders are better off or worse off with the elimination of the double taxation of dividends.

PROBLEMS

1. Financial data are shown below on two companies. What differences are reflected in these data that give insight into dividend policy and valuation?

	Cleveland Machine Tool Company			**Fox Electronics Company**		
	Earnings per Share	Dividends per Share	Range P/E Ratio	Earnings per Share	Dividends per Share	Range P/E Ratio
1980	$3.02	$1.50	12–18	$1.18	$0.15	25–32
1979	3.19	1.50	9–14	1.02	0.10	25–35
1978	3.10	1.25	13–18	0.81	0.10	30–40
1977	2.90	1.25	10–17	0.72	0.10	30–40
1976	1.06	1.25	13–17	0.48	0.05	35–45
1975	2.03	1.25	14–18	0.41	0.05	40–50
1974	2.87	1.25	15–23	0.29	0.05	45–55
1973	2.13	1.25	11–16	0.20	0.04	40–60
1972	1.32	1.00	8–13	0.14	0.00	30–45
1971	2.21	1.00	10–15	0.13	0.00	40–50

[26]See Litzenberger and Van Horne, "Elimination of the Double Taxation of Dividends and Corporate Financial Policy," *Journal of Finance,* 33 (June 1978), 737–49.

2. Malkor Instruments Company treats dividends as a residual decision. It expects to generate $2 million in net earnings after taxes in the coming year. The company has an all-equity capital structure and its cost of equity capital is 10 percent. The company treats this cost as the opportunity cost of retained earnings. Because of flotation costs and underpricing, the cost of common-stock financing is higher, it is 11 percent.

(a) How much in dividends (out of the $2 million in earnings) should be paid if the company has $1.5 million in projects whose expected return exceeds 10 percent?

(b) How much in dividends should be paid if it has $2 million in projects whose expected return exceeds 10 percent?

(c) How much in dividends should be paid if it has $3 million in projects whose expected return exceeds 11 percent? What else should be done?

3. The Beta-Alpha Company expects with some degree of certainty to generate the following net income and to have the following capital expenditures during the next five years (in thousands):

Year	Net Income	Capital Expenditures
1	$2,000	$1,000
2	1,500	1,500
3	2,500	2,000
4	2,300	1,500
5	1,800	2,000

The company currently has one million shares of common stock outstanding and pays dividends of $1 per share.

(a) Determine dividends per share if dividend policy is treated as a residual decision.

(b) Determine the amounts of external financing that will be necessary if the present dividend per share is maintained.

(c) Determine dividends per share and the amounts of external financing that will be necessary if a dividend-payout ratio of 50 percent is maintained.

(d) Under which of the three dividend policies are aggregate dividends maximized? External financing minimized?

4. The Mann Company belongs to a risk class for which the appropriate equity capitalization rate is 10 percent. It currently has outstanding 100,000 shares selling at $100 each. The firm is contemplating the declaration of a $5 dividend at the end of the current fiscal year, which just began. Answer the following questions based on the Modigliani and Miller model and the assumption of no taxes.

(a) What will be the price of the stock at the end of the year if a dividend is not declared? What will it be if one is?

(b) Assuming that the firm pays the dividend, has net income of $1 million, and makes new investments of $2 million during the period, how many new shares must be issued?

(c) Is the MM model realistic with respect to valuation? What factors might mar its validity?

5. The University of Northern California pays no taxes on the dividend income and capital gains received on its various endowment funds. Over the years, it has steadily bought the stock of IVM Corporation for its alumni fellowship fund. The alumni campaign is such that the bulk of alumni giving occurs in the months of June and December. Coincidentally, IVM pays a semiannual dividend in these months. In the past, the university has not paid attention as to whether it bought the stock before or after the ex-dividend dates of June 10 and December 10. (Before the ex-dividend date, the investor is entitled to the dividend; after, he is not.) The feeling has been that the stock will decline by the amount of the dividend on the ex-dividend date, so it really doesn't matter when the stock is purchased.

However, Shirley McDonald, the finance officer of the university, has just completed a study which shows that over the years IVM's stock price on average declined by only 70 percent of the dividend per share on the ex-dividend date. She attributes this occurrence to the fact that a number of investors are interested in capital gains, which are taxed at a lower rate than dividends. As a result, these investors buy the stock after the ex-dividend date, and the impact of their purchases causes the stock to decline by less than the amount of the dividend. (See footnote 18 in this chapter.) In view of this finding, should the university change the timing of its purchase of IVM stock? If so, how should it change?

6. Faisano Baking Corporation currently pays no dividends and is evaluating the appropriate dividend-payout ratio, if any. The company has an all-equity capital structure, and over the years its capital expenditures have approximately equaled its earnings plus depreciation charges. As a result, any dividend that is paid eventually will have to come from a common-stock offering. On the basis of a careful empirical study, Faisano has found a net preference in the market for current dividends. It estimates that it could change the market price of its stock by the following formula due to this consideration alone:

$$\text{Price change} = 0.5(\text{Dividend-payout ratio}) - 0.6(\text{Dividend-payout ratio})^2$$

where the dividend-payout ratio is expressed in decimal form. (For example, a payout ratio of 50 percent is 0.50.) However, any new sale of stock will have an adverse effect on share price owing to flotation costs and underpricing. Faisano estimates that this factor, in isolation from the previous factor, will lower share price according to the following formula:

$$\text{Price change} = -0.05 \, (\text{Dividend-payout ratio})$$

where again the ratio is expressed in decimal form.

The company is considering dividend-payout ratios in increments of 0.10, going from 0 to 1.00. On the basis of this information, determine the optimal dividend-payout ratio.

7. The Eureka Mining Company consists of one mine, which has a remaining useful life of five years. The owners feel that no new shafts should be sunk for at least this long; indeed, they probably will not continue in this business after five years. Since the initiation of the company, total cash flows have been paid out in dividends. All of the firm's stockholders were original investors, have a marginal

tax rate of 40 percent, and require an after-tax return of 10 percent. The mine will generate the following income during each of the next five years:

Net operating income	$25,000
Less: Depreciation and depletion	5,000
Net income before taxes	$20,000
Less: Taxes @ 22%	4,400
Net income	$15,600

Compute the total market value of Eureka if all available funds were paid in dividends at the end of the year they became available.

SELECTED REFERENCES

BAR-YOSEF, SASSON, AND RICHARD KOLODNY, "Dividend Policy and Capital Market Theory," *Review of Economics and Statistics*, 58 (May 1976), 181–90.

BLACK, FISCHER, AND MYRON SCHOLES, "The Effects of Dividend Yield and Dividend Policy on Common Stock Prices and Returns," *Journal of Financial Economics*, 1 (May 1974), 1–22.

BRENNAN, MICHAEL, "A Note on Dividend Irrelevance and the Gordon Valuation Model," *Journal of Finance*, 26 (December 1971), 1115–23.

BRITTAIN, JOHN A., *Corporate Dividend Policy*. Washington, D.C.: Brookings Institution, 1966.

ELTON, EDWIN J., AND MARTIN J. GRUBER, "Marginal Stockholder Tax Rates and the Clientele Effect," *Review of Economics and Statistics*, 52 (February 1970), 68–74.

FAMA, EUGENE F., "The Empirical Relationships between the Dividend and Investment Decisions of Firms," *American Economic Review*, 64 (June 1974), 304–18.

FAMA, EUGENE F., AND HARVEY BABIAK, "Dividend Policy: An Empirical Analysis," *Journal of the American Statistical Association*, 63 (December 1968), 1132–61.

GORDON, MYRON J., *The Investment, Financing and Valuation of the Corporation*. Homewood, Ill.: Richard D. Irwin, 1962.

GORDON, M. J., AND L. I. GOULD, "The Cost of Equity Capital with Personal Income Taxes and Flotation Costs," *Journal of Finance*, 33 (September 1978), 1201–12.

GRABOWSKI, HENRY G., AND DENNIS C. MUELLER, "Life-Cycle Effects on Corporate Returns on Retentions," *Review of Economics and Statistics*, 57 (November 1975), 400–409.

HIGGINS, ROBERT C., "The Corporate Dividend-Saving Decision," *Journal of Financial and Quantitative Analysis*, 7 (March 1972), 1527–41

———, "Dividend Policy and Increasing Discount Rate: A Clarification," *Journal of Financial and Quantitative Analysis*, 7 (June 1972), 1757–62.

KEANE, SIMON M., "Dividends and the Resolution of Uncertainty," *Journal of Finance & Accounting*, 1 (Autumn 1974), 389–93.

KRAINER, ROBERT E., "A Pedagogic Note on Dividend Policy," *Journal of Financial and Quantitative Analysis*, 6 (September 1971), 1147–54.

LINTNER, JOHN, "Distribution of Income of Corporations among Dividends, Retained Earnings, and Taxes." *American Economic Review*, 46 (May 1956), 97–113.

———, "Dividends, Earnings, Leverage, Stock Prices and the Supply of Capital to Corporations," *Review of Economics and Statistics*, 44 (August 1962), 243–69.

LITZENBERGER, ROBERT H., AND JAMES C. VAN HORNE, "Elimination of the Double Taxation of Dividends and Corporate Financial Policy." *Journal of Finance,* 33 (June 1978), 737–49.

MEHTA, DILEEP R., "The Impact of Outstanding Convertible Bonds on Corporate Dividend Policy," *Journal of Finance,* 31 (May 1976), 489–506.

MILLER, MERTON H., AND FRANCO MODIGLIANI, "Dividend Policy, Growth, and the Valuation of Shares," *Journal of Business,* 34 (October 1961), 411–33.

——, "Some Estimates of the Cost of Capital to the Electric Utility Industry," *American Economic Review,* 56 (June 1966), 333–91.

MILLER, MERTON H., AND MYRON S. SCHOLES, "Dividends and Taxes." Working paper, University of Chicago, August 1978.

PETTIT, R. RICHARDSON, "Dividend Announcements, Security Performance, and Capital Market Efficiency," *Journal of Finance,* 27 (December 1972), 993–1007.

——, "The Impact of Dividend and Earnings Announcements: A Reconciliation," *Journal of Business,* 49 (January 1976), 86–96.

——, "Taxes, Transaction Costs and the Clientele Effect of Dividends," *Journal of Financial Economics,* 5 (November 1977), 419–36.

PETTWAY, RICHARD H., AND R. PHIL MALONE, "Automatic Dividend Reinvestment Plans of Nonfinancial Corporations," *Financial Management,* 2 (Winter 1973), 11–18.

POGUE, THOMAS F., "A Cross-Section Study of the Relationship between Dividends and Investment," *Yale Economic Essays,* 2 (Fall 1971), 181–218.

PORTERFIELD, JAMES T. S., *Investment Decisions and Capital Costs,* Chap. 6. Englewood Cliffs, N.J.: Prentice-Hall, 1965.

PYE, GORDON, "Preferential Tax Treatment of Capital Gains, Optimal Dividend Policy, and Capital Budgeting," *Quarterly Journal of Economics,* 86 (May 1972), 226–42.

STIGLITZ, JOSEPH E., "On the Irrelevance of Corporate Financial Policy," *American Economic Review,* 64 (December 1974), 851–66.

VAN HORNE, JAMES C., AND JOHN G. MCDONALD, "Dividend Policy and New Equity Financing," *Journal of Finance,* 26 (May 1971), 507–19.

WALTER, JAMES E., "Dividend Policies and Common Stock Prices," *Journal of Finance,* 11 (March 1956), 29–41.

——, *Dividend Policy and Enterprise Valuation.* Belmont, Calif.: Wadsworth, 1967.

WATTS, ROSS, "Comments," *Journal of Business,* 49 (January 1976), 97–106.

——, "The Information Content of Dividends," *Journal of Business,* 46 (April 1973), 191–211.

12
dividend policy of the firm

Given its approximate long-run investment requirements, the firm is able to adopt a long-run dividend-payout ratio. This ratio should be determined in keeping with the objective of maximizing shareholder wealth. As discussed in the preceding chapter, its determination will depend upon the expected magnitude of acceptable investment opportunities, the perceived value to investors of dividends as opposed to capital gains, and the difference in cost between common-stock financing and the retention of earnings. Although the dividend-payout ratio is a major aspect of the dividend policy of the firm, there are other aspects that may affect valuation. In this chapter, we consider the stability of dividends, certain factors that influence the dividend-payout ratio from the standpoint of the firm, stock dividends and stock splits, the repurchase of stock, and the procedural and legal elements of dividend policy.

STABILITY OF DIVIDENDS

In addition to the percentage of dividend payout of a company over the long run, investors may value stable dividends over this period. All other things being the same, the market price of the stock of a company may be higher if it

347

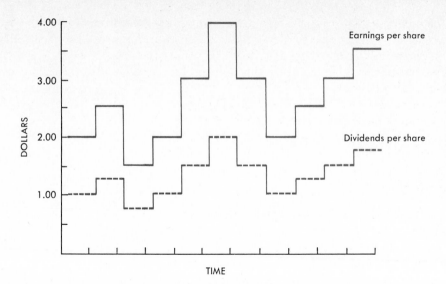

figure 12-1
Hypothetical dividend
policy of Company A

pays a stable dividend over time than if it pays out a fixed percentage of earnings. To illustrate, suppose Company A has a long-run dividend-payout ratio of 50 percent of earnings. Suppose further that it has the policy of paying out this percentage every year, despite the fact that its earnings are cyclical. The dividends of Company A are shown in Figure 12-1. Company B, on the other hand, has exactly the same earnings and a long-run dividend-payout ratio of 50 percent, but it maintains a relatively stable dividend over time. It changes the absolute amount of dividend only in keeping with the underlying trend of earnings. The dividends of Company B are shown in Figure 12-2.

Over the long run, the total amount of dividends paid by these two firms is the same. However, the market price per share of Company B may be

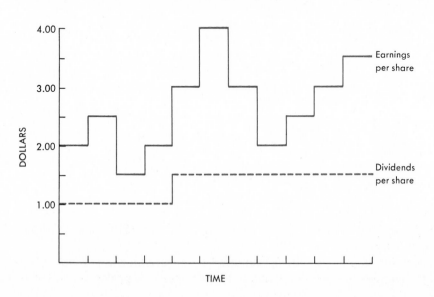

figure 12-2
Hypothetical dividend
policy of Company B

higher than that of Company A, all other things being the same. Investors may well place a positive utility on dividend stability and pay a premium for the company that offers such stability. To the extent that investors value dividend stability, the overall dividend policy of Company B would be better than that of Company A. This policy includes not only the percentage of dividend payout in relation to earnings but also the manner in which the actual dividends are paid. Rather than vary dividends directly with changes in earnings per share, Company B raises the dividend only when reasonably confident a higher dividend can be maintained.

Valuation of Stability

There are several reasons why investors may value stable dividends and pay a premium for the stock of the company providing such stability. These include the informational content of dividends, the desire of investors for current income, and certain legal considerations.

Informational Content   As we said in the preceding chapter, dividends may serve to resolve uncertainty in the minds of investors. When earnings drop and a company does not cut its dividend, the market's confidence in the stock may be bolstered over what it would be if the dividend were cut. The stable dividend may convey to investors management's view that the future of the company is better than the drop in earnings suggests. Thus management may be able to influence the expectations of investors through the informational content of dividends. Management, however, cannot "fool" the market permanently. If there is a downward trend in earnings, a stable dividend will not convey forever an impression of a rosy future. Moreover, if a firm is in an unstable business with wide swings in earnings, a stable dividend cannot give the illusion of underlying stability.

Current Income Desires   A second factor favoring stable dividends is that investors who desire a specific periodic income will prefer a company with stable dividends to one with unstable dividends, even though both companies may have the same pattern of earnings and long-run dividend payout. Although the investor can always sell a portion of his stock for income when the dividend is not sufficient to meet his current needs, many investors have an aversion to "dipping into principal." Moreover, there are transaction and inconvenience costs. Finally, when a company reduces its dividend, earnings usually are down and the market price of the stock depressed. As a result, the investor would have to sell his stock on unfavorable terms. Overall, it would seem that income-conscious investors place a positive utility on stable dividends.

Legal Considerations   Finally, a stable dividend may be advantageous from the legal standpoint of permitting certain institutional investors to invest in the stock. Various governmental bodies prepare legal lists of securities in which pension funds, savings banks, trustees, insurance companies, and others may invest. In order to qualify, a company must have an uninterrupted

Source: Economic Report of the President

figure 12-3
Corporate profits after tax with inventory valuation and capital consumption adjustments and corporate dividends

pattern of dividends. A cut in, or omission of, the dividend may result in the removal of a company from these legal lists.

The arguments presented in support of the notion that stable dividends have a positive effect upon the market price of the stock are only suggestive. There is little in the way of empirical evidence to shed light on the question. Although studies of individual stocks often suggest that stable dividends buffer the market price of the stock when earnings turn down, there have been no comprehensive studies of a large sample of stocks dealing with the relationship between dividend stability and valuation. Nevertheless, most companies strive for stability in their dividend payments. This occurrence is illustrated in Figure 12-3, where total corporate dividends and profits after taxes and after adjustments for inventory valuation and depreciation are shown for the post-World War II period. Overall, corporations behave in a manner that is consistent with a belief that stable dividends have a positive effect on value. From the standpoint of public policy, dividend stability acts as a built-in stabilizer, for it tends to cushion the effect of changes in income on aggregate demand over economic cycles.[1]

Target Payout Ratios

It would appear that a number of companies follow the policy of a target dividend-payout ratio over the long run. Lintner contends that dividends are adjusted to changes in earnings, but only with a lag.[2] When earnings increase to a new level, dividends are increased only when it is felt

[1]See John A. Brittain, *Corporate Dividend Policy* (Washington, D.C.: Brookings Institution, 1966), p. 212.

[2]See John Lintner, "Distribution of Income of Corporations," *American Economic Review,* 46 (May 1956), 97–113.

that the increase in earnings can be maintained. In addition, there appears to be a definite reluctance on the part of companies to cut the absolute amount of their cash dividend. Both of these factors explain the lag in dividend changes behind changes in earnings. Given a lag relationship, retained earnings will increase relative to dividends in an economic upturn. In a contraction, however, retained earnings will decrease relative to dividends. Empirically, the lag of dividend changes behind changes in earnings has been verified by several investigators, using Lintner's target payout ratio model.[3]

To illustrate the use of a target payout ratio and stable dividends, consider the case of Coleman Company. This company makes outdoor recreation equipment and central heating and air-conditioning units. These lines of business are somewhat cyclical, with resulting swings in earnings. However, the company maintained stable and increasing dividends in the sixties and seventies; it seems to raise dividends once management and the board of directors are confident that the earnings can be sustained. The dividends per share and earnings per share for the company are shown in Figure 12-4. (A change to the Lifo method of inventory valuation reduced 1974 net income by 60 cents a share.)

Regular and Extra Dividends

One way for a company to increase its cash distribution in periods of prosperity is to declare an *extra* dividend in addition to the *regular* quarterly or semiannual dividend. By declaring an extra dividend, the company at-

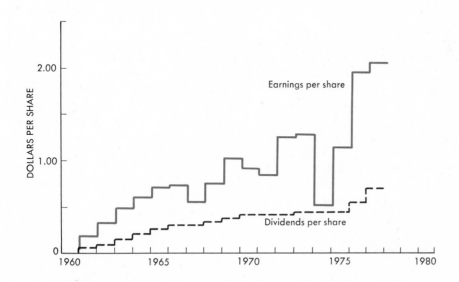

figure 12-4
**Coleman company
dividends and earnings
per share**

[3]See Brittain, *Corporate Dividend Policy*, Chaps. 2–7; and Eugene F. Fama and Harvey Babiak, "Dividend Policy: An Empirical Analysis," *Journal of the American Statistical Association*, 63 (December 1968), 1132–61.

tempts to prevent investors from expecting that the dividend represents an increase in the established dividend rate. The declaration of an extra dividend is particularly suitable for companies with fluctuating earnings. General Motors, for example, frequently declares extra dividends in good car years. The use of the extra dividend enables the company to maintain a stable record of regular dividends but also to distribute to stockholders some of the rewards of prosperity. By paying extra dividends only when earnings are higher than usual, the company will not lead investors to count on the increased dividends in future periods. However, a company cannot pay extra dividends continuously without conveying to the market some impression of permanency. As soon as a certain level of dividends is recurrent, investors begin to expect that level regardless of the distinction between regular and extra dividends.

OTHER CONSIDERATIONS

So far, we have related the dividend policy of a firm to the investment opportunities of that firm, to the magnitude and stability of earnings, to the possible preference of investors for dividends relative to capital gains, and to the fact that common stock is a more expensive form of financing than is the retention of earnings. However, a number of other considerations influence a company in the dividend policy it undertakes. These considerations tend to be of a more practical nature than those discussed so far.

Liquidity

The liquidity of a company is an important consideration in many dividend decisions. As dividends represent a cash outflow, the greater the cash position and overall liquidity of a company, the greater its ability to pay a dividend. A company that is growing and profitable may not be liquid, for its funds may go into fixed assets and permanent working capital. Because the management of such a company usually desires to maintain some liquidity cushion to give it flexibility and a protection against uncertainty, it may be reluctant to jeopardize this position in order to pay a large dividend. The liquidity of the company, of course, is determined by the firm's investment and financing decisions. The investment decision determines the rate of asset expansion and the firm's need for funds; and the financing decision determines the way in which this need will be financed.

Ability to Borrow

A liquid position is not the only way to provide for flexibility and thereby protect against uncertainty. If a firm has the ability to borrow on comparatively short notice, it may be relatively flexible. This ability to borrow can be in the form of a line of credit or a revolving credit from a bank, or simply the informal willingness on the part of a financial institution to extend credit. In addition, flexibility can come from the ability of a firm to go to the capital markets with a bond issue. The larger and more established a company, the better its access to the capital markets. The greater the ability of the firm to borrow, the greater its flexibility, and the greater its ability to pay a cash dividend. With ready access to debt funds, management should be less concerned with the effect that a cash dividend has upon its liquidity.

Control

If a company pays substantial dividends, it may need to raise capital at a later time through the sale of stock in order to finance profitable investment opportunities. Under such circumstances, the controlling interest of the company may be diluted if controlling stockholders do not or cannot subscribe for additional shares. These stockholders may prefer a low dividend payout and the financing of investment needs with retained earnings.

Control can work two ways, however. In the case of a company being sought by another company or by individuals, a low dividend payout may work to the advantage of the "outsiders" seeking control. The outsiders may be able to convince stockholders that the company is not maximizing shareholder wealth and that they (the outsiders) can do a better job. Consequently, companies in danger of being acquired may establish a high dividend payout in order to please stockholders.

Nature of Stockholders

When a firm is closely held, management usually knows the dividend desires of its stockholders and may act accordingly. If most stockholders are in high tax brackets and prefer capital gains to current income, the firm can establish a low dividend payout. The low payout, of course, would be predicated upon having profitable investment opportunities in which to employ the retained earnings. The corporation with a large number of stockholders does not know the dividend desires of its stockholders. It can judge these desires only in a market context.

Timing of Investment Opportunities

A company may have profitable investment opportunities, but these opportunities may occur too sporadically for the company to be justified in retaining earnings. For example, a firm may know that it will need to build a major extension on its existing plant in about six years. If it retains earnings to finance this plant expansion, the funds will not be used for some period of time. During this period, the company will invest the funds in short-term securities yielding less than the required rate of return on retained earnings. However, shareholder wealth might be maximized by paying out the inter-

mediate earnings as dividends and raising the capital six years later with a
stock issue. The sale of stock is a more desirable means than retained earnings by which to raise a large block of capital at one time.

Restrictions in Bond Indenture or Loan Agreement

The protective convenants in a bond indenture or loan agreement
often include a restriction on payment of dividends.[4] This restriction is employed by the lender(s) to preserve the company's ability to service debt.
Usually, it is expressed as a maximum percentage of cumulative earnings.
When such a restriction is in force, it naturally influences the dividend policy
of the firm. There are times when the management of a company welcomes a
dividend restriction imposed by lenders because it does not then have to
justify to stockholders the retention of earnings. It need only point to the
restriction.

Inflation

Inflation also may have an influence upon dividend policy. With
rising prices, funds generated from depreciation are not sufficient to replace
and/or restore existing assets as they wear out or become obsolete.[5] Consequently, a case can be made for retaining earnings simply to preserve the
earning power of the firm. This decision must be based upon considerations
taken up in the preceding chapter concerning investment policy and
valuation.

STOCK DIVIDENDS AND STOCK SPLITS

In this section, we discuss stock dividends and stock splits. In an economic
sense, the two are very similar, although typically they are used for different
purposes. Only from an accounting standpoint is there a significant
difference.

Stock Dividends

A stock dividend simply is the payment of additional stock to stockholders. It represents nothing more than a recapitalization of the company; a
stockholder's proportional ownership remains unchanged. To illustrate,

---

[4]For a more detailed examination of these restrictions, see Chapter 18.

[5]See James C. Van Horne and William F. Glassmire, Jr., "The Impact of Unanticipated
Changes in Inflation on the Value of Common Stocks," *Journal of Finance,* 27 (December 1972),
1081–92.

suppose a company had the following capital structure before issuing a stock dividend:

Common stock ($5 par, 400,000 shares)	$ 2,000,000
Capital surplus	1,000,000
Retained earnings	7,000,000
Net worth	$10,000,000

Now, suppose the company pays a 5 percent stock dividend, amounting to 20,000 additional shares of stock, and that the fair market value of the stock is $40 a share. For each twenty shares of stock owned, the stockholder receives an additional share. The balance sheet of the company after the stock dividend would be

Common stock ($5 par, 420,000 shares)	$ 2,100,000
Capital surplus	1,700,000
Retained earnings	6,200,000
Net worth	$10,000,000

With a stock dividend, $800,000, ($40 × 20,000 shares), is transferred from retained earnings to the common-stock and capital surplus accounts. Because the par value stays the same, the increase in number of shares is reflected in a $100,000 increase in the common-stock account ($5 par × 20,000 shares). The residual of $700,000 goes into the capital surplus account. The net worth of the company remains the same.

Because the number of shares of stock outstanding is increased by 5 percent, earnings per share of the company are reduced proportionately. Suppose that total net profit after taxes were $1 million. Before the stock dividend, earnings per share would be $2.50, ($1 million/400,000). After the stock dividend, earnings per share are $2.38, ($1 million/420,000). Thus the stockholder has more shares of stock but lower earnings per share. His proportion of total earnings available to common-stock holders remains unchanged.

Value to Investor If the company pays no cash dividend, what does the stockholder receive with a stock dividend? In theory, he receives nothing but an additional stock certificate. His proportionate ownership of the company is unchanged. Presumably, the market price of the stock will drop, all other things being equal, so that the total market value of his holdings stays the same. For example, if he held 100 shares of stock previously, and market price per share were $40, the total value of his holdings would be $4,000. After the stock dividend, the price of the stock should drop by $40(1 − 1.00/1.05), or by $1.90. The total value of his holdings then would be $38.10 × 105, or $4,000.

Under these conditions, the stock dividend does not represent a thing of value to the stockholder. He simply has an additional stock certificate evidencing ownership.

To the extent that the investor wishes to sell a few shares of stock for income, the stock dividend may make it easier for him to do so. Without the stock dividend, of course, he could also sell a few shares of his original holdings for income. In either case, the sale of stock represents the sale of principal and is subject to the capital gains tax. However, some investors may not look upon the sale of a stock dividend as a sale of principal. To them, the stock dividend represents a windfall gain; they can sell it and still retain their original holdings. The stock dividend may have a favorable psychological effect on these stockholders.

The stock dividend can also be a thing of value to the investor if the company maintains the same cash dividend per share after the stock dividend as before. Suppose an investor owns 100 shares of a company paying a $1 dividend and that the company declares a 10 percent stock dividend and, at the same time, announces that the cash dividend per share will remain unchanged. The investor then will have 110 shares; and total cash dividends will be $110 rather than $100, as before. In this case, a stock dividend increases his total cash dividends. Whether this increase in cash dividend has a positive effect upon shareholder wealth will depend upon the tradeoff between current dividends and retained earnings, which we discussed in the last chapter. Clearly, the stock dividend in this case represents a decision by the firm to increase modestly the amount of cash dividends.

Use of the stock dividend *per se* may convey some information. Stock dividends typically are associated with growth companies. Under these circumstances, the dividend may connote to investors that management expects earnings to continue to grow and to more than offset the dilution in earnings per share arising from the increase in the total number of shares. The underlying effect on value is growth, however, and not the stock dividend itself.

Advantages and Disadvantages   Frequently, a stock dividend is employed to "conserve cash." Instead of increasing the cash dividend as earnings rise, a company may desire to retain a greater portion of its earnings and declare a stock dividend. The decision then is to lower the dividend-payout ratio, for as earnings rise and total cash dividends remain the same, the payout ratio will decline. Whether shareholder wealth is increased by this action will depend upon considerations taken up in the preceding chapter. The decision to retain a higher proportion of earnings, of course, could be accomplished without a stock dividend. However, the stock dividend may tend to please certain investors by virtue of its informational content as well as its psychological impact. In addition, if the cash dividend per share is kept the same, total cash dividends will increase in keeping with the increase in the number of shares.

In the discussion of advantages so far, the decision to issue a stock dividend has been based upon the availability of profitable investment opportunities. The percentage of cash dividend payout was reduced in order to finance a portion of these opportunities with retained earnings. Certain companies, however, have employed the stock dividend as a means of replacing the cash dividend because of financial difficulty. In these situations, the stock dividend should not connote the prospect of favorable earnings, but financial deterioration, and it should be so evaluated. It is doubtful whether many investors are fooled by the substitution.

The use of a stock dividend by a firm may also serve to keep the market price of the stock within a popular trading range. Certain companies do not like to see the market price of their stocks above a certain amount—say $60 a share—because a high price will not appeal to small investors. Consequently, they will endeavor to keep the price below a desired ceiling either by using stock dividends or, more commonly, by means of stock splits. Increasing the total number of shares outstanding may increase the total number of stockholders, resulting in a greater overall popularity of the stock.

The principal disadvantage of stock dividends to the firm is that they are much more costly to administer than cash dividends. This added cost flows to bank trust departments or others who administer the stock dividend and works to the obvious disadvantage of the company and its stockholders.

Stock Splits

With a stock split, the number of shares are increased through a proportional reduction in the par value of the stock. Suppose that the capital structure of a company before a two-to-one stock split were

Common stock ($5 par, 400,000 shares)	$ 2,000,000
Capital surplus	1,000,000
Retained earnings	7,000,000
Net worth	$10,000,000

After the split, the capital structure is

Common stock ($2.50 par, 800,000 shares)	$ 2,000,000
Capital surplus	1,000,000
Retained earnings	7,000,000
Net worth	$10,000,000

With a stock dividend, the par value is not reduced; whereas with a split, it is. As a result, the common-stock, capital surplus, and retained earnings accounts remain unchanged. The net worth, of course, also stays the same; the only change is in the par value of the stock. Except in accounting treatment, the stock dividend and stock split are very similar. A stock split, however, is usually reserved for occasions when a company wishes to achieve a substantial reduction in the market price per share. The principal purpose of a split is to place the stock in a more popular trading range.

As was true of the stock dividend, the stock split does not represent a thing of value to the investor. He has more shares than before, but his proportional ownership of the company remains unchanged. The market price of the stock should decline proportionately, so that the total value of his holdings stays the same. Again, however, the split may have a favorable informational content. The announcement of the split may indicate to investors that management believes that earnings will continue to grow. As a result, the market price per share may increase upon the announcement of the split, or the rumor of an announcement, and remain higher. However, the underlying cause for the increase in market price is growth and not the split itself.

Very seldom will a company maintain the same cash dividends per share after a split as it did before. However, it may increase the effective dividends to stockholders. For example, suppose a company splits its stock two for one and establishes a dividend rate of $1.20 a share, whereas before the rate was $2.00 a share. A stockholder owning 100 shares before the split would receive $200 in cash dividends per annum. After the split, he would own 200 shares and would receive $240 in dividends. The market price of the stock (on an after-split basis) may react favorably to the increase in cash dividends.

Reverse Split   Rather than increasing the number of shares of stock outstanding, a company may want to reduce the number. This reduction can be accomplished with a *reverse split*. In our example above, suppose that there were a one-to-four reverse split, instead of the two-to-one straight stock split. For each four shares held, the stockholder would receive one share in exchange. The par value per share would become $20, and there would be 100,000 shares outstanding rather than 400,000. Reverse stock splits are employed to increase the market price per share when the stock is considered to be selling at too low a price. Many companies have an aversion to seeing the price of their stock fall below $10 per share. If, due to financial difficulty or other reasons, the price should fall into this range, the market price per share can be increased with a reverse split. The reverse split is regarded by many as an admission by a company that it is in financial difficulty. However, financial difficulty is not always the reason for the split, and the stock market's reaction to it depends primarily upon the company's past and expected future earnings.[6]

REPURCHASE OF STOCK

In recent years, a number of companies have repurchased a portion of their outstanding common stock. There are several reasons for it. Some companies repurchase stock in order to have it available for stock options. In this way,

[6]See Richard R. West and Alan B. Brouilette, "Reverse Stock Splits," *Financial Executive*, 38 (January 1970), 12–17.

the total number of shares is not increased with the exercise of the options.

Another reason for repurchase is to have shares available for the acquisition of other companies. In certain situations, companies no longer wishing to be publicly owned "go private" by purchasing all the stock of the outside stockholders. In still other situations, however, stock is repurchased with the full intention of retiring it. Under these circumstances, repurchase of stock may be treated as a substitute for dividends.

Repurchasing as Part of a Dividend Decision

If a firm has excess cash and insufficient profitable investment opportunities to justify the use of these funds, it may be in the shareholders' interests to distribute the funds. The distribution can be accomplished either by the repurchase of stock or by paying the funds out in increased dividends. In the absence of personal income taxes and transaction costs, it should make no difference theoretically to stockholders which of the two alternatives is chosen. With repurchase, fewer shares remain outstanding, and earnings per share rise. As a result, the market price per share should rise as well. In theory, the capital gain arising from repurchase should equal the dividend that otherwise would have been paid.

To illustrate, suppose that a company has the following earnings and market price per share:

Net profit after taxes	$2,000,000
Number of shares outstanding	500,000
Earnings per share	$4.00
Market price per share, ex-dividend	$60.00
Price/earnings ratio	15

Suppose further that the company is considering the distribution of $1.5 million, either in cash dividends or in the repurchase of its own stock. If investors are expecting the cash dividend, the value of a share of stock before the dividend is paid will be $63—that is, $3 a share in expected dividends ($1.5 million/500,000) plus the $60 market price. Suppose, however, that the firm chooses to repurchase its stock and makes a tender offer to stockholders at $63 a share. It then will be able to repurchase $1.5 million/$63, or 23,810 shares. Earnings per share will be

$$EPS = \$2,000,000/476,190 = \$4.20$$

If the price/earnings ratio stays at 15, the total market price per share will be $63 ($4.20 × 15), the same total value as under the dividend alternative. Thus the amount of distribution to stockholders is $3 per share, whether dividends or repurchase of stock (and subsequent capital gain) is used. If stockholders are indifferent between dividends and capital gains, the value of the stock is not influenced by the way the funds are returned to stockholders.

We have seen in the preceding chapter, however, that this indifference is open to question. If investors have a systematic preference either for current dividends or for capital gains, the value of the firm may be affected by the method of distribution.

The benefit arising from the repurchase of stock is that the total number of shares is reduced so that earnings per share (and dividends per share if a constant dividend-payout ratio is maintained) are increased. If the price/earnings ratio remains unchanged, the market price of the stock will increase.

In our example, the equilibrium repurchase price to offer was $63 a share. If a lower price were offered, stockholders who sold their shares would suffer a decrease in wealth relative to those who retained their stock. A higher price would result in a redistribution of wealth in favor of those who sold their shares. The equilibrium price the firm should offer in a repurchase is[7]

$$P^* = P_x + \frac{D}{S}$$

(12-1)

where P_x = market price per share on an ex-dividend basis

D = aggregate amount the firm wishes to distribute

S = number of shares outstanding prior to the distribution

With a differential tax rate on dividends and capital gains, however, repurchase of stock offers a considerable tax advantage over payment of dividends. The market-price increase resulting from a repurchase of stock is subject to the capital gains tax; whereas dividends are taxed at the higher ordinary income tax rate. It is important to recognize that if an investor manufactures a "homemade" dividend by selling off sufficient stock to match the cash dividend that otherwise would have been paid, the proceeds realized are not entirely subject to the capital gains tax. Only the excess of the price realized over original cost is subject to taxation. Capital gains arising from the repurchase are not taxed on the remainder of the investor's holdings until such stock is actually sold. In essence, the bulk of the capital gains tax is postponed. For tax reasons, then, the investor usually is better off financially if the firm elects to distribute unused funds via the stock repurchase route than through cash dividends.[8]

---

[7]See Edwin Elton and Martin Gruber, "The Effect of Share Repurchases on the Value of the Firm," *Journal of Finance,* 23 (March 1968), 136–37.

[8]If existing stockholders are equivalent with respect to tax treatment, their wealth is enhanced by an amount equal to the difference between the marginal income tax rate and marginal capital gains tax rate, times the aggregate amount of cash the firm wishes to distribute (ibid., pp. 138–39). Elton and Gruber go on to explore modifications of this amount due to the postponement and incidence of the capital gains tax, and to various types of costs associated with paying a dividend and undertaking a repurchase. With the heterogeneous tax treatment of stockholders, the preferred method of distribution will depend upon the composition of stockholders.

The repurchase of stock is particularly advantageous when the firm has a large amount of unused funds to distribute. To pay the funds out through an extra dividend would result in a substantial tax to stockholders. The tax effect could be alleviated somewhat by paying the funds out as extra dividends over a period of time, but this action might result in investors' counting on the extra dividend. The firm must be careful not to undertake a steady program of repurchase in lieu of paying dividends. The Internal Revenue Service is likely to regard such a program as an attempt to allow stockholders to avoid the payment of taxes on dividends; accordingly, it may impose a penalty.[9] Hence it is important that the repurchase of stock be somewhat of a "one-shot" nature and not be used as a substitute for regular dividends or even for recurring extra dividends.

Investment or Financing Decision?

Some regard the repurchase of stock as an investment decision instead of a dividend decision. Indeed, in a strict sense, it is. However, stock held in the treasury does not provide an expected return as other investments do. No company can exist by investing only in its own stock. The decision to repurchase should involve distribution of unused funds when the firm's investment opportunities are not sufficiently attractive to employ those funds, either now or in the foreseeable future. Therefore the repurchase of stock cannot be treated as an investment decision as we define the term.

Repurchase may be regarded as a financing decision, however, provided its purpose is to alter the capital structure proportions of the firm. By issuing debt and repurchasing stock, a firm can immediately change its debt-to-equity ratio toward a greater proportion of debt. In this case, the repurchase of stock is a financing decision, because the alternative is not to pay out dividends. Only when there is excess cash can the repurchase of stock be treated as a dividend decision.

Method of Repurchase

The two most common methods of repurchase are through a tender offer and through the purchase of stock in the marketplace. With a tender offer, the company makes a formal offer to stockholders to purchase so many shares, typically at a set price. This bid price is above the current market

---

[9]One should recognize that the tax consequences involved in the repurchase of stock are complex and, in places, ambiguous. In most cases, the monies received by stockholders tendering their shares are subject to the capital gains tax. Under certain circumstances, however, the distribution can be treated as ordinary income to the redeeming stockholder. If the stockholder's percentage of ownership of the company after the tender is greater than 0.80 of his ownership percentage prior to the tender, the repurchase can be treated as ordinary income by the Internal Revenue Service. This problem can be avoided, however, if the company obtains an advance ruling from the IRS that the repurchase of stock is not equivalent to a dividend.

price; stockholders can elect to either sell their stock at the specified price or continue to hold it. Typically the tender-offer period is between two and three weeks. If stockholders tender more shares than originally sought by the company, the company may elect to purchase all or part of the excess. However, it is under no obligation to do so. In general, the transaction costs to the firm in making a tender offer are much higher than those incurred in the purchase of stock in the open market. The principal costs involve the fee paid to the investment banker who manages the repurchase and the fees paid to soliciting dealers.

In open-market purchases, a company buys its stock through a brokerage house in the same manner as any other investor. Usually, the brokerage fee is negotiated. If the repurchase program is gradual, its effect is to drive up the price of the stock. Also, certain Security and Exchange Commission rules restrict the manner in which a company bids for its shares. As a result, it takes an extended period of time for a company to accumulate a relatively large block of stock. For these reasons, the tender offer is more suitable when the amount of stock the company seeks is large.

Before the company repurchases stock, it is important that stockholders be informed of the company's intentions. In a tender offer, these intentions are announced by the offer itself. Even here, however, it is important that the company not withhold other information. For example, it would be unethical for a mining company to withhold information of a substantial ore discovery while making a tender offer to repurchase shares.

In open-market purchases, it is especially important to disclose the company's repurchase intentions. Otherwise, stockholders may sell their stock not knowing that a repurchase program is under way that will increase earnings per share. Given full information about the amount of repurchase and the objective of the company, the stockholder can sell his stock if he so chooses. Without proper disclosure, the selling stockholder may well be penalized.[10] When the amount of stock repurchased is substantial, a tender offer is particularly suitable, for it gives all stockholders equal treatment.

PROCEDURAL AND LEGAL ASPECTS

Declaration of Dividends

When the board of directors of a corporation declares a cash dividend, it specifies a *date of record*. At the close of business that day, a list of stockholders is drawn up from the stock transfer books of the company. Stockholders on the list are entitled to the dividend, whereas stockholders who come on the books after the date of record are not entitled to the

---

[10]For a discussion of the ethics surrounding repurchase, see Richard Stevenson, "Corporate Stock Reacquisitions," *Accounting Review*, 41 (April 1966), 312–17.

dividend. To illustrate, suppose the members of the board of directors of United Chemical Company meet on May 8 and declare a dividend of 25 cents a share payable June 15 to stockholders of record on May 31. If Jennifer Doakes owns the stock on May 31, she is entitled to the dividend even though she might sell her stock prior to the dividend actually being paid on June 15.

However, there is a problem in the sale of stock in the days immediately prior to the date of record. The reason is that the buyer and the seller of the stock have several days to settle; that is, to pay for the stock or to deliver it in the case of the seller. As a result, the company may not be notified of the stock transfer in sufficient time. For this reason, the brokerage community has a rule whereby a new stockholder is entitled to the dividend only if he purchases the stock four business days prior to the date of record. If the stock is purchased after that time, the stockholder is not entitled to the dividend. The date itself is known as the *ex-dividend date.* In our example, the date of record was May 31. If this were a Friday, four business days before would be May 27, and this would be the ex-dividend date. In order to receive the dividend, a new stockholder must purchase the stock on May 26 or before. If purchased May 27 or after, the stock is said to be ex-dividend. That is, it is without the 25-cent dividend.

In the absence of a differential tax on capital gains and dividends, the market price of the stock should decline by the amount of the dividend when the stock goes ex-dividend. With a more favorable tax treatment of capital gains, however, there is an incentive to purchase the stock after it goes ex-dividend, and this occurrence may cause the market price of the stock to decline by less than the amount of the dividend. (See footnote 18 in the preceding chapter.) Because other factors influence the market price of the stock, this effect is sometimes difficult to measure. Once a dividend is declared, stockholders become creditors of the company until the dividend is actually paid; the declared but unpaid dividend is a current liability of the company.

Automatic Dividend Reinvestment Plans

In recent years, a number of large companies have instigated automatic dividend reinvestment plans (ADR plans). Under these plans, stockholders can reinvest the dividends that they would receive in the stock of the company. The stock involved can be either existing stock or newly issued stock. In the case of existing stock, a bank acting as trustee accumulates funds from all stockholders wishing to reinvest and then purchases shares in the open market. The stockholder must bear the brokerage costs, but these costs are relatively low because the trustee buys stock in volume.

When the stock is newly issued, the company merely sells additional shares. There is no fee to the stockholder in this case. From the standpoint of the company, an ADR plan enables it to raise new equity capital on a slow but steady basis. Many large companies, such as AT&T, have had favorable experiences with ADR plans. Such plans allow them to build their equity base without incurring the flotation costs and underpricing associated with a common-stock offering. However, the companies still must absorb the costs of administering the plan.[11] It is important to recognize that just because a stockholder elects to reinvest his dividends in the company, he still must pay taxes on the dividend income.

Legal Aspects

Although the legal restrictions we discuss below are unimportant in most dividend decisions, some companies are affected by them. We have already considered one type of legal restriction—namely, the restriction on dividends imposed in a bond indenture or loan agreement. Other legal restrictions have to do with capital impairment, insolvency, and excess accumulation of cash.

Capital Restriction   Although state laws vary considerably, most states prohibit the payment of dividends if these dividends impair capital. *Capital* is defined in some states as the par value of the common stock. For example, if a firm had one million shares outstanding with a $2 par value, total capital would be $2 million. If the net worth of a company were $2.1 million, the company could not pay a cash dividend totaling $200,000 without impairing capital.

Other states define capital to include not only the par value of the common stock but also the capital surplus. Under such statutes, dividends can be paid only out of retained earnings. The purpose of the capital impairment laws is to protect creditors of a corporation. For a relatively new corporation, these laws may afford creditors a degree of protection. However, for established companies that have been profitable in the past and have built up retained earnings, substantial losses will usually have been incurred before the restriction has an effect. By this time, the situation may be sufficiently hopeless that the restriction gives creditors little protection.

Insolvency   Some states prohibit the payment of cash dividends if the company is insolvent. *Insolvency* is defined either in a legal sense, as liabilities exceeding assets, or in a technical sense, as the firm's being unable to pay its creditors as obligations come due. Because the ability of the firm to pay its obligations is dependent upon its liquidity rather than upon its capital, the technical insolvency restriction gives creditors a good deal of protection. When cash is limited, a company is restricted from favoring stockholders to the detriment of creditors.

Excess Accumulation of Cash   The Internal Revenue Code prohibits the undue retention of earnings. Although *undue retention* is defined vaguely, it

---

[11]For a discussion of ADR plans, see Richard H. Pettway and R. Phil Malone, "Automatic Dividend Reinvestment Plans for Nonfinancial Corporations," *Financial Management,* 2 (Winter 1973), 11–18.

usually is thought to be retention significantly in excess of the present and future investment needs of the company. The purpose of the law is to prevent companies from retaining earnings for the sake of avoiding taxes. For example, a company might retain all its earnings and build up a substantial cash and marketable-securities position. The entire company then could be sold, and stockholders would be subject only to a capital gains tax. If the IRS can prove unjustified retention, it can impose penalty tax rates on the accumulation. Whenever a company does build up a substantial liquid position, it has to be sure that it can justify the retention of these funds to the IRS. Otherwise, it may be in order to pay the excess funds out to stockholders as dividends.

SUMMARY

The stability of dividends is felt by many to have a positive effect upon the market price of the stock. Stable dividends may tend to resolve uncertainty in the minds of investors, particularly when earnings per share drop. They also may have a positive utility to investors interested in current periodic income. Many companies appear to follow the policy of a target dividend-payout ratio, increasing dividends only when it is felt that an increase in earnings can be sustained. The use of an extra dividend permits a cyclical company to maintain a stable record of regular dividends while paying additional dividends whenever earnings are unusually high.

Other considerations that affect the cash-dividend policy of the firm include the liquidity of the company; its ability to borrow; the desire to maintain control; the nature of the company's stockholders; the timing of investment opportunities; dividend restrictions in a bond indenture or loan agreement; and the impact of inflation on the replacement of assets.

A stock dividend represents the payment of additional stock to stockholders. It is used frequently as a means to conserve cash and to reduce the cash dividend-payout ratio of the firm. Theoretically, the stock dividend does not represent a thing of value to the stockholder unless cash dividends per share remain unchanged or are increased. However, stock dividends may have informational content with respect to earnings and may serve to keep the market price per share in a popular trading range. A much more effective device for reducing market price per share is a stock split. With a split, the number of shares is increased by the terms of the split—for example, a three-for-one split means that the number of shares is tripled.

A company's repurchase of its own stock should be treated as a dividend decision when the firm has funds in excess of present and foreseeable future investment needs. It may distribute these funds either by dividends or by the repurchase of a stock. In the absence of a tax differential between dividends and capital gains, the monetary value of the two alternatives should be about the same. With the tax differential, there is a considerable tax advantage to the repurchase of stock. Because of objections by the Internal Revenue Service, however, repurchase of stock cannot be used in lieu of regular dividends. Repurchases can be accomplished either with a tender offer or through purchases in the open market. In either case, the repurchase intentions of the company should be made clear to stockholders.

Finally, we discussed the procedures by which dividends are declared, automatic dividend reinvestment plans, and various legal restrictions on the payment of dividends which on occasion may influence the dividend policy of the firm.

PROBLEMS

1.

The Sherill Corporation capital structure Dec. 30, 19X1	
Common stock ($1 par, 1,000,000 shares)	$1,000,000
Capital surplus	300,000
Retained earnings	1,700,000
Net worth	$3,000,000

The firm earned $300,000 after taxes in 19X1, and paid out 50 percent of this in cash dividends. The price of the firm's stock on December 30 was $5.

(a) If the firm declared a stock dividend of 3 percent on December 31, what would be the reformulated capital structure?

(b) Assuming the firm paid no stock dividend, what would be earnings per share for 19X1? How much would dividends per share be?

(c) Assuming a 3 percent stock dividend, what would EPS and DPS be for 19X1?

(d) What would the price of the stock be after the 3 percent dividend?

2.

Zoppo Manufacturers capital structure Dec. 30, 19X1	
Common stock ($100 par, 300,000 shares)	$ 30,000,000
Excess over par	15,000,000
Retained earnings	55,000,000
Net worth	$100,000,000

On December 31, Zoppo split the stock 2-for-1 and then declared a 10 percent stock dividend. The price of the stock on December 30 was $500. Reformulate the capital structure of the firm.

3. The Sampson Company is owned by several wealthy New York businessmen, all of whom are in the 70 percent marginal income tax bracket. The firm earned $3,500,000 after taxes this year. With one million shares outstanding, earnings per share were thus $3.50. The stock has recently traded at $72 per share, among the current shareholders. Two dollars of this value is accounted for by investor anticipation of a cash dividend. As financial manager of Sampson, you have contemplated the alternative of repurchasing the company stock by means of a tender offer at $72 per share.

(a) How much stock could the firm repurchase if this alternative were selected?
(b) Ignoring taxes, which alternative should be selected?
(c) Considering taxes, which alternative should be selected?
(d) What might preclude the firm from choosing the preferred alternative?

4. The Axalt Corporation and the Baxalt Corporation have had remarkably similar earnings patterns over the last five years. In fact, both firms have had identical earnings per share. Further, both firms are in the same industry, produce the same product, and face the same business and financial risks. In short, these firms are carbon copies of each other in every respect but one: Axalt pays out a constant percentage of its earnings (50 percent) in dividends, while Baxalt has paid a constant cash dividend. The financial manager of the Axalt Corporation has been puzzled however by the fact that the price of his firm's stock has been generally lower than the price of Baxalt's stock, even though in some years Axalt's dividend was substantially larger than Baxalt's.

(a) What might account for this condition?
(b) What might be done by both companies to increase the market prices of their stock?

	Axalt			Baxalt		
Year	EPS	Div.	Mkt. Price	EPS	Div.	Mkt. Price
19X1	$1.00	.50	$6	$1.00	.23	$4⅞
19X2	.50	.25	4	.50	.23	4⅜
19X3	− .25	nil	2	− .25	.23	4
19X4	.30	.15	3	.30	.23	4¼
19X5	.50	.25	3½	.50	.23	4½

5. The Xavier Cement Company has hired you as a financial consultant to advise the company with respect to its dividend policy. The cement industry has been very stable for some time, and the firm's stock has not appreciated significantly in market value for several years. However, the rapidly growing southwestern market provides an excellent opportunity for this old, traditionally midwestern cement manufacturer to undertake a vigorous expansion program into a new market area. To do so, the company has decided to sell common stock for equity capital in the near future. The company expects its entrance into the southwestern market to be extremely profitable—returning approximately 25 percent on

investment each year. Below you will find data on earnings, dividends, and common-stock prices.

	19X1	19X2	19X3	19X4	Anticipated 19X5
Earn./share	$ 4.32	$ 4.17	$ 4.61	$ 4.80	$ 4.75
Cash avail./share	$ 6.00	$ 5.90	$ 6.25	$ 6.35	$ 6.25
Dividend/share	$ 2.90	$ 2.80	$ 3.00	$ 3.20	?
Payout ratio	67%	67%	65%	67%	?
Avg. market price	$60.00	$58.00	$60.00	$67.00	$66.00
P/E ratio	14/1	14/1	13/1	14/1	14/1

What dividend policy recommendations would you make to the company? Specifically, what payout would you recommend for 19X5? Justify your position.

6. The Davis Company, a large manufacturing concern, is a rapidly growing corporation. It has consistently earned over 20 percent on its investment in assets, and prospects for the future appear to be equally good. In the past, the company has retained about 30 percent of its earnings, paying out 70 percent in dividends. The firm's management has justified this payout policy on two grounds: (1) that a company exists for purposes of paying dividends to stockholders, and (2) that the dividends paid by the company have a favorable effect on the price of the company's stock.

   (a) Evaluate the management's justification of its dividend policy in light of the fact that most of the firm's stockholders are middle-aged businesspersons in rather high marginal income tax brackets.

   (b) What other factors would you, as a financial manager, take into consideration in deciding the appropriate dividend policy in addition to those considered by the Davis management?

7. The Carales Copper Company declared a 25 percent stock dividend on March 10 to stockholders of record on April 1. The market price of the stock is $50 per share. You own 160 shares of the stock.

   (a) If you sold your stock on March 20, what would be the price per share, all other things the same?

   (b) After the stock dividend is paid, how many shares of stock will you own?

   (c) At what price would you expect the stock to sell on April 2, all other things the same?

   (d) What will be the total value of your holdings before and after the stock dividend, all other things the same?

8. On February 2, 1980, the board of directors of International Zinc and Iron Corporation met and declared a 20-cent-per-share cash dividend payable March 20 to stockholders of record on March 1.

   (a) If you wished to buy the stock before it went ex-dividend, by what date would you need to make your purchase?

   (b) If you already own the stock but the company declares bankruptcy on March 10, what happens to your dividend?

Bar-Yosef, Sasson, and Lawrence D. Brown, "Reexamination of Stock Splits Using Moving Averages," *Journal of Finance,* 32 (September 1977), 1069–80.

Bierman, Harold, Jr., and Richard West, "The Acquisition of Common Stock by the Corporate Issuer," *Journal of Finance,* 21 (December 1966), 687–96.

Brittain, John A., *Corporate Dividend Policy,* Washington, D.C.: Brookings Institution, 1966.

Copelan, Thomas E., "Liquidity Changes Following Stock Splits," *Journal of Finance,* 34 (March 1979), 115–42.

Elton, Edwin J., and Martin J. Gruber, "The Cost of Retained Earnings—Implications of Share Repurchase," *Industrial Management Review,* 9 (Spring 1968), 87–104.

——, "The Effect of Share Repurchases on the Value of the Firm," *Journal of Finance,* 23 (March 1968), 135–50.

——, "Marginal Stockholder Tax Rates and the Clientele Effect," *Review of Economics and Statistics,* 52 (February 1970), 68–74.

Fama, Eugene F., Lawrence Fisher, Michael Jensen, and Richard Roll, "The Adjustment of Stock Prices to New Information," *International Economic Review,* 10 (February 1969), 1–21.

Ferris, Kenneth R., Arie Melnik, and Alfred Rappaport, "Factors Influencing the Pricing of Stock Repurchase Tenders," *Quarterly Review of Economics and Business,* 18 (Spring 1978), 31–39.

Griffin, Paul A., "Competitive Information in the Stock Market: An Empirical Study of Earnings, Dividends and Analysts Forecasts," *Journal of Finance,* 31 (May 1976), 631–50.

Hausman, W. H., R. R. West, and J. A. Largay, "Stock Splits, Price Changes, and Trading Profits: A Synthesis," *Journal of Business,* 45 (January 1971), 69–77.

Johnson, Keith B., "Stock Splits and Price Changes," *Journal of Finance,* 21 (December 1966), 675–86.

Lintner, John, "Distribution of Income of Corporations," *American Economic Review,* 46 (May 1956), 97–113.

Millar, James A., "Split or Dividend: Do the Words Really Matter?" *Accounting Review,* 52 (January 1977), 52–55,

Pettway, Richard H., and R. Phil Malone, "Automatic Dividend Reinvestment Plans for Nonfinancial Corporations," *Financial Management,* 2 (Winter 1973), 11–18.

Stevenson, Richard, "Corporate Stock Reacquisitions," *Accounting Review,* 41 (April 1966), 312–17 .

Stewart, Samuel S., Jr., "Should a Corporation Repurchase Its Own Stock?" *Journal of Finance,* 31 (June 1976), 911–21.

West, Richard R., and Harold Bierman, Jr., "Corporate Dividend Policy and Preemptive Security Issues," *Journal of Business,* 42 (January 1968), 71–75.

West, Richard R., and Alan B. Brouilette, "Reverse Stock Splits," *Financial Executive,* 38 (January 1970), 12–17.

management of liquidity and current assets

13

working-capital management and efficient market considerations

INTRODUCTION

In Parts I through III, we considered the valuation of the firm under varying assumptions as to the perfection of capital markets. While the discussion involved investment in assets and financing in general, the implied focus was on fixed assets and long-term financing. By tradition perhaps more than anything else, a split has evolved between consideration of current assets (short-term financing) and fixed assets (long-term financing). *Current assets,* by accounting definition, are assets normally converted into cash within one year. Working-capital management is usually described as involving the administration of these assets—namely, cash and marketable securities, receivables, and inventories—and the administration of current liabilities. Administration of *fixed assets* (assets normally not converted into cash within the year), on the other hand, is usually considered to fall within the realm of capital budgeting, whereas administration of long-term financing involves capital structure considerations.

In our view, this split is unfortunate, for it has tended to cloud the valuation of the firm as a whole. There is no question but that from the standpoint of the day-to-day operations of the typical financial manager, the management of current assets and liabilities occupies the bulk of his attention. Unfortunately, this repetitive concentration has tended to result in a myopic approach to such management. Most of the work dealing with working-capital management has been confined to the left-hand side of the balance sheet, where it has been directed to optimizing the levels of cash and marketable securities, of receivables, and of inventories. For the most part, the optimization process is in isolation of the optimization of other current assets and of the overall valuation of the firm.

The separation in treatment of current and fixed assets is often justified on the basis of differences in their nature. Fixed assets are said to be "lumpy" in the sense that they involve the commitment of funds to a specific asset over an extended period of time, during which the asset is thought to have limited marketability. In contrast, current assets are often viewed as a continuum of possible investment levels as opposed to investment in a specific form or type of liquid assets, receivable, or inventory. While this distinction has some validity, we feel it has been exaggerated and has resulted in an isolation of current-asset decisions from fixed-asset decisions and from the overall valuation of the firm. On the liability side, much less distinction exists in theory as well as in practice between current and long-term liabilities. Here the important variable is maturity, and the breakdown between current and long-term liabilities is arbitrary.

Conceptually, it does not make sense to divorce the various components of working-capital management from the more fundamental decisions of investment and financing. In practice, however, we must recognize that many firms do separate working-capital management from other aspects of financial management. In recent years, there have evolved some highly sophisticated models for cash, receivables, and inventory management. Here the benefits associated with a particular level of current asset are balanced against the risk-adjusted cost of maintaining it. While these models provide efficient decision rules, virtually all of them optimize in a partial equilibrium sense. It is clear that what is needed is an understanding of current-asset and liability decisions in light of the overall valuation of the firm.

In this chapter, we endeavor to present this conceptual understanding. In this regard, we categorize the various components of working-capital management according to the avenues by which they impact valuation. These categories are liquidity, receivables and inventories, and current liabilities. As the chapter unfolds, we will see that decisions reached in these areas determine the amount of working capital the firm maintains. However, the latter emerges as a by-product; it does not represent an active decision in itself. The discussion in this chapter is purposely general so as to provide a conceptual overview for judging working-capital decisions in relation to the valuation of the firm. Hopefully, this overview will give a better perspective for decisions involving specific current assets and liabilities, which we examine in the remaining chapters of this part and in Part V.

LIQUIDITY AND ITS ROLE

Liquidity may be defined as the ability to realize value in money, the most liquid of assets. It has two dimensions: (1) the time necessary to convert an asset into money; and (2) the degree of certainty associated with the conversion ratio, or price, realized for the asset. While most assets have a degree of liquidity, we will focus on the most liquid assets of the firm—cash and marketable securities. Liquidity management, then, involves determining the total amount of these two types of assets the firm will hold.[1] Implied is that we hold constant the credit policies and procedures of the firm, its inventory management and control, and the administration of its fixed assets, for decisions here affect the overall liquidity of the firm. Thus a narrow definition of liquidity is taken in order to simplify our discussion of certain principles.

Liquidity When Perfect Capital Markets Exist

Recall from Parts I through III that under the assumptions of perfect capital markets, a firm could not alter its value by varying its capital structure, its dividend policy, and the diversification of the assets it holds. If we invoke these assumptions again, the degree of liquidity of the firm also would be a matter of indifference to equityholders. Presumably, investors would manage their portfolios of common stocks and other assets, as well as their liabilities, in such a way as to satisfy their utility for liquidity. As a result, the liquidity of individual firms would not be a factor enhancing shareholder wealth. In essence, the argument is that the firm is unable to do something for investors that they cannot do for themselves. The same argument applies to the irrelevance of capital structure decisions (where investors are able to undertake "homemade" leverage by borrowing on their own), of dividend decisions (where investors are able to manufacture "homemade" dividends by selling a portion of their holdings), and of diversification of asset decisions (where investors are able to diversify on their own).

Implied in the assumptions of perfect capital markets is that if the firm should become technically insolvent,[2] and unable to pay its bills, creditors are able to step in instantaneously and realize value either by liquidating

---

[1]The split between the two types of assets is taken up in the subsequent chapter.

[2]*Technical insolvency* occurs whenever a firm is unable to meet its cash obligations. It differs from *insolvency* in a legal sense, which is defined as the point at which the assets of the firm are less than its liabilities, and, as a result, it has a negative net worth. See James E. Walter, "Determination of Technical Insolvency," *Journal of Business*, 30 (January 1957), 30–43.

assets, by running the company themselves, or by effecting a costless reorganization. If the assets are sold, assumed is that they are employed productively without delay or inefficiency in other areas of the economy. When we allow for the costs of bankruptcy, a market imperfection, liquidity may become a desirable characteristic affecting value.

Recall from our earlier discussion of bankruptcy costs in Chapter 9 that there are two dimensions to such costs. The first is the "shortfall" arising from the liquidation of assets at "distress" prices below their economic values. The second is the out-of-pocket fees paid to lawyers, trustees in bankruptcy, referees, receivers, liquidators, and so forth. Embodied in the "shortfall" phenomenon is the fact that considerable delays are involved in bankruptcy proceedings during which time the firm and its value can continue to deteriorate. With respect to out-of-pocket costs, certain studies show that administrative costs approximate 20 percent of the estate.[3] Although the documentation of bankruptcy costs is sketchy, there appear to be a number of inefficiencies in bankruptcy proceedings which make administrative costs high.

Liquidity Management with Bankruptcy Costs

In effect, bankruptcy costs represent a drain in the system to suppliers of capital. This drain obviously works to the disadvantage of equityholders, who have a residual claim on assets in liquidation. Moreover, creditors may pass on all or part of the ex ante costs of bankruptcy in the form of higher interest rates on loans than would be the case in the absence of such costs. This obviously also works to the disadvantage of equityholders. Investors are unable to diversify away the costs of bankruptcy. However, the firm can reduce the probability of bankruptcy by maintaining liquidity.

This reduction may benefit stockholders, particularly if by avoiding bankruptcy and its associated costs in one period through maintaining liquidity, future states are likely to prevail where bankruptcy does not occur. Under these circumstances, bankruptcy costs could be avoided altogether, and considerable benefits would accrue to stockholders as residual owners of the firm. Thus the firm may be able to do something for stockholders that they cannot do for themselves. If bankruptcy is merely postponed, bankruptcy costs will eventually be incurred. Whether or not stockholders benefit in this case depends on the circumstances, but it is clear that if they do benefit it will be to a much lesser degree than in the previous case.

As liquidity is increased, the probability of technical insolvency can be reduced. The benefits associated with this reduction will depend on the magnitude of bankruptcy costs avoided. To illustrate with a simple example, suppose we have a two-period model. Assume the initial probabilities of insolvency and the bankruptcy costs shown in the upper panel of Table 13-1.

---

[3]See, for example, David T. Stanley and Marjorie Girth, *Bankruptcy: Problem, Process, Reform* (Washington, D.C.: Brookings Institution, 1971).

table 13-1
Illustration of bankruptcy costs

Period 1			Period 2		
State	Probability	Present Value of Bankruptcy Costs	State	Probability	Present Value of Bankruptcy Costs
Zero Liquidity					
Insolvency	0.2	$1,000			
Insolvency	0.2	$500			
Solvency	0.6	0	Insolvency	0.1	$500
			Solvency	0.9	0
$20,000 Liquidity					
Insolvency	0.1	$750			
Solvency	0.9	0	Insolvency	0.1	$1,000
			Insolvency	0.2	$500
			Solvency	0.7	0
$40,000 Liquidity					
Insolvency	0.1	$750			
Solvency	0.9	0	Insolvency	0.2	$700
			Solvency	0.8	0

Let us suppose further that if insolvency occurs, creditors will initiate bankruptcy proceedings and liquidate the company. As a result, bankruptcy costs will be incurred. We assume then that all of the costs of bankruptcy are borne by equityholders.[4] The upper panel of the table gives the probability of insolvency in periods 1 and 2, together with the present values of bankruptcy costs, under the assumption that no liquidity is maintained. Note that in period 1 there are two states in which insolvency occurs, each with a different present value of bankruptcy costs. The expected value of present-value bankruptcy costs for the situation of zero liquidity is

$$(.2)(\$1,000) + (.2)(\$500) + (.6)(.1)(\$500) = \$330 \qquad (13\text{-}1)$$

Suppose now that the firm were considering maintaining initial liquidity levels of $20,000 and $40,000 and that these levels changed the probabilities of insolvency and bankruptcy costs to those figures shown in the middle and lower panels of Table 13-1, respectively. The expected value of present-value bankruptcy costs when the firm maintains an initial liquidity level of $20,000 is

$$(.1)(\$750) + (.9)(.1)(\$1,000) + (.9)(.2)(\$500) = \$255 \qquad (13\text{-}2)$$

[4]This is due to debtholders' charging higher interest rates than would otherwise be the case. In practice, some type of sharing of bankruptcy costs may occur between debtholders and equityholders. For ease of illustration, however, we assume that such costs are borne entirely by equityholders.

while that for a $40,000 initial liquidity level is

$$(.1)(\$750) + (.9)(.2)(\$700) = \$201 \tag{13-3}$$

Thus, by increasing liquidity from zero to $20,000, the expected value of present-value bankruptcy costs can be lowered from $330 to $255. By increasing it from $20,000 to $40,000, the expected value is lowered from $255 to $201. In this situation, then, there are positive benefits associated with maintaining liquidity; it lowers the probability of insolvency in period 1 as well as the joint probability of bankruptcy occurring during the two periods.

Benefits Relative to Cost

Against the benefits associated with maintaining liquidity, one must balance the cost. In the final analysis, liquidity must be raised through financing. In a general sense, its cost might be thought to be the differential in interest earned on the investment of funds in liquid assets and the cost of financing. If the firm could both borrow and lend at the same interest rate, there would be no "cost" to maintaining whatever level of liquidity was desired to reduce the probability of technical insolvency. If imperfections exist in the capital markets which result in the borrowing rate exceeding the lending rate, however, there is a "cost" to maintaining liquidity. Under these conditions, a tradeoff exists between the benefits associated with liquidity and the cost of maintaining it. The optimal level of liquidity then could be determined by marginal analysis.

While quantification of this tradeoff is complex,[5] our purpose has been to explore the problem in concept. The important thing to remember is that justification for maintaining cash and marketable securities depends on the presence of certain market imperfections which render financial markets less than perfect. In particular, one needs to concentrate on bankruptcy costs and differences in the borrowing and lending rates of the firm. Even with these imperfections, however, the firm could avoid or at least reduce the possibility of bankruptcy if it had ready access to external financing. Instead of using a liquidity buffer, it would simply raise funds externally to offset a downside deviation in operating cash flows. In this way the firm would be able to meet its creditor and contractual debt obligations, but it would not need to maintain liquidity in order to do so. However, if there are flotation costs associated with external financing, this alternative becomes less attractive.[6] In addition to out-of-pocket flotation costs, there may be imperfections that cause delays in the ability of the firm to bring about external financing.

[5]A state-preference approach to the problem is shown in James C. Van Horne, "Corporate Liquidity and Bankruptcy Costs" (Research paper, Stanford Graduate School of Business, 1975).

[6]For an analysis of this issue as well as that of liquidity in general, see James H. Scott, Jr., "The Effects of Investment in Marketable Securities on Corporate Valuation" (Research paper, Graduate School of Business, Columbia University, August 1976).

Both of these factors would strengthen the case for liquidity to reduce the possibility, and hence the cost, of bankruptcy.

Thus the important thing in establishing a case for a firm maintaining any liquidity is the presence of market imperfections which make liquidity a thing of value. If the various imperfections discussed can be approximated, it is possible to determine in theory at least the appropriate level of liquid assets the firm should maintain. While we will propose more practical means for looking at the problem in subsequent chapters, it is important to keep in mind the valuation of liquid assets in a market context. In the absence of specific imperfections in financial markets, liquidity management is not a thing of value to shareholders.

RECEIVABLES AND INVENTORIES

Receivables and inventories can, and should, be evaluated from much the same perspective as fixed assets, whose evaluation we took up in Part III. Many capital-budgeting projects embody receivables and inventories as well as a fixed-asset component. Examples include a new distribution system where a new warehouse is involved and a new-product decision where manufacturing facilities must be added. As discussed earlier, the thing that tends to differentiate receivables and inventories from fixed assets is that much of the analysis of the former is framed in terms of overall levels, whereas analysis of the latter is framed in terms of specific assets. From the standpoint of the overall valuation of the firm, however, this distinction is unimportant. Capital-budgeting projects can be evaluated as a package of assets.

Analysis in a Market Context

If an overall market valuation approach is employed to analyze risky investments, the package can be judged using the capital-asset pricing model. Recall from the applications of this model in Chapters 7 and 8 that the appropriate discount rate for a risky investment proposal is

$$R_k = i + \frac{R_m - i}{\sigma_m^2}(r_{km}\sigma_k\sigma_m)$$

(13-4)

where R_k = required rate of return for investment project k

i = risk-free rate

R_m = expected rate of return on the market portfolio

σ_m = standard deviation of the probability distribution of possible returns for the market portfolio

σ_k = standard deviation of the probability distribution of possible returns for project k

r_{km} = correlation between rates of return for proposal k and the market portfolio

figure 13-1
Required rate of
return for an
investment in
receivables and/or
inventories

The term $(r_{km}\sigma_k\sigma_m)$ is the covariance of returns for project k with those of the market portfolio, whereas $(R_m - i)/\sigma_m^2$ represents the market equilibrium relationship between excess returns and risk. As we know from before, Eq. (13-4) can be expressed as

$$R_k = i + (R_m - i)\beta_k \qquad (13\text{-}5)$$

where β_k is a measure of the responsiveness of excess market returns on the project to excess returns on the market portfolio. This term is known as the beta of the asset, and it portrays the degree of systematic risk. According to the capital-asset pricing model, the relevant risk of an investment project is its systematic risk. This is the risk that remains in the firm's stock after efficient diversification.

The reader is referred to Chapter 7 for an illustration of how this approach may be used in practice. Our purpose here is to suggest that the same principles that hold for the valuation of fixed assets hold for the valuation of receivables and inventories. According to the assumptions embodied in the capital-asset pricing model, an investment project should have the same required rate of return regardless of the particular firm that undertakes it. This is illustrated in Figure 13-1, where the market-determined relationship between expected return and systematic risk is shown by the diagonal line. For a level of systematic risk equal to, say, y, the required return is found by tracing up to the diagonal line and then over to the vertical axis to point x. Thus the project requires an expected return of x or greater in order for it to be acceptable. Just because a particular project has the same required rate of return for all firms does not mean that it is equally valuable to all of them. Due to expertise and operating efficiencies, some firms will be able to generate greater profitability from the project than will other firms.

Projects that are comprised entirely of receivables, or of inventories, can be evaluated using this approach. An example of the former is a decision of whether or not to lower credit standards, where the latter might involve a decision to stock a greater number of parts. The advantage of the approach is that it allows consideration of projects with greatly different risks. A separate required rate of return is determined for each project, and this return is based on the systematic risk of the project in a market context. The lower the risk, the lower the required rate of return.

This is particularly important when it comes to projects comprised heavily of receivables and/or inventories. As these assets frequently are less risky than fixed assets, they would require a lower return. The virtue of the approach is in specifying a required rate of return low enough to take account of the project's inherent safety.

The Effect of Imperfections

In Chapter 7, we contrasted the evaluation of risky investments in a capital-asset pricing model context relative to a firm-risk context. In this regard, we suggested that to the extent the assumptions associated with perfect capital markets do not hold in practice, residual risk, or the risk remaining after systematic risk is taken into account, becomes important. When market imperfections, such as bankruptcy costs, exist, rational investors become concerned with the total risk of the firm, not just its systematic risk. Total risk, of course, is comprised of both systematic and residual risk. We then suggested the use of dual investment hurdle rates—the required return in a capital-asset pricing model context and the required return in a total firm-risk context. The more the real-world conditions involved approximate those of perfect capital markets, the greater the reliance that would be placed on the capital-asset pricing model approach; whereas the greater the imperfections that can be identified, the greater the reliance that would be placed on the total firm-risk approach.

In general, we might expect to find fewer imperfections involved in connection with a receivable investment than we would in connection with an inventory and/or a fixed-asset investment, and in certain cases fewer imperfections involved in connection with an inventory investment than in connection with a fixed-asset investment. Receivables are a financial asset rather than a real asset. In general, fewer imperfections are evident in financial markets than in product markets. If financial markets were perfect, the firm could not expect to earn an excess return on the investment in receivables. That is, it could not expect to earn a return above the required return line in Figure 13–1. Under these circumstances, it would make no difference whether receivables were held as an investment or sold in the market.[7] Only with imperfections in financial markets can excess returns

[7]See John J. Pringle and Richard A. Cohn, "Steps toward an Integration of Corporate Financial Planning," in *Management of Working Capital* (New York: West Publishing, 1974) pp. 369–75.

above the required return be earned by the firm on its investment in receivables.

In contrast to receivables, inventories represent a real asset, the same as fixed assets. However, there is reason to believe that there may be somewhat fewer imperfections in the product market for inventories than in that for fixed assets. Obviously, there are a number of exceptions to this statement, but inventories are portable and have other characteristics that give rise to fewer imperfections. The important thing to be gleaned from this discussion is that if a case can be made for the use of the capital-asset pricing model approach for evaluating fixed assets, an equally strong if not stronger case can be made for its use with receivables and inventories.

On the basis of this approach, as well as possible allowance for residual risk, decisions can be reached on investment projects of which receivables and inventories are a part. Decisions of this sort over time will determine the level of investment in these two assets. Together with a decision concerning liquidity, which was discussed in the previous section, the current assets of the firm are established. More will be said about this later. We want to turn now to the liability side of the balance sheet and examine the last facet of what has been "characterized" working-capital management.

CURRENT LIABILITIES

For purposes of present analysis, we assume that the firm has an established policy with respect to payment for purchases, labor, taxes, and other expenses. As a result, payables and accruals represent passive decision variables; they change in keeping with changes in the level of production or service offered and, in the case of taxes payable, with a change in income before taxes. In a sense, this component of current liabilities represents built-in financing; it tends to rise as the firm expands and fall as the firm contracts. (In Chapter 17, this assumption is relaxed and we analyze payables and accruals as nonpassive decision variables.)

In contrast, the other component of current liabilities, which we call the active component, should be determined as part of more basic decisions involving determination of the maturity composition and other conditions of the firm's debt. By other conditions, we mean such things as whether or not the debt is secured, the type of security, the type of call feature, and whether or not it is convertible. Determination of the total amount of debt the firm should maintain was taken up in Chapters 9 and 10 when we examined the capital structure of the firm. Our concern now is with the type of debt that should be used.

The Value Implications of Debt Maturity and Other Conditions

If perfect financial markets are assumed, not only is the debt-versus-equity question irrelevant but so are questions about the maturity and other conditions of the debt. Under this assumption, all of the firm's financial liabilities would have the same cost on a certainty-equivalent basis.[8] This statement follows from our previous discussion of arbitrage in efficient financial markets. As the argument is a familiar one by now, we need not repeat it. If imperfections exist in financial markets, however, different financial liabilities may have different certainty-equivalent costs. Such imperfections as taxes, transaction costs, flotation costs, bankruptcy costs, costs of information, and legal constraints on investing by certain institutions may make the maturity and other conditions of a firm's debt relevant considerations when it comes to their impact on value. For example, if flotation costs are roughly the same for all maturities, there will be an incentive for the firm to issue longer-term debt, all other things the same. The reason is that this financing policy would reduce the number of times the firm had to issue debt and incur flotation costs. On the other hand, the presence of bankruptcy costs might cause certain secured debt instruments to be used, whereas they would not be used in the absence of such costs.[9]

While we would not expect the impact of market imperfections with respect to maturity and other conditions of debt to be as important as they are for the question of debt-versus-equity, nonetheless some effect may exist which causes different financial liabilities to have somewhat different certainty-equivalent costs. With different certainty-equivalent costs, the firm would not be indifferent as to the type of debt instrument it issued.

Unfortunately, the differential impact of various financial liabilities has not received nearly the attention in the literature as has the debt-versus-equity question. There has been a reasonable amount of research on the call feature and some on the maturity structure of corporate debt.[10] While most of this work supports the notion of efficient markets, the empirical tests involved are not precise enough to pick out the subtle effects of market imperfections. There has been virtually no work on the effect of different types of secured positions on the value of debt. With bankruptcy costs, we would expect in theory at least that variations in the type of secured position would have an effect on the debt's value. The same principle would apply to the various protective covenants included in the loan agreement or bond indenture. These covenants give the lender greater flexibility to effect changes should the borrower's financial condition deteriorate.[11]

Clearly, much more work needs to be done on the subject. In this book, we allow for the possibility that differences in maturity and other conditions *may* result in differences, although slight, in the certainty-equivalent costs to a company of the various debt instruments available. We

[8]See Pringle and Cohn, "Steps toward an Integration," for a discussion of this point.

[9]In Chapter 18, this idea is discussed in more detail.

[10]See Chapter 21 for a review of the work on the call feature, and Chapter 17 for a discussion of maturity.

[11]For a discussion of the various protective covenants, see Chapter 18. See also James C. Van Horne, "Optimal Initiation of Bankruptcy Proceedings by Debt Holders," *Journal of Finance,* 31 (June 1976), 897–910.

assume, therefore, that these factors may be relevant considerations when it comes to structuring the financial liabilities of the firm. To assume otherwise would negate the need to examine the features of various financial instruments. In Part V, we explore the various real-world conditions associated with short- and intermediate-term debt in the hope of obtaining a better understanding of their valuation implications.

The important thing to realize in closing this section is that the amount of current liabilities the firm maintains is the result of more fundamental decisions concerning the maturity composition of its debt. Any debt with a maturity of one year or less, by accounting definition, is a current liability. However, the active component of current liabilities should not be determined in isolation, but rather as part of an overall determination of the best combination of financial liabilities for the firm. The amount of debt that falls into current liabilities is incidental.

IMPLICATIONS FOR WORKING CAPITAL

In the preceding sections of this chapter, we have presented a conceptual overview for reaching decisions concerning cash and marketable securities, receivables, inventories, and current liabilities. This overview was in keeping with an objective of maximizing the overall value of the firm. Once decisions are reached concerning these areas, the level of working capital, by definition, is also determined. However, the latter is not determined in any active decision sense, but rather falls out as a residual from the decisions made above.

Thus, working capital—current assets less current liabilities—has no economic meaning in the sense of implying some type of normative behavior. According to this line of reasoning, it is largely an accounting artifact. Working-capital management, then, is a misnomer; the working capital of the firm is not managed. Instead, the term is used to describe a category of management decisions affecting specific types of current assets and current liabilities. In turn, those decisions should be rooted in the overall valuation of the firm.

SUMMARY

In this chapter, we took up the valuation of the firm as it pertains in particular to the current assets and liabilities of the firm. We argued that in theory it does not make sense to separate decisions involving specific current assets and liabilities from the overall investment and financing decisions of the firm. Thus the distinction between current and fixed assets and between current and long-term liabilities is largely an accounting one. In practice, however, there are some characteristics associated with current assets that differentiate them somewhat from fixed assets, and these were explored.

The various components of working capital were categorized along functional lines and analyzed in keeping with the valuation of the firm in a market context. These components were liquidity, receivables and inventories, and current liabilities. We saw that theoretical justification for maintaining liquidity rests on the presence of bankruptcy costs. Given these costs, liquidity management can be a thing of value. Receivables and inventories can be evaluated in much the same manner as fixed assets by using the capital-asset pricing model. The advantage of this approach is that it allows determination of a required rate of return in keeping with the inherent safety, or lack thereof, of receivables and inventories.

The last area of concern was the current liabilities of the firm. The amount of current liabilities the firm maintains falls out as a by-product of fundamental decisions involving capital structure, and the maturity and other conditions of the debt. We then touched on the degree of imperfections in the market for financial liabilities and the implications of such imperfections. Once decisions are reached in these three areas, the level of working capital of the firm emerges as a residual.

In the subsequent chapters of Part IV, we explore the cash and marketable securities, receivables, and inventories of the firm in more detail. The analysis will purposely be partial equilibrium in nature, since most of the analytical work to date has been in this vein and managerial decisions are framed in this manner. However, the conceptual overview presented in this chapter will transcend our discussion. Hopefully, it will provide the reader with the ability to transform, or link, the decision-making problems presented in the subsequent chapters to their valuation underpinnings.

PROBLEMS

1. The Andersen Corporation has a sales level of $280,000 with a 10 percent net profit margin before interest and taxes. To generate this sales volume, the firm maintains a fixed-asset investment of $100,000. At present, the firm maintains $50,000 in current assets.

   (a) Determine the asset turnover for the firm. Compute the rate of return on assets.
   (b) What would be the rate of return if management assumed a more conservative attitude and increased current assets by $50,000?
   (c) What would be the rate of return if management assumed a less conservative attitude and decreased current assets by $25,000?
   (d) Appraise the significance of increases and decreases in the level of current assets.

2. The Amos Company has determined that the distribution of expected net cash flows (available to meet current liabilities) for the next three months is approximately normal with a mean of $500,000 and a standard deviation of $350,000. The firm now earns 16 percent on its investment in nonliquid assets; by investing in marketable securities, it could earn only 4 percent. It has been estimated that

lengthening the maturity of the firm's outstanding debt ($6 million) could reduce the outflow of cash in the following manner:

Added Length of Maturity	Reduced Cash Outflow
One year	$250,000
Two years	375,000
Three years	450,000
Four years	500,000
Five years	535,715
Six years	562,500
Seven years	583,333

Lengthening the maturity by five years or less would cost the company an additional 1 percent annually, while lengthening it by six or seven years would result in a 2 percent annual increase in interest costs.

(a) Assuming that the management of the Amos Company is willing to tolerate a 5 percent probability of running out of cash, by how much should it increase its liquid assets (or decrease cash outflows)?

(b) There are three alternatives that will reduce the probability of running out of cash to 5 percent:
 (1) Increase liquid assets
 (2) Lengthen maturity of debt
 (3) A combination of (1) and (2)
 Which alternative is best from the standpoint of management?

3. The George T. Booker Company is considering increasing its inventory investment in glass fibers by $200,000 in order to give customers better service. It has found in the past that the sale of such fibers closely parallels the Gross National Product. On the basis of this observation, Mr. Booker, the company's president, feels that the underlying risk of the inventory investment is "about that of a typical stock listed on the New York Stock Exchange."

 At present the rate on Treasury bills is 6 percent, and in recent years the average return on Standard & Poor's 500-stock index has been 12 percent. The Booker Company has an all-equity capital structure and intends to finance all new investment proposals entirely with equity.

(a) On the basis of this information, what is the required rate of return on the investment?

(b) On what does this required return depend? Is it a realistic acceptance criterion to employ?

4. The Zakuta Fish Company is in a cyclical and risky business. By maintaining liquidity, it lowers the possibility of going into bankruptcy. It is estimated that if bankruptcy were to occur, there would be a $100,000 present-value shortfall in what suppliers of capital would realize from the book value of the assets. This "cost" of bankruptcy is attributable to legal expenses and the sale of assets at distress prices. By maintaining the following levels of liquidity, the probabilities of bankruptcy occurring are:

Level of Liquidity	Probability of Bankruptcy
$25,000	0.30
50,000	0.20
75,000	0.15
100,000	0.12
125,000	0.10
150,000	0.08
175,000	0.06
200,000	0.05
225,000	0.04
250,000	0.03

Liquidity is increased by borrowing and it is held in the form of marketable securities. Marketable securities yield less than the interest rate the company must pay on short-term borrowings. The present-value differential amounts to $1,500 for each $25,000 borrowed. If we assume no taxes, and no other explicit or implicit costs associated with debt, what is the optimal level of liquidity?

SELECTED REFERENCES

BIERMAN, H., K. CHOPRA, AND J. THOMAS, "Ruin Considerations: Optimal Working Capital and Capital Structure," *Journal of Financial and Quantitative Analysis*, 10 (March 1975), 119–28.

BUDIN, MORRIS, AND ROBERT J. VAN HANDEL, "A Rule-of-Thumb Theory of Cash Holdings by Firm," *Journal of Financial and Quantitative Analysis*, 10 (March 1975), 85–108.

KEOWN, ARTHUR J., and JOHN D. MARTIN, "A Chance Constrained Goal Programming Model for Working Capital Management," *Engineering Economist*, 22 (Spring 1977), 153–74.

KNIGHT, W. D., "Working Capital Management—Satisficing versus Optimization," *Financial Management*. 1 (Spring 1972), 33–40.

MEHTA, DILEEP R., *Working Capital Management*. Englewood Cliffs, N.J.: Prentice-Hall, 1974.

MERVILLE, L. J., AND L. A. TAVIS, "Optimal Working Capital Policies: A Chance-Constrained Programming Approach," *Journal of Financial and Quantitative Analysis*, 8 (January 1973), 47–60.

MORRIS, JAMES R., "A Model for Corporate Debt Maturity Decisions," *Journal of Financial and Quantitative Analysis*, 11 (September 1976), 339–58.

SCOTT, JAMES H., "The Effects of Investment in Marketable Securities on Corporate Valuation." Research paper, Graduate School of Business, Columbia University, August 1976.

SILVERS, J. B., "Liquidity, Risk and Duration Patterns in Corporate Financing," *Financial Management*, 5 (Autumn 1976), 54–64.

SMITH, KEITH V., *Management of Working Capital*. New York: West Publishing, 1974.

STANCILL, JAMES McN., *The Management of Working Capital*. Scranton, Pa.: Intext, 1971.

TINSLEY, P. A., "Capital Structure, Precautionary Balances, and Valuation of the Firm: The Problem of Financial Risk," *Journal of Financial and Quantitative Analysis*, 5 (March 1970), 33–62.

VAN HORNE, JAMES C., "A Risk-Return Analysis of a Firm's Working-Capital Position," *Engineering Economist*, 14 (Winter 1969), 71–89.

WALKER, ERNEST W., "Towards a Theory of Working Capital," *Engineering Economist,* 9 (January-February 1964), 21–35.

WALTER, JAMES E., "Determination of Technical Solvency," *Journal of Business,* 30 (January 1957), 30–43.

YARDINI, EDWARD E., "A Portfolio-Balance Model of Corporate Working Capital," *Journal of Finance,* 33 (May 1978), 535–52.

14

management of cash and marketable securities

INTRODUCTION

Our concern in the preceding chapter was with the valuation implications for liquidity, receivables and inventories, and current liabilities. In this and the subsequent two chapters, we examine the firm's investment in specific current assets. Our purpose is to investigate ways in which these assets can be managed efficiently so as to contribute to the overall objective of the firm. This chapter is devoted to cash management and the investment of excess funds in marketable securities. In the last twenty-five years, we have witnessed ever-increasing sophistication in cash management by corporations. The trend has been toward reducing cash—the firm's most liquid asset—to a minimum; the funds released are invested in earning assets. This trend can be attributed to rising interest rates on securities, which make the opportunity cost of holding cash more expensive, to innovations in cash management, and to economies of scale in cash management as corporations grow larger.

Keynes has identified three motives for holding cash: the transactions motive, the precautionary motive, and the speculative motive.[1] The transactions motive is the need for cash to meet payments arising in the ordinary course of business. These payments include such things as purchases, labor, taxes, and dividends. The precautionary motive for holding cash has to do with maintaining a cushion or buffer to meet unexpected contingencies. The more predictable the cash flows of the business, the less precautionary balances that are needed. Ready borrowing power to meet emergency cash drains also reduces the need for this type of balance. It is important to point out that not all of the firm's transactions and precautionary balances need be held in cash; indeed, a portion may be held in marketable securities—near-money assets.

The speculative motive relates to the holding of cash in order to take advantage of expected changes in security prices. When interest rates are expected to rise and security prices to fall, this motive would suggest that the firm should hold cash until the rise in interest rates ceases. When interest rates are expected to fall, cash may be invested in securities; the firm will benefit by any subsequent fall in interest rates and rise in security prices. For the most part, companies do not hold cash for the purpose of taking advantage of expected changes in interest rates. Consequently, we concentrate only upon the transactions and precautionary motives of the firm, with these balances held both in cash and in marketable securities.

The Function of Cash Management

Cash management involves managing the monies of the firm in order to attain maximum cash availability and maximum interest income on any idle funds. At one end, the function starts at the point at which a customer writes a check to pay the firm on its accounts receivable. The function ends at the point at which a supplier, an employee, or the government receives payment by the firm on an account payable or accrual. All activities between these two points fall within the realm of cash management. Efforts by the firm to affect the point at which a customer pays its bill fall within accounts receivable management. On the other hand, the decision by the firm as to when to pay a bill involves accounts payable and accrual management.

The cash management function usually is carried out by the treasurer's office of a company. Instrumental in the process is a cash budget, which is a forecast, usually monthly, of receipts and disbursements. As the preparation of a cash budget is discussed in Chapter 26, where we consider the tools of financial analysis and control, it will not be taken up here. The cash budget tells us the likely availability of cash with respect to both timing and magnitude. In other words, it tells us how much cash we are likely to

---

[1]John Maynard Keynes, *The General Theory of Employment, Interest, and Money* (New York: Harcourt, Brace & Jovanovich, 1936), pp. 170–74.

have, when, and for how long. As suggested in Chapter 26, it is important to take uncertainty into account, and this can be done by preparing multiple cash budgets under alternative assumptions. Thus the cash budget serves as a foundation for cash planning and control.

In addition to the cash budget, the firm needs to have systematic information on cash as well as some kind of control system. Usually the information is computer based as opposed to manually based. In either case, it is important to obtain frequent reports, preferably daily or even more often, on cash balances in the bank by account, on the cash disbursed, on the average daily balances, and on the marketable security position of the firm as well as a detailed report of changes in this position.[2] Also, it is useful to have information on major anticipated cash receipts and cash disbursements. All of this information is essential if a firm is to manage its cash in an efficient manner.

MANAGING COLLECTIONS

In this section, we analyze various collection and disbursement methods by which a firm can improve its cash management efficiency. These methods constitute two sides of the same coin; they exercise a joint impact on the overall efficiency of cash management. The general idea is to collect accounts receivable as soon as possible while paying accounts payable as late as is consistent with maintaining the firm's credit standing with suppliers. We consider first the acceleration of collections, or reducing the delay between the time a customer pays his bill and the time the check is collected and becomes usable funds for the firm. A number of methods have been employed to speed up this collection process and maximize available cash. These methods are designed to do one or all of the following: (1) speed the mailing time of payments from customers to the firm; (2) reduce the time during which payments received by the firm remain uncollected funds; and (3) speed the movement of funds to disbursement banks.

The second item represents float, and this entails two aspects. The first is the time it takes a company to process checks internally. This interval extends from the moment a check is received to the moment it is deposited with a bank for credit to the company's account. The second aspect of float involves the time consumed in clearing the check through the banking system. A check becomes collected funds when it is presented to the drawee bank and actually paid by that bank. In order to streamline the availability of credit, the Federal Reserve System has established a schedule specifying

---

[2]For a method of daily cash forecasting that uses statistical techniques to estimate cash-flow patterns, see Bernell K. Stone and Robert A. Wood, "Daily Cash Forecasting: A Simple Method for Implementing the Distribution Approach," *Financial Management,* 6 (Fall 1977), 40–50.

availability for all checks deposited with it for collection. This schedule is based upon the average time required for a check deposited with a particular Federal Reserve bank to be collected in a particular geographical area of the country. However, the maximum period for which credit is deferred is two days. This means that even if a check is not actually collected through the Federal Reserve System within two days, it becomes collected funds because the Federal Reserve carries the float. Float is important to the financial manager because usually a company cannot make withdrawals on a deposit until the checks in that deposit are collected. As the name of the game is usable funds, the financial manager wants to reduce float as much as possible. In what follows, we examine various ways to speed up the collection process so as to have more usable funds.

Concentration Banking

Concentration banking is a means of accelerating the flow of funds of a firm by establishing strategic collection centers. Instead of a single collection center located at the company headquarters, multiple collection centers are established. The purpose is to shorten the period between the time a customer mails in his payment and the time when the company has the use of the funds. Customers in a particular geographic area are instructed to remit their payments to a collection center in that area. The selection of the collection centers usually is based upon the geographic areas served and the volume of billings in a given area. When payments are received, they are deposited in the collection center's local bank. Surplus funds are then transferred from these local bank accounts to a concentration bank or banks. A bank of concentration is one with which the company has a major account—usually a disbursement account. For example, a company headquartered in New York City might have but one concentration bank, a New York bank. Concentration banking is one way to reduce the size of the float, the difference between the amount of deposit and the amount of usable funds in a bank.

An Illustration   To illustrate concentration banking and the transfer of funds, we examine the case of an actual large company with over twenty collection centers. At the time of the study, each collection center billed customers in its area and made daily deposits in its local bank of payments received from customers. On the average, the checks deposited in a bank were collected in one and one-fourth days. In other words, the company had use of the funds one and one-fourth days after deposit. In each of its local banks, the company maintained sufficient collected balances to compensate the bank for the costs of servicing the account.

A daily *wire transfer* arrangement was used to transfer collected balances in excess of compensating balances to one of several concentration banks. The managers of the collection centers initiated the transfer on the basis of a daily report of estimated collected balances from their local banks.

Because the wire transfers were made through the Federal Reserve System, the funds transferred became available immediately at the concentration banks.

This method of transfer differs from a *depository transfer check* arrangement for the movement of funds, whereby a depository check is drawn on the local bank, payable to a concentration bank. Funds are not immediately available at the concentration bank, for the check must be collected through the usual channels. Whereas a transfer check costs considerably less than a wire transfer, it is not as fast. The delay must be analyzed in relation to the difference in cost. For small transfers, a wire transfer may be too costly compared with a depository transfer check. In other words, the earnings possible on investing the released funds may not cover the differential in cost.

The advantage of a system of decentralized billings and collections over a centralized system is twofold. (Recall that we compare a system of multiple collection centers with a single collection center located at company headquarters.)

1. The time required for mailing is reduced. Because the collection center bills customers in its area, these customers usually receive their bills earlier than if the bills were mailed from the head office. In turn, when customers pay their bills, the mailing time to the nearest collection center is shorter than the time required for the typical remittance to go to the head office. The company estimated that there was a saving of approximately one day in mailing time from the customer to the company.

2. The time required to collect checks is reduced, because remittances deposited in the collection center's local bank usually are drawn on banks in that general area. The company estimated that the average collection period would be two days if all remittances were deposited in the company's head office bank, compared with one day under the present system. At the margin, then, the company was able to speed up the collection of customer checks by one day.

Thus the company was able to accelerate overall collections by two days; one day was gained by reducing the mailing time and one day by reducing the time during which deposited checks remain uncollected. At the time of the study, average daily remittances by customers were $2.1 million. By saving two days in the collection process, approximately $4.2 million in funds were released for investment elsewhere. With a high level of interest rates, it is not difficult to see the opportunity cost of tying up funds. However, profits from the investment of the released funds must be compared with any additional costs of a decentralized system over a centralized one. Also, it is important to consider any differences between the two systems in total compensating balances. The greater the number of collection centers, the greater the number of local bank accounts that must be maintained.

Another means of accelerating the flow of funds is a lock-box arrangement. With concentration banking, remittances are received by a collection center and deposited in the bank after processing. The purpose of a lock-box arrangement is to eliminate the time between the receipt of remittances by the company and their deposit in the bank. A lock-box arrangement usually is on a regional basis, with the company choosing regional banks according to its billing patterns. Before determining the regions to be used, a feasibility study is made of the availability of checks that would be deposited under alternative plans. In this regard, operation research techniques have proved useful in the selection of lock-box sites.[3] If a company divided the country into five sections on the basis of a feasibility study, it might pick New York City for the Northeast, Atlanta for the Southeast, Chicago for the Midwest, Dallas for the Southwest, and San Francisco for the West Coast.

The company rents a local post office box and authorizes its bank in each of these cities to pick up remittances in the box. Customers are billed with instructions to mail their remittance to the lock box. The bank picks up the mail several times a day and deposits the checks in the company's account. The checks are microfilmed for record purposes and cleared for collection. The company receives a deposit slip and a list of payments, together with any material in the envelope. This procedure frees the company from handling and depositing the checks.

The main advantage of a lock-box system is that checks are deposited at banks sooner and become collected balances sooner than if they were processed by the company prior to deposit. In other words, the lag between the time checks are received by the company and the time they actually are deposited at the bank is eliminated. The principal disadvantage of a lock-box arrangement is the cost. The bank provides a number of services additional to the usual clearing of checks and requires compensation for them, usually preferring increased deposits. Because the cost is almost directly proportional to the number of checks deposited, lock-box arrangements usually are not profitable if the average remittance is small.

The appropriate rule for deciding whether or not to use a lock-box system, or, for that matter, concentration banking, is simply to compare the added cost of the most efficient system with the marginal income that can be generated from the released funds. If costs are less than income, the system is profitable; if not, the system is not a profitable undertaking. The degree of profitability depends primarily upon the geographical dispersion of customers, the size of the typical remittance, and the earnings rate on the released funds. Although there is disagreement as to what earnings rate to

---

[3]See Ferdinand K. Levy, "An Application of Heuristic Problem Solving to Accounts Receivable Management," *Management Science*, 12 (February 1966), 236–44; and Robert F. Calman, *Linear Programming and Cash Management/CASH ALPHA* (Cambridge, Mass.: M.I.T. Press, 1968), Chap. 4.

use, the most appropriate rate for our purpose is the rate on marketable securities. Because a decision as to the total amount of liquid assets to maintain was considered in Chapter 13, our present decision affects mainly the proportion of cash to marketable securities, not their sum. Thus the opportunity cost of tying up funds in cash is the return forgone on marketable securities.

management of cash and
marketable securities

Other Procedures

Frequently, firms give special attention to the handling of large remittances so that they may be deposited in a bank as quickly as possible. This special handling may involve personal pickup of these checks or the use of airmail or special delivery. When a small number of remittances account for a large proportion of total deposits, it may be worthwhile to initiate controls to accelerate the deposit and collection of these large checks. Instead of processing all checks for collection through the Federal Reserve System, some commercial banks offer special services where high-dollar-volume checks are presented directly to the drawee bank. The benefit is a speedup in collection of these checks, and it is passed on to the bank customer in having usable funds more quickly.

In addition to these techniques, the firm should exercise tight control over interbank transfers of cash and transfers between various units of the company, such as divisions or subsidiaries. Excessive funds may be tied up in various divisions of the firm.

Some companies maintain too many bank accounts, thereby creating unnecessary pockets of idle funds. A company that has an account in every city where it has either a sales office or a production facility might be able to reduce cash balances considerably if it were to eliminate some of these accounts. The banking activities of a sales office can often be handled from a larger account with little loss in service or availability of funds. Even though small accounts may create a degree of goodwill with bankers, they make little sense in the overall cash management of the firm. By closing such unnecessary accounts, a firm may be able to release funds that it then can put to profitable use.

CONTROL OF DISBURSEMENTS

In addition to accelerating collections, effective control of disbursements can result in a faster turnover of cash. Whereas the underlying objective of collections is maximum acceleration, the objective in disbursements is to slow them down as much as possible. The combination of fast collections and slow disbursements will result in maximum availability of funds.

One way of maximizing cash availability is "playing the float." In the case of disbursements, float is the difference between the total dollar amount of checks drawn on a bank account and the balance shown on the bank's books. It is possible, of course, for a company to have a negative balance on its books and a positive bank balance, because checks outstanding have not been collected from the account on which they are drawn. If the size of float can be estimated accurately, bank balances can be reduced and the funds invested to earn a positive return.

For a company with multiple banks, it is important to be able to shift funds quickly to those banks from which disbursements are made, to prevent excessive balances from building up temporarily in a particular bank. Operating procedures for disbursements should be well established. If cash discounts are taken on accounts payable, procedures should aim toward eliminating or minimizing the loss of discounts due to clerical inefficiencies. The timing of payments is important. For maximum use of cash, payments should be made on the due dates, not before and not after.

A company can delay disbursements through the use of drafts. Unlike an ordinary check, the draft is not payable on demand. When it is presented to the issuer's bank for collection, the bank must present it to the issuer for acceptance. The funds then are deposited by the issuing firm to cover payment of the draft. The advantage of the draft arrangement is that it delays the time the firm actually has to have funds on deposit to cover the draft. Consequently, it allows the firm to maintain smaller deposits at its banks. A possible disadvantage of a draft system is that certain suppliers may prefer checks. Also, banks do not like to process drafts because they require special attention, usually manual. As a result, banks typically impose a much higher service charge to process them than they do to process ordinary checks.

When a company has multiple bank accounts located throughout the country, the opportunities for "playing the float" expand. Taking advantage of inefficiencies in the check-clearing processes of the Federal Reserve System and of certain commercial banks as well as inefficiencies in the postal system, a firm may maximize the time the checks it writes remain outstanding. Various models have been proposed to maximize disbursement float through the selection of geographically optimal disbursing banks.[4] The idea is to locate disbursing banks and to draw checks on them in such a way as to maximize the time a check will remain outstanding. For example, a check payable to a supplier in Arizona might be drawn on a bank in Portland, Maine. The solution depends on the location of and the amount of billings from suppliers, procedural delays in the banking system associated with various supplier location–disbursing bank location combinations, and the cost of banking services whether it be compensating balances or fees.

By maximizing disbursement float, the firm can reduce the amount of cash it holds and employ these funds in more profitable ways. However, one firm's gain is another firm's loss. Maximizing disbursement float means that suppliers will not have collectible funds as early as would otherwise be the

---

[4]See Lawrence J. Gitman, D. Keith Forrester, and John R. Forrester, Jr., "Maximizing Cash Disbursement Float," *Financial Management,* 5 (Summer 1976), 15–24, for such an approach. The authors treat the problem as a warehouse location problem and solve it heuristically.

case. To the extent that they look with disfavor on such payment habits, supplier relations may be hurt. If so, this factor must be taken into account in planning disbursements.

Payroll Disbursements

Many companies maintain a separate account for payroll disbursements. In order to minimize the balance in this account, one must predict when the payroll checks issued will be presented for payment. If payday falls on a Friday, for example, not all of the checks will be cashed on that day. Consequently, the firm need not have funds on deposit to cover its entire payroll.[5] Even on Monday, some checks will not be presented due to delays in their deposit. Based upon its experience, the firm should be able to construct a distribution of when, on the average, checks are presented for collection. An example is shown in Figure 14-1. With this information, the firm can approximate the funds it needs to have on deposit to cover payroll checks.

However, this information is not enough. The firm also needs to know the magnitude of possible deviations from expected outcomes. On the first day, Friday, suppose the firm expects the probability distributions of possible outcomes shown in Figure 14-2. The actual balance maintained will depend upon the risk tolerances of management. If management is willing to tolerate insufficient cash with a 2 percent probability, it would maintain approximately 39 percent of the total payroll on deposit on Friday. The outcome on the second day depends upon what happened the first day. For example, if a small percentage of employees present checks for collection on Friday, the percentage presented for collection on Monday and succeeding days will be larger than would otherwise be the case. Consequently, it is necessary to develop a series of conditional probabilities of outcomes, given the outcome on preceding days. If transfers from the general account can be consummated rapidly, there is no reason why a firm cannot predict ahead one day at a time.

figure 14-1
**Percentage of payroll
checks collected**

[5]See James McN. Stancill, *The Management of Working Capital* (Scranton, Pa.: Intext, 1971), pp. 19–22.

figure 14-2
Probability distribution of payroll collected the first day

As a result, the complexity of the problem is reduced; only one probability distribution need be projected at a time. Similar to the payroll account, many firms establish a separate account for dividends. Here too the idea is to predict when such checks will be presented for payment so as to minimize the cash balance in the account.[6]

Electronic Transfers and Banking

In recent years, we have witnessed substantial changes in the way bills are paid. This progress has come about because of changes in financial institution regulation and because of advances in computer information systems as well as in electronic communications. Regulatory changes have focused on permitting greater competition among financial institutions. Commercial banks have been authorized to offer a variety of savings accounts and time deposits not only to individuals but to businesses and to state and local governments. On the other hand, nonbank deposit institutions have been allowed to issue accounts that have most of the attributes of checking accounts. For both types of institutions, the purpose of savings deposits has been extended to allow their partial use as a payments mechanism. Preauthorized transfers between checking and savings accounts have permitted customers to make more efficient use of their checking accounts and to draw interest on idle funds.

The second aspect of the changing environment is the increased sophistication in computer applications to cash management and in electronic funds transfers. As individuals, we all are aware of plastic cards with magnetic coding which can be used to obtain cash, to transfer funds from one account to another, to pay bills, to borrow, and to do other things. These transactions can occur at a financial institution, at an unmanned electronic payments machine that is open twenty-four hours a day, and at certain retail stores. With respect to the last, one is able to pay for a purchase with such a card, as funds are transferred electronically from the customer to the store.

[6]See Stancill, *Management of Working Capital*, pp. 20–21.

The advantage to the retailer is obvious; he is assured that the payment for the purchase is good and it is immediate. Retailers also can reduce the possibility of bad checks by using guarantee systems that a number of banks offer. With such a system, a customer's check is scanned electronically and verified by computer. Because the bank guarantees the checks it verifies, the retailer is not exposed to bad-check losses. Electronic banking also is used to automatically deposit payrolls to employee accounts, to make dividend and other payments, and to transfer funds nationally and internationally. The net result is faster and more efficient financial services.

Because electronic banking is capital intensive, the cost per transaction is reduced as volume increases. Indeed this has occurred in recent years; and a good deal of the savings is passed along to users of financial services. The reason the customer benefits is that competition among financial institutions and large retailers that provide financial services is intense. For the firm, electronic banking means less time in the collection of receivables, more efficient control of cash, and, perhaps, a reduction in servicing costs.

Thus the use of electronic banking techniques can result in greater economization of money balances. In turn, the movement toward these techniques depends in part on the level of interest rates in financial markets. The greater the interest rate, of course, the greater the opportunity cost of holding cash and the more attractive electronic banking techniques become, all other things the same. However, the use of a new cash management technique typically involves significant start-up costs. As a result, once a new method is in place, there is a tendency to keep it even if interest rates should decline somewhat thereafter. Therefore the shifting to new cash techniques is not linearly related to interest rates prevailing in financial markets, but rather is a ratchet type of function.

As mentioned earlier, optimizing cash availability involves accelerating collections as much as possible and delaying payments as long as is realistically possible. Because delaying payments may damage the firm's credit standing, the resulting cost to the firm must be taken into account. In the future, we can expect to see further improvements in electronic money-payment transactions. As we move toward a "checkless society," the time funds remain uncollected becomes shorter. In a checkless society where transfers are made through computers, payments will be immediate. There will be no uncollected funds, for one party's account will be debited the instant another's is credited. Although the firm's deposits will be collected faster, so too will the checks it writes. Whether it gains or loses will depend upon the typical float on checks deposited relative to the float on checks written.

Compensating Balances and Fees

Establishing a minimum level of cash balances depends in part upon the compensating balance requirements of banks. These requirements are set on the basis of the profitability of the accounts. A bank begins by calculating the average collected balances shown on the bank's books over a period of time. As brought out before, this balance often is higher than the cash balance shown on the company's books. From the average collected balance, the bank subtracts the percentage of deposits it is required to maintain at the Federal Reserve, around 16 percent. The residual constitutes the earnings base on which income is generated. Total income is determined by multiplying the base times the earnings rate of the bank. This rate fluctuates in keeping with money-market conditions.

Once the income from an account is determined, the cost of the account must be computed. Most banks have a schedule of costs on a per item basis for such transactions as transfers and processing checks. The account is analyzed for a typical month during which all transactions are multiplied times the per item cost and totaled. If the total cost is less than the total income from the account, the account is profitable; if more, it is unprofitable. The minimum average level of cash balances required is the point at which the account is just profitable. Because banks differ in the earnings rate they use as well as in their costs and method of account analysis, the determination of compensating balances varies. The firm, therefore, may be wise to shop around and determine the bank that requires the lowest compensating balances for a given level of activity. If a firm has a lending arrangement with a bank, the firm may well be required to maintain balances in excess of those required to compensate the bank for the activity in its account. Because we consider compensation for a lending arrangement in Chapter 17, no discussion of this form of compensation will be undertaken at this time.

In recent years, there has been a marked trend toward paying cash for services rendered by a bank instead of maintaining compensating balances. The advantage to the firm is that it may be able to earn more on funds used for compensating balances than the fee for the services. The higher the interest rate in the financial markets, the greater the opportunity cost of compensating balances and the greater the advantage of service charges. It is an easy matter to determine if the firm would be better off with service charges as opposed to maintaining compensating balances. One simply compares the charges with the earnings on the funds released. Some banks resist placing normal services, such as clearing checks, on a fee basis. Nevertheless, an increasing number of bank services are being offered on such a basis. Indeed, competition dictates it. The balances maintained at a bank and the services the bank performs should be analyzed carefully. If deposits are more than compensating, funds may be tied up unnecessarily.[7] Where a service offered can

---

[7]Linear programming has been used to structure a firm's banking relations and to determine a minimum level of cash balances. See Calman, *Linear Programming and Cash Management/CASH ALPHA*. The objective function of his model is to minimize the total cost of the banking system to the firm, subject to various levels of activities requiring banking services. Gerald A. Pogue, Russell B. Faucett, and Ralph N. Bussard, "Cash Management: A Systems Approach," in *Management of Working Capital*, ed. Keith V. Smith (New York: West Publishing, 1974), pp. 77–90, approach the problem in a similar manner, as does Bernell K. Stone, "Allocating Credit Lines, Planned Borrowing, and Tangible Services over a Company's Banking System," *Financial Management*, 4 (Summer 1975), 65–78, although additional factors are considered. For an extensive linear-programming model that deals with cash management of the firm as a whole, see Yair E. Orgler, *Cash Management* (Belmont, Calif.: Wadsworth, 1970), Chaps. 3–6.

better be paid for by a fee, the firm should be alert to take advantage of the situation and reduce its compensating balances.

BALANCING CASH AND MARKETABLE SECURITIES

Given the overall level of transactions and precautionary balances, we wish to consider the appropriate split between cash and marketable securities. Because these securities can be converted into cash on very short notice, they serve the precautionary need of the firm to hold cash. The level of cash, which in turn determines the level of marketable securities given our assumptions, should be the *greater* of two constraints. The first is the compensating balance requirement of a commercial bank. This requirement is expressed in terms of an average cash balance over some period of time rather than a minimum below which cash cannot fall. The second constraint is self-imposed, and it is determined by the need for cash, the predictability of this need, the interest rate on marketable securities, and fixed cost of effecting a transfer between marketable securities and cash. This constraint should be determined apart from the first constraint, and, as suggested, the optimal level of cash is the greater of the two constraints. Because we have already discussed the determination of the compensating balance constraint, we turn now to the second constraint.

If the future were known with certainty, it would be an easy matter to determine the optimal split between cash and marketable securities. Projected cash would be invested as long as the interest earnings exceeded transactions and inconvenience costs, and as long as the delays in conversion between cash and marketable securities did not hinder the firm in paying its bills. If transactions and inconvenience costs were zero and conversion between the two assets were instantaneous, the firm would hold no cash. It simply would sell securities to pay its bills. When transactions and inconvenience costs are positive, however, the firm will want to hold cash when the expected holding period for investment is not long enough to earn sufficient interest to offset them. By the same token, with conversion delays, the firm may need to hold cash. Thus, even if future cash flows were known with certainty, a firm would probably hold some cash.

Inventory Model

Under conditions of certainty, one simple model for determining the optimal average amount of transaction cash is the economic order quantity formula (EOQ) used in inventory management (see Chapter 16). It provides a useful conceptual foundation for the cash management problem.[8] In the

---

[8]The model was first applied to the problem of cash management by William J. Baumol, "The Transactions Demand for Cash: An Inventory Theoretic Approach," *Quarterly Journal of Economics*, 66 (November 1952), 545–56. It has been further refined and developed by a number of others.

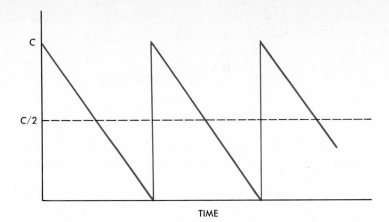

figure 14-3
Inventory model
applied to cash
management

TIME

model, the carrying cost of holding cash, namely the interest forgone on marketable securities, is balanced against the fixed cost of transferring marketable securities to cash, or vice versa. The model is illustrated by the sawtooth lines in Figure 14-3.

In the figure, we assume that the firm has a steady demand for cash over some period of time, say one month. The firm obtains cash during this period by selling marketable securities. Suppose it starts out with C dollars in cash, and when this amount is expended, it replenishes it by selling C dollars of marketable securities. Thus the transfer of funds from securities to cash occurs whenever cash touches zero. If a cushion is desired or if there are lead times to effect a transaction, the threshold for initiating a transfer can be higher. The principle is the same regardless of whether or not a cushion is used.

The objective is to specify the value of C that minimizes total costs—that is, the sum of the fixed costs associated with transfers and the opportunity cost of earnings forgone by holding cash balances. These costs can be expressed as

$$b\left(\frac{T}{C}\right) + i\left(\frac{C}{2}\right)$$

(14-1)

where b is the fixed cost of a transaction that is assumed to be independent of the amount transferred, T is the total demand for cash over the period of time involved, and i is the interest rate on marketable securities for the period involved (assumed to be constant). T/C represents the number of transactions during the period, and when it is multiplied times the fixed cost per transaction, we obtain the total fixed cost for the period. $C/2$ represents the average cash balance, and when it is multiplied times the interest rate, we obtain the earnings forgone by virtue of holding cash. The larger the C, the larger the average cash balance, $C/2$, and the smaller the average investment in securities and earnings from these securities. Thus there is a higher opportunity cost

of interest income forgone. However, the larger the C, the fewer the transfers,
T/C, that occur and the lower the transfer costs. The object is to balance
these two costs so that total costs are minimized.

The optimal level of C is found to be

$$C^* = \sqrt{\frac{2bT}{i}}$$

(14-2)

when the derivative of Eq. (14-1) with respect to C is set equal to zero. Thus
cash will be demanded in relation to the square root of the dollar volume of
transactions. This phenomenon implies that as the level of cash payments
increases, the amount of transaction cash the firm needs to hold increases by
a lesser percentage. In other words, economies of scale are possible. The
implication is that the firm should try to pool individual bank accounts into as
few as possible in order to realize economies in cash management. This does
not mean that the firm cannot maintain control over the pooled accounts.
Accounting records are kept for each of the accounts and control is maintained; the accounts are pooled only to take advantage of economies of scale
available in cash management.

We see also in Eq. (14-2) that C^* varies directly with the fixed cost, b,
and inversely with the interest rate on marketable securities, i.[9] The greater
the fixed cost of transfers between cash and marketable securities, the fewer
the transfers that will take place and the higher the cash balance, all other
things the same. The greater the interest rate, the greater the opportunity cost
of holding cash and the lower the cash balance, all other things the same.
However, in both cases, the relationship is dampened by the square-root sign.

To illustrate the use of the EOQ formula, consider a firm with estimated cash payments of $6 million for a one-month period where these
payments are expected to be steady over the period. The fixed cost per
transaction is $100 and the interest rate on marketable securities is 6 percent
per annum, or 0.5 percent for the one-month period. Therefore,

$$C = \sqrt{\frac{2bT}{i}} = \sqrt{\frac{2(100)(6,000,000)}{.005}} = \$489,898$$

Thus the optimal transaction size is $489,898 and the average cash balance
$489,898/2 = \$244,949$. This means the firm should make $6,000,000/$489,898
$= 12 +$ transactions of marketable securities to cash during the month.

It is useful now to consider in more detail the two costs involved. The
interest rate is fairly straightforward; it simply represents the rate of interest

[9]For a study involving the effect changing interest rates have on the relative level of
cash held by the firm, see Morris Budin and Robert J. Van Handel, "A Rule-of-Thumb Theory of
Cash Holdings by Firms," *Journal of Financial and Quantitative Analysis*, 10 (March 1975),
85–108.

on securities that would be sold to replenish cash. In most cases, this is the rate on short-term money-market instruments and not the average rate of return on all marketable securities. The fixed cost associated with a transaction is more difficult to measure because it consists of both explicit and implied costs. Included are the fixed component of transaction costs, the time it takes the treasurer or other official to place an order with an investment banker, the time he consumes in recording the transaction, the secretarial time needed to type the transaction and the purchase order, the time needed to record the transaction on the books, and the time needed to record the safekeeping notification. Given a number of transactions, the procedures for placing an order can be streamlined to reduce the average fixed cost per transaction. Nevertheless, these costs do exist and too often are either overlooked or underestimated.

One limitation to the use of the EOQ model is that cash payments are assumed to be steady over the period of time specified. Only if this assumption is a reasonable approximation of the situation is the model applicable. When cash payments become lumpy, it may be appropriate to reduce the period for which calculations are made so that expenditures during the period are relatively steady. The EOQ model can be applied also when receipts are continuous and there are discontinuous large payments. The decision to be made then would be the optimal purchase size of marketable securities.

Another limitation to the use of the model is that cash payments are seldom completely predictable. For modest degrees of uncertainty, one need only add a cushion so that a transfer from marketable securities to cash is triggered at some level of cash above zero. In general, the EOQ model gives the financial manager a benchmark for judging the optimal cash balance. It does not have to be used as a precise rule governing his behavior. The model merely suggests what would be the optimal balance under a set of assumptions. The actual balance may be more if the assumptions do not entirely hold.

Stochastic Models

In those cases where the uncertainty of cash payments is large, the EOQ model may not be applicable and other models should be used to determine optimal behavior. If cash balances fluctuate randomly, one can apply control theory to the problem. Assume that the demand for cash is stochastic and unknown in advance. We then can set control limits such that when cash reaches an upper limit a transfer of cash to marketable securities is consummated, and when it hits a lower limit a transfer from marketable securities to cash is triggered. As long as the cash balance stays between these limits, no transactions take place.

How the limits are set depends in part upon the fixed costs associated with a securities transaction and the opportunity cost of holding cash. As before, we assume these costs are known and that the fixed cost of selling a

marketable security is the same as that for buying it. In essence, we want to
satisfy the demand for cash at the lowest possible total cost. Although there
are a number of applications of control theory to the problem, we discuss a
relatively simple one. The Miller-Orr model specifies two control limits—h
dollars as an upper bound and zero dollars as a lower bound.[10] The model is
illustrated in Figure 14-4 under the simplifying assumption that there is no
underlying trend in the cash balance over time.

We see in the figure that when the cash balance touches the upper
bound, $h - z$ dollars of marketable securities are bought and the new balance
becomes z dollars. When the cash balances touches zero, z dollars of marketable securities are sold and the new balance again becomes z. This is illustrated in the figure. The minimum bound can be set at some amount higher
than zero, and h and z would move up in the figure. However, we will use zero
as the lower bound for purposes of illustration, recognizing that a firm can set
the lower bound at some positive amount. This obviously would be necessary
if there were delays in transfer.

The solution for the optimal values of h and z depend not only upon
the fixed and opportunity costs but also upon the degree of likely fluctuation
in cash balances. The optimal value of z, the return-to-point for security
transactions, is

$$z = \sqrt[3]{\frac{3b\sigma^2}{4i}} \tag{14-3}$$

where b = fixed cost associated with a security transaction
σ^2 = variance of daily net cash flows
i = interest rate per day on marketable securities

figure 14-4
**Control limit model
applied to cash
management**

[10]See Merton H. Miller and Daniel Orr, "A Model of the Demand for Money by Firms,"
Quarterly Journal of Economics, 80 (August 1966), 413–35.

The optimal value of h is simply $3z$. With these control limits set, the model minimizes the total costs (fixed and opportunity) of cash management. Again, the critical assumption is that cash flows are random. The average cash balance cannot be determined exactly in advance, but it is approximately $(z + h)/3$. As experience unfolds, however, it can be easily calculated.[11]

The Miller-Orr model is one of a number of control-limit models designed to deal with the cash management problem under the assumption of stochastic cash flows. As long as cash remains within specified limits, no transactions take place.[12] Thus we have considered two models for determining the optimal level of cash. The EOQ model assumes cash flows are predictable, while the control-limit model assumes they are random. The average cash balance suggested by the second model will be higher than that suggested by the first for obvious reasons.

A Probability Approach

Usually the cash flows of a firm are neither completely predictable nor completely stochastic. Rather they are predictable within a range. When there is only moderate uncertainty, the EOQ model can be modified to incorporate into it a precautionary balance to buffer against uncertainty. For many firms, their cash position is reasonably predictable over the near term, and therefore the EOQ model can be employed with some degree of confidence. For these firms, a stochastic model serves primarily as a benchmark for determining cash balances under an extreme assumption with respect to predictability. As we know, the average cash balance will be considerably higher when this model is employed as opposed to the EOQ one. Thus, when average cash balances of a company are as high as or higher than those dictated by a stochastic model, and cash flows are reasonably predictable, we know the cash balance is too high. If in fact cash flows are relatively unpredictable, however, a stochastic model can be used to make automatic transfers between cash and marketable securities.

When cash flows are not reasonably predictable or reasonably unpredictable, a probabilistic approach may be employed. For example, end-of-period cash balances, exclusive of the purchase or sale of marketable securities, can be estimated for various cash-flow outcomes to form a probability distribution. The period used should be short—perhaps a few days or no longer than a week. This probabilistic information, together with

[11]In a second article, Miller and Orr, "The Demand for Money by Firms: Extension of Analytic Results," *Journal of Finance,* 23 (December 1968), 735–59, extend the model to allow for two types of securities—long-term and short-term.

[12]Peter A. Frost, "Banking Services, Minimum Cash Balances, and the Firm's Demand for Money," *Journal of Finance,* 25 (December 1970), 1029–39, extends the stochastic cash management model to incorporate varying levels of banking services. If the bank's supply function of services varies with the level of deposits, Frost contends that the minimum cash balance and the transaction balance must be determined simultaneously.

information about the fixed cost of a transfer between cash and marketable securities and the return on investment in marketable securities, is all we need to determine the proper initial balance between cash and marketable securities.

For various possible cash-flow outcomes, the expected net earnings associated with different initial levels of marketable securities can be determined. The greater the amount of securities held, of course, the greater the probability that some of those securities will have to be sold in order to meet a cash shortfall. The expected net earnings for a particular level of marketable securities is the gross interest earned on the marketable security position, less the expected fixed cost of selling securities to meet a cash shortfall and less the expected loss of interest income associated with the sale of those securities.

When calculations are undertaken for various possible levels of initial marketable security holdings, one obtains the expected net earnings associated with each level. Typically, expected net earnings rise as the level of marketable securities is increased from zero or from some low amount. With subsequent increases, however, the probability that marketable securities will have to be sold in order to meet a cash shortfall increases, as do the expected fixed costs of transfer and expected losses (in an opportunity sense) of interest income. Beyond a point, the latter more than offset the interest income on the initial marketable security holdings. The optimal level of marketable securities is the level where expected net earnings are maximized.

As the mechanics involved in such probabilistic formulations are familiar by now, we do not illustrate the probability model approach to cash management. The reader should be able to visualize the approach. Again, probability models may be used when the cash flows of the firm are neither relatively predictable nor relatively unpredictable.

Optimal Level of Cash

Depending on the situation, one of the models discussed above—the EOQ model, a stochastic model, or a probability model—can be used to determine the proper level of cash. Many of the assumptions can be modified depending upon the circumstances. Where these optimization models do not offer improvement over simpler decision rules, they should not be used.[13] Their purpose is to assist one in determining the appropriate level of investment in marketable securities. Given the level of total liquid assets, deter-

[13]For an analysis of the potential savings arising from the use of such models vis-à-vis simple heuristic cash management rules, see Hans G. Daellenbach, "Are Cash Management Optimization Models Worthwhile?" *Journal of Financial and Quantitative Analysis,* 9 (September 1974), 607–26. Only if fixed transaction costs are relatively large does Daellenbach find the use of optimization models to be worthwhile.

mination of an appropriate level of cash will also determine the level of investment in marketable securities.

Usually, the optimal level of average cash balances will be the greater of two constraints: the compensating balance requirement imposed by a bank, and the average level of cash suggested by an appropriate cash-marketable securities model. In most cases, the former will exceed the latter. However, when the fixed costs of a security transaction are high, the opportunity cost of holding cash is low, and/or cash flows are subject to great fluctuation, the average cash balance suggested by an appropriate model may be higher than that required by the bank. Therefore, average balances in excess of those considered compensating should be maintained.

In addition to these considerations, the optimal level of cash may be affected by whether a bank allows services to be paid for on a fee basis as opposed to compensating balances. If there is a fee schedule, the firm needs to compare the fee to be charged with the earnings available on the funds that would otherwise be tied up in compensating balances. Where the earnings are greater, a case can be made for the payment for bank services on a fee basis. Under this circumstance, the optimal level of cash balances can be determined by an appropriate cash-marketable securities model. However, to the extent that the firm can use the cash balance so determined as partial or full compensation to the bank for the services rendered, the fees that are paid will be reduced or eliminated altogether. As a result, a case can be made for the simultaneous consideration of all of these factors when determining an optimal cash balance.[14]

INVESTMENT IN MARKETABLE SECURITIES

Once the firm has determined an optimal cash balance, the residual of its liquid assets are invested in marketable securities. In the models examined, we assumed a given yield and no risk of fluctuations in market price. These assumptions are realistic for very short-term, high-grade securities used as a buffer to replenish cash. However, firms frequently hold securities with lesser characteristics for less immediate needs. In this section, then, we examine the types of marketable securities available to a company as near-money investments, allowing for varying yields and for fluctuations in market price. First, however, we need to explore the reasons for differences in yields on different securities. These yield differentials exist because of differences in default risk, in marketability, in length of time to maturity, and in taxability.[15]

[14]See Frost, "Banking Services, Minimum Cash Balances, and the Firm's Demand for Money."

[15]Callability also affects the yield to maturity. Because the marketable securities position of most firms is confined to short-term securities, it usually is not an important factor. The call feature, however, is analyzed in Chapter 21 from the standpoint of an issuer of long-term debt.

Default Risk

When we speak of default risk, we mean the risk that the borrower will not satisfy the contractual obligation to make principal and interest payments. Investors are said to demand a risk premium to invest in other than default-free securities.[16] The greater the possibility that the borrower will default on his obligation, the greater the financial risk and the premium demanded by the marketplace. Treasury securities are usually regarded as default-free, and other securities are judged in relation to them. For example, U.S. government agency issues might be rated next to Treasury securities in credit-worthiness. For all practical purposes, these securities are default-free. The credit-worthiness of other obligations is frequently judged on the basis of security ratings. Moody's Investors Service and Standard & Poor's, for example, grade corporate and municipal securities as to their quality. The greater the default risk of the borrower, the greater the yield of the security should be, all other things held constant. By investing in riskier securities, the firm can achieve higher returns, but it faces the familiar tradeoff between expected return and risk.

Marketability

Marketability of a security relates to the ability of the owner to convert it into cash. There are two dimensions: the price realized and the amount of time required to sell the asset. The two are interrelated in that it is often possible to sell an asset in a short period of time if enough price concession is given. For financial instruments, marketability is judged in relation to the ability to sell a significant volume of securities in a short period of time without significant price concession. The more marketable the security, the greater the ability to execute a large transaction near the quoted price. In general, the lower the marketability of a security, the greater the yield necessary to attract investors. Thus the yield differential between different securities of the same maturity is caused not only by differences in default risk but also by differences in marketability.

Maturity

The relationship between yield and maturity can be studied graphically by plotting yield and maturity for securities differing only in the length of time to maturity. In practice, this means holding constant the degree of default risk. For example, we could study the yield-maturity relationship for default-free Treasury securities. An example of the yield-maturity rela-

---

[16]For an extended discussion of default-risk premiums and of the empirical tests involving such premiums, see James C. Van Horne, *Financial Market Rates and Flows* (Englewood Cliffs, N.J.: Prentice-Hall, 1978), Chap. 6.

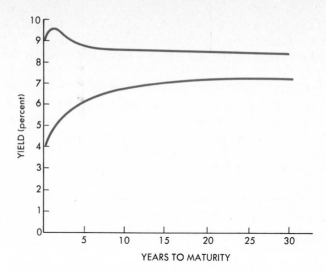

figure 14-5
Examples of Treasury
yield curves

tionship for Treasury securities on two separate dates is shown in Figure 14-5. Maturity is plotted on the horizontal axis and yield on the vertical; their relationship is described by a yield curve fitted to the observations.

Generally, when interest rates are expected to rise, the yield curve is upward-sloping, whereas it is humped and somewhat downward-sloping when they are expected to fall significantly. However, the yield differential between short- and long-term securities is greater for the steepest upward-sloping yield curve than the negative difference is for the steepest downward-sloping yield curve. In other words, there is a tendency toward positive-sloped yield curves. Most economists attribute this tendency to the presence of risk for those who invest in long-term securities vis-à-vis short-term securities. In general, the longer the maturity, the greater the risk of fluctuation in the market value of the security. Consequently, investors need to be offered a risk premium to induce them to invest in long-term securities. Only when interest rates are expected to fall significantly are they willing to invest in long-term securities yielding less than short- and intermediate-term securities.[17]

Some firms try to take advantage of an upward-sloping yield curve by "riding the yield curve," which involves selling securities before they mature. By investing in 182-day Treasury bills, for example, and selling them before maturity, a firm may be able to obtain a significantly higher return for the holding period than by holding the bills to maturity. If 182-day bills yield 6 percent and 91-day bills 5 percent, and the firm buys the 182-day bills now and sells them 91 days later at a yield of 5 percent, its return per annum for the holding period is 7.2 percent. This example assumes that the yield curve does not change over the holding period. Ignoring transaction costs, the investor

---

[17]For a much deeper discussion of this concept, see Van Horne, *Financial Market Rates and Flows*, Chap. 4.

buys the 182-day bills at a price of $97, at which price they yield 6 percent to maturity, and sells them 90 days later for $98.75, where they yield 5 percent to maturity. Thus he realizes a holding-period yield of $(1.75/97)(365/91) = 7.2$ percent.

A second aspect of "riding the yield curve" involves taking advantage of expected shifts in interest rates. If interest rates are expected to fall, the firm will invest in long-term securities because these securities tend to have the greatest increase in market price when interest rates are falling. When the interest rate cycle is thought to have bottomed out, long-term securities will be sold and the firm will invest in very short-term securities, to assure a minimum of market-price decline if interest rates rise. Playing the yield curve in this manner involves risk, because expectations may prove to be wrong. Consequently, a firm that holds marketable securities as near-money investments to meet possible cash drains should be careful not to undertake such an operation on too large a scale.

Taxability

Another factor affecting observed differences in market yields is the differential impact of taxes. The interest income on all but one category of securities is taxable to taxable investors. Interest income from state and local government securities is tax-exempt; as a result, they sell in the market at lower yields to maturity than Treasury and corporate securities of the same maturity. A differential impact on yields arises also because interest income is taxed at the ordinary tax rate, while capital gains on securities held more than one year are taxed at the more favorable capital gains tax rate. As a result, fixed-income securities that sell at a discount because of a low coupon rate in relation to prevailing yields are attractive to taxable investors. The reason is that part of the yield to maturity is a capital gain. Because of the desirability of discount fixed-income securities, their yield to maturity tends to be lower than the yield on comparable securities with higher coupon rates. The greater the discount, the greater the capital gains attraction and the lower its yield relative to what it would be if the coupon rate were such that the security sold at par.

We have considered four factors that explain yield differentials on different securities: default risk, marketability, maturity, and taxability. By analyzing securities in terms of these concepts, one is able to determine what one has to give up in order to obtain a higher yield. In this way, a systematic analysis of marketable securities is possible so that a portfolio is formed in keeping with the objectives of the firm.

Types of Marketable Securities

In this section, we describe briefly the more prominent marketable securities available for investment. Space prohibits the discussion of longer-term investments in this book, although corporations do invest excess funds in long-term securities that mature in the near future. Our concern is with various money-market instruments which, by definition, are highly marketable and subject to little default risk. In addition, the usual definition restricts the maturity of a money-market instrument to less than a year.

Treasury Securities U.S. Treasury obligations constitute the largest segment of the money markets. The principal securities issued are bills, tax-anticipation bills, notes, and bonds. Treasury bills are auctioned weekly by the Treasury with maturities of 91 days and 182 days. In addition, nine-month and one-year bills are sold periodically. Treasury bills carry no coupon but are sold on a discount basis. Denominations range from $10,000 to $1 million. These securities are extremely popular with companies as short-term investments, in part because of the large amount outstanding. The market is very active, and the transaction costs involved in the sale of Treasury bills in the secondary market are small.

The original maturity on Treasury notes is one to ten years, whereas the original maturity on Treasury bonds is over ten years. With the passage of time, of course, a number of these securities have maturities of less than one year and serve the needs of short-term investors. Notes and bonds are coupon issues, and there is an active market for them. Overall, Treasury securities are the safest and most marketable investments. Therefore they provide the lowest yield for a given maturity of the various instruments we consider.

Agency Securities Obligations of various agencies of the federal government are guaranteed by the agency issuing the security, but not by the U.S. government as such. Principal agencies issuing securities are the Federal Housing Administration and the Government National Mortgage Association (Ginnie Mae). In addition, there are a number of government-sponsored, quasi-private agencies. The securities of these agencies are not guaranteed by the federal government, nor is there any stated "moral" obligation. In the final analysis, however, there is an implied backing. It would be hard to imagine the federal government allowing them to fail. Major government-sponsored agencies include the Banks for Cooperatives, Federal Intermediate Credit Banks, Federal Land Banks, Federal Home Loan Banks, and the Federal National Mortgage Association (Fannie Mae). The first three agencies are part of the Farm Credit Bank System, which issues consolidated systemwide discount short-term notes and bonds in behalf of these agencies. Over time, consolidated borrowings will replace borrowings by the individual agencies.

Although agency issues are being increasingly accepted by the investment community, they still provide a modest yield advantage over Treasury securities of the same maturity. These securities have a fairly high degree of marketability; they are sold in the secondary market through the same security dealers as are Treasury securities. With the sharp increase in agency financing in recent years, marketability has been enhanced considerably. While interest income on these securities is subject to federal income taxes, for the Farm Credit agencies it is not subject to state and local income taxes. Maturities range from several days to approximately fifteen years.

However, about one-half of the securities outstanding mature in less than a year.

Bankers' Acceptances   Bankers' acceptances are drafts that are accepted by banks, and they are used in the financing of foreign and domestic trade. The credit-worthiness of bankers' acceptances is judged relative to the bank accepting the draft, not the drawer. Acceptances generally have maturities of less than six months and are of very high quality. They are traded in an over-the-counter market dominated by five principal dealers. The rates on bankers' acceptances tend to be slightly higher than rates on Treasury bills of like maturity; and both are sold on a discount basis.

Commercial Paper   Commercial paper consists of short-term unsecured promissory notes issued by finance companies and certain industrial concerns. Commercial paper can be sold either directly or through dealers. Many large sales finance companies have found it profitable, because of the volume, to sell their paper directly to investors, thus bypassing dealers. Among companies selling paper on this basis are the C.I.T. Financial Corporation, Ford Motor Credit Company, General Motors Acceptance Corporation (GMAC), and Sears Roebuck Acceptance Corporation.

Paper sold through dealers is issued by industrial companies and smaller finance companies. The dealer organization for commercial paper is dominated by three firms. Overall, the total volume of paper sold through dealers is considerably less than the total volume sold directly. Dealers screen potential issuers very carefully as to their credit-worthiness. In a sense, the dealer stands behind the paper he places with investors.

Rates on commercial paper are somewhat higher than rates on Treasury bills of the same maturity and about the same as the rates available on bankers' acceptances. Paper sold directly, however, generally commands a lower yield than paper sold through dealers. Usually, commercial paper is sold on a discount basis, and maturities generally range from 30 to 270 days. Most paper is held to maturity, for there is essentially no secondary market. However, direct sellers of commercial paper will often repurchase the paper on request. Arrangements may also be made through dealers for repurchase of paper sold through them. Commercial paper is sold only in fairly large denominations, usually of at least $25,000.

Repurchase Agreements   In an effort to tap important sources of financing, government security dealers offer repurchase agreements to corporations. The repurchase agreement, or "repo," as it is called, is the sale of short-term securities by the dealer to the investor whereby the dealer agrees to repurchase the securities at a specified future time. The investor receives a given yield while he holds the security. The length of the holding period itself is tailored to the needs of the investor. Thus, repurchase agreements give the investor a great deal of flexibility with respect to maturity. Rates on repurchase agreements are related to the rates on Treasury bills, federal funds, and loans to government security dealers by commercial banks. There is little marketability to the instrument, but the usual maturity is only a few days.

Because the instrument involved is a U.S. Treasury security, there is no default risk.

Negotiable Certificates of Deposit   Negotiable time certificates of deposit are a short-term investment that originated in 1961. The certificate (CD) is evidence of the deposit of funds at a commercial bank for a specified period of time and at a specified rate of interest. The most common denomination is $100,000, so its appeal is limited to large investors. Money-market banks quote rates on CD's; these rates are changed periodically in keeping with changes in other money-market rates. The maximum rate that banks are allowed to pay, however, is regulated by the Federal Reserve System under Regulation Q. Yields on CD's are greater than those on Treasury bills and repos and about the same as those on bankers' acceptances and commercial paper. Original maturities of CD's generally range from 30 to 360 days. A fair secondary market has developed for the CD's of the large money-market banks, so such CD's are marketable. Default risk is that of the bank failing, a possibility that is low in most cases.

Portfolio Management

The decision to invest excess cash in marketable securities involves not only the amount to invest but also the type of security in which to invest. To some extent, the two decisions are interdependent. Both should be based upon an evaluation of expected net cash flows and the certainty of these cash flows. If future cash-flow patterns are known with reasonable certainty, the portfolio may be arranged so that securities will be maturing on approximately the dates when the funds will be needed. Such a cash-flow pattern gives the firm a great deal of flexibility in maximizing the average return on the entire portfolio, for it is unlikely that significant amounts of securities will have to be sold unexpectedly.

To illustrate, suppose that the liquidity position of a firm, net of transactions cash and compensating balance requirement needs, were expected to fluctuate in the manner shown by the dotted line in Figure 14-6. While the figure shows only four months, we assume that the dotted line is not expected to decline below $900,000 over the next twelve months. Based on these projections, an appropriate investment strategy might be that shown by the horizontal bars in the figure. The bottom portion is represented by a 360-day investment in a certificate of deposit, followed by a Federal Home Loan Bank bond with about ten months to final maturity. Next the firm has invested in 91-day Treasury bills and these are expected to be renewed, or rolled over, at maturity. The other investments shown in the figure are designed to match the fluctuating pattern of cash flows shown. Finally, the remaining areas under the dotted line are assumed to be filled as much as possible with repurchase agreements. With "repos," maturities of only one or a few days can be tailored to the availability of funds for investment. Overall, then, the firm is able to match the maturities of its investments in marketable securities with its expected cash-flow patterns. In this way, it is able to

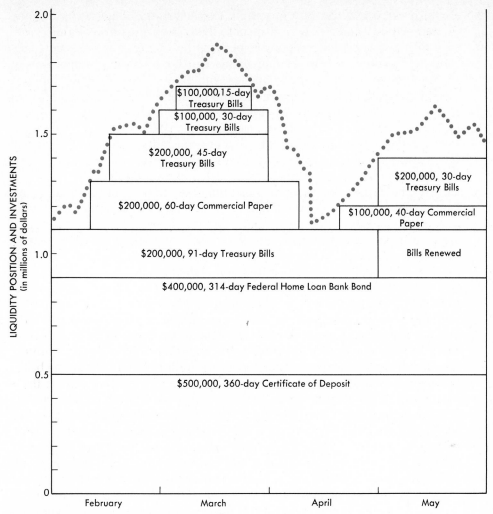

figure 14-6
**Investment strategy in relation to projected
liquidity position**

maximize its return on investment insofar as maturity decisions alone will
allow.

The key, of course, is the degree of certainty one has in the cash-flow
projections. With a high degree of certainty, the maturity of a marketable
security becomes its most important characteristic.[18] As illustrated in Figure
14-6, maturities can be arranged so as to tightly fit the availability of funds
and, hence, interest income can be maximized. However, if future cash flows

---

[18]This statement assumes that all the securities considered are of reasonably high
quality from the standpoint of default risk. Otherwise they would not fall within the usual
definition of a marketable security.

are fairly uncertain, the most important characteristics of a security become its marketability and risk with respect to fluctuations in market value. Treasury bills and short-term repos are perhaps best suited for the emergency liquidity needs of a firm. Higher yields can be achieved by investing in longer-term, less marketable securities with greater risk. Although the firm should always be concerned with risk and marketability, some possibility of loss of principal is tolerable provided the expected return is high enough. In addition to risk and marketability, transaction costs are a factor with uncertain cash flows. If securities must be sold unexpectedly, transaction costs will be incurred and their incurrence will result in a lower net return. Thus the firm faces the familiar tradeoff between risk and profitability.

The larger the security portfolio, the more chance there is for specialization and economies of operation. A large enough security portfolio may justify a staff whose sole responsibility is managing the portfolio. Such a staff can undertake research, plan diversification, keep abreast of market conditions, and continually analyze and improve the firm's position. When investment is made a specialized function of the firm, the number of different securities considered for investment is likely to be diverse. Moreover, continual effort can be devoted to achieving the highest yield possible in keeping with the cash needs of the firm. Trading techniques in such a firm tend to be very sophisticated. For companies with smaller security positions, however, there may be no economic justification for a staff. Indeed, a single individual may handle investments on a part-time basis. For this type of company, the diversity of securities in the portfolio will probably be limited.

Although diversification of the short-term marketable security portfolio of a firm might be desirable, there is far less opportunity for such diversification than there is with a portfolio of common stocks.[19] *Diversification* is usually defined as the reduction of the dispersion of possible returns from a portfolio relative to the expected return from the portfolio. This reduction is achieved by investing in securities not having high degrees of covariance among themselves. Unfortunately, there is a high degree of correlation in the price movements of money-market instruments over time. Consequently, they are ill suited for purposes of diversification. As a result, the objective of most firms is to maximize overall return subject to maintaining sufficient liquidity to meet cash drains. Because of differences in the ability to diversify, the management of a firm's marketable security portfolio differs considerably from the management of a portfolio of common stocks.

SUMMARY

The firm has three motives for holding liquid assets: the transactions motive, the precautionary motive, and the speculative motive. Our concern is with only the first two of these motives. In the management of cash, we should

---

[19]See Chapter 3 for a review of portfolio analysis and selection.

attempt to accelerate collections and handle disbursements so that maximum cash is available. Collections can be accelerated by means of concentration banking, a lock-box system, and certain other procedures. Disbursements should be handled so as to give maximum transfer flexibility and the optimum timing of payments.

Given the total level of liquid assets, comprised of cash and marketable securities, the firm must determine the optimal split between these two assets. The optimal level of cash, which in turn determines the optimal level of marketable securities, is the greater of (1) the compensating balance requirement of a commercial bank, and (2) the optimal level determined by an appropriate model. The first constraint is rather straightforward and its determination was discussed in depth. With respect to the second constraint, the optimal level of cash depends upon the predictability of future cash flows, their volatility, the fixed cost of a security transaction, and the carrying cost of holding cash—that is, the interest rate forgone on marketable securities. Several models were examined for determining an optimal level of average cash balances under varying assumptions as to the predictability and pattern of future cash flows.

There are a number of marketable securities in which the firm can invest. These securities can be evaluated in relation to their default risk, marketability, maturity, and taxability. Depending upon the cash-flow pattern of the firm and other considerations, a portfolio can be selected in keeping with these characteristics. Specific securities considered included Treasury securities, government agency securities, bankers' acceptances, commercial paper, repurchase agreements, and certificates of deposit. It was shown that the management of a firm's portfolio of marketable securities is considerably different from the management of a portfolio of common stocks.

PROBLEMS

1. Speedway Owl Company franchises Gas and Go stations in North Carolina and Virginia. All payments by franchisees for gasoline and oil products are by check, which average in total $420,000 a day. At present, the overall time between a check being mailed by the franchisee to Speedway Owl and the company having available funds at its bank is six days.

   (a) How much money is tied up with respect to this interval of time?

   (b) To reduce this delay, the company is considering picking up the checks daily from the stations by means of a car. In all, three cars would be needed and three additional people hired. The cost of this daily pickup would be $93,000 on an annual basis. This procedure would reduce the overall delay by two days. Currently, the opportunity cost of funds is 9 percent, that being the interest cost on bank borrowings. Should the company inaugurate the pickup plan?

   (c) Rather than mail checks to its bank, the company is considering delivering them by messenger service. This procedure will reduce the overall delay by one day and cost $10,300 on an annual basis. Should the company undertake this plan?

2. The Zindler Company currently has a centralized billing system. Payments are made by all customers to the central billing location. It requires, on the average, four days for customers' mailed payments to reach the central location. Further, an additional one and one-half days are required to process payments before a deposit can be made. The firm has a daily average collection of $500,000.

The company has recently considered the possibility of initiating a lock-box system. It has been estimated that such a system would reduce the time required for customers' mailed payments to reach the receipt location by two and one-half days. Further, the processing time could be reduced by an additional day, because each lock-box bank would pick up mailed deposits twice daily.

(a) Determine the reduction in cash balances that can be achieved through the use of a lock-box system.

(b) Determine the opportunity cost of the present system, assuming a 5 percent return on short-term instruments.

(c) If the annual cost of the lock-box system will be $75,000, should such a system be initiated?

3. The List Company, which can earn 7 percent on money-market instruments, currently has a lock-box arrangement with a New Orleans bank for its southern customers. The bank handles $3 million a day in return for a compensating balance of $2 million.

(a) The List Company has discovered that it could divide the southern region into a southwestern region (with $1 million a day in collections, which could be handled by a Dallas bank for a $1 million compensating balance) and a southeastern region (with $2 million a day in collections, which could be handled by an Atlanta bank for a $2 million compensating balance). In each case, collections would be one-half day quicker than with the New Orleans arrangement. What would be the annual savings (or cost) of dividing the southern region?

(b) In an effort to retain the business, the New Orleans bank has offered to handle the collections strictly on a fee basis (no compensating balance). What would be the maximum fee the New Orleans bank could charge and still retain List's business?

4. The Frazini Food Company has a weekly payroll of $150,000, paid on Friday. On average, its employees cash their checks in the following manner:

Day Check Cleared on Company's Account	Percent of Checks Cashed
Friday	20
Monday	40
Tuesday	25
Wednesday	10
Thursday	5

As treasurer of the company, how would you arrange your payroll account? Are there any problems involved?

5. The Schriver Company plans to have $1 million in steady cash outlays for next year. The firm believes that it will face an opportunity interest rate of 5 percent

and will incur a cost of $100 each time it borrows (or withdraws). Cash outlays are expected to be steady over the year. Using the inventory model:

(a) Determine the transactions demand for cash (the optimal borrowing or withdrawal lot size) for the Schriver Company.
(b) What is the total cost for the use of cash needed for transactions demand?
(c) What will be the cash cycle for the firm (in days)?
(d) What would be the average cash balance for the firm?

6. Assume that the Schriver Company (problem 5) began the year with $1 million in cash.

(a) How much would initially be invested in securities?
(b) How much would be invested in securities after 231 days?

7. The Verloom Berloop Tulip Bulb Company has experienced a stochastic demand for its product with the result that cash balances fluctuate randomly. The standard deviation of daily net cash flows, σ, is $1,000. The company wishes to make the transfer of funds from cash to marketable securities and vice versa as automatic as possible. It has heard that this can be done by imposing upper and lower bound control limits. The current interest rate on marketable securities is 6 percent. The fixed cost associated with each transfer is $100 and transfers are instantaneous.

(a) What are the optimal upper and lower bound control limits? (Assume a 360-day year.) *Hint:* On a calculator, treat the $1,000 as $1 and solve for the cube root by trial and error. Move the decimal point of the final answer two places to the right.
(b) What happens at these control limits?

8. Assuming an upward-sloping yield curve for marketable securities, devise a profit-maximizing maturity schedule for investment in marketable securities by Joey Brown Stereo Company based on the following considerations. The company wishes to maintain cash balances of $100,000 at all times. There are no transaction costs for investing in or selling marketable securities. In the absence of any investment in marketable securities, cash balances are expected to be:

January	$300,000	July	$400,000
February	500,000	August	300,000
March	600,000	September	200,000
April	500,000	October	200,000
May	700,000	November	100,000
June	800,000	December	100,000

Why might such a schedule be in the best interests of the company?

9. Research Project
Examine quotations in the *Wall Street Journal* for each of the following money-market instruments:

(a) Treasury bills
(b) Bankers' acceptances
(c) Certificates of deposit
(d) Commercial paper

(e) Government agency issues

Evaluate the yield-risk tradeoff for each instrument. Consider the appropriateness of each of these securities for the corporation's short-term investment account.

SELECTED REFERENCES

BARRO, ROBERT J., "Integral Constraints and Aggregation in an Inventory Model of Money Demand," *Journal of Finance,* 31 (March 1976), 77–88.

BAUMOL, WILLIAM J., "The Transactions Demand for Cash: An Inventory Theoretic Approach," *Quarterly Journal of Economics,* 65 (November 1952), 545–56.

BAXTER, NEVINS D., "Marketability, Default Risk, and Yields on Money-Market Instruments," *Journal of Financial and Quantitative Analysis,* 3 (March 1968), 75–85.

BUDIN, MORRIS, AND A. T. EAPEN, "Cash Generation in Business Operations: Some Simulation Models," *Journal of Finance,* 25 (December 1970), 1091–1107.

BUDIN, MORRIS, AND ROBERT J. VAN HANDEL, "A Rule-of-Thumb Theory of Cash Holdings by Firms," *Journal of Financial and Quantitative Analysis,* 10 (March 1975), 85–108.

CALMAN, ROBERT F., *Linear Programming and Cash Management/CASH ALPHA.* Cambridge, Mass.: M.I.T. Press, 1968.

DAELLENBACH, HANS G., "Are Cash Management Optimization Models Worthwhile?" *Journal of Financial and Quantitative Analysis,* 9 (September 1974), 607–26.

ELTON, EDWIN J., AND MARTIN J. GRUBER, *Finance as a Dynamic Process,* Chap. 3. Englewood Cliffs, N.J.: Prentice-Hall, 1975.

EPPEN, GARY D., AND EUGENE F. FAMA, "Cash Balance and Simple Dynamic Portfolio Problems with Proportional Costs," *International Economic Review,* 10 (June 1969), 110–33.

——, "Solutions for Cash-Balance and Simple Dynamic-Portfolio Problems," *Journal of Business,* 41 (January 1968), 94–112.

——, "Three-Asset Cash Balance and Dynamic Portfolio Problems," *Management Science,* 17 (January 1971), 311–19.

FROST, PETER A., "Banking Services, Minimum Cash Balances and the Firm's Demand for Money," *Journal of Finance,* 25 (December 1970), 1029–39.

GITMAN, LAWRENCE J., D. KEITH FORRESTER, AND JOHN R. FORRESTER, JR., "Maximizing Cash Disbursement Float," *Financial Management,* 5 (Summer 1976), 15–24.

LEVY, FERDINAND K., "An Application of Heuristic Problem Solving to Accounts Receivable Management," *Management Science,* 12 (February 1966), 236–44.

MEHTA, DILEEP R., *Working Capital Management,* Chaps. 6–8. Englewood Cliffs, N.J.: Prentice-Hall, 1974.

MILLER, MERTON H., AND DANIEL ORR, "The Demand for Money by Firms: Extension of Analytic Results," *Journal of Finance,* 23 (December 1968), 735–59.

——, "A Model of the Demand for Money by Firms," *Quarterly Journal of Economics,* 80 (August 1966), 413–35.

ORGLER, YAIR E., *Cash Management.* Belmont, Calif.: Wadsworth, 1970.

SEARBY, FREDERICK W., "Use Your Hidden Cash Resources," *Harvard Business Review,* 46 (March-April 1968), 74–75.

SMITH, KEITH V., *Management of Working Capital,* Sec. 2. New York: West Publishing, 1974.

STANCILL, JAMES McN., *The Management of Working Capital,* Chaps. 2 and 3. Scranton, Pa.: Intext, 1971.

STONE, BERNELL K., "Cash Planning and Credit-Line Determination with a Financial Statement Simulator: A Cash Report on Short-Term Financial Planning," *Journal of Financial and Quantitative Analysis,* 8 (November 1973), 711–30.

———, "Allocating Credit Lines, Planned Borrowing, and Tangible Services over a Company's Banking System," *Financial Management,* 4 (Summer 1975), 65–78.

STONE, BERNELL K., AND ROBERT A. WOOD, "Daily Cash Forecasting: A Simple Method for Implementing the Distribution Approach," *Financial Management,* 6 (Fall 1977), 40–50.

VAN HORNE, JAMES C., *Financial Market Rates and Flows.* Englewood Cliffs, N.J.: Prentice-Hall, 1978.

———, "Interest-Rate Risk and the Term Structure of Interest Rates," *Journal of Political Economy,* 73 (August 1965), 344–51.

15
management of accounts receivable

Accounts receivable represent the extension of open-account credit by one firm to other firms and to individuals. For most companies, accounts receivable are an extremely important investment and require careful analysis. The purpose of this chapter is to examine this vital function and the means by which receivables can be managed efficiently. We consider first the credit and collection policies of the firm as a whole and then discuss credit and collection procedures for the individual account.

Actually, the two facets are closely related. For example, credit policy involves a tradeoff between the profits on sales that give rise to receivables on one hand and the cost of carrying these receivables plus bad-debt losses on the other. Credit analysis is instrumental in determining the amount of credit risk to be accepted. In turn, the amount of risk accepted affects the slowness of receivables, and the resulting investment in receivables, as well as the amount of bad-debt losses. Collection procedures also affect these factors. Thus the credit and collection procedures of the firm are essential to the firm's overall credit and collection policies.

Although the level of accounts receivable is affected importantly by the influence of economic conditions on credit sales, it is determined also by policy decisions. Economic conditions, of course, are largely beyond the control of the financial manager. As with other current assets, however, he can vary the level of receivables in keeping with the tradeoff between profitability and risk. By increasing the level of receivables through lowering quality standards, for example, the financial manager hopes to stimulate demand, which, in turn, should lead to higher profits. However, there is a cost to carrying the additional receivables as well as a greater risk of bad-debt losses. It is this tradeoff we wish to examine.

The policy variables we consider include the quality of the trade accounts accepted, the length of the credit period, the cash discount given, any special terms given, such as seasonal datings, and the collection program of the firm. Together, these elements largely determine the average collection period and the proportion of bad-debt losses. We analyze each element in turn, holding constant certain of the others as well as any exogenous variables that affect the average collection period and the percentage of bad-debt losses. In addition, we assume that the evaluation of risk is sufficiently standardized so that degrees of risk for different accounts can be compared objectively.

Credit Standards

Credit policy can have a significant influence upon sales. If competitors extend credit liberally and we do not, our policy may have a dampening effect upon the marketing effort. Trade credit is one of many factors that influence the demand for a firm's product. Consequently, the degree to which trade credit can promote demand depends upon what other factors are being employed. In theory, the firm should lower its quality standard for accounts accepted as long as the profitability of sales generated exceeds the added costs of the receivables. What are the costs of relaxing credit standards? One type of cost is the enlarged credit department and the clerical expenses involved in checking additional accounts and servicing the added volume of receivables. We assume for now that these costs are deducted from the profitability of additional sales to give a net profitability figure for computational purposes. Another cost comes from the increased probability of bad-debt losses. However, we postpone consideration of this cost to a subsequent section; we assume for now that there are no bad-debt losses.

Finally, there is the opportunity cost of the additional receivables, resulting from (1) increased sales and (2) a slower average collection period. If new customers are attracted by the relaxed credit standards, collecting from these customers is likely to be slower than collecting from existing customers. In addition, a more liberal extension of credit may cause certain existing customers to be less conscientious in paying their bills on time.

To determine the profitability of a more liberal extension of credit, we must know the profitability of additional sales, the added demand for products arising from the relaxed credit standards, the increased slowness of the average collection period, and the required return on investment. Suppose a firm's product sells for $10 a unit, of which $7 represents variable costs before taxes, including credit department costs. Moreover, suppose the firm is operating at less than full capacity and that an increase in sales can be accommodated without any increase in fixed costs. Therefore the contribution margin of an additional unit of sales is the selling price less variable costs involved in producing the unit, or $10 − $7 = $3.

At present, annual credit sales are running at a level of $2.4 million, and there is no underlying trend in such sales. Now suppose the firm is considering a more liberal extension of credit, which will result in a slowing in the average collection period from one to two months.[1] However, existing customers are not expected to alter their payment habits. The relaxation in credit standards is expected to produce a 25 percent increase in sales, to $3 million annually.[2] This $600,000 increase represents 60,000 additional units if we assume that the price per unit stays the same. Finally, assume that the opportunity cost of carrying the additional receivables is 20 percent before taxes.

Given this information, our evaluation is reduced to a tradeoff between the added profitability on the additional sales and the opportunity cost of carrying the additional receivables, and we are able to make the calculations shown in Table 15-1.[3] We see that with $3 million in sales, which represents a 25 percent increase over the present level, and with a receivable turnover ratio of six times a year as opposed to twelve, the new level of receivables will be $500,000. This represents an increment of $300,000 over the present level of $200,000. Inasmuch as the profitability on additional sales, $180,000, exceeds the required return on the additional receivables, $60,000, the firm would be well advised to relax its credit standards. An optimal credit policy would involve extending trade credit more liberally until the marginal profitability on additional sales equals the required return on the additional investment in receivables.

[1]It should be pointed out that if there is either an upward or a downward trend in sales, the average collection period and receivable turnover ratio will not provide an accurate estimate of the new level of receivables outstanding. This problem is investigated at length in Chapter 25 where we explore the use of the average collection period and aging of accounts receivable. For ease of understanding of our example above, we assume that there is no trend in sales either before a credit policy decision or after the decision.

[2]In estimating the effect of a change in credit policy on demand, it is important to take into account the reaction of competitors to this change. Their reaction will affect demand over the long run.

[3]For simplicity, we assume that the additional sales do not require additional inventories to be held. If this is not the case, the additional inventories associated with a new credit policy should be added to the additional receivables, and the opportunity cost computed on the basis of the combined increase.

table 15-1
Profitability versus required return

Profitability of additional sales	=	$3 × 60,000 units = $180,000
Present level of receivables	=	(Annual sales/Receivable turnover)
		$2.4 million/12 = $200,000
Level of receivables after change in credit policy	=	$3 million/6 = $500,000
Additional receivables	=	$300,000
Opportunity cost of additional receivables	=	0.20 × $300,000 = $60,000

Obviously there are many practical problems in effecting a change in credit policy, particularly in estimating the outcomes. In our example, we have worked with only the expected values of additional demand and of the slowing of the average collection period. It is possible, and desirable, to attach probability distributions to the increased demand and to the increased slowness in receivables and evaluate a range of possible outcomes. For simplicity of discussion, however, we shall not incorporate these dimensions into our example.

Another assumption is that we can produce 60,000 additional units at a variable cost of $7 a unit; that is, we do not have to increase our plant. After some point, we are no longer able to meet additional demand with existing plant and would need to add plant. This occurrence would necessitate a change in analysis, for there would be a large block of incremental costs at the point where the existing plant could produce no more units. One implication to all of this is that the firm should vary its credit quality standards in keeping with the level of production. As capacity is approached, quality standards might be increased. When production sags and the firm operates at a level below capacity, the lowering of credit quality standards becomes more attractive, all other things the same. Implied also in our analysis is that the conditions described will be permanent. That is, increased demand as a function of lowering credit quality standards as well as price and cost figures will remain unchanged. If the increase in sales that results from a change in credit policy were a one-shot as opposed to a continuing occurrence, we would need to modify our analysis accordingly.

Credit Terms

Credit Period Credit terms involve both the length of the credit period and the discount given. The terms "2/10, net 30" mean that a 2 percent discount is given if the bill is paid before the tenth day after the date of invoice; payment is due by the thirtieth day. The credit period, then, is thirty days. Although the customs of the industry frequently dictate the terms given, the credit period is another means by which a firm may be able to affect product demand—hoping to increase demand by extending the credit period. As before, the tradeoff is between the profitability of additional sales and the required return on the additional investment in receivables. Assume for the purpose of illustration that our example involves lengthening the credit period from thirty to sixty days instead of relaxing credit standards. Assume also that by lengthening the credit period, the firm expects sales to increase by 25 percent and the average collection period to increase from one to two months. Because the quality of account being accepted is the same, we assume that there is no change in bad-debt losses—in other words, there are no losses. The analysis is the same as in Table 15-1. As seen, such a policy would be advantageous to the company because the profitability on additional sales—$180,000— exceeds the required return on the additional investment in receivables— $60,000.

Discount Given Varying the discount involves an attempt to speed up the payment of receivables. To be sure, the discount also may have an effect upon demand and upon bad-debt losses. However, we assume that the discount offered is not regarded as a means of cutting price and thereby affecting demand,[4] and that the discount offered does not affect the amount of bad-debt losses. Holding constant these factors, we must determine whether a speedup in collections would more than offset the cost of an increase in the discount. If it would, the present discount policy should be changed.

Suppose, for example, that the firm has annual credit sales of $3 million and an average collection period of two months, and that the sales terms are net 45 days, with no discount given. Assume further that the annual turnover of receivables is six times. Consequently, the average receivable balance is $500,000. Now, suppose that by instigating terms of 2/10, net 45, the average collection period is reduced to one month and that 50 percent of the customers (in dollar volume) take advantage of the 2 percent discount. The opportunity cost of the discount to the firm is .02 × 0.5 × $3 million, or $30,000 annually. However, the turnover of receivables has improved to twelve times a year, so that average receivables are reduced from $500,000 to $250,000.

Thus the firm realizes $250,000 from accelerated collections. The value of the funds released is their opportunity cost. If we assume a 20 percent rate of return, the opportunity saving is $50,000. In this case the opportunity saving arising from a speedup in collections is greater than the cost of the discount. Consequently, the firm should adopt a 2 percent discount. If the speedup in collections had not resulted in sufficient opportunity savings to offset the cost of discount, the discount policy should not be changed. It is

---

[4] If a price effect does occur, it will depend upon the elasticity of demand. The greater the discount, the lower the effective price to the customer who takes discounts and the greater his demand. However, the relevant range of discount changes is quite small. Unless demand is highly elastic, the effect on demand will be small.

possible, of course, that discounts other than 2 percent may result in an even greater difference between the opportunity savings and the cost of the discount.

Discount Period   In addition to the size of the discount offered, the length of the discount period also may affect the average collection period. Here the effect is not as clear as before. When a firm lengthens the discount period, two forces influence the average collection period. If the credit period is held constant, certain customers will be tempted to take the discount where previously they did not do so. This practice will tend to shorten the average collection period. On the other hand, customers who have been taking the discount and paying at the end of the discount period will now postpone payment until the end of the new discount period, thereby lengthening the average collection period. Whether the first force dominates the second will depend upon the mix of payment habits of the firm's customers. Given estimates of the likely effect of a change in the discount period on the average collection period, the firm can balance this effect with the increased dollar cost associated with more customers taking the discount. For all practical purposes, the discount period is variable within only a narrow range. The minimum period for mailing invoices and receipt of checks is about ten days. To increase it significantly beyond ten days defeats its purpose. In reality, then, the discount period is not an important decision variable.

Seasonal Datings   Another aspect of the credit terms given to customers involves seasonal datings. During periods of slack sales, firms will sometimes sell to customers without requiring payment for some time to come. This extension of the credit period is known as seasonal dating. Seasonal datings may be employed to stimulate demand from customers who cannot pay until later in the season. Because datings can be tailored to the cash flow of the customer, they can play an important role in selling the goods. Again, we should compare the profitability of additional sales with the required return on the additional investment in receivables to determine whether datings are an appropriate means by which to stimulate demand.

Datings also can be used to avoid inventory carrying costs. If sales are seasonal and production is steady throughout the year, there will be buildups in finished goods inventory during certain times of the year. Storage involves warehousing costs; therefore, it may be profitable to give datings in order to move the goods and avoid these costs. If warehousing costs plus the required rate of return on investment in inventory exceed the required rate of return on the additional receivables, it is worthwhile to give datings.

Default Risk

In the above examples, we assumed no bad-debt losses. Our concern in this section is not only with the slowness of collection but also with the portion of the receivables defaulting. Different credit policies will involve both of these factors. Suppose that we are considering the present credit

policy (sales of $2,400,000) together with two new ones and that these policies
are expected to produce the following results:

	Present Policy	Policy A	Policy B
Additional demand (percentage)	0	25	35
Average collection period	1 month	2 months	3 months
Default losses (percentage)	1	3	6

We assume that after six months an account is turned over to a collection
agency and that, on the average, 1 percent of the total receivable volume
under the present credit policy is never received by the firm, 3 percent is never
received under policy A, and 6 percent is never received under policy B.

If we go through the same type of calculations as in the earlier
example, we obtain the results shown in Table 15-2 for policies A and B. The
profitability of the two credit policies in relation to the required return on
investment can be summarized as follows:

	Policy A	Policy B
Profitability of additional sales less additional bad-debt losses, Present Policy to Policy A	$114,000	
Profitability of additional sales less additional bad-debt losses, Policy A to Policy B		$(32,400)
Required return on additional investment	60,000	62,000
	$ 54,000	$(94,400)

Consequently, we would want to adopt Policy A but would not want
to go so far in relaxing our credit standards as Policy B. As we see, the
marginal benefit is positive in moving from the present policy to Policy A, but
negative in going from Policy A to Policy B. It is possible, of course, that a
relaxation of credit standards that fell on one side or the other of Policy A
would provide an even greater marginal benefit; the optimal policy is the one
that provides the greatest marginal benefit.

Another approach to the problem might be to combine the
probability of bad-debt losses with the probability of slowness of collection
for each customer. Such an approach would be practical only if the size of the
account is reasonably large. For a customer with a $10,000 receivable, we
might formulate the probability distribution of expected collections shown in
Table 15-3.

table 15-2
Profitability versus required return and bad-debt losses

	Policy *A*	Policy *B*
Annual sales	$3,000,000	$3,240,000
Turnover of receivables	6	4
Level of receivables after change in credit policy	$ 500,000	$ 810,000
Additional receivables	$ 300,000	$ 310,000
Opportunity cost of additional receivables (20%)	$ 60,000	$ 62,000
Additional sales above present sales (units)	60,000	
Additional sales above Policy *A* sales (units)		24,000
Profitability of additional sales	$ 180,000	$ 72,000
Bad-debt losses (percent of annual sales)	$ 90,000	$ 194,000
Additional bad-debt losses above present losses ($24,000)	$ 66,000	
Additional bad-debt losses above Policy *A* losses ($90,000)		$ 104,400
Profitability of additional sales less additional bad-debt losses	$ 114,000	$ (32,400)

For this customer, there is a .05 probability that the account will not be paid after six months and that it will be charged off as a bad-debt loss.[5] For other customers, we could construct similar probability distributions. If the probability distributions were independent, a total probability distribution could be obtained simply by totaling the expected collections for each month

table 15-3
Possible time of receipt: single account

Time Received after Billing	Probability	Expected Collections
1 month	0.50	$ 5,000
2 months	0.20	2,000
3 months	0.10	1,000
4 months	0.05	500
5 months	0.05	500
6 months	0.05	500
Bad-debt loss	0.05	500
	1.00	$10,000

[5]Cyert, Davidson, and Thompson have made an interesting application of Markov chains to estimating the probability of a bad-debt loss for an account at various future dates. R. M. Cyert, H. J. Davidson, and G. L. Thompson, "Estimation of the Allowance for Doubtful Accounts by Markov Chains," *Management Science*, 8 (April 1962), 287–303. For similar applications, see William Beranek, *Analysis for Financial Decisions* (Homewood, Ill.: Richard D. Irwin, 1963), pp. 308–20; and Edwin J. Elton and Martin J. Gruber, *Finance as a Dynamic Process* (Englewood Cliffs, N.J.: Prentice-Hall, 1975), Chap. 4.

table 15-4
Possible time of receipts: all accounts

Time Received after Billing	Probability	Expected Collections
1 month	0.60	$300,000
2 months	0.15	75,000
3 months	0.10	50,000
4 months	0.05	25,000
5 months	0.04	20,000
6 months	0.02	10,000
Bad-debt loss	0.04	20,000
	1.00	$500,000

for all accounts.[6] For our hypothetical firm, the probability distribution for all accounts, totaling $500,000, might be that shown in Table 15-4. By calculating probability distributions for all accounts at different times of the year and comparing actual results with expected results, we could obtain fairly exact information as to the average investment in receivables and the average collection period for these receivables.

Collection Policy

The overall collection policy of the firm is determined by the combination of collection procedures it undertakes. These procedures include such things as letters sent, phone calls, personal calls, and legal action, and they are described later in this chapter. One of the principal policy variables is the amount expended on collection procedures. Within a range, the greater the relative amount expended, the lower the proportion of bad-debt losses and the shorter the average collection period, all other things the same.

The relationships, however, are not linear. Initial collection expenditures are likely to cause little reduction in bad-debt losses. Additional expenditures begin to have a significant effect in reducing the amount of bad-debt losses. Beyond a point, however, additional expenditures tend to have little effect in further reducing these losses. The hypothesized relationship between expenditures and bad-debt losses is shown in Figure 15-1. Likewise, the relationship between the average collection period and the level of collection expenditures is likely to be similar to that shown in the figure.

If sales are independent of the collection effort, the appropriate level of collection expenditure again involves a tradeoff—this time between the level of expenditure on the one hand and the reduction in the cost of bad-debt

[6]For an examination of the predictive accuracy of expected bad-debt ratios for customers under varying degrees of correlation between default losses for such customers, see James C. T. Mao and Carl Erik Sarndal, "Controlling Risks in Accounts Receivable Management," *Journal of Business Finance & Accounting,* 1 (Autumn 1974), 395–403.

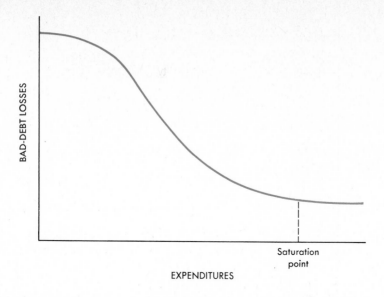

figure 15-1
Relationship between
amount of bad-debt
losses and collection
expenditures

losses and reduction in receivables on the other. Suppose that we are considering the present collection program in relation to two new ones and that the programs are expected to produce these results:

	Present Program	Program A	Program B
Annual collection expenditures	$116,000	$148,000	$200,000
Average collection period	2 months	1½ months	1 month
Percentage of default	3	2	1

Assume that present sales are $2.4 million and that they are not expected to change with changes in the collection effort. If we go through the same type of reasoning as we did for the discount policy where receivables were reduced and for bad-debt losses, we obtain the results in Table 15-5. In the last three rows of the table, we see that the opportunity saving resulting from a speedup in collections plus the reduction in bad-debt losses exceeds the additional collection expenditures in going from the present program to Program A, but not in going from Program A to Program B. As a result, the firm should adopt Program A but not increase collection expenditures to the extent of Program B.

In the example above, we have assumed that demand is independent of the collection effort. In most cases, however, sales are likely to be affected adversely if the collection efforts of the firm become too intense and customers become increasingly irritated. If they do, we must take into account the relationship between the collection effort and demand. Reduction in demand can be incorporated into the marginal analysis of collection expenditures in the same manner as was the increase in demand accompanying a

table 15-5
Evaluation of collection programs

	Present Program	Program A	Program B
Annual sales	$2,400,000	$2,400,000	$2,400,000
Turnover of receivables	6	8	12
Average receivables	$ 400,000	$ 300,000	$ 200,000
Reduction in receivables from present level		$ 100,000	
Reduction in receivables from Program A level			$ 100,000
Return on reduction in receivables (20 percent)		$ 20,000	$ 20,000
Bad-debt losses (percent of annual sales)	$ 72,000	$ 48,000	$ 24,000
Reduction in bad-debt losses from present losses		$ 24,000	
Reduction in bad-debt losses from Program A losses			$ 24,000
Opportunity saving on reduced receivables plus reduction in bad-debt losses		$ 44,000	$ 44,000
Additional collection expenditures from present expenditures		$ 32,000	
Additional collection expenditures from Program A expenditures			$ 52,000

relaxation in credit standards. In addition, if the collection effort has an effect on the percentage of total sales taking a cash discount, this factor must be considered. With increased collection efforts, for example, more customers might take the cash discount.

Credit and Collection Policies—Summary

We see that the credit and collection policies of a firm involve several decisions as to (1) the quality of account accepted, (2) the credit period, (3) the cash discount given, (4) any special terms such as seasonal datings, and (5) the level of collection expenditures. In each case, the decision should involve a comparison of what is to be gained by a change in policy with the cost of the change. Optimal credit and collection policies would be those that resulted in the marginal gains equaling the marginal costs.

To maximize profits arising from credit and collection policies, the firm should vary these policies jointly until an optimal solution is achieved. That solution will determine the best combination of credit standards, credit period, cash discount policy, special terms, and level of collection expenditures. In this regard, sensitivity analysis might be used to judge the impact of a change in policies upon profits. Once functional relationships have been specified for the relationship between a particular policy and marginal sales, average collection period, and bad-debt losses, the policy can be varied from one extreme to the other, holding constant other factors. This variation gives insight into the impact of a change in policy upon profits.

For most policy variables, profits increase at a decreasing rate up to a point and then decrease as the policy is varied from no effort to an extreme effort. This relationship is depicted in Figure 15-2 for the quality of account rejected. When there are no credit standards, that is, when all applicants are accepted, sales are maximized. However, the maximization of sales is offset by large bad-debt losses as well as by the opportunity cost of carrying a very large receivable position. As credit standards are initiated and applicants rejected, revenue from sales declines but so do the average collection period and bad-debt losses. Because the latter two decline initially at a faster rate than do sales, profits increase. As credit standards are tightened increasingly, however, sales revenue declines at an increasing rate. At the same time, the average collection period and bad-debt losses decrease at a decreasing rate. Fewer and fewer bad credit risk are eliminated. Because of the combination of these influences, total profits of the firm increase at a diminishing rate with stricter credit standards up to a point, after which they decline. The optimal

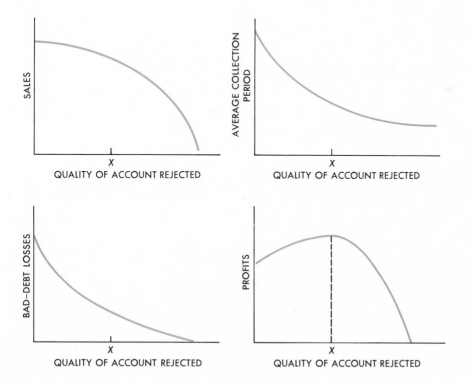

figure 15-2
Relationship of sales, average collection period, bad-debt losses, and profits to the quality of account rejected

policy with respect to credit standards is represented by point X in the figure. In turn, this policy determines the level of accounts receivable held by the firm.[7]

To the extent that decisions with respect to credit standards, the credit period, the discount given, special terms offered, and the level of collection expenditures exercise a joint influence upon profits, this interdependency must be recognized in formulating the functional relationships. With assumed relationships specified, the firm can use sensitivity analysis to experiment with different credit and collection policies in order to determine the optimal set of policies. The optimal set establishes the credit terms given, the collection procedures followed, and the cutoff point on quality of account accepted.[8]

In cases where some of the underlying parameters change, sensitivity analysis proves valuable in formulating new credit and collection policies. For example, if the marginal profit per unit of sales declines due to increased competition, the optimal set of policies is likely to change. Lower profits per unit of sale may not justify the present level of receivables carried nor the present loss rate. As a result, new credit and collection policies might be in order. Through sensitivity analysis, management could determine the new set of policies that will maximize profit.

The analysis in the last several sections has purposely been rather general, to provide insight into the important concepts of credit and collection policies. Obviously a policy decision should be based upon a far more specific evaluation than that contained in the examples above. Estimating the increased demand and increased slowness of collections that might accompany a relaxation of credit standards is extremely difficult. Nevertheless, management must make estimates of these relationships if it is to appraise its existing policies realistically.

EVALUATING THE CREDIT APPLICANT

Having established the terms of sale to be offered, the firm must evaluate individual credit applicants and consider the possibilities of a bad debt or slow payment. The credit evaluation procedure involves three related steps:

---

[7]For a present-value approach to evaluating credit policy decisions, see Yong H. Kim and Joseph C. Atkins, "Evaluating Investments in Accounts Receivable: A Wealth Maximizing Framework," *Journal of Finance,* 33 (May 1978), 403–12.

[8]Greer develops a model to maximize profits based upon the number of credit applicants accepted by a creditor. Functional relationships are derived linking the number of accounts accepted to most of the factors we discussed. By differentiating the profit function with respect to the number of applicants accepted and setting the expression equal to zero, one can solve for the number of applicants that maximizes profits. Although somewhat unrealistic for trade credit, the model is useful for a retail company trying to determine a credit policy for charge accounts. Carl C. Greer, "The Optimal Credit Acceptance Policy," *Journal of Financial and Quantitative Analysis,* 2 (December 1967), 399–415.

obtaining information on the applicant; analyzing this information to deter-mine the applicant's credit-worthiness; and making the credit decision. The credit decision, in turn, establishes whether credit should be extended and what the maximum amount of credit should be.

Sources of Information

Though there are a number of sources of credit information, there necessarily are expenses incurred in collecting it. For some accounts, especially small ones, the cost of collecting comprehensive credit information may outweigh the potential profitability of the account. The firm extending credit may have to be satisfied with a limited amount of information on which to base a decision. Later in this chapter, we present a sequential investigation process whereby a firm may weigh the cost of collecting and analyzing additional information in relation to the expected benefits to be derived from it. In addition to cost, the firm must consider the time it takes to investigate a credit applicant. A shipment to a prospective customer cannot be delayed unnecessarily pending an elaborate credit investigation. Thus the amount of information collected needs to be considered in relation to the time and expense required. Depending upon these considerations, the credit analyst may use one or more of the following sources of information.

Financial Statement   One of the most desirable sources of information for credit analysis is a financial statement that the seller may request from his customer at the time of the prospective sale. Some companies are perfectly willing to provide statements to suppliers, whereas others may refuse to do so. There is frequently a correlation between a company's refusal to provide a statement and weaknesses in its financial position. When possible, it is help-ful to obtain interim statements, particularly for companies having seasonal patterns of sales. Needless to say, audited statements are far better than unaudited figures.

Credit Ratings and Reports   In addition to financial statements, credit rat-ings are available from various mercantile agencies. Dun & Bradstreet, Inc., is perhaps the best known and most comprehensive of these agencies. It provides credit ratings to subscribers for a vast number of business firms throughout the nation. A key to its individual ratings is shown in Figure 15-3. As we see in the figure, D & B ratings give the credit analyst an indication of the estimated size of net worth and a credit appraisal for companies of a particular size, ranging from "high" to "limited." D & B also indicates when the information available is insufficient to provide a rating for a given business.

In addition to its rating service, D & B provides credit reports on business firms. These reports contain a brief history of the company and its principal officers, the nature of the business, certain financial information, and a trade check of suppliers as to the length of their experience with the company and as to whether payments are discount, prompt, or past due. The

figure 15-3
Dun & Bradstreet key to ratings

quality of the D & B reports varies with the information available externally and the willingness of the company being checked to cooperate with the D & B reporter. In addition to Dun & Bradstreet, there are a number of credit agencies that specialize in a particular line of business or in geographic areas, such as New York or Chicago.

Bank Checking   Another source of information for the firm is a credit check through a bank. Many banks have large credit departments that undertake, as a service, credit checks for their customers. By calling or writing the bank(s) of account of the company being checked, a firm's bank is able to obtain information as to the average cash balance carried, loan accommodations, experience, and sometimes financial information. Because banks generally are more willing to share information with other banks than with a direct inquirer, it usually is best for the firm to initiate the credit check through its own bank rather than to inquire directly.

Trade Checking   Credit information frequently is exchanged among companies selling to the same customer. Through various credit organizations, credit people in a particular area become a closely knit group. A company is able to check other suppliers as to their experience with an account. Useful information includes the length of time they have had the account, the maximum credit extended, the amount of the line of credit, and whether payments are prompt or slow. In addition, there are various clearing houses of credit information. The largest of these is the National Association of Credit Management; credit information is provided by this agency in the form of a report. The report shows the type of supplier, the terms of trade, the recent high credit, the total amount owed on the account, and an aging of this amount according to the times in the past when various components of the total were billed. In addition, an overall aging is given for all reported accounts for each of the previous six months. Such information is extremely valuable in determining the experience of other suppliers with a customer.

The Company's Own Experience   In addition to these sources, a company's own experience with an account is extremely important. A study of the promptness of past payments, including any seasonal patterns, for example, is very useful. Frequently, the credit department will make written assessments of the quality of the management of a company to whom credit may be extended. These assessments are very important, for they pertain to the first of the famous "three C's" of credit: *character, collateral,* and *capacity*. For a *prospective* customer, the salesman is frequently able to supply useful information based on his impressions of the management and operations. Caution is necessary in interpreting this information, however, because a salesman has a natural bias toward granting credit and making the sale.

Credit Analysis and Decision

Having collected credit information, the firm must undertake a credit analysis of the applicant and determine if the company falls above or below the minimum quality standard. If financial statements are provided, the analyst should undertake a ratio analysis, a source and use of funds analysis, and perhaps other analyses, as described in Chapters 25 and 26. As suggested in Chapter 25, empirical studies may be undertaken to determine which financial ratios have the greatest predictive power. The analyst will be particularly interested in the applicant's liquidity and ability to pay bills on time.

In addition to analyzing financial statements, the credit analyst will consider the character and strength of the company and its management, the business risk associated with its operation, and various other matters. He then attempts to determine the ability of the applicant to service trade credit. In this regard, he assesses the probability of an applicant's not paying on time and of a bad-debt loss. On the basis of this information together with information about the profit margin of the product or service being sold, a decision is reached as to whether or not to extend credit.

One tool finding increasing utilization in this regard is *discriminant analysis*. This statistical technique is described in the Appendix to this chapter, so we will not go into a detailed description here. On the basis of a weighted overall score provided by this technique, an applicant is judged to be a "good" or a "bad" credit risk. Discriminant analysis has been used with success in consumer credit and other forms of installment lending, where various characteristics of an individual are quantitatively rated and a credit decision made on the basis of the total score. Numerical rating systems also are being used by companies extending trade credit.[9] With the overall growth of trade credit, a number of companies are finding it worthwhile to screen out "clear" accept and reject applicants. In other words, routine credit decisions are made on the basis of a numerical score. Marginal applicants, which fall between "clear" accept or reject signals, can then be analyzed in detail by the credit analyst.[10] In this way, a company is able to achieve greater efficiency in its credit investigation process, utilizing trained credit analysts to the best advantage.

Sequential Investigation Process

Most credit investigations involve a sequential analysis where the collection of information and its analysis are interrelated. In general, the riskier the credit applicant, the more information the analyst will want to have. The cost of acquiring this information, however, must be balanced against the expected benefits to be derived from the order. A credit decision for an individual account may take one of three courses of action: accept, reject, or obtain additional information.[11] For the last alternative, the expected value of additional information must exceed the cost of acquiring it.

To illustrate a sequential investigation process, suppose the following stages of credit investigation were open to a company:

1. Consult past experience to see if the firm has had previous experience with the account and, if it has, what has been that experience.
2. Order a Dun & Bradstreet report on the applicant and evaluate it.
3. Undertake credit checks with banks and trade creditors.

Stages 2 and 3 could be broken down into additional steps. For example, a firm might first seek a credit rating from Dun & Bradstreet and, on the basis of

---

[9]See Sylvia Lane, "Submarginal Credit Risk Classification," *Journal of Financial and Quantitative Analysis,* 7 (January 1972), 1379–85; William P. Poggess, "Screen-Test Your Credit Risks," in *Working Capital Management,* ed. Keith V. Smith (New York: West Publishing, 1974), pp. 109–20; and Robert O. Edmister and Gary G. Schlarbaum, "Credit Policy in Lending Institutions," *Journal of Financial and Quantitative Analysis,* 9 (June 1974), 335–56.

[10]In addition to the Appendix, see Dileep R. Mehta, *Working Capital Management* (Englewood Cliffs, N.J.: Prentice-Hall, 1974), Chap. 1, for a detailed discussion of this technique. For a discussion of the updating of the underlying sample used in a credit scoring system, see Michael S. Long, "Credit Screening System Selection," *Journal of Financial and Quantitative Analysis,* 11 (June 1976), 313–28.

[11]This section draws upon Dileep Mehta, "The Formulation of Credit Policy Models," *Management Science,* 15 (October 1968), 30–50.

that rating, decide whether or not to order a report. For stage 3 it might check banks first and then, depending upon the outcome of the bank check, check trade creditors. Moreover, the number of trade creditors checked might be a sequential function. An additional stage might be a personal interview by the credit analyst with the company placing the order. For simplicity of illustration, we consider only three stages but recognize that the sequential investigation process could be expanded to take account of additional stages.

These three stages are broken down into various quality categories. For stage 1, an order is classified into one of the following categories, depending upon what the investigation of past experience reveals:

a. Good. A good account is one in which the customer consistently pays within the credit period.
b. Fair. This rating is given to a customer who frequently pays beyond the credit period but usually is no more than forty-five days delinquent. Moreover, the customer keeps the firm informed and pays according to plan.
c. Poor. A poor account is one where the customer is often more than forty-five days delinquent. In addition, the customer does not keep the firm informed and usually is inconsistent in payments.
d. New. A new order.

When a report is ordered from Dun & Bradstreet, the credit analyst evaluates it and the financial statements contained therein. On the basis of this evaluation, he assigns a letter rating of either A, B, C, or D. A is the highest grade and indicates that the prospects for the customer paying within the credit period are excellent. On the other end of the spectrum, D is the lowest rating and indicates that there is a high degree of probability the customer either will be delinquent in payment or will not pay at all. Similarly, for stage 3, a letter rating of A through D is assigned on the basis of credit checks with banks and trade creditors. In the investigation process, it is important that each stage be treated as independent of the preceding stage. In other words, credit checks should be evaluated independently of the evalution of the D & B report.

When an order is received, the credit department must make a decision as to whether or not to accept it. It would of course be desirable to undertake stages 1 through 3 for all orders, but each involves a cost. To investigate past experience, someone must check the credit file and accounts receivable ledger and categorize the applicant into one of four quality categories. For stage 2, the firm must pay for the D & B report. In addition, the credit analyst must devote time to analyzing the report and to assigning a letter rating. This analysis also involves a cost. The last stage, credit checkings, involves a considerable cost, for the credit analyst must either call or write bank(s) and trade creditors and inquire of their experience. Additionally, he must analyze the information and assign a letter rating. Suppose that the costs for the various stages of investigation are the following:

		Cost
Stage 1	Past experience	$ 1
Stage 2	D & B report	8
Stage 3	Credit checkings	15

These costs will be compared shortly with the expected value of information provided by each stage.

Expected Benefits and Costs

First, however, we must establish the expected benefits to be derived from an order. Assume that the firm makes but one product and that the marginal profit from each unit sold is $10 and the marginal cost to produce it $15. Moreover, suppose that the required return on investment in receivables is 15 percent on a before-tax basis. Given this information, the firm must estimate the average collection period, the average collection costs, and the probability of bad-debt loss for each of the possible quality categories. These estimates should be based upon actual experience during a sample period in which the firm undertakes all stages of investigation for each credit applicant but extends open-book credit to all. As experience unfolds for an account, the firm records the collection period, the collection cost, and whether or not it was a bad debt. On the basis of experience with a number of accounts over the sample period, it computes an average collection period, average collection costs, and the percentage of bad debt for each quality category of applicants. An example of this information for stage 1 is presented in Table 15-6. If future orders are not expected to differ significantly from the orders constituting the sample, the firm may use the information in this table to assess the profitability of an order.[12]

table 15-6

Estimates of collection period, collection costs, and bad debts for stage 1

Stage	Average Collection Period	Average Collection Costs	Probability of Bad-Debt Loss
Past experience:			
Good	28.5 days	0.775	0.0175
Fair	52.5	2.775	0.1560
Poor	87.0	9.000	0.3375
New account	59.3	3.560	0.2060

[12]It is essential that future orders correspond closely to those in the sample; otherwise, the estimates of profitability of an order will not be reliable.

It now is possible to compute the expected cost of accepting an order:

Acceptance cost = Probability of bad debt(Variable cost per unit)X
+ (Required return)(Average collection period/
360)(Variable cost per unit)X + Average
collection cost   (15-1)

where X is the number of units ordered. For our hypothetical example,

Acceptance cost = (Probability of bad debt)(15X) + 0.15(Average collection
period/360)(15X) + Average collection cost

Recall that variable costs were assumed to be $15 per unit and the required
rate of return 15 percent. Thus the acceptance cost embodies the costs of
bad-debt losses, carrying receivables, and collection. Because collection
costs are assumed to be fixed, they do not vary with the size of the order.
The expected cost of rejecting an order is

Rejection cost = (1 − Probability of bad debt) (Marginal profit
per unit) X   (15-2)

which, for our example, is

Rejection cost = (1 − Probability of bad debt)10X

The rejection cost is simply the probability of payment times the marginal
profit forgone on the order.

To illustrate the calculation of acceptance and rejection costs, suppose that there is an order for X units and that as a matter of policy the firm
always investigates past experience. The expected costs of acceptance and
rejection for a poor account are

Acceptance cost = 0.3375(15X) + 0.15(87/360)(15X) + $7.00
= 5.606X + $9.00
Rejection cost = 0.6625(10X) = 6.625X

Similarly, we can compute the expected costs of acceptance and rejection
for the other quality categories in the first stage. These costs are shown in
Figure 15-4.

From the information in Figure 15-4, we can determine that for the
poor category, the cost of acceptance exceeds the cost of rejection for orders
of eight units or less. When X ≥ 9, however, the cost of acceptance is less.
If past experience (stage 1) were the only stage of investigation, an order that
fell into the poor category would be rejected if it were for eight units or less
and accepted if it were for nine units or more. For the good, fair, and new-
order categories, the cost of acceptance is less than the cost of rejection for

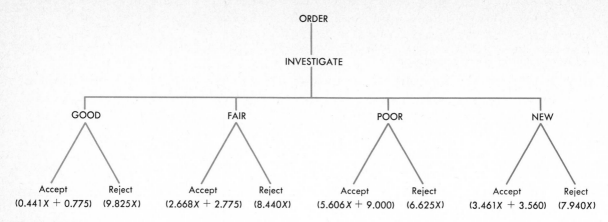

figure 15-4
Investigation of past experience cost structure

all $X \geq 1$. Therefore an order that fell into any of these categories would be accepted if examining past experience were the only stage of investigation.

Sequential Stages of Investigation

With additional stages of investigation, however, we must decide whether to investigate further or to accept or reject the order on the basis of the information we have. A decision to go on to the next stage of investigation depends upon the benefits expected to be derived from the additional information in relation to its cost. In a nutshell, we want to establish whether the added information will improve our chances of making a correct decision.[13]

Stage 2 involves analyzing a D & B report. Assume for now that only the first two stages of investigation are open to the company. On the basis of an evaluation of the D & B report, the credit analyst assigns a letter grade ranging from A through D. When this information is combined with that in the preceding stage, the probabilities as well as the average collection periods, average collection costs, and probabilities of bad-debt losses change. New estimates of them should be based upon the sample discussed earlier. Suppose that on the basis of this sample, the firm found the conditional probabilities, average collection periods, average collection costs, and probabilities of bad-debt losses to be those shown in Table 15-7. Note that when the combination of past experience and D & B report analysis is less desirable, the factors shown in the last three columns are worse.

Similar to Figure 15-4, the expected costs of acceptance and rejection can be determined for the combinations shown in Table 15-7; and they are shown in Table 15-8. Given this information, we are able to determine

---

[13]The new information has value only if we change our previous accept-reject decision on the basis of it. See Harold Bierman, Jr., Charles P. Bonini, and Warren H. Hausman, *Quantitative Analysis for Business Decisions,* 5th ed. (Homewood, Ill.: Richard D. Irwin, 1977), Chaps. 5–8.

table 15-7
Estimates of collection period, collection costs, and
bad-debt loss for D & B report analysis, given the
investigation of past experience

Good Past Experience D & B Report	Conditional Probability of Occurrence	Average Collection Period	Average Collection Cost	Probability of Bad-Debt Loss
A	0.70	25 days	0.50	0.00
B	0.15	30	1.00	0.02
C	0.10	40	1.50	0.07
D	0.05	50	2.50	0.15
Fair Past Experience D & B Report				
A	0.20	30 days	1.00	0.03
B	0.40	45	2.00	0.10
C	0.25	60	3.50	0.20
D	0.15	90	6.00	0.40
Poor Past Experience D & B Report				
A	0.05	40 days	1.50	0.05
B	0.25	60	3.50	0.15
C	0.35	80	8.00	0.30
D	0.35	120	15.00	0.55
New Order D & B Report				
A	0.20	32 days	1.20	0.04
B	0.30	48	2.40	0.12
C	0.30	65	4.00	0.22
D	0.20	95	7.00	0.48

whether the firm should go beyond the investigation of past experience to analyze a D & B report. The crux of the decision involves comparing the expected benefits derived from the additional information with the cost of acquiring it. In turn, the magnitude of benefits depends upon the size of the order.

An Illustration

To illustrate the investigation process, assume that an order for ten units is received and that the firm has investigated its past experience and found it to be poor. For a cost of $8, it can go to the next stage of investigation

table 15-8
Costs of acceptance and rejection
for D & B report analysis

Good Past Experience D & B Report	Cost of Acceptance	Cost of Rejection
A	0.16X + 0.50	10.0X
B	0.49X + 1.00	9.8X
C	1.30X + 1.50	9.3X
D	2.56X + 2.50	9.3X
Fair Past Experience **D & B Report**		
A	0.64X + 1.00	9.7X
B	1.78X + 2.00	9.0X
C	3.38X + 3.50	8.0X
D	6.56X + 6.00	6.0X
Poor Past Experience **D & B Report**		
A	1.00X + 1.50	9.5X
B	2.63X + 3.50	8.5X
C	5.00X + 8.00	7.0X
D	9.00X + 15.00	4.5X
New Order **D & B Report**		
A	0.90X + 1.20	9.6X
B	2.10X + 2.40	8.8X
C	3.71X + 4.00	7.8X
D	7.79X + 7.00	5.2X

and analyze a D & B report. The question is whether it is worthwhile for it to do so. From Figure 15-4, we know the order would be accepted if past experience were the only stage of investigation—the reason is that for orders of nine or more units, the cost of acceptance is less than the cost of rejection. We now must determine if the additional information arising from a D & B report analysis will cause us to change our decision. Only if it will does the additional information have value. The cost of acceptance and the cost of rejection for an order of ten units, given poor past experience, can be derived from Table 15-8; and they are found to be:

D & B Report Grade	Cost of Acceptance	Cost of Rejection
A	$ 11.50	$95.00
B	26.30	85.00
C	58.00	70.00
D	105.00	45.00

Thus, if ten units are ordered, the cost of acceptance exceeds the cost of rejection only if the D & B analysis grade turns out to be *D*. Under these circumstances, the firm would reject the order, whereas before the order would have been accepted. Consequently, there is value in obtaining the additional information. The expected net benefit is the difference between the cost of acceptance avoided and the cost of rejection incurred, times the conditional probability of occurrence. For our example, the expected net benefit is

$$(105.00 - 45.00)0.35 = \$21.00$$

Inasmuch as this figure exceeds the cost of investigation of $8, an analysis of a D & B report should be undertaken. When $X = 9$, it also is found that the expected benefits associated with a stage 2 investigation exceed the $8 cost.

There still remains the question of whether it is worthwhile to undertake a D & B report analysis if the order is for eight units or less. Here the order would be rejected on the basis of past experience alone. We must determine if additional information will cause us to change that decision. If the order were for five units, the expected costs of acceptance and rejection would be:

D & B Report Grade	Cost of Acceptance	Cost of Rejection
A	$ 6.50	$47.50
B	16.65	42.50
C	33.00	35.00
D	60.00	22.50

If a D & B report analysis were undertaken, the firm could avoid the cost of rejection for cases of grades *A*, *B*, and *C*. However, it would incur the lesser cost of acceptance in all three cases. Because the order would be rejected on the basis of past experience alone, there is no benefit to be derived from grade *D*, inasmuch as the cost of acceptance exceeds the cost of rejection. Again, the value of additional information comes only if it causes us to change a decision. The expected net benefit to the firm is determined by multiplying the differences between the costs of rejection and acceptance for the first three cases times their respective conditional probabilities of occurrence:

$$(47.50 - 6.50)0.05 + (42.50 - 16.65)0.25 + (35.00 - 33.00)0.35 = \$9.21$$

Because the expected net benefit exceeds the cost of undertaking a D & B report analysis, the investigation of a D & B report is worthwhile. However, when an order is for four units, the expected benefit, $7.50, is less than the cost of investigation of $8.00. Therefore an order for four units from a poor account should be rejected.

As a general decision rule, then, the firm should reject any order for five units or less if an investigation of past experience reveals the account to have been poor. No further investigation should be undertaken. If the order is for six or more units, however, the firm should undertake an analysis of a D & B report because the expected benefit of the additional information exceeds its cost. Depending upon the outcome of this investigation, the order will be either accepted or rejected.[14]

Similarly, decision rules can be formulated for other categories of past experience. For good past experience, the cost of acceptance in Table 15-8 is less than the cost of rejection for all $X \geq 1$. Therefore there is no benefit to be derived from further investigation. The previous acceptance decision will not be changed. As a result, the firm should accept all orders where an investigation of past experience reveals that experience to have been good.

For an account judged to be fair by past experience, the cost of acceptance exceeds the cost of rejection in Table 15-8 only if the D & B report analysis grade turns out to be D. Under these circumstances, the expected net benefit is

$$(6.56X + 6.00 - 6.0X)0.15$$

For an analysis of a D & B report to be worthwhile, the expected net benefit must exceed the cost of investigation of $8.00. To be indifferent, we must have the following equality:

$$(6.56X + 6.00 - 6.0X)0.15 = 8.00$$

Transposing and solving for X:

$$0.56X + 6.00 = 8.00/0.15$$
$$0.56X = 53.33 - 6.00$$
$$X = 84.5$$

Thus, only if the order size is eighty-five units or more will an analysis of a D & B report benefit the firm. If an order judged to be fair by past experience is for less than eighty-five units, it should be accepted without such analysis.

[14]This decision rule and the others presented assume a linear utility function with respect to money. As discussed in Chapter 2, there is a serious question as to whether a manager behaves in this fashion. If his utility function could be specified, the sequential investigation process could be expressed in utile values in a manner similar to the analysis in Chapter 2. However, given the relatively small size of investment in the individual account, a linear utility function is not unreasonable to assume.

For a new account, the cost of acceptance exceeds the cost of rejection only for grade *D* in Table 15-8. The expected benefit is

$$(7.79X + 7.00 - 5.2X)0.20$$

To be indifferent, the expected benefit must equal the cost of investigation:

$$(7.79X + 7.00 - 5.2X)0.20 = 8.00$$

Transposing and solving for X:

$$2.59X + 7.00 = 8.00/0.20$$
$$2.59X = 40.00 - 7.00$$
$$X = 12.7$$

Consequently, only if the order size is thirteen units or more should the firm analyze a D & B report for a new order. If the order is for less than this number, it should be accepted without credit investigation.

Our example could be extended to take account of the last stage of investigation—a checking of banks and trade suppliers. However, because our example is already rather long, we shall limit it to the first two stages of the investigation process. Because the desirability of additional information diminishes with each successive stage, one can visualize that the number of times where the additional information would be worthwhile would be less for credit checkings than for the D & B report analysis. One final point has to do with the procedure used to solve the problem. For purposes of illustration, we have solved it in descending stages of analysis. However, it often makes more sense to work backward from the last stage to the first. Those readers familiar with dynamic programming have probably already discovered that the problem lends itself to this optimization technique.

Implications   The sequential investigation process presented illustrates one means by which a firm can reach a credit decision with a minimum of investigation cost. Rather than perform all stages of investigation regardless of the size of the order and the firm's past experience, the firm should undertake investigation in stages and go to a new stage only when the expected net benefits of the additional information exceed the cost of acquiring it. When past experience has been favorable, there may be little need for further investigation. We saw that decision rules can be established whereby an order is investigated only if it meets certain size constraints and falls into a particular category in the preceding stage of investigation. Because the stages of credit investigation are sequential, added sophistication is introduced only when it is beneficial to do so. In this manner, the firm can make optimal credit decisions with respect to acceptance, rejection, or further investigation.

The decision rules used in a sequential investigation process will vary according to the marginal profit and marginal cost of the product, the cost of bad debts, the average collection period, and the average collection costs. To the extent that these factors change over time, the firm will need to formulate new decision rules. As experience changes and the sample on which estimates are made is no longer valid, the firm will need to revise its probability estimates and its estimates of costs and bad-debt losses in Tables 15-6 and 15-7. Perhaps the most suitable means for review is to extend credit to all applicants on a periodic basis. With this experience recorded, new estimates of the average collection period and costs, the probability of bad-debt losses, and the probabilities of occurrence can be formulated. The more stable the experience over time, the less frequent the need for periodic review.[15] If the underlying system is basically unstable, however, a sequential investigation process is not well suited for the problem at hand. Yet, for most situations it represents a meaningful application of decision theory to credit analysis.

Line of Credit

Another means of control for repeat orders is to establish a line of credit for an individual account. A line of credit is a maximum limit on the amount the firm will permit to be owing at any one time. In essence, it represents the maximum risk exposure that the firm will allow itself to undergo for an account. In the sequential investigation method illustrated above, single orders were evaluated. With a line of credit, multiple orders are assumed. The principle, however, is the same. Likely profits from present and future sales must be balanced against the likely collection period, collection costs, and probability of bad-debt losses over time. The latter three depend upon the magnitude of the line of credit offered rather than upon the size of order. As before, probability concepts can be applied in order to analyze the tradeoff between expected benefits and expected costs and to determine an appropriate line of credit for the customer.

The establishment of a credit line streamlines the procedure for shipping goods, for one need only determine whether an order brings the amount owed by a customer in excess of the line. If not, the order is shipped; if so, an incremental credit decision must be reached. The line itself must be reevaluated periodically in order to keep abreast of developments in the account. What was a satisfactory risk exposure today may be more or less than satisfactory a year from today. Despite comprehensive credit procedures, there will always be special cases that must be dealt with individually. Here, too, however, the firm can streamline the operation by defining responsibilities clearly.

---

[15]For the development of an optimal updating schedule, see Long, "Credit Screening System Selection," pp. 316–27.

Collection Procedures

In addition to credit procedures for the individual account, the firm must establish clear-cut collection procedures for past due or delinquent accounts. The initial question to be answered is, How past due should an account be allowed to go before collection procedures are initiated? Because a receivable is only as good as the likelihood that it will be paid, a firm cannot afford to wait too long before initiating collection procedures. On the other hand, if it initiates procedures too soon, it may anger reasonably good customers who, for some reason, fail to make payments by the due date. Procedures, whatever they are, should be firmly established. Initially, a letter is usually sent, followed, perhaps, by additional letters that become ever more serious in tone. Next may come a telephone call from the credit manager and then, perhaps, one from the company's attorney. Some companies have collection personnel who make personal calls on the account.[16]

If all else fails, the account may be turned over to a collection agency. The agency's fees are quite substantial—frequently, one-half the amount of the receivable—but such a procedure may be the only feasible alternative, particularly for a small account. Direct legal action is costly, sometimes serves no real purpose, and may only force the account into bankruptcy. When payment cannot be collected, compromise settlements may provide a higher percentage of collection.[17]

Similar to our analysis of the amount of collection expenditures in the aggregate, the amount spent on an individual account must be evaluated in relation to the likely benefits. In short, the firm should not spend $25 to collect a $15 account. The expected benefits should exceed the collection costs. Suppose that Z-REX Corporation was owed $1,000 from a delinquent customer. With a $60 collection expenditure, Z-REX expects the following:

Collection	Probability	Expected Outcome
$ 0	0.5	$ 0
100	0.2	20
200	0.1	20
300	0.1	30
400	0.1	40
		$110

[16]For an evaluation of alternative collection policies using the Markov process, see Mehta, *Working Capital Management,* Chap. 2.

[17]For an extended discussion of these settlements, see Chapter 24.

Because the expected value of benefits, $110, exceeds the amount expended, $60, the collection effort provides an expected value of net benefits of $50. Of course, other collection efforts may result in even higher net benefits and they should be explored. Past experience may tell a firm what the optimal collection procedure is relative to profitability.

Credit Insurance

To protect against unusual bad-debt losses in extending trade credit, a firm may take out credit insurance. Although the firm cannot insure against losses normally incurred in the industry (known as primary losses), it can insure against above-normal losses. Insurance companies usually restrict coverage to certain acceptable risks, as determined by Dun & Bradstreet ratings. In addition, these companies usually insist upon *coinsurance,* the participation of the collecting firm in a portion of the bad-debt loss—usually 10 to 20 percent. The insistence upon coinsurance safeguards the insurance company from the firm's becoming excessively liberal in the granting of credit. The cost of credit insurance varies directly with the risk of the accounts accepted and is calculated as a percentage of sales. The decision to use credit insurance depends upon the probability of extreme credit losses and the ability of the firm to bear these losses, as well as the amount of premiums.

Use of Electronic Data-Processing Equipment

Computers have been used a great deal in credit management. Their use provides certain essential up-to-date information needed for analysis. All of the information previously placed on receivable ledgers can be placed in computer storage. As a result, the credit department has very quick access to this information. At frequent intervals, it can obtain a trial balance that gives a summary of all billings, payments, discounts taken, and amounts still owed. Also, it can obtain an aging of accounts showing the total amounts owed the firm, the portion that is current, the portion that is up to thirty days past due, that which is thirty to sixty days past due, and so forth.

In addition, the computer can be programmed to provide complete reports on all delinquent accounts, and delinquency letters can be sent out mechanically at regular intervals. Frequent reports on past-due accounts, which were not possible before the computer, alert the credit manager to problems as they develop. As a result, he is able to stay on top of them and take corrective action. Formerly, the situation might have deteriorated during the information lag. Management also may want to be informed when an account approaches the line of credit established for it, and computers can provide this information easily.

The computer helps the credit manager by providing timely and accurate information on the status of accounts. The payment history of a customer can be drawn from storage and printed out in seconds. Included in this history is information such as the date the account was opened, the amount owed currently, the customer's credit line, any numerical credit ratings, and the promptness of past payments. Special reports can be prepared that involve categorization or comparisons. For example, if several companies in the same industry are slow in their payments at a particular time of the year, management might want to know the firm's experience with all other companies in that particular industry. Such information enables the credit manager to analyze and deal with the problem more effectively. In another situation, management might wish to compare incoming orders from a particular customer with his payment history. This information also can be provided quickly.

Indeed, the computer can provide a vast array of detailed information, previously impractical to obtain, that may be useful not only to the credit manager but to other management as well. In addition to processing data, the computer can be programmed to make certain routine credit decisions. In particular, small orders from good accounts can be approved by the computer without the order ever going to a credit analyst. All in all, electronic data processing can make a significant contribution to the credit department. With a large volume of receivables, many firms find computer processing to be the only feasible means by which to handle receivables.

SUMMARY

Credit and collection policies encompass the quality of accounts accepted, the credit period extended, the cash discount given, certain special terms, and the level of collection expenditures. In each case, the credit decision involves a tradeoff between the additional profitability and the cost resulting from a change in any of these elements. For example, by liberalizing the quality requirements for accounts, the firm might hope to make more on the additional sales than the cost of carrying the additional receivables plus the additional bad-debt losses. To maximize profits arising from credit and collection policies, the firm should vary these policies jointly until an optimal solution is obtained. This variation can be accomplished through simulation once the functional relationships are specified. The firm's credit and collection policies, together with its credit and collection procedures, determine the magnitude and quality of its receivable position.

In evaluating a credit applicant, the credit analyst is concerned with obtaining financial and other information about the applicant, analyzing this information, and reaching a credit decision. A sequential analysis process using decision theory was presented whereby the firm can reach a decision with respect to accepting an order, rejecting it, or obtaining additional information. Obtaining additional information is justified only when the expected benefits of the information exceed its cost. In turn, expected benefits arise only if the information allows us to correct a previously wrong decision. Because the stages of investigation are sequential, added sophistication in credit analysis is undertaken only when it is profitable to do so.

If the account is new, the firm must decide whether or not to accept the order. With repeat orders, the firm usually must decide upon the maximum credit to extend. This maximum, known as a line of credit, is based upon the credit-worthiness of the applicant. Collection procedures should be firmly established and applied consistently. The length of time an account may be delinquent before collection procedures are initiated will depend upon the billing terms and the nature of the account. To protect against unusual credit losses, a firm may take out credit insurance. We reviewed briefly some of the applications of electronic data processing to credit management. The uses of the computer are many and increasing in importance.

APPENDIX
Application of Discriminant Analysis to the Selection of Accounts

Discriminant analysis is a statistical tool that can help us decide which prospective accounts to accept or reject, on the basis of certain relevant variables.[18] This type of analysis is similar to regression analysis but assumes that the observations come from two or more different universes. In our case, these universes consist of good and bad accounts. Suppose that we start with an evaluation of only two characteristics of trade credit applicants: the quick, or acid-test, ratio and the ratio of net worth to total assets. For purposes of experiment, we extend open-book credit to all new credit applicants for a sample period. For each account, we record the quick ratio of the firm, its net worth/total assets ratio, and whether or not after a length of time it defaults in payment. If the account defaults, it is classified as a bad account; if it pays in a reasonable period of time, it is classified as a good account. With this information, we are able to undertake a linear discriminant analysis with two independent variables. We wish to determine the predictive value of these variables for the behavior of the dependent variable, whether the account is good or bad.

Suppose that we plot quick ratios and net worth/total assets ratios for each account on a scatter diagram, obtaining the results shown in Figure 15-5. The circles represent bad accounts; the squares represent good accounts. Using the two independent variables, our objective is to find the linear boundary line that discriminates best between good and bad accounts. We need to find the parameters, or weights, of the following discriminant function:

$$f_i = a_1(X_1) + a_2(X_2) \tag{15A-1}$$

---

[18]For a discussion of discriminant analysis, see T. W. Anderson, *An Introduction to Multivariate Statistical Analysis* (New York: John Wiley, 1958); Robert A. Eisenbeis and Robert B. Avery, *Discriminant Analysis and Classification Procedures* (Lexington, Mass.: Heath, 1972); and Donald F. Morrison, *Multivariate Statistical Methods* (New York: McGraw-Hill), 1967).

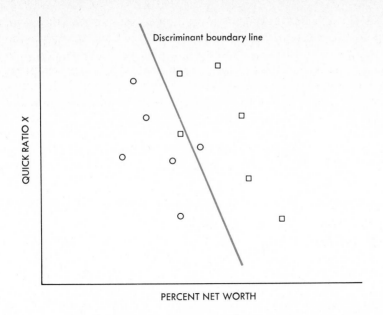

figure 15-5
Discriminant analysis
of accounts receivable

where X_1 is the quick ratio of the firm, X_2 is its net worth to total assets ratio, and a_1 and a_2 are the parameters or weights we wish to compute. Our purpose is to obtain parameter values such that the average or mean value of f_g in Eq. (15A-1) for good accounts will be significantly larger than the average value of f_b for bad accounts. This notion is illustrated in Figure 15-6, where the discriminant function value is along the horizontal axis and the probability of occurrence is along the vertical. In the figure, two universes of credit applicants are shown, good to the right and bad to the left. The average value, f_b, for bad accounts is seen to be much lower than the average value, f_g, for good

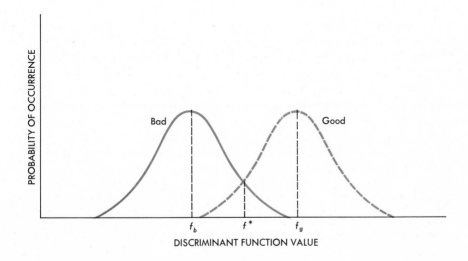

figure 15-6
Universes of good and
bad accounts

accounts. However, we see also that there is an area of overlap between the two universes. In general, the smaller the area of overlap, the better the ability of discriminant analysis to predict good and bad accounts. In other words, it is desirable that the averages or means of the two distributions, f_b and f_g, be as far apart as possible.

The coefficients a_1 and a_2 in Eq. (15A-1) can be computed mathematically from the sample data by

$$a_1 = \frac{Szzdx - Sxzdz}{SzzSxx - Sxz^2} \tag{15A-2}$$

$$a_2 = \frac{Sxxdz - Sxzdx}{SzzSxx - Sxz^2} \tag{15A-3}$$

where Sxx and Szz represent the variances of variables X_1 and X_2, respectively, and Sxz is the covariance of variables X_1 and X_2. The difference between the average of X_1's for good accounts and the average of X_1's for bad accounts is represented by dx. Similarly, dz represents the difference between the average of X_2's for good accounts and the average of X_2's for bad accounts. When we solve for a_1 and a_2, we obtain the parameters of the linear discriminant function in Eq. (15A-1). The ratio a_1/a_2 determines the slope of the discriminant boundary line.

We now need to determine the minimum cutoff value of the function. The idea is to refuse credit to those accounts with values of f below the cutoff value and extend credit to those with f values above the cutoff value. In theory, we wish to find the discriminant function value in Figure 15-6 denoted by f^*. Using this value for cutoff purposes will minimize the prediction of good accounts when they are bad and the prediction of bad accounts when they are good. To determine the cutoff value in practice, we start by calculating the f_i for each account, given the parameters of Eq. (15A-1). For our example, suppose that we obtained the f_i values, arranged in ascending order of magnitude, shown in Table 15-9.

We see that there is an area of overlap for accounts 6, 12, 11, and 4. We know that the cutoff value must lie between 1.65 and 1.91. For simplicity, we may want to use the midpoint, 1.78, as our cutoff value. Given the cutoff value, we are able to draw the discriminant boundary line in Figure 15-5 that discriminates best between good and bad accounts. We note, however, that two of the accounts, 11 and 12, are misclassified, given this cutoff value. Account 11 is classified as a good account when, in fact, it was bad; while account 12 is classified as a bad account when, in fact, it was good. Rather than assign a strict cutoff value, it may be better to allow for misclassification and designate the area between 1.65 and 1.91 as uncertain, requiring further analysis. In theory, this area would correspond to the area of overlap in Figure 15-6.

If we have reason to believe that new credit applicants will not differ significantly from the relationships found for the sample accounts, discriminant analysis can be used as a means for selecting and rejecting credit sale customers. If we use a minimum cutoff value, we will reject all sales in which the f_i value for the credit applicant is less than 1.78 and accept all sales in which the f_i value exceeds 1.78. If a range is used, we will accept all sales in which the prospective customer has an f_i value in excess of 1.91 and reject applicants with f_i values below 1.65. For applicants with f_i values lying between these two values, we might want to obtain additional credit information, along with information as to the profitability of the sale, before making a decision.

table 15-9
Values of f_i

Account Number	Good or Bad	f_i
7	Bad	0.81
10	Bad	0.97
2	Bad	1.36
3	Bad	1.44
6	Bad	1.65
12	Good	1.77
11	Bad	1.83
4	Good	1.91
1	Good	2.12
8	Good	2.19
5	Good	2.34
9	Good	2.48

Although the example we used is simple, it illustrates the potential of discriminant analysis in selecting or rejecting credit applicants. Discriminant analysis can be extended to include a number of other independent variables. In fact, additional independent variables should be added as long as the benefits of greater predictability exceed the costs of collecting and processing the additional information. As before, the idea with more than two independent variables is to determine a set of weights, $a_1, a_2, a_3, \ldots, a_n$, for the various independent variables employed such that the weighted average, or total score, f_i

$$f_i = a_1 X_1 + a_2 X_2 + a_3 X_3 + \cdots + a_n X_n \qquad (15A\text{-}4)$$

for the good accounts is as different as possible from that for the bad accounts. Given the optimal set of weights or parameters, one then calculates the total score, f^*, which best discriminates between good and bad accounts.

To illustrate, suppose that we were concerned with four independent variables: the quick ratio, X_1; the net worth/total assets ratio, X_2; the cash-flow/total debt ratio, X_3; and the net profit margin ratio, X_4. Suppose that the optimal parameters, or weights, for a_1, a_2, a_3, and a_4 were found to be 2, 5, 13, and 22, respectively. If a new credit applicant had a quick ratio of 1.5, a net worth to total assets ratio of 0.4, a cash-flow to total debt ratio of 0.2, and a net profit margin of 0.05, its total credit score would be

$$f_i = 2(1.5) + 5(0.4) + 13(0.2) + 22(0.05) = 8.7$$

This score is then compared with the optimal discriminant function, or cutoff, value determined on the basis of a sample. If 8.7 exceeds the predetermined cutoff value, the account is accepted. If 8.7 is less than the cutoff value, the account is rejected. Thus the method is the same whether two independent variables are used or more than two are used.

For discriminant analysis to have predicted value, the credit applicants being analyzed must correspond to the sample applicants on whom the discriminant-function parameters are based. With the passage of time, the underlying characteristics change. What was once an important financial ratio for predictive purposes may be less important today. In most applications, there is a decay in the validity of the discriminant function over time. As the system decays, there is a tendency to extend credit to more bad customers and to reject more potentially good customers.[19] After a point, the discriminant-function system is no longer worthwhile from the standpoint of credit decisions and the firm would be better off with no system. Therefore, as experience provides new information it is important to assess the validity of the parameters or weights. Where the parameters are no longer realistic, a new sample should be drawn and new parameters generated.

While a linear discriminant function does not fit the data, it is possible to develop nonlinear functions. In particular, the quadratic function has been used with success. While problems other than those discussed exist in the application of discriminant analysis to finance, space does not permit us to explore them here. For the reader interested in such applications, excellent discussions are available which explore underlying problems in discriminant analysis as they relate to research in finance.[20]

In summary, discriminant analysis is a flexible and practical means for evaluating new credit applicants as well as for monitoring existing accounts. Because the information is processed on a high-speed computer, time spent on clerical work and credit analysis can be reduced. Credit analysts can concentrate on only those marginal accounts falling in an uncertain area. Discriminant analysis offers an efficient means by which a company can meet the mounting demands on its credit department.

---

[19]For a discussion of the optimal updating of the credit-screening system, see Michael S. Long, "Credit Screening System Selection," *Journal of Financial and Quantitative Analysis,* 11 (June 1976), 313–28.

[20]See Robert A. Eisenbeis, "Pitfalls in the Application of Discriminant Analysis in Business, Finance, and Economics," *Journal of Finance,* 32 (June 1977), 875–900; and O. Maurice Joy and John O. Tollefson, "On Financial Applications of Discriminant Analysis," *Journal of Financial and Quantitative Analysis,* 10 (December 1975), 723–40.

1. In order to increase sales from their present annual level of $240,000, the Heap Corporation is considering a more liberal credit policy. Currently, the firm has an average collection period of thirty days; however, it is believed that as the collection period is lengthened, sales will increase by the following amounts:

Credit Policy	Increase in Average Collection Period	Increase in Sales
A	15 days	$10,000
B	30	15,000
C	45	17,000
D	60	18,000

The firm has the following cost pattern at present:

Price of the only product manufactured	$1.00
Variable costs per unit (before taxes)	.60
Average costs per unit (current)	.80

If the firm has a pretax opportunity cost of 20 percent, which credit policy should be pursued? (Assume a 360-day year.)

2. If the only information available to the Heap Corporation (problem 1) was that an increase in the average collection period by sixty days would increase sales by $18,000, would the firm increase the collection period?

3. The Heap Corporation (problem 1) has estimated that the following pattern of bad-debt experience will prevail if it initiates more liberal credit terms:

Increase in Average Collection Period	Percent Default
15 days	3%
30	6
45	10
60	15

The current bad-debt loss is 1 percent. Given the other assumptions in problem 1, which credit policy should be pursued?

4. Recalculate problem 3, assuming the following pattern of bad-debt experience:

Increase in Average Collection Period	Percent Default
15 days	1.5%
30	2.0
45	4.0
60	8.0

5. The Chickee Corporation has a 12 percent opportunity cost of funds and cur-
    rently sells on terms of net 10, EOM. This means that goods shipped before the
    end of the month must be paid for by the 10th of the following month. The firm has
    sales of $10 million a year, which are 80 percent on credit and spread evenly over
    the year. Currently, the average collection period is sixty days. If Chickee offered
    terms of 2/10, net 30, 60 percent of its customers would take the discount, and
    the collection period would be reduced to forty days. Should Chickee change its
    terms from net/10, EOM to 2/10, net 30?

6. The Pottsville Manufacturing Corporation is considering extending trade credit
    to the San Jose Company. Examination of the records of San Jose has produced
    the following financial statements.

San Jose Company balance sheet (in millions)

	19X1	19X2	19X3
Assets:			
Current Assets:			
Cash	$ 1.5	$ 1.6	$ 1.6
Receivables	1.3	1.8	2.5
Inventories (at lower of cost or market)	1.3	2.6	4.0
Other	.4	.5	.4
Total current assets	$ 4.5	$ 6.5	$ 8.5
Fixed assets:			
Buildings (net)	2.0	1.9	1.8
Machinery and equipment (net)	7.0	6.5	6.0
Total fixed assets	$ 9.0	$ 8.4	$ 7.8
Other assets	1.0	.8	.6
Total assets	$14.5	$15.7	$16.9
Liabilities:			
Current liabilities:			
Notes payable (8½%)	$ 2.1	$ 3.1	$ 3.8
Trade payables	.2	.4	.9
Other payables	.2	.2	.2
Total	$ 2.5	$ 3.7	$ 4.9
Term loan (8%)	4.0	3.0	2.0
Total	$ 6.5	$ 6.7	$ 6.9
Net worth			
Common stock	5.0	5.0	5.0
Preferred stock(6½%)	1.0	1.0	1.0
Retained earnings	2.0	3.0	4.0
Total liabilities and net worth	$14.5	$15.7	$16.9

The San Jose Company has a Dun & Bradstreet rating of 4A-2. A bank check
indicates that the firm generally carries balances in the low seven figures. A trade
credit check of five suppliers to San Jose reveals that the firm takes its discounts
from the three creditors offering 2/10, net 30 terms, though it is about fifteen
days slow in paying the two firms offering terms of net 30.

San Jose Company income statement
(in millions)

	19X1	19X2	19X3
Net credit sales	$15.0	$15.8	$16.2
Cost of goods sold	11.3	12.1	13.0
Gross profit	$ 3.7	$ 3.7	$ 3.2
Operating expenses	1.1	1.2	1.2
Net profit before taxes	$ 2.6	$ 2.5	$ 2.0
Tax	1.3	1.2	1.0
Profit after taxes	$ 1.3	$ 1.3	$ 1.0
Dividends	.3	.3	.0
	$ 1.0	$ 1.0	$ 1.0

   Analyze the San Jose Company's application for credit. What positive factors are present? What negative factors are present?

7. It has been determined that the San Jose Company (problem 6) will purchase about $1 million worth of supplies from Pottsville (problem 6) each year. Further, it has been estimated that San Jose will meet its credit obligations to Pottsville according to the following distribution:

Payment Schedule	Probability
Payment on time (net 30)	0.15
Payment one month late	0.34
Payment two months late	0.30
Payment three months late	0.20
No payment (bad debt)	0.01

   If the marginal profit on each unit sold to San Jose is $5 (price = $100 per unit), should credit be extended? (Assume that no sales would be made to San Jose unless credit were extended. Further assume that Pottsville has an opportunity cost of funds of 2 percent per month, not compounded.)

8. Matlock Gauge Company makes wind and current gauges for pleasure boats. The gauges are sold throughout the Southeast to boat dealers, and the average order size is $50. The company sells to all registered dealers without a credit analysis. Terms are net forty-five days and the average collection period is sixty days, which is regarded as satisfactory. However, Jane Sullivan, vice-president–finance, is concerned because of the increasing number of bad-debt losses on new orders. With credit ratings from local and regional credit agencies, she feels she would be able to classify new orders into one of three risk categories. Past experience shows the following:

	Order Category		
	Low Risk	Medium Risk	High Risk
Bad-debt loss	3%	7%	24%
Percent of category orders to total orders	30	50	20

The cost of producing and shipping the gauges and of carrying the receivables is 78 percent of sales. The cost of obtaining credit-rating information and of evaluating it is $4 per order. Surprisingly, there does not appear to be any association between the risk category and the collection period; the average for each of the three risk categories is around sixty days. Based on this information, should the company obtain credit information on new orders instead of selling to all new accounts without credit analysis?

9. On the basis of their past trade credit experience, the McDougal Corporation rates customers Good, Fair, or Poor. The cost of a past experience check is $1 and of a Dun & Bradstreet report $8. The marginal profit per item to McDouglas is $5, the marginal cost is $10, and the required return is 20 percent before taxes. Assuming McDougal runs a past experience check as a matter of policy, the following data may be estimated:

Past Experience	Proportion	Avg. Collection Period	Avg. Collection Cost	Prob. of Bad Debt
Good	40%	35 days	$ .25	0.03
Fair	30	60	1.50	0.20
Poor	30	100	4.00	0.40

(a) Determine the costs of acceptance and rejection for each classification and the order size at which the two cross.

If a Dun & Bradstreet report were obtained, the analyst would classify each account as Yes or No, with the following data:

Experience	Dun & Bradstreet	Prob.	Avg. Collection Period	Avg. Collection Cost	Prob. of Bad Debt
Good	Yes	70%	30 days	$ .20	0.01
	No	30	47	.37	0.08
Fair	Yes	50	40	.80	0.10
	No	50	80	2.20	0.30
Poor	Yes	30	60	2.00	0.20
	No	70	117	4.86	0.49

(b) Determine the costs of acceptance and rejection for each of the above. In each case, at what order size would a D & B become desirable?

(c) On the basis of the above analysis, formulate the firm's policy in regard to each type of order.

(*Note:* This problem involves lengthy computations. The typical time involved is about one and one-half hours.)

SELECTED REFERENCES

BENISHAY, HASKEL, "Managerial Controls of Accounts Receivable—A Deterministic Approach," *Journal of Accounting Research,* 3 (Spring 1965), 114–33.

——, "A Stochastic Model of Credit Sales Debt," *Journal of the American Statistical Association,* 61 (December 1966), 1010–28.

BROSKY, JOHN J., *The Implicit Cost of Trade Credit and Theory of Optimal Terms of Sale.* New York: Credit Research Foundation, 1969.

CYERT, R. M., H. J. DAVIDSON, AND G. L. THOMPSON, "Estimation of the Allowance for Doubtful Accounts by Markov Chains," *Management Science,* 8 (April 1962), 287–303.

DYL, EDWARD A., "Another Look at the Evaluation of Investment in Accounts Receivable," *Financial Management,* 6 (Winter 1977), 67–70.

EDMISTER, ROBERT O., AND GARY G. SCHLARBAUM, "Credit Policy in Lending Institutions," *Journal of Financial and Quantitative Analysis,* 9 (June 1974), 335–56.

EISENBEIS, ROBERT A., "Pitfalls in the Application of Discriminant Analysis in Business, Finance and Economics," *Journal of Finance,* 32 (June 1977), 875–900.

GREER, CARL C., "The Optimal Credit Acceptance Policy," *Journal of Financial and Quantitative Analysis,* 2 (December 1967), 399–415.

HERBST, ANTHONY F., "Some Empirical Evidence on the Determinants of Trade Credit at the Industry Level of Aggregation," *Journal of Financial and Quantitative Analysis,* 9 (June 1974), 377–94.

JOY, MAURICE O., AND JOHN O. TOLLEFSON, "On the Financial Applications of Discriminant Analysis," *Journal of Financial and Quantitative Analysis,* 10 (December 1975), 723–40.

KIM, YONG H., AND JOSEPH C. ATKINS, "Evaluating Investments in Accounts Receivable: A Wealth Maximization Framework," *Journal of Finance,* 33 (May 1978), 403–12.

LANE, SYLVIA, "Submarginal Credit Risk Classification," *Journal of Financial and Quantitative Analysis,* 7 (January 1972), 1379–85.

LEWELLEN, WILBUR G., "Finance Subsidiaries and Corporate Borrowing Capacity," *Financial Management,* 1 (Spring 1972), 21–32.

LEWELLEN, W. G., AND R. O., EDMINISTER, "A General Model for Accounts Receivable Analysis and Control," *Journal of Financial and Quantitative Analysis,* 8 (March 1973), 195–206.

LEWELLEN, W. G., AND R. W. JOHNSON, "Better Way to Monitor Accounts Receivable," *Harvard Business Review,* (May-June 1972), pp. 101–9.

LONG, MICHAEL S., "Credit Screening System Selection," *Journal of Financial and Quantitative Analysis,* 11 (June 1976), 313–28.

MAO, JAMES C. T., "Controlling Risk in Accounts Receivable Management," *Journal of Business Finance & Accounting,* 1 (Autumn 1974), 395–403.

MARRAH, GEORGE L., "Managing Receivables," *Financial Executive,* 38 (July 1970), 40–44.

MEHTA, DILEEP, "The Formulation of Credit Policy Models." *Management Science,* 15 (October 1968), 30–50.

——, "Optimal Credit Policy Selection: A Dynamic Approach," *Journal of Financial and Quantitative Analysis,* 5 (December 1970), 421–44.

————, *Working Capital Management*, Chaps. 1–3. Englewood Cliffs, N.J.: Prentice-Hall, 1974.

OH, JOHN S., "Opportunity Cost in the Evaluation of Investment in Accounts Receivable," *Financial Management*, 5 (Summer 1976), 32–36.

SCHIFF, MICHAEL, AND ZVI LIEBER, "A Model for the Integration of Credit and Inventory Management," *Journal of Finance*, 29 (March 1974), 133–40.

SCHWARTZ, ROBERT, A., "An Economic Model of Trade Credit," *Journal of Financial and Quantitative Analysis*, 9 (September 1974), 643–58.

SHAPIRO, ALAN, "Optimal Inventory and Credit Granting Strategies under Inflation and Depreciation," *Journal of Financial and Quantitative Analysis*, 7 (January 1973), 37–46.

SMITH, KEITH V., *Management of Working Capital*, Sec. 3. New York: West Publishing, 1974.

STONE, BERNELL K., "The Payments-Pattern Approach to the Forecasting and Control of Accounts Receivable," *Financial Management*, 5 (Autumn 1976), 65–82.

WELSHANS, MERLE T., "Using Credit for Profit Making," *Harvard Business Review*, 45 (January-February 1967), 141–56.

16
inventory management

Inventories, like receivables, represent a significant portion of most firms' assets and, accordingly, require substantial investments. In order that these investments not become unnecessarily large, inventories must be managed efficiently. Our purpose is to investigate briefly the means by which efficient management can be achieved and to relate these methods to financial management.

Inventories provide an important link in the production and sale of a product. For a company engaged in manufacturing, a certain amount of inventory is necessary in the production of the product; this inventory is known as "goods in process." Although other types of inventory—namely, in-transit, raw-materials, and finished-goods inventory—are not necessary in the strictest sense, they are important if the firm is to be at all flexible. For example, inventory in transit, that is, inventory between various stages of production or storage, permits efficient production scheduling and utilization of resources. Without this type of inventory, each stage of production would be dependent upon the preceding stage's finishing its operation on a unit of production. As a result, there probably would be delays and considerable idle time in certain stages of production. Thus there is an incentive for the firm to maintain large in-transit inventory.

Raw-materials inventory gives the firm flexibility in its purchasing. Without it, the firm must exist on a hand-to-mouth basis, buying raw material strictly in keeping with its production schedule. Moreover, the purchasing department often is able to take advantage of quantity discounts. By so doing, raw-materials inventory may be bloated temporarily. Finished-goods inventory allows the firm flexibility in its production scheduling and in its marketing. Production does not need to be geared directly to sales. Large inventories also allow efficient servicing of customer demands. If a certain product is temporarily out of stock, present as well as future sales to the customer may be lost. Thus there is an incentive to maintain large stocks of all three types of inventory.

The advantages of increased inventories, then, are several. The firm can effect economies of production and purchasing and can fill customer orders more quickly. In short, the firm is more flexible. The obvious disadvantages are the total cost of holding the inventory, including storage and handling costs, and the required return on capital tied up in the investment in inventory. Inventories, like accounts receivable, should be increased as long as the resulting savings exceed the total cost of holding the added inventory. The balance finally reached depends upon the estimates of actual savings, the cost of carrying additional inventory, and the efficiency of inventory control. Obviously, this balance requires coordination of the production, marketing, and finance areas of the firm in keeping with an overall objective.

INVENTORY CONTROL

For a given level of inventory, the efficiency of inventory control affects the flexibility of the firm. Two essentially identical firms with the same amount of inventory may have significantly different degrees of flexibility in operations due to differences in inventory control. Inefficient procedures may result in an unbalanced inventory—the firm may frequently be out of certain types of inventory, and overstock other types, necessitating excessive investment. These inefficiencies ultimately have an adverse effect upon profits. Turning the situation around, differences in the efficiency of inventory control for a given level of flexibility affect the level of investment required in inventories. The less efficient the inventory control, the greater the investment required. Similarly, excessive investment in inventories impacts profits adversely. Thus the effects of inventory control on flexibility and on the level of investment required in inventories represent two sides of the same coin. Our purpose in the subsequent sections is to examine various principles of inventory control.

Economic Order Quantity

The economic order quantity (EOQ) is an important concept in the purchase of raw materials and in the storage of finished-goods and in-transit inventories. In our analysis, we wish to determine the optimal order quantity for a particular item of inventory, given its forecasted usage, ordering cost, and carrying cost. Ordering can mean either the purchase of the item or its production. Assume for the moment that the usage of a particular item of inventory is known with certainty. Moreover, assume that this usage is stationary or steady throughout the period of time being analyzed. In other words, if usage is 2,600 items for a six-month period, 100 items would be used each week. While the EOQ model can be modified to take account of increasing and decreasing usage over time,[1] we do not get into this added degree of complexity.

We assume that ordering costs, O, are constant regardless of the size of the order. In the purchase of raw materials or other items, these costs represent the clerical costs involved in placing an order as well as certain costs of receiving and checking the goods once they arrive. For finished-goods inventories, ordering costs involve scheduling a production run. For in-transit inventories, ordering costs are likely to involve nothing more than record keeping. The total ordering cost for a period is simply the number of orders for that period, times the cost per order.

Carrying costs per period, C, represent the cost of inventory storage, handling, and insurance, together with the required rate of return on the investment in inventory. These costs are assumed to be constant per unit of inventory, per unit of time. Thus the total carrying cost for a period is the average number of units of inventory for the period, times the carrying cost per unit. In addition, we assume for now that inventory orders are filled without delay. Because out-of-stock items can be replaced immediately, there is no need to maintain a buffer or safety stock. Though the assumptions made up to now may seem overly restrictive, they are necessary for an initial understanding of the conceptual framework that follows. Subsequently, we will relax some of them.

If the usage of an inventory item is perfectly steady over a period of time and there is no safety stock, average inventory (in units) can be expressed as

$$\text{Average inventory} = \frac{Q}{2} \tag{16-1}$$

where Q is the quantity (in units) ordered and is assumed to be constant for the period. The above problem is illustrated in Figure 16-1. Although the

---

[1]For such a modification, see Dileep R. Mehta, *Working Capital Management* (Englewood Cliffs, N.J.: Prentice-Hall, 1974), pp. 81–89.

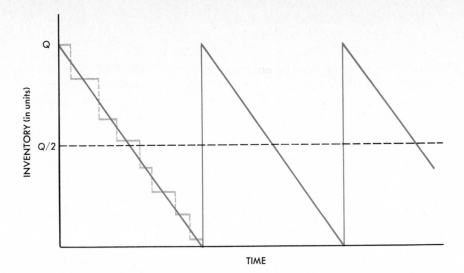

figure 16-1
Order quantity example

quantity demanded is a step function, we assume for analytical purposes that it can be approximated by a straight line. We see that zero inventory always indicates that further inventory must be ordered.

The carrying cost of inventory is the carrying cost per unit, times the average number of units of inventory, or $CQ/2$. The total number of orders for a period of time is simply the total usage (in units) of an item of inventory for that period, S, divided by Q. Consequently, total ordering costs are represented by the ordering cost per order, times the number of orders, or SO/Q. Total inventory costs, then, are the carrying costs plus ordering costs, or

$$T = \frac{CQ}{2} + \frac{SO}{Q}$$

(16-2)

We see from Eq. (16-2) that the higher the order quantity, Q, the higher the carrying costs but the lower the total ordering costs. The lower the order quantity, the lower the carrying costs but the higher the total ordering costs. We are concerned with the tradeoff between the economies of increased order size and the added cost of carrying additional inventory.

In order to determine the optimal order quantity, Q^*, we differentiate Eq. (16-2) with respect to Q and set the derivative equal to zero, obtaining[2]

[2]The steps are

$$\frac{dT}{dQ} = \frac{C}{2} - \frac{SO}{Q^2} = 0$$

$$CQ^2 - 2SO = 0$$

$$Q^2 = \frac{2SO}{C}$$

$$Q = \sqrt{\frac{2SO}{C}}$$

$$Q^* = \sqrt{\frac{2SO}{C}}$$

This equation is known as the economic lot-size formula.[3] To illustrate its use, suppose that usage of an inventory item is 2,000 units during a 100-day period, ordering costs are \$100 an order, and the carrying costs are \$10 per unit per 100 days. The optimal economic order quantity, then, is

$$Q^* = \sqrt{\frac{2(2,000)(100)}{10}} = 200 \text{ units}$$

With an order quantity of 200 units, the firm would order (2,000/200), or ten times, during the period under consideration, or every ten days. We see from Eq. (16-3) that Q^* varies directly with total usage, S, and order cost, O, and inversely with the carrying cost, C. However, the relationship is dampened by the square-root sign in both cases. As usage increases, the optimal order size and the average level of inventory increase by a lesser percentage. In other words, economies of scale are possible.

In our example, we have assumed that inventory can be ordered with no delay. However, there is usually a time lapse in procurement between the time a purchase order is placed and the time the inventory is actually received, or in the time it takes to manufacture an item after an order is placed. This lead time must be considered. If it is constant and known with certainty, however, the optimal order quantity is not affected. In the above example, the firm would still order 200 units at a time and place ten orders during the specified time period, or every ten days. If the lead time for delivery were three days, the firm simply would place its order seven days after delivery of the previous order.

The EOQ function is illustrated in Figure 16-2. In the figure, we plot ordering costs, carrying costs, and total costs—the sum of the first two costs. We see that whereas carrying costs vary directly with the size of the order, ordering costs vary inversely with the size of the order. The total cost line declines at first as the fixed costs of ordering are spread over more units. The

---

[3]This formula also holds if there is a variable component to order costs, provided the component is a linear function of order size. Given a linear relationship, total variable costs for the period of time being analyzed are VS, where V is variable cost per unit ordered. Total costs then become

$$T = \frac{CQ}{2} + VS + \frac{SO}{Q}$$

When we differentiate this expression with respect to Q, we see that VS does not enter in and that the optimal order quantity is

$$\sqrt{\frac{2SO}{C}}$$

figure 16-2
Economic order
quantity relationship

total cost line begins to rise, however, when the decrease in average ordering cost is more than offset by the additional carrying costs. Point X, then, represents the economical order quantity, which minimizes the total cost of inventory.

The EOQ formula taken up in this section is a very useful tool for inventory control. In purchasing raw materials or other items of inventory, it tells us the amount to order and the best timing of our orders. For finished-goods inventory, it enables us to exercise better control over the timing and size of production runs. In general, the EOQ model gives us a rule for deciding when to replenish inventories and the amount to replenish. All inventory models, no matter how complex, address themselves to this problem of the timing and magnitude of replenishment.

Quantity Discounts

Frequently, the firm is able to take advantage of quantity discounts in ordering. Because these discounts affect the price per unit, they also influence the economic order quantity. However, the basic EOQ framework should still be used as a point of departure for analyzing the problem. In our example, we assumed 2,000 units of usage during a 100-day period, order costs of $100 an order, and carrying costs of $10 per unit per 100 days, resulting in an economic order quantity of 200 units. Suppose now that a quantity discount of $0.10 a unit in price is available if the firm increases its order size to 250 units, whereas currently it enjoys no discount. To determine whether or not the discount is worthwhile, we must analyze the benefits in relation to costs involved.

The savings available to the firm in lower purchase price are

$$\text{Savings} = \text{Discount per unit} \times \text{Usage}$$
$$= 0.10 \times 2{,}000 = \$200 \qquad (16\text{-}4)$$

The cost is the additional carrying cost less savings in ordering costs that result from fewer orders being placed. The additional carrying cost, where Q' is the new order size required, is

$$\frac{(Q' - Q^*)C}{2} = \frac{(250 - 200)10}{2} = \$250$$

The saving in ordering costs is

$$\frac{SO}{Q^*} - \frac{SO}{Q'} = \frac{(2{,}000)(100)}{200} - \frac{(2{,}000)(100)}{250} = \$200$$

Therefore the net increase in costs is $250 - $200, or $50, for going from an order quantity of 200 units to 250 units. Because the net cost is less than the benefits to be derived, $200, the firm should use an order quantity of 250 units. Similarly, other problems involving quantity discounts can be analyzed in this manner. The economic order quantity formula serves as a point of departure for balancing the benefits against the costs of a change in order size.

UNCERTAINTY AND SAFETY STOCKS

In practice, the demand or usage of inventory is not generally known with certainty; usually it fluctuates during a given period of time. Typically, the demand for finished-goods inventory is subject to the greatest fluctuation. In contrast, the usage of raw-materials inventory and in-transit inventory, both of which depend upon the production scheduling, is much more predictable. In addition to demand or usage, the lead time required to receive delivery of inventory once an order is placed is usually subject to some variation. Owing to these fluctuations, it is not feasible to allow expected inventory to fall to zero before a new order is expected to be received, as could be done when usage and lead time were known with certainty.

Most firms maintain some margin of safety, or safety stock; otherwise, they may be unable to satisfy the demand for an item of inventory at a particular time. There are opportunity costs to being out of stock. In the case of finished-goods inventory, the customer is likely to become irritated and may take his business elsewhere. In the case of raw-materials and in-transit inventories, the cost of being out of stock is a stoppage in production and the resulting inefficiencies that occur. While this opportunity cost is measured more easily than that associated with finished-goods inventory, a stockout of the latter has a cost; and the firm must recognize it.

Proper Level of Safety Stock

The decision to maintain a safety stock involves balancing the cost of stockouts with the cost of carrying additional inventory. If we know the probability distribution of future demand or usage, we can assess this balance. Suppose, for example, that the usage of an inventory item over a ten-day period is expected to be the following:

Usage (in units)	50	100	150	200	250	300	350
Probability	0.04	0.08	0.20	0.36	0.20	0.08	0.04

Moreover, assume an economic order quantity of 200 units every ten days, steady usage, 200 units of inventory on hand at the beginning of the period, and three days lead time required to procure inventory. This lead time is known with certainty, and a new order is always placed at the end of the eighth day for delivery at the end of the eleventh day. If the firm carries no safety stock, there will be no stockouts if usage is 200 units or less. However, if usage proves to be 250 units instead of 200 units, there will be a stockout of 50 units. Similarly, if usage is 300 units or 350 units, there will be stockouts of 100 units and 150 units, respectively.

If we know the cost per unit of stockout, we can calculate the expected cost of stockouts and then compare this cost with the cost of carrying additional inventory. Included in the stockout cost are the loss of profit associated with the order not being filled as well as the intangible loss of customer goodwill. The extreme with respect to dissatisfaction is that the customer will cease to do business with the firm altogether. Suppose that we are able to estimate the stockout cost and that it is $6 a unit, and that the average carrying cost for the ten-day period is $1 per unit. In Table 16-1, we show the expected stockout cost, carrying cost, and total cost for various levels of safety stock. We see that the optimal safety stock is 50 units, the level at which the total cost is lowest. Rather than estimate a cost of stockout, some firms simply specify a maximum probability of running out of stock. If the hypothetical firm in our example did not want the probability of stockout to be more than 5 percent, it would maintain a safety stock of 100 units. In this way, it could meet all demand except that for 350 units, where there is a 4 percent probability of occurrence.

Order Point Formula

Because the probabilistic analysis taken up in the preceding section is cumbersome, many people find it unfeasible for a multiperiod problem. Instead, they propose using an order point, whereby an order is placed once

table 16-1
Expected costs associated with various safety stocks

Safety Stock	Stockout	Stockout Cost ($6 per unit)	Probability	Expected Stockout Cost	Carrying Cost	Total Cost
150 units	0	$ 0	0	$ 0	$150	$150
100 units	50	300	0.04	12	100	112
50 units	100	600	0.04	24		
	50	300	0.08	24		
				$ 48	50	98
0 units	150	900	0.04	36		
	100	600	0.08	48		
	50	300	0.20	60		
				$144	0	144

inventory reaches so many units.[4] The firm specifies an acceptable stockout percentage and then calculates an order point based upon this percentage, as well as upon other factors. The optimal order point is the level of inventory at which we should order the economic order quantity of additional stock. It is the point at which forecasted usage of an item of inventory, given a stockout tolerance, would just exhaust the existing inventory during the lead time required to procure additional inventory.

$$\text{Order point*} = S(L) + F\sqrt{SR(L)} \qquad (16\text{-}5)$$

where S is the usage, L is the lead time required to obtain additional inventory once an order is placed, R is the average number of units per order, and F is a stockout acceptance factor.

If 300 units were ordered during a period of time, with twenty orders, R would be fifteen. The stockout acceptance factor is based upon the probability distribution of usage. If demand or usage is distributed according to a Poisson distribution,[5] F can be determined as in Figure 16-3. For example, if the stockout acceptance percentage is specified as 10 percent, we see from the figure that this percentage corresponds to an acceptance factor of 1.29.

To illustrate the use of Eq. (16-5), suppose that we consider a problem in which usage, S, is 100 units per month, lead time, L, is one-half month, the average number of units per customer order, R, is five, and the acceptable stockout percentage is 10 percent. The optimal order point, then, would be

$$100(\tfrac{1}{2}) + 1.29\sqrt{(100)(5)(\tfrac{1}{2})} = 70 \text{ units}$$

[4]See Arthur Snyder, "Principles of Inventory Management," *Financial Executive*, 32 (April 1964), 13–21. This section is based upon his article, although the concept of an order point is found in most of the literature on inventory theory.

[5]A discussion of the Poisson probability distribution can be found in most statistic texts.

figure 16-3
Stockout acceptance
factor

Thus the firm should reorder when inventory reaches 70 units. We note that the order point includes a safety stock, which is determined by the stockout acceptance percentage we specify. If there were no safety stock, the order point would be at 50 units, or one-half of one month's usage. The one-half month takes into account the lead time required to actually receive inventory once an order is placed. The order point formula given in Eq. (16-5) minimizes the investment in inventory relative to an acceptable level of stockout. The concept of the order point can be extended to situations where usage is normally distributed[6] or distributed according to some other distribution.

The concept itself is illustrated in Figure 16-4 in conjunction with an economic order quantity. If demand is reasonably steady over a long period of time, the firm might employ the EOQ formula and order the same amount of inventory whenever the level of inventory touched the order point. In the figure, the order quantity is represented by the vertical distances and is the same for each order. The lead time for actual delivery of inventory is assumed to be known with certainty and to be the same for each order. However, usage is assumed to be subject to uncertainty. As a result, the time intervals T_1, T_2, T_3, and T_4 are not equal; and the low points in the level of inventory are not the same. Indeed, during period T_2, inventory reaches zero and the firm is out of stock until the new order is received.

The inventory system illustrated in Figure 16-4 is known as a "two-bin system," in which a constant replenishment order is placed whenever a critical level of inventory is reached. One might think of it as using stock from the regular bin and when this bin is exhausted, using stock from the safety bin and at the same time placing a replenishment order. The system combines the economic order quantity with the order point concept to produce an optimal

[6]For an analysis of the order point when usage is assumed to be normally distributed, see Harold Bierman, Jr., Charles P. Bonini, and Warren H. Hausman, *Quantitative Analysis for Business Decisions*, 5th ed. (Homewood, Ill.: Richard D. Irwin, 1977), Chap. 17.

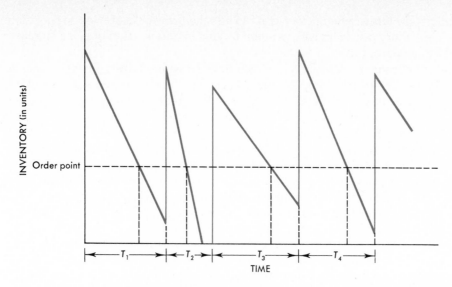

figure 16-4
Order-point example

control system when the firm is faced with lead times and uncertain usage. We see that if the size of the order point is reduced, less inventory is held on the average, and carrying costs are reduced. However, the probability of stockout is increased. Likewise, when the order quantity is reduced, carrying costs are reduced and the probability of stockout increased. Because total costs are affected by both the order point and the order quantity, an optimal control system must embody both of these factors.

OTHER CONSIDERATIONS

The control system we have described is straightforward in that given information about demand, order costs, and carrying costs, we are able to determine an optimal level of average inventory. However, other factors sometimes come into play. For one thing, a company may not always be able to count on obtaining an order within a reasonable period of time. A major supplier may experience a strike, with the result that production is shut down and no orders are shipped. In anticipation of a strike, the firm may overorder so that it will have inventory on hand to see it through the likely duration of the strike. This anticipatory buying often happens in the case of steel before the major labor contract with the steelworkers expires. In another situation, a supplier may be operating at full capacity with long and uncertain lags before an order is received. Here, too, the firm may engage in anticipatory buying and build an unusually large safety stock.

Moreover, a supplier may announce a price increase effective some time in the future. To take advantage of the existing price, the firm may buy items in excess of its immediate needs. In fact, during a period of rapid inflation, firms have an incentive to carry larger inventories than would otherwise be the case. By investing in real assets of this sort, they gain in monetary terms when prices rise.[7] While the firm will not want to speculate on inventory price changes, prudent buying in anticipation of price increases may be appropriate.

In the models presented, we have considered only the overall level of inventory of the firm. Yet most firms have multiple items of inventory, oftentimes in the thousands. In general, the greater the number of separate items, the greater the overall level of inventory the firm needs to carry. This arises because of economies of scale in inventory control, as implied by the square-root sign in the EOQ formula (Eq. (16-3)). In some situations, marketing considerations may dominate the inventory management decision. Some firms want to carry a complete product line in all stores in the belief that overall demand will be enhanced. This contrasts with a policy of carrying only those items that involve a reasonable demand.

The considerations discussed above must often be factored into the analysis of the proper level of overall inventory the firm should maintain. These considerations are apart from the formulas and probabilistic approaches presented for inventory control and safety stocks. As a result, the overall level of inventory of a firm may be higher than that dictated by earlier considerations.

INVENTORY AND THE FINANCIAL MANAGER

The inventory control methods that have been described in this chapter give us a means for determining an optimal level of inventory, as well as how much should be ordered and when. These tools are necessary for managing inventory efficiently and balancing the advantages of additional inventory against the cost of carrying this inventory. With the use of computers, great improvements in inventory control have been made and are continuing to be made. Unfortunately, a review of the many applications of operations research to inventory management is beyond the scope of this book.

Although inventory management usually is not the direct operating responsibility of the financial manager, the investment of funds in inventory is an important aspect of financial management. Consequently, the financial manager must be familiar with ways to control inventories effectively so that capital may be allocated efficiently. The greater the opportunity cost of funds invested in inventory, the lower the optimal level of average inventory and the lower the optimal order quantity, all other things held constant. This statement can be verified by increasing the carrying costs, C, in Eq. (16-3). The EOQ model also can be useful to the financial manager in planning for inventory financing.

When demand or usage of inventory is uncertain, the financial manager may try to effect policies that will reduce the average lead time required to receive inventory once an order is placed. The lower the average lead time, the lower the safety stock needed and the lower the total investment in

[7]For a further discussion of this point, see Chapter 25.

inventory, all other things held constant. The greater the opportunity cost of
funds invested in inventory, the greater the incentive to reduce this lead time.
In the case of purchases, the purchasing department may try to find new
vendors that promise quicker delivery or place pressure on existing vendors
for faster delivery. In the case of finished goods, the production department
may be able to schedule production runs for faster delivery by producing a
smaller run. In either case, there is a tradeoff between the added cost involved
in reducing the lead time and the opportunity cost of funds tied up in
inventory.

The financial manager also is concerned with the risks involved in
carrying inventory. The major risk is that the market value of specific inventories will be less than the value at which they were acquired. Certain types of
inventory are subject to obsolescence, whether it be in technology or in
consumer tastes. A change in technology may make an electronic component
worthless. On the other hand, a change in dress styles may cause a retailer to
sell dresses at substantially reduced prices. Still other inventories are subject
to physical deterioration over time. Agricultural products, for example, cannot be held indefinitely. With deterioration, of course, inventories will have
to be sold at lower and lower prices, all other things the same. In other
situations, the principal risk is that of fluctuations in market price. Some
items of inventory, such as copper, are subject to rather wide price swings.
The financial manager is perhaps in the best place to objectively analyze the
risks associated with the firm's investment in inventories. These risks must be
considered in determining the appropriate level of inventory the firm should
carry.

The opportunity cost of funds is the link by which the financial
manager ties inventory management to the overall objective of the firm. In
this regard, inventory can be treated as an asset to which capital is committed
like any capital-budgeting project. Different items of inventory may involve
different risks, and these differences can be incorporated into an analysis of
risk similar to that for capital budgeting. As discussed in Chapter 13, the
essential difference between a capital asset and inventory is that the former
typically involves a discrete investment, while the latter represents a continuum of possible investments. Our discussion in this chapter has focused on
determining an optimal *level* of investment. We know that the greater the
efficiency with which the firm manages its inventory, the lower the required
investment and the greater the shareholder wealth, all other things the same.

SUMMARY

The optimal level of inventories should be judged in relation to the flexibility
inventories afford. If we hold constant the efficiency of inventory management, the lower the level of inventories, the less the flexibility of the firm.
The higher the amount of inventories, the greater the flexibility of the firm. In
evaluating the level of inventories, management must balance the benefits of

economies of production, purchasing, and increased product demand against the cost of carrying the additional inventory. Of particular concern to the financial manager is the cost of funds invested in inventory, which is a function of the risk of the specific inventories involved.

The efficiency of inventory control very much affects the flexibility of the firm, given a level of inventory. Conversely, given a degree of flexibility, efficiency affects the level of inventory investment. In this chapter, we have examined several tools of inventory control. One is the economic order quantity (EOQ), whereby we determine the optimal size of order to place, on the basis of the demand or usage of the inventory, the ordering costs, and the carrying costs. Under conditions of uncertainty, the firm usually must provide for a safety stock, owing to fluctuations in demand for, or usage of, inventory. Another tool—the order-point formula—tells us the optimal point at which to reorder a particular item of inventory. Together, these tools provide the means for determining an optimal average level of inventory for the firm.

In certain instances, other considerations play a role in determining an optimal level of inventory. The firm may want to purchase in anticipation of a strike at a major supplier's plant or in anticipation of an increase in price by a supplier. In some instances, marketing considerations dominate the inventory decision. Finally, the firm generally will need to maintain a higher overall level of inventory the greater the number of specific items in that inventory.

PROBLEMS

1. A college book store is attempting to determine the optimal order quantity for a popular book on financial management. The store sells 5,000 copies of this book a year at a retail price of $12.50, although the publisher allows the store a 20 percent discount from this price. The store figures that it costs $1 per year to carry a book in inventory and $100 to prepare an order for new books.

   (a) Determine the total costs associated with ordering one, two, five, ten, and twenty times a year.
   (b) Determine the economic order quantity.

2. The Hedge Corporation manufactures only one product, planks. The single raw material used in making planks is the dint. For each plank manufactured, twelve dints are required. Assume that the company manufactures 150,000 planks per year, that demand for planks is perfectly steady throughout the year, that it costs $200 each time dints are ordered, and that carrying costs are $8 per dint per year.

   (a) Determine the economic order quantity of dints.
   (b) What are total inventory costs for Hedge (carrying costs plus ordering costs)?
   (c) How many times per year would inventory be ordered?

3. Vostick Filter Company is a distributor of air filters to retail stores. It buys its filters from several manufacturers. Filters are ordered in lot sizes of 1,000, and each

order costs $40 to place. Demand from retail stores is 20,000 filters per month,

and carrying cost is $0.10 a filter per month.

(a) What is the optimal order quantity with respect to so many lot sizes?
(b) What would be the optimal order quantity if the carrying cost were $0.05 a filter per month?
(c) What would be the optimal order quantity if ordering costs were $10?

4. Favorite Foods, Inc., buys 50,000 boxes of ice cream cones every two months to service steady demand for the product. Order costs are $100 per order and carrying costs are $0.40 per box.

(a) Determine the optimal order quantity.
(b) The vendor now offers Favorite Foods a quantity discount of $0.02 per box if it buys cones in order sizes of 10,000 boxes. Should Favorite Foods avail itself of the quantity discount?

5. The Seguro Corporation has determined that its only raw material has an economic order quantity of 1,000 units every thirty days. Further, the firm knows with certainty that a four-day lead time is required for ordering. It has been estimated that the following inventory usage distribution will prevail each month:

Usage (in units)	900	950	1,000	1,050	1,100	1,150	1,200	1,250
Probability	0.06	0.14	0.30	0.16	0.13	0.10	0.07	0.04

If stockouts would cost the firm $10 per unit, and the average monthly carrying cost is $1 per unit:

(a) Determine the optimal safety stock.
(b) What is the probability of being out of stock?

6. The Apex Company has a policy of reordering raw materials when inventory levels reach a certain point. The firm has determined that it uses 50,000 units of inventory per month, that a lead time of ten days is required, that 5,000 orders necessitating equal raw-materials usage are filled on the average each month, and that the stockout-acceptance percentage is 10 percent (demand is Poisson distributed).

(a) What is the optimal order point?
(b) What would be the order point with no safety stock?

7. In order to reduce production start-up costs, Bodden Truck Company is considering longer runs of the same truck. Estimated savings from the increase in efficiency are $260,000 per year. However, inventory turnover will decrease from eight times a year to six times a year. Costs of goods sold are $48 million on an annual basis. If the required rate of return on investment in inventories is 15 percent, should the company instigate the new production plan?

8. Wilstat is contemplating a change in inventory policy. Currently, the firm has an inventory turnover of twenty-four times a year. Sales have been holding steady at $240,000 per year. Variable costs are 70 percent of the total sales dollar. The company feels that if it were to increase inventories, it could avoid certain stockouts that now occur and, as a result, increase sales. The required rate of return before taxes is 20 percent. The company estimates the following relationship between inventory turnover and sales:

Inventory turnover	24	12	6	4	3
Sales	$240,000	$252,000	$261,000	$266,000	$270,000

Using the marginal analysis procedure developed in the preceding chapter (accounts receivable), determine the optimal inventory policy.

SELECTED REFERENCES

BIERMAN HAROLD, JR., CHARLES P. BONINI, AND WARREN H. HAUSMAN, *Quantitative Analysis for Business Decisions,* 5th ed., Chaps. 17–19. Homewood, Ill.: Richard D. Irwin, 1977.

BUFFA, E. S., AND W. H. TAUBERT, *Production-Inventory Systems: Planning and Control,* rev. ed. Homewood, Ill.: Richard D. Irwin, 1972.

HALEY, CHARLES W., AND ROBERT C. HIGGINS, "Inventory Control Theory and Trade Credit Financing," *Management Science,* 20 (December 1973), 464–71.

HAUSMAN, WARREN H., AND L. JOSEPH THOMAS, "Inventory Control with Probabilistic Demand and Periodic Withdrawals," *Management Science,* 18 (January 1972), 265–75.

HILLIER, FREDERICK S., AND GERALD J. LIEBERMAN, *Introduction to Operations Research,* 2nd ed. San Francisco: Holden-Day, 1974.

MAGEE, JOHN F., "Guides to Inventory Policy," I–III, *Harvard Business Review,* 34 (January-February 1956), 49–60; (March-April 1956), 103–16; and (May-June 1956), 57–70.

MEHTA, DILEEP R., *Working Capital Management,* Chaps. 4–5. Englewood Cliffs, N.J.: Prentice-Hall, 1974.

SCHIFF, MICHAEL, AND ZVI LIEBER, "A Model for the Integration of Credit and Inventory Management," *Journal of Finance,* 29 (March 1974), 133–40.

SHAPIRO, ALAN, "Optimal Inventory and Credit-Granting Strategies under Inflation and Devaluation," *Journal of Financial and Quantitative Analysis,* 7 (January 1973), 37–46.

SMITH, KEITH V., *Management of Working Capital,* Sec. 4. New York: West Publishing, 1974.

SNYDER, ARTHUR, "Principles of Inventory Management," *Financial Executive,* 32 (April 1964), 13–21.

STANCILL, JAMES McN., *The Management of Working Capital,* Chap. 5. Scranton, Pa.: Intext, 1971.

WAGNER, HARVEY M., *Principles of Operation Research,* 2nd ed. Englewood Cliffs, N.J.: Prentice-Hall, 1975.

short- and intermediate-term financing

17
unsecured short-term financing

CONCEPTUAL CONSIDERATIONS FOR THE TYPE OF FINANCING

In Chapter 13, we considered the current liabilities of the firm as part of its overall financing decision. Involved was not only the question of debt versus equity but also questions about the maturity composition of the debt and about conditions associated with the debt. (An example of the latter is whether or not the debt is secured and, if so, the type of security.) Decisions reached with respect to these issues determine the amount of current liabilities of the firm. We suggested that if capital markets were perfect, stockholders would be indifferent as to the maturity and type of debt the firm employed. Put another way, the firm would be unable to affect the value of its equity by altering the maturity composition and types of debt contracts employed. Accordingly, there would be no reason to proliferate the types and maturities of debt; one debt strategy would be as good as the next.

If imperfections exist in financial markets, however, it will be in the stockholders' interest that the firm "package" its debt instruments in such a way as to take advantage of these imperfections. The more important imperfections affecting debt financing are flotation costs, bankruptcy costs, costs of information, and restrictions on lenders. Since these imperfections were described earlier in Parts II and III, we touch now on their implications for the problem at hand.

If flotation costs are fixed, either in whole or in part, this creates a bias toward less frequent financing, larger offerings of debt each time, and longer maturities. In other words, the presence of fixed costs results in economies of scale with respect to debt offerings. The existence of bankruptcy costs creates a bias in favor of lower levels of debt obligations coming due in the near future, that is, longer maturities. To the extent that there are costs of information, these costs affect the sources of financing the firm is able to tap. If the cost of information is somewhat fixed to either the lender or the borrower, this creates a bias toward fewer types of debt arrangements. For example, a medium-sized firm may be unable to sell its debt in a public offering simply because the cost of information to ultimate investors is sufficiently high as to make debt issues of less than $10 million unfeasible. Instead, the firm will go to a commercial bank or an institutional lender such as an insurance company where it need negotiate with only one party. If the relationship is continuous over time, the cost of information per financing can be reduced. Thus, economies of scale in information affect the sources of debt financing the firm is able to tap.

Restrictions, or institutional constraints, on lenders affect the type of loans they can make. These constraints may be caused by such things as legal restrictions or tax differences, or they may simply be self-imposed. Commercial banks tend to make short- to intermediate-term loans, for example, owing to regulations on their investment behavior. To the extent that a firm is small and, because of the cost-of-information argument, restricted to bank financing, the maturity composition of its debt may be shorter than would otherwise be the case. Other examples of imperfections could be cited, but these examples are sufficient to give one an idea as to the direction of their impact.

In Part V, we assume implicitly that imperfections exist in financial markets, without necessarily arguing that they are substantial. As a result, the way the firm "packages" its debt financing is important. That is, by varying the maturity composition and conditions of its debt, the firm may be able to affect its value, although the impact is likely to be modest. For our purposes in this chapter, the most important aspect of a firm's debt is its maturity.

Hedging Approach to Maturity Composition

If the firm adopts a hedging approach to financing, each asset would be offset with a financing instrument of the same approximate maturity. This approach to financing is similar to hedging in the commodity futures market. For example, a miller having a contract to deliver processed grain three months from now at an established price may purchase a futures contract for delivery of the grain he needs three months hence. Thus the miller hedges against the uncertainty of changes in the price of grain by having a contract to buy grain on approximately the same date in the future as he will need it. With a hedging approach to financing, short-term or seasonal variations in current assets would be financed with short-term debt; the permanent component of current assets would be financed with long-term debt or equity. This policy is illustrated in Figure 17-1.

If current assets fluctuate in the manner shown in the figure, only the short-term fluctuations shown at the top of the figure would be financed with short-term debt. To finance short-term requirements with long-term debt would necessitate the payment of interest for the use of funds during times when they were not needed. This occurrence could be illustrated if we drew a straight line to represent the total amount of long-term debt and equity across the seasonal humps at the top of Figure 17-1. It is apparent that financing would be employed in periods of seasonal lull when it was not needed. With a hedging approach to financing, the borrowing and payment schedule for short-term financing would be arranged so as to correspond to the expected swings in current assets. Fixed assets and the permanent component of current assets would be financed with long-term debt, equity, and the permanent component of current liabilities.

A hedging approach to financing suggests that apart from current installments on long-term debt, a firm would show no current borrowings at the seasonal troughs in Figure 17-1. Short-term borrowings would be paid off with surplus cash. As the firm moved into a period of seasonal funds needs, it would borrow on a short-term basis, again paying the borrowings off as surplus cash was generated. In this way, financing would be employed only when it was needed. Permanent funds requirements would be financed with long-term debt and equity. In a growth situation, permanent financing would be increased in keeping with increases in permanent funds requirements.

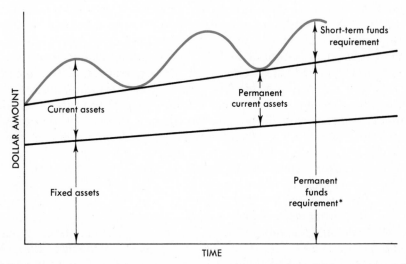

figure 17-1
**Funds requirement—
hedging financing
policy**

*Financed by long-term debt, equity, and the permanent component of current liabilities (accounts payable and accruals)

Although an exact synchronization of the schedule of expected future net cash flows and the payment schedule of debt is appropriate under conditions of certainty, it usually is not under uncertainty. Net cash flows will deviate from expected flows in keeping with the business risk of the firm. As a result, the schedule of maturities of the debt contracts is very important in the risk-profitability tradeoff. We assume that the firm will not arrange its debt obligations so that the composite maturity schedule calls for payments of principal and interest before expected net cash flows are available. The question, however, is, What margin of safety should be built into the maturity schedule in order to allow for adverse fluctuations in cash flows? This depends on the tradeoff between risk and profitability.

The Relative Risks and Costs Involved   In general, the shorter the maturity schedule of a firm's debt obligations, the greater the risk that it will be unable to meet principal and interest payments. On the other hand, the longer the maturity schedule, the less risky the financing of the firm, all other things the same.

To illustrate, suppose a company borrows on a short-term basis in order to build a new plant. The cash flows from the plant are not sufficient in the short run to pay off the loan. As a result, the company bears the risk that the lender may not choose to renew the loan at maturity. This risk could be reduced by financing the plant on a long-term basis where the expected cash flows were sufficient to retire the debt in an orderly manner. Thus the risk associated with committing funds to a long-term asset and borrowing short is that the firm may not be able to renew its borrowings. If the company should fall on hard times, creditors may regard renewal as too risky and may demand immediate payment. This, in turn, will cause the firm to either contract or go into bankruptcy.

In addition to this sort of risk, there is also the uncertainty associated with interest costs. When the firm finances with long-term debt, it knows precisely what its interest costs will be over the time period it needs the funds. If it finances with short-term debt, however, it is uncertain as to its interest costs upon refinancing. In a sense, then, the uncertainty of interest costs represents risk to the borrower. We know that short-term interest rates fluctuate far more than long-term interest rates. During the 1970s for example, the interest rate on short-term commercial paper issued by corporations ranged from approximately 4 percent to over 12 percent. A firm caught in a period of rising interest rates may pay an overall interest cost on short-term debt that is higher than what it would have paid using long-term debt. Therefore the absence of knowledge of future short-term interest costs may represent risk to a company.

A mitigating factor is the possible covariance of short-term interest costs with operating income. With covariance, when operating income is high it will be offset by higher interest costs, thereby dampening the rise in net income. When operating income is low, net income will benefit from the lower interest costs that occur at that time.[1] Therefore net income would be somewhat lower in periods of economic prosperity and somewhat higher in periods of economic contraction than would otherwise be the case. What does "otherwise be the case" mean? In our context, it means financing with long-term debt where interest costs are constant over time. It is only if the financing is short-term and rolled over at maturity that interest costs vary over time and there is the possibility for covariance with the firm's operating income. Therefore, while a long-term financing policy will reduce the uncertainty of interest costs over the life of a project, such a policy can increase the overall uncertainty with respect to the firm's net income.

The practical question, of course, is, What is the covariance of interest rates with a firm's operating income? There is some evidence germane to this question. For the first twenty-five years of the post–World War II period, there was a tendency for interest rates to rise and fall in keeping with the business cycle; they rose in periods of economic expansion and fell during recessions. Likewise, overall corporate profits varied in this manner. However, in the 1970s, inflation became an increasingly difficult problem and was a factor responsible for the 1970–71 and the 1974–75 recessions. During these times, particularly 1974–75, interest rates remained high owing to the high levels of inflation. As a result, interest costs for short-term borrowers were high at the same time that corporate profits were depressed. One is left with an unclear picture of the covariance over time of corporate operating income with interest rates. The financial manager simply cannot count on fluctuations in short-term interest rates dampening the effect of fluctuations in operating income on net income. At times, interest rate fluctuations have accentuated fluctuations in net operating income. Nonetheless, the possible covariance of operating income with interest rates is a factor that should be considered in maturity of debt structure decisions.

Taking all the above factors into account, we can say that in general the longer the maturity schedule of a firm's debt in relation to its expected net cash flows, the less the risk. The major risk in this regard is the possible inability to refinance short-term debt at its maturity. There is also the uncertainty associated with interest costs upon the "rollover" of short-term borrowings, which can either dampen or accentuate fluctuations in the firm's operating income.

Differences in risks between short- and long-term financing must be balanced against differences in interest costs. The longer the maturity schedule of a firm's debt, the more costly the financing is likely to be. For one thing, the explicit cost of long-term financing usually is more than that of short-term financing. In periods of high interest rates, however, the rate on short-term corporate borrowings may exceed that on long-term borrowings. Over a reasonable period of time, however, the firm typically pays more for

[1]This proposition is advanced by James R. Morris, "On Corporate Debt Maturity Strategies," *Journal of Finance,* 31 (March 1976), 29–37.

long-term borrowings, particularly if they are negotiated privately. In addition to the generally higher costs of long-term borrowings, the firm may well pay interest on debt over periods of time when the funds are not needed. Thus there usually is an inducement to finance funds requirements on a short-term basis.[2]

Consequently, we have the familiar tradeoff between risk and profitability. The margin of safety, or lag between expected net cash flows and payments on debt, will depend upon the risk preferences of management. In turn, its decision as to the maturity breakdown of the firm's debt will determine the portion of current assets financed by current liabilities and the portion financed on a long-term basis.

To allow for a margin of safety, management might decide upon the proportions of short-term and long-term financing shown in Figure 17-2. Here we see that the firm finances a portion of its expected seasonal funds requirement on a long-term basis. If the expected net cash flows do occur, it will pay interest on debt during seasonal troughs when the funds are not needed. Thus the firm can reduce the risk of cash insolvency by increasing the maturity schedule of its debt.

With this general framework in mind, we are now able to examine in detail specific methods of short-term financing. The major sources are trade credit, accruals, commercial paper, and short-term loans. The first three as well as unsecured short-term loans are considered in this chapter; secured short-term loans are taken up in the next. We wish to see how these sources of

figure 17-2
Funds requirement:
margin of safety

[2]For an analysis of the optimal mix of short- and long-term debt to finance cyclical funds requirements where these requirements are known, as are the costs of the two methods of financing, see D. J. Aigner and C. M. Sprenkle, "On Optimal Financing of Cyclical Cash Needs," *Journal of Finance,* 28 (December 1973), 1249–54.

short-term financing may be used to finance seasonal and temporary fluctuations in funds requirements, as well as the more permanent needs of the firm.

TRADE CREDIT FINANCING

Trade credit is a form of short-term financing common to almost all businesses. In fact, it is the largest source of short-term funds for business firms collectively. In an advanced economy, most buyers are not required to pay for goods upon delivery but are allowed a short deferment period before payment is due. During this period, the seller of the goods extends credit to the buyer. Because suppliers generally are more liberal in the extension of credit than are financial institutions, trade credit is an important source of funds for small companies in particular.

There are three types of trade credit: open account, notes payable and trade acceptances. By far the most common type is the open-account arrangement. With this arrangement, the seller ships goods to the buyer along with an invoice that specifies the goods shipped, the price, the total amount due, and the terms of the sale. Open-account credit derives its name from the fact that the buyer does not sign a formal debt instrument evidencing the amount that he owes the seller. The seller extends credit based upon his credit investigation of the buyer (see Chapter 15).

In some situations, promissory notes are employed instead of open-account credit. In this case, the buyer is asked to sign a note that evidences his debt to the seller. The note itself calls for the payment of the obligation at some specified future date. Promissory notes have been used in such lines of business as furs and jewelry. This arrangement is employed where the seller wants the buyer to recognize his debt formally. For example, a seller might request a promissory note from a buyer if the latter's open account became past due.

A trade acceptance is another arrangement by which the indebtedness of the buyer is recognized formally. Under this arrangement, the seller draws a draft on the buyer ordering him to pay the draft at some date in the future. The seller will not release the goods until the buyer accepts the time draft.[3] When the buyer accepts the draft, he designates a bank at which the draft will be paid when it comes due. At that time, the draft becomes a trade acceptance; and, depending upon the credit-worthiness of the buyer, it may possess some degree of marketability. If the trade acceptance is marketable, the seller of the goods can sell it at a discount and receive immediate payment for the goods. At final maturity, the holder of the acceptance presents it to the designated bank for collection.

---

[3]If the instrument is a sight draft, the buyer is ordered to pay the draft upon presentation. Under this arrangement, trade credit is not extended.

Because the use of promissory notes and trade acceptances is rather limited, the subsequent discussion will be confined to open-account trade credit. With this type of credit, the terms of the sale are an important consideration. These terms, which are specified in the invoice, may be placed in several broad categories according to the net period within which payment is expected and according to the terms of the cash discount.

COD and CBD—No Extension of Credit   COD terms mean cash on delivery of the goods. The only risk that the seller undertakes in this type of arrangement is that the buyer may refuse the shipment. Under such circumstances, the seller will be stuck with the shipping costs. Occasionally, a seller might ask for cash before delivery (CBD) to avoid all risk. Under either COD or CBD terms, the seller does not extend credit. CBD terms must be distinguished from progress payments, which are very common in certain industries. With progress payments, the buyer pays the manufacturer at various stages of production prior to the actual delivery of the finished product. Because large sums of money are tied up in work in progress, aircraft manufacturers request progress payments from airlines in advance of the actual delivery of aircraft.

Net Period—No Cash Discount   When credit is extended, the seller specifies the period of time allowed for payment. For example, the terms "net 30" indicate that the invoice or bill must be paid within thirty days. If the seller bills on a monthly basis, it might require such terms as "net/15 EOM," which means that all goods shipped before the end of the month must be paid for by the fifteenth of the following month.

Net Period with Cash Discount   In addition to extending credit, the seller may offer a cash discount if the bill is paid during the early part of the net period. The terms "2/10, net 30" indicate that the buyer is offered a 2 percent discount if the bill is paid within ten days; if he does not pay within ten days, he must pay the full amount of the bill within thirty days. A cash discount differs from a trade discount and from a quantity discount. With a trade discount, one type of customer (a wholesaler for example) is given a lower price on goods purchased than is another type of customer, say a retailer. With a quantity discount, a customer is given a discount if the shipment is above a certain amount. Under most circumstances, a cash discount is offered as an incentive to the buyer to pay early. In Chapter 15, we considered the question of the optimal cash discount to be offered by a seller.

Datings   Datings are used frequently in a seasonal business, where the seller wishes to encourage customers to place their orders before a heavy selling period. For example, a manufacturer of lawn mowers may give seasonal datings specifying that any shipment to a dealer in the winter or spring does not have to be paid for until summer. The arrangement is beneficial to the seller because, with earlier orders, he can gauge his demand more realistically and schedule production more efficiently. Also, the seller does not have to store certain finished-goods inventory. The advantage of datings to the buyer is that he does not have to pay for the goods until he is able to sell them. Under this arrangement, credit is extended for a longer than normal period of time.

Trade Credit as a Means of Financing

We have seen that trade credit is a source of funds, because the buyer does not have to pay for goods until after they are delivered. If the firm automatically pays its bills a certain number of days after the date of invoice, trade credit becomes a built-in source of financing that varies with the production cycle. As the firm increases its production and corresponding purchases, accounts payable increase and provide part of the funds needed to finance the increase in production. As production decreases, accounts payable tend to decrease. Although the variation of accounts payable with production may not be directly proportional, on account of shortages or gluts in inventory on hand, there is a strong degree of correspondence.

If a firm adheres strictly to the practice of paying its bills at a given time after invoice, trade credit is not a discretionary source of financing. It is entirely dependent upon the purchasing plans of the firm, which, in turn, are dependent upon its production cycle. In examining trade credit as a discretionary form of financing, we want to consider specifically situations in which (1) a firm does not take a cash discount but pays on the last day of the net period, and (2) a firm pays its bills beyond the net period.

Payment on the Final Due Date

In this section, we assume that the firm forgoes a cash discount but does pay its bill on the final due date of the net period. If no cash discount is offered, there is no cost for the use of credit during the net period. By the same token, if a firm takes the discount, there is no cost for the use of trade credit during the discount period. However, if a cash discount is offered and it is not taken, there is a definite opportunity cost. For example, if the terms of sale are 2/10, net 30, the firm has the use of funds for an additional twenty days if it does not take the cash discount but pays on the final day of the net period. In the case of a $100 invoice, it would have the use of $98 for twenty days. The annual interest cost is[4]

$$\frac{2}{98} \times \frac{360}{20} = 36.7 \text{ percent}$$

Thus we see that trade credit can be a very expensive form of short-term financing when a cash discount is offered.

---

[4]For ease of calculation, 360 rather than 365 is used as the number of days in the year.

The cost of trade credit declines the longer the net period is in relation to the discount period. For example, had the terms in the above example been 2/10, net 60, the annual interest cost would have been

$$\frac{2}{98} \times \frac{360}{50} = 14.7 \text{ percent}$$

The relationship between the annual interest cost of trade credit and the number of days between the end of the discount period and the end of the net period is shown in Figure 17-3. In the figure, we assume 2/10 discount terms. We see that the cost of trade credit decreases at a decreasing rate as the net period increases. The point is that if a firm does not take a cash discount, its cost of trade credit declines the longer it is able to postpone payment.

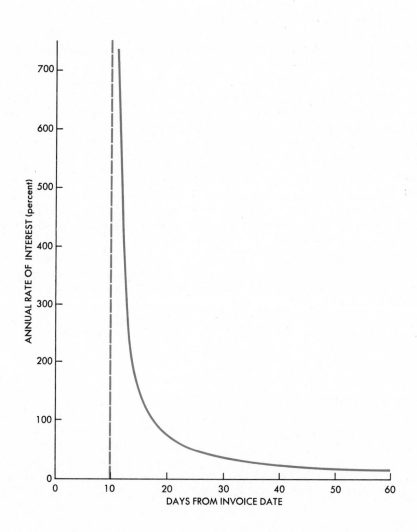

figure 17-3
Annual rate of interest on accounts payable with terms of 2/10, net 30

Stretching Accounts Payable

In the preceding section, we assumed that payment was made at the end of the due period. However, a firm may postpone payment beyond this period; we shall call this postponement "stretching" accounts payable or "leaning on the trade." The cost of stretching accounts payable is twofold: the cost of the cash discount forgone and the possible deterioration in credit rating. In Chapter 15, we discussed the rating system of such credit agencies as Dun & Bradstreet. If a firm stretches its payables excessively so that trade payables are significantly delinquent, its credit rating will suffer. Suppliers will view the firm with apprehension and may insist upon rather strict terms of sale if, indeed, they sell at all. Also, banks and other lenders do not regard excessive slowness in the trade very favorably in assessing a company. Although it is difficult to measure, there is certainly an opportunity cost to a deterioration in a firm's credit reputation.

Notwithstanding the possibility of a deteriorating credit rating, it may be possible to postpone certain payables beyond the net period without severe consequences. Suppliers are in business to sell goods, and trade credit may be a very important sales tool. A supplier may well be willing to go along with a certain stretching of his payables, particularly if the risk of bad-debt loss is negligible. If the funds requirement of the firm is seasonal, suppliers may not view the stretching of payables in an unfavorable light during periods of peak requirements, provided that the firm is current in the trade during the rest of the year. However, there may be an indirect charge for this extension of credit in the form of higher prices. The firm should be particularly careful to consider this possibility in evaluating the cost of stretching accounts payable.

Periodic and reasonable stretching of payables is not necessarily bad *per se*. It should be evaluated objectively in relation to its cost and in relation to alternative sources of short-term credit. When a firm does stretch its payables, effort should be made to keep suppliers fully informed of its situation. Many suppliers will allow a firm to stretch payables if the firm is honest with the supplier and consistent in its payments. Sometimes a firm with seasonal funds requirements is able to obtain a dating from a supplier. When a firm obtains a dating, it does not stretch its payables; as long as it pays the bill by the final date, no deterioration in its credit ratings is likely.

Advantages of Trade Credit

The firm must balance the advantages of trade credit as a discretionary source of financing without any explicit cost against the cost of forgoing a cash discount and the opportunity cost associated with a possible deterioration in credit reputation if it stretches its payables. There are several advantages of trade credit as a form of short-term financing. Probably the major advantage is its ready availability. The accounts payable of most firms represent a continuous form of credit. There is no need to arrange financing formally; it is already there. If the firm is now taking cash discounts, additional credit is readily available by not paying existing accounts payable until the end of the net period. There is no need to negotiate with the supplier; the decision is entirely up to the firm. In the case of stretching accounts payable, it will become necessary, after a certain degree of postponement, to negotiate with the supplier.

In most other types of short-term financing, it is necessary to negotiate formally with the lender over the terms of the loan. The lender may impose restrictions on the firm and seek a secured position. Restrictions are possible with trade credit, but they are not nearly as likely. With other sources of short-term financing, there may be a lead time between the time the need for funds is recognized and the time the firm is actually able to borrow them. Trade credit is a more flexible means of financing. The firm does not have to sign a note, pledge collateral, or adhere to a strict payment schedule on the note. A supplier views an occasional delinquent payment with a far less critical eye than does a banker or other lender.

The advantages of using trade credit must be weighted against the cost. As we have seen, the cost may be very high when all factors are considered. Many firms utilize other sources of short-term financing in order to be able to take advantage of cash discounts. The savings in cost over other forms of short-term financing, however, must offset the flexibility and convenience of trade credit. For certain firms, moreover, there simply are no alternative sources of short-term credit.

Who Bears the Cost?

It is important to recognize that trade credit involves a cost for the use of funds over time. In the previous sections, it was implied that there is no explicit cost to trade credit if the buyer pays the invoice during the discount period or during the net period, if no cash discount is given. Although this supposition is valid from the standpoint of marginal analysis, it overlooks the fact that somebody must bear the cost of trade credit, for the use of funds over time is not free. The burden may fall on the supplier, the buyer, or both parties. The supplier may be able to pass the cost on to the buyer in the form of higher prices.

In the case of a product for which demand is elastic, however, the supplier may be reluctant to increase prices and may end up absorbing most of the cost of trade credit. Under other circumstances, the supplier is able to pass the cost on to the buyer. The buyer should determine who is bearing the cost of trade credit; if he finds that he is bearing the cost, he may want to consider other suppliers to see if he can do better elsewhere. In addition, the buyer should recognize that the cost of trade credit changes over time. In periods of rising interest rates and tight money, suppliers may raise the price of their products to take account of the rising cost of carrying receivables. This rise in price should not be confused with other rises caused by changing supply and demand conditions in the product markets.

ACCRUAL ACCOUNTS AS SPONTANEOUS FINANCING

Perhaps even more than accounts payable, accrual accounts represent a spontaneous source of financing. The most common accrual accounts are for wages and taxes. In both cases, the expense is incurred or accrued but not paid. Usually a date is specified indicating when the accrual must be paid. In the case of taxes, payment is quarterly on income taxes and semiannually on property taxes. Wages must typically be paid either weekly, every other week, bimonthly, or monthly. Like accounts payable, accruals tend to expand with the scope of the operation. As sales increase, labor costs typically increase—and with them, accrued wages increase. As profits increase, accrued taxes increase in almost direct proportion.

In a sense, accruals represent costless financing. In the case of wages, services are rendered but employees are not paid, and do not expect to be paid, until the end or after the end of the pay period. The lapse is established by the company; however, unions and competing employers in the labor market influence its length. Similarly, taxes are not expected to be paid until their due date. Thus accruals represent an interest-free source of financing.

Unfortunately for the company, they do not represent discretionary financing. In the case of taxes, the government is the creditor and it likes to be paid on time. For the company in extreme financial difficulty, such taxes can be postponed for a short while, but there is a penalty charge. Similarly, the payment of wages can be postponed if a company is in dire financial straits. However, such a postponement brings hardships on employees and hurts morale. Employees may respond with absenteeism or reduced efficiency or may simply seek employment elsewhere. Therefore a company must be extremely careful in postponing wages. Full information should be conveyed to employees and a firm date established as to when they will be paid. While such a measure is one of last resort, many a company on the brink of cash-flow disaster finds itself having to postpone wages as well as all other payments.

Accrued Wages and Pay Period Changes

Accrued wages are partially discretionary in that a company can change the frequency of wage payments and thereby affect the amount of financing. Assuming the interval of time between the last working day of a pay period and payday stays the same, the less frequent the paydays the more the financing. To illustrate, suppose a company had a weekly payroll of $400,000 with an average amount accrued of $200,000. If the company were to increase its pay period from one to two weeks, the payroll at the end of the period would be $800,000. The average amount of accrued wages would now be $400,000 ($800,000 divided by two). Therefore the company increases its interest-free financing by $200,000.

The longer the pay period, the greater the amount of accrued wage financing. Obviously it would be desirable from the standpoint of a company to have as long a pay period as possible. However, competition for labor from other employers and union pressures limit the feasible range of options. Moreover, an increase in the pay period is usually "one-shot" in that it is not possible to repeat with a subsequent increase. In most cases, the maximum pay period is no more than one month. In summary, then, accruals are a discretionary source of financing only within a very narrow range.

MONEY-MARKET CREDIT

Large, well-established companies sometimes borrow on a short-term basis through commercial paper and other money-market instruments. Commercial paper consists of unsecured short-term negotiable promissory notes sold in the money market. Because these notes are unsecured and are a money-market instrument, only the most credit-worthy companies are able to use commercial paper as a source of short-term financing.

Commercial Paper Market

The commercial paper market is composed of two parts: the dealer market and the direct placement market.[5] Industrial firms, utilities, and medium-sized finance companies sell commercial paper through dealers. The dealer organization is composed of a half-dozen major dealers, who purchase commercial paper from the issuer and, in turn, sell it to investors. The typical commission a dealer earns is one-eighth percent, and maturities on dealer-placed paper generally range from one to six months. The market is a highly organized and sophisticated one; paper is sold in denominations ranging from $25,000 to several million dollars. Although the dealer market has been characterized in the past by a significant number of issuers who borrow on a seasonal basis, the trend definitely is toward financing on a revolving or more permanent basis.

Since the 1920s, a number of large sales finance companies, such as General Motors Acceptance Corporation, have bypassed the dealer organization in favor of selling their paper directly to investors. These issuers tailor both the maturity and the amount of the note to the needs of investors, most of which are large corporations with excess cash. Maturities on directly placed paper can range from as little as a few days up to nine months. Unlike many industrial issuers, finance companies use the commercial paper market as a permanent source of funds. With the development of the direct-placement market, pockets of idle investment funds have been tapped for

---

[5]For a discussion of commercial paper from the standpoint of a short-term investor, see Chapter 14.

short-term financing purposes. Directly placed paper has recently accounted for 60 to 80 percent of the total commercial paper outstanding.

Characteristics for the Borrower The principal advantage of commercial paper as a source of short term financing is that it is generally cheaper than a short-term business loan from a commercial bank. Usually, the rate on prime commercial paper is 0.25 percent to 2 percent lower than the prime rate for bank loans to the highest-quality borrower. The differential tends to increase in periods of easy money and to decrease in periods of tight money. It is important to recognize that commercial paper rates fluctuate considerably in keeping with money-market conditions. In assessing commercial paper as a means of financing, the firm should weigh the relative cost and availability in comparison with alternative sources of funds. In this comparison, the cost of bank credit should be adjusted upward for compensating-balance requirements.

Many companies consider commercial paper a desirable supplement to bank credit. Ideally, a company would borrow heavily through commercial paper when the interest-rate differential was wide and borrow more from banks when the differential narrowed. This strategy would result in the lowest average interest cost and the maximum flexibility. However, commercial banks do not look favorably on credit requests only in periods of tight money. Switching from commercial paper to bank borrowings is possible, but a company must be careful not to impair relations with its bank. The commercial paper market is highly impersonal. If a firm cannot borrow from a commercial bank, it is at the mercy of the market. Therefore it is important to maintain lines of credit at commercial banks in order to backstop adverse money-market conditions.

In addition to cost advantages, another reason commercial paper is used is that the legal limitations on the size of a loan that a commercial bank can extend preclude satisfying the requirements of the large finance companies. For example, the maximum loan a national bank can make to a single borrower is 10 percent of its capital and surplus. The total borrowing requirements of the three largest sales finance companies exceed the legal lending limits of the fifty largest banks in this country. Consequently, these companies must turn to other sources of short-term financing—namely, direct investors.

Bankers' Acceptances

For a company engaged in foreign trade, bankers' acceptances can be an important source of financing. To illustrate their use, suppose an American company wishes to import $100,000 worth of electronic components from a company in Japan. The two companies agree that a ninety-day time draft will be used in settlement of the trade. The American company arranges a letter of credit with its bank whereby the bank agrees to honor drafts drawn on the company as presented through a Japanese bank. The Japanese company ships the goods and at the same time draws a draft ordering the American company to pay in ninety days. It then takes the draft to its Japanese bank. By prearrangement, the draft is sent to the American bank and is accepted by that bank. At that time it becomes a bankers' acceptance. In essence, the bank accepts responsibility for payment, thereby substituting its credit-worthiness for that of the drawee—the American company.

If the bank is large and well known, and most banks accepting drafts are, the instrument becomes highly marketable upon acceptance. As a result, the drawer, the Japanese company, does not have to hold the draft until the final due date; it can sell the draft in the market. The draft is sold for less than its face value. The discount involved represents the interest payment to the investor. At the end of ninety days, the investor presents the acceptance to the accepting bank for payment and receives $100,000. At this time, the American company is obligated to have funds on deposit to cover the draft. In the manner illustrated, the American company finances its import for a ninety-day period. Presumably, the Japanese exporter would charge a lower price if he were paid upon shipment, whereas with a time draft the price is $100,000. In this sense, the American company is the borrower.

The presence of an active and viable bankers' acceptance market makes possible the financing of foreign trade at interest rates approximating those on commercial paper. While acceptances can be used to finance domestic trade, only a small portion of the total bankers' acceptances outstanding are domestic. However, the principles by which the acceptance is created are exactly the same as with a foreign trade. In recent years, bankers' acceptances have grown tremendously in importance. While in the 1960s, outstandings were only $3–$4 billion, they have recently been $25 billion. This compares with commercial paper outstandings of about $60 billion. The growth in bankers' acceptances is attributable to a sharp growth in foreign trade, particularly with the Far East, and to companies' increasing recognition of the usefulness of this form of financing.

SHORT-TERM LOANS

For expository purposes, it is convenient to separate business loans into two categories: unsecured loans and secured loans. Almost without exception, finance companies do not offer unsecured loans, simply because a borrower who deserves unsecured credit can borrow at a lower cost from a commercial bank. Consequently, our discussion of unsecured loans will involve only commercial banks. Secured loans will be examined in the next chapter.

Short-term, unsecured bank loans typically are regarded as "self-liquidating" in that the assets purchased with the proceeds generate sufficient cash flows to pay the loan in less than a year. At one time, banks confined their lending almost exclusively to this type of loan. Fortunately, banks now provide a wide variety of business loans, tailored to the specific needs of the borrower. Still, the short-term, self-liquidating loan is an important source of business financing. It is particularly popular in financing seasonal buildups in accounts receivable and inventories. Unsecured short-term loans may be extended under a line of credit, under a revolving-credit agreement, or on a transaction basis. The debt itself is evidenced formally by a promissory note signed by the borrower, showing the time and amount of payment and the interest to be paid.

Line of Credit

A line of credit is an arrangement between a bank and its customer with respect to the maximum amount of unsecured credit the bank will permit the firm to owe at any one time. Usually, credit lines are established for a one-year period and are subject to one-year renewals. Frequently, lines of credit are set for renewal after the bank receives the audited annual report and has had a chance to review the progress of the borrower. For example, if the borrower's year-end statement date is December 31, a bank may set its line to expire some time in March. At that time, the bank and the company would meet to discuss the credit needs of the firm for the coming year in light of its past year's performance. The amount of the line is based upon the bank's assessment of the credit-worthiness of the borrower and upon his credit needs. Depending upon changes in these conditions, a line of credit may be adjusted at the renewal date, or before, if conditions necessitate a change.

The cash budget, perhaps, gives the best insight into the borrower's short-term credit needs. For example, if maximum or peak borrowing needs over the forthcoming year are estimated at $800,000, a company might seek a line of credit of $1 million to give it a margin of safety. Whether the bank will go along with the request, of course, will depend upon its evaluation of the credit-worthiness of the firm. If the bank agrees, the firm then may borrow on a short-term basis—usually ninety days—up to the full $1 million line. Because banks tend to regard borrowing under lines of credit as seasonal or temporary financing, they usually require that the borrower be out of bank debt at some time during the year. Frequently, the borrower will be required to "clean up" bank debt for at least thirty days during the year. The understanding between the bank and the borrower with respect to a "cleanup," of course, is subject to negotiation. The "cleanup" itself is evidence to the bank that the loan is truly seasonal in nature and not a portion of the permanent financing of the firm.

Despite its many advantages to the borrower, a line of credit does not constitute a legal commitment on the part of the bank to extend credit. The borrower is usually informed of the line by means of a letter indicating that the bank is willing to extend credit up to a certain amount. An example of such a letter is shown in Figure 17-4. This letter is not a legal obligation of the bank to extend credit. If the credit-worthiness of the borrower should deteriorate over the year, the bank may not want to extend credit and would not be required to do so. Under most circumstances, however, a bank feels bound to honor a line of credit.

March 23, 1980

Mr. Joseph A. Ralberg
Vice President & Treasurer
Barker Manufacturing Corporation
Palo Alto, California

Dear Mr. Ralberg:

Based upon our analysis of your year-end audited statements,
we are pleased to renew your $1 million unsecured line of
credit for the forthcoming year. Borrowings under this
line will be at a rate of one-half percent ($\frac{1}{2}$%) over the
prime rate.

This line is subject to only the understanding that your
company will maintain its financial position and that it
will be out of bank debt for at least 45 days during the
fiscal year.

Yours very truly,

John D. Myers
Vice President

figure 17-4
Sample letter
extending line of
credit

Revolving-Credit Agreement

A revolving-credit agreement represents a legal commitment on the part of the bank to extend credit up to a maximum amount. While the commitment is in force, the bank must extend credit to the borrower any time he wishes to borrow, provided total borrowings do not exceed the maximum amount specified. If the revolving credit is for $1 million, and $700,000 is already owing, the borrower can borrow an additional $300,000 at any time. For the privilege of having this formal commitment, the borrower usually is required to pay a commitment fee on the unused portion of the revolving credit. For example, if the revolving credit is for $1 million, and borrowing for the year averages $400,000, the borrower will be required to pay a commitment fee on the $600,000 unused portion. If the fee is 0.5 percent, the cost of this privilege will be $3,000 for the year. Revolving-credit agreements frequently extend beyond one year. Because lending arrangements of more than a year must be regarded as intermediate rather than short-term credit, we shall examine revolving credits more extensively in Chapter 18. The purpose of introducing them at this time is to illustrate the formal nature of the arrangement in contrast to the informality of a line of credit.

Transaction Loans

Borrowing under a line of credit or under a revolving-credit arrangement is not appropriate when the firm needs short-term funds for only one purpose. For example, a contractor may borrow from a bank in order to complete a job. When the contractor receives payment for the job, he pays the loan. For this type of loan, a bank evaluates each request by the borrower as a separate transaction. In these evaluations, the cash-flow ability of the borrower to pay the loan is usually of paramount importance.

Eurodollar Loans

In addition to the lending arrangements discussed, banks also extend Eurodollar loans to multinational companies. These loans range in maturity from one day to several years. A *Eurodollar* is defined as a dollar deposit held in a bank outside the United States. Since the late fifties, an active market has developed for these deposits. Foreign banks and foreign branches of U.S. banks, mostly in Europe, bid actively for Eurodollar deposits, paying interest rates that fluctuate in keeping with supply and demand conditions. These deposits are in large denominations, frequently $100,000 or more. The banks use the Eurodollar deposits they receive to make dollar loans to prime borrowers. These loans are made at a rate in excess of the deposit rate; the differential varies according to the relative risk of the borrower. All loans are unsecured. Essentially, the borrowing and lending of Eurodollars represent a wholesale operation, with far fewer costs than are usually associated with banking. The market itself is free from government restrictions and is truly international in scope.

The Eurodollar market serves as an important source of short-term financing for the working-capital requirements of the multinational company. Many American firms arrange for lines of credit and revolving credits from Eurodollar banks. For the latter arrangement, the firm pays a commitment fee the same as it does for a domestic revolving credit. The interest rate on loans is based upon the Eurodollar deposit rate and bears only an indirect relationship to the prime rate. Typically, rates on loans are quoted in terms of the London interbank offering rate, commonly called the LIBO rate. The greater the risk, the greater the spread above the LIBO rate. One should realize that the LIBO rate is usually much more volatile than the U.S. prime rate, owing to the sensitive nature of supply and demand conditions for Eurodollar deposits. Consequently, it is more difficult to project the cost of a Eurodollar loan than that of a domestic loan. Nevertheless, no compensating balances are required, thus enhancing the attractiveness of this kind of financing.

Interest Rates

Unlike interest rates on such impersonal money-market instruments as Treasury bills, bankers' acceptances, and commercial paper, most business loans are determined through personal negotiation between the borrower and the lender(s). In some measure, banks try to vary the interest rate charged according to the credit-worthiness of the borrower; the lower the credit-worthiness, the higher the interest rate. Interest rates charged also vary in keeping with money-market conditions. One measure that varies with underlying market conditions is the *prime* rate. The prime rate is the lowest rate typically charged on business loans to large, well-established, and financially sound companies.[6] The rate itself is usually set by large money-market banks and is relatively uniform throughout the country. In the past, the rate changed only slowly over time in keeping with underlying changes in market conditions. This phenomenon is evident in Figure 17-5 up to the mid-1960s.

figure 17-5

Relationship between callable new issues of Aa utility bonds and the prime rate

[6]In order to attract loans from companies that issue short-term commercial paper, certain banks offer special interest rates. These rates are based upon the bank's internal cost of funds and may be lower than the prime rate. The idea is to provide the commercial paper borrower with a supplementary source of funds. The interest rate charged is frequently changed in keeping with changing money-market conditions.

After the mid-1960s, the prime rate changed much more rapidly. Several factors were responsible. For one thing, there was a greater volatility in overall market rates of interest. The early- to mid-sixties was a period of unprecedented stability in interest rates. This stability has not been witnessed since. Another factor is the cost of funds to banks. Over the years, time deposits and other liabilities on which interest is paid have increased significantly in relation to demand deposits. As a result, fluctuations in market rates of interest cause greater volatility in the cost of funds to banks than was true in years gone by. One way for banks to keep up with rapidly changing market rates of interest is simply to adjust the prime rate more frequently. Indeed this has happened in recent years, as evidenced in Figure 17-5.

Another means for coming to grips with the problem is with a floating prime rate. Initiated in 1971 by the First National City Bank of New York, the floating prime is geared to the rate on some money-market instrument. For example, the rate might be established as 1 percent above the commercial paper rate, with adjustments occurring on a weekly basis. The differential between the floating prime rate and the money-market rate is periodically adjusted depending on relative conditions in the money markets vis-á-vis the market for bank loans. The floating prime not only has resulted in those banks adjusting their prime rates more frequently than before but has brought pressure on "nonfloating" prime banks to change their rates more frequently than might otherwise be the case. All of these factors have resulted in frequent changes in the prime rate in recent years, as evidenced in Figure 17-5.

Rates above Prime   Given a prime rate for companies of the highest credit-worthiness, other borrowers are charged rates above the prime. For example, a bank might extend a line of credit to a company at a rate of 0.5 percent above prime. If the prime rate is 7.5 percent, the borrower will be charged an interest rate of 8 percent. If the prime rate changes to 7 percent, the borrower will pay 7.5 percent.

The interest-rate differential between the prime rate and the rate charged to a borrower will depend upon the relative bargaining power of the borrower and the bank. Supposedly, this differential should reflect only the borrower's credit-worthiness in relation to that of a "prime-risk" borrower. However, other factors influence the differential. The balances maintained and other business the borrower has with a bank (such as trust business) may be important considerations. A good customer who has maintained very attractive balances in the past may be able to obtain a more favorable interest rate than will a firm of equal credit-worthiness that has carried rather meager balances. Also, the cost of servicing a loan is a factor determining the differential in rate from prime. Certain collateral loans are costly to administer, and this cost must be passed on to the borrower either in the interest rate charged or in a special fee.

Although the prime rate reflects national credit conditions, many banks extend credit only in a specific geographic area. To the extent that credit conditions in that area differ from national conditions, the interest-rate differential from the prime rate will be affected. In addition, a bank that is aggressively seeking a relationship with a company may be willing to extend credit at a rate slightly lower than it might charge normally.

Thus the interest rate charged on a short-term loan will depend upon the prevailing prime rate, the credit-worthiness of the borrower, his present and prospective relationship with the bank, and, sometimes, upon other considerations. Because of the fixed costs involved in credit investigation and in the processing of a loan, we would expect the interest rate on small loans to be higher than the rate on large loans.

Methods of Computing Interest Rates   There are two ways in which interest on a loan may be paid: on a collect basis and on a discount basis. When paid on a collect basis, the interest is paid at the maturity of the note; when paid on a discount basis, interest is deducted from the initial loan. To illustrate, suppose we have a $10,000 loan at 8 percent interest for one year. The effective rate of interest on a collect note is

$$\frac{\$800}{\$10,000} = 8.00 \text{ percent}$$

On a discount basis, the effective rate of interest is not 8 percent but

$$\frac{\$800}{\$9,200} = 8.70 \text{ percent}$$

When we pay on a discount basis, we have the use of only $9,200 for the year but must pay back $10,000 at the end of that time. Thus the effective rate of interest is higher on a discount note than on a collect note. We should point out that most bank business loans are on a collect-note basis.

Compensating Balances

In addition to charging interest on loans, commercial banks often require the borrower to maintain demand-deposit balances at the bank in direct proportion to either the amount of funds borrowed or the amount of the commitment. These minimum balances are known as compensating balances. The amount required in the compensating balance varies according to the particular bank and the borrower, but many banks require balances equal to 15 percent of a line of credit. If the line is $1 million, the borrower will be required to maintain average balances of at least $150,000 during the year. The effect of a compensating-balance requirement is to raise the effective cost of borrowing if the borrower is required to maintain balances above the amount the firm would maintain ordinarily.

To the extent that a compensating-balance requirement does not require the borrower to maintain balances above those that it would maintain ordinarily, such a requirement does not raise the effective cost of borrowing. However, if balances above the ordinary must be maintained, the effective cost of borrowing is raised.[7] For example, suppose we borrow $1 million at 8 percent and are required to maintain $100,000 more in balances than we would ordinarily. We would then have use of only $900,000 of the $1 million loan. The effective annual interest cost is $80,000/$900,000 = 8.88 percent, rather than 8 percent.

Compensating-balance requirements may increase the liquidity position of the borrower from the bank's point of view. As a last resort, the bank can exercise its legal right of offset and apply the balances on deposit to pay off the loan or a portion of the loan. The compensating balance required of a firm may vary somewhat in keeping with credit availability in general. When money is tight and loan demand high, commercial banks are able to enforce higher compensating-balance requirements than they are when credit is readily available. In most cases, compensating-balance requirements range between 10 and 20 percent. Like most other things, the requirement is negotiated between the borrower and the lender.

There is some indication that the notion of compensating balances for loans is lessening in importance. Increasingly, banks are becoming more profit- as opposed to deposit-oriented and, accordingly, are "fine tuning" their profitability analyses of customer relationships. This movement has led a number of banks to prohibit the use of balances to support both account activity and lending arrangements. With the rapid and significant fluctuation in the cost of funds to banks in recent years, some banks are making loans without compensating-balance requirements. The interest rate charged is higher and more in line with the bank's incremental cost of obtaining funds. The movement toward more sophisticated profitability analysis is likely to reduce further, though certainly not eliminate, the imposition of compensating-balance requirements in connection with lending arrangements.

SUMMARY

Given the fact that imperfections exist in financial markets, it makes sense that the financial manager is concerned with the type of debt that is issued. By "packaging" debt instruments in such a way as to take advantage of imperfections, the firm can maximize shareholder wealth. While a debt instrument has a number of features, one of the most important is its maturity. In general, short-term debt is less costly than long-term debt, but it is also more risky. Thus a decision as to the maturity composition of the firm's debt involves a tradeoff between profitability and risk. A number of types of short-term financing are available.

[7]For an analysis of the relationship between interest cost, compensating balances, activity in the account, and loan costs to the bank, see Bernell K. Stone, "The Cost of Bank Loans," *Journal of Financial and Quantitative Analysis*, 7 (December 1972), 2077–86.

Trade credit can be an important source of short-term financing. However, it is a discretionary source only if a firm does not have a strict policy with respect to the number of days after invoice a bill is paid. When a cash discount is offered but not taken, the cost of trade credit is the cash discount forgone. However, the longer the period between the end of the discount period and the time the bill is paid, the less this opportunity cost. "Stretching" accounts payable involves postponement of payment beyond the due period. The opportunity cost of stretching payables is the possible deterioration in the firm's credit rating. The firm must balance the costs of trade credit against its advantages and the costs of other short-term credit. The major advantage of trade credit is the flexibility it gives the firm.

Like accounts payable, accruals represent a spontaneous source of financing. With accruals, however, there is even less discretion available to the firm than there is with trade credit financing. The principal accrual items are wages and taxes, and both are expected to be paid on established dates. In the interim, however, interest-free financing is available to the company and, for an ongoing company, this financing is continuous. A company can increase the amount of its accrued wages by lessening the frequency of paydays. However, the pay period can only be lengthened within a narrow range.

Commercial paper is used only by well-established, high-quality companies. The evidence of debt is an unsecured short-term promissory note that is sold in the money market. Commercial paper is sold either through dealers or directly to investors. The latter method is used by large sales finance companies, and about two-thirds of commercial paper is placed in this manner. The principal advantage of commercial paper is that its yield typically is less than the rate of interest a company would have to pay on a bank loan. Bankers' acceptance financing is another type of money-market credit. While usually associated with a foreign trade transaction, the acceptance is highly marketable and can be a very desirable source of short-term funds.

Short-term loans can be divided into two types, unsecured loans and secured loans. Unsecured credit is usually confined to bank loans under a line of credit, under a revolving-credit agreement, or on a transaction basis. In addition, banks are a source of Eurodollar loans. Interest rates on business loans are a function of the existing prime rate, the credit-worthiness of the borrower, and the profitability of the relationship to the bank. Typically, banks require balances to compensate for a lending arrangement. If the borrower is required to maintain balances above those that it would maintain ordinarily, the effective cost of borrowing is increased.

PROBLEMS

1. Determine the annual percentage interest cost for each of the following terms of sale, assuming the firm does not take the cash discount but pays on the final day of the net period (assume a 360-day year):

(a) 1/20, net 30 ($500 invoice)

(b) 2/30, net 60 ($1,000 invoice)

(c) 2/5, net 10 ($100 invoice)

(d) 3/10, net 30 ($250 invoice)

2. Does the dollar size of the invoice affect the annual interest cost of not taking discounts? Illustrate with an example.

3. Recompute problem 1, assuming a ten-day stretching of the payment date. What is the major advantage of stretching? What are the disadvantages?

4. The Dud Company purchases raw materials on terms of 2/10, net 30. A review of the company's records by the owner, Mr. Dud, revealed that payments are usually made fifteen days after purchases are received. When asked why the firm did not take advantage of its discounts, the bookkeeper, Mr. Grind, replied that it cost only 2 percent for these funds, whereas a bank loan would cost the firm 10 percent.

(a) What mistake is Grind making?

(b) What is the real cost of not taking advantage of the discount?

(c) If the firm could not borrow from the bank and was forced to resort to the use of trade-credit funds, what suggestion might be made to Grind that would reduce the annual interest cost?

5. On January 1, Faville Car Company, a large car dealer, gave its employees a 10 percent pay increase in view of the substantial profits the preceding year. Before the increase, the weekly payroll was $50,000. Profits were $274,000 the preceding year, but only $200,000 was previously used in estimating quarterly tax payments. The company is in the 46 percent marginal tax bracket and intends to pay the additional taxes on April 15. What is the combined effect of these two changes on accruals?

6. The Halow Harp and Chime Company is negotiating a new labor contract. Among other things, the union is demanding that the company pay its workers weekly as opposed to twice a month. The payroll currently is $260,000 per payday and accrued wages average $130,000. What is the annual cost of the union's demand if the company's opportunity cost of funds is 9 percent?

7. The Fox Company is able to sell $1 million of commercial paper every three months at a rate of 7 percent and a placement cost of $3,000 per issue. The dealers require Fox to maintain $200,000 in bank balances, which would otherwise not be held. Fox has a 40 percent tax rate. What is the after-tax cost of funds from commercial paper to Fox?

8. The Sphinx Supply Company needs to increase its working capital by $100,000. It has decided that there are essentially three alternatives of financing available. They are:

(a) Forgo cash discounts, granted on a basis of 3/10, net 30.

(b) Borrow from the bank at 8 percent. This alternative would necessitate maintaining a 25 percent compensating balance.

(c) Issue commercial paper at 7 1/2 percent. The cost of placing the issue would be $500 each six months.

Assuming the firm would prefer the flexibility of bank financing, and provided the additional cost of this flexibility is no more than 1 percent, which alternative should be selected?

9. Bork Corporation wishes to borrow $100,000 for one year and must choose one of the following alternatives:

   (a) An 8 percent loan on a discount basis with 20 percent compensating balances required
   (b) A 9 percent loan on a discount basis with 10 percent compensating balances required
   (c) A 10 1/2 percent loan on a collect basis with no compensating-balance requirement

   Which alternative should Bork Corporation choose if it is concerned with the effective interest rate?

10. Commercial paper has no stipulated interest rate. It is sold on a discount basis, and the amount of the discount determines the interest cost to the issuer. On the basis of the following information, determine the percentage interest cost on an annual basis for each of the following issues. (Assume a 360-day year.)

Issue	Face Value	Price	Time to Maturity
(a)	$ 25,000	$24,500	60 days
(b)	100,000	96,500	180
(c)	50,000	48,800	90
(d)	75,000	71,300	270
(e)	100,000	99,100	30

11. At the end of the first quarter, Fishbein Electronics Company expects the following net operating cash inflows or outflows on a quarterly basis over the next three years (in millions):

Quarter	Cash Inflow or (Outflow)
I, 1st year (actual)	$3.8
II, 1st year	(5.3)
III, 1st year	(2.6)
IV, 1st year	1.9
I, 2nd year	4.2
II, 2nd year	(3.9)
III, 2nd year	(4.7)
IV, 2nd year	2.2
I, 3rd year	4.1
II, 3rd year	(4.8)
III, 3rd year	(3.7)
IV, 3rd year	2.4

These cash flows are exclusive of any new financing that might be required. The company currently has a cash balance of $1 million and wishes to maintain at least this much in the future.

(a) How much long-term financing would you recommend for the company?
(b) Approximately how much short-term financing will be required?

BROSKY, JOHN J., *The Implicit Cost of Trade Credit and Theory of Optimal Terms of Sale.* New York: Credit Research Foundation, 1969.

CRANE, DWIGHT B., AND WILLIAM L. WHITE, "Who Benefits from a Floating Prime Rate?" *Harvard Business Review,* 50 (January-February 1972), 121–29.

GUPTA, MANAK C., "Optimal Financing Policy for a Firm with Uncertain Fund Requirements," *Journal of Financial and Quantitative Analysis,* 8 (December 1973), 831–47.

HAYES, DOUGLAS A., *Bank Lending Policies: Domestic and International,* 2nd ed. Ann Arbor: University of Michigan, 1977.

MORRIS, JAMES R., "On Corporate Debt Maturity Strategies," *Journal of Finance,* 31 (March 1976), 29–37.

NADIRI, M. I., "The Determinants of Trade Credit in the U.S. Total Manufacturing Sector," *Econometrica,* 37 (July 1969), 408–23.

NADLER, PAUL S., "Compensating Balances and the Prime at Twilight," *Harvard Business Review,* 50 (January-February 1972), 112–20.

RICKS, DAVID A., *International Dimensions of Corporate Finance,* Chap. 9. Englewood Cliffs, N.J.: Prentice-Hall, 1978.

SCHWARTZ, ROBERT A., "An Economic Analysis of Trade Credit," *Journal of Financial and Quantitative Analysis,* 9 (September 1974), 643–58.

SILVERS, J. B., "Liquidity, Risk and Duration Patterns of Corporate Financing," *Financial Management,* 5 (Autumn 1976), 54–64.

SMITH, KEITH V., *Management of Working Capital,* Sec. 5. New York: West Publishing, 1974.

STONE, BERNELL K., "Allocating Credit Lines, Planned Borrowing, and Tangible Services over a Company's Banking System," *Financial Management,* 4 (Summer 1975), 65–78.

———, "The Cost of Bank Loans," *Journal of Financial and Quantitative Analysis,* 7 (December 1972), 2077–86.

18
secured loans and term financing

In this chapter, we extend our examination of short-term loans to consider secured types of lending arrangements. The principal characteristic of short-term loans is that they are self-liquidating over a period of time of less than a year. Frequently, these types of loans are employed to finance seasonal and temporary funds requirements. Intermediate-term financing, on the other hand, is employed to finance more permanent funds requirements, such as underlying buildups in receivables and inventories, as well as to provide flexibility in a period of uncertainty. In the second part of the chapter, we examine various types of intermediate-term loans. In the following chapter, we consider lease financing, another means of intermediate-term financing.

SECURED LENDING ARRANGEMENTS

Many firms cannot obtain credit on an unsecured basis, either because they are new and unproven or because their ability to service debt is not regarded as adequate by bankers. In order to make a loan, lenders require security so as to reduce their risk of loss. With security, lenders have two sources of loan

payment: the cash-flow ability of the firm to service the debt and, if that
source fails for some reason, the collateral value of the security. Most lenders
will not make a loan unless the firm has sufficient expected cash flows to
make proper servicing of debt probable. To reduce their risk further, however, they require security as well.

We know that secured lending arrangements are more costly to
administer than unsecured loans and that the incremental cost is passed on to
the borrower in the form of fees and/or higher interest costs than would
otherwise be the case. The question that might be asked is, Why is it in either
party's interest to create the additional cost? The answer is that the market for
loans is a competitive one. If a borrower can obtain unsecured credit elsewhere at less total cost, he will do so. Beyond a point in risk, however, all
lenders in the market will want some type of safeguard beyond the general
credit standing of the company. This safeguard can come in the form of
security and/or a set of protective covenants which afford the lender the
ability to take corrective steps prior to maturity if the borrower's financial
condition should deteriorate. We discuss protective covenants later in the
chapter, whereas our focus now is on secured loans. In both cases, however, it
is important to recognize that the conditions imposed on a borrower are
determined in competitive financial markets. A lender simply cannot demand
security and expect to get it unless the borrower has no other alternatives![1]
The use of security is negotiated in keeping with conditions in the overall
market for loans.

Collateral Value

The excess of the market value of the security pledged over the
amount of the loan determines the lender's margin of safety. If the borrower is
unable to meet his obligation, the lender can sell the security to satisfy the
claim. If the security is sold for an amount exceeding the amount of the loan
and interest owed, the difference is remitted to the borrower. If the security is
sold for less, the lender becomes a general, or unsecured, creditor for the
amount of the difference. Because secured lenders do not wish to become
general creditors, they usually seek security with a market value sufficiently
above the amount of the loan to minimize the likelihood of their not being
able to sell the security in full satisfaction of the loan. However, the degree of
security protection a lender seeks varies with the credit-worthiness of the
borrower, the security the borrower has available, and the financial institution making the loan.

[1]See James H. Scott, Jr., "Bankruptcy, Secured Debt, and Optimal Capital Structure,"
Journal of Finance, 32 (March 1977), 1–19, for an extension of this notion. In addition, Scott posits
that a firm can increase its value to its shareholders by issuing secured debt. The reason advanced
is that with a secured lending arrangement, the present value of expected payments to unsecured
creditors is reduced. Essentially, equityholders sell the right to be first in order of priority in the
event of bankruptcy. As this right is valuable, equityholders are said to obtain value for it in some
form of side payment from the secured lender.

The value of the collateral to the lender varies according to several factors. Perhaps the most important is marketability. If the collateral can be sold quickly in an active market without depressing the price, the lender is likely to be willing to lend an amount that represents a fairly high percentage of the collateral's stated value. On the other hand, if the collateral is a special-purpose machine designed specifically for a company with no viable secondary market, the lender may choose to lend nothing at all. The life of the collateral also is important. If the collateral has a life that closely parallels the life of the loan, it will be more valuable to the lender than collateral that is much longer term in nature. As the collateral is liquidated into cash, the proceeds may be used to pay down the loan. Therefore a lender will prefer short-term collateral for short-term loans and long-term collateral for long-term loans. Still another factor is the basic riskiness associated with the collateral. The greater the fluctuation in its market value and/or the greater the uncertainty on the part of the lender concerning market value, the less desirable the collateral from the standpoint of the lender. Thus marketability, life, and riskiness determine the attractiveness of various types of collateral to a lender and, hence, the amount of financing available to a company. Before taking up specific short-term secured lending arrangements, we must briefly examine the means by which a lender protects himself under the Uniform Commercial Code.

Article 9 of the Code deals with security interests of lenders, the specific aspect with which we are concerned.[2] Whenever a lender requires collateral of a borrower, he obtains a *security interest* in the collateral. The collateral may be accounts receivable, inventory, equipment, or other assets of the borrower. The security interest in the collateral is created by a *security agreement,* also known as a *security device*. This agreement is signed by the borrower and the lender and contains a description of the collateral. In order to "perfect" a security interest in the collateral, the lender must file a copy of the security agreement or a financing statement with a public office of the state in which the collateral is located. Frequently, this office is that of the secretary of state. The filing gives public notice to other parties that the lender has a security interest in the collateral described. Before accepting collateral as security for a loan, a lender will search the public notices to see if the collateral has been pledged previously in connection with another loan. Only the lender with a valid security interest in the collateral has a prior claim on the assets and can sell the collateral in settlement of his loan.

Assignment of Accounts Receivable

Accounts receivable represent one of the most liquid assets of the firm, and, consequently, they make desirable security for a loan. From the standpoint of the lender, the major difficulties with this type of security are the cost of processing the collateral and the risk of fraud. To illustrate the

[2]See Lester E. Denonn, "The Security Agreement," *Journal of Commercial Bank Lending,* 50 (February 1968), 32–40.

nature of the arrangement, we trace through a typical assignment of accounts-receivable loan. A company may seek a receivable loan from either a commercial bank or a finance company. Because the interest rate charged by a bank usually is less than that charged by a finance company, the firm will generally try to borrow first from a bank.

Quality and Size of Receivables   In evaluating the loan request, the lender will analyze the quality of the firm's receivables in order to determine the amount he is willing to lend against these receivables. The greater the quality of the accounts the firm maintains, the greater the percentage the lender is willing to advance against the face value of the receivables pledged. A lender does not have to accept all the borrower's accounts receivable; usually, he will reject accounts that have low credit ratings or that are unrated. Also, government and foreign accounts usually are ineligible unless special arrangements are made. Depending upon the quality of the receivables accepted, a lender typically advances between 50 percent and 80 percent of their face value.

The lender is concerned not only with the quality of receivables but also with their size. The lender must keep records on each account receivable that is pledged; the smaller the average size of the accounts, the more it costs per dollar of loan to process them. Consequently, a firm that sells low-priced items on open account will generally be unable to obtain a receivable loan regardless of the quality of the accounts. The cost of processing the loan is simply too high. Occasionally a "bulk" assignment of receivables will be used to circumvent the problem. With a "bulk" assignment, the lender does not keep track of the individual accounts but records only the total amounts in the accounts assigned and the payments received. Because preventing fraud is difficult with a "bulk" assignment, the percentage advance against the face value of receivables is likely to be low—perhaps 25 percent.

Procedure   Suppose a lender has decided to extend a loan to a firm on the basis of a 75 percent advance against the face value of accounts receivable assigned. The firm then sends in a schedule of accounts showing the name of the account, the date of billing(s), and the amounts owed. An example of an assignment schedule is shown in Figure 18-1. The lender will sometimes require evidence of shipment, such as an invoice. Having received the schedule of accounts, the lender has the borrower sign a promissory note and a security agreement. The firm then receives 75 percent of the face value of the receivables shown on the schedule of accounts.

A receivable loan can be on either a nonnotification or a notification basis. Under the former arrangement, the customer of the firm is not notified that his account has been pledged to the lender. When the firm receives payment on the account, it forwards this payment, together with other payments, to the lender. The lender checks the payments against its record of accounts outstanding and reduces the amount the borrower owes by 75 percent of the total payments. The other 25 percent is credited to the borrower's regular checking account. With a nonnotification arrangement, the lender must take precautions to make sure the borrower does not with-

SCHEDULE OF ACCOUNTS ASSIGNED

The undersigned hereby assigns to **WELLS FARGO BANK** the following accounts:

(LIST NAMES OR REFER TO ATTACHED)	GROSS AMOUNT	
Accounts receivable totalling _____		
evidenced by _____		
for (dates) _____ Attached hereto and made a part hereof		
TOTAL		

The above accounts are assigned to **WELLS FARGO BANK** and a security interest is granted in accordance with the terms and conditions of the existing Continuing Security Agreement between undersigned and **WELLS FARGO BANK**, to which reference is made.

Date _____

Signed _____

By: _____

Schedule No. S _____

N503   —100/PAD—217—006

figure 18-1
Accounts-receivable assignment form

hold a payment check, using the funds himself. With a notification arrangement, the account is notified of the assignment, and remittances are made directly to the lender. Under this arrangement, the borrower cannot withhold payments. Most firms naturally prefer to borrow on a nonnotification basis; however, the lender reserves the right to place the arrangement on a notification basis.

An accounts-receivable loan is a more or less continuous financing arrangement. As the firm generates new receivables that are acceptable to the lender, they are assigned, adding to the security base against which the firm is able to borrow. New receivables replace the old, and the security base and the amount of loan fluctuate accordingly. A receivable loan is a very flexible means of secured financing. As receivables build up, the firm is able to borrow additional funds to finance this buildup. Thus it has access to "built-in" financing. Many banks do not require compensating balances for receivable loans. Because the borrower frequently is rapidly growing, the burden of this requirement is felt to be unreasonable. Compensation comes in the form of a higher rate. Also, a "cleanup" of the loan is not required, because it is regarded as a more or less permanent source of financing.

Factoring Receivables

In the assignment of accounts receivable, the firm retains title to the receivables. When a firm *factors* its receivables, however, it actually sells them to a factor. The sale may be either with or without recourse, depending upon the type of arrangement negotiated. The factor maintains a credit department and makes credit checks on accounts. Based upon its credit investigation, the factor may refuse to buy certain accounts that it deems too risky. By factoring, a firm frequently relieves itself of the expense of maintaining a credit department and making collections. Any account that the factor is unwilling to buy is an unacceptable credit risk unless, of course, the firm wants to assume this risk on its own and ship the goods. Factoring arrangements are governed by a contract between the factor and the client. The contract frequently is for one year with an automatic provision for renewal and can be canceled only with prior notice of thirty to sixty days. Although it is customary in a factoring arrangement to notify the customer that his account has been sold and that payments on the account should be sent directly to the factor, in some instances notification is not made. The customer continues to remit payments to the firm, which, in turn, endorses them to the factor. These endorsements are frequently camouflaged to prevent the customer from learning that his account has been sold.

Factoring Costs For bearing risk and servicing the receivables, the factor receives a fee of around 1 to 3 percent of the face value of the receivables sold. This fee will vary according to the typical size of individual accounts, the volume of receivables sold, and the quality of the accounts. The typical fee is somewhat over 1 percent. We must recognize that the receivables sold to the factor will not be collected from the various accounts for a period of time. If the firm wishes to receive payment for the sale of its receivables before they are actually collected, it must pay interest on the advance. Advancing payment is a lending function of the factor in addition to his functions of risk bearing and of servicing the receivables. For this additional function, the factor requires compensation.

For example, if the receivables sold total $10,000, and the factoring fee is 2 percent, the factor will credit the firm's account with $9,800. If the firm wants to draw on this account before the receivables are collected, however, it will have to pay an interest charge—say 1 percent a month—for the use of the funds. If it wishes a cash advance of the full $9,800, and the receivables are collected, on the average, in one month, the interest cost will be approximately 0.01 × $9,800, or $98.[3] Thus the total cost of factoring is composed of a factoring fee plus an interest charge if the firm draws upon its account before the receivables are collected. If the firm does not draw on its account until the receivables are collected, there is no interest charge. A third alternative is for the firm to leave its funds with the factor beyond the time when the receivables are collected and to receive interest on the account from the factor.

Flexibility The typical factoring arrangement is continuous. As new receivables are acquired, they are sold to the factor, and the firm's account is credited. The firm then draws upon this account as it needs funds. Sometimes the factor will allow the firm to overdraw its account during periods of peak

[3]The actual cash advance would be $9,800 less the interest cost, or $9,702.

needs and thereby borrow on an unsecured basis. Under other arrangements, the factor may withhold a reserve from the firm's account as a protection against losses. The principal sources of factoring are commercial banks, factoring subsidiaries of bank holding companies, and certain old-line factors. While the business originally was confined to the last and to New York City, the entry of banks in the 1960s expanded considerably the scope, reputation, and geography of the factoring business.

Factoring, like the assignment of accounts receivable, affords the firm flexibility in its financing. As sales increase and the firm needs funds, financing becomes available automatically. This eliminates the uncertainty associated with the collection cycle. Consequently, the cash flows of the firm are more predictable. While some people attach a stigma to the company that factors, in many quarters it is regarded as a perfectly acceptable method of financing. Its principal shortcoming is that it can be expensive. We must bear in mind, however, that the factor often relieves the firm of credit checkings, the cost of processing receivables, and collection expenses. For a small firm, the savings may be quite significant. All in all, factoring has found increasing acceptance as a means of financing, showing substantial growth in volume during the last fifteen years.

Inventory Loans

Inventories also represent a reasonably liquid asset and are therefore suitable as security for a short-term loan. As with a receivable loan, the lender determines a percentage advance against the market value of the collateral. This percentage varies according to the quality of the inventory. Certain inventories, such as grains, are very marketable and when properly stored resist physical deterioration. The margin of safety required by the lender on a loan of this sort is fairly small, and the advance may be as high as 90 percent. On the other hand, the market for a highly specialized piece of equipment may be so narrow that a lender is unwilling to make any advance against its reported market value. Thus not every kind of inventory can be pledged as security for a loan. The best collateral is inventory that is relatively standard and for which a ready market exists apart from the marketing organization of the borrower.

Lenders determine the percentage that they are willing to advance by considering marketability, perishability, market-price stability, and the difficulty and expense of selling the inventory to satisfy the loan. The cost of selling some inventory may be very high indeed. The lender does not want to be in the business of liquidating collateral, but he does want to assure himself that the collateral has adequate value in case the borrower defaults in the payment of principal or interest. As is true with most secured loans, however, the actual decision to make the loan will depend upon the cash-flow ability of the borrower to service debt. There are a number of different ways a lender can obtain a secured interest in inventories, and we consider each in turn. In the case of the first methods (floating lien, chattel mortgage, and trust receipt), the inventory remains in the possession of the borrower. In the last two methods (terminal warehouse and field warehouse receipts), the inventory is in the possession of a third party.

Floating Lien   Under the Uniform Commercial Code, the borrower may pledge his inventories "in general" without specifying the kind of inventory involved. Under this arrangement, the lender obtains a floating lien on all inventory of the borrower. This lien is very general and difficult to police on the part of the lender. Frequently, a floating lien is requested only as additional protection and does not play a major role in determining whether or not the loan will be made. Even if the lender does regard the collateral as important, he usually is willing to make only a moderate advance because he cannot exercise tight control over the collateral. The floating lien can be made to cover both receivables and inventories, as well as the collection of receivables. This modification gives the lender a lien on a major portion of a firm's current assets. In addition, the lien can be made to encompass almost any length of time so that it includes future as well as present inventory as security.[4]

Chattel Mortgage   With a chattel mortgage, inventories are identified specifically either by serial number or by some other means. While the borrower holds title to the goods, the lender has a lien on inventory. This inventory cannot be sold unless the lender gives his consent. Because of the rigorous identification requirements, chattel mortgages are ill suited for inventory with rapid turnover and/or inventory that is not easily identified because of size or other reasons. They are well suited, however, for certain capital assets, such as machine tools.

Trust Receipt Loans   Under a trust receipt financing arrangement, the borrower holds the inventory and proceeds from the sale of inventory in trust for the lender. This type of lending arrangement, known also as floor planning, has been used extensively by automobile dealers, equipment dealers, and consumer durable goods dealers. To illustrate trust receipt financing, suppose an automobile manufacturer ships cars to a dealer who, in turn, finances the payment for these cars through a finance company. The finance company pays the manufacturer for the cars shipped. The dealer signs a trust receipt security agreement, which specifies what can be done with the inventory. The car dealer is allowed to sell the cars but must turn the proceeds of the sale over to the lender in payment of the loan. Inventory in trust, unlike inventory under a floating lien, is specifically identified by serial number or by other means. In our example, the finance company periodically audits the cars the dealer has on hand. The serial numbers of these cars are checked against those shown in the security agreement. The purpose of the audit is to see if the dealer has sold cars without remitting the proceeds of the sale to the finance company.

[4]For further discussion, see J. Carson Quarles, "The Floating Lien," *Journal of Commercial Bank Lending*, 53 (November 1970), 51–58.

As the dealer buys new cars from the automobile manufacturer, a new trust receipt security agreement is signed that takes account of the new inventory. The dealer then borrows against this new collateral, which he holds in trust. Although there is tighter control over collateral with a trust receipt agreement than with a floating lien, there is still the risk of inventory being sold without the proceeds being turned over to the lender. Consequently, the lender must exercise judgment in deciding to lend under this arrangement. A dishonest dealer can devise numerous ways to fool the lender.

Many durable goods manufacturers finance the inventories of their distributors or dealers. Their purpose is to encourage dealers or distributors to carry reasonable stocks of goods. It is reasoned that the greater the stock, the more likely the dealer or distributor is to make a sale. Because the manufacturer is interested in selling his product, financing terms are often more attractive than they are with an "outside" lender.

Terminal Warehouse Receipt Loans   A borrower secures a terminal warehouse receipt loan by storing inventory with a public, or terminal, warehousing company.[5] The warehouse company issues a warehouse receipt, which evidences title to specified goods that are located in the warehouse. An example of a warehouse receipt is shown in Figure 18-2. The warehouse receipt gives the lender a security interest in the goods, against which he makes a loan to the borrower. Under such an arrangement, the warehouseman can release the collateral to the borrower only when authorized to do so by the lender. Consequently, the lender is able to maintain strict control over the collateral and will release collateral only when the borrower pays a portion of the loan. For his own protection, the lender usually requires the borrower to take out an insurance policy with a loss-payable clause in favor of the lender.

Warehouse receipts may be either nonnegotiable or negotiable. A nonnegotiable warehouse receipt is issued in favor of a specific party—in this case, the lender—who is given title to the goods and has sole authority to release them. A negotiable warehouse receipt can be transferred by endorsement. Before goods can be released, however, the negotiable receipt must be presented to the warehouseman. A negotiable receipt is useful when title to the goods is transferred from one party to another while the goods are in storage. With a nonnegotiable receipt, the release of goods can be authorized only in writing. Most lending arrangements are based upon nonnegotiable receipts.

Field Warehouse Receipt Loans   In a terminal warehouse receipt loan, the goods are located in a public warehouse. Another arrangement, known as field warehousing, permits loans to be made against inventory that is located

---

[5]For an excellent discussion of warehouse receipts, see Robert W. Rogers, "Warehouse Receipts and Their Use in Financing," *Bulletin of the Robert Morris Associates*, 46 (April 1964), 317–27.

figure 18-2
Warehouse receipt

on the borrower's premises. Under this arrangement, a field warehousing company sets off a designated storage area on the borrower's premises for the inventory pledged as collateral. The field warehousing company has sole access to this area and is supposed to maintain strict control over it. (The goods that serve as collateral are segregated from the borrower's other inventory.) The field warehousing company issues a warehouse receipt as described in the preceding section, and the lender extends a loan based upon the collateral value of the inventory. The field warehouse arrangement is a useful means of financing when it is not desirable, either because of the expense or because of the inconvenience, to place the inventory in a public warehouse. Field warehouse receipt lending is particularly appropriate when a borrower must make frequent use of inventory. Because of the need to pay the field warehousing company's expenses, the cost of this method of financing can be relatively high.

It is important to recognize that the warehouse receipt, as evidence of collateral, is only as good as the issuing warehousing company. When administered properly, a warehouse receipt loan affords the lender a high degree of control over the collateral. However, there have been sufficient examples of fraud to show that the warehouse receipt does not always evidence actual value. The warehouseman must exercise strict control. A grain elevator that is alleged to be full may, in fact, be empty. Upon close examination, we may find that barrels reported to contain chemical concentrate actually contain water.[6]

INTERMEDIATE-TERM DEBT

Typically, intermediate-term financing is self-liquidating. For this reason, it resembles short-term financing. However, intermediate-term financing also can satisfy more permanent funds requirements and, in addition, can serve as an interim substitute for long-term financing. If a firm wishes to float long-term debt or issue common stock but conditions are unfavorable in the market, the firm may seek intermediate-term debt to bridge the gap until long-term financing can be undertaken on favorable terms. Thus intermediate-term debt may give a firm flexibility in the timing of long-term financing. It also can provide flexibility when the firm is uncertain as to the size and nature of its future funds requirements. As uncertainty is resolved, intermediate-term financing can be replaced by a more appropriate means of financing. The most important use of intermediate-term financing, however, is to provide credit when the expected cash flows of the firm are such that the debt can be retired steadily over a period of several years and the size of the need precludes long-term financing. Even though it is sometimes linked to a particular asset, such as a piece of equipment, intermediate-term financing must be considered in relation to the firm's total funds requirements.

In this section, we examine various forms of intermediate-term debt. We begin by considering bank term loans, perhaps the most important source of intermediate-term financing for the firm.

Bank Term Loans

An ordinary term loan is a business loan with an original, or final, maturity of more than one year, repayable according to a specified schedule. For the most part, these loans are repayable in periodic installments; for example, quarterly, semiannually, or yearly. The payment schedule of the

---

[6]For a lively discussion of the various ways frauds have taken place against secured lenders, see Monroe R. Lazere, "Swinging Swindles and Creepy Frauds," *Journal of Commercial Bank Lending,* 60 (September 1977), 44–52.

loan usually is geared to the borrower's cash-flow ability to service the debt. Typically, this schedule calls for equal periodic installments, but it may be irregular with respect to amounts or may simply call for repayment in a lump sum at final maturity. Sometimes the loan is amortized in equal periodic installments except for the final payment, known as a "balloon" payment, which is larger than any of the others.

Most bank term loans are written with original maturities in the three- to seven-year range. Some banks are willing to make longer-term loans, but only rarely will a bank make a term loan with a final maturity of more than ten years. In recent years, however, banks have been making longer-term loans. Whereas a five-year loan once was considered dangerous to a bank's liquidity, term loans in this final maturity area are now common.

The final maturity of a term loan does not always convey the length of time the loan is likely to remain outstanding. In some cases, the bank as well as the company expects the loan to be renewed successively with maturity. These loans are known as "evergreen" loans and are typically characterized by credits to companies in growth phases. Despite the expectation of "evergreen" refunding upon maturity, the bank is not legally obligated to extend the loan. As a result, most requests for extensions and additional credit are analyzed afresh based on changed conditions from the time of the original loan. What was thought to be an "evergreen" loan may turn out to be a "deciduous" one if the financial condition and performance of the borrower deteriorate.

Generally, the interest rate on a term loan is higher than the rate on a short-term loan to the same borrower. For example, if a firm could borrow at the prime rate on a short-term basis, it might pay 0.25 percent to 0.50 percent more on a term loan. The interest rate on a term loan can be set in one of two ways: (1) a fixed rate that is effective over the life of the loan may be established at the outset, or (2) a variable rate may be set that is adjusted in keeping with changes in the prime rate.

In addition to interest costs, the borrower is required to pay the legal expenses that the bank incurs in drawing up the loan agreement. Also, a commitment fee may be charged for the time during the commitment period when the loan is not taken down. For an ordinary term loan, these additional costs usually are rather small in relation to the total interest cost of the loan. A typical fee on the unused portion of a commitment is 0.50 percent, with a range of 0.25 percent to 0.75 percent. This means that if the commitment fee were 0.50 percent on a commitment of $1 million and the company took down all of the loan three months after the commitment, it would owe the bank $1 million $\times$ .005 $\times$ 3/12 = $1,250. In addition to the commitment fee, an indirect cost to the borrower is the need to maintain compensating balances, which we discussed in Chapter 17.

The principal advantage of an ordinary bank term loan is flexibility. The borrower deals directly with the lender, and the loan can be tailored to the borrower's needs through direct negotiation. The bank usually has had previous experience with the borrower, so it is familiar with the company's situation. Should the firm's requirements change, the terms and conditions of the loan may be revised. It is considerably more convenient to negotiate with a single lender or a reasonably small group of lenders than with a large number of public security holders, as there are with a bond issue. In addition, the borrower can deal confidentially with a bank, or, for that matter, with any private lending institution, and does not have to reveal certain financial information to the public.

In many instances, bank term loans are made to small businesses that do not have access to the capital markets and cannot readily float a public issue. In addition, the ability to sell a public issue varies over time in keeping with the tone of the capital markets. In the 1970s, most companies of moderate size but with good growth potential were unable to go to the public market with a debt issue. In the 1960s, a number of these companies found a receptive market, particularly if an option relating to common stock were involved. Finally, large companies that are able to go to the public market may find it quicker and more convenient to seek a bank term loan than to float a public issue. A term loan can be arranged in several weeks, whereas a public issue takes a good deal longer.

Revolving Credits

As we said in Chapter 17, a revolving credit is a formal commitment by a bank to lend up to a certain amount of money to a company over a specified period of time. The actual notes evidencing debt are short-term, usually ninety days; but the company may renew them or borrow additionally, up to the specified maximum, throughout the duration of the commitment. Many revolving-credit commitments are for three years, although it is possible for a firm to obtain a shorter commitment. As with an ordinary term loan, the interest rate is usually 0.25 to 0.50 percent higher than the rate at which the firm could borrow on a short-term basis under a line of credit. When a bank makes a revolving-credit commitment, it is legally bound under the loan agreement to have funds available whenever the company wants to borrow. The borrower usually must pay for this availability in the form of a commitment fee, perhaps 0.50 percent per annum, on the difference between the amount borrowed and the specified maximum.[7]

Because most revolving-credit agreements are for more than one year, they are regarded as intermediate-term financing. This borrowing arrangement is particularly useful at times when the firm is uncertain about its funds requirements. A revolving-credit agreement has the features of both a short-term borrowing arrangement and a term loan, for the firm can borrow a

---

[7]For an analysis of the optimal amount of revolving credit to establish, see Paul D. Berger and William K. Harper, "Determination of an Optimal Revolving Credit Agreement," *Journal of Financial and Quantitative Analysis*, 8 (June 1973), 491–97. In the article, the authors examine the tradeoff between the commitment fee cost, which is a linear function of the amount of the revolving credit, and the risk of borrowing needs exceeding the amount of revolving credit established.

fixed amount for the entire duration of the commitment. Thus the borrower has flexible access to funds over a period of uncertainty and can make more definite credit arrangements when the uncertainty is resolved. Revolving-credit agreements can be set up so that at the maturity of the commitment, borrowings then owing can be converted into a term loan at the option of the borrower. To illustrate, suppose a company introduces a new product and is faced with a period of uncertainty over the next several years. To provide maximum financial flexibility, the company might arrange a three-year revolving credit that is convertible into a five-year term loan at the expiration of the revolving-credit commitment. At the end of three years, the company, hopefully, would know its funds requirements better. If these requirements are permanent, or nearly so, the firm might wish to exercise its option and take down the term loan.

Insurance Company Term Loans

Insurance companies and certain other institutional lenders, as well as banks, extend term loans to companies. The former establish protective covenants much as a bank does. However, there are important differences in the maturity of the loan extended and in the interest rate charged. In general, life insurance companies are interested in term loans with final maturities in excess of ten years. Because these companies do not have the benefit of compensating balances or other business from the borrower, and because their loans usually have a longer maturity than bank term loans, typically the rate of interest is higher. To the insurance company, the term loan represents an investment and must yield a return commensurate with the costs involved in making the loan, the risk, the maturity, and prevailing yields on alternative investments. Because an insurance company is interested in keeping its funds employed without interruption, it normally has a prepayment penalty, whereas ordinarily the bank does not. One of the simpler prepayment formulas calls for a premium of 0.25 percent for each year remaining to maturity.

Insurance company term loans generally are not competitive with bank term loans. Indeed, they are complementary, for they serve different maturity ranges. Sometimes a bank and an insurance company will participate in the same loan. The bank may take the early maturities, perhaps the first five years, with the insurance company taking the remaining maturities. Including an insurance company in the credit permits a longer maturity range than the bank can provide, and the bank can offer a lower interest rate on the early maturities. A term loan of this sort may serve both the intermediate- and long-term funds requirements of the firm.

Equipment Financing

Equipment represents another asset of the firm that may be pledged to secure a loan. If the firm either has equipment that is marketable or is purchasing such equipment, it is usually able to obtain some sort of secured financing. Because such loans usually are for more than a year, we consider them as intermediate-term financing. As with other secured loans, the lender is concerned with the marketability of the collateral. Depending upon the quality of the equipment, he will make a percentage advance against the equipment's market value. Frequently, the repayment schedule for the loan is set in keeping with the depreciation schedule of the equipment. For example, a trucking company will usually depreciate its tractors over four years and its trailers over six years. A lender might set a four-year installment payment schedule for a loan secured by tractors and a six-year schedule for a loan secured by trailers. In setting the repayment schedule, the lender wants to be sure that the market value of the tractor or trailer always exceeds the balance of the loan.

The excess of the expected market value of the equipment over the amount of the loan represents the margin of safety, which will vary according to the specific situation. In the case of the rolling stock of a trucking company, the collateral is movable and reasonably marketable. As a result, the advance may be as high as 80 percent. Less marketable equipment, such as that with a limited use, will not command as high an advance. A certain type of lathe, for example, may have a thin market, and a lender might not be willing to advance more than 50 percent of its reported market value. Some equipment is of such a special-purpose nature that it has no value for collateral purposes. Frequently, the lender either will have its own appraiser or will hire an appraiser to estimate the approximate value of a piece of equipment if it should have to be sold. As with other collateral, the lender is interested not only in the estimated market price of the equipment but also in the cost of selling it.

Sources of Equipment Financing   Sources of equipment financing include commercial banks, finance companies, and the sellers of equipment. Because the interest charged by a finance company on an equipment loan is usually higher than that charged by a commercial bank, a firm will turn to a finance company only if it is unable to obtain the loan from a bank. The seller of the equipment may finance the purchase either by holding the secured note itself or by selling the note to its captive finance subsidiary. The interest charge will depend upon the extent to which the seller uses financing as a sales tool. If he uses it extensively, he may charge only a moderate interest rate and may make up for part of the cost of carrying the notes by charging higher prices for the equipment. The borrower must consider this possibility in judging the true cost of financing. Equipment loans may be secured either by a chattel mortgage or by a conditional sales contract arrangement.

Chattel Mortgage   A chattel mortgage is a lien on property other than real estate. The borrower signs a security agreement, which gives the lender a lien on the equipment specified in the agreement. In order to perfect the lien, the lender files a copy of the security agreement or a financing statement with a public office of the state in which the equipment is located. Given a valid lien, the lender can sell the equipment if the borrower defaults in the payment of principal or interest on the loan.

Conditional Sales Contract   With a conditional sales contract arrangement, the seller of the equipment retains title to it until the purchaser has satisfied all the terms of the contract. The buyer signs a conditional sales contract security agreement under which he agrees to make periodic installment payments to the seller over a specified period of time. These payments usually are monthly or quarterly. Until the terms of the contract are satisfied completely, the seller retains title to the equipment. Thus the seller receives a down payment and a promissory note for the balance of the purchase price upon the sale of the equipment. The note is secured by the contract, which gives the seller the authority to repossess the equipment if the buyer does not meet all the terms of the contract.

The seller may either hold the contract himself or sell it, simply by endorsing it, to a commercial bank or finance company. The bank or finance company then becomes the lender and assumes the security interest in the equipment. If the buyer should default under the terms of the contract, the bank or finance company could repossess the equipment and sell it in satisfaction of its loan. Often the vendor will sell the contract to a bank or finance company with recourse. Under this arrangement, the lender has the additional protection of recourse to the seller in case the buyer defaults.

PROTECTIVE COVENANTS AND LOAN AGREEMENTS

When a lender makes a term loan or revolving-credit commitment, it provides the borrower with available funds for an extended period of time. Much can happen to the financial condition of the borrower during that period. In order to safeguard itself, the lender requires the borrower to maintain its financial condition and, in particular, its current position at a level at least as favorable as when the commitment was made. The provisions for protection contained in a loan agreement are known as protective convenants.

The loan agreement itself simply gives the lender legal authority to step in should the borrower default under any of the provisions. Otherwise, he would be locked into a commitment and would have to wait until maturity before being able to effect corrective measures. If the borrower should suffer losses or other adverse developments, he will default under a well-written loan agreement; the lender then will be able to act. The action usually takes the form of working with the company to straighten out its problems. Seldom will a lender demand immediate payment, although he has the legal right to do so in cases of default. More typically, the condition under which the borrower defaults is waived or the loan agreement is amended. The important thing is that the lender has the authority to act, even though he may negotiate with the borrower in order to resolve the problem.

The formulation of the different restrictive provisions should be tailored to the specific loan situation. These provisions are the tools by which the lender fashions the overall protection of his loan. No one provision is able by itself to provide the necessary safeguards, but together with the other provisions, it is designed to assure overall liquidity and ability to pay a loan. The important protective convenants of a loan agreement may be classified as follows: (1) general provisions used in most loan agreements, which are variable to fit the situation; (2) routine provisions used in most agreements, which usually are not variable; and (3) specific provisions that are used according to the situation. Although we focus on a bank loan agreement, the protective covenants used and the philosophy underlying their use are the same for a bond indenture, which is described in Chapter 21.

General Provisions

The *working-capital requirement* is probably the most commonly used and most comprehensive provision in a loan agreement. Its purpose is to preserve the company's current position and ability to pay the loan. Frequently, a straight dollar amount, such as $2 million, is set as the minimum working capital the company must maintain during the duration of the commitment. When the lender feels that it is desirable for a specific company to build working capital, it may increase the minimum working-capital requirement throughout the duration of the loan. The establishment of a working-capital minimum normally is based upon the amounts of present working capital and projected working capital, allowing for seasonal fluctuations. The requirement should not restrict the company unduly in the ordinary generation of profit. However, should the borrower incur sharp losses or spend too much for fixed assets, purchase of stock, dividends, redemption of long-term debt, and so forth, it would probably breach the working-capital requirement.

The *cash dividend and repurchase-of-stock restriction* is another important restriction in this category. Its purpose is to limit cash going outside the business, thus preserving the liquidity of the company. Most often, cash dividends and repurchase of stock are limited to a percentage of net profits on a cumulative basis after a certain base date, frequently the last fiscal year-end prior to the date of the term-loan agreement. A less flexible method is to restrict dividends and repurchase of stock to an absolute dollar amount each year. In most cases, the prospective borrower must be willing to undergo a cash dividend and repurchase-of-stock restriction. If tied to earnings, this restriction still will allow adequate dividends as long as the company is able to generate satisfactory profits.

The *capital-expenditures limitation* is third in the category of general provisions. Capital expenditures may be limited to a fixed dollar amount each year. However, it probably is more common to limit annual capital expenditures either to depreciation or to a percentage thereof. The capital-expenditures limitation is another tool used by the lender to assure the maintenance of the borrower's current position. By limiting capital expenditures directly, the bank can be more sure that it will not have to look to liquidation of fixed assets for payment of its loan. Again, however, the provision should not be so restrictive as to prevent the adequate maintenance and improvement of facilities.

A *limitation on other indebtedness* is the last general provision. This limitation may take a number of forms, depending upon the circumstances. Frequently, a loan agreement will prohibit a company from incurring any other long-term debt. This provision protects the lender, inasmuch as it prevents future lenders from obtaining a prior claim on the borrower's assets. Usually a company is permitted to borrow within reasonable limits for seasonal and other short-term purposes arising in the ordinary course of business.

Routine Provisions

The second category of restrictions includes routine, usually invariable, provisions found in most loan agreements. Ordinarily, the loan agreement requires the borrower to furnish the bank with financial statements and to maintain adequate insurance. Additionally, the borrower normally is required not to sell a significant portion of its assets and is required to pay, when due, all taxes and other liabilities, except those contested in good faith. A provision forbidding the pledging or mortgaging of any of the borrower's assets is almost always included in a loan agreement; this important provision is known as a negative pledge clause.

Ordinarily, the company is required not to discount or sell its receivables. Moreover, the borrower generally is prohibited from entering into any leasing arrangement of property, except up to a certain dollar amount of annual rental. The purpose of this provision is to prevent the borrower from taking on a substantial lease liability, which might endanger its ability to pay the loan. A lease restriction also prevents the firm from leasing property instead of purchasing it and thereby getting around the limitations on capital expenditures and debt. Usually, too, there is a restriction on other contingent liabilities.

In addition to these restrictions, there typically is a restriction on the acquisition of other companies. This restriction often is a straight prohibition of such mergers unless specifically approved by the lender. It is possible to have other kinds of restrictions on mergers, but a flat prohibition is most prevalent. The provisions in this "routine" category appear as a matter of routine in most loan agreements. Although somewhat mechanical, they are important because they close many loopholes and provide a tight, comprehensive loan agreement.

Special Provisions

Special provisions are used in specific loan agreements by the banker in order to achieve a desired total protection of his loan. For instance, a loan agreement may contain a definite understanding regarding the use of the loan proceeds, so that there will be no diversion of funds to purposes other than those contemplated when the loan was negotiated. A provision for limiting loans and advances often is found in a bank term-loan agreement. Closely allied to this restriction is a limitation on investments, which is used to safeguard liquidity by preventing certain nonliquid investments.

If one or more executives are essential to a firm's effective operation, a bank may insist that the company carry life insurance on their lives. Proceeds of the insurance may be payable to the company or directly to the bank, to be applied to the loan. An agreement may also contain a management clause under which certain key individuals must remain actively employed in the company during the time the loan is owing. Aggregate executive salaries and bonuses are sometimes limited in the loan agreement to prevent excessive compensation of executives, which might reduce profits. This provision closes another loophole; it prevents large stockholders who are officers of the company from increasing their own salaries in lieu of paying higher dividends, which are limited under the agreement.

Negotiating Restrictions and the Option Pricing Theory

The provisions described above represent the most frequently used protective convenants in a loan agreement. From the standpoint of the lender, the aggregate impact of these provisions should be to safeguard the financial position of the borrower and its ability to pay the loan. Under a well-written agreement, the borrower cannot get into serious financial difficulty without defaulting under the agreement, thereby giving the lender legal authority to take action. Although the lender is instrumental in establishing the restrictions, the restrictiveness of the protective covenants is subject to negotiation between the borrower and the lender. The final result will depend upon the relative bargaining power of each of the parties involved.[8]

From our discussion in Chapters 4 and 9 concerning the application of the option pricing theory, it is easy to visualize the debtholder-equityholder relationship as being essentially an option arrangement. Looking at the relationship in this manner affords a better understanding of a lender's desire for protective covenants. To illustrate, suppose a firm has a single debt issue outstanding which is denoted by the obligation of the company to pay D at time T.[9] If the total value of the company at time T, which we denote by V, exceeds D, debtholders will be paid the face value of the obligation. If V is

---

[8]For a linear-programming approach to analyzing the opportunity costs of protective covenants, see James Van Horne, "A Linear-Programming Approach to Evaluating Restrictions under a Bond Indenture or Loan Agreement," *Journal of Financial and Quantitative Analysis,* 1 (June 1966), 68–83. In the article, the dual-variable values are taken as measures of the opportunity costs of protective covenants. Through sensitivity analysis, one can evaluate the effect on the optimal solution of given changes in the protective-covenant restrictions.

[9]This example is based on James C. Van Horne, "Optimal Initiation of Bankruptcy Proceedings by Debt Holders," *Journal of Finance,* 31 (June 1976), 897–910. See also Fischer Black and John C. Cox, "Valuing Corporate Securities: Some Effects of Bond Indenture Provisions," *Journal of Finance,* 31 (May 1976), 351–67; and Fischer Black and Myron Scholes, "The Pricing of Options and Corporate Liabilities," *Journal of Political Economy,* 81 (May-June 1973), 649–51.

less than D, however, the firm is assumed to default. Therefore the value of the debt obligation at time T is Min. (D,V). This merely states that debtholders receive the lesser of the contractual amount of the debt obligation or the value of the firm if this obligation cannot be entirely paid at time T. In other words, in default the ownership of the firm passes to the debtholders and they realize a value on their claim which is less than the contractual amount.

On the other hand, the value of the common stock at time T is Max. $(V - D, 0)$. Equityholders are the residual owners of the company and are entitled to any value of the firm that remains after the debt has been paid, $V - D$. In the event the debt cannot be paid in its entirety because V is less than D, they receive nothing. In this sense, the equityholders have an option on the total value of the firm at time T. If V exceeds D, they exercise this option so to speak, and they receive the total value of the firm at time T less the debt claim. (The face value of the debt can be thought of as the exercise price of the option.) If V is less than D, however, the option is worth zero. Now we know from Chapter 4 that with an option the greater the variance of the distribution of possible values of the firm at time T, the greater the value of the option, all other things the same. Put another way, it is the variance of the value of the associated asset—in this case the firm—that gives an option value. The same principles that apply to options on stock apply here.

In the context of our example, it behooves the equityholders to increase the risk of the firm in order to increase the variance of its total value. By undertaking more risky ventures, the value of the equityholders' option increases. While greater risk works to the advantage of equityholders, it is at the expense of the option writer, the debtholders. In fact, the increase in value of the equityholders' option means a corresponding decrease in the value of debt. Expressed differently, there is a transfer in wealth from debtholders to equityholders. The same thing occurs when the capital structure is changed by issuing new debt and repurchasing stock. As illustrated in Chapter 9, the probability of default increases and, as a result, the value of existing debt declines. In essence, the stockholders expropriate some of the wealth of the old debtholders. (New debtholders are not affected because they lend money on the basis of the new, and more risky, capital structure.)

If a lender recognizes the possibility that the equityholders may substantially alter the riskiness of the firm or issue new debt after a loan is made, he will probably want to institute some safeguards against these occurrences before making the loan. This can be done by imposing protective covenants of the sort described earlier. If the firm should breach any of these restrictions, default occurs and the lender can then declare the loan immediately payable. The obvious advantage to the lender of protective covenants is the additional ability it affords him to force bankruptcy. With bankruptcy, ownership of the firm effectively passes to the debtholders and they can seize upon the value of the firm at that time. Therefore lenders are in a position to preclude equityholders from increasing the risk of the company or issuing new debt at their expense. They have only to write protective covenants that will trigger default.

When protective covenants are initially formulated, the key question from the standpoint of the lender is the potential benefits of such covenants. One way to conceptually judge the benefits is in terms of the present value of the debt with and without a particular covenant. If the present value of the existing debt is no higher with the addition of a particular protective covenant than it is without it, the covenant does not really benefit the lender.[10] Decisions by the firm that affect the overall riskiness of its assets can be restrained, but not altogether precluded, by such protective covenants as the working-capital provision, the capital expenditures restrictions, and a restriction on the sale of assets. Limitations on the issuance of additional debt are important because only in this way can existing lenders preclude new lenders from coming in with the same claim on assets or with a superior one.

Conceptually, then, the purpose of these restrictions should be to protect against a transfer of value from the debtholders to the equityholders. As stated before, the benefit to the debtholders of protective covenants is the ability to initiate bankruptcy proceedings earlier than would otherwise be the case. In this way, they can limit the increase in risk allowed before default is triggered, thereby limiting the potential transfer of value to the equityholders.

Still it is important to remember that protective covenants are negotiated between the borrower and the lender. What the lender might want, the borrower might not want to give up. Both parties wish to preserve their flexibility. For the lender, this means very restrictive protective covenants so that with increases in risk, default is triggered and he is completely in the driver's seat. For the borrower, it means as nearly as possible an absence of protective covenants. However, as discussed in Chapter 9, there are monitoring costs associated with the writing of protective covenants and with their enforcement.[11] These costs ultimately are borne by the equityholders, so it is in their interests to see that monitoring activities are administered efficiently. The greater the safeguards to the lender, the greater his protection and the lower the interest rate, all other things the same. However, the incremental protection afforded the lender increases at a decreasing rate. On the other hand, monitoring costs increase as more safeguards are added, and probably at an increasing rate. Therefore it is neccesary to strike a balance that embraces this tradeoff. The final position will be a compromise between the borrower and the lender, and one that is influenced by relative conditions in the financial markets and by the costs of monitoring. As the latter were discussed in detail in Chapter 9, when we considered the theory of capital structure, a further discussion here would be redundant.

---

[10]For an approach to determining the incremental present value of the debt associated with a protective covenant using a multiperiod state preference model, see Van Horne, "Optimal Initiation of Bankruptcy Proceedings," pp. 908–9.

[11]See Michael C. Jensen and William H. Meckling, "Theory of the Firm: Managerial Behavior, Agency Cost and Ownership Structure," *Journal of Financial Economics,* 3 (October 1976), 305–60, for a discussion of these as well as other agency costs.

Many firms are unable to obtain unsecured credit and are required to pledge security. In giving a secured loan, the lender looks first to the cash-flow ability of the company to service debt and, if this source of loan repayment should fail, to the collateral value of the security. To provide a margin of safety, a lender usually will advance somewhat less than the market value of the collateral. The percentage advance varies according to the quality of the collateral pledged and the control the lender has over this collateral. Accounts receivable and inventory are the principal assets used to secure short-term business loans. Receivables may either be pledged to secure a loan or sold to a factor. Inventory loans can be under a general lien, under a trust receipt, or under terminal warehouse or field warehouse receipt arrangements.

Intermediate-term financing generally is thought to include maturities of one to five years. There are a number of sources of intermediate-term financing. Commercial banks, insurance companies, and other institutional investors make term loans to business firms. Banks also provide financing under a revolving-credit arrangement, which represents a formal commitment on the part of the bank to lend up to a certain amount of money over a specified period of time. On a secured basis, firms can obtain intermediate-term financing by pledging equipment that they own or are purchasing. Banks, finance companies, and sellers of the equipment are active in providing this type of secured financing.

Lenders who offer unsecured credit usually impose restrictions on the borrower. These restrictions are called protective covenants and are contained in a loan agreement. If the borrower defaults under any of the provisions of the loan agreement, the lender may initiate immediate corrective measures. The use of protective covenants can be viewed in the option pricing model framework of debtholders versus equityholders. This framework was illustrated, as was the influence of monitoring costs.

PROBLEMS

1. The Barnes Corporation has just acquired a large account. As a result, it needs an additional $75,000 in working capital immediately. It has been determined that there are three feasible sources of funds:

   (a) Trade credit: the company buys about $50,000 of materials per month on terms of 2/30, net 90. Discounts are taken.

   (b) Bank loan: the firm's bank will lend $100,000 at 9 percent. A 20 percent compensating balance will be required.

   (c) A factor will buy the company's receivables ($100,000 per month), which have a collection period of sixty days. The factor will advance up to 75 percent of the face value of the receivables for an annual charge of 8 percent. The factor will also charge a 2 percent fee on all receivables purchased. It has been estimated that the factor's services will save the company a credit department expense and bad-debt expense of $1,500 per month.

Which alternative should be selected?

2. The Selby Gaming Manufacturing Company has experienced a severe cash squeeze and must raise $200,000 over the next ninety days. The company has already pledged its receivables in support of a loan. However, it still has $570,000 in unencumbered inventories. Determine which of the following financing alternatives is better:

   (a) The Cody National Bank of Reno will lend against finished goods, provided they are placed in a public warehouse under its control. As the finished goods are released for sale, the loan is reduced by the proceeds of the sale. The company currently has $300,000 in finished-goods inventories and would expect to replace finished goods that are sold out of the warehouse with new finished goods so that it could borrow the full $200,000 for ninety days. The interest rate is 10 percent and, in addition, the company will need to pay warehousing costs of $3,000. Finally, it will experience a reduction in efficiency as a result of this arrangement. Management estimates that the lower efficiency will reduce before-tax profits by $5,000.

   (b) The Zarlotti Finance Company will lend the company the money under a floating lien on all of its inventories. The rate is 23 percent, but no additional expenses will be incurred.

3. The Bone Company has been factoring its accounts receivable for the past five years. The factor charges a fee of 2 percent and will lend up to 80 percent of the volume of receivables purchases for an additional 3/4 percent per month. The firm typically has sales of $500,000 per month, 70 percent of which are on credit. By using the factor, two savings are effected:

   (a) $2,000 per month that would be required to support a credit department, and

   (b) A bad-debt expense of 1 percent on credit sales.

   The firm's bank has recently offered to lend the firm up to 80 percent of the face value of the receivables shown on the schedule of accounts. The bank would charge 8 percent per annum interest plus a 2 percent processing charge per dollar of receivables lending. The firm extends terms of net 30, and all customers who pay their bills do so by the thirtieth of the month. Should the firm discontinue its factoring arrangement in favor of the bank's offer if the firm borrows, on the average, $100,000 per month on its receivables?

4. The Kedzie Cordage Company needs to finance a seasonal bulge in inventories of $400,000. The funds are needed for six months. The company is considering the following possibilities:

   (a) Warehouse receipt loan from a finance company. Terms are 12 percent with an 80 percent advance against the value of the inventory. The warehousing costs are $7,000 for the six-month period. The residual financing requirement, which is $400,000 less the amount advanced, will need to be financed by forgoing cash discounts on its payables. Standard terms are 2/10, net 30. However, the company feels it can postpone payment until the fortieth day without adverse effect.

(b) A floating lien arrangement from the supplier of the inventory at an effective interest rate of 20 percent. The supplier will advance the full value of the inventory.

(c) A field warehouse loan from another finance company at an interest rate of 10 percent. The advance is 70 percent and field warehousing costs amount to $10,000 for the six-month period. The residual financing requirement will need to be financed by forgoing cash discounts on payables as in the first alternative.

Which is the least costly method of financing the inventory needs of the firm?

5. On January 1, Sharpe Razor Corporation is considering a four-year, $3 million term loan from the Fidelity First National Bank. The loan is payable at the end of the fourth year and would involve a loan agreement containing a number of protective covenants. Among these restrictions are the following: the company must maintain working capital of $3 million at all times; it cannot take on any more long-term debt; its total liabilities cannot be more than 0.6 of its total assets; and capital expenditures in any year are limited to depreciation plus $3 million. The company's balance sheet at December 31, before the term loan, is:

Current assets	$ 7 million	Current liabilities	$ 3 million
Net fixed assets	10	Long-term debt (due in 5 years)	5
		Net worth	9
	$17 million		$17 million

The proceeds of the term loan will be used to increase Sharpe's investment in inventories and receivables in response to introducing a new "closer-to-the-face" razor blade. The company anticipates a subsequent need to grow at a rate of 24 percent a year, equally divided between current assets and net fixed assets. Profits after taxes of $1.5 million are expected this year, and these profits are expected to grow by $250,000 per year over the subsequent three years. The company pays no dividends and does not intend to pay any over the next four years. Depreciation in the past year was $2.5 million, and this is expected to grow over the next four years at the same rate as the increase in net fixed assets.

Under the loan agreement, will the company be able to achieve its growth objectives?

6. The McDonald Company wishes to buy a $1.2 million piece of equipment over a two-year period. The bank has offered to lend the required money on the basis of a two-year note with a $600,000 amortization payment at the end of each year. The loan would require a compensating balance equal to 15 percent of the outstanding balance and would bear an interest rate of 10 percent. The seller of the equipment has offered McDonald a conditional sales contract with two equal annual payments. How large could the payments be before McDonald would find the bank loan more attractive?

7. The Dale Boot Company is contemplating investing in a project that will generate the following net cash flows (after taxes):

Year	0	1	2	3
Net cash flow (end of year)	− 4,000,000	+ 1,000,000	+ 2,000,000	+ 3,000,000

The company has decided to finance the project through intermediate-term debt and is considering two possibilities:

(a) Utilize an additional $4 million of the firm's three-year revolving bank credit. Currently $3 million of the $8 million commitment is in use. The bank charges 1 percent over prime and a 1/2 percent commitment fee on the unused portion. Interest is paid at the end of the year. No additional compensating balances are required. The company expects the prime rate, now 7 percent, to increase to 8 percent at the end of year 1, and to remain at that level through year 3.

(b) Privately place a $4 million unsecured note with California-Sierra Mutual Life Insurance Co. The interest cost is 8 1/4 percent with a 0.5 percent placement fee. The note calls for principal payments of $1 million at the end of years 1 and 2, and $2 million at the end of year 3. Which financing arrangement is preferred? Why?

8. Max-Fli Toy Company currently has a total value of $10 million. The face value of the debt outstanding is $7 million, and it is represented by discount bonds which all mature in four years. The standard deviation of the continuously compounded rate of return on the total value of the firm is 0.30. The short-term risk-free rate is currently 6 percent.

(a) Using the Black-Scholes option model, Eq. (4-2) in Chapter 4, determine the value of the equity and the value of the debt. (This problem can be solved with the use of a relatively sophisticated calculator or with the use of tables.)

(b) If the company goes into a new riskier toy line which increases the standard deviation to 0.50, what will be the effect on the value of the debt?

(c) How can the debtholders protect themselves?

9. *Research Project*
Examine several bond indentures and/or loan agreements (if available). What major restrictions are imposed? Do you note any differences in the restrictions outlined in bond indentures as opposed to those in loan agreements? Why might these differences exist? Do you find any correlation between the maturity length of the instrument and the number (and degree) of the restrictions? What might account for your findings?

SELECTED REFERENCES

ABRAHAM, ALFRED B., "Factoring—The New Frontier for Commercial Banks," *Journal of Commercial Bank Lending,* 53 (April 1971), 32–43.

BERGER, PAUL D., AND WILLIAM K. HARPER, "Determination of an Optimal Revolving Credit Agreement," *Journal of Financial and Quantitative Analysis,* 8 (June 1973), 491–98.

BLACK, FISCHER, AND JOHN C. COX, "Valuing Corporate Securities: Some Effects of Bond Indenture Provisions," *Journal of Finance,* 31 (May 1976), 351–67.

BULOW, J. I., AND J. B. SHOVEN, "The Bankruptcy Decision," *Bell Journal of Economics,* 9 (Autumn 1978), 437–56.

DENONN, LESTER E., "The Security Agreement," *Journal of Commercial Bank Lending,* 50 (February 1968), 32–40.

HAYES, DOUGLAS A., *Bank Lending Policies: Domestic and International.* Ann Arbor: University of Michigan, 1977.

JENSEN, MICHAEL C., AND WILLIAM H. MECKLING, "Theory of the Firm: Managerial Behavior, Agency Cost and Ownership Structure," *Journal of Financial Economics,* 3 (October 1976), 305–60.

LAZERE, MONROE R., "Swinging Swindles and Creepy Frauds," *Journal of Commercial Bank Lending,* 60 (September 1977), 44–52.

MIDDLETON, J. WILLIAM, "Term Lending—Practical and Profitable," *Journal of Commercial Banking Lending,* 50 (August 1968), 31–43.

QUARLES, J. CARSON, "The Floating Lien," *Journal of Commercial Bank Lending,* 53 (November 1970), 51–58.

QUILL, GERALD D., JOHN C. CRESCI, AND BRUCE D. SHUTER, "Some Considerations about Secured Lending," *Journal of Commercial Bank Lending,* 59 (April 1977), 41–56.

ROGERS, ROBERT W., "Warehouse Receipts and Their Use in Financing," *Bulletin of the Robert Morris Associates,* 46 (April 1964), 317–27.

SCOTT, JAMES H., JR., "Bankruptcy, Secured Debt, and Optimal Capital Structure," *Journal of Finance,* 32 (March 1977), 1–19.

SMITH, CLIFFORD W., JR., AND JAROLD B. WARNER, "On Financial Contracts and Optimal Capital Structure: An Analysis of Bond Covenants." Research paper, University of Rochester, May 1978.

VAN HORNE, JAMES, "A Linear-Programming Approach to Evaluating Restrictions under a Bond Indenture or Loan Agreement," *Journal of Financial and Quantitative Analysis,* 1 (June 1966), 68–83.

VAN HORNE, JAMES C., "Optimal Initiation of Bankruptcy Proceedings by Debt Holders," *Journal of Finance,* 31 (June 1976), 897–910.

ZIMMERMAN, CHARLES S., "An Approach to Writing Loan Agreement Covenants," *Journal of Commercial Bank Lending,* 58 (November 1975), 2–17.

19
lease financing

A lease is a means by which a firm can acquire the economic use of an asset for a stated period of time.[1] For many companies, a lease represents an important source of financing. In recent years, the reporting of the lease obligation for accounting purposes has undergone substantial change. For some companies, the accounting treatment of the lease is a major issue; and we consider the present rules later on in the chapter. However, our principal concern is with the cash-flow evaluation of the lease contract. In this regard, our focus is on financial leases. A *financial lease* is a noncancelable contractual commitment on the part of a lessee to make a series of payments to a lessor for the use of an asset. The lessee acquires most of the economic values associated with outright ownership of the asset, even though the lessor retains title to it. With a financial lease, the total payments the lessee agrees to make must exceed the purchase price of the asset.[2]

[1]The development of most of this chapter assumes that the reader has covered Parts II and III.

[2]See Richard F. Vancil, "Lease or Borrow: New Method of Analysis," *Harvard Business Review,* 39 (September-October 1961), 122–36.

Because of the contractual nature of a financial lease obligation, it must be regarded as a form of financing. It is used in place of other methods of financing to acquire the use of an asset. An alternative method of financing might be to purchase the asset and finance its acquisition with debt. Both the lease payment and the payment of principal and interest on debt are fixed obligations that must be met. Inability to meet these obligations will result in financial embarrassment. Thus, lease financing and debt financing are very similar from the standpoint of analyzing the ability of the firm to service fixed obligations.

In lease financing, the nature of the obligations of the lessor and the lessee is specified in the lease contract. This contract contains

1. The basic lease period during which the lease is noncancelable.
2. The timing and amounts of periodic rental payments during the basic lease period.
3. Any option to renew the lease or to purchase the asset at the end of the basic lease period. Otherwise the lessor takes possession of the asset and is entitled to any residual value associated with it.
4. Provision for the payment of the costs of maintenance and repairs, taxes, insurance, and other expenses. With a "net lease," the lessee pays all of these costs. Under a "maintenance lease," the lessor maintains the asset and pays the insurance.

FORMS OF LEASE FINANCING

There are three main types of lease financing: a sale and leaseback arrangement, the direct acquisition of an asset under a lease, and leveraged leasing. Virtually all lease-financing arrangements fall into one of these three categories. In this section, we briefly describe these categories; in the subsequent sections, we present a framework for the analysis of lease financing and we discuss the basic valuation implications.

Sale and Leaseback

Under a sale and leaseback arrangement, a firm sells an asset it owns to another party, and this party leases it back to the firm. Usually, the asset is sold at approximately its market value. The firm receives the sales price in cash and the economic use of the asset during the basic lease period. In turn, it contracts to make periodic lease payments and, of course, gives up title to the asset.[3] As a result, the lessor realizes any residual value the asset might have at the end of the lease period, whereas before this would have been realized

---

[3]For an evaluation of the sale and leaseback arrangement in the economic context of wealth transfers between bondholders and shareholders associated with such arrangements, see E. Han Kim, Wilbur G. Lewellen, and John J. McConnell, "Sale-and-Leaseback Agreements and Enterprise Valuation," *Journal of Financial and Quantitative Analysis*, forthcoming.

by the firm. Lessors engaged in sale and leaseback arrangements include insurance companies, other institutional investors, finance companies, and independent leasing companies.

Direct Leasing

Under direct leasing, a company acquires the use of an asset it did not own previously. For example, a firm simply may lease an asset from the manufacturer: IBM leases computers; Kearney & Trecker Corporation leases machine tools. Indeed, a number of capital goods are available today on a lease-financed basis. There are a wide variety of direct leasing arrangements available to meet the various needs of the firm. The major types of lessors are manufacturers, finance companies, banks, independent leasing companies, special-purpose leasing companies, and partnerships. For leasing arrangements involving all but the first, the vendor sells the asset to the lessor and he, in turn, leases it to the lessee. In certain cases, economies of scale are possible in the purchase of capital assets by the lessor. These economies may be passed on to the lessee in the form of lower lease payments.

Since 1963, commercial banks have been allowed to engage in direct leasing; their entry represented an important development in the leasing industry. Independent leasing companies finance the purchase of a wide variety of equipment. In doing so, they frequently borrow from banks, securing the loan with the assignment of the lease payments. Special-purpose leasing companies confine their operations to certain types of assets; computer leasing companies, for example, mainly lease computer hardware and peripheral equipment. In recent years, high-tax-bracketed individuals have formed partnerships for the purpose of purchasing equipment and leasing it to companies. The tax shield afforded by the investment tax credit, accelerated depreciation charges and interest paid on borrowings may be more valuable to them than to a corporation. As a result, both the lessor and the lessee may benefit. Much more will be said about this when we take up the economic benefits associated with leasing.

Leveraged Leasing

In recent years, a special form of leasing has developed in conjunction with the financing of assets requiring large capital outlays. It is known as *leveraged leasing*. In contrast to the two parties involved in the forms of leasing previously described, there are three parties involved in leveraged leasing: (1) the lessee, (2) the lessor, or equity participant, and (3) the lender. We examine each in turn.[4]

[4]For a discussion of leveraged leasing, see Edward A. Dyl and Stanley A. Martin, Jr., "Setting Terms for Leveraged Leasing," *Financial Management*, 6 (Winter 1977), 20–27; Robert C. Wiar, "Economic Implications of Multiple Rates of Return in the Leveraged Lease Context," *Journal of Finance*, 28 (December 1973), 1275–86; and E. Richard Packham, "An Analysis of the Risks of Leveraged Leasing," *Journal of Commercial Bank Lending*, 57 (March 1975), 2–29.

From the standpoint of the lessee, there is no difference between a leveraged lease and any other type of lease. The lessee contracts to make periodic payments over the basic lease period and, in return, is entitled to the use of the asset over that period of time. The role of the lessor, however, is changed. The lessor acquires the asset in keeping with the terms of the lease arrangement. This acquisition is financed in part by an equity investment by the lessor of, say, 20 percent (hence the name *equity participant*). The remaining 80 percent is provided by a long-term lender or lenders. The loan is usually secured by a mortgage on the asset, as well as by the assignment of the lease and lease payments.[5] The lessor, however, is the borrower.

As owner of the asset, the lessor is entitled to deduct all depreciation charges associated with the asset, as well as utilize the entire investment tax credit. The cash-flow pattern for the lessor typically involves (1) a cash outflow at the time the asset is acquired, which represents its equity participation less the investment tax credit; (2) a period of cash inflows represented by lease payments and tax benefits, less payments on the debt (principal and interest); and (3) a period of net cash outflows where, because of declining tax benefits, the sum of lease payments and tax benefits falls below the debt payments due. If there is any residual value at the end of the lease period, this of course represents a cash inflow to the lessor.

To illustrate, suppose that A. B. Chance Company leased an asset from the Vanier-First Corporation. The asset cost $500,000, and lease payments of $115,000 are required at the end of each of the next five years. The lessor puts up $100,000 in "equity participation" and borrows the remaining $400,000 through mortgage bonds which are placed with a group of large individual investors. These bonds bear an interest rate of 10 percent, and loan payments of $105,519 are required at the end of each of the next five years. These payments embody both principal and interest, the latter of which is deductible for tax purposes. Depreciation is on the sum-of-the-years'-digits basis where 5/15, 4/15, 3/15, 2/15, and 1/15 of the purchase price of the asset are deductible at the end of each of the five years. We assume that an investment tax credit of $33,333 is realized at the time the asset is acquired. (For assets with useful lives of at least five but less than seven years, only two-thirds of the investment is eligible for the 10 percent investment tax credit. Therefore the investment tax credit = $500,000 × 0.10 × 2/3 = $33,333.) Finally, let us assume no residual value at the end of the lease period and a marginal tax rate for the lessor of 40 percent.

Given these considerations, the cash flows to the lessor are shown in Table 19-1. In the last column, we see that the cash flow is negative at time 0, followed by positive flows for years 1–3, and negative flows for years 4 and 5. The declining cash flows are of course due to decreasing tax benefits, which in turn are caused by the decrease in depreciation and in interest payments.

In some leveraged lease situations, the negative cash flow in later periods is sufficiently large so that the sum total of cash flows for all years is

[5]Sometimes in addition the lessee guarantees the debt.

table 19-1
Illustration of cash flows to lessor in a leveraged lease

End of Year	(1) Initial Equity Participation ($100,000) less Investment Tax Credit ($33,333)	(2) Lease Payment Receipt	(3) Depreciation	(4) Loan Interest Payment
0	$(66,667)			
1	—	$115,000	$166,667	$40,000
2	—	115,000	133,333	33,448
3	—	115,000	100,000	26,241
4	—	115,000	66,667	18,313
5	—	115,000	33,333	9,593

negative. This gives rise to the possibility of multiple internal rates of return when the lessor goes to compute his return.[6] (This problem and the need to determine the "economic" return were addressed in Appendix A in Chapter 5.) It is important to note that the reversal in signs for cash flows to the lessor from positive to negative is one of the distinguishing features of a leveraged lease.

The leveraged lease may at first seem more complicated than either the sale and leaseback arrangement or direct leasing. However, it reduces to certain basic concepts, which, from the standpoint of the lessee, can be analyzed in the same manner as for any lease. Therefore we will not treat it separately in the rest of this chapter. It should be emphasized, however, that leveraged leasing has increasingly been used in the financing of large capital assets, and its growth has paralleled that of project financing.

ACCOUNTING TREATMENT OF LEASES

The accounting treatment of leases has undergone sweeping change over the past two decades. Where once leases were not disclosed, disclosure was gradually required in the footnotes to the financial statement. With only minimal disclosure, however, leasing was attractive to certain firms as an "off–balance sheet" method of financing. While there was no evidence that such financing had a favorable effect on valuation, all other things the same, many a company proceeded on the assumption that "off–balance sheet" financing was a good thing. Then came the Financial Accounting Standards Board Statement No. 13 in 1976 with an explicit ruling that called for the capitalization on the balance sheet of certain types of leases.[7] In essence, this

[6]For a discussion of this problem as well as the presentation of a possible approach, see Wiar, "Economic Implications of Multiple Rates of Return in the Leveraged Lease Context."

table 19-1 (cont.)

(5)	(6)	(7)	(8)
Taxable Income (2) − (3) − (4)	Taxes* (5) × 0.4	Total Loan Payment	Cash Flows (1) + (2) − (6) − (7)
			$(66,667)
$(91,667)	$[36,667]	$105,519	46,148
(51,781)	[20,712]	105,519	30,193
(11,241)	[4,496]	105,519	13,977
30,020	12,008	105,519	(2,527)
72,074	28,830	105,519	(19,349)

*Brackets indicate a tax credit.

statement says that if the lessee acquires essentially all of the economic benefits and risks of the leased property, then the value of the asset along with the corresponding lease liability must be shown on the balance sheet.

Capital and Operating Leases

Leases that conform in principle to this definition are called *capital leases*. More specifically, a lease is regarded as a capital lease if it meets any one of the following conditions:

1. The lease transfers title to the asset to the lessee by the end of the lease period.
2. The lease contains an option to purchase the asset at a bargain price.
3. The lease period is equal to or greater than 75 percent of the estimated economic life of the asset.
4. At the beginning of the lease the present value of the minimum lease payments equals or exceeds 90 percent of the fair value of the leased property to the lessor (minus any investment tax credit realized by the lessor).

If any of these conditions is met, the lessee is said to have acquired most of the economic benefits and risks associated with the leased property and, therefore, a capital lease is involved. If a lease does not meet one of these conditions, it is classified as an *operating lease*. Essentially, operating leases give the lessee the right to use the leased property over a period of time, but they do not give the lessee all of the benefits and risks that are associated with the asset.

[7]*Statement of Financial Accounting Standards No. 13, Accounting for Leases* (Stamford, Conn.: Financial Accounting Standards Board, November 1976).

Determining the Value of a Capital Lease   With a capital lease, the lessee must report the value of the leased property on the asset side of the balance sheet. The amount reflected is the present value of the minimum lease payments over the lease period. If executory costs, such as insurance, maintenance, and taxes, are a part of the total lease payment, these are deducted and only the remainder is used for purposes of calculating the present value. The discount rate employed is the lower of (1) the lessee's incremental borrowing rate or (2) the lessor's implicit interest rate if in fact that rate can be determined.

To illustrate these computations, suppose that Gonzalez Gear Company wishes to lease a stamping machine that calls for lease payments of $15,336 due at the beginning of each of the next eight years. (The lease payments are due in advance.) The company's incremental borrowing rate is 8 percent. The cost of the machine to the lessor is $100,000, and the machine is not expected to have any residual value at the end of the lease period. However, the lessor will avail itself of the 10 percent investment tax credit and thereby realize $10,000 in tax savings at the time the asset is placed in service. Therefore the lessor's out-of-pocket cost is $90,000. The implicit interest rate realized by the lessor can be determined by solving the following equation for r:

$$\$90,000 = \sum_{t=0}^{7} \frac{\$15,336}{(1 + r)^t} \tag{19-1}$$

Because lease payments are made in advance, the first payment can be thought of as being due at time 0 with seven other payments due in yearly intervals. As a result, we turn to Table A-2 at the end of the book for the present-value discount factors for an even stream of cash flows over seven years. To the discount factor we must add 1 because the payment at time 0 is not discounted. For an interest rate of 9 percent, we see that the discount factor shown in Table A-2 is 5.0329, to which we add 1 to obtain a discount factor of 6.0329. Dividing $90,000 by 6.0329, we obtain $14,918. As this amount is less than the lease payment, we know the implicit interest rate must be higher. For 10 percent, the discount factor is 4.8684, to which we add 1 to obtain 5.8684. Dividing $90,000 by 5.8684, we obtain $15,336, exactly the lease payment. Therefore the lessor's implicit interest rate is 10 percent. By trial and error, then, we can determine the lessor's implied interest rate provided we know the purchase price of the asset and certain other information. Usually interpolation is involved, and this can be done in the manner described in Chapter 2.

As the lessor's implicit interest rate for our example is higher than the lessee's incremental borrowing rate of 8 percent, the latter would be used in determining the capitalized value of the lease. In most instances this will be the case. However, the lessee insofar as is practical must try to determine the lessor's implicit interest rate. When the implicit rate is less than the lessee's incremental borrowing rate, it must be used as the discount rate. Given the amount of the lease payments and the discount rate to employ, one can easily determine the amount that should be recorded on the balance sheet for a capital lease. For our example, the present value at time 0, after the initial lease payment, is

$15,336 for seven years at 8%
(5.2064 discount factor) = $79,845

Recording the Capital Lease on the Balance Sheet   This amount should be recorded on the lessee's balance sheet as an asset. (However, if the fair value of the leased property is lower than the present value of the minimum lease payments, then the fair value would be shown.) The associated lease obligation would be shown on the liability side of the balance sheet, with the present value of payments due within one year being reflected as current liabilities and the present value of payments due after one year being shown as noncurrent liabilities. The leased property may be combined with similar information on assets that are owned, but there must be a disclosure in a footnote with respect to the value of the leased property and its amortization. A hypothetical balance sheet might look like the following:

Assets		Liabilities	
Gross fixed assets*	$3,000,000	Current:	
Less accumulated depreciation and amortization	1,000,000	Obligations under capital leases	$90,000
		Noncurrent:	
Net fixed assets	$2,000,000	Obligations under capital leases	$270,000

*Gross fixed assets include leased property of $500,000. Accumulated depreciation and amortization includes $140,000 in amortization associated with such property.

Here we see in the footnote that the capitalized value of leases of the company is $500,000 less $140,000 in amortization, or $360,000 in total. The liability is split with $90,000 current and $270,000 due beyond one year. In addition to this information, more-detailed information is required in footnotes. Relevant information here includes: the gross amounts of leased property by major property categories (these can be combined with those for owned assets); the total future minimum lease payments; a schedule by years of future lease payments required over the next five years; the total minimum sublease rentals to be received; the existence and terms of purchase or renewal options and of escalation clauses; rentals that are contingent on some factor other than the passage of time; and any restrictions imposed in the lease agreement.

Disclosure of Operating Leases   For operating leases, some of the same disclosure is required as in the case of capital leases, but it can be in footnotes. For noncancelable leases having remaining terms in excess of one year, the lessee must disclose: total future minimum lease payments; a schedule by

table 19-2
Illustration of the "interest" method to reduce
the lease obligation

Beginning of Year	Lease Payment	Principal Payment	Principal Amount Owing at Beginning of Year	Annual Interest at 8%
1	$15,336	$15,336	$79,845	0
2	15,336	8,949	70,896	$6,387
3	15,336	9,664	61,232	5,672
4	15,336	10,438	50,794	4,898
5	15,336	11,272	39,522	4,064
6	15,336	12,174	27,348	3,162
7	15,336	13,148	14,200	2,188
8	15,336	14,200	0	1,136

year for the next five years; the total sublease rentals to be received; the basis for contingent rental payments; the existence and terms of purchase and renewal options and of escalation clauses; and any lease agreement restrictions. The last two categories are included in a general description of the leasing arrangement.

Amortizing the Capital Lease and Reducing the Obligation

A capital lease must be amortized and the liability reduced over the lease period. The method of amortization can be the lessee's usual depreciation method for assets that are owned. In our earlier example, if the firm normally depreciates its assets on a straight-line basis, the annual amortization over the eight-year lease period would be ($79,845 + $15,336)/8 = $11,898. The $79,845 represents the present value of seven future lease payments, whereas the $15,336 represents the initial lease payment. The amortization of $11,898 annually means that at the beginning of year 2, the value of the leased property is shown as $79,845 − $11,898 = $67,947; at the beginning of year 3, as $67,947 − $11,898 = $56,049; and so on. It should be pointed out that the period of amortization is always the lease term even if the economic life of the asset is longer. If the latter occurs, the asset would have an expected residual value which would go to the lessor.

FASB No. 13 also requires that the capital lease obligation be reduced over the lease period by the "interest" method. Under this method, each lease payment is broken down into two components—the payment of principal and the payment of interest. The obligation is reduced by the amount of the principal payment. To illustrate, recall in our example that the firm had the obligation to pay $15,336 at the beginning of each year, that its incremental borrowing rate was 8 percent, and that this rate is used as the discount rate.[8]

In Table 19-2, the calculation of interest and principal payments are shown. At the beginning of year 1, which represents the beginning of the lease period, the lease payment is represented entirely by a payment of principal. After that, interest is involved but the proportional amount declines over the lease period.

The Reporting of Earnings   For income-reporting purposes, FASB No. 13 requires that both the amortization of the leased property and the annual interest embodied in the lease payment be treated as an expense. This expense then is deducted in the same way that any expense is to obtain net income. For our example, we would have the following lease expense at the end of each of the eight years (as opposed to the beginning):

End of Year	Amortization of Asset (Straight Line)	Annual Interest (from Table 19-2)	Annual Lease Expense
1	$11,898	$6,387	$18,285
2	11,898	5,672	17,570
3	11,898	4,898	16,796
4	11,898	4,064	15,962
5	11,898	3,162	15,060
6	11,897	2,188	14,085
7	11,897	1,136	13,033
8	11,897	0	11,897

This treatment differs from that for the operating lease where only the lease payment itself is deductible as an expense. It also differs from the way all leases were treated prior to FASB No. 13 where, again, only the lease payment was deductible.

Tax Treatment

It is important to recognize that the treatment of capital leases for tax purposes differs from that for income statement purposes. FASB No. 13 did not change the tax treatment of leases. For the most part, companies continue to report the lease payment as an expense for tax purposes. In other words, a company does not deduct the amortization of the asset and the interest as the expense of a capital lease for tax purposes. It deducts the annual lease payment.

However, the Internal Revenue Service is concerned that the lease contract truly represent a lease and not an installment sale. Therefore it may

---

[8]If the fair value of the leased property is less than the present value of the net lease payments, using the incremental borrowing rate as the discount rate, then the interest rate used for amortization purposes is the rate of discount that equates the present value of the minimum lease payments with the fair value.

check to see whether the length of the lease approximates the economic life of the asset (say 75 percent of the life of the asset or more.) It also may check to see that the lessor earns a reasonable return and that any renewal or repurchase option to the lessee be on the basis of market values prevailing at the lease's expiration. In essence, the IRS wants to assure itself that the contract does not represent a purchase of the asset where payments are much more rapid than would be allowed with depreciation. As lease payments are deductible for tax purposes, such a contract would allow the lessor to effectively "depreciate" the asset more quickly than allowed under a straight purchase. As long as the lease contract corresponds to our earlier definition of a lease where, among other things, the basic lease period approximates the economic life of the asset, the full lease payment is deductible for tax purposes. This distinction between the accounting and tax treatments becomes important when we evaluate lease financing in a cash-flow context where the taxes paid are the important consideration and not the effect on reported income. To this topic we now turn.

TO LEASE OR TO BORROW

Whether lease financing or borrowing is favored will depend upon the patterns of cash outflows for each financing method and upon the opportunity cost of funds. A number of different methods may be used to compare the two alternatives.[9] In this section, we illustrate some of the more important, using a hypothetical example. We assume that the firm has decided to invest in a project on the basis of considerations taken up in Part II. In other words, the investment worthiness of the project is evaluated separately from the specific method of financing to be employed.[10] We assume also that the firm has determined an appropriate capital structure and that this structure calls for financing the project with a fixed-income obligation—either debt or lease financing. Our concern is with determining the least costly alternative.

An additional assumption is that only the lease payment is deductible for tax purposes. Therefore the considerations taken up in the preceding section for determining expenses to report for accounting statement purposes are not a factor in the cash-flow evaluation that follows. Finally, for ease of

---

[9]For a survey of how companies analyze the lease, see Paul F. Anderson and John D. Martin, "Lease vs. Purchase Decisions: A Survey of Current Practice," *Financial Management*, 6 (Spring 1977), 33–40. The authors found that the most frequently used method was the internal-rate-of-return one.

[10]For an analysis in which the leasing contract is viewed as an investment rather than a financing decision, see Robert W. Johnson and Wilbur G. Lewellen, "Analysis of the Lease-or-Buy Decision," *Journal of Finance*, 27 (September 1972), 815–24. They hold that the lease is a long-term acquisition of services and that the relevant comparison is lease versus buy, not lease versus borrow. For a comparison of various methods for analyzing leasing versus borrowing, see Richard S. Bower, "Issues in Lease Financing," *Financial Management*, 2 (Winter 1973), 25–34.

illustration we assume initially that the leased property has no residual value at the end of the lease period. However, it should be recognized that for a lease to qualify as a "true" lease for tax purposes, the leased property generally must have a residual value of at least 20 percent of original cost or the remaining useful life of the property must equal or exceed 20 percent of its original estimated useful life. Later in the chapter, we consider residual value and show how this consideration can be factored into our analysis.

Example

For comparative purposes, each method of analysis we consider will be illustrated with the same example. Suppose a firm has decided to acquire an asset costing $200,000 and having an expected economic life of ten years, after which the asset is not expected to have any residual value. Once the investment decision is made, the question becomes, Is it better to finance the asset by leasing or by borrowing? If leasing is used, the lessor requires that cost of the asset be completely amortized over the ten-year period and that it yield an 8 percent return. As is customary, lease payments are to be made in advance—that is, at the end of the year prior to each of the ten years. The amount of annual lease payment may be calculated by solving the following equation for x:

$$\$200{,}000 = \sum_{t=0}^{9} \frac{x}{(1.08)^t}$$

$$\$200{,}000 = x + 6.2469x$$

$$x = \frac{\$200{,}000}{7.2469}$$

$$x = \$27{,}598 \tag{19-2}$$

Because lease payments are made in advance, we solve for the annual lease payment that equates the cost of the asset, $200,000, with the present value of one lease payment at time 0, plus the present value of nine lease payments at the end of each of the next nine years. Because the discount rate is 8 percent, we find in Table A-2 at the end of the book that the present-value discount factor for an even stream of cash flows for nine years, discounted at 8 percent, is 6.2469. Therefore the annual lease payment necessary to amortize the cost of the asset completely and to return the lessor 8 percent is $27,598.

If the asset is purchased, the firm is able to deduct depreciation charges for tax purposes as well as avail itself of the investment tax credit. If straight-line depreciation is used, annual depreciation charges are $20,000. The investment tax credit is available at the time the asset is placed into service. For a moment of digression, this credit was conceived in 1962 to provide an incentive to corporations and individuals to invest in capital assets. The credit was later repealed, reinstated, and repealed, and reinstated once again in 1971 in a countercyclical manner designed to stimulate or dampen modernization, depending on the phase of the economy. Since 1971, it has remained in effect. The maximum permanent credit available at the time of this writing was 10 percent on qualified property with a useful life of seven or more years; the effective percentage is less if the useful life is less than seven years.

Back to our example then, assume that a 10 percent credit is applicable and the asset is placed in service at the time of purchase. As a result, $20,000 is deductible at time 0. This deduction effectively lowers the purchase price by $20,000 to $180,000, if the asset is purchased.[11] Assume also that (1) if the firm were to borrow it would be able to do so at a 10 percent rate, (2) the effective income tax rate is 50 percent for the firm involved, and (3) the operating costs borne by the firm are the same whether the asset is purchased or leased.

Present-Value Analysis of Alternatives

The first method of analysis we consider is a comparison of the present values of cash outflows for each of the alternatives. According to this method, whichever alternative has the lowest present value is the most desirable. Recall that the firm will make annual lease payments of $27,598 if the asset is leased. Because these payments are an expense, they are deductible for tax purposes. However, they are deductible only in the year for which the payment applies. For example, the $27,598 payment at the end of year 0 represents a prepaid expense and is not deductible for tax purposes until year 1. Similarly, the other nine payments are not deductible until the following year.

As leasing is analogous to borrowing, an appropriate discount rate for discounting the after-tax cash flows might be the after-tax cost of borrowing. The use of this rate assumes that the firm's future taxable income will be sufficient so as to fully utilize the tax shield associated with lease payments. It also assumes that the tax rate will not change. While these assumptions are not unreasonable approximations of reality for many firms, it is important to point out that there is disagreement as to the appropriate discount rate to employ.[12]

Given the assumptions above, we are able to derive a schedule of cash outflows after taxes and compute their present value. These computations are shown in Table 19-3. The present value of the total cash outflows under the leasing alternative is seen to be $117,208. This figure, then, must be compared with the present value of cash outflows under the borrowing alternative.

---

[11]We assume at this time that the firm is able to use the tax credit in its entirety to offset taxes it would otherwise pay. As we shall see later in the chapter, some firms are unable to completely utilize the tax credit, and this affects the relative desirability of leasing.

[12]See Bower, "Issues in Lease Financing," p. 31; and Myron J. Gordon, "A General Solution to the Buy or Lease Decision: A Pedagogical Note," *Journal of Finance,* 29 (March 1974), 245–46.

table 19-3
Schedule of cash outflows: leasing alternative

End of Year	(1) Lease Payment	(2) Tax Shield	(3) Cash Outflow after Taxes (1) − (2)	(4) Present Value of Cash Outflows (5%)
0	$27,598	—	$27,598	$ 27,598
1–9	27,598	$13,799	13,799	98,081
10	—	13,799	(13,799)	(8,471)
				$117,208

If the asset is purchased, the firm is assumed to finance it entirely with a 10 percent unsecured term loan. Moreover, we assume that the loan payment schedule is of the same configuration as the lease payment schedule. In other words, loan payments are assumed to be payable at the beginning as opposed to the end of each year. This assumption places the loan on an equivalent basis with the lease and allows us to compare "apples" with "apples," as most lease arrangements call for payment in advance.[13] Recall that if the asset is purchased, an investment tax credit of $20,000 is available at the outset. Therefore the effective cost of the asset and the amount to be financed is $200,000 − $20,000 = $180,000. A loan of this amount is taken out at time 0 and is payable over ten years with annual payments of $26,631 at the beginning of each year.[14] The proportion of interest in each payment depends upon the unpaid balance of the principal amount owing during the year. For example, the principal amount owing during year 1 is $180,000 − $26,631 = $153,369; the annual interest for that year is $15,337.[15] Table 19-4 shows the amount of debt payments, and the proportion represented by interest.

Given annual interest and depreciation, we are able to compute the cash outflows after taxes for the borrowing alternative; these outflows are shown in Table 19-5. Because both depreciation and interest are deductible for tax purposes, they provide a tax shield equal to their sum times the tax rate. When this shield is deducted from the total payment of $26,631, we obtain the cash outflow after taxes at the end of each year. Finally, we compute the present value of these outflows, and they are found to total $102,781. As this present value is less than that for the lease alternative, $117,208, the firm should acquire the asset through debt financing.

---

[13]If the loan payments were payable at the end of the year while lease payments were payable at the beginning, the earlier payments under the lease alternative would in theory at least release capacity for raising funds by other means of financing earlier than under the debt alternative. See Richard S. Bower, Frank C. Herringer, and J. Peter Williamson, "Lease Evaluation," *Accounting Review*, 41 (April 1966), 257–65.

[14]This amount is computed in the same manner as in Eq. (19-2), using 10 percent instead of 8 percent as the discount factor. At the end of year 9, nothing is owing.

[15]For ease of illustration, we round to the nearest dollar throughout. This results in the final debt payment in Table 19-4 being slightly more than would otherwise be the case.

table 19-4
Schedule of debt payments

End of Year	Interest Plus Principal Payments	Principal Amount Owing at End of Year	Annual Interest
0	$26,631	$153,369	0
1	26,631	142,075	$15,337
2	26,631	129,652	14,208
3	26,631	115,986	12,965
4	26,631	100,954	11,599
5	26,631	84,418	10,095
6	26,631	66,229	8,442
7	26,631	46,221	6,623
8	26,631	24,212	4,622
9	26,633	0	2,421

This conclusion arises despite the fact that the implied interest rate embodied in the lease payments, 8 percent, is less than the explicit interest rate on the debt, 10 percent. The major relative advantage of purchasing the asset and financing it with debt is the realization of the investment tax credit at the outset. This credit effectively reduces the purchase price and the amount of debt to be incurred. In the case of the lease, the lessor is entitled to the investment tax credit. This advantage may be passed off in part to the lessee in the form of lease payments lower than would otherwise be the case. While the lower interest rate embodied in the lease payments in our example reflects this occurrence, it is not sufficient to cause the lease alternative to be more attractive. Also with a lease, the lessor can if it chooses assign the

table 19-5
Schedule of cash outflows: debt alternative

End of Year	(1) Loan Payment	(2) Interest	(3) Straight-Line Depreciation	(4) Tax Shield [(2) + (3)]0.5	(5) Cash Outflows after Taxes (1) − (4)	(6) Present Value of Cash Flows (5%)
0	$26,631	0	0	0	$26,631	$ 26,631
1	26,631	$15,337	$20,000	$17,669	8,962	8,535
2	26,631	14,208	20,000	17,104	9,527	8,641
3	26,631	12,965	20,000	16,483	10,148	8,766
4	26,631	11,599	20,000	15,800	10,831	8,911
5	26,631	10,095	20,000	15,048	11,583	9,076
6	26,631	8,442	20,000	14,221	12,410	9,261
7	26,631	6,623	20,000	13,312	13,319	9,466
8	26,631	4,622	20,000	12,311	14,320	9,692
9	26,633	2,421	20,000	11,211	15,422	9,941
10	0	0	20,000	10,000	(10,000)	(6,139)
						$102,781

table 19-6

Schedule of cash outflows: debt alternative with
sum-of-the-years'-digits depreciation

End of Year	(1) Loan Payment	(2) Interest	(3) SYD Depreciation	(4) Tax Shield [(2) + (3)]0.5	(5) Cash Outflows after Taxes (1) − (4)	(6) Present Value of Cash Outflows (5%)
0	$26,631	0	0	0	$26,631	$26,631
1	26,631	$15,337	$36,364	$25,851	780	743
2	26,631	14,208	32,727	23,468	3,163	2,869
3	26,631	12,965	29,091	21,028	5,603	4,840
4	26,631	11,599	25,455	18,527	8,104	6,667
5	26,631	10,095	21,818	15,957	10,674	8,363
6	26,631	8,442	18,182	13,312	13,319	9,939
7	26,631	6,623	14,545	10,584	16,047	11,404
8	26,631	4,622	10,909	7,786	18,845	12,755
9	26,633	2,421	7,272	4,847	21,786	14,043
10	0	0	3,637	1,819	(1,819)	(1,117)
						$97,137

investment tax credit to the lessee. The lessee would then reduce its taxes by the amount of the credit and the lessor would be entitled to none of it. However, the lessor would then want higher lease payments to offset the loss of the tax credit. More will be said about how lease payments are determined by the lessor when we take up the economics of leasing in the last section of the chapter. For now, our concern is with the analysis of the alternatives and not with the underlying economics.

Another factor that favors the debt alternative is the deductibility of interest payments for tax purposes. Because the amount of interest embodied in a "mortgage-type" debt payment is high at first and declines with successive payments, the tax benefits associated with these payments follow the same pattern over time. From a present-value standpoint, this pattern benefits the firm relative to the pattern of lease payments, which typically are constant over time. (The reader should compare Table 19-3 with Table 19-4 for amplification of this point.)

Accelerated Depreciation   In our example, we assumed straight-line depreciation. If the company uses accelerated depreciation, it obtains a greater tax shield in the early years and a lower one in later years. As a result, cash outflows after taxes in the early years are reduced relative to cash outflows in later years, and the present value under the borrowing alternative is decreased. For example, if sum-of-the-years'-digits depreciation is employed, we get the results shown in Table 19-6. The present value of cash outflows under the borrowing alternative becomes $97,137, in contrast with $102,781 when straight-line depreciation is used. Thus, accelerated depreciation makes borrowing more attractive than it is with straight-line depreciation. It should be pointed out, however, that a lessor also is able to use accelerated depreciation. In turn, the lessor may pass on some of the benefits inherent in its use to the lessee in the form of lower lease payments.

Residual Value   Recall that we assumed the project had no residual value at the end of ten years. If it were expected to have an after-tax residual value, this value should be treated as a cash inflow at the end of year 10. To illustrate, suppose that in our original example, the asset was expected to have a residual value of $40,000 at the end of year 10. Put another way, the economic life of the project is longer than the lease term, namely twelve and one-half years versus ten years. As a result, straight-line depreciation over the ten-year lease period is $16,000 as opposed to $20,000 per year. Using the same format as in Table 19-5, the schedule of cash outflows for the debt alternative is shown in Table 19-7.

Assumed in the table is that the asset will be sold at its book value at the end of the year 10 and that the firm will realize $40,000 in cash.[16] The table shows that the debt alternative is more favorable than before, having a total present value of cash outflows of $93,667 as opposed to $102,781 before. In most cases, the presence of a residual value makes the borrowing alternative more attractive than would otherwise be the case. However, its presence also makes the asset more attractive to the lessor, who may pass on some of the benefits in the form of lower lease payments. It should be noted that if there is no residual value, the Internal Revenue Service may treat the lease as a purchase, which usually works to the disadvantage of the lessor.

A final consideration is the fact that the residual value is seldom known with certainty. The economic value of an asset at the end of a period of time is usually subject to considerable uncertainty whether it be sold or continue to be employed in the firm. One way to treat the problem is with a probability distribution of residual values. Another way is to analyze the asset in terms of the value of services that are expected over its remaining life where these values are subject to a stochastic process.[17] As such an approach is beyond the scope of this book, we do not consider it. In closing, however, it is important to stress the importance of factoring residual value into one's analysis if, in fact, a significant residual value is expected to occur.

Internal-Rate-of-Return Analysis

Instead of computing the present value of cash outflows for the two financing alternatives, we could compute the internal rates of return. This approach avoids the problem of having to choose a rate of discount. In general, businessmen feel more comfortable in comparing percentages than

---

[16]If the asset is sold for other than its book value, a capital gain or loss will be involved and the analysis needs to be modified for the capital gains tax effect. See Chapter 5 for further discussion of the tax effect.

[17]Such an approach is contained in Michael J. Brennan and Alan Kraus, "The Equilibrium Valuation of Lease Contracts" (Research paper, University of British Columbia, August 1977).

table 19-7

Schedule of cash outflows: debt alternative with
a residual value and straight-line depreciation

End of Year	(1) Loan Payment	(2) Interest	(3) Depreciation	(4) Tax Shield [(2) + (3)]0.5	(5) Residual Value	(6) Cash Outflows after Taxes (1) − (4) − (5)	(7) Present Value of Cash Outflows (5%)
0	$26,631	0	0	0		$26,631	$26,631
1	26,631	$15,337	$16,000	$15,669		10,962	10,440
2	26,631	14,208	16,000	15,104		11,527	10,455
3	26,631	12,965	16,000	14,483		12,148	10,494
4	26,631	11,599	16,000	13,800		12,831	10,556
5	26,631	10,095	16,000	13,048		13,583	10,643
6	26,631	8,442	16,000	12,221		14,410	10,753
7	26,631	6,623	16,000	11,312		15,319	10,887
8	26,631	4,622	16,000	10,311		16,320	11,046
9	26,633	2,421	16,000	9,211		17,422	11,230
10	0	0	16,000	8,000	$40,000	(48,000)	(29,468)
							$93,667

they do in comparing present values. For these reasons as well as others presented later, the author has a preference for the internal-rate-of-return method of analysis. Variations of this method have been used by Beechy, Doenges, Findlay, Mitchell, Roenfeldt and Osteryoung, Wyman, and Long.[18]

To begin with consideration of the lease, the after-tax cost of leasing can be determined by solving the following equation for r:

$$A_o - \sum_{t=0}^{n-1} \frac{L_t}{(1+r)^t} + \sum_{t=1}^{n} \frac{T(L_{t-1} - P_t)}{(1+r)^t} - ITC = 0 \qquad (19\text{-}3)$$

where A_o = cost of the asset to be leased

n = number of periods to the end of the lease

L_t = lease payment at the end of period t

T = corporate tax rate

P_t = depreciation in period t that would be applicable if the asset were owned

ITC = amount of investment tax credit

In this construct, the cost of leasing is the rate of discount that equates the present value of lease payments, net of their tax shields, together with the tax shields for depreciation and the investment tax credit, which would occur if the asset were purchased, with the cost of the asset. In other words, the cost of leasing includes not only the lease payments but the depreciation tax deductions as well as investment tax credit forgone by virtue of leasing the asset as opposed to purchasing it. These two tax benefits, which are associated with owning an asset, represent opportunity costs if the asset is leased. As we shall see in the last section of this chapter, they represent the focal point around which lease financing by the firm should be negotiated.

Using our previous example and assuming straight-line depreciation, the information necessary to solve for the after-tax cost of leasing is shown in Table 19-8. The last column represents the cash-flow stream. When we solve for the rate of discount that equates the negative cash flows with the positive ones in this column, we find it to be 7.11 percent. This figure then serves as the after-tax cost of lease financing, and it should be compared with the after-tax cost of debt financing to determine which method results in the lower cost of financing. The after-tax cost of debt financing is merely the before-tax cost

[18]Thomas H. Beechy, "Quasi-Debt Analysis of Financial Leases," *Accounting Review*, 44 (April 1969), 375–81; Beechy, "The Cost of Leasing: Comment and Correction," *Accounting Review*, 45 (October 1970), 769–73; Conrad R. Doenges, "The Cost of Leasing," *Engineering Economist*, 17 (Fall 1971), 31–44; M. Chapman Findlay III, "A Sensitivity Analysis of IRR Leasing Models," *Engineering Economist*, 20 (Summer 1975), 231–42; G. B. Mitchell, "After-Tax Cost of Leasing," *Accounting Review*, 45 (April 1970), 308–14; Rodney L. Roenfeldt and Jerome S. Osteryoung, "Analysis of Financial Leases," *Financial Management*, 2 (Spring 1973), 74–87; Harold E. Wyman, "Financial Lease Evaluation under Conditions of Uncertainty," *Accounting Review*, 48 (July 1973), 489–93; and Michael S. Long, "Leasing and the Cost of Capital," *Journal of Financial and Quantitative Analysis*, 12 (November 1977), 579–86. Most of these articles are summarized and analyzed in Bower, "Issues in Lease Financing."

table 19-8
Schedule of cash flows—lease analysis

End of Year	(1) Cost of Asset	(2) L_t Lease Payment	(3) P_t Depreciation	(4) Tax Shield $T(L_{t-1} - P_t)$	(5) Investment Tax Credit	(6) Cash Flow (1) − (2) + (4) − (5)
0	$200,000	$27,598	—	—	$20,000	$152,402
1	—	27,598	$20,000	$3,799	—	(23,799)
2	—	27,598	20,000	3,799	—	(23,799)
3	—	27,598	20,000	3,799	—	(23,799)
4	—	27,598	20,000	3,799	—	(23,799)
5	—	27,598	20,000	3,799	—	(23,799)
6	—	27,598	20,000	3,799	—	(23,799)
7	—	27,598	20,000	3,799	—	(23,799)
8	—	27,598	20,000	3,799	—	(23,799)
9	—	27,598	20,000	3,799	—	(23,799)
10	—	—	20,000	3,799	—	3,799

times 1 minus the tax rate. With the before-tax interest cost of 10 percent and a tax rate of 0.5 for our example problem, the after-tax cost of debt financing is $10.00(1 - 0.5) = 5.00$ percent. According to this method of analysis, then, borrowing is the preferred alternative because its effective yield is less than that for the leasing alternative. If depreciation were on an accelerated basis or if there were a residual value, borrowing would be even more attractive —the same as illustrated when we took up the present-value method of analysis.

In summary, the internal-rate-of-return method of analysis permits a simple comparison of the after-tax costs of the lease and borrowing alternatives. Whichever alternative has the lowest rate would be selected according to this method. Again, this assumes that decisions have already been reached with respect to acquiring the asset and to financing it with a fixed-income type of instrument—either debt or a lease. Implied is that either method of financing has the same effect on the capacity of the firm to raise additional funds.

Bower-Herringer-Williamson Method

In yet another approach to evaluating lease versus borrowing, Bower, Herringer, and Williamson (BHW) divide the payments streams into two parts: the cash flows associated with financing and the cash flows associated with tax savings.[19] As in our present-value example, they assume that the loan payment schedule is of the same configuration as the lease payment schedule. This assumption places the loan on an equivalent basis with the lease.

[19]"Lease Evaluation," pp. 257–65.

Analyzing the cash flows associated with financing first, Bower, Herringer, and Williamson measure the incremental impact of a loan by subtracting the present value of lease payments from the present value of loan payments, where both are discounted at the debt rate. For our example problem, the present value of loan payments in Table 19-4 is $180,000 if a 10 percent discount rate is used. Recall that the investment tax credit of $20,000 reduced the amount of debt financing from $200,000 to $180,000. The present value of the lease payments is determined by discounting the lease payments in column (1) of Table 19-3 by 10 percent, and it is found to be $186,535. Given these present values, the *financial disadvantage* of leasing is determined as follows:

Present value of loan payments	$180,000
Present value of lease payments	186,535
Financial advantage (disadvantage)	$ (6,535)

The next step is to determine the incremental present value of the tax savings associated with leasing. If we use the straight-line depreciation example, we begin by subtracting the tax shield for the borrowing alternative in Table 19-5 from that for the leasing alternative in Table 19-3. The difference represents the decrease in the firm's tax payments, which is associated with leasing as opposed to borrowing. The calculations are shown in Table 19-9. When these decreases in tax payments are discounted by the cost-of-capital rate, we obtain what BHW call the *operating advantage* of the lease. If the cost of capital is, say, 13 percent, the present value of the decreased tax payments is found to be −$7,233 for our example problem.

The decision to lease or borrow is made on the basis of whether the operating advantage of the lease exceeds its financial disadvantage. If so, lease financing should be used; if not, debt financing should be employed. In our case, there is an actual operating disadvantage associated with leasing. Therefore the latter holds and debt financing should be employed, according to this analysis.

The BHW method of analysis is similar to the *basic interest rate* approach of Richard F. Vancil.[20] Like BHW, Vancil separates the financing effect of leasing from its tax-savings effect. Holding constant the amount of financing, he discounts the tax savings associated with the noninterest portions of the two payments streams by the cost of capital. Whichever financing alternative has the lower present value is preferred.

A critical factor in both the BHW and the Vancil approaches is the discount rate employed. As discussed earlier, a case can be made for using the after-tax cost of debt. BHW justify the use of the cost of capital as the

[20]"Lease or Borrow: New Method of Analysis," *Harvard Business Review,* 39 (September-October 1961), 138–59.

table 19-9

Calculation of decrease in tax payments with leasing—
BHW Method

End of Year	(1) Leasing Tax Shield*	(2) Borrowing Tax Shield†	(3) Decrease in Tax Payments with Leasing (1) − (2)	(4) Present Value of Decreases (13%)
1	$13,799	$17,669	−$3,870	−$3,425
2	13,799	17,104	−3,305	−2,588
3	13,799	16,483	−2,684	−1,860
4	13,799	15,800	−2,001	−1,227
5	13,799	15,048	−1,249	−678
6	13,799	14,221	−422	−203
7	13,799	13,312	487	207
8	13,799	12,311	1,488	560
9	13,799	11,211	2,588	862
10	13,799	10,000	3,799	1,119
				−$7,233

*From Table 19-3.
†From Table 19-5.

discount rate on the basis that investors and creditors, in their valuation of the firm, recognize the difference in tax savings between the two methods. Because investors and creditors determine the overall value of the firm, BHW view the average cost of capital as the appropriate discount rate. Whether investors and creditors evaluate differences in tax savings in this manner is open to doubt. In addition, there is the conceptual problem of the cost of capital depending in part upon the decision to lease or borrow. An inconsistency arises in using the cost of capital as the discount rate to evaluate this decision. While the problem is not important when the project being financed is relatively small, the problem is important if the project is large. In essence, the tax savings that result from a financing decision are evaluated as though they were an investment.

An Assessment

Because of these problems, a case can be made for the use of the internal-rate-of-return method proposed in the preceding section. By comparing effective yields for the two financing alternatives, one does not have to choose a discount rate. This approach avoids intermingling investment and financing decisions by treating the problem as one of financing alone. Nonetheless, if differences in taxes are valued in the market at an implied interest rate higher than the effective interest yield computed, the method will give biased results. To the extent that these differences are valued at a rate that approximates the firm's cost of capital, the BHW method would be preferred.

Under most circumstances, the two methods will provide identical decisions.

This concludes our presentation of various methods for analyzing leasing versus borrowing. In recent years, a number of articles have been written on this subject, and no attempt is made in this chapter to present all views. By and large, however, the methods proposed are variations of the three methods presented. In the final section of this chapter, we explore reasons why lease financing might be a thing of value for the corporation and discuss how one can focus one's analysis on the factors that give rise to such value. First, however, we wish to consider a special lease situation and how it might be analyzed using the methods of analysis already described.

Analysis of an Asset That Can Only Be Leased

Occasionally, the firm must evaluate an asset that can only be acquired by leasing. For example, use of certain dock facilities by ocean freighters can be obtained only through a long-term lease. The purchase alternative is not available. In situations of this sort, the firm does not choose between leasing or borrowing; the only decision is whether or not to lease. As a result, the investment and financing decisions are inextricably intertwined.

Although no method of analysis is entirely satisfactory, perhaps the best approach is to determine the merit of the project as an investment. The first step is to compute the cash-equivalent price of the lease alternative, beginning by establishing an interest rate that is consistent with other current leasing arrangements. The cash-equivalent price is the present value of all required lease payments, discounted by this rate. The next step is to compute the present value of expected future cash benefits associated with the project, discounted at the required rate of return. Obviously these benefits should be estimated only for the duration of the lease period. If the present value of the expected future cash benefits exceeds the cash-equivalent price, the project is worthwhile, and the firm should enter into the lease.[21] If the present value of the cash benefits is less than the cash-equivalent price, the project should be rejected.

If the project is accepted, obviously it can be financed only by leasing. Implied then in our method of analysis is that lease financing does not alter the firm's cost of capital. In other words, the firm must be able to balance this method of financing with others so that it maintains a desired capital structure. If, for some reason, this balancing is not possible, perhaps because the project is large, then the effect of financing the project on the firm's cost of capital must be taken into account.

---

[21]We assume that the acceptance of the project does not change the business-risk complexion of the firm (see Part II). Under no circumstances should the lease payments be deducted from the expected cash benefits and the project judged on the basis of whether or not the present value of the residuals is positive.

We have saved our discussion of the economics of leasing until the last. Hopefully the reader has acquired an understanding of leasing and how it might be analyzed in relation to debt financing. In this section, we focus on the factors that give rise to leasing's being a thing of value in the capital markets. These are shown to be differences in effective taxes paid by lessors and lessees and differences in the protection afforded the lender and the lessor in bankruptcy. In the end, we will show how a firm can concentrate its evaluation on these factors to determine whether lease financing is appropriate for its situation.

Lease Financing in Perfect Capital Markets

It is useful to begin by assuming that capital markets are perfect. As taken up in Part III and in other parts of the book, this implies that there are no transaction costs, information is costless and readily available to all, securities are infinitely divisible, there are no bankruptcy costs, and there are no taxes. Under these assumptions, and the implied perfect competition among financial markets that results, it can be shown that the debt and lease obligations of a firm will be valued by secured lenders and lessors in the same manner.[22] The costs of debt and lease financing will therefore be the same, and the firm would be indifferent between the two as methods of financing.

When we relax the assumptions of perfect capital markets, however, debt and lease instruments may not be valued in the same manner. As a result, their costs to the firm may differ. The introduction of transaction costs, information costs, and less than infinite divisibility of securities results in impediments to arbitraging between financial instruments. However, these imperfections do not have a systematic effect in the sense that they favor leasing or favor debt financing all of the time. Rather, arbitrage between the markets is impeded, and consequently it may be possible for the firm to take "advantage" of the situation by issuing one type of instrument or the other. However, the advantage is likely to be small and extremely difficult to predict in practice. Therefore we do not concentrate on these imperfections. In contrast, the presence of bankruptcy costs and taxes affect things in a systematic manner and their effect is predictable as to direction. To these factors we now turn.

---

[22]In James C. Van Horne, "The Cost of Leasing with Capital Market Imperfections," *Engineering Economist*, 23 (Fall 1977), 1–12, this is demonstrated using a state-preference model. As the model is complicated, it is not presented here. However, the conclusion logically follows from all of our earlier discussion of the impact of the perfect market assumption on the valuation of financial instruments.

One "advantage" to a lease relative to debt from the standpoint of a supplier of capital is that the lessor enjoys a superior position in liquidation. [23] Because the lessor owns the asset, he is able to take it back when conditions of default occur. Although the lender can secure his loan with the asset involved, it is more difficult and costly to gain possession of it in the event of default. As we know from our analysis of capital structure decisions and liquidity decisions earlier in the book, there are costs associated with the initiation of bankruptcy proceedings. In addition to out-of-pocket costs, there are delays to the secured lender in taking over the asset involved; these delays have an obvious opportunity cost. Neither the out-of-pocket costs nor the delays affect the lessor nearly to the extent that they do the secured lender.

The riskier the firm that seeks financing, the greater the incentive for the supplier of capital to make the arrangement a lease rather than a loan. While many suppliers of capital are either lenders or lessors but not both, others engage in both types of accommodations. A case in point is the bank holding company. The author is familiar with situations where loans have been converted to leases when the risk of default has increased significantly. The purpose, of course, is to improve one's position should liquidation become necessary. In the total scheme of things, there is less "external drain" due to bankruptcy costs with lease financing than there is with debt financing. To the extent that any of the ex ante costs of bankruptcy avoided by leasing instead of borrowing are passed on to the lessee in the form of lower lease payments than would otherwise be the case, the firm might have an incentive to lease as opposed to borrow.[24]

Although the superior position of the lessor in bankruptcy relative to that of the lender is one reason for the development of the leasing industry, it is not the dominant one. But it is important and should not be overlooked, as it often distinguishes a lease from a loan in the eyes of a supplier of capital. Moreover, the importance of this factor varies over time. As the default risk of companies in general increases, as it might in a recession, this factor becomes more important. As a result, the incentive for lease financing increases, and we would expect to see a greater amount of it.

The Effect of Differing Taxes

The dominant economic reason for the existence of leasing, however, is differences in the tax benefits associated with the ownership of an asset among companies, financial institutions, and individuals. The greater the divergence in tax benefits from owning an asset among economic units in an

---

[23]See Chapter 24 for a discussion of bankruptcy proceedings.

[24]This advantage may be offset by the fact that leasing sometimes introduces an additional intermediary with a resulting increment in administrative costs.

economy, the greater the attraction of lease financing overall, all other things the same. We know from our previous discussion that the tax benefits associated with owning an asset are the investment tax credit, which is realized when the asset is placed into service, and the tax shield afforded by the deduction of depreciation over the depreciable life of the asset.

If the effective tax benefits associated with owning an asset were the same for all economic units in the economy, and if capital markets were perfect in every other way, debt and lease obligations would be valued in the same manner. As a result, their costs would be the same. If the lessor did not pass on all of the tax benefits associated with the ownership of the asset to the prospective lessee in the form of lower lease payments than would otherwise be the case, the prospective lessee could simply purchase the asset and finance it with debt. In this way, it could avail itself of all of the tax benefits. Therefore it is not the existence of taxes *per se* which gives rise to leasing being a thing of value, but it is due to a situation where different companies, financial institutions, and individuals have different abilities to realize the tax benefits associated with owning an asset.

Such differences are due to (1) different tax rates among economic units in the economy and (2) different levels of past and current income among economic units. Examples of the former include differences in personal and corporate income tax rates, as well as differences in tax rates among various individuals and corporations. An example of the latter is a company with a tax-loss carry-forward which pays little or no taxes on profits. Another example is a situation where the investment tax credit is so large that it exceeds the taxes that the firm would otherwise pay. As a result, part of the tax credit goes unutilized.

To the extent that a firm that pays little or no taxes is able to lease an asset from another party that pays high taxes, it may be able to avail itself of part of the tax benefits associated with ownership through lease payments that are lower than they would otherwise be. In turn, the lessor is able to use the full tax credit which might not otherwise be available to it. As a result, both parties gain.

Example of the Analysis of Divergent Tax Benefits   To illustrate, suppose that W. Barclay and Company, a food producer and processor, wishes to acquire the use of a large and highly sophisticated crop bundler, which has an economic life of eight years. No salvage value is expected at the end of that time. The machine and electronic accessories cost $1 million and are subject to a 10 percent investment tax credit, or $100,000 at the outset. Unfortunately, Barclay has had several loss years and currently has a tax-loss carry-forward of $200,000, which can be applied against future profits up to five years. If unutilized, the investment tax credit may be carried forward for a period up to seven years.

Suppose further that Barclay has entered into a contract to supply corn at a price that guarantees Barclay a profit over the next eight years.

These before-tax profits are as follows, and they are expected with a high degree of certainty:[25]

			Profit (in thousands)				
19_1	19_2	19_3	19_4	19_5	19_6	19_7	19_8
$100	$120	$140	$170	$200	$250	$300	$300

Barclay is considering financing the machine either with debt or with lease financing, both from the Third National Bank of Wabash, Indiana. If debt, the rate would be 10 percent and the loan would be payable $170,404 annually at the beginning of each of the next eight years.[26] In other words, payments are due in advance, the same as with leasing. The schedule of debt payments is shown in Table 19-10. Because of the advanced payments, the amount owed at time 0 is $1,000,000 − $170,404 = $829,596.

Assume that the tax rate for corporations is 22 percent on the first $25,000 in income and 48 percent on amounts in excess of $25,000. (While the present graduation of tax rates has more steps and, seemingly, is ever changing, for simplicity of illustration we have used a one-step graduation.) Given this assumption, we show in Table 19-11 the tax and loan payment cash outflows for Barclay and Company over the next eight years. Because no taxes are expected to be paid until the eighth year, the investment tax credit of $100,000 expires and, consequently, goes unutilized. Moreover, because of

table 19-10

Schedule of debt payments for Barclay and Company example

End of Year	Interest Plus Principal Payments	Principal Amount Owing at End of Year	Annual Interest
19_0	$170,404	$829,596	0
19_1	170,404	742,152	$82,960
19_2	170,404	645,963	74,215
19_3	170,404	540,155	64,596
19_4	170,404	423,767	54,016
19_5	170,404	295,740	42,377
19_6	170,404	154,910	29,574
19_7	170,404	0	15,491

[25]Profit projections assume the machine in question is acquired, but they do not include financing charges associated with its acquisition or depreciation charges.

[26]This amount is computed in the same manner as Eq. (19-2), using a 10 percent rate and eight years.

the previous tax-loss carry-forward as well as negative profits for the first several years, the company is unable to fully utilize the tax advantages associated with depreciation and interest payments on the debt. As shown, part of the tax-loss carry-forward expires in 19-5, so the firm loses altogether some of the tax advantage. In other words, the tax benefit is not merely postponed, which works to one's disadvantage on a present-value basis, but part of it is lost forever.

In contrast, the Third National Bank, which has agreed to make the loan at a 10 percent rate, is not similarly affected. The bank is very profitable, and its marginal tax rate is 48 percent. If it were to buy the asset and lease it to Barclay and Company, it would be able to reap the full advantage of the investment tax credit and accelerated depreciation. Therefore the bank is willing to charge a rate of interest lower than 10 percent.

Suppose, for example, that the bank agreed to charge an implied rate of interest of 7 percent. This corresponds to annual lease payments of $156,512, payable at the beginning of each of the next eight years.[27] The after-tax cash flows to the bank arising from such a lease are shown in Table 19-12. The cash flows are composed of the lease receipts less the taxes paid. The internal rate of return for the cash flows shown in the last column of the table is 7.24 percent. Thus, with an initial cash outlay of $818,614 ($1 million less the initial lease receipt and less the tax credit), the bank is able to earn a return of 7.24 percent after taxes.

This return compares with an after-tax return of $.10 (1 - .48) = 5.20$ percent for a loan involving an initial cash outlay of $829,596, ($1 million less the initial loan payment of $170,404). Obviously it is better off with the lease even though the implied interest rate embodied in the lease receipts is much less than the explicit interest rate on the loan. The reason is that the bank is able to avail itself of the investment tax credit and the tax benefits associated with accelerated depreciation. These are not available to it in the case of a loan.[28]

Barclay and Company also benefits from the lease arrangement in that the present value of its incremental cash outflows is lower than it is with the loan. In Table 19-13, the cash outflows under the lease arrangement are shown.[29] When the cash outflows in column (8) are related to the purchase price of $1 million at time 0, the internal rate of return is found to be 10.34 percent. This rate compares with an internal rate of return for the cash outflows under the loan arrangement (column (10) of Table 19-11) of 11.29 percent. Thus Barclay is better off with lease financing than it is with debt financing.

[27]As before, this amount is computed using Eq. (19-2).

[28]In this analysis, we ignore the fact that in the event of bankruptcy, the bank enjoys a better position as a lessor than it does as a lender. This factor makes leasing even more attractive.

[29]One might note that while part of the loss carry-forward expires, much less expires than in the case of the loan (Table 19-11).

table 19-11
Cash outflows for Barclay and Company using a loan

End of Year	(1) Loan Payment	(2) Interest	(3) Depreciation SYD	(4) Expected Profit before Interest and Depreciation	(5) Expected Profit after Interest and Depreciation (4) − (2) − (3)
19_0	$170,404	0			
19_1	170,404	$82,960	$222,222	$100,000	$(205,182)
19_2	170,404	74,215	194,444	120,000	(148,659)
19_3	170,404	64,596	166,667	140,000	(91,263)
19_4	170,404	54,016	138,889	170,000	(22,905)
19_5	170,404	42,377	111,111	200,000	46,512
19_6	170,404	29,574	83,333	250,000	137,093
19_7	170,404	15,491	55,555	300,000	228,954
19_8	—	—	27,778	300,000	272,222

The relative advantage is due to the fact that the company is unable to avail itself of the investment tax credit and some of the accelerated depreciation tax benefits associated with owning the asset. This is caused by the company's poor earnings in the past and the low earnings projected in the near future. As the Third National Bank is able to avail itself of all the tax benefits associated with ownership, it is willing to pass some of them on to Barclay and Company in the form of lower lease payments than would otherwise be the case. In this situation, the company should go with lease as opposed to debt financing.

A Summing Up

This example illustrates how both the lessee and the lessor can gain through a lease-financing arrangement. While the example is purposely extreme, it illustrates the principal economic foundation for the existence of

table 19-12
Cash flows to the lessor—Third National Bank

End of Year	(1) Purchase of Asset	(2) Investment Tax Credit	(3) Lease Receipts	(4) Accelerated Depreciation	(5) Taxes [(3) − (4)]0.48 − (2)	(6) Cash Flows after Taxes (1) + (3) − (5)
19_0	($1,000,000)	$100,000	$156,512	—	($24,874)	($818,614)
19_1			156,512	$222,222	(31,541)	188,053
19_2			156,512	194,444	(18,207)	174,719
19_3			156,512	166,667	(4,874)	161,386
19_4			156,512	138,889	8,459	148,053
19_5			156,512	111,111	21,792	134,720
19_6			156,512	83,333	35,126	121,386
19_7			156,512	55,555	48,459	108,053
19_8			—	27,778	(13,333)	13,333

table 19-11 (cont.)

(6)	(7)	(8)	(9)	(10)
Tax-Loss Carry-Forward Utilized	Remaining Tax-Loss Carry-Forward	Expected Taxable Income	Expected Taxes†	Cash Outflows (1) + (9)
	$200,000			$170,404
—	405,182	0	—	170,404
—	553,841	0	—	170,404
—	645,104	0	—	170,404
—	668,009	0	—	170,404
$ 46,512	468,009*	0	—	170,404
137,093	262,827*	0	—	170,404
228,954	33,873	0	—	170,404
33,873	0	$238,349	$107,908	107,908

*At the end of five years, the unutilized carry-forward expires.
†22 percent on first $25,000; 48 percent on profits above that.

leasing and the leasing industry. Again, this reason is differences among companies, financial institutions, and individuals in their ability to realize the tax benefits associated with owning an asset. Leasing permits the firm with little such ability to realize a greater portion of these benefits than it is able to do on its own. How much greater a realization depends upon the supply and demand for lease financing among economic units in the economy.

A lessor is unlikely to give up all of the tax benefits because realization of such benefits by the company seeking financing depends on its favor-

table 19-13
Cash outflows for Barclay and Company using a lease

End of Year	(1) Lease Payment	(2) Expected Profit before Lease Payments	(3) Expected Profit after Lease Payments (2) − (1)	(4) Tax-Loss Carry-Forward Utilized	(5) Remaining Tax Loss Carry-Forward	(6) Expected Taxable Income	(7) Expected Taxes†	(8) Cash Outflow (1) + (7)
19_0	$156,512				$200,000			$156,512
19_1	156,512	$100,000	$ (56,512)	—	256,512	0	0	156,512
19_2	156,512	120,000	(36,512)	—	293,024	0	0	156,512
19_3	156,512	140,000	(16,512)	—	309,536	0	0	156,512
19_4	156,512	170,000	13,488	$13,488	296,048	0	0	156,512
19_5	156,512	200,000	43,488	43,488	109,536*	0	0	156,512
19_6	156,512	250,000	93,488	93,488	16,048*	0	0	156,512
19_7	156,512	300,000	143,488	16,048	0	$127,440	$ 54,671	211,183
19_8	—	300,000	300,000	0	0	300,000	137,500	137,500

*At the end of five years, the unutilized carry-forward expires.
†22 percent on first $25,000; 48 percent on profits above that.

able tax situation. By the same token, competition among lessors will assure that part of the benefits will be transferred to the lessee in the form of lower lease payments than would otherwise be the case. The exact sharing of the tax benefits is negotiable, but it will depend on equilibrium conditions in the capital markets. Our example showed how a firm can concentrate its analysis on the important tax considerations when approaching the question of whether to lease or borrow.

For the consistently profitable company, lease financing may make little sense. To the extent that a third-party lessor is involved, an added financial intermediary is introduced. This additional intermediation adds administrative costs which ultimately must be borne by the lessee. As a result, lease financing may be more costly than debt financing. For the marginally profitable firm or for the firm that has had a temporary setback and expects to pay little in the way of taxes in the near future, however, lease financing may prove very beneficial. The economic benefits passed off to the lessee are reflected in the amount of periodic lease payments relative to the cost of the asset involved, or simply in the implied interest cost of the lease. By concentrating on this cost and the economic benefits associated with leasing relative to those for borrowing, the firm is able to determine whether lease financing is promising. It also is able to better "shop around" among lessors and to negotiate the lease. In this way, the decision will be grounded in sound economic reasoning as opposed to the "sales pitch" used by many a leasing company to sell its financial service.

In the United States, a sophisticated market has developed in the leasing of such large and expensive assets as airplanes, ships, railroad cars, and computers. Commercial banks, because of their profitability and relatively high tax brackets, have come to dominate the field as lessors. As would be expected, the lessees of such assets are primarily companies that have relatively low profitability and are unable to take full advantage of the tax benefits. Perhaps the most important illustration of this arrangement is the lease financing of jet airplanes by airlines. The profitability of these companies has been relatively low or negative in recent years, and therefore they are unable to take full advantage of the tax benefits available, particularly the investment tax credit. Lease financing enables them to realize a significant portion of these benefits. In addition to commercial banks, partnerships of high-tax-bracketed individuals are frequently formed to buy an asset and lease it to a company. This form of arrangement has grown in importance in recent years, and we can expect it to continue.

Although divergent tax situations among companies, financial institutions, and individuals are the principal foundation on which the leasing industry rests, we should not lose track of the superior position of the lessor relative to that of the lender in bankruptcy. This factor also has contributed to the growth of lease financing. Together these factors are reflected in differences in the "true" cost between lease and debt financing, a comparison that the reader should now be in a position to make.

Lease financing involves the acquisition of the economic use of an asset through a contractual commitment to make periodic lease payments to a lessor who owns the asset. Because of this contractual obligation, leasing is regarded as a method of financing similar to borrowing. Leasing can involve the direct acquisition of an asset under a lease, a sale and leaseback arrangement whereby the firm sells an asset it owns and leases it back from the buyer, or a leveraged lease.

The accounting treatment of leases has changed dramatically over the past two decades. Leases that convey most of the economic benefits and risks associated with ownership are known as capital leases. Noncancelable leases not meeting this criterion are called operating leases. For a capital lease, the capitalized value of the leased property must be shown on the balance sheet as an asset, with the obligation shown as a liability. Moreover, the reported lease expense is the amortization of the leased property plus the implied interest rate embodied in the lease payments, not the amount of the lease payment. For the operating lease, however, the reported lease expense is the latter. Also, for tax purposes the lease payment is what is deductible as an expense.

Several cash-flow methods were analyzed for evaluating lease financing in relation to debt financing. The decision to lease or borrow can be made on the basis of which alternative has the lowest present value of cash outflows or the lowest after-tax internal rate of return. Because the latter does not require specifying a discount rate, it is preferred by many. Another method of analysis calls for the separation of differences in explicit financing costs from differences in taxes, with the two methods of financing compared according to their present values. Consideration also was given to situations in which leasing is the only means by which an asset can be acquired.

In the final section, we took up the economics of leasing. The foundation for the growth in leasing was shown to be (1) differences in the protection afforded the lessor and the lender in the event of bankruptcy, and (2) differences in the ability of companies, financial institutions, and individuals to take advantage of the tax benefits associated with owning an asset. The impact of both of these factors varies over time with changes in perceived default risk, in bankruptcy costs, in federal, state, and local tax rates, and in the overall profitability of companies. As a result, the relative importance of lease financing in the economy can change over time.

Of the two factors, the second is by far the more important, and we concentrated our attention on it. It was shown that firms that pay low taxes may be able to reap significant economic benefit from lease as opposed to debt financing. By leasing an asset from a lessor that pays substantial taxes, the firm is able to realize part of the tax benefits associated with the investment tax credit and accelerated depreciation through lease payments that are lower than would otherwise be the case. It was shown that both parties can gain by the lease arrangement at the expense of the federal government.

PROBLEMS

1. Given the following information, compute the annual lease payment that a lessor will require. (Lease payments are in advance.)

   (a) Purchase price of $260,000, interest rate of 13 percent, five-year lease period, and no residual value
   (b) Purchase price of $138,000, interest rate of 6 percent, nine-year lease period, and a near certain residual value of $20,000
   (c) Purchase price of $773,000, interest rate of 9 percent, ten-year lease period, and no residual value

2. Conrad Reduction Company has just leased a press that calls for annual lease payments of $40,000 payable in advance. The lease period is nine years and the leased property is classified as a capital lease. The company's incremental borrowing rate is 7 percent, whereas the lessor's implied interest rate is 12 percent. The company depreciates all of its owned assets on a straight-line basis. On the basis of this information, compute:

   (a) The value of the leased property to be shown on the balance sheet after the initial lease payment
   (b) The annual lease expense in each year as it will appear on the accounting income statement

3. The Carver Paper Company has decided to acquire a $300,000 pulp quality control device, which has a useful life of ten years after which no salvage value is expected. The device would be depreciable on a sum-of-the-years'-digits basis with 10/55 depreciation in the first year, 9/55 in the second, down to 1/55 in the last year. The investment tax credit is in effect, and a 10 percent credit is applicable at the time the device is acquired and placed into service.

   The company is trying to determine whether it is better to finance the acquisition with debt or with a lease arrangement. If debt, the interest rate would be 10 percent and debt payments would be due at the very beginning of each of the ten years. The company is in a 50 percent tax bracket. If the acquisition is financed with a lease, lease payments of $33,000 would be required at the beginning of each year. What is the present value of cash outflows for each of these financing alternatives, using the after-tax cost of debt? Which alternative is preferable?

4. The Kraus Corporation, which has a 40 percent tax rate, wishes to acquire a $100,000 stamping machine, which would be depreciated on a straight-line basis with an eight-year life and no salvage value. An investment tax credit of 10 percent is available at the time the asset is acquired. It would be possible to lease the machine for $15,000 per year, payable in advance; it also would be possible to borrow at a 10 percent rate. Using an internal-rate-of-return analysis, determine the better alternative.

5. In problem 4, describe what would happen if sum-of-the-years'-digits instead of straight-line depreciation were used. (Merely explain; do not work out.) Describe what would happen if the tax rate were 60 percent instead of 40 percent.

6. Northern Star Engine Company has decided to buy a special generator costing $1.2 million. It can finance the project with a ten-year mortgage bond issue. The interest rate would be 12 percent, and the loan is payable at the beginning of each of the ten years. In essence, the first payment serves as a down payment. The company's marginal tax rate is 33 1/3 percent, and an investment tax credit of 10 percent is available at the outset. The company uses straight-line depreciation, but the asset has an economic life of fifteen years. At the end of ten years, however, the company expects to sell the asset at its then existing book value.

   In addition to financing the project with debt, Northern Star is considering a sale and leaseback arrangement with Sunburst Finance Company. The generator would be sold, and lease payments of $160,000 per year would be required at the beginning of each of the next ten years. On the basis of the present value of cash outflows, which of the two financing alternatives is better?

7. Pacific-Baja Shipping Company is considering leasing dock facilities in Valdez, Alaska. It would use the facilities for four years in connection with supplying heavy-duty equipment and other cargo to the area. The Port of Valdez Authority leases the facilities at an annual cost of $200,000 payable at the beginning of each year. While the Port Authority has not stated the implied interest rate embodied in the lease payments, officials of Pacific-Baja believe a 9 percent rate would be appropriate. Over the four years, the company expects the project to show net cash flows of $180,000 in the first year, $250,000 in the second, $320,000 in the third, and $240,000 in the last year. (For simplicity assume these cash flows are realized at the end of each of the years.) The project is subject to considerable risk, and it has been determined that the required after-tax rate of return is 18 percent.

   Should the company undertake the project and lease the dock facilities or should it reject the project?

8. The Xenia-Youngstown Zipper Company (XYZ) has decided to invest in a computer-controlled measuring device costing $120,000. The device has an economic life of seven years, after which no salvage value is expected. The company must determine whether it is better to finance the acquisition through debt or leasing. XYZ expects profits before taxes of $10,000 next year, $20,000 the following year, $30,000 the third year, and $40,000 each year thereafter (before depreciation on the device). It has a high degree of confidence in these estimates. The tax rate is 22 percent on the first $25,000 in profits and 48 percent on amounts over that. The company has had break-even operations during the previous three years. Finally, the machine is subject to a 10 percent investment tax credit.

   If the machine is financed with debt, the Atticks National Bank of Youngstown is willing to extend a loan for the full purchase price at an 11 percent rate of interest payable in equal annual amounts over seven years. The bank also has a leasing division and has indicated that it is willing to lease finance the acquisition for XYZ over the seven-year period. The bank is and has been quite profitable, and it is in a 48 percent tax bracket. Describe in words whether lease or debt financing is likely to be more favorable for XYZ? Why? Is the bank likely to want to accommodate the company more on a lease basis or on a debt basis?

SELECTED REFERENCES

ANDERSON, PAUL F., *Financial Aspects of Industrial Leasing Decisions: Implications for Marketing.* East Lansing: Division of Research, Graduate School of Business Administration, Michigan State University, 1977.

ANDERSON, PAUL F., AND JOHN D. MARTIN, "Lease vs. Purchase Decisions: A Survey of Current Practice," *Financial Management,* 6 (Spring 1977), 41–47.

BEECHY, THOMAS H., "The Cost of Leasing: Comment and Correction," *Accounting Review,* 45 (October 1970), 769–73.

———, "Quasi-Debt Analysis of Financial Leases," *Accounting Review,* 44 (April 1969), 375–81.

BOWER, RICHARD S., "Issues in Lease Financing," *Financial Management,* 2 (Winter 1973), 25–34.

BOWER, RICHARD S., FRANK C. HERRINGER, AND J. PETER WILLIAMSON, "Lease Evaluation," *Accounting Review,* 41 (April 1966), 257–65.

BRENNAN, MICHAEL J., AND ALAN KRAUS, "The Equilibrium Valuation of Lease Contracts." Research paper, University of British Columbia, August 1977.

COOPER, KERRY, AND ROBERT H. STRAWSER, "Evaluation of Capital Investment Projects Involving Asset Leases," *Financial Management,* 4 (Spring 1975), 44–49.

DOENGES, R. CONRAD, "The Cost of Leasing," *Engineering Economist,* 17 (Fall 1971), 31–44.

DYL, EDWARD A., AND STANLEY A. MARTIN, JR., "Setting Terms for Leveraged Leasing," *Financial Management,* 6 (Winter 1977), 20–27.

FERRARA, WILLIAM L., "Should Investment and Financing Decisions Be Separated?" *Accounting Review,* 41 (January 1966), 106–14.

FERRARA, WILLIAM L., AND JOSEPH F., WOJDAK, "Valuation of Long-Term Leases," *Financial Analysis Journal,* 25 (November-December 1969), 29–32.

FINDLAY, M. CHAPMAN, III, "A Sensitivity Analysis of IRR Leasing Models," *Engineering Economist,* 20 (Summer 1975), 231–42.

GORDON, MYRON J., "A General Solution to the Buy or Lease Decision: A Pedagogical Note," *Journal of Finance,* 29 (March 1974).

JOHNSON, ROBERT W., AND WILBUR G., LEWELLEN, "Analysis of the Lease-or-Buy Decision," *Journal of Finance,* 27 (September 1972), 815–23.

KALATA, JOHN J., DENNIS G. CAMPBELL, AND IAN K. SHUMAKER, "Lease Financing Reporting," *Financial Executive* (March 1977), 34–40.

KELLER, THOMAS F., AND RUSSELL J. PETERSON, "Optimal Financial Structure, Cost of Capital, and the Lease-or-Buy Decision," *Journal of Business Finance & Accounting,* 1 (Autumn 1974), 405–14.

KIM, E. HAN, WILBUR G. LEWELLEN, AND JOHN J. MCCONNELL, "Sale and Leaseback Agreements and Enterprise Valuation," *Journal of Financial and Quantitative Analysis,* forthcoming.

LEWELLEN, WILBUR G., MICHAEL S. LONG, AND JOHN J. MCCONNELL, "Asset Leasing in Competitive Capital Markets," *Journal of Finance,* 31 (June 1976), 787–98.

LONG, MICHAEL S., "Leasing and the Cost of Capital," *Journal of Financial and Quantitative Analysis,* 12 (November 1977), 579–86.

MCGUGAN, VINCENT J., AND RICHARD E. CAVES, "Integration and Competition in the Equipment Leasing Industry," *Journal of Business,* 47 (July 1974), 382–96.

MILLER, MERTON H., AND CHARLES W. UPTON, "Leasing, Buying, and the Cost of Capital Services," *Journal of Finance,* 31 (June 1976), 787-98.

MITCHELL, G. B., "After-Tax Cost of Leasing," *Accounting Review,* 45 (April 1970), 308-14.

MYERS, STEWART C., DAVID A. DILL, AND ALBERTO J. BAUTISTA, "Valuation of Financial Lease Contracts," *Journal of Finance,* 31 (June 1976), 799-820.

OFFER, AHARON R., "The Evaluation of the Lease versus Purchase Alternatives," *Financial Management,* 5 (Summer 1976), 67-74.

ROENFELDT, RODNEY L., AND JEROME S. OSTERYOUNG, "Analysis of Financial Leases," *Financial Management,* 2 (Spring 1973), 74-87.

SCHALL, LAWRENCE D., "The Lease-or-Buy and Asset Acquisition Decisions," *Journal of Finance,* 29 (September 1974), 1203-14.

SORENSEN, IVAR W., AND RAMON E. JOHNSON, "Equipment Financial Leasing Practices and Costs: An Empirical Study," *Financial Management,* 6 (Spring 1977), 33-40.

VANCIL, RICHARD F., "Lease or Borrow: New Method of Analysis," *Harvard Business Review,* 39 (September-October 1961), 122-36.

VAN HORNE, JAMES C., "The Cost of Leasing with Capital Market Imperfections," *Engineering Economist,* 23 (Fall 1977), 1-12.

WIAR, ROBERT C., "Economic Implications of Multiple Rates of Return in the Leverage Lease Context," *Journal of Finance,* 28 (December 1973), 1275-86.

WYMAN, HAROLD E., "Financial Lease Evaluation under Conditions of Uncertainty," *Accounting Review,* 48 (July 1973), 489-93.

part VI

long-term financing

20
financing externally and common stock

In Part III, the focus of our analysis was primarily on the theoretical aspects of long-term financing—both external and internal. By and large, methods of financing were categorized broadly into the equity and nonequity portions of the capital structure of the firm. In this part, we explore in detail the specific methods of external long-term financing. We are concerned with the way a firm employs these various methods, their features, various valuation concepts, and, when appropriate, the integration of certain aspects of a method into the theory discussed previously. This chapter explores the role of investment banking in long-term financing, the institutional aspects of common stock, and the issuance of common stock through a rights offering to existing shareholders. In Chapter 21, we take up long-term bond issues, private placements, and preferred stock, while in Chapter 22 our concern is with convertible securities and warrants.

FINANCIAL FLOWS

The raising of funds externally automatically involves a company in the financial markets. Because conditions in these markets affect the cost and availability of alternative methods of financing, obviously the financing decision is affected. By virtue of their interdependence with this decision, the investment and dividend decisions are affected as well. Consequently, it is important that the financial manager keep abreast of financial market conditions. The more frequent the need of the firm to finance externally, of course, the closer the attention that he will need to pay. Extensive evaluation of interest rates and equity returns in financial markets is beyond the scope of this book; however, such an analysis is available in a supplementary volume.[1]

When a business firm finances its investment in real assets externally, it ultimately obtains funds from savings-surplus economic units in the economy. A savings-surplus unit can be either a business, a household, or a government whose current savings (current income less current consumption) exceeds its investment in real assets for the period under consideration. A savings-deficit unit, on the other hand, is one whose investment in real assets exceeds its current savings. If the investment in real assets always equaled the current savings for all economic units in an economy, there would be no need for any economic unit to obtain funds externally or for money and capital markets. In a modern economy, the investment in real assets for most economic units differs from their savings. Some units save more than they invest; others invest more than they save. As a result, we have money and capital markets. The more diverse these economic units are in their patterns of investment in real assets and savings, the greater the need for financial markets and the greater the amount of financial assets in the economy. Although *ex post* investment must equal *ex post* savings for the economy as a whole, there can be considerable divergence between savings and investment for the individual economic unit.

One of the functions of the money and capital markets is to allocate efficiently the flow of funds from savings-surplus economic units to savings-deficit units. The allocation of these funds occurs primarily on the basis of interest rates—the price of money. The efficiency of a country's money and capital markets is instrumental in the channeling of savings to the most promising investment opportunities and in the growth and development of a viable economy. The more varied the vehicles by which savings can flow from ultimate savers to ultimate users of funds, the more efficient the financial markets of an economy tend to be. In this regard, we are concerned specifically with the way business firms obtain funds—in particular long-term funds—to finance the excess of their investment in real assets over current savings for the period.

Our emphasis will be on the *primary* market for corporate securities; that is, the sale of new securities by the firm to investors. This market differs from the *secondary* market, where existing securities are bought and sold among investors. It is important to understand that a viable secondary market enhances the efficiency of the primary market because it provides market-

---

[1]James C. Van Horne, *Financial Market Rates and Flows* (Englewood Cliffs, N.J.: Prentice-Hall, 1978).

ability to the original investor. As a result, the primary security is more attractive than it would be in the absence of a secondary market. The secondary market also gives management of a company information about the costs of debt and equity funds, providing the backdrop for the valuation concepts advanced in this book. We do not want to leave the impression that the secondary market is unimportant. Our focus in this chapter is simply upon understanding the role of the primary market as it pertains to corporate securities.

INVESTMENT BANKING

The efficient functioning of financial markets requires a number of financial institutions.[2] One of these institutions is the investment banker, who acts as middleman in the distribution of new securities to the public. His principal function is to buy the securities from the company and then resell them to investors. For this service, the investment banker receives the difference, or spread, between the price he pays for the security and the price at which the securities are resold to the public. Because most companies make only occasional trips to the capital market, they are not specialists in the distribution of securities. To sell securities on their own would be both costly and risky. On the other hand, investment banking firms have the know-how, the contacts, and the sales organization necessary to do an efficient job of marketing securities to investors. Because they are continually in the business of buying securities from companies and selling them to investors, investment bankers can perform this service at a lower cost than can the individual firm.

Competitive Bidding Versus Negotiated Offering

A security offering through an investment banker to investors other than the firm's own stockholders (known as a public offering) can be either on a competitive bid basis or on a negotiated basis. When new securities are sold by competitive bidding, the company issuing the securities invites bids from investment bankers. Frequently, two or more investment banking firms join together for purposes of bidding on a security issue; the combination is known as a syndicate. The purpose underlying the formation of a syndicate is to spread the risk and to obtain a larger overall selling organization. The issuing company specifies the date that sealed bids will be received, and competing syndicates submit bids at the specified time and place. The syndicate with the highest bid wins the security issue. At that time, it pays the

[2]For a theoretical discussion of the efficiency of financial markets and savings flows, see ibid., Chapters 1 and 2.

company the difference between its good-faith deposit and the bid price and then attempts to resell the issue at a higher price to investors.

With a negotiated offering, the company issuing the securities selects an investment banking firm and works directly with that firm in determining the essential features of the issue. Together, they discuss and negotiate a price for the security and the timing of the issue. Depending upon the size of the issue, the investment banker may invite other firms to join it in sharing the risk and selling the issue. If a company has satisfactory experience with an investment banking firm, it usually will use the same firm for subsequent security issues.

From the standpoint of the issuing company, the key consideration in deciding between a competitive offering and a negotiated offering is the likely net price paid to it. Advocates of competitive offerings argue that the competition between bidding syndicates results in a higher price to the company and a lower profit spread to the investment banker than does a negotiated offering. For this reason, certain types of companies are required to issue securities on a competitive bid basis. For example, Rule 50 of the Public Utility Holding Company Act of 1935 mandates that registered utility holding companies receive at least two bids. (Because of depressed markets in the 1970s, the Securities and Exchange Commission granted a number of exemptions to this rule.) In addition to federal regulations, many state public utility commissions require that public utilities in their states issue securities by competitive bidding, unless an exemption is sought by the utility and approved by the commission. In addition, railroads are required by the Interstate Commerce Commission to use competitive bidding in the sale of their securities.

Advocates of negotiated offerings argue that such underwritings allow the investment banker more time to locate investors and to place the issue, which in turn results in a more favorable price than is possible under a competitive bidding situation. In particular, this is said to be important in times of "demoralized" markets where security prices are falling, as well as in the case of a very large issue. In a "demoralized" market, certain investment bankers may refuse to enter into a competitive bid syndicate. Their absence, together with the reluctance of others to bid aggressively, could result in a lower net price to the company than would be the case with a negotiated offering. Also, with a negotiated offering, a syndicate can be formed of those investment banking firms having the strongest selling organizations, whereas with a competitive offering, this selling power may be dispersed.[3]

Empirical testing of competitive versus negotiated offerings has shown somewhat mixed results. Various studies of municipal bonds suggest that the issuer receives a higher net price with competitive bids than with a

---

[3]See George G. C. Parker and Daniel Cooperman, "Competitive Bidding in the Underwriting of Public Utilities Securities," *Journal of Financial and Quantitative Analysis,* 5 (December 1978), 885–902.

negotiated offering.[4] With respect to corporate bonds, several authors have found underwriter spreads to be lower for competitive bid offerings than for negotiated offerings.[5] Moreover, certain studies have shown the relative advantage to vary with the degree of market uncertainty, with negotiated offerings being more advantageous to the issuer in periods of unstable market conditions than they are in periods of stable market conditions.[6] This follows from our discussion above. Still other studies have found a lack of relationship between the type of offering and flotation costs, and between the type of offering and the net cost to the issuer.[7] Overall then, the empirical evidence is mixed, though the majority of it shows underwriter compensation to be less for a competitive bid situation. However, the relative advantage appears to change with the tone of the market.

Functions of the Investment Banker—Underwriting

One of the key functions the investment banker performs is that of bearing risk. When an investment banker buys a security issue, he *underwrites* the sale of the issue by giving the company a check for the purchase price. At that time, the company is relieved of the risk of not being able to sell the issue to investors at the established price. If the issue does not sell well, either because of an adverse turn in the market or because it is overpriced, the underwriter, and not the company, takes the loss. Thus the investment banker insures, or underwrites, the risk of adverse market price fluctuations during the period of distribution.

Typically, the investment banker with whom a company discusses the offering does not handle the underwriting alone. In order to spread risk

[4]Reuben A. Kessel, "A Study of the Effects of Competition in the Tax-Exempt Bond Market," *Journal of Political Economy,* 79 (August 1971), 706–38; Richard R. West, "New Issue Concessions on Municipal Bonds: A Case of Monopsony Pricing," *Journal of Business,* 38 (April 1965), 135–48; and West, "Determinants of Underwriters' Spreads on Tax-Exempt Bond Issues," *Journal of Financial and Quantitative Analysis,* 2 (September 1967), 241–63.

[5]Avery B. Cohan, *Cost of Flotation and Long-Term Corporate Debt* (Chapel Hill: University of North Carolina Press, 1961); and Louis H. Ederington, "Uncertainty, Competition, and Costs of Corporate Bond Underwriting," *Journal of Financial Economics,* 2 (March 1975), 71–94.

[6]Gary D. Tallman, David F. Rush, and Ronald W. Melicher, "Competitive versus Negotiated Underwriting Costs of Regulated Industries," *Financial Management,* 3 (Summer 1974), 49–55; Louis H. Ederington, "Uncertainty, Competition, and Costs"; and Louis H. Ederington, "Negotiated versus Competitive Underwritings of Corporate Bonds," *Journal of Finance,* 31 (March 1976), 17–28.

[7]Keith B. Johnson, T. Gregory Morton, and M. Chapman Findlay III, "An Empirical Analysis of the Flotation Cost of Corporate Securities," *Journal of Finance,* 30 (September 1975), 1129–33; Dennis E. Logue and Robert A. Jarrow, "Negotiation vs. Competitive Bidding in the Sale of Securities by Public Utilities," *Financial Management,* 7 (Autumn 1978), 31–39: and Parker and Cooperman, "Competitive Bidding in the Underwriting of Public Utilities Securities."

and obtain better distribution, he invites other investment bankers to participate in the offering. The originating house usually is the manager and has the largest participation. Other investment bankers are invited into the syndicate, and their participations are determined primarily on the basis of their ability to sell securities.[8] For the risk-bearing function of the offering, these investment bankers are compensated by an underwriting profit.

Underwriting Commission   To illustrate the compensation of investment bankers, we turn to an example. Figure 20-1 shows the cover of the prospectus for a $400 million issue of 7⅞ percent debentures of the Standard Oil

figure 20-1
**Example of a
prospectus**

[8]For a discussion of the traditions by which syndicates are formed, see Samuel L. Hayes III, "Investment Banking: Power Structure in Flux," *Harvard Business Review,* 49 (March-April 1971), 136–52.

Company of Indiana. The issue was on a negotiated basis, with Morgan Stanley & Co. as manager putting together a syndicate of some two hundred investment banking firms. Morgan Stanley's participation was by far the largest, being $80 million. Other participations ranged from $8 million down to $250,000. We see in the figure that the syndicate bought the debentures from the company for $395 million, or $987.50 a bond. In turn, it priced the bonds to the public at $996.25 per bond, or $398.5 million. The spread of $8.75 per bond, or $3.5 million in total, represents the gross commission to the syndicate for underwriting the issue, for selling it, and for covering the various expenses incurred.

Of the total spread of $8.75 per bond, $3.75, or 43 percent, represents the gross underwriting profit. The remaining 57 percent represents the selling concession, which we discuss shortly. This breakdown between underwriting and selling profits is typical for corporate bonds. A portion of the gross underwriting profit goes to the originating house as manager of the offering. Although this figure is not given for the issue, the typical fee is 15 to 20 percent of the total spread. After the bonds are sold, total underwriting profits less expenses and managers' fee are distributed to members of the syndicate on the basis of their percentage participation. It should be noted that the amount of underwriting profit to a member of a syndicate after expenses and the managers' fee is not large. In our example, it probably is less than $2 a bond. The principal reward from participation comes from selling the securities.

With respect to underwriter risk, each member of the syndicate is liable for his percentage participation in the unsold securities of the syndicate, regardless of the number of securities the individual member sells. If a member of a syndicate has a 20 percent participation in an offering involving 40,000 bonds, and 10,000 remain unsold at the termination of the syndicate, the member would be responsible for 2,000 bonds. His liability would be the same whether he had sold 20,000 bonds or none.

Best Efforts Offering   Instead of underwriting a security issue, an investment banker may sell the issue on a *best efforts* basis. Under this arrangement, the investment banker agrees only to sell as many securities as he can at an established price. The investment banker has no responsibility for securities that are unsold. In other words, he bears no risk. Investment bankers frequently are unwilling to underwrite a security issue of a small company. For these companies, the only feasible means by which to place securities may be through a best efforts offering.[9]

Making a Market   On occasion, the underwriter will make a market for a security after it is issued. In the case of a public offering of common stock for the first time, making a market is extremely important to investors. In making

---

[9]For a theoretical analysis of a best efforts offering relative to an underwritten one from the standpoint of the firm seeking the "best" contract with an investment banker, see Gershon Mandelker and Artur Raviv, "Investment Banking: An Economic Analysis of Optimal Underwriting Contracts," *Journal of Finance*, 32 (June 1977), 638–94.

a market, the underwriter maintains a position in the stock and stands ready to buy and sell it at bid and ask prices he quotes. These quotations are based upon underlying supply and demand conditions. With a secondary market, the stock has greater liquidity to investors; this appeal enhances the success of the original offering.

Selling the Securities

The second major function of the investment banker is that of selling the securities to investors. As we discussed earlier, investment bankers are invited into syndicates and their participations are determined primarily on the basis of their ability to distribute securities. For this function, an investment banker is rewarded by a selling concession of so many dollars a bond. In the case of the Standard Oil Company of Indiana offering, the selling concession was $5 per bond, or 57 percent of the total spread of $8.75. The ultimate seller can be either a member of the underwriting syndicate or a qualified outside security dealer. In order to earn the full concession, however, he must be a member of the syndicate. An outside security dealer must purchase the bond(s) from a member, obtaining only a dealer concession, which is less than the full selling concession. In our example, the outside dealer concession was $2.50 per bond out of a total selling concession of $5.00.

In a negotiated offering, the underwriters begin to line up prospective buyers before the actual offering date. A preliminary prospectus stating certain facts about the issue and the company is printed and given to interested investors. At this time, a price has not been established for the securities; the prospectus is known as a "red herring" because it contains, printed in red, a statement to the effect that a registration statement has been filed with the Securities and Exchange Commission but has not as yet been approved. Upon approval of the registration, the offering price to the public is established, and a final prospectus is printed. At that time, security salesmen seek orders from investors. If the issue is priced fairly, it will be sold within a matter of a day or two or, perhaps even within a few hours. Sometimes "hot" issues are sold out in advance to preorder subscribers. Upon the sale of all the securities, the underwriting syndicate is dissolved.

Advising

In a negotiated offering, such as our example, the originating house is able to advise the company on a wide variety of matters pertinent to the success of the offering. For a company that makes infrequent trips to the capital markets, this advice can be valuable, for the matters considered include the timing of the issue, its pricing, and features that are desirable to assure a successful sale. Because of his expertise and experience in the market, the investment banker is able to recommend the best package of terms for the particular issue under consideration. When the sale of securities is by competitive bid, the issuer does not receive the benefit of this advice because the underwriter enters the picture only after the bid is accepted and the price determined. Advice from investment bankers may be of a continuing nature, with the company consulting a certain investment banker or a group of bankers regularly.

Pricing the Issue

In a negotiated offering, the issuing company and the investment banker determine the price. The investment banker would like to see a price low enough to assure a successful sale, but he is aware that if the price is too low, the issuing company will be dissatisfied. An investment banker can ill afford dissatisfied customers, for news of such dissatisfaction spreads quickly in the financial community. Moreover, the issuing company must agree to the price recommended by the underwriter. Otherwise, of course, there can be no offering.

In the case of bonds, the issue will be priced in relation to the price of other new issues of the same grade. For example, if the bond being issued were rated Baa, comparisons would be made with other Baa new issues. The underwriter and the issuing company must assess the tone of the market with respect to expectations as to future interest rates. In addition to recent interest rate movements in the money and capital markets, they consider the forthcoming supply of new issues, the expected future of the economy, and expectations as to monetary and fiscal policy. Typically, a new issue will have to be sold at a lower price and higher yield to maturity than a seasoned issue of the same maturity and grade. In a competitive bidding situation, the syndicate will consider these same factors in determining the bid it will submit.[10] The syndicate wants to submit a bid high enough to win the issue but low enough to be able to sell the issue to investors. For the negotiated issue, the underwriter wants a price that is high enough to satisfy the issuer but low enough to make the probability of a successful sale to investors reasonably high.

For a common-stock issue, the problem of pricing is perhaps more difficult because of the greater volatility of the stock market. When a company already has stock outstanding that is held by the public, the principal factor that governs the price of any new issue is the market price of the existing stock. The new issue will need to be underpriced in order to sell, however. The degree of underpricing will depend upon the volatility of the stock and the tone of the market. When it becomes known in the marketplace that a company is going to offer new stock, downward pressure usually is exerted on the market price of the outstanding stock. Pressure usually develops on the day the new issue is announced, or before, if rumors of the new issue are out. This pressure contributes to the problem of underpricing

---

[10]See Ernest Bloch, "Pricing a Corporate Bond Issue: A Look Behind the Scenes," *Essays in Money and Credit*, Federal Reserve Bank of New York, December 1964, pp. 72–76.

the issue. With a negotiated offering where stock already is held by the public, the price usually is not established until the night before the offering.

If a company is issuing stock to the public for the first time, the pricing problem is much more difficult because there is no current market price to serve as a benchmark. For privately held companies that are going public, a comparison with similar companies usually is made to determine the appropriate price/earnings ratio. For this comparison, regression studies and other types of statistical analyses may be helpful. However, some companies may be so specialized that comparison with other companies is very difficult. The pricing of these issues is usually resolved by consideration of such essentials as present earnings, the growth rate, the volatility of earnings, and the company's underlying risk to investors.[11]

It is important to recognize that there exists a tradeoff between the price per share to the public and the underwriting spread. The higher the price, the greater the risk that the investment banker will be unable to sell the entire issue or that the distribution period will be prolonged. As a result of this greater risk, greater compensation is needed in the form of the spread between the price paid to the company and the reoffering price to the public.[12] The important thing to the company, of course, is the net price it is paid by the underwriter. In addition to this factor, it has been found that the underwriter spread varies inversely with the number of bidders and with the size of the issue. The first relationship is attributable to increased competition, while the second is due to economies of scale in underwriting.[13]

Flotation Costs The flotation costs of a new issue of securities tend to vary with the size and the type of the issue. These costs include the underwriting spread, registration expenses, and other out-of-pocket expenses. In general, the larger the issue, the lower the cost of flotation as a percentage of gross proceeds. Because certain company expenses—printing and legal fees in particular—essentially are fixed, the larger the issue, the lower their percentage cost. The underwriter also has certain "fixed" expenses. Thus the larger the issue, the smaller the underwriting expense percentagewise. Additionally and more importantly, there usually is an inverse relationship between the size of an issue and the quality of the issuing company. Also, the relative cost of flotation tends to be highest for a common-stock issue and lowest for a debt issue—a fact not surprising in view of the differences in underwriting risk.[14]

---

[11]For an analysis of the price performance and return to investors on new issues of common stock, see J. G. McDonald and A. K. Fisher, "New-Issue Stock Price Behavior," *Journal of Finance,* 27 (March 1972), 97–102.

[12]For an empirical investigation of this tradeoff with respect to unseasoned issues of common stock, see Dennis E. Logue and John R. Lindvall, "The Behavior of Investment Bankers: An Econometric Investigation," *Journal of Finance,* 29 (March 1974), 203–15.

[13]For a theoretical investigation of the relationship between underwriter uncertainty in bidding for an issue, the offer price, and the underwriter spread, as well as an empirical test of the interrelationship, see Ederington, "Uncertainty, Competition, and Costs."

[14]Johnson, Morton, and Findlay, "An Empirical Analysis of the Flotation Cost of Corporate Securities," used a large sample of corporate bond and common-stock issues during the

Both the federal and state governments regulate the sale of new securities to the public. A company issuing securities must comply with these regulations. Of the two regulatory bodies, the federal authority is far more encompassing in its influence.

Federal Regulation   With the collapse of the stock market in 1929 and the subsequent Depression, there came a cry for the protection of investors from misinformation and fraud. Congress undertook extensive investigations and, in the end, proposed federal regulation of the securities industry. The Securities Act of 1933 dealt with the sale of new securities and required the full disclosure of information to investors. The Securities Exchange Act of 1934 dealt with the regulation of securities already outstanding. Moreover, it created the Securities and Exchange Commission to enforce the two acts.

Most corporations selling securities to the public must register the issue with the SEC. Certain types of corporations, such as railroads, are exempt because they are regulated by other authorities. In addition, a corporation selling less than $500,000 in new securities is required to file only a limited amount of information with the SEC. Also, if the issue is entirely sold to citizens of a single state, it does not necessarily fall under the SEC. Other corporations, however, must file a detailed registration statement, which contains such information as the nature and history of the company, the use of the proceeds of the security issue, financial statements, the management and directors and their security holdings, competitive conditions and risks, legal opinions, and a description of the security being issued. Along with the registration statement, the corporation must file a copy of the *prospectus,* which is a summary of the essential information in the registration statement. As mentioned previously, this prospectus is known as a "red herring" because it has not yet been approved by the SEC. The prospectus must be available to prospective investors and others who request it.

The SEC reviews the registration statement and the prospectus to see that all the required information is presented and that it is not misleading. If the SEC is satisfied with the information, it approves the registration, and the company then is able to sell the securities. If not, it issues a *stop order,* which prevents the sale of the securities. Most deficiencies can be corrected by the company, and approval will usually be given eventually, except in cases of fraud or misrepresentation. For serious violations of the 1933 Securities Act, the SEC is empowered to go to court and seek an injunction. It should be

---

years 1971 and 1972 to test certain explanatory variables. With flotation costs as the dependent variable, they found that the size of the issuer was the most significant variable in both cases (the larger the issuer, the lower the flotation costs percentagewise). For bond issues, other significant variables were a surrogate for seasoning, a risk surrogate, whether or not warrants were attached, and variables for the type of offering (direct placement, underwriting, or best efforts). For stock issues, other significant variables were the type of offering (underwriting or rights offering), and variables reflecting seasoning.

pointed out that the SEC is not concerned with the investment value of the securities being issued, only with the presentation of complete and accurate information. The investor must make his own decision based upon that information. The security being issued may well be a highly speculative one subject to considerable risk. As long as the information is correct, the SEC will not prevent its sale.

The minimum period required between the time a registration statement is filed and the time it becomes effective is twenty days, sometimes known as a "cooling-off" period. During this time, investors can evaluate the information in the prospectus and reach a decision. The usual time lapse, however, is longer, around forty days.

The SEC regulates the sale of securities in the secondary markets in addition to the sale of new issues. In this regard, it regulates the activities of the security exchanges, the over-the-counter market, investment bankers and brokers, the National Association of Security Dealers, and investment companies. In its regulatory capacity, the SEC seeks to prevent manipulative practices by investment dealers and by officers and directors of the company, abuses by insiders (officers and directors) in transactions involving the company's stock, fraud by any party, and other abuses affecting the investing public.

State Regulation   Individual states have security commissions that regulate the issuance of new securities in their states. Like the SEC, these commissions seek to prevent the fraudulent sale of securities. The laws providing for state regulation of securities are known as "blue-sky" laws, because they attempt to prevent the false promotion and sale of securities representing nothing more than "blue sky." State regulations are particularly important when a security issue is sold entirely to people within the state and is not subject to SEC scrutiny. In addition, it can be important when the amount of the issue is less than $500,000 and subject to only limited SEC scrutiny. Unfortunately, the laws of the individual states vary greatly in their effectiveness. Some states are strict, but others are fairly permissive, with the result that misrepresentative promotion can thrive.

INSTITUTIONAL ASPECTS OF COMMON STOCK

The common stockholders of a corporation are its residual owners; collectively, they own the company and assume the ultimate risk associated with ownership. Their liability, however, is restricted to the amount of their investment. In the event of liquidation, these stockholders have a residual claim on the assets of the company after the claims of all creditors and preferred stockholders are settled in full. Common stock, like preferred stock, has no maturity date, and a stockholder can liquidate his investment by selling his stock in the secondary market.

Features of Common Stock

Authorized, Issued, and Outstanding Shares   The corporate charter of a company specifies the number of *authorized* shares of common stock, the maximum that the company can issue without amending its charter. Although amending the charter is not a difficult procedure, it does require the approval of existing stockholders, which takes time. For this reason, a company usually likes to have a certain number of shares that are authorized but unissued. These unissued shares allow flexibility in granting stock options, pursuing mergers, and splitting the stock. When authorized shares of common stock are sold, they become *issued* stock. *Outstanding* stock is the number of shares issued that actually are held by the public; the corporation can buy back part of its issued stock and hold it as *Treasury* stock.

Par Value   A share of common stock can be authorized either with or without par value. The par value of a stock is merely a stated figure in the corporate charter and is of little economic significance. However, a company should not issue stock at a price less than par value, because stockholders are liable to creditors for the difference between the price they paid and the par value. Consequently, the par values of most stocks are set at fairly low figures relative to their market values. Suppose a company sold 10,000 shares of new common stock at $45 a share and that the par value of the stock was $5 per share. The equity portion of the balance sheet would be:

Common stock ($5 par value)	$ 50,000
Capital surplus	400,000
Net worth	$450,000

Stock can be authorized without par value, in which case the stock is carried on the books at the market price at which it is sold or at some stated value. The difference between the issuing price and the stated value is reflected as capital surplus.

Book Value and Liquidating Value   The book value of a share of stock is the net worth of a corporation less the par value of preferred stock outstanding, divided by the number of shares outstanding. Suppose the equity portion of the balance sheet of a company is as follows:

Preferred stock ($100 par value)	$10,000,000
Common stock ($5 par value)	5,000,000
Capital surplus	10,000,000
Retained earnings	16,000,000
Net worth	$41,000,000

The book value of a share of common stock is $31 million/1 million shares = $31 per share. Theoretically, the book value of a share of stock should correspond to the liquidating value of the company, but this situation seldom occurs. Only if the assets of a corporation can be liquidated for the book values shown on the financial statement will book value per share correspond to the liquidating value per share. Even then, if liquidating costs are high, the liquidating value per share will be less than book value per share. For most companies, the liquidating value per share is less than book value per share because many of the assets can be liquidated only at distress prices. However, some companies carry certain assets—notably, land and mineral rights—at modest values on their books relative to the market value of the asset. For these companies, the liquidating value per share may be significantly higher than the book value. Sometimes investors calculate the net working capital per share in order to obtain a more conservative estimate of the possible liquidating value of a company.

Rights of Stockholders

Right to Income   Common stockholders are entitled to share in the earnings of the company only if cash dividends are paid. Stockholders prosper from the market value appreciation of their stock, but they are entirely dependent upon the board of directors for the declaration of dividends that give them income from the company. Thus we see that the position of a common stockholder differs markedly from that of a creditor. If the company fails to pay contractural interest and principal payments to creditors, the creditors are able to take legal action to assure that payment is made or the company is liquidated. Stockholders, on the other hand, have no legal recourse to a company for not distributing profits. Only if management, the board of directors, or both are engaged in fraud may they take their case to court and, possibly, force the company to pay dividends.

Voting Power   Inasmuch as the common stockholders of a company are its owners, they are entitled to elect a board of directors. In a large corporation, stockholders usually exercise only indirect control through the board of directors they elect. The board, in turn, selects the management; and management actually controls the operations of the company. With a proprietorship, partnership, or small corporation, the owners usually control the operations of the business directly. With a large corporation, however, there may be times when the goals of management differ from those of the common stockholders. The only recourse of a stockholder to management is through the board of directors.

Because common stockholders often are widely dispersed geographically and, therefore, disorganized, management can often exercise effective control of a large corporation if it controls only a small percentage of the stock outstanding. By proposing a slate of directors that is favorable to its own interests, management is able to maintain control. An outside stockholder, however, does have the right to expect that the directors will administer the affairs of the corporation properly in his behalf. If the directors act in a manner that results in personal gain, a stockholder can sue to recover. These suits are known as *derivative suits*. However, derivative suits are infrequent, partly because many states require that the stockholder bear the legal expenses of the corporation if he loses the suit. Thes laws were instigated to prevent stockholders from undertaking derivative suits at the least provocation.

Proxies   Each common stockholder is entitled to one vote for each share of stock he owns. Because most stockholders do not attend the annual meeting, they may vote by proxy. A proxy is simply a form by which the stockholder assigns his right to vote to another person or persons. The SEC regulates the solicitation of proxies and also requires companies to disseminate information to its stockholders through proxy mailings. Prior to the annual meeting, management solicits proxies from stockholders to vote for the recommended slate of directors and for any other proposals requiring stockholder approval. If stockholders are satisfied with the company, they generally sign the proxy in favor of management, giving written authorization to management to vote their shares. If a stockholder does not vote his shares, the number of shares voted at the meeting and the number needed to constitute a majority are lower. Because of the proxy system and the fact that management is able to mail information to stockholders at the company's expense, management has a distinct advantage in the voting process. As a result, it usually is able to perpetuate existing practices if it so chooses.

However, outsiders can seize control of a company through a proxy contest. Obviously, outsiders would not attempt a takeover if management controlled a large percentage of shares outstanding. When an outside group undertakes a proxy raid, it is required to register its proxy statement with the Securities and Exchange Commission to prevent the presentation of misleading or false information. The outside group attempts to persuade stockholders to sign a proxy giving them the authority to vote the stockholders' shares.

In a proxy contest, the odds favor existing management to win the contest. It has both the organization and the use of the company's resources to carry on the proxy fight. Insurgents are likely to be successful only when the earnings performance of the company has been bad and management obviously ineffective. The lower the rate of return, profit margins, dividend payout, and percentage of stock owned by management, the greater the probability of success for the insurgents.[15] In recent years, proxy contests have been relatively infrequent. To a certain extent, they have been replaced by tender offer takeover bids, a topic considered in Chapter 23.

Voting Procedures   Depending upon the corporate charter, the board of directors is elected either under a *majority voting system* or under a

---

[15]See Richard M. Duvall and Douglas V. Austin, "Predicting the Results of Proxy Contests," *Journal of Finance*, 20 (September 1965), 464–71. They use discriminant analysis with the four variables mentioned above to predict the results.

cumulative voting system. Under the former system, each stockholder has one vote for each share of stock he owns, and he must vote for each director position that is open. For example, if a stockholder owns 100 shares, he will be able to cast 100 votes for each director's position open. Because each person seeking a position on the board must win a majority of the total votes cast for that position, the system precludes minority interests from electing directors. If management can obtain proxies for over 50 percent of the shares voted, it can select the entire board.

Under a cumulative voting system, a stockholder is able to accumulate his votes and cast them for less than the total number of directors being elected. His total number of votes is the number of shares he owns times the number of directors being elected. For example, if a stockholder owns 100 shares, and twelve directors are to be elected, he will be entitled to cast 1,200 votes. He can cast these votes for whatever number of directors he chooses, the maximum being 1,200 votes for one director.

A cumulative voting system, in contrast to the majority system, permits minority interests to elect a certain number of directors. The minimum number of shares necessary to elect a specific number of directors is determined by

$$\frac{\text{Total shares outstanding times specific number of directors sought}}{\text{Total number of directors to be elected plus one}} + 1 \quad \text{(20-1)}$$

For example, if there are 3 million shares outstanding, the total number of directors to be elected is fourteen, and if a minority group wishes to elect two directors, it will need at least the following number of shares:

$$\frac{3,000,000 \times 2}{14 + 1} + 1 = 400,001$$

As is evident, cumulative voting gives minority interests a better opportunity to be represented on the board of directors of a corporation. Because the system is more democratic, a number of states require that companies in the state elect directors in this way. Even with cumulative voting, however, management sometimes can preclude minority interests from obtaining a seat on the board of directors by reducing the number of directors. For example, suppose the minority group above actually owns 400,001 shares. With fourteen directors to be elected, the group can elect two directors. However, if the board is reduced to six members, the minority group can elect no directors because the minimum number of shares needed to elect a single director is

$$\frac{3,000,000 \times 1}{6 + 1} + 1 = 428,572$$

Another method used to thwart a minority interest from obtaining representation is to stagger the terms of the directors so that only a portion is elected each year. For example, if a firm had twelve directors and the term was four years, only three would be elected each year. As a result, a minority group would need considerably more shares voted in its favor to elect a director than it would if all twelve directors came up for election each year.

Right to Examine Books A stockholder is legally entitled to inspect the books and records of a corporation. However, this access is limited, for most corporations feel that the audited financial statement is sufficient to satisfy the requirement. To obtain more specific information, the stockholder may have to take his case to court in order to prove the necessity for obtaining this information. Stockholders are also entitled to a list of the stockholders of the corporation and their addresses. This list is vital to an insurgent group in a proxy contest. However, management may engage in delaying tactics by contending that the stockholder list will be misused. In these situations, the stockholder may have to go to court and demonstrate sufficient cause for obtaining the information. Upon a court order, management is required to provide the list.

Classified Common Stock

A company may have more than one class of common stock. Its common stock can be classified with respect to the claim on income and as to voting power. For example, the Class A common of a company may have no voting privilege but may be entitled to a prior claim to dividends, while the Class B common has voting rights but a lower claim to dividends. Usually, the promoters of a corporation and its management will hold the Class B common stock, whereas the Class A common is sold to the public. Actually, the Class A shares in this example are no more than a form of preferred stock. However, the Class A stock usually is given some voting power, but not as much as the Class B stock per dollar of investment. One incentive is that the New York Stock Exchange will not list a nonvoting stock, and other exchanges will do so only with reluctance.

Suppose, for example, that the Class A and Class B common stockholders of a company are entitled to one vote per share, but that the Class A stock is issued at an initial price of $20 a share. If $2 million is raised in the original offering through the issuance of 80,000 shares of Class A common for $1.6 million and 200,000 shares of Class B common for $400,000, the Class B stockholders will have over twice the number of votes as the Class A holders, despite the fact that their original investment is only one quarter as large. Thus the Class B holders have effective control of the company. Indeed, this is the purpose of classified stock.

For this control, the Class B holders must be willing to give something up in order to make the Class A stock attractive to investors. Usually, they take a lower claim to dividends and a lower claim on assets. An appropriate balance must be struck between voting power and the claim to dividends and assets if the company is to bargain effectively for Class A equity funds.

Sometimes the Class B common simply is given to the promoters of a corporation without any cash investment on their part.

Ford Motor Company Example Perhaps the most famous example of a company with classified common stock is the Ford Motor Company. At December 31, 1977, the issued shares of capital stock for the company were:

	Shares Issued
Class B (voting)	14,639,759
Common stock (voting)	104,214,399
	118,854,158

The Class B stock is owned by members of the Ford family and constitutes 40 percent of the total voting power of the company. The common is held by the general public and has 60 percent of the voting power of the company. The common stock was originally owned by the Ford Foundation, but the stock has been sold to the general public. A holder of common stock of Ford is entitled to one vote for each share he owns. A holder of Class B common is entitled to that number of votes per share that will make the voting power of the Class B common 40 percent of the total voting power of the corporation. At December 31, 1977, this number was

$$\frac{104{,}214{,}399}{14{,}639{,}759} \times \frac{0.40}{0.60} = 4.75 \text{ votes}$$

Each shareholder of Class B stock was entitled to 4.75 votes per share at the end of 1977. Thus members of the Ford family retain substantial voting power in the company despite the fact that they hold far fewer shares than does the general public. All shares of common and Class B stock share equally in dividends and equally in their claim on assets in the event of liquidation.[16] The use of classified capital stock in this case affects only the voting power.

Venture Capital

Venture capital represents funds invested in a new enterprise. While debt funds sometimes are provided, for the most part common stock is involved. Almost always this stock is not registered for a period of years. Known as *letter stock,* the stock cannot be sold until the issue is registered. Therefore the investor has no liquidity for a period of time. His hope is that the company will thrive and that after five years or so it will be of sufficient size and profitability so that stock can be sold in the public market. In turn,

[16]*Annual Report,* Ford Motor Company, 1977 and *Prospectus* to Ford Motor Company Stock, November 20, 1963.

the venture capitalist hopes to be in a position to sell his stock for many times what he paid for it. While this is one scenario, other scenarios unfortunately are possible. The risks associated with a new venture are many and the frequency of failure high. With failure, the investor loses everything. The probability of possible returns for most venture capital investments is highly skewed to the right. That is, there is a fairly good chance that the investor will lose all his investment, but there also is some probability that his investment will increase in value ten or even fifty fold. The possibility of very substantial returns is what makes venture capital investments attractive.

However, the attractiveness to the venture capitalist, and hence the availability of venture capital, changes over time. In general, the relative availability of venture capital is closely tied to the tone of the stock market. When the market is buoyant and price/earnings ratios are high, venture capitalists are interested in making investments. The reason is that they can look to a viable and active stock market for ultimate payout. One could argue that it is not the present tone of the market but the expected tone several years hence that is important. However, expectations of future market conditions are heavily influenced by present market conditions. On the other hand, when the stock market is in the doldrums, venture capital funds tend to dry up.

Thus the 1960s were characterized by considerable interest in venture capital investments, particularly up to 1968. On average, interest was much lower in the 1970s. Even in the 1970s, however, it ebbed and flowed with changes in the stock market.

In general, new venture proposals in the high-technology area find a more receptive ear from the venture capitalist than does a new venture in a mundane industry. The reason is simple. In high technology, there is the perceived possibility of substantial growth and ultimate capital gains. Thus there are a number of venture capital firms in the Greater Boston and San Francisco areas, owing to the hotbed of electronic activities in these areas. In addition, however, there are a number of venture capitalists in New York, Chicago, and Dallas. Perhaps the most prominent venture capitalist in the post–World War II era was Laurence Rockefeller, who was actively involved in a number of young and ultimately successful companies.

The sources of venture capital are several. The traditional source, wealthy individuals, while still important is no longer the dominant source. Individuals make venture capital investments directly or indirectly. In a direct investment, the individual or partnership of individuals screens applicants, investigates the investment, and reaches a decision. With an indirect approach, the first step is undertaken by a finder or broker who presents situations and a certain amount of analysis to the investor. Institutional investors, such as pension funds, trusts, and life insurance companies, frequently have venture capital groups or divisions. The intent is to invest a certain portion of the overall portfolio, usually less than 5 percent, in new ventures. Some of these investors have local offices in areas of the country where high-technology companies are prevalent. Also, bank holding companies are a source of venture capital. In a number of instances, banks establish a small business investment company (SBIC) to engage in venture capital investing. The interest of banks in venture capital increased with the advent of the bank holding company concept where a number of nonbank financial services were placed under the holding company umbrella.

In summary, there are various sources of venture capital financing. In all cases, however, the enterprise seeking financing must provide the venture capitalist with the expectation of sizable returns to offset the substantial risks that are involved with any new venture. While not available to all new enterprises for this reason, venture capital can play an extremely important role in the financing of some companies.

SELLING COMMON STOCK THROUGH A PRIVILEGED SUBSCRIPTION

Instead of selling a security issue to the general public, many firms offer the securities first to existing shareholders on a privileged-subscription basis. Frequently, the corporate charter requires that a new issue of common stock or an issue of securities convertible into common be offered first to existing shareholders because of their preemptive right.

Preemptive Right

Under a preemptive right, an existing common stockholder has the right to preserve his proportionate ownership in the corporation. If the corporation issues additional common stock, he must be given the right to subscribe to the new stock so that he maintains his pro rata interest in the company. Suppose an individual owns 100 shares of a corporation and the company decides to increase by 10 percent the number of shares outstanding through a new common-stock offering. If the stockholder has a preemptive right, he must be given the option to buy ten additional shares so that he can preserve his proportionate ownership in the company. Various states differ with respect to laws regarding preemptive rights. However, the majority of the states provide that a stockholder has a preemptive right unless the corporate charter otherwise denies it.

Offering through Rights

When a company sells securities by privileged subscription, each stockholder is mailed one right for each share of stock he holds. With a common-stock offering, the rights give him the option to purchase additional shares according to the terms of the offering. The terms specify the number of rights required to subscribe for an additional share of stock, the subscription price per share, and the expiration date of the offering. The holder of rights has three choices: he can exercise them and subscribe for additional shares; he can sell them, because they are transferable; or he can simply do nothing and let them expire. The last usually occurs only if the value of a right is negligible and/or if the stockholder owns but a few shares of stock. Generally, the subscription period is about three weeks. If a stockholder wishes to by a share of additional stock but does not have the necessary number of rights, he may purchase additional rights. For example, suppose a person now owns eighty-five shares of stock in a company, and the number of rights required to purchase one additional share is ten. Given his eighty-five rights, he can purchase only eight full shares of stock. He can, however, buy the ninth share by purchasing an additional five rights.

In a rights offering, the board of directors establishes a date of record. Investors that buy the stock prior to that date receive the right to subscribe to the new issue. The stock is said to sell with *rights-on* through the date of record. After the date of record, the stock is said to sell *ex-rights*; that is, the stock is traded without the rights attached. An investor who buys the stock after this date does not receive the right to subscribe to additional stock.

financing externally and common stock

Value of Rights

The market value of a right is a function of the present market price of the stock, the subscription price, and the number of rights required to purchase an additional share of stock. The theoretical market value of one right after the offering is announced but while the stock is still selling rights-on is

$$R_o = \frac{P_o - S}{N + 1}$$

(20-2)

where R_o = market value of one right when stock is selling rights-on
  P_o = market value of a share of stock selling rights-on
  S = subscription price per share
  N = number of rights required to purchase one share of stock

For example, if the market price of a stock is $100 a share and the subscription price $90 a share, and it takes four rights to buy an additional share of stock, the theoretical value of a right when the stock is selling rights-on would be

$$R_o = \frac{100 - 90}{4 + 1} = \$2$$

(20-3)

We note that the market value of the stock with rights-on contains the value of one right.

When the stock goes ex-rights, the market price theoretically declines, for investors no longer receive the right to subscribe to additional shares. The theoretical value of one share of stock when it goes ex-rights is

$$P_x = \frac{(P_o \times N) + S}{N + 1}$$

(20-4)

where P_x = market price of stock when it goes ex-rights. For our example,

$$P_x = \frac{(100 \times 4) + 90}{4 + 1} = \$98 \qquad (20\text{-}5)$$

From this example we see that, theoretically, the right does not represent a thing of value to the stockholder. His stock is worth $100 before the date of record; after the date of record, it is worth $98 a share. The decline in market price is offset exactly by the value of the right. Thus, theoretically, the stockholder does not benefit from a rights offering; the right represents merely a return of capital. Another way to look at a rights offering is to equate it with a stock dividend to existing stockholders coupled with a new stock issue to which these stockholders have the first right to subscribe.[17] The fall in stock price caused by the right offering $P_o - P_x$, is the same as the fall in price caused by a stock dividend. In neither case does the stockholder receive a thing of value.

The theoretical value of a right when the stock sells ex-rights is

$$R_x = \frac{P_x - S}{N} \qquad (20\text{-}6)$$

where R_x = the market value of one right when the stock is selling ex-rights. If, in our example, the market price of the stock is $98 when it goes ex-rights,

$$R_x = \frac{98 - 90}{4} = \$2 \qquad (20\text{-}7)$$

or the same value as before.

It is important to recognize that the actual value of a right may differ somewhat from its theoretical value on account of transaction costs, speculation, and the irregular exercise and sale of rights over the subscription period. There is an old adage on Wall Street that says a stockholder should sell his rights early in the subscription period because at that time they have the maximum value. The high value, as the reasoning goes, is due to hesitation on the part of many stockholders either to exercise or to sell their rights in the early days of the subscription period. This hesitation is said to reflect a "wait and see" attitude. As a result, there is a shortage of rights early in the subscription period; and the market price of the right rises relative to its theoretical value. The opposite occurs near the end of the subscription period; stockholders are said to unload rights.

Although this behavior may seem logical enough, empirical studies have not revealed any distinct price pattern of rights over the subscription period.[18] One reason is that arbitrage limits the deviation of actual value from

---

[17]Haim Levy and Marshall Sarnat, "Risk, Dividend Policy, and the Optimal Pricing of a Rights Offering," *Journal of Money, Credit and Banking*, 3 (November 1971), 840–41. See also Simon M. Keane, "The Significance of the Issue Price in Rights Issues," *Journal of Business Finance*, 4, No. 3 (1972), 40.

[18]See Robert M. Soldofsky and Craig R. Johnson, "Rights Timing," *Financial Analysis Journal*, 23 (July-August 1967), 101–114.

theoretical value. If the price of a right is significantly higher than its theoretical value, stockholders will sell their rights and purchase the stock in the market. Such action will exert downward pressure on the market price of the right and upward pressure on its theoretical value. The latter occurs because of the upward pressure on the market price of the stock. If the price of the right is significantly lower than its theoretical value, arbitragers will buy the rights, exercise their option to buy stock, and then sell the stock in the market. This occurrence will exert upward pressure on the market price of the right and downward pressure on its theoretical value. These arbitrage actions will continue as long as they are profitable.

In the rights formulas presented, it is assumed implicitly that the relative earning power and risk complexion of the firm do not change as a result of the investment of funds raised in the offering. Implied also is that the firm's capital structure does not change—that is, it employs the same financing mix as before. If these conditions do not hold, the market price of the common stock may well behave in a manner out of keeping with its previously computed theoretical value.

The Success of the Offering

One of the most important aspects of a successful rights offering is the subscription price. If the market price of the stock should fall below the subscription price, stockholders obviously will not subscribe to the stock, for they can buy it in the market at a lower price. Consequently, a company will set the subscription price at a value lower than the current market price to reduce the risk of the market price's falling below it. We know that the stock should fall in price when it goes ex-rights. Its new theoretical value is determined by Eq. (20-4); and we see that it depends importantly upon N, the number of rights required to purchase one share of stock. The greater the N, the less the theoretical price decline when the stock goes ex-rights. Thus the risk that the market price will fall below the subscription price is inversely related to N.[19] To illustrate, suppose the following were true:

	Company A	Company B
Market value per share rights-on, P_o	$60.00	$60.00
Subscription price, S	$46.00	$46.00
Number of rights needed to purchase one share, N	1	10
Theoretical value of one share ex-rights, P_x	$53.00	$58.73

[19]See Levy and Sarnat, "Risk, Dividend Policy, and the Optimal Pricing of a Rights Offering," pp. 840–49.

We see that Company A will have a greater decline in value per share when its stock goes ex-rights than will Company B. All other things the same, there is a greater probability, or risk, that Company A's stock will fall below the subscription price of $46 than there is that Company B's stock will fall below it.

Amount of Discount   Apart from the number of rights required to purchase one share, the risk that the market price of a stock will fall below the subscription price is a function of the volatility of the company's stock, the tone of the market, expectations of earnings, and other factors. To avoid all risk, a company could set the subscription price so far below the market price that there is virtually no possibility that the market price will fall below it. The greater the discount from the current market price, the greater the value of the right, and the greater the probability of a successful sale of stock, all other things the same.[20] As long as the stockholder does not allow his rights to expire, theoretically he neither gains nor loses by the offering. Therefore it might seem feasible to set the subscription price at a substantial discount in order to assure a successful sale.

However, the greater the discount, the more shares that will have to be issued to raise a given amount of money, and the greater the dilution in earnings per share. This dilution may be a relevant consideration, for the investment community analyzes closely the growth trend in earnings per share. Significant underpricing of the new issue may excessively dampen the growth trend in earnings per share and result in a lower price/earnings ratio in the market. Although theoretically the stockholder should be equally well off regardless of the subscription price set, in practice the market value of his stock holdings may suffer if there is excessive dilution in reported earnings per share. Obviously this would be an imperfection in the market, but imperfections on occasion can be important.

Moreover, if the firm wishes to maintain the same dividend per share, underpricing, which results in more shares being issued, will increase the total amount of dividends the company will need to pay and lower its coverage ratio. The disadvantages of underpricing must be balanced against the risk of the market price's falling below the subscription price. The primary consideration in setting the subscription price is to reduce the probability of this occurrence to a tolerable level. If, then, the subscription price results in

---

[20]Peter W. Bacon, "The Subscription Price in Rights Offerings," *Financial Management,* 1 (Summer 1972), 59–64, in a test of rights offerings for the 1965–68 period, found at least some support for the notion that the relative size of the subscription discount influenced positively the success of the offering, as measured by the ratio of the number of shares subscribed for to the number of shares offered. In studying a large sample of rights offerings for Canadian companies over the 1956–74 period, Cecil R. Dipchand, "The Canadian Experience with Inherent Stock Splits of Rights Issues," *Financial Management,* 6 (Summer 1977), 34–41, found no statistically significant relationship between the size of the subscription discount and the success of the offering. However, he did find a significant relationship between discount size and the volatility of share price, as reflected by the stock's beta.

excessive dilution, the company should consider a public issue, wherein the amount of underpricing usually is less. For most rights offerings, the subscription price discount from the current market price ranges between 10 and 20 percent.

Other Factors   There are other factors that influence the success of a rights offering. The size of the capital outlay in relation to a stockholder's existing ownership of the stock is important. Stockholders are likely to be more willing to subscribe to an issue amounting to a 10 percent addition to the stock they now hold than to an issue amounting to a 50 percent addition. The mix of existing stockholders may also be a factor. If a substantial number of stockholders hold only a few shares, the success of the offering may be less than if most stockholders held units of 100 shares. The breakdown between institutional and individual investors may also bear upon the success of the rights offering. The current trend and tone of the stock market are extremely important. If the trend is upward and the market is relatively stable in this upward movement, the probability of a successful sale is quite high. The more uncertain the stock market, the greater the underpricing that will be necessary in order to sell the issue. In fact, there are times when the market is so unstable that an offering will have to be postponed.

Standby Arrangement and Oversubscriptions

A company can ensure the complete success of a rights offering by having an investment banker or a group of investment bankers "stand by" to underwrite the unsold portion of the issue. For this standby commitment, the underwriter charges a fee that varies with the risk involved in the offering. Often the fee consists of two parts: a flat fee, and an additional fee for each unsold share of stock that the underwriter has to buy. From the standpoint of the company issuing the stock, the greater the risk of an unsuccessful sale, the more desirable a standby arrangement, although it also is more costly.[21]

Another means of increasing the probability that the entire issue will be sold is through oversubscriptions. With this device, each stockholder is given not only the right to subscribe for his proportional share of the total offering but also the right to oversubscribe for any unsold shares. Oversubscriptions are then awarded on a *pro rata* basis relative to the number of unsold shares. For example, suppose a rights offering calls for 500,000 shares to be sold and that stockholders subscribe for 460,000 shares. However, certain subscribing stockholders wish to purchase more shares, and their oversubscriptions total 100,000 shares. As a result, each stockholder over-

---

[21]For an analysis of an underwriter's risk in a standby agreement, see Levy and Sarnat, "Risk, Dividend Policy, and the Optimal Pricing of a Rights Offering," pp. 842–45. For an excellent analysis of its use from the standpoint of the company, see Keane, "Significance of the Issue Price in Rights Issues," pp. 40–45.

subscribing is awarded four-tenths of a share for each share oversubscribed. This results in the entire issue being sold. Although the use of the oversubscription increases the chances that the issue will be entirely sold, it does not assure this occurrence as does the standby agreement. It is possible that the combination of subscriptions and oversubscriptions will fall short of the amount of stock the company desires to sell.

Privileged Subscription versus Public Issue

By offering stock first to existing stockholders, the company taps investors who are familiar with the operations of the company. As a result, a successful sale is probable. The principal sales tool is the discount from the current market price, whereas with a public issue, the major selling tool is the investment banking organization. When the issue is not underwritten with a standby arrangement, the flotation costs of a rights offering are lower than the costs of an offering to the general public. Therefore, there is less drain in the system from the standpoint of existing stockholders.[22] Moreover, many stockholders feel that they should be given the first opportunity to buy new common shares. Also, a public offering will tend to result in a wider distribution of shares which may be desirable to the company.

Offsetting these advantages to some degree may be the fact that a rights offering will have to be sold at a lower price than will an issue to the general public. If a company goes to the equity market with reasonable frequency, this means that there will be somewhat more dilution with rights offerings than there will be with public issues. While this consideration is not relevant theoretically, many companies wish to minimize dilution and will choose the public offering. To the extent that there are information, legal, and institutional imperfections that influence this choice, existing shareholder wealth may be enhanced by a decision to go the public issue route. Examples of imperfections include financial reporting that masks the "true" trend in earnings per share, restraints on a company issuing stock at below its book value, and possible institutional incentives for a company to sell stock at as high a price per share as possible. While these factors may have an effect on shareholder wealth, we would expect their effect to be slight. Still these factors may loom important in the minds of management and may favor a public issue.

---

[22]Clifford W. Smith, Jr., "Alternative Methods for Raising Capital," *Journal of Financial Economics*, 5 (November 1977), 273–307, analyzes empirically flotation costs for underwritings, rights offerings with standby arrangements, and pure rights offerings. He found that the total average cost as a percent of proceeds was slightly higher for the underwriting, 6.17 percent, than it was for the rights offering with a standby arrangement, 6.05 percent, and both were significantly higher than the cost for a pure rights offering, 2.45 percent. The differences were most dramatic for issues of $100 million or more where the total cost as a percent of proceeds was but 0.13 percent for the pure rights offering compared with approximately 4 percent for both the underwriting and the rights offering with a standby arrangement.

When companies finance their long-term needs externally, they may obtain funds from the capital markets. If the financing involves a public offering, the company usually will use the services of an investment banking firm. The investment banker's principal functions are risk-bearing, or underwriting, and selling the securities. For these functions, the investment banking firm is compensated by the spread between the price it pays for the securities and the price at which it resells the securities to investors. With a negotiated offering, the investment banker provides an additional service in advising the company as to the pricing and timing of the issue and as to procedures and features involved in the issue. With an offering on a competitive bid basis, the issue is sold to the investment banker or syndicate of investment bankers that submits the highest bid.

The common stockholders of a corporation are its owners. As such, they are entitled to share in the residual earnings of the company if cash dividends are paid. As owners, however, they have only a residual claim on assets in the event of liquidation. Common stockholders are also entitled to a voice in management through the board of directors they elect. These directors can be elected under a majority voting system or a cumulative voting system; the latter system allows minority interests to obtain representation on the board of directors. The use of different classes of common stock allows the promoters and management of a corporation to retain voting control without having to make a large capital contribution. An important source of common-stock financing for some high-technology companies is venture capital, which represents money invested in a new enterprise.

A company may give its existing stockholders the first opportunity to purchase a new security issue on a privileged-subscription basis. This type of issue is known as a rights offering, because existing stockholders receive one right for each share of stock they hold. A right represents an option to buy the new security at the subscription price, and it takes a specified number of rights to purchase the security. Depending upon the relationship between the current market price of the stock and the subscription price, a right usually will have a market value. Both security offerings to the general public and offerings on a privileged-subscription basis must comply with federal and state regulations. The enforcement agency for the federal government is the Securities and Exchange Commission, whose authority encompasses both the sale of new securities and the trading of existing securities in the secondary market.

PROBLEMS

1. Caldacci Copper Company needs to raise $75 million in long-term debt funds. The company is negotiating the offering through First Columbia Corporation. First Columbia believes it can bring together a syndicate of investment bankers

to underwrite and sell the issue. The bonds will be given a coupon rate so that they may be priced to the public at their face value of $1,000. The selling concession will be $6 per bond; in addition, administrative expenses of $115,000 will be incurred. Typically, First Columbia requires a managers' fee of 15 percent of the total spread. To sell this issue, it feels that the underwriting commission, net of expenses and management fees, must be 25 percent of the total spread.

(a) What will be the total spread? The total spread per bond?
(b) What will be the net proceeds of the issue to Caldacci Copper?
(c) What is the selling concession as a percentage of the total spread?
(d) What are the total costs of issuing the securities as a percentage of the net proceeds to the company?

2. At last year-end, the long term capitalization of Belgravia Furniture Company consisted of the following:

Long-term bonds, 9%	$ 3,400,000
Preferred stock, 8%, $50 par value	2,000,000
Common stock, $5 par value	1,000,000
Capital surplus	500,000
Retained earnings	4,000,000
	$10,900,000

During the current year, the company earned $2.5 million before interest and taxes. Its dividend payout rate with respect to profits after taxes was 40 percent, and the company's tax rate is 46 percent. At the current year-end, it issues 50,000 additional shares of common stock at a price to the public of $38 per share. The underwriters' spread is $3 a share. What is the long-term capitalization of the company at the current year-end?

3. The Homex Company wishes to raise $5 million in additional equity capital. After consideration is given to the potential difficulty of selling the shares, the investment banker decides that the selling concession should be between 3 percent and 4 percent of the value of the issue. When the risks of underwriting are evaluated, it is decided that the selling concession should constitute between 50 percent and 60 percent of the gross spread. If the management fee (which constitutes part of the underwriting profit) is taken to be 15 percent of the gross spread, answer the following questions:

(a) Assuming that the selling concession is set at 4 percent of gross proceeds and 50 percent of the gross spread, what would be the dollar value of the management fee, net underwriting profit, selling concession, and gross spread on the Homex underwriting?
(b) Rework (a), assuming that the selling concession were set at 3 percent of gross proceeds and 60 percent of the gross spread.
(c) Assuming that the managing underwriter underwrote 25 percent and sold 20 percent of the issue, what would be his total compensation under case (a) above? Under case (b)?

4. The Tabbot Corporation, a rather new and speculative concern, wishes to sell stock. Its investment banker, the First Salem Corporation, offers the following two alternatives:

(1) First Salem will make a firm underwriting of 1 million shares at $4.00 per share to the public, with a gross spread of 8 percent.

(2) First Salem will attempt, for a $200,000 fee, a best efforts distribution at $4.50 per share to the public, with a gross spread of 8 percent on those shares sold. First Salem expects sales at this price to have an approximately normal distribution, with a mean of 900,000 shares and a standard deviation of 100,000 shares.

  (a) What are the expected proceeds to Tabbot under each alternative?
  (b) What is the approximate probability that the best efforts distribution will yield more to Tabbot than the firm underwriting?

5. D. Sent, a disgruntled stockholder of the Zebec Corporation, desires representation on the board. The Zebec Corporation, which has ten directors, has 1 million shares outstanding.

  (a) How many shares would Sent have to control to be assured of one directorship under a majority voting system?
  (b) Recompute (a), assuming a cumulative voting system.
  (c) Recompute (a) and (b), assuming the number of directors was reduced to five.

6. Joe Miller has formed a company that can earn a 12 percent return after taxes, although no investment has yet been made. Joe plans to take $100,000 in $1 par value stock for his promotion efforts. All financing for the firm will be in stock, and all earnings will be paid in dividends.

  (a) Suppose that Joe desires to keep 50 percent control of the company after he has acquired new financing. He can do this by taking his stock in the form of $1 par value Class B, with two votes per share; while selling $1 par value Class A stock. However, the investors would require a dividend formula that would give them a 10 percent dividend return. How many Class A shares would be issued? What dividend formula would meet the investors' requirements? What dividend payment would be left for Joe's Class B shares?
  (b) Suppose that if Joe were willing to lose control of the company he could have just one class of common stock and sell the same amount to the public as he could Class A stock in (a) above. In such a case, the investors would only require an 8 percent rate of return. What would be the dividend formula and Joe's return in this case? Comparing this answer with that obtained in (a) above, what is Joe paying to retain control?
  (c) Rework (b) above under the assumption that the investors require a 9 percent dividend return. What must Joe do?

7. Two different companies are considering rights offerings. The current market price per share is $48 in both cases. In order to allow for fluctuations in market price, Company X wants to set a subscription price of $42 while Company Y feels a subscription price of $41.50 is in order. The number of rights necessary to purchase an additional share is 14 in the case of Company X and 4 in the case of Company Y.

  (a) Which company has the larger stock issue relatively? Is it the larger stock issue in absolute terms?
  (b) In which case is there less risk that the market price will fall below the subscription price?

8. The stock of the Dunbar Company is selling for $150 per share. If the company were to issue rights to subscribe for one additional share of stock, at $125 a share, for each nine held, compute the following:

   (a) The theoretical value of a right when the stock is selling rights-on
   (b) The theoretical value of one share of stock when it goes ex-rights
   (c) The theoretical value of a right when the stock sells ex-rights and the actual market price goes to $143 per share

9. The stock of the National Corporation is selling for $50 per share. The company then issues rights to subscribe to one new share at $40 for each five shares held.

   (a) What is the theoretical value of a right when the stock is selling rights-on?
   (b) What is the theoretical value of one share of stock when it goes ex-rights?
   (c) What is the theoretical value of a right when the stock sells ex-rights at $50?
   (d) Joe Speculator has $1,000 at the time National stock goes ex-rights at $50 per share. He feels that the price of the stock will rise to $60 by the time the rights expire. Compute his return on his $1,000 if he (1) buys National stock at $50, or (2) buys the rights at the price computed in (c) above assuming his price expectations are valid.

10. Instead of a rights offering, National Corporation (see problem 9) could undertake a public offering at $45 per share with a 6 percent gross spread. National currently has 1 million shares outstanding and earns $4 million a year. All earnings are paid in dividends. In either case, National would sell enough shares to raise $1 million, which would be invested at an after-tax return of 10 percent.

    (a) Compute the earnings per share, dividends per share, and market price of the stock (assuming a 12.5 P/E ratio) for (1) the rights offering and (2) the public offering alternatives.
    (b) Mr. Brown owns one share of National stock. On a rights offering, he will sell the right (assume for $2), thereby reducing his investment to $48. On a public offering, he would not buy any more shares. Compute Mr. Brown's earnings and dividend return on his investment and his price gain or loss on his investment under each of the two financing alternatives facing National.

SELECTED REFERENCES

BACON, PETER W., "The Subscription Price in Rights Offerings," *Financial Management* (Summer 1972), 59–64.

BEAR, ROBERT M., AND ANTHONY J. CURLEY, "Unseasoned Equity Financing," *Journal of Financial and Quantitative Analysis*, 10 (June 1975), 311–26.

BLOCH, ERNEST, "Pricing a Corporate Bond Issue: A Look behind the Scenes," *Essays in Money and Credit*, pp. 72–76. New York: Federal Reserve Bank of New York, 1964.

DIPCHAND, CECIL R., "The Canadian Experience with Inherent Stock Splits of Rights Issues," *Financial Management*, 6 (Summer 1977), 34–41.

DOUGALL, HERBERT E., AND JACK E. GAUMNITZ, *Capital Markets and Institutions.* Englewood Cliffs, N.J.: Prentice-Hall, 1975.

DUVALL, RICHARD M., AND DOUGLAS V. AUSTIN, "Predicting the Results of Proxy Contests," *Journal of Finance*, 20 (September 1965), 467–71.

EDERINGTON, LOUIS H., "Negotiated versus Competitive Underwritings of Corporate Bonds," *Journal of Finance*, 30 (September 1975), 1129–33.

——, "Uncertainty, Competition, and Costs in Corporate Bond Underwriting," *Journal of Financial Economics*, 2 (March 1975), 71–94.

EIBOTT, PETER, "Trends in the Value of Individual Stockholdings," *Journal of Business*, 47 (July 1974), 339–48.

EVANS, G. H., JR., "The Theoretical Value of a Stock Right," *Journal of Finance*, 10 (March 1955), 55–61.

FIRTH, MICHAEL, "The Information Content of Large Investment Holdings," *Journal of Finance*, 30 (December 1975), 1265–82.

HAYES, SAMUEL L., III, "Investment Banking: Power Structure in Flux," *Harvard Business Review*, 49 (March-April 1971), 136–52.

JOHNSON, KEITH B., T. GREGORY MORTON, AND M. CHAPMAN FINDLAY III, "An Empirical Analysis of the Flotation Cost of Corporate Securities 1971–1972," *Journal of Finance*, 30 (September 1975), 1129–33.

KEANE, SIMON M., "The Significance of the Issue Price in Rights Issues," *Journal of Business Finance*, 4, No. 3 (1972), 40–45.

LEVY, HAIM, AND MARSHALL SARNAT, "Risk, Dividend Policy, and the Optimal Pricing of a Rights Offering," *Journal of Money, Credit, and Banking*, 3 (November 1971), 840–49.

LOGUE, DENNIS E., "On the Pricing of Unseasoned Equity Issues: 1965–1969," *Journal of Financial and Quantitative Analysis*, 8 (January 1973), 91–104.

LOGUE, DENNIS E., AND ROBERT A. JARROW, "Negotiation vs. Competitive Bidding in the Sale of Securities by Public Utilities," *Financial Management*, 7 (Autumn 1978) 31–39.

LOGUE, DENNIS E., AND JOHN R. LINDVALL, "The Behavior of Investment Bankers: An Econometric Investigation," *Journal of Finance*, 29 (March 1974), 203–16.

McDONALD, J. G., AND A. K. FISHER, "New Issue Stock Price Behavior," *Journal of Finance*, 27 (March 1972), 97–102.

MANDELKER, GERSHON, AND ARTHUR RAVIV, "Investment Banking: An Economic Analysis of Optimal Underwriting Contracts," *Journal of Finance*, 32 (June 1977), 683–94.

MORRIS, JAMES R., "A Model for Corporate Debt Maturity Decisions," *Journal of Financial and Quantitative Analysis*, 11 (September 1976), 339–57.

NELSON, J. RUSSELL, "Price Effects in Rights Offerings," *Journal of Finance*, 20 (December 1965), 647–50.

PARKER, GEORGE G. C., AND DAVID COOPERMAN, "Competitive Bidding in the Underwriting of Public Utilities Securities," *Journal of Financial and Quantitative Analysis*, 5 (December 1978), 885–902.

SMITH, CLIFFORD W., JR., "Alternative Methods for Raising Capital," *Journal of Financial Economics*, 5 (November 1977), 273–307.

SOLDOFSKY, ROBERT M., "Classified Common Stock," *Business Lawyer* (April 1968), pp. 899–902.

SOLDOFSKY, ROBERT M., AND CRAIG R. JOHNSON, "Rights Timing," *Financial Analysts Journal*, 23 (July-August 1967), 101–4.

STOLL, HANS R., "The Pricing of Security Dealer Services: An Empirical Study of NASDAG Stocks," *Journal of Finance*, 33 (September 1978), 1153–72.

——, "The Supply of Dealer Services in Securities Markets," *Journal of Finance*, 33 (September 1978), 1133–52.

TALLMAN, GARY D., DAVID F. RUSH, AND RONALD W. MELICHER, "Competitive versus Negotiated Underwriting Costs for Regulated Industries," *Financial Management*, 3 (Summer 1974), 49–55.

THOMPSON, HOWARD E., "A Note on the Value of Rights in Estimating the Investor Capitalization Rate," *Journal of Finance*, 28 (March 1973), 157–60.

VAN HORNE, JAMES C., *Financial Market Rates and Flows*. Englewood Cliffs, N.J.: Prentice-Hall, 1978.

——, "Implied Fixed Costs in Long-Term Debt Issues," *Journal of Financial and Quantitative Analysis,* 8 (December 1973), 821–34.

——, "New Listings and Their Price Behavior," *Journal of Finance,* 25 (September 1970), 783–94.

WESTON, C. R., "Adjustment to Future Dividend Rates in the Prediction of Ex-Rights Prices," *Journal of Business Finance & Accounting,* 1 (Autumn 1974), 335–41.

WIESEN, JEREMY L., *Regulating Transactions in Securities.* St. Paul, Minn.: West Publishing, 1975.

YOUNG, ALAN, AND WAYNE MARSHALL, "Controlling Shareholder Servicing Costs," *Harvard Business Review,* 49 (January-February 1971), 71–78.

21

long-term debt and preferred stock

In Chapters 9 and 10, the theoretical aspects of fixed-income securities were analyzed in conjunction with the use of equity capital. Our discussion was framed in terms of fixed-income securities in general rather than in terms of specific types of instruments, as we considered the question of the optimal split between debt and equity. In this chapter, we examine the wide spectrum of long-term debt instruments available to the firm, consider certain conceptual and valuation issues associated with long-term debt, and evaluate the use of preferred-stock financing. From the standpoint of common stockholders, preferred stock represents a form of leverage and must be evaluated in much the same way as debt.

FEATURES OF DEBT

The holders of a company's long-term debt, of course, are creditors. Generally, they cannot exercise control over the company and do not have a voice in management. However, if the company violates any of the provisions of the debt contract, these holders may be able to exert some influence upon the direction of the company. In addition to not having voting power, holders of long-term debt do not participate in the residual earnings of the company; instead, their return is fixed. Also, a debt instrument has a specific maturity, whereas a share of common or preferred stock does not. In liquidation, the claim of debtholders is before that of preferred and common stockholders. Depending upon the nature of the debt instrument, however, there may be differences in the priority of claim among the various creditors of a company.

Some Definitions

The fixed return of a long-term debt instrument is denoted by the *coupon rate*. For example, an 8.5 percent debenture indicates that the issuer will pay the bondholder $85 per annum for every $1,000 face value bond he holds. The yield to maturity on a bond is determined by solving for the rate of discount that equates the present value of principal and interest payments with the current market price of the bond. (See the Appendix to Chapter 2 for the mathematics of bond interest.) The yield on a bond is the same as the internal rate of return for an investment project.

With a bond issue to the public, a qualified *trustee* is designated by the company to represent the interests of the bondholders. The obligations of a trustee are specified in the Trust Indenture Act of 1939, administered by the Securities and Exchange Commission. His responsibilities are: to authenticate the bond issue as to its legality at the time of issuance; to watch over the financial condition and behavior of the borrower to make sure all contractual obligations are carried out; and to initiate appropriate actions if the borrower does not meet any of these obligations. The trustee is compensated directly by the corporation; this compensation adds to the cost of borrowing.

The legal agreement between the corporation issuing the bonds and the trustee, who represents the bondholders, is defined in the *indenture*. The indenture contains the terms of the bond issue as well as the restrictions placed upon the company. These restrictions, known as *protective covenants*, are very similar to those contained in a term-loan agreement. Because we analyzed protective covenants in detail in Chapter 18, it is not necessary to describe these restrictions here. The terms contained in the indenture are established jointly by the borrower and the trustee. (If the issue is a negotiated underwriting, the underwriter also will be involved.) If the corporation defaults under any of the provisions of the indenture, the trustee, on behalf of the bondholders, can take action to correct the situation. If not satisfied, he then can call for the immediate payment of all outstanding bonds.

Retirement

The retirement of bonds may be accomplished in a number of ways. For example, bonds may be retired by payment at final maturity, by conversion if the bonds are convertible, by calling the bonds if there is a call feature, or by periodic repayment. Periodic repayment of the debt is possible if the bond issue is either a sinking-fund issue or a serial bond issue. Conversion is taken up in the next chapter, and the calling of bonds is examined later in this chapter. We turn now to a discussion of sinking-fund and serial bonds.

Sinking Funds   If a bond issue has a sinking fund, the corporation makes periodic sinking-fund payments to the trustee. In turn, the trustee uses these funds to purchase or redeem bonds and retire them. This operation generally is favorable to bondholders because it tends to support the market price of the bonds and assures the steady repayment of the issue. The trustee can retire bonds in two ways. He can purchase them in the open market. To prevent the purchase of bonds at too high a price, however, most sinking-fund bond issues provide for a *call price,* which enables the trustee to call the bonds for redemption. Usually, bonds are called on a lottery basis by their serial numbers, which are published in the *Wall Street Journal* and other papers. The trustee will purchase the bonds in the open market as long as the market price is less than the call price; when the market price exceeds the call price, he will call the bonds.

The amount of required sinking-fund payment may be either fixed or variable, depending upon the terms in the indenture. Under the former arrangement, the corporation makes fixed, equal periodic payments to the trustee. As the bonds are retired, the interest on the oustanding bonds becomes less and less. These fixed sinking-fund payments do not necessarily have to retire all the bonds by final maturity. For example, a $20 million, twenty-year bond issue might call for annual sinking-fund payments of only $500,000. Thus a $10 million "balloon" payment at final maturity would be required to retire the remaining bonds.

Variable periodic sinking-fund payments are those that are not equal in amount. These payments may be tied to the earnings of the corporation, so that the greater the earnings, the greater the sinking-fund payment. This type of arrangement obviously is appealing to a company and its stockholders. In periods of poor earnings, the company is not constrained by the need to make a fixed sinking-fund payment. Bondholders, of course, would prefer fixed payments, because these payments assure a steady reduction of the debt over time. If the borrower cannot meet these payments, he would be in clear default under the terms of the indenture. This default enables the trustee to take corrective actions. The amount of sinking-fund payment may vary also with the number of years to final maturity. For some bond issues, the amount of sinking-fund payment may increase over the years; for others, it may decrease. Variable sinking-fund payments are employed less often than are fixed payments.

Serial Bonds   All sinking-fund bonds in an issue mature on the same date, although specific bonds are retired before that date. Serial bonds, however, mature periodically until final maturity. For example, a $20 million issue of serial bonds might have $1 million of the bonds maturing each year for twenty years. With a serial bond issue, the investor is able to choose the maturity that best suits his needs. Thus a bond issue of this type appeals to a wider group of investors than an issue in which all the bonds have the same maturity.

TYPES OF DEBT FINANCING

Debentures

The term *debenture* usually applies to the unsecured bonds of a corporation; the investor looks to the earning power of the corporation as his security. Because these general credit bonds are not secured by specific property, in the event of liquidation the holder becomes a general creditor. Although the bonds are unsecured, debenture holders are protected by the restrictions imposed in the indenture. One of the more important of these restrictions is a negative pledge clause, which precludes the corporation from pledging its assets to other creditors. This provision safeguards the investor in that the borrower's assets will not be impaired in the future. Because debenture holders must look to the general credit of the borrower to meet principal and interest payments, only well-established and credit-worthy companies are able to issue debentures.

Subordinated Debentures

Subordinated debentures represent debt that ranks behind senior debt with respect to the claim on assets. In the event of liquidation, subordinated debenture holders would receive settlement only if all senior creditors were paid the full amount owed them. However, these holders still would rank ahead of preferred stockholders in the event of liquidation. The existence of subordinated debentures works to the advantage of senior holders, because these holders are able to assume the claims of the subordinated debenture holders. To illustrate, suppose a corporation is liquidated for $600,000 and that it had $400,000 in straight debentures outstanding, $400,000 in subordinated debentures outstanding, and $400,000 in obligations owed to general creditors. One might suppose that the straight debenture holders and the general creditors would have an equal and prior claim in liquidation—that is, each would receive $300,000. However, the straight debenture holders are entitled to the subordinated debenture holders' claims, giving them $800,000 in total claims. As a result, they are entitled to two-thirds of the liquidating value, or $400,000, whereas general creditors are entitled to only one-third, or $200,000.

Because subordinated debentures are subordinate to all existing and future debt, senior creditors regard them as equity when evaluating the financial condition of the company. In fact, subordinated debt usually is employed to increase the equity base and support further borrowing. Finance companies have made extensive use of this type of debt in their capital structures. The popularity of the instrument stems in part from the fact that interest payments are deductible for tax purposes, whereas dividends on preferred stock, the closest substitute method of financing, are not.

Because of the nature of the claim, a straight subordinated debenture issue has to provide a yield significantly higher than a regular debenture issue in order to be attractive to investors. Frequently, however, subordinated debentures are convertible into common stock and therefore may sell at a yield that actually is less than what the company would have to pay on an ordinary debenture. From the standpoint of a creditor, the equity base of the firm is the same whether the issue remains as subordinated debentures or is converted into common stock.

Mortgage Bonds

A mortgage bond issue is secured by a lien on specific assets of the corporation—usually fixed assets. The specific property securing the bonds is described in detail in the mortgage, which is the legal document giving the bondholder a lien on the property. As with other secured lending arrangements, the market value of the collateral should exceed the amount of the bond issue by a reasonable margin of safety. If the corporation defaults in any of the provisions of the bond indenture, the trustee, on behalf of the bondholders, has the power to foreclose. In a foreclosure, the trustee takes over the property and sells it, using the proceeds to pay the bonds. If the proceeds are less than the amount of the issue outstanding, the bondholders become general creditors for the residual amount.

A company may have more than one bond issue secured by the same property. For example, a bond issue may be secured by a *second mortgage*. In the event of foreclosure, the first-mortgage bondholders must be paid the full amount owed them before there can be any distribution to the second-mortgage bondholders. For the obvious reason of lack of appeal to investors, second-mortgage bonds seldom are used.

A mortgage may be either *closed-end* or *open-end*. When a mortgage is closed, additional bonds cannot be issued under that lien. In order to raise additional funds through mortgage bonds, the company must mortgage additional properties. The result is frequently a hodgepodge of mortgage bond issues outstanding. Under an open-end mortgage, however, the company can issue additional bonds under an existing lien. This arrangement allows the company to issue various series of bonds at different times under the same lien. In this respect, it gives the company considerable flexibility in its financing. In order to protect the position of the bondholders of earlier series, certain restrictions usually are imposed that limit the amount of additional debt. These restrictions include a maximum percentage on the amounts of bonds in relation to the value of the property securing these bonds and a minimum earning power of the company in relation to the bonds outstanding. Public utilities and railroads have used open-end mortgages rather extensively.

Some mortgage bond issues have an *after-acquired clause.* Under this clause, the lien covers acquisitions of property after the initial bond issue. The after-acquired clause affords investors additional protection, because any property acquired in the future is added to the lien. If the mortgage is open-end, which is almost always the case in this situation, the after-acquired clause does not restrict the company from additional mortgage financing. It merely assures existing bondholders that future bondholders will have no better claim on assets than they now do. It is important to recognize that even with a mortgage bond issue, investors look to the earning power of the corporation as the primary test of credit-worthiness.

Income Bonds

With an income bond, a company is obligated to pay interest only when it is earned. There may be a cumulative feature in the issue where unpaid interest in a particular year accumulates. If the company does generate earnings, it will have to pay the cumulative interest to the extent that earnings permit. However, the cumulative obligation usually is limited to no more than three years. As should be evident, this type of security offers the investor a rather weak promise of a fixed return. Nevertheless, the income bond is still senior to preferred and common stock as well as to any subordinated debt. Moreover, the interest payment is deductible for tax purposes, unlike preferred-stock dividends. Because income bonds are not popular with investors, they have been used principally in reorganizations.

Equipment Trust Certificates

Although equipment trust financing is a form of lease financing, the certificates themselves represent an intermediate- to long-term fixed-income investment. This method of financing is used by railroads to finance the acquisition of "rolling stock." Under this method, the railroad arranges with a trustee to purchase equipment from a railway equipment manufacturer. The railroad signs a contract with the manufacturer for the construction of specific equipment. When the equipment is delivered, equipment trust certificates are sold to investors. The proceeds of this sale, together with the down payment by the railroad, are used to pay the manufacturer for the equipment. Title to the equipment is held by the trustee, who in turn leases the equipment to the railroad. Lease payments are used by the trustee to pay a fixed return on the certificates outstanding—actually a dividend—and to retire a specified portion of the certificates at regular intervals. Upon the final lease payment by the railroad, the last of the certificates is retired, and title to the equipment passes to the railroad.

The duration of the lease varies according to the equipment involved, but fifteen years is rather common. Because rolling stock is essential to the operation of a railroad and it has a ready market value, equipment trust certificates enjoy a very high standing as fixed-income investments. As a result, railroads are able to acquire cars and locomotives on favorable financing terms. In addition to railroads, airlines use a form of equipment trust certificate to finance jet aircraft. Usually these certificates are sold to institutional investors; however, some issues are sold to the public.

Industrial Development and Pollution Control Bonds

With industrial development and pollution control bonds, a local government establishes an agency for a project. In the case of the former type of bond, the project usually is the construction of a plant—the local government endeavors to attract industry to the area and thereby increase employment. In the case of the latter type of bond, the project usually is the addition of pollution control equipment to an existing plant. For example, such equipment might be a "scrubber" for the smoke generated by an electric utility. If the project conforms to federal regulations, the agency is empowered to issue municipal securities whose interest is tax exempt to finance the project. The agency leases the plant and/or equipment to the corporation. The bonds issued are backed by the lease payments and, hence, by the credit-worthiness of the company involved. The bonds, however, are not backed by the general taxing power of the municipality.

The advantage of this arrangement to the company is that the borrowing rate is lower (because the bonds are tax exempt) than when the company borrows directly to finance the project. Most of the savings in borrowing costs are passed on to the company through lease payments which are lower than would otherwise be the case. Therefore the company enjoys lower financing costs than it would with direct financing. Despite this attraction, it should be noted that in recent years the U.S. Department of Treasury has taken steps to curtail sharply this type of financing. It is clear that the ultimate intention is to eliminate such financing altogether. It represents borrowing by corporations and not by municipalities, for whom the tax-exempt feature was intended.

Convertible Bonds

A convertible bond is one that may be converted at the option of the holder into a certain number of shares of common stock of the corporation. The number of shares into which the bond is convertible is specified in the bond, and these shares remain unissued until actual conversion. Because we consider convertible securities in depth in Chapter 22, they are not discussed at this time.

Project Financing

The term *project financing* is used to describe a variety of financing arrangements for large individual investment projects. Often a separate legal entity is formed which owns the project. Suppliers of capital then look to the earnings stream of the project for repayment of their loan or for the return on their equity investment. With the energy problems of recent years, there has come the need to finance not only large explorations of gas, oil, and coal but also tankers, port facilities, refineries, and pipelines. Other projects include alumina plants, fertilizer plants, and nuclear plants. These projects require huge amounts of capital, but such financing is often beyond the reach of a single company. Sometimes a consortium of companies is formed to finance the project. Part of the capital comes from equity participations by the companies, and the rest comes from lenders and/or lessors.

If the loan or lease is on a nonrecourse basis, the lender or lessor pays exclusive attention to the size of the equity participation and to the economic feasibility of the project. In other words, the lender or lessor can only look to the project for payout, so the larger the equity cushion and the greater the confidence that can be placed in the projections, the better the project. Sometimes the project's sponsors guarantee its completion, which simply assures the lendor or lessor that the project will be completely built. After its completion, however, the supplier of capital is on his own. Repayment must come from the project's earnings, so the economic feasibility of the project continues to be of major concern.[1] In still another type of arrangement, each sponsor may guarantee his share of the project's obligations. Under these circumstances, the lender or lessor places emphasis on the credit-worthiness of the sponsors as well as on the economic feasibility of the project.

For the sponsors of the project, there are several types of sharing rules. In a "take-or-pay" arrangement, each sponsor agrees to purchase a specific percentage of the output of the project and to pay that percentage of the operating costs of the project plus debt-servicing charges. When pipelines are involved, the type of sharing rule is frequently a "through put" arrangement. Here each sponsor is required to ship through the facility a certain amount, or percentage, of product. If the total shipped is insufficient to cover the expenses of running the facility, sponsors are assessed additional amounts to cover the shortfall. The amount of assessment is proportional to their participation. The maturity of the loan or lease corresponds to the likely ability of the project to generate cash over time. Although the financing need not be long-term, in most cases it extends over a period of eight or more years.

Actually, the term *project financing* conveys nothing more than the financing of a large project. The methods of financing are no different from those we have studied. They include debt and lease financing. What is different is the size and complexity of the financing. It is tailored to the needs of the sponsors as well as to the needs of potential suppliers of capital. Tax considerations become very important in tailoring the financing to the best advantage of all parties. In addition, certain environmental restrictions must be observed, and these influence the type of financing undertaken. When the project is located on foreign soil, political risks arise. These may be reduced

---

[1]For further discussion of these two kinds of arrangements, see Grover R. Castle, "Project Financing—Guidelines for the Commercial Banker," *Journal of Commercial Bank Lending,* 57 (April 1975), 14–30.

by guarantees from the Export-Import Bank or from some other government agency. Nonetheless, foreign projects are complicated by different laws and political risks than those that prevail for domestic projects.

As indicated earlier, project financing has become significant in recent years because of the need to finance large energy-related investments. Their size necessitates financing apart from the sponsoring company's main line of business. This is particularly true when several sponsors enter into a consortium in order to spread risk. The key, then, is that the project stands alone in the sense that the sponsoring companies are liable for no more than their equity participations. With the continuing energy needs and the large amounts of capital financing such needs require, project financing is likely to become increasingly important in the future.

FREQUENCY OF DEBT FINANCING

Once the firm has decided on an appropriate capital structure, its long-term debt requirements are determined by a forecast of its investment needs. Given these requirements over some interval of time, say three years, the question becomes, What is the optimal size and frequency of debt issues? For purposes of illustrating a method for determining the optimal size and frequency, assume for now that the amount of long-term debt required is known with certainty and that the use of these funds is steady over the interval involved. Assume further that the company wishes to go to the market with debt issues of the same size over this interval. The situation described is not unusual for such steady users of debt as public utilities. The idea is to determine the optimal size of debt issue, S, which in turn determines the frequency of financing. For example, if the total amount of debt financing required over the next three years were $60 million and the optimal value of S were found to be $15 million, the company would finance four times, or once every nine months. We turn now to a specific model for determining the optimal issue size.

An Issue Size Model

If interest rates over the interval y were not expected to change, the optimal debt issue size could be determined using the economic order quantity formula employed in inventory management.[2] The essential ingredients

---

[2] See Chapter 16. The model also is used in conjunction with cash management in Chapter 14. See James C. Van Horne, "Implied Fixed Costs in Long-Term Debt Issues," *Journal of Financial and Quantitative Analysis,* 8 (December 1973), 821–34, on which this section is based. See also Harold Bierman, Jr., "The Bond Issue Size Decision," *Journal of Financial and Quantitative Analysis,* 1 (December 1966), 1–14, for an additional application of the model to the problem at hand. Bierman modifies the basic approach outlined above to allow for bank borrowings. This allowance gives the firm the ability to finance funds gaps on a short-term basis.

of the model are the flotation costs and the carrying costs. The flotation costs of a debt issue usually include a fixed and a variable component. If the variable component is a constant percentage of the amount of funds raised, total flotation costs over the interval y can be expressed as

$$\text{Flotation costs} = \frac{FD}{S} + VD$$

(21-1)

where F is the fixed cost per issue of long-term debt, D is the total amount of funds raised during the interval y, D/S is the number of issues during the interval, and V is the variable cost of flotation per dollar of funds raised. Fixed costs include such things as executive and other time consumed in the offering, legal fees, accounting costs, registration costs, and printing costs; while variable costs pertain mainly to underwriting costs.

In addition to flotation costs, a carrying cost is involved. Because the use of funds is steady over the period, there are excess funds over parts of the period. Excess funds are assumed to be invested in short-term securities. The carrying cost can be thought of as the difference between the rate paid on the long-term debt and the rate the company is able to earn on the temporary investment of excess funds in short-term securities such as Treasury bills. We assume for now that interest rates on the two types of instruments are not only known but constant over the interval y.[3] Thus, total carrying costs for the interval are $(S/2)(L - B)$, where $S/2$ is the average investment in short-term securities, L is the rate of interest on long-term debt issues, and B is the rate of interest earned on Treasury bills. Both of these rates are expressed in terms of the interval of time involved.

Our objective is to minimize total costs over the interval y where these costs are depicted by

$$\Theta = \frac{FD}{S} + VD + \frac{S(L - B)}{2}$$

(21-2)

Differentiating this expression with respect to S and setting the derivative equal to zero, we obtain

$$S^* = \sqrt{\frac{2FD}{L - B}}$$

(21-3)

which is simply the economic lot-size formula. Given our assumptions, it tells us the issue size that minimizes total fixed and carrying costs over interval y.[4]

---

[3]This assumption is relaxed later in this section when we consider changing interest rates.

[4]Robert H. Litzenberger and David P. Rutenberg, "Size and Timing of Corporate Bond Flotations," *Journal of Financial and Quantitative Analysis,* 7 (January 1972), 1343–60, extend this basic model to consider situations in which the firm's annual demand for long-term debt funds is stochastic and stationary, deterministic and nonstationary, and stochastic and nonstationary. As a point of reference, demand in the above problem is assumed to be deterministic and stationary.

To illustrate its use, suppose that Bartlow Manufacturing Company
estimates that it will need $50 million in long-term debt funds over the next
three years, that the fixed component of flotation costs is $100,000, and that
the long-term interest rate on debt issued is 9 percent, while the rate on
short-term securities is 7 percent. $L - B$ then becomes $(.09 - .07)3$, or .06.
(It is necessary to convert annual rates to correspond to the 3-year interval.)
Given these factors, the optimal issue size is

$$S^* = \sqrt{\frac{(2)(100,000)(50,000,000)}{.06}} = \$12,909,270$$

With an optimal issue size of $12,909,270, the company should issue long-
term debt about every 9.3 months.[5]

Allowance for Changing Interest Rates

One obvious deficiency in the model outlined above is that interest
rates on long-term debt and short-term securities are assumed to be constant
throughout the interval. If interest rates are expected to change, both the
timing and the frequency of debt financing are affected. For example, suppose interest rates were expected to rise steadily over the interval. Under
these circumstances the firm should increase the size of debt issued currently,
all other things the same. On the other hand, if interest rates were expected
to fall, it should postpone the issue or decrease its size, all other things the
same. With a change in interest rates, not only is the interest cost of long-term
debt affected, but the relationship between the rate the company pays and
what it is able to earn on short-term securities (the carrying cost) may be
affected as well. Not to take account of expected changes in these two factors
is likely to result in a suboptimal decision.

Thus the firm should balance the fixed cost of issuing debt against
expectations of the future course of interest rates as well as against carrying
costs in deciding on the optimal size of debt issue. Because the rate of interest at which long-term debt is issued affects not only interest costs during
interval y but also interest costs through maturity, the relevant consideration
is the present value of all future interest payments.[6] (An appropriate discount
rate might be the average of the interest rates on the company's long-term
debt expected to prevail over interval y.)

The objective of the firm should be to minimize the sum of fixed
costs, carrying costs, and the present value of interest payments. This sum
is represented as

$$\Theta = \frac{FD}{S} + VD + \sum_{x=0}^{(D/S)-1} \left[\frac{C_x}{D/S} \right] \frac{S}{2} + \sum_{x=0}^{(D/S)-1} \left[\frac{P_x}{D/S} \right] S \qquad (21\text{-}4)$$

[5]This duration is determined by

$$36 \text{ months}/(50,000,000/12,909,270) = 9.3 \text{ months}$$

[6]We assume here that the issue is not called. Also assumed is that a debt issue is priced
at face value so that the coupon rate equals the rate of interest in the market.

where F = fixed cost per long-term debt issue

D = total demand for long-term debt funds during interval y

S = issue size

D/S = number of issues during interval y

$\dfrac{C_x}{D/S}$ = rate on long-term debt less rate on short-term investments expected to prevail $[x/(D/S)]$ [y years] in the future, expressed in terms of $[1 - x/(D/S)]$ [y years] to maturity

$\dfrac{P_x}{D/S}$ = present value of all future interest payments per \$1 of long-term debt issued $[x(D/S)]$ [y years] in the future, discounted to the time of issuance[7]

The reader may find the expression of carrying cost and present value of interest costs to be somewhat puzzling. In these expressions, we simply need to specify the time of issuance. If $D/S = 1$, for example, the firm would borrow only once during interval y—at the outset—and the third and fourth terms would become $(C_o)(S/2)$ and $(P_o)(S)$, respectively. If $D/S = 2$, the third term would become $(C_o)(S/2) + C_{1/2(y\ years)}(S/2)$, where $C_{1/2(y\ years)}$ is the carrying cost expected to prevail one-half the way through interval y. The fourth term would be $P_o(S) + P_{1/2(y\ years)}(Q)$. Similarly, the carrying cost and present value of ½ (y years) interest costs can be determined for other values of D/S. Thus the first term on the right in Eq. (21-4) represents fixed costs over the interval y, the second term variable flotation costs over the interval, the third term is total carrying costs over the interval, and the last term is the total present value of all expected future interest payments on debt issued during the interval. The objective, of course, is to minimize Θ.

Once expectations are introduced, the EOQ formula becomes very difficult to differentiate. Perhaps the best method for determining the optimal issue size is simply to set S in Eq. (21-4) equal to 1, 2, 3, 4, 5, . . . , n, solve for each of these S's and select the issue size that results in the minimum Θ. If expectations of future interest rates are stochastic, then $C_x/(D/S)$ and $P_x/(D/S)$ become stochastic and the problem can best be handled by simulation.

In summary, Eq. (21-4) provides a general framework by which the financial manager can approach the question of the optimal issue size for long-term debt. The model is meant not as a substitute for experience but as a supplement to such experience in guiding the financial manager in the debt issue size decision. In particular, it places in proper perspective the fixed cost of an issue and the fact that the funds raised may not be used immediately. The firm needs to balance the fixed cost of an issue against the carrying cost of holding excess liquidity and against expectations as to the future course of interest rates. Where the assumptions of the model are not appropriate, it can be modified to accommodate different assumptions as to the demand for

---

[7]We assume that the length of time to maturity is the same for all issues.

CALL PROVISION AND REFUNDING

Nearly all corporate bond issues provide for a call feature, which gives the corporation the option to buy back the bonds at a stated price before their maturity. The call price usually is above the par value of the bond and decreases over time. For example, a bond with twenty years to maturity might be callable at $105 ($1,050 per $1,000 face value bond) the next four years, $104 the following four years, and so on until the final four years, when it is callable at $101. Frequently, the call price in the first year is established at one year's interest above the face value of the bond. If the coupon rate is 8 percent, the initial call price may be $108 ($1,080 per $1,000 face value).

There are two types of call provision, according to when they can be exercised. Some issues state that the call privilege can be exercised immediately after issuance; with other issues, the call privilege is deferred for a period of time. The most widely used deferred call periods are five years for public utility bonds and ten years for industrial bonds. During this deferment period, the investor is protected from a call by the issuer. In recent years, virtually all issues of corporate bonds have involved a deferred call as opposed to an immediate call feature.

The call provision gives the company flexibility in its financing. If interest rates should decline significantly, it can call the bonds and refinance the issue at a lower interest cost. Thus the company does not have to wait until the final maturity to refinance. In addition, the provision may be advantageous to the company if it finds any of the protective covenants in the bond indenture to be unduly restrictive. By calling the bonds before maturity, the company can eliminate these restrictions. Of course, if the issue is refinanced with bonds, similar restrictions may be imposed.

Value of Call Privilege

Although the call privilege is beneficial to the issuing corporation, it works to the detriment of investors. If interest rates fall and the bond issue is called, they can invest in other bonds only at a sacrifice in yield to maturity. Consequently, the call privilege usually does not come free to the borrower. Its cost, or value, is measured at the time of issuance by the difference in yield on the callable bond and the yield that would be necessary if the security

---

[8]For a somewhat different approach to the problem, see James R. Morris, "A Model for Corporate Debt Maturity Decisions," *Journal of Financial and Quantitative Analysis,* 11 (September 1976), 339–57. Using a dynamic programming model, Morris balances expectations of the future course of interest rates against flotation costs to obtain an optimal maturity structure for a firm's debt and, hence, the optimal timing of debt issues.

were noncallable. This value is determined by supply and demand forces in the market for callable securities. In equilibrium, the value of the call feature will be just sufficient to bring the demand for callable securities by investors into balance with the supply of callable securities by borrowers. In the equilibrating process, both borrowers and investors are influenced by expectations as to the future course of interest rates.

When interest rates are high and expected to fall, the call feature is likely to have significant value. Investors are unwilling to invest in callable bonds unless such bonds yield more than bonds that are noncallable, all other things the same. In other words, they must be compensated for assuming the risk that the bonds might be called. On the other hand, borrowers are willing to pay a premium in yield for the call privilege in the belief that yields will fall and that it will be advantageous to refund the bonds. In equilibrium, both the marginal borrower and the marginal investor will be indifferent as to whether the bond issue is callable or noncallable.[9]

When interest rates are low and expected to rise, the call privilege may have a negligible value in that the company might pay the same yield if there were no call privilege. For the privilege to have value, interest rate expectations must be such that there is a possibility that the issue will be called. If interest rates are very low and not expected to fall further, there is little probability that the bonds will be called. The key factor is that the borrower has to be able to refund the issue at a profit. In order for him to do so, interest rates have to drop significantly; for the issuer must pay the call price, which is usually at a premium above par value, as well as the flotation costs involved in refinancing. If there is no probability that the borrower can refund the issue at a profit, the call privilege is unlikely to have a value.[10]

Empirical evidence with respect to the yield differential between immediate callable and deferred callable bonds suggests that the call privilege has the most value, and the most cost to the corporation when

---

[9]See Gordon Pye, "The Value of the Call Option on a Bond," *Journal of Political Economy,* 74 (April 1966), 200–203.

Jess B. Yawitz and William J. Marshall, "Why Firms Issue Callable Bonds: A Bias in the Tax Laws," *Journal of Finance,* forthcoming, maintain that taxes play a critical role in the equilibration process. When a bond is called, the call premium is treated as a capital gain from the standpoint of the investor, but as an expense to be deducted from ordinary income by the corporation. Since the former tax is less than the latter on average, Yawitz and Marshall contend that the total taxes paid by the investor and the corporation are less for a callable bond that is called than for a noncallable bond. The present value of the reduction in tax payments represents a net gain and is said to be shared between the investor and the corporation.

[10]Zvi Bodie and Robert A. Taggart, Jr., "Future Investment Opportunities and the Value of the Call Provision on a Bond," *Journal of Finance,* 33 (September 1978), 1187–1200, argue that the use of a call provision is more than a zero-sum game between the lender and the borrower based on interest-rate expectations. They maintain that the provision has an option value to stockholders. With future investment opportunities, the call provision allows the firm to re-negotiate its debt to reflect the value of an additional investment. Otherwise, debtholders would share in the benefits to the extent there is a chance that the firm will default in its debt obligation.

interest rates are high and are expected to fall.[11] By the same token, the call privilege has the greatest potential benefit to the corporation at these times. However, for this privilege, the corporation must pay a cost at the time the bonds are sold.

Valuation in an Option Pricing Context   The call feature, of course, represents an option to the corporation. Consequently, much of the thinking that went into our discussion of the option pricing theory in Chapter 4 applies here. However, rather than the variance of a common-stock's value determining the value of the option, in this case it is the variance of future interest rates. The greater the expected volatility of future interest rates, the greater the value of the call option. This principle stems from the fact that it is the variance of the value of the associated asset that determines the value of the option. From the standpoint of the company issuing the debt, it will want to have a call policy that minimizes the value of the bonds to the bondholders, thereby maximizing the value of the firm to its equityholders.[12] With such a call policy, the bond issue will be called when interest rates are low but will not be called when they are high.

This concept, which is essentially the same as that stated earlier, is illustrated in Figure 21-1. In the figure, we assume that the call option pertains only to a given future date. In other words, the option can be exercised at only

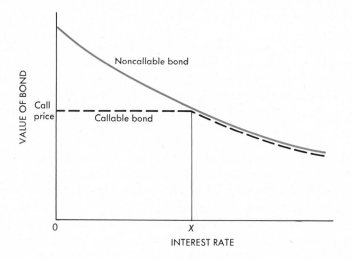

figure 21-1
Valuation of callable bond on the option date

[11]See references on Jen and Wert, Johnson and Klein, Kolodny, Pye, and Winn and Hess at the end of this chapter.

[12]For an analysis of the valuation of the call option under the assumption that interest rates follow a Gauss-Wiener process, see Michael J. Brennan and Eduardo S. Schwartz, "Savings Bonds, Retractable Bonds and Callable Bonds," *Journal of Financial Economics,* 5 (1977), 67–88. For an analysis of the call policy for a convertible security in an option pricing model context, see Jonathan Ingersoll, "An Examination of Corporate Call Policies on Convertible Securities," *Journal of Finance,* 32 (May 1977), 463–78.

one time, this being the option date. The value of the bond appears on the vertical axis, and the interest rate in the market on the horizontal axis. For a noncallable bond, value decreases at a decreasing rate as the interest rate increases. For a callable bond, however, value is constrained on the upside by the call price. This occurs for lower levels of interest rates—to the left of X on the horizontal axis. In this range, the difference between the value of a noncallable bond and the value of a callable bond represents the value of the option on the option date. If interest rates are such that the bond's value as a noncallable bond is less than the call price, the company obviously will not call the issue. As a result, the value of the callable bond is the same as that of a noncallable bond for interest rates higher than X on the horizontal axis. The key to valuation of the option is the likelihood that interest rates will be less than X on the horizontal axis on the option date. This, in turn, depends on the variance of the distribution of possible interest rates. The greater the variance, the greater the expected value of call option to the company.

In summary, we see that the principles of the option pricing theory apply to the valuation of the call feature. The greater the variance or uncertainty of future interest rates, the greater the value of the option to the corporation and, in efficient financial markets, the greater its cost to the company. We turn now to the question of refinancing an existing bond issue, given a call feature on the bond.

Refunding a Bond Issue

In this section, we analyze the profitability of a company refunding a bond issue before its maturity. By *refunding*, we mean calling the issue and replacing it with a new issue of bonds. In this regard, we focus our attention on only one reason for refunding—profitability, which, in turn, is due to interest rates having declined since the bonds were issued. However, there are other reasons that, on occasion, prompt companies to refund outstanding bonds. Sometimes a company will refund a bond issue simply to eliminate overly restrictive protective covenants in the bond indenture. This assumes, of course, that the protective covenants in the new bond indenture will be less onerous. Another reason, and usually an unfortunate one, is to show higher reported profits in an accounting sense. The difference between the purchase price of the old bonds and their book value is treated as income in the year in which the bonds are called.[13] For example, if a bond had a book value of $1,000 and interest rates rose so that it could be acquired in the market at a discount, say at $900, the reported income on the transaction would be $100. However, the bond needs to be replaced with one that bears a higher interest

---

[13]For an analysis of refunding bonds selling at a discount as well as at a premium, see Gene Laber, "Repurchases of Bonds through Tender Offers: Implications for Shareholder Wealth," *Financial Management*, 7 (Summer 1978), 7–13; and John Caks, "Corporate Debt Decisions: A New Analytical Framework," *Journal of Finance*, 33 (December 1978), 1297–1315.

rate. As a result, the present value of interest payments will be higher and the company generally will be worse off in an economic sense.[14] Presumably, the motivation is to "fool the market" in the short run at the expense of higher interest costs in the long run. However, it is doubtful that even in the short run the market is fooled. Therefore we will concentrate on the economic motivation for refunding.

A Refunding Example   The refunding decision can be regarded as a form of capital budgeting; there is an initial cash outlay followed by future interest savings. These savings are represented by the difference between the annual cash outflow required under the old bonds and the net cash outflow required on the new, or refunding, bonds. Calculating the initial cash outlay is more complex. Consequently, it is best to use an example to illustrate the method of evaluation.[15]

Suppose that a company currently has a $20 million, 8 percent debenture issue outstanding and that the issue still has twenty years to final maturity. In addition, assume that interest rates are significantly lower now than at the time of the original offering. As a result, the company can now sell a $20 million issue of twenty-year bonds at a coupon rate of 7 percent that will net it $19,600,000 after the underwriting spread.

For federal income tax purposes, the unamortized issuing expense of the old bonds, the call premium, and the unamortized discount of the old bonds, if they were sold at a discount, are deductible as expenses in the year of the refunding. Assume that the old bonds were sold originally at a slight discount from par value and that the unamortized portion now is $200,000. Moreover, the legal fees and other issuing expenses involved with the old bonds have an unamortized balance of $100,000. Finally, let us assume a call price on the old bonds of $105, issuing expenses on the new bonds of $150,000, a federal income tax rate of 50 percent, and a thirty-day period of overlap. The period of overlap is the lag between the time the new bonds are sold and the time the old bonds are called. This lag occurs because most companies wish to have the proceeds from the new issue on hand before they call the old issue. Otherwise, there is a certain amount of risk associated with calling the old issue and being at the mercy of the bond market in raising new funds. During the period of overlap, the company pays interest on both bond issues.

Framework for Analysis   With this rather involved background information in mind, we can calculate the initial cash outflow and the future cash benefits. The net cash outflow at the time of the refunding is as follows:

---

[14]A. J. Kalotay, "On the Advanced Refunding of Discounted Debt," *Financial Management,* 7 (Summer 1978), 14–18, shows that if there is essentially no tax obligation associated with the reported gain but income taxes otherwise are paid, refunding of discount debt may be profitable. However, very few situations are of this sort.

[15]This example draws upon Oswald D. Bowlin, "The Refunding Decision: Another Special Case in Capital Budgeting," *Journal of Finance,* 21 (March 1966), 55–68.

Cost of calling old bonds (call price $105)		$21,000,000
Net proceeds of new bond issue		19,600,000
Difference		$ 1,400,000
Expenses:		
Issuing expense of new bonds	$ 150,000	
Interest expense on old bonds during overlap period	133,333	283,333
Gross cash outlay		$ 1,683,333
Less tax savings:		
Interest expense on old bonds during overlap period	133,333	
Call premium	1,000,000	
Unamortized discount on old bonds	200,000	
Unamortized issuing expenses on old bonds	100,000	
Total	$1,433,333	
Tax savings (50% of amount above)		716,667
Net cash outflow		$ 966,666

The annual net cash benefits may be determined by calculating the difference between the net cash outflow required on the old bonds and the net cash outflow required on the new or refunding bonds. The annual net cash outflow on the old bonds is:

Interest expense 8%		$1,600,000
Less tax savings:		
Interest expense	$1,600,000	
Amortization of bond discount ($200,000/20)	10,000	
Amortization of issuing costs ($100,000/20)	5,000	
Total	$1,615,000	
Tax savings (50% of amount above)		807,500
Annual net cash outflow—old bonds		$ 792,500

The annual net cash outflow on the new bonds is:

Interest expense 7%		$1,400,000
Less tax savings:		
Interest expense	$1,400,000	
Amortization of bond discount ($400,000/20)	20,000	
Amortization of issuing costs ($150,000/20)	7,500	
Total	$1,427,500	
Tax savings (50% of amount above)		713,750
Annual net cash outflow—new bonds		$ 686,250
Difference between annual net cash outflows ($792,500 − $686,250)		$ 106,250

Discounting   Thus, for an initial net cash outflow of $966,666, the company can achieve annual net cash benefits of $106,250 over the next twenty years. Because the net cash benefits occur in the future, they must be discounted back to present value. But what discount rate should be used? Certain authors advocate the use of the cost of capital. However, a refunding operation differs from other investment proposals. Once the new bonds are sold, the net cash benefits are known with certainty. From the standpoint of the corporation, the refunding operation is essentially a riskless investment project. The only risks associated with the cash flows are that of the firm defaulting in the payment of principal or interest. Because a premium for default risk is embodied in the market rate of interest, most agree that the appropriate discount rate is the cost of debt.[16]

However, there is disagreement as to whether the before-tax or the after-tax cost should be used. Myron J. Gordon argues that the before-tax cost of debt is the appropriate discount rate, even though the cash flows are after-tax.[17] The logic of his position is that the opportunity cost of the funds employed in the refunding is that which investors in the company require. Since an investor can earn the before-tax rate by buying the refunding bonds directly. Gordon argues that this rate is the appropriate opportunity cost.

Aharon R. Ofer and Robert A. Taggart, Jr., show that this is true only if the net refunding outlay is financed with equity.[18] If additional bonds are issued to finance the refunding outlay, stockholders will realize additional tax savings through the corporation, and the relevant discount rate becomes the after-tax cost of the refunding bonds. If the after-tax cost of the refunding bonds in our example, 3.5 percent, is used as the discount rate under the assumption that the initial outlay of $966,666 is financed with the sale of additional bonds, the net-present value of the refunding operation is found to be $543,400. As this amount is positive, the refunding operation would be worthwhile.[19] If the before-tax cost of the new bonds of 7 percent is used as the discount rate, the net-present value is found to be $158,947. Again the refunding operation would be worthwhile.[20] However, the worth of the operation obviously is less.

---

[16]For a discussion of this issue, see Thomas H. Mayor and Kenneth G. McCoin, "The Rate of Discount in Bond Refunding," *Financial Management*, 3 (Autumn 1974), 54–58.

[17]"A General Solution to the Buy or Lease Decision: A Pedagogical Note," *Journal of Finance*, 29 (March 1974), 245–50.

[18]"Bond Refunding: A Clarifying Analysis," *Journal of Finance*, 32 (March 1977), 21–30. Ofer and Taggert also analyze the favorable effect of a refunding on the firm's debt capacity. They propose a means for analyzing the tax savings that result from the increase in debt capacity.

[19]We recall from Chapter 5 that the net-present value is the present value of net cash benefits less the initial cash outflow.

[20]For a study of the present values associated with actual bond refundings undertaken by public utilities, see A. M. Sibler, "Some Evidence on the Cash Flow Effects of Bond Refunding," *Financial Management*, 3 (Autumn 1974), 50–53.

Finally, two points should be raised with respect to the calculations in our example. First, most firms refund an existing issue with a new bond issue of a longer maturity. In our example, we assumed that the new bond issue has the same maturity as that of the old bond issue. The analysis needs to be modified somewhat when the maturity dates are different. The usual procedure is to consider only the net cash benefits up to the maturity of the old bonds. A second assumption in our example was that neither issue involved sinking-fund bonds or serial bonds. If either issue calls for periodic reduction of the debt, we must adjust our procedure for determining future net cash benefits.

An Alternative Approach

Another way to look at the bond refunding decision is to replicate the net cash outflows of the old bond issue and then determine the price at which the new bond would sell in the current market. If the new bond can be sold at a price in excess of the call price, bond refunding is favorable; whereas if below, it is not. If favorable, the firm will end up issuing new bonds with a higher present value than the call price of the old bonds. Since the stream of future net cash outflows is the same, the refunding action will transfer present value from creditors to equityholders.[21] Expressed differently, the firm's leverage, as depicted by the stream of debt-servicing outflows, remains the same but the firm exchanges one bond issue for another. In so doing, it receives cash for the difference between the sales price of the new bond and the call price of the old. Equityholders obviously are better off.

To illustrate, suppose a company currently has a $5 million, 10 percent debenture issue outstanding that has twenty-five years to maturity with a call price of $108. For simplicity, we assume that interest on the bonds is paid annually. In order to replicate the coupon and principal payment stream, the company must issue a bond with a coupon rate of 10 percent and a maturity of twenty-five years. Suppose that such an issue currently can be sold to the public at a yield to maturity of 8 percent. The present value of a 10 percent, $5 million issue yielding 8 percent to maturity in twenty-five years is determined by

$$x = \frac{\$500,000}{(1.08)} + \frac{\$500,000}{(1.08)^2} + \cdots + \frac{\$500,000}{(1.08)^{25}} + \frac{\$5,000,000}{(1.08)^{25}} = \$6,067,470 \qquad (21\text{-}5)$$

Suppose that the underwriting spread is 1 percent, so that the net proceeds of the new issue to the company are $6,067,470 (1 − .01) = $6,006,795. Moreover,

[21]This approach is used by Gordon Pye, "The Value of the Call Option on a Bond," *Journal of Political Economy*, 74 (April 1966), 200–205; and by Jess B. Yawitz and James A. Anderson, "The Effect of Bond Refunding on Shareholder Wealth," *Journal of Finance*, 32 (December 1977), 1738–46.

assume a tax rate of 50 percent, and an overlap period of one month.[22] Thus the net cash inflow at the time of the refunding is:

Net proceeds of new bond issue		$6,006,795
Cost of calling old bonds (call price $108)		5,400,000
Difference		$ 606,795
Expenses:		
Interest expense on old bonds during overlap period		41,667
Gross cash inflow		$ 565,128
Plus tax savings:		
Interest expense on old bonds during overlap period	$ 41,667	
Call premium	400,000	
Total	$441,667	
Tax savings (50% of amount above)		220,833
Net cash inflow		$ 785,961

Therefore, with the same contractual stream of cash outflows to service debt over the next twenty-five years as before, the company can realize present cash of $785,961. The refunding obviously is worthwhile.

We see then that there are different ways the bond refunding decision might be approached. While the latter method is appropriate if the firm intends to replicate the debt-service stream of payments, it is not if this is not the case. Generally, companies will issue new bonds at coupon rates approximating current yields in the market. As a result, the cash outflow stream will not be precisely replicated, even if more bonds are issued. For this reason, the alternative method presented here may not be practical in most situations. Still it serves as a conceptual way to deal with a refunding decision and, under most circumstances, gives accurate answers even if the input data are not precise.

Timing of Refunding

We must recognize that just because a refunding operation is found to be worthwhile, it should not necessarily be undertaken right away. If interest rates are declining, and this decline is expected to continue, management may prefer to delay the refunding. At a later date, the refunding bonds can be sold at an even lower rate of interest, making the refunding operation even more worthwhile. The decision concerning timing must be based upon expectations of future interest rates. In determining whether or not to postpone

---

[22]For simplicity, we assume that there is no unamortized discount or unamortized issuing expenses on the old bonds and no issuing expenses on the new bonds.

refunding, the financial manager should also consider the dispersion and shape of the probability distribution of possible future interest rates.

    Several writers have used dynamic programming models to deal with the optimal timing of a bond refunding. Weingartner[23] and Elton and Gruber[24] have viewed the problem as a multiperiod decision process, in which future interest rates are deterministic. Bierman[25] uses a two-period model in which probabilities of future interest rates are generated through Markov chains to decide whether to refund now or wait. Kalymon[26] extends this approach to the multiperiod case, in which future interest rates in each period are determined by a Markovian stochastic process. In an efficient market context, Kraus[27] presents a dynamic programming formulation involving a single refunding and a single-state variable. The essential feature of all of these models is that they provide guidelines for deciding each period whether to keep the existing bond or to refund it and issue a new bond. In this regard, the models supplement intuitive judgments as to the future course of interest rates.

PRIVATE PLACEMENTS

Rather than sell securities to the public, a corporation can sell the entire issue to a single institutional investor or a small group of such investors. This type of sale is known as a private or direct placement, for the company negotiates directly with the investor over the terms of the offering, eliminating the function of the underwriter. Some issues of common stock are placed privately, but the vast majority of private placements involve debt issues. Consequently, in the discussion that follows we shall be concerned only with the direct placement of debt issues. In recent years, private placements have accounted for approximately one-third of the net issuance of bonds by corporations.

[23]H. Martin Weingartner, "Optimal Timing of Bond Refunding," *Management Science,* 13 (March 1967), 511–24.

    [24]Edwin J. Elton and Martin J. Gruber, *Finance as a Dynamic Process* (Englewood Cliffs, N.J.: Prentice-Hall, 1975), Chap. 2.

    [25]Harold Bierman, Jr., "The Bond Refunding Decision as a Markov Process," *Management Science,* 12 (August 1966), 545–51. In another paper, Harold Bierman, Jr., and Amir Barnea, "Expected Short-Term Interest Rates in Bond Refunding," *Financial Management,* 3 (Spring 1974), 75–80, use future interest rates reflected in the current term structure of interest rates to determine whether it is desirable to wait one or more periods to refund.

    [26]Basil A. Kalymon, "Bond Refunding with Stochastic Interest Rates," *Management Science,* 18 (November 1971), 171–83.

    [27]Alan Kraus, "The Bond Refunding Decision in an Efficient Market," *Journal of Financial and Quantitative Analysis,* 8 (December 1973), 793–806. Kraus shows that in this context the relevant time frame for expectations can be reduced to one period. The decision then is whether to refund immediately or to refund one period hence.

Features

One of the more frequently mentioned advantages of a private placement is the speed of the commitment. A public issue must be registered with the SEC, documents prepared and printed, and extensive negotiations undertaken; all this requires a certain lead time. In addition, the public issue always involves risks with respect to timing. With a private placement, the terms can be tailored to the needs of the borrower, and the financing can be consummated much more quickly. Because the issue is negotiated, the exact timing in the market is not a critical problem. The fact that there is but a single investor or small group of investors is attractive if it becomes necessary to change any of the terms of the issue. It is much easier to deal with a single investor than with a large group of public security holders. A possible disadvantage in this regard, however, is that a single investor may monitor the company's operations in much greater detail than will a trustee for the purchasers of a public issue.

Another advantage of a privately placed debt issue is that the actual borrowing does not necessarily have to take place all at once. The company can enter into an arrangement whereby it can borrow up to a fixed amount over a period of time. For this nonrevolving credit arrangement, the borrower usually will pay a commitment fee. This type of arrangement gives the company flexibility, allowing it to borrow only when it needs the funds. With a public issue, it is necessary to sell the entire issue at one time. Because the private placement does not have to be registered with the SEC, the company avoids making available to the public the detailed information required by the SEC.

Private placements allow medium-sized and sometimes small companies to sell a bond issue, whereas with a public offering the flotation costs would be prohibitive. Institutional investors are willing to invest in bonds of smaller companies, provided the company is credit-worthy. It is doubtful that institutional investors would seek an issue of less than $100,000 (and many insist upon a higher minimum), but we must remember that a $5 million bond issue is considered small as a public offering.

Cost of Issue

There are two costs to consider in comparing a private placement of debt with a public offering: the initial cost and the interest cost. Because the negotiations usually are direct, private placement involves no underwriting or selling expenses. Frequently, however, a company seeks the services of an investment banker for advice in planning and negotiating the issue. Investment bankers have become increasingly involved as agents in private placements, thus offsetting to a certain degree the loss of underwriting and selling business. However, overall, the initial total cost of a private placement is significantly less than that of a public offering.

The second aspect of the cost of a private placement of debt is the interest cost. Fragmentary evidence here indicates that the yield on private placements is significantly above that on public offerings. In addition to interest costs, institutional investors sometimes will request an equity "sweetener," such as warrants, to entice them to invest in the debt issue of a company. Although the exact cost of this "sweetener" is difficult to measure, it certainly adds to the total cost of a private placement.

In summary, it would seem that the initial cost of a private placement of debt is less than that of a public offering. However, the interest cost and any additional compensation appear to be higher. For a long-term debt issue, the total cost is likely to be somewhat higher for a private placement than for a public offering. However, the difference in cost must be compared with the advantages of the private placement.

PREFERRED STOCK

Preferred stock is a hybrid form of financing, combining features of debt and common stock. In the event of liquidation, a preferred stockholder's claim on assets comes after that of creditors but before that of common stockholders. Usually, this claim is restricted to the par value of the stock. For example, if the par value of a share of preferred stock is $100, the investor will be entitled to a maximum of $100 in settlement of the principal amount. Although preferred stock carries a stipulated dividend, the actual payment of a dividend is a discretionary, rather than a fixed, obligation of the company. The omission of a dividend will not result in a default of the obligation or insolvency of the company. The board of directors has full power to omit a preferred-stock dividend if it so chooses.

The maximum return to preferred stockholders usually is limited to the specified dividend, and these stockholders ordinarily do not share in the residual earnings of the company. Thus, if an investor owns 100 shares of 6 percent preferred stock, $100 par value, the maximum return he can expect in any one year, usually, is $600; and this return is at the discretion of the board of directors. The corporation cannot deduct this dividend on its tax return; this fact is the principal shortcoming of preferred stock as a means of financing. In view of the fact that interest payments on debt are deductible for tax purposes, the company that treats a preferred-stock dividend as a fixed obligation finds the explicit cost to be rather high.

Cumulative Feature

Almost all preferred stocks have a cumulative feature, providing for unpaid dividends in any one year to be carried forward. Before the company can pay a dividend on its common stock, it must pay the dividends *in arrears* on its preferred stock. For example, suppose that the board of directors of a company omitted the preferred-stock dividend on its 8 percent cumulative preferred stock for three consecutive years. If the stock has a $100 par value, the company would be $24 per share in arrears on its preferred stock. Before it can pay a dividend to its common stockholders, it must pay preferred stockholders $24 for each share of preferred stock held. It should be emphasized that just because preferred-stock dividends are in arrears, there is no guarantee that they will ever be paid. If the corporation has no intention of paying a common-stock dividend, there is no need to clear up the arrearage on the preferred. The preferred-stock dividend typically is omitted for lack of earnings, but the corporation does not have to pay a dividend if earnings are restored.

If the preferred-stock dividends are in arrears, and the company wishes to pay a common-stock dividend, it may choose not to clear up the arrearage but to make an exchange offering to preferred stockholders. For example, suppose that the dividend arrearages on an issue of $100 par value preferred stock are $56 and that the market price of the stock is $74 a share. The company might offer preferred stockholders common stock in the company, valued at $110, for each share of preferred stock held. Although theoretically the preferred stockholder is asked to give up $156 ($110 par value plus $56 dividend arrearages), the exchange offering promises him $110 relative to a current preferred-stock market value of only $74 per share. In order to eliminate the preferred stock, the company must obtain the approval of a required percentage of the stock outstanding, often two-thirds. Consequently, it probably will make its exchange offering contingent upon obtaining the required acceptance. If the incentive is attractive enough, preferred stockholders probably will accept the offer despite the fact that they are not satisfied to the full extent of the arrearages.

If a preferred stock is noncumulative, dividends not paid in one year do not carry forward. As a result, a company can pay a common-stock dividend without regard to any dividends it did not pay in the past on its preferred stock. From the standpoint of an investor, a noncumulative preferred stock is little more than an income bond. In fact, there is somewhat less uncertainty with income bonds, for the conditions under which interest will be paid are specified clearly, and bondholders have a prior claim on assets. Because of the obvious disadvantage to investors, noncumulative preferred-stock issues are rare, although they may be used in reorganizations.

Participating Feature

A participating feature allows preferred stockholders to participate in the residual earnings of the corporation according to some specified formula. For example, the preferred stockholder might be entitled to share equally with common stockholders in any common-stock dividend beyond a certain amount. Suppose that a 6 percent preferred stock ($100 par value) were participating, so that the holders were entitled to share equally in any common-stock dividends in excess of $6 a share. If the common-stock dividend is $7, the preferred stockholder will receive $1 in extra dividends for each share of stock owned. The formula for participation can vary greatly. The essential feature is that preferred stockholders have a prior claim on income and an opportunity for additional return if the dividends to common stockholders exceed a certain amount. Unfortunately for the investor, practically all preferred-stock issues are nonparticipating, with the maximum return limited to the specified dividend rate.

Voting Power

Because of their prior claim on assets and income, preferred stockholders normally are not given a voice in management unless the company is unable to pay preferred-stock dividends during a specified period of time. For example, arrearages on four quarterly dividend payments might constitute such a default. Under such circumstances, preferred stockholders as a class will be entitled to elect a specific number of directors. Usually, the number is rather small in relation to the total. Moreover, by the time the preferred stockholders are able to obtain a voice in management, the company probably is in considerable financial difficulty. Consequently, the voting power that preferred stockholders are granted may be virtually meaningless.

Depending upon the agreement between the preferred stockholders and the company, they may obtain voting power under other conditions as well. The company may default under certain restrictions in the agreement similar to those found in a loan agreement or a bond indenture. One of the more frequently imposed restrictions is that dividends on common stock are prohibited if the company does not satisfy certain financial ratios. We note, however, that default under any of the provisions of the agreement between the corporation and its preferred stockholders does not result in the obligation's becoming immediately payable, as does default under a loan agreement or bond indenture. The preferred stockholders merely are given a voice in management and assurance that common-stock dividends will not be paid during the period of default. Thus, preferred stockholders do not have nearly the same legal power in default as do debtholders.

Retirement of Preferred Stock

Preferred stock, like common stock, has no maturity, However, most preferred-stock issues are not regarded as a means of perpetual financing, because provision for retirement of the stock invariably is made.

Call Feature   Practically all preferred-stock issues have a stated call price, which is above the original issuance price and may decrease over time. Like the call feature on bonds, the call feature on preferred stock affords the company flexibility. Because the market price of a straight preferred stock tends to fluctuate in keeping with interest-rate cycles, the value of the preferred-stock call feature is determined by the same considerations as is the call feature for bonds, which we discussed earlier. However, with long-term debt, unlike with preferred stock, there is a final maturity that assures the eventual retirement of the issue. Without a call feature on preferred stock, the corporation would be able to retire the issue only by the often more expensive and less efficient methods of purchasing the stock in the open market, inviting *tenders* of the stock from preferred stockholders at a price above the market price, or offering the preferred stockholders another security in its place.

Sinking Fund   Many preferred-stock issues provide for a sinking fund, which partially assures an orderly retirement of the stock. The trustee of the preferred-stock issue may use the sinking-fund payments to either buy stock in the open market or call a portion of it. In either case, the stock is retired. A sinking fund is advantageous to investors because the retirement process exerts upward pressure on the market price of the remaining shares. Also, the coverage ratio on the preferred-stock dividend is improved as the number of shares outstanding is reduced. The sinking fund works to the disadvantage of common stockholders because it represents another prior charge and, therefore, contributes to the financial risk of the company from their standpoint. A preferable arrangement for them would be a sinking-fund requirement wherein payments were variable in relation to earnings. Because the sinking fund is beneficial to preferred stockholders, the company should be able to sell the issue at a lower dividend yield than if it provided for no sinking fund. Overall, sinking funds are used much less with preferred stock than with bonds.

Convertibility   Certain preferred-stock issues are convertible into common stock at the option of the holder. Upon conversion, of course, the preferred stock is retired. Because practically all convertible securities have a call feature, the company can force conversion by calling the preferred stock if the market price of the preferred is significantly above the call price. Convertible preferred stock is used frequently in the acquisition of other companies. In part, its use stems from the fact that the transaction is not taxable for the company that is acquired or its stockholders at the time of the acquisition. It becomes a taxable transaction only when the preferred stock is sold. We shall examine convertible securities in much more detail in the next chapter.

Financing with Preferred Stock

Nonconvertible preferred stock is not used extensively in financing; only public utilities employ it with any degree of regularity.[28] One of the principal drawbacks to its use is the fact that the preferred dividend is not tax

[28]For an older review of preferred-stock financing, see Donald E. Fisher and Glenn A. Wilt, Jr., "Nonconvertible Preferred Stock as a Financing Instrument," *Journal of Finance,* 23 (September 1968), 611–24. One reason for the use of preferred stock by utilities is that the Securities and Exchange Commission stated in 1952 that the capital structure of an electric utility should not exceed 60 percent debt, and that common stock should not be less than 30 percent. Thus the 10 percent residual could be filled by preferred stock. Another reason is that a public utility is able to pass off the higher explicit cost of preferred stock, as compared with that of debt, in the rates it charges. Public utility commissions allow utilities to base their rates on their overall measured cost of capital.

deductible. With a 46 percent tax rate, the explicit cost of preferred stock is almost twice that of bonds. As an investment, however, preferred stock may be more attractive to the corporate investor than bonds because 85 percent of the dividends received is not subject to taxation. As a result, many preferred stocks sell at a lower yield than do the bonds of the same company, despite their lower priority of claim.

The advantage of preferred-stock financing is that it is a flexible financing arrangement. The dividend is not a legal obligation on the part of the corporation issuing the securities; if earnings turn bad and the financial condition of the company deteriorates, the dividend can be omitted. With debt financing, interest must be paid regardless of whether earnings are good or bad. To be sure, companies that are accustomed to paying dividends on their common stock certainly regard the preferred dividend as a fixed obligation. Nevertheless, under dire circumstances, a company that omits its common-stock dividend can also omit its preferred dividend.

Another advantage of a straight preferred-stock issue is that it has no final maturity; in essence, it is a perpetual loan. Also, the majority of preferred-stock issues do not require sinking-fund payments. Thus a preferred-stock issue gives a corporation flexibility by allowing it not to make principal payments or plan for refinancing. Moreover, from the standpoint of creditors, preferred stock adds to the equity base of the company and thereby strengthens its financial condition. The additional equity base enhances the ability of the company to borrow in the future. Although the explicit cost of preferred stock is considerably higher than that of bonds, the implied benefits discussed above may offset this cost. In addition, the implicit cost of preferred-stock financing, from the standpoint of investors penalizing the price/earnings ratio of the common stock, may be somewhat less than that of debt financing. To the extent that investors are apprehensive over legal bankruptcy, they would regard debt as a riskier form of leverage. Unlike creditors, preferred stockholders cannot force a company into legal bankruptcy.[29]

SUMMARY

Our concern in this chapter has been with the various features and types of fixed-income securities. The decision to use such securities in the capital structure and the amount to be employed was considered in Chapters 9 and 10. The principal features of debt include the fixed return, the priority of claim on assets, the call privilege, and the method of retirement of the debt.

[29]Gordon Donaldson, "In Defense of Preferred Stock," *Harvard Business Review*, 40 (July-August 1962), 123–36, defends rigorously the use of preferred stock as a means of financing under certain circumstances. He argues that when a company has utilized its debt capacity, it may be able to finance further with preferred stock because the preferred-stock capacity of a company is distinct from its debt capacity.

We saw that periodic reduction of the debt can be accomplished by issuing either sinking-fund bonds or serial bonds.

In financing with long-term debt, the company must bargain with investors over the terms of the debt instrument. If the company wishes to include terms that are not beneficial to investors, it must be prepared to pay a higher yield in order to sell the instrument. For example, if debentures are subordinated, investors will demand a higher yield than if the issue involves straight debentures. Another interesting aspect of the bargaining process between the borrower and investors relates to the call privilege. If interest rate expectations in the market are such that investors think that the issue may be called, the company will have to pay a higher yield for the privilege of being able to call it. As with any option, the value of it depends upon variability; in the case of the call option, it is the variance of future interest rates that is important. Given a call feature on a bond, a method was proposed for analyzing the refunding of the bond issue before maturity. This method treats the refunding operation as a riskless capital-budgeting project. An alternative method also was considered where the cash payment stream on the old bonds is replicated and attention is focused on the net cash provided by the refunding. Also examined was the timing of a refunding.

The size and frequency of long-term debt issues depend upon the fixed cost associated with an issue, upon the difference in yield between the rate of interest paid on the debt issue and the rate on short-term securities, and upon interest rate expectations. We examined a model for evaluating the tradeoff between these factors. Rather than offer securities to the general public, a company may place them privately with an institutional investor. With a private placement, the company negotiates directly with the investor; there is no underwriting and no registration of the issue with the SEC. The private placement has the virtue of flexibility and affords the medium-sized and even the small company the opportunity to sell its securities.

Preferred stock is a hybrid form of security having characteristics of both debt and common stock. The payment of dividends is not a legal but a discretionary obligation, although many companies regard the obligation as fixed. Preferred stockholders' claims on assets and income come after those of creditors but before those of common stockholders. The return on their investment is almost always limited to the specified dividend; very seldom do preferred stockholders participate in the residual earnings of the company. Although they may have some voting power, this power generally is restricted to situations where the company has evolved itself into financial difficulty.

Because preferred stock has no final maturity, almost all recent issues have had call features that give the corporation financial flexibility. Retirement of the preferred stock can also be accomplished by a sinking fund, by convertibility, or by an exchange offering. The principle disadvantage of preferred stock is that the dividend is not tax deductible. Offsetting in some measure the difference in explicit after-tax costs between preferred-stock and debt financing are implicit benefits associated with debt capacity and financial flexibility. Despite these implicit benefits, however, preferred stock is little used as a method of financing.

PROBLEMS

1. The Lemand Corporation has $10 million of 8 percent mortgage bonds outstanding under an open-end indenture. The indenture allows additional bonds to be issued as long as all of the following conditions are met:

   (a) Pretax interest coverage [(income before taxes + bond interest)/bond interest] remains greater than 4.

   (b) Net depreciated value of mortgaged assets remains twice the amount of mortgage debt.

   (c) Debt/equity ratio remains below 0.5.

   The Lemand Corporation has net income after taxes of $2 million and a 50 percent tax rate, $40 million in equity, and $30 million in depreciated assets, covered by the mortgage, which are depreciated at $2 million per year. Assuming that 50 percent of the proceeds of a new issue would be added to the base of mortgaged assets and that the company has no sinking-fund payments until next year, how much more 8 percent debt could be sold?

2. The Hirsch Corporation is in bankruptcy. Mortgaged assets have been sold for $5 million and other assets have yielded $10 million. Hirsch has $10 million in mortgage bonds, $5 million in subordinated (to the mortgage bonds) debentures, $15 million owed to general creditors, and $10 million par value of common stock. How would distribution of the $15 million in liquidating value be made?

3. Western States Electric Company needs to raise $200 million in long-term debt funds over the next three years. As the capital improvements that these funds will finance cannot be postponed and their cost is known, the $200 million figure is a certainty. Moreover, the use of funds will be steady over the three-year interval. The rate of interest on Treasury bills is currently 7 percent, and the company can raise long-term debt at 8½ percent interest. Western States does not expect these rates to change over the three-year period. In a study of flotation costs about a year ago, the company found that fixed costs associated with an individual issue total $100,000.

   (a) If the size of debt issue were to be the same for each issue, what is the optimal issue size over the three-year period? What is the optimal frequency between financings?

   (b) From the formula for optimal issue size, what would happen if fixed costs increased?

   (c) What would happen if the rate on the long-term debt rose relative to the rate on Treasury bills?

4. The Laster Corporation wishes to borrow $10 million for ten years. It can issue either a noncallable bond at 8 percent interest or a bond callable at the end of five years for 9 percent. For simplicity, we assume that the bond will be called only at the end of year 5 and that both bonds are sold at par. The interest rate that is likely to prevail five years hence for a five-year bond can be described by a normal probability distribution with an expected value of 7 percent and a standard deviation of 1 percent.

   (a) What is the probability that the absolute amount of total interest payments under the callable bonds and later issuance of five-year bonds will be less than that under the noncallable ten-year bonds?

(b) If the company can earn 14 percent before taxes on its funds, what is the probability that the callable bond alternative has a greater pretax present value than the noncallable bond alternative?

5. Five years ago, Zapada International issued $50 million of 10 percent, 25-year debentures at a price of $990 per bond. The call price was originally $1,100 per bond the first year after issuance, and this price declined by $10 each subsequent year. Zapada now is calling the bonds in order to refund them at a lower interest rate.

   (a) Ignoring taxes, what is the bondholder's return on investment for the five years? (Assume that interest is paid once a year and that the investor owns one bond.)

   (b) If the bondholder can now invest $1,000 in a 20-year bond of equivalent risk that provides 8 percent interest, what is his overall return over the 25-year holding period? How does this compare with the return on the Zapada bonds had they not been called? (Assume again that interest is paid once a year.)

6. The U.S. Zither Corporation has $50 million of 10 percent debentures outstanding, which are due in 25 years. USZ could refund these bonds in the current market with new 25-year bonds, sold to the public at par ($1,000) with a 9 percent coupon; total gross spread would be 2½ percent of the issue. The old bonds have an unamortized discount of $1 million, unamortized legal fees and other expenses of $100,000, and a call price of 107. The tax rate is 50 percent. There is a two-month overlap, and issuing expenses are $200,000. Compute the present value of the refunding, using the after-tax rate on the new bonds. Is the refunding worthwhile?

7. The Kramer Corporation wishes to raise $10 million of debt for twenty years. It can sell bonds publicly with an 8 percent coupon and a 1.50 percent gross spread, or it can place an 8½ percent note privately, with no other costs. Assuming that the Kramer Corporation would not repay the principal of either loan until maturity, would make annual interest payments, and is able to earn 12 percent before taxes on funds it employs in very safe investments, which plan would have the higher present value to the firm?

8. *Research Project*
   Obtain copies of several bond indentures. Pay particular attention to the restrictive covenants concerning such things as dividends, working capital, additional debt, and nature of the business. Try to relate the cost of debt to the firm to the relative restrictiveness of these provisions. Does management pay extra for discretion? If it does, can these covenants truly be said to be nonquantifiable? How would you go about finding a measure of degree of restriction so that tradeoffs with interest could be made?

9. The Riting Railroad needs to raise $9.5 million for capital improvements. It is considering a new preferred-stock issue and feels that it could issue 8%, $100 par value stock that would yield 9 percent to investors. Flotation costs for an issue this size amount to 5 percent of the total amount of preferred stock sold; these costs are deducted from gross proceeds in determing the net proceeds to the company. (Ignore any tax considerations.)

   (a) At what price per share will the preferred stock be offered to investors? (Assume the issue will never be called.)

(b) How many shares must be issued to raise $9.5 million for Riting Railroad?

10. Northern California Public Service Company is considering refunding its preferred stock. The dividend rate on this stock is $4 and it has a par value of $50 a share. The call price is $52 a share and 500,000 shares are outstanding. George Arroya, vice-president—finance, feels the company can issue new preferred stock in the current market at an interest rate of 7 percent. With this rate, the new issue could be sold at par; the total par value of the issue would be $25 million. Flotation costs of $780,000 are tax deductible, but the call premium is not tax deductible; the company's marginal tax rate is 50 percent. There is expected to be a ninety-day period of overlap between the time the new preferred stock is issued and the time the old preferred stock is retired. Should the company refund its preferred stock?

11. Lost Horizon Silver Mining Company has 200,000 shares of $7 cumulative preferred stock outstanding, $100 par value. The preferred stock has a participating feature. If dividends on the common stock exceed $1 per share, preferred stockholders receive additional dividends per share equal to one-half of the excess. In other words, if the common-stock dividend were $2, preferred stockholders would receive an additional dividend of $0.50. The company has 1 million shares of common outstanding. What would dividends per share be on the preferred stock and on the common stock if earnings available for dividends in three successive years were (a) $1,000,000, $600,000, and $3,000,000; (b) $2,000,000, $2,400,000, and $4,600,000; and (c) $1,000,000, $2,500,000, and $5,700,000. (Assume all of the available earnings are paid in dividends, but nothing more is paid.)

SELECTED REFERENCES

ANG, JAMES S. "The Two Faces of Bond Refunding," *Journal of Finance,* 30 (June 1975), 869–74.

BIERMAN, HAROLD, JR., "The Bond Refunding Decision as a Markov Process," *Management Science,* 12 (August 1966), 545–51.

BIERMAN, HAROLD, JR., AND AMIR BARNEA, "Expected Short-Term Interest Rates in Bond Refunding," *Financial Management,* 3 (Spring 1974), 75–79.

BILDERSEE, JOHN S., "Some Aspects of the Performance of Non-Convertible Preferred Stocks," *Journal of Finance,* 28 (December 1973), 1187–1202.

BODIE, ZVI, AND ROBERT A. TAGGART, JR., "Future Investment Opportunities and the Value of the Call Provision on a Bond," *Journal of Finance,* 33 (September 1978), 1187–1200.

BOWLIN, OSWALD D., "The Refunding Decision: Another Special Case in Capital Budgeting," *Journal of Finance,* 21 (March 1966), 55–68.

BRENNAN, MICHAEL J., AND EDUARDO S. SCHWARTZ, "Savings Bonds, Retractable Bonds and Callable Bonds," *Journal of Financial Economics,* 5 (1977), 67–88.

BROWN, BOWMAN, "Why Corporations Should Consider Income Bonds," *Financial Executive,* 35 (October 1967), 74–78.

CAKS, JOHN, "Corporate Debt Decisions: A New Analytical Framework," *Journal of Finance,* 33 (December 1978), 1297–1315.

DONALDSON, GORDON, "In Defense of Preferred Stock," *Harvard Business Review,* 40 (July-August 1962), 123–36.

ELSAID, HUSSEIN H., "The Function of Preferred Stock in the Corporate Financial Plan," *Financial Analysis Journal* (July-August 1969), 112–17.

ELTON, EDWIN J., AND MARTIN J. GRUBER, "Dynamic Programming Applications in Finance," *Journal of Finance*, 26 (May 1971), 473–505.

——, "The Economic Value of the Call Option," *Journal of Finance*, 27 (September 1972), 891–902.

EMERY, DOUGLAS R., "Overlapping Interest in Bond Refunding: A Reconsideration," *Financial Management*, 7 (Summer 1978), 19–20.

FISHER, DONALD E., AND GLENN A. WILT, JR., "Nonconvertible Preferred Stock as a Financing Instrument, 1950–1965," *Journal of Finance*, 23 (September 1968), 611–24.

INGERSOLL, JONATHAN, "An Examination of Corporate Call Policies on Convertible Securities," *Journal of Finance*, 32 (May 1977), 463–78.

JEN, FRANK C., AND JAMES E. WERT, "The Deferred Call Provision and Corporate Bond Yields," *Journal of Financial and Quantitative Analysis*, 3 (June 1968), 157–69.

——, "The Effect of Call Risk on Corporate Bond Yields," *Journal of Finance*, 22 (December 1967), 637–51.

JOHNSON, RODNEY, AND RICHARD KLEIN, "Corporate Motives in Repurchases of Discounted Bonds," *Financial Management*, 3 (Autumn 1974), 44–49.

KALOTAY, A. J., "On the Advanced Refunding of Discounted Debt," *Financial Management*, 7 (Summer 1978), 14–18.

KALYMON, BASIL A., "Bond Refunding with Stochastic Interest Rates," *Management Science*, 18 (November 1971), 171–83.

KOLODNY, RICHARD, "The Refunding Decision in Near Perfect Markets," *Journal of Finance*, 29 (December 1974), 1467–78.

KRAUS, ALAN, "The Bond Refunding Decision in an Efficient Market," *Journal of Financial and Quantitative Analysis*, 8 (December 1973), 793–806.

LABER, GENE, "Repurchases of Bonds through Tender Offers: Implications for Shareholder Wealth," *Financial Management*, 7 (Summer 1978), 7–13.

LITZENBERGER, ROBERT H., AND DAVID P. RUTENBERG, "Size and Timing of Corporate Bond Flotations," *Journal of Financial and Quantitative Analysis*, 8 (January 1972), 1343–59.

MAYOR, THOMAS H., AND KENNETH G. McCOIN, "The Rate of Discount in Bond Refunding," *Financial Management*, 3 (Autumn 1974), 54–58.

OFER, AHARON R., AND ROBERT A. TAGGART, JR., "Bond Refunding: A Clarifying Analysis," *Journal of Finance*, 32 (March 1977), 21–30.

PINCHES, GEORGE E., "Financing with Convertible Preferred Stock, 1960–1967," *Journal of Finance*, 25 (March 1970), 53–63.

PINCHES, GEORGE E., AND KENT A. MINGO, "A Multivariate Analysis of Industrial Bond Ratings," *Journal of Finance*, 28 (March 1973), 1–18.

——, "The Role of Subordination and Industrial Bond Ratings," *Journal of Finance*, 30 (March 1975), 201–6.

PYE, GORDON, "The Value of Call Deferment on a Bond: Some Empirical Results," *Journal of Finance*, 22 (December 1967), 623–36.

——, "The Value of the Call Option on a Bond," *Journal of Political Economy*, 74 (April 1966), 200–205.

SHAPIRO, ELI, AND CHARLES R. WOLF, *The Role of Private Placements in Corporate Finance.* Boston: Division of Research, Graduate School of Business Administration, Harvard University, 1972.

SIBLER, A. M., "Some Evidence on the Cash Flow Effects of Bond Refunding," *Financial Management*, 3 (Autumn 1974), 50–53.

STEVENSON, RICHARD A., "Retirement of Non-Callable Preferred Stock," *Journal of Finance,* 25 (December 1970), 1143–52.

VAN HORNE, JAMES C., *Financial Market Rates and Flows,* Chaps. 6 and 7. Englewood Cliffs, N.J.: Prentice-Hall, 1978.

——, "Implied Fixed Costs in Long-Term Debt Issues," *Journal of Financial and Quantitative Analysis,* 8 (December 1973), 821–34.

WEINGARTNER, H. MARTIN, "Optimal Timing of Bond Refunding," *Management Science,* 13 (March 1967), 511–24.

WEINSTEIN, MARK I., "The Seasoning Process of New Corporate Bond Issues," *Journal of Finance,* 33 (December 1978), 1343–54.

WINN, WILLIS J., AND ARLEIGH HESS, JR., "The Value of the Call Privilege," *Journal of Finance,* 14 (May 1959), 182–95.

YAWITZ, JESS B., AND JAMES A. ANDERSON, "The Effect of Bond Refunding on Shareholder Wealth," *Journal of Finance,* 32 (December 1977), 1738–46.

YAWITZ, JESS B., AND WILLIAM J. MARSHALL, "Why Firms Issue Callable Bonds: A Bias in the Tax Laws," *Journal of Finance,* forthcoming.

22

financing with options: the warrant and the convertible security

INTRODUCTION

Both convertible securities and warrants—the subject of this chapter—are forms of options. We know from Chapter 4 that an option is merely an instrument that gives its owner the right to buy or sell the common stock of a company within a specific period of time. The price paid for the stock, or the price at which it is sold, is known as the *exercise price,* and it is stated in the contract. For example, we might have a "call" option to buy one share of stock of ABC Corporation at $10 through December 31 of the current year.[1] Thus the option has an exercise price of $10 and an expiration date of December 31. The option itself may be traded in a market. If it is, its value will be closely related to the value of the associated stock—the two securities are close substitutes with respect to market price movements.

[1]In contrast, a "put" option entitles the holder to sell stock at a specified exercise price through the expiration date. In the remainder of our discussion, we will be concerned only with call options.

We also know from Chapter 4 that the value of the option should bear a relationship to the certain other variables. It is useful to review them briefly. Obviously the higher the current price of the stock and/or the lower the exercise price of the option, the greater the value of the option. Increased volatility of the common stock works to the advantage of the option holder. This is because the downside risk of the option is bounded at zero. Therefore an increase in variance expands the upside potential of the option while the downside risk continues to be bounded at zero. The result is an increase in the option's value. Also we saw in Chapter 4 that the longer the length of time to the expiration of the option, the more valuable it becomes, all other things the same. Moreover, the higher the short-term, risk-free interest rate, the greater the value of the option, holding all else constant. Finally, the higher the dividend on the common stock, the lower the value of the option. This is due to the fact that option holders are not entitled to dividends, nor is their option readjusted to reflect the payment of dividends to the common stockholders. All of the factors discussed above govern the value of an option in the marketplace. While the principal determinant of an option's price is the value of the associated common stock, these additional factors exert a moderate influence on option valuation.

We discovered in Chapter 4 that the relationship between the value of the stock and the value of the option is affected by the ability of market participants to hold a fully hedged, risk-free position. This can be accomplished by buying stock and writing options or buying options and shorting stock. By holding such a combination, movements upward or downward in the price of the stock are offset by opposite movements in the value of the option position. With efficient financial markets, a risk-free hedged position should return only the risk-free rate. To the extent that returns in excess of the risk-free rate can be earned, individuals will have an incentive to take such positions. The impact of their buying and selling of stocks and options to establish hedged positions will affect relative prices in such a way as to drive out any excess returns that might be earned. Black and Scholes have provided a precise formula for determining the equilibrium value of an option under these conditions;[2] and this model was illustrated in Chapter 4. In equilibrium, then, excess returns should not be possible, and stocks and options should be priced in the market in such a way that one is not overvalued or undervalued relative to the other.

With this general discussion of options in mind, we now examine two specific types of options frequently employed by business firms in their financing—the warrant and the convertible security. As we shall see, the warrant is a pure call option, although the number of shares of stock a warrant will purchase can be more than or less than one. Virtually all of our discussion on option valuation in Chapter 4 is directly applicable here. Not

---

[2]Fischer Black and Myron Scholes, "The Pricing of Options and Corporate Liabilities," *Journal of Political Economy*, 81 (May-June 1973), 637–54.

wishing to be redundant, we mainly explore the use of warrants as a financing vehicle. Convertible securities are somewhat different in that they represent a hybrid security—part bond or preferred stock and part common stock. As a result, their valuation is somewhat different from that of a straight option and we will need to spend more time on them.

641

financing with options:
the warrant and the
convertible security

THE USE OF WARRANTS

A *warrant* is an option to purchase a specified number of shares of common stock at a stated price. When the holder exercises the option, he surrenders the warrant. Warrants are often employed as "sweeteners" to a public issue of bonds or debt that is privately placed. The investor obtains not only the fixed return associated with debt but also an option to purchase common stock at a stated price. If the market price of the stock should rise, this option can be valuable. As a result, the corporation should be able to obtain a lower interest rate than it would otherwise. For companies that are marginal credit risks, the use of warrants may make the difference between being able and not being able to raise funds through a debt issue. In addition to a "sweetener" to debt financing, warrants also are used in the founding of a company as compensation to underwriters and venture capitalists.

Features

The warrant itself contains the provisions of the option. It states the number of shares the holder can buy for each warrant he holds. For example, the Greyhound Corporation warrants provide an option to purchase one share of common stock for each warrant held; Braniff Airways warrants provide for the purchase of 3.18 shares for each warrant held. Another important provision is the price at which the warrant is exercisable. For example, Greyhound warrants are exercisable at $30 a share. The exercise price can be either fixed or "stepped up" over time. The Textron Inc., warrants, for example, were exercisable at $10.00 a share until May 1, 1979, after which they have been exercisable at $11.25.

Finally, the warrant must specify the date on which the option expires. Certain warrants, such as those of Alleghany Corporation, are perpetual, having no expiration date. Most warrants, however, have a stated expiration date. Warrants may be either detachable or nondetachable. Detachable warrants may be sold separately from the bond. Consequently, the bondholder does not have to exercise his option in order to obtain the value of the warrant. He simply can sell the warrant in the marketplace. Many detachable warrants are listed on the American Stock Exchange, on the Chicago Board Options Exchange, and on regional exchanges. A nondetachable warrant cannot be sold separately from the bond; it can be detached only when the bondholder exercises his option and purchases stock.

Because a warrant is only an option to purchase stock, the warrant holder is not entitled to any cash dividends paid on the common stock, nor does he have voting power. If the common stock is split or a stock dividend is declared, the option price of the warrant usually is adjusted to take this change into account.

For accounting reporting purposes, a company with warrants outstanding is required to report earnings per share in such a way that the financial statement reader can visualize the potential dilution. More specifically, it must report earnings per share on two bases. The first is *primary* earnings per share, which are simply earnings available to common stockholders divided by the actual number of shares outstanding. The second is *fully diluted* earnings per share, which are earnings available to common stockholders divided by the total number of shares outstanding plus the number of shares that would be added if all warrants were exercised and all convertible securities were converted. For companies with sizable financing with options, the difference between the two earnings-per-share figures can be substantial.

Exercise of Warrants

When warrants are exercised, the common stock of the company is increased. Moreover, the debt that was issued in conjunction with the warrants remains outstanding, assuming the warrants are detachable. At the time of the issue of the warrants, the exercise price usually is set in excess of the market price of the common stock. The premium often is 15 percent or so above the stock's value. For example, if the share price were $40 and the holder could purchase one share of common stock for each warrant held, this would translate into an exercise price of $46.

To illustrate the infusion of new capital into a company with the exercise of warrants, suppose that ABC Corporation has just raised $25 million in debt funds with warrants attached. The debentures carry a 9 percent coupon rate, and with each debenture ($1,000 face value) the investor receives one warrant entitling him to purchase four shares of common stock at $30 a share. The capitalization of the company before financing, after financing, and after complete exercise of the option is as follows (in millions):

	Before Financing	After Financing	After Exercise
Debentures		$25	$25
Common stock ($10 par value)	$10	10	11
Capital surplus			2
Retained earnings	40	40	40
Net worth	$50	$50	$53
Total capitalization	$50	$75	$78

We assume that the retained earnings of the company remain unchanged and that the debenture issue has neither matured nor been called. Exercising their options, the warrant holders purchase 100,000 shares of stock at $30 a share, or $3 million in total. Consequently, the total capitalization of the company is increased by that amount.

A company cannot force the exercise of the warrant option as it can force the exercise of the conversion option by calling a convertible security. Consequently, it is unable to control when the warrant will be exercised and when there will be an infusion of new equity capital into the corporation. Only the expiration date sets a limit on how long the warrants can remain outstanding and unexercised.

Valuation of Warrants

The theoretical value of a warrant can be determined by

$$NP_s - E \qquad (22\text{-}1)$$

where N = the number of shares that can be purchased with one warrant

E = the option price associated with the purchase of N shares

P_s = the market price of one share of stock

Note that this formula is exactly the same as that discussed in Chapter 4 for the valuation of an option where $N = 1$. On October 16, 1978, the common stock of American Airlines closed at $17¼ per share. The exercise price for American Airlines warrants was $14, which enabled the holder to purchase one share of common stock for each warrant held. Consequently, the theoretical value of an American Airlines warrant on October 16, 1978, was

$$(1)(17¼) - 14 = \$3¼$$

However, most warrants sell at prices in excess of their theoretical values. For example, the American Airlines warrants closed at $7½ on October 16, 1978. The reasons for this occurrence were discussed in Chapter 4 and they relate to the volatility of the common stock, to the length of time to the expiration of the warrant, and to the time value of money. The typical relationship between the market value of a warrant and the value of the associated common stock is shown in Figure 22-1. The theoretical value of the warrant is represented by the colored line in the figure, and the actual market value of the warrant by the dashed line. When the market value of the associated stock is less than the exercise price, the theoretical value of the warrant is zero. When the value of the associated common stock is greater than the exercise price, the theoretical value of the warrant is positive, as depicted by the solid diagonal line.

The shorter the length of time to the expiration of the option, the more convex the market value line. With only a few days to expiration, the market

figure 22-1
Relation between
theoretical and market
values of a warrant

value line will approach the theoretical value line. The same relationship holds as the dividend on the common stock increases. Because the investor in the warrant does not participate in dividends paid on the common, the greater the dividend, the less attractive the warrant in relation to its associated stock. As a result, the greater the dividend, the more the actual value line would approach the theoretical value line. All of these factors are familiar from our consideration of option valuation in Chapter 4. Rather than repeat our discussion of why options typically sell at premiums over their theoretical values, the reader is referred to that chapter. We turn now to convertible securities, a subject requiring a more extended discussion.

CONVERTIBLE SECURITIES

A *convertible security* is a bond or a share of preferred stock that can be converted at the option of the holder into the common stock of the same corporation. Once converted into common stock, the stock cannot be exchanged again for bonds or preferred stock. The ratio of exchange between the convertible security and the common stock can be stated in terms of either a *conversion price* or a *conversion ratio*. To illustrate, the American Hospital Supply Corporation's 5¾ percent convertible subordinated debentures ($1,000 face value), issued in December 1974, have a conversion price of $29.50, meaning that each debenture is convertible into 33.9 shares of common stock. We simply divide the face value of the security by the conversion price to obtain the conversion ratio, $1,000/$29.50 = 33.9 shares. The conversion privilege can be stated in terms of either the conversion price or the conversion ratio.

The conversion terms are not necessarily constant over time. Many convertible issues provide for increases or "step-ups" in the conversion price at periodic intervals. For example, a $1,000 face value bond might have a conversion price of $100 a share for the first five years, $110 a share for the second five years, $120 for the third five, and so on. In this way, the bond converts into fewer shares of common stock as time goes by. Usually, the conversion price is adjusted for any stock splits or stock dividends that occur after the securities are sold. If the common stock were split two for one, for example, the conversion price would be halved. This provision protects the convertible bondholder and is known as an antidilution clause.

Conversion Value and Premium

The *conversion value* of a convertible security is the conversion ratio of the security times the market price per share of the common stock. If American Hospital Supply Corporation stock were selling for $40, the conversion value of one convertible subordinated debenture would be 33.9 × $40, or $1,356.

The convertible security provides the investor with a fixed return, in the case of a bond, or with a specified dividend, in the case of preferred stock. In addition, he receives an option to convert the security into common stock, and he thereby participates in the possibility of capital gains associated with being a residual owner of the corporation. Because of this option, the company usually is able to sell the convertible security at a lower yield than it would have to pay on a straight bond or preferred-stock issue. At the time of issuance, the convertible security will be priced higher than its conversion value. The differential is known as the *conversion premium*. For example, the American Hospital Supply Corporation's convertible subordinated debentures were sold to the public for $1,000 a bond. The market price of the common stock at the time of issuance of the convertibles was approximately $26. Therefore the conversion value of each bond was 33.9 × $26 = $881.40, and the differential of $118.60 between this value and the issuing price represented the conversion premium. Frequently, this premium is expressed as a percentage; in our example the conversion premium is $118.60/$881.40 = 13.5 percent.

Almost without exception, convertible securities provide for a *call price*. As was true with the straight bond or preferred stock, the call feature enables the corporation to call the security for redemption. Few convertible securities, however, are ever redeemed. Instead, the purpose of the call usually is to force conversion when the conversion value of the security is significantly above its call price.

How Should A Convertible Be Analyzed?

Because a convertible security is a bond or preferred stock at the time of issuance but is usually common stock later, it poses a certain amount of difficulty for the analyst examining the financial condition of the company.

Convertible subordinated debt or convertible preferred stock can be treated as a part of the equity base by a lender when he evaluates the financial condition of the issuer. In the event of liquidation, it makes no difference to the lender if the issue is actually converted; for in either case he has a prior claim. The situation is different, however, in the case of a convertible bond that is not subordinated. As long as the bond is not converted, its holder would be a general creditor in the event of liquidation. Consequently, lenders tend to regard the convertible bond as debt until actual conversion takes place. For this reason, there is a strong incentive for the company to make the issue subordinated.

Investors in a company's common stock tend to recognize the *potential* dilution in their position before actual conversion takes place. To illustrate the dilution effect, suppose that a company issues $20 million in 7 percent convertible debentures and that the conversion price is $20 a share. The total number of additional shares upon conversion would be $20 million/$20 = 1 million shares. Assume further that the company has 3 million common shares outstanding and no other debt, that it expects earnings before interest and taxes two years from now to be $10 million, and that the income tax rate is 50 percent. Earnings per share before and after conversion would be:

	Convertible Debentures Outstanding	Debentures Converted
Earnings before interest and taxes	$10,000,000	$10,000,000
Interest 7% debentures	$ 1,400,000	—
Profit before taxes	$ 8,600,000	$10,000,000
Taxes	$ 4,300,000	$ 5,000,000
Profit after taxes	$ 4,300,000	$ 5,000,000
Shares outstanding	3,000,000	4,000,000
Earnings per share	$1.43	$1.25

We see that upon future conversion, there is dilution in earnings per share in this example. We note also that upon conversion, the company no longer has to pay interest on the debentures; this factor has a favorable influence upon earnings per share. If earnings were low enough of course, the elimination of interest payments could result in an increase in earnings per share. However, this occurrence is the exception rather than the rule.

As with warrants, we should point out that it is necessary for companies to report earnings per share on a fully diluted basis. Full dilution means the maximum possible dilution if all convertible securities were converted into common stock and all warrants or options to purchase common stock were exercised. As a result of this requirement, the common-stock investor is not likely to overlook the potential dilution inherent in a company's financing with convertible securities and warrants.

Convertible securities, in most cases, are employed as deferred common-stock financing.[3] Technically these securities represent debt or preferred stock, but in essence they are delayed common stock. Companies that issue convertibles expect them to be converted in the future. By selling a convertible security instead of common stock, they create less dilution in earnings per share, both now and in the future. The reason is that the conversion price on a convertible security is higher than the issuing price on a new issue of common stock.

To illustrate, suppose that the current market price of the common stock of ABC Corporation is $40 per share. If the company raises capital with an issue of common stock, it will have to underprice the issue in order to sell it in the market. Suppose that the company is able to sell the stock through underwriters and to realize net proceeds of $36 per share. If the company wishes to raise $18 million, the issue would involve 500,000 shares of additional stock. On the other hand, if ABC Corporation sells a convertible issue, it is able to set the conversion price above the current market price per share. If the conversion premium is 15 percent, the conversion price would be $46 per share. Assuming an $18 million issue of convertibles, the number of shares of additional stock after conversion would be

$$\frac{\$18 \text{ million}}{\$46} = 391,305$$

We see that potential dilution with a convertible issue is less than that with a common issue because fewer shares are being added.

As a financing strategy, management may wish to finance with convertible securities as opposed to common stock when its estimates of the firm's future are more favorable than those of the market. By so doing, it obtains lesser dilution for existing stockholders than it would if it financed with common stock. Once management's expectations are realized, the stock presumably will rise in price. Of course, the merit of such a strategy depends upon management's estimates of the future being more accurate than those of the market. When the stock is depressed in price, however, it may be wise to avoid both common-stock and convertible financing. This situation will be discussed later in the chapter when we consider the timing of a convertible issue.

Another advantage to the company in using convertible securities is that the interest rate or preferred dividend rate typically is lower than the rate

---

[3]For presentation of a different concept of convertible financing, see Wilbur G. Lewellen and George A. Racette, "Convertible Debt Financing," *Journal of Financial and Quantitative Analysis*, 8 (December 1973), 777–92. The authors argue that the principal benefit of convertible financing is the tax deductibility of interest payments. As a result, they conclude that convertibles are an inefficient source of financing, inferior to that of straight debt.

the company would have to pay on a straight bond or a straight preferred-stock issue. The conversion feature makes the issue more attractive to investors. The greater the value of the conversion feature to investors, the lower the yield the company will need to pay in order to sell the issue. For companies with relatively low credit ratings but good prospects of growth, it may be extremely difficult to sell a straight issue of bonds or preferred stock. However, the market may regard a convertible issue of these companies in a favorable light, not because of its quality as a bond or as preferred stock but because of its quality as common stock.

Forcing or Stimulating Conversion

Companies usually issue convertible securities with the full expectation that these securities will be converted within a certain length of time. The investor can exercise his option voluntarily at any time and exchange the convertible security for common stock. However, he may prefer to hold the security, for its price will increase as the price of the common stock increases. In addition, he receives regular interest payments or preferred-stock dividends. For the convertible security in which the common stock pays no dividend, it is to the convertible security holder's advantage never to convert voluntarily. In other words, the investor should delay conversion as long as possible. On the other hand, it is in the company's interest, in behalf of existing stockholders, to force conversion as soon as possible. In this way, the cost of paying interest on the convertible debenture or dividends on the convertible preferred stock can be avoided.[4] However, when a company pays a common-stock dividend, it may be in the interest of the convertible security holder to convert voluntarily.

In order to force conversion, companies issuing convertible securities usually must call the issue. To do so, the market price of the security must be higher than the call price, so that investors will convert rather than accept the lower call price. Many companies regard a 20 percent premium of conversion value over call price as a sufficient cushion for possible declines in market price and for enticing investors to convert their securities. Suppose that the conversion price of a convertible debenture ($1,000 face value) were $50 and that the call price were $1,080. For the conversion value of the bond to equal the call price, the market price of the stock must be $1,080/20, or $54 a share. If the bonds are called when the market price is $54, many investors might choose to accept the call price rather than convert.[5] The company then would

[4]See Jonathan E. Ingersoll, Jr., "A Contingent-Claims Valuation of Convertible Securities," *Journal of Financial Economics,* 4 (January 1977), 297–301; and M. J. Brennan and E. S. Schwartz, "Convertible Bonds: Valuation and Optimal Strategies for Call and Conversion," *Journal of Finance,* 32 (December 1977), 1699–1715.

[5]Under the usual conditions associated with the option pricing model and with Modigliani-Miller's irrelevance of capital structure position, Ingersoll, "Contingent-Claims Valuation of Convertible Securities," demonstrates for the company that pays no common-stock dividend that the optimal time to force conversion is when the conversion value just equals the call price. However, the author recognizes that this is at odds with the practice of most com-

649

financing with options:
the warrant and the
convertible security

have to redeem many of the bonds for cash, in part defeating the purpose of the original financing. In order to assure almost complete conversion, it might wait to call the debentures until the conversion value of the bond is 20 percent above the call price, a value that corresponds to a common-stock market price of approximately $65 a share. At this price, the investor would suffer a significant opportunity loss if he accepted the call price.[6]

Other means are available to a company for "stimulating," as opposed to "forcing," conversion. By establishing an acceleration or "step-up" in the conversion price at steady intervals in the future, there is persistent pressure on bondholders to convert, assuming the conversion value of the security is relatively high. For example, if the conversion price is scheduled to increase from $50 to $56 at the end of next month, convertible bondholders have an incentive to convert prior to that time, all other things the same. If the holder waits, he receives fewer shares of stock. Recognize that the "step-up" provision must be established at the time the convertible issue is sold. It cannot be used for purposes of stimulating conversion at a particular moment in time. Another means for stimulating conversion is to increase the dividend on the common stock, thereby making the common more attractive.[7] In certain cases, the dividend income available on the associated common may exceed interest income on the convertible security. Although the two stimulants discussed above enhance conversion, invariably a portion of the convertible bondholders will not convert, owing to the downside protection of the bond, the superior legal claim on assets, and other reasons. Consequently, calling the issue may be the only means for assuring that the issue will be substantially converted.

The Risk of an Overhanging Issue

If a company is unable to force or stimulate conversion because the market price of the stock has not risen sufficiently to entice the investor to convert, the convertible issue is said to be "overhanging." With an overhanging issue, the company is constrained in its ability to obtain new financing. It is difficult to sell another convertible security issue until the present one is converted. The overhanging issue creates apprehension in the market over the investment worthiness of any new issue of convertibles and may even create apprehension over the worthiness of a nonconvertible security offering.

---

panies, who wait until the conversion value is substantially in excess of the call price before calling the issue. He cites as a possible explanation market imperfections. See also Brennan and Schwartz, "Convertible Bonds," for further discussion of the optimal time to convert and to call.

[6]For a discussion of ways a company can notify bondholders of the call and to assure that a very high percentage exercise their option, see Alexander B. Miller, "How to Call Your Convertibles," *Harvard Business Review,* 49 (May-June 1971), 66-70.

[7]For an analysis of voluntary conversion by the security holder in the presence of a conversion price "step-up" and/or dividends being paid on the common stock, see Ingersoll, "Contingent-Claims Valuation of Convertible Securities," pp. 314-19.

The risk of an overhanging issue and the loss of flexibility associated with such an issue may offset, at least in part, the advantage in issuing price of the convertible security over a common-stock offering. With a common-stock offering, the firm obtains equity capital now. With a convertible security issue, it is uncertain when, if ever, the security will convert and the company will obtain equity capital. If it were not for this factor, the lesser dilution associated with a convertible issue as opposed to a common-stock issue would always make the convertible issue more attractive.

Because issuing companies usually wish to force conversion within a reasonable length of time as well as avoid an overhanging issue, the convertible security is best suited for a growth company. The faster the increase in the market price of the company's stock, of course, the quicker the company will be in a position to force conversion. To illustrate, suppose R-Tronics, Inc., is able to sell a 6 percent convertible bond at a price of $1,000 to the public, with a conversion price of $50 and a call price of $1,060. This call price corresponds to a market price per share of $53. Suppose further that the price of the company's stock at the time of issuance is $44 per share. If R-Tronics has the policy of forcing conversion only when the conversion value of the bond is 20 percent in excess of the call price, it will need to wait until the stock rises to approximately $64 per share ($53 × 1.2). If the company is expected to have an annual growth in earnings per share of 30 percent in the foreseeable future, and if the price/earnings ratio is not expected to change, it will take less than eighteen months from the time of issuance for the stock to reach $64 per share. On the other hand, if the growth rate were expected to be only 5 percent per annum, it would take almost eight years for the stock to reach a value of $64 per share.

Thus there is considerable question whether a company that envisions only modest growth should finance with convertible securities. With a growth rate of 5 percent in the example above, it takes an extremely long period of time before it is possible to force conversion. During this time, the company is less flexible in additional financing than it would be if it could "clear the decks" and force conversion. Moreover, investors have come to expect companies that issue convertible securities to be able to force conversion within several years after issuance. Not to be able to do so during this time is a sign that the stock has not performed as well as the company had expected originally. Thus a company with prospects for little or no growth would be ill advised to use convertible securities as a method of financing. They are best suited for the growth company.

Conversion Premiums and Timing

For most issues of convertibles, the conversion premium ranges from 10 to 20 percent. Recall that this premium is the percentage by which the issuing price of the convertible exceeds its conversion value. If a convertible bond were sold for $1,000 with a conversion price of $50, and if the market price of common at the time of issuance were $43 a share, the conversion

651

financing with options:
the warrant and the
convertible security

premium would be $7/$43, or 16.3 percent. For a growth company, the conversion premium can be in the upper part of the 10–20 percent range, or perhaps even higher in the case of a super-growth stock. For companies with more moderate growth, however, the conversion premium may be closer to 10 percent. The range itself is established mainly by market tradition, in keeping, however, with the idea that the stock should be expected to rise in price so that it exceeds the conversion price within a reasonable period of time. The greater the growth in market price per share, the more quickly will the market price exceed the conversion price, all other things the same. Thus the super-growth company is able to command a higher conversion premium in the market than is a company with only moderate growth potential.

The higher the conversion premium, of course, the lower the dilution. If the company sets too high a conversion price, however, the issue will have to be sold as essentially a fixed-income security with a yield commensurate with what the company would pay on a straight debt or preferred-stock issue. Under such circumstances, the issue cannot be considered delayed equity financing. The ability of the firm to force conversion simply is too uncertain. For this reason, there are practical limits as to how high a conversion premium can be set. For most situations, it is 20 percent or less.

The appropriate timing of a convertible issue must be evaluated in relation to the market for the company's common stock. If it is a poor time to sell common stock because of a depressed market price, it usually is also a poor time to sell a convertible, even though the convertible issue can be sold at a conversion price higher than the price at which a common-stock issue can be sold. This is due both to the depressed market price of the stock and to variations in the conversion premium with market psychology. Because the dilution associated with a convertible issue depends directly upon its conversion price, which in turn is primarily a function of the market price of the stock, it is obvious that considerable dilution occurs when the stock is depressed in price. In addition to this influence, the conversion premium at which the issue can be sold is likely to be lower when the stock is depressed than when it is buoyant. Because the conversion premium is a function of expected growth, and because investors are less likely to expect growth when the stock is depressed than when it is strong, the conversion premium normally will be lower in a depressed market. These factors will result in greater dilution, the more depressed the market price of the stock. Thus we see that the appropriate timing of a convertible issue follows very closely the market behavior of the company's stock.

VALUE OF CONVERTIBLE SECURITIES

The value of a convertible security to an investor is twofold: its value as a bond or preferred stock, and its potential value as common stock. (Because the principles of valuation of a convertible bond and a convertible preferred stock are nearly the same, our subsequent discussion will refer to convertible bonds.) The investor obtains a hedge when he purchases a convertible bond. If the market price of the stock rises, the value of the convertible is determined largely by its conversion value. However, if the market for the stock turns down, the investor still holds a bond whose value provides a floor below which the price of the convertible is unlikely to fall.

Bond Value

The bond value of a convertible security is the price at which a straight bond of the same company would sell in the open market. It can be determined by solving the following equation for B:[8]

$$B = \sum_{t=1}^{n} \frac{I}{(1 + i)^t} + \frac{F}{(1 + i)^n} \qquad (22\text{-}2)$$

where B = straight bond value of the convertible

I = annual interest payments determined by the coupon rate

F = face value of the bond

n = years to final maturity

i = market yield to maturity on a straight bond of the same company

For example, suppose that ABC Company has outstanding a 6 percent convertible debenture issue with a final maturity twenty years hence. Suppose further that if the company is to sell a straight twenty-year debenture in the current market, the bond will have to yield 8 percent to maturity to be attractive to investors. For a twenty-year bond with a 6 percent coupon to yield 8 percent to maturity, the bond has to sell at a discount. More specifically, the market price has to be $804 for each $1,000 face value bond.[9] Thus the bond-value floor of ABC's convertible bond would be $804. This floor suggests that if the price of the common stock were to fall sharply, the price of the convertible would fall only to $804. At that price, the security would sell as a straight bond in keeping with prevailing bond yields for that grade of security.

---

[8] In this equation, we assume that interest payments are annual and paid at the end of the year. If payments are semiannual, the equation should be modified according to the discussion in the Appendix to Chapter 2.

[9] Solving for Eq. (22-2)

$$B = \sum_{t=1}^{20} \frac{\$60}{(1.08)^t} + \frac{\$1,000}{(1.08)^{20}} = \$804$$

Fortunately, we need only consult a bond table to determine the market price. Given any three of the four variables above—namely, years to maturity, coupon rate, yield to maturity, and market price—we can determine quickly the fourth variable from the table. An example of a bond table is shown in the Appendix to Chapter 2, where we take up the mathematics of bond interest.

The bond-value floor of a convertible is not constant over time. It varies with (1) interest-rate movements in the capital markets and (2) changes in the financial risk of the company involved. If interest rates in general rise, the bond value of a convertible will decline. For example, if the yield to maturity on a straight bond in our example increases from 8 to 9 percent, the bond value of the convertible will drop from $804 to $726. Moreover, the company's credit rating can either improve or deteriorate over time. If it improves, and the company is able to sell a straight bond at a lower yield to maturity, the bond value of the convertible security will increase, all other things held constant. However, if the company's credit standing deteriorates and the yield on a straight bond increases, the bond-value floor will decline. Unfortunately for the investor, when the market price of the stock falls because of poor earnings, the company may have financial difficulty, in which case its credit standing will suffer. As a result, the straight bond value of the convertible may decline along with the decline in its conversion value, giving the investor less downside protection than he might have expected originally.[10]

Premiums

Convertible securities usually sell at premiums over both their bond value and their conversion value. Recall that the conversion value of a convertible is simply the current market price per share of the company's common stock times the number of shares into which the security is convertible. The fact that the convertible bond provides the investor with a degree of downside protection, given the qualifications mentioned above, usually results in its selling at a market price somewhat higher than its conversion value. How much higher will depend largely upon the probability that the conversion value of the security will fall below its bond value. Suppose, in our example, that the conversion price is $50 a share and the current market price of the common stock is $60 a share. The conversion value of the $1,000 face value bond will be $1,200. If the stock falls to $25 a share, the conversion value of the bond will plummet to $500. Assuming a straight bond value of $804, however, the market price of the convertible would not be expected to fall below $804. Consequently, the investor can reduce his risk by investing in a convertible security rather than in the common stock of a corporation. In general, the more volatile the price movements of the stock, the more valuable is the downside protection afforded by the bond-value floor. For this reason as well as for additional reasons discussed later, the market price of a convertible security usually is above its conversion value. The difference is known as the *premium-over-conversion value*.

___

[10]Mathematically, the straight bond value of a convertible security will rise over time, all other things held constant, if the face value of the convertible is above the straight bond value at the time of issuance. At final maturity, the straight bond value, of course, will equal the face value of the convertible. See the Appendix to Chapter 2.

653

financing with options:
the warrant and the
convertible security

Moreover, a convertible bond usually will sell at a *premium-over-bond value,* primarily because of the conversion feature. Unless the market price of the stock is very low relative to the conversion price, the conversion feature usually will have value, in that investors may eventually find it profitable to convert the securities. To the extent that the conversion feature does have value, the convertible will sell at a premium over its straight bond value. The higher the market price of the common relative to the conversion price, the greater this premium.

Relation between Premiums

The tradeoff between the two premiums depicts the value of the option to investors and is illustrated in Figure 22-2. On the horizontal axis is the market price of the common and on the vertical the value of the convertible security. It should be pointed out that the two axes are on different scales. If the conversion ratio were 20 to 1, for example, the horizontal axis might be in units of $10 while the vertical axis was in units of $200. The diagonal line, which starts at the origin, represents the conversion value of the bond, while the horizontal line represents its straight bond value. The curved line represents the market price of the convertible security. The distance between this line and the bond-value line is the premium over bond value, while the distance between the market-price line and the conversion value line represents the premium-over-conversion value. Note the similarity

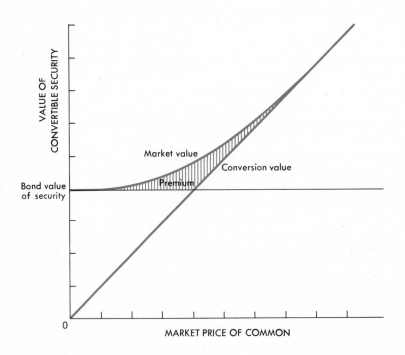

figure 22-2
Relation between bond value and conversion value premiums

of this figure with that for the value of an option in the form of a warrant—Figure 22-1.

We see that at relatively high common-stock price levels, the value of the convertible as a bond is insignificant. Consequently, its premium-over-bond value is high, whereas its premium-over-conversion value is negligible. The security sells mainly for its stock equivalent. Investors are unwilling to pay a significant premium-over-conversion value for the following reasons. First, the greater the premium of market price of the convertible over its bond value, the less valuable the bond-value protection to the investor. If the bond-value floor of a convertible bond is $900, for example, there is considerably more downside protection if the market price of the convertible is $1,000 than if it is $2,000. Second, when the conversion value is high, the convertible may be called; and if it is, the investor will want to convert rather than redeem the bond for the call price. Upon conversion, of course, the bond is worth only its conversion value.

On the other hand, when the market value of the convertible is close to its straight bond value, the conversion feature has little value. At this level, the convertible security is valued primarily as a straight bond. Under these circumstances, the market price of the convertible is likely to exceed its conversion value by a substantial premium.

The principal reason for premiums in market price over both conversion value and bond value is the unusual appeal of a convertible as both a bond and a common stock. It offers the holder protection on the downside together with participation in upward movements in stock price. Thus the distribution of possible outcomes is skewed to the right, and this characteristic finds favor with risk-averse investors. We note in Figure 22-2 that the premiums over both conversion value and bond value exist only within a range. At the far right of the figure, the convertible sells mainly for its common-stock equivalent and there is no premium-over-conversion value. There is, of course, a substantial premium-over-bond value. At the far left, the convertible sells as a bond with no premium-over-bond value but a substantial premium-over-conversion value.

Because of the skewed nature of the distribution of possible outcomes, the convertible security like any option should have more value the greater the volatility in the market price of the common. The investor has the downside protection of the bond-value floor in Figure 22-2 coupled with unlimited upside potential; thus the greater the dispersion of the probability distribution of possible common-stock market prices, the higher the expected value of return. In turn, this leads to a higher value for the option, which in this case is a convertible security. All of this follows, of course, from our discussion of option valuation in Chapter 4.

Other Reasons for Premiums

Although we have concentrated on the main reasons for premiums, other factors appear to have at least a modest influence on the premiums. The influence of some of these factors stems from the presence of certain impediments to the perfect market assumptions invoked earlier in our discussion of options. For one thing, a convertible security sometimes is attractive to investors who operate on margin. In the past, the margin requirement on stock, which is set by the Federal Reserve, has been higher than that on convertible securities. This meant that market participants were able to borrow more for investment in convertible securities than they were for investment in stock. Thus the greater collateral-value attractiveness of convertibles resulted in a greater demand for convertibles than for stock; this demand, in turn, exerted upward pressure on the premiums. At the time of this writing, however, the margin requirement was the same for both types of securities, namely, 50 percent. This means that the maximum loan a person could obtain from a bank or investment house was 50 percent of the market value of the convertible securities or stock pledged. Therefore the two types of securities had the same degree of collateral-value attractiveness.

Lower transaction costs on convertible bonds relative to those on common stocks also enhance the attractiveness of these bonds. An investor who wishes to acquire common stock of a company would incur lower transaction costs by purchasing a convertible bond and converting it into common stock than he would by purchasing the stock outright. This attraction should exert upward pressure on the premiums-over-conversion value and over-bond value. Yet another influence that may raise premiums is that certain institutional investors, such as life insurance companies, are restricted with respect to investing in common stock.[11] By investing in convertible bonds, they gain the benefits of a common-stock investment without actually investing in common stock.

The duration of the convertible option also should affect the premiums. In general, the longer the duration, the more valuable the option.[12] Unlike other options, however, the duration until expiration is uncertain owing to the fact that the company can force conversion if the price of the common stock is high enough. The longest duration is the maturity of the security, but the actual duration typically is much shorter. Another factor is the dividend on the common. The greater the dividend, the greater the attraction of the common vis-à-vis the convertible security and the lower the premiums, all other things the same. All of these influences affect the premiums at which convertible securities sell. While they tend to be less important than the influences discussed in the previous section, they need to be considered nonetheless in determining the value of a convertible security.

[11]See Eugene F. Brigham, "An Analysis of Convertible Debentures: Theory and Some Empirical Evidence," *Journal of Finance,* 21 (March 1966), 153.

[12]See Roman L. Weil, Jr., Joel E. Segall, and David Green, Jr., "Premiums on Convertible Bonds," *Journal of Finance,* 23 (June 1968), 445–47. See also Walter and Que, "Valuation of Convertible Bonds."

In this chapter, we have examined two types of options under which the holder can obtain common stock. The conversion feature enables the investor to convert a debt instrument or preferred stock into common stock, whereas a warrant attached to a bond enables the holder to purchase a specified number of shares of common stock at a specified price. With a warrant, the exercise of the option does not result in the elimination of the bonds. Convertibles tend to be used more than warrants in financing.

Normally, warrants are employed as a "sweetener" to a public or private issue of debt. The market value of a warrant usually is higher than its theoretical value when the market value of the stock is close to the option price, because this situation gives an opportunity for favorable leverage to the investor. When the market price of the stock is high relative to the option price, warrants tend to sell at about their theoretical values. In addition to the market price of the associated common stock, other factors were discussed that appear to affect the value of warrants.

The value of the convertible in the marketplace is determined primarily by its value as a straight bond or preferred stock and its conversion value as common stock. For the corporation, convertibles represent delayed common-stock financing, and the timing of a convertible issue must be analyzed by the company in relation to the market for its common stock. There will be less dilution, for a given amount of financing, with a convertible issue than with a common-stock issue, assuming, of course, that the issue eventually converts. Offsetting in some measure this advantage is the risk of an "overhanging" issue, which occurs when the company is unable to force conversion because the market price of the stock has not risen sufficiently to raise the conversion value of the security significantly above the call price.

The premiums at which a convertible security sells above its conversion value and above its bond value are due to: the security's downside protection as a bond and its upside potential as stock (the same in principle as with any option); the volatility of the common stock; the dividend on the common; the duration of the convertible option; and certain institutional imperfections that affect investors.

PROBLEMS

1. Using Eq. (22-1), compute the theoretical value of each of the following warrants:

	N	P	E
(a)	5	$100	$400
(b)	10	10	60
(c)	2.3	4	10
(d)	3.54	$27\frac{1}{8}$	35.40

2. (a) Compute the theoretical value of each of the following five warrants as a ratio of their exercise price:

	N	P	E
A	1	$10	$20
B	1	20	20
C	1	30	20
D	1	40	20
E	1	50	20

(b) Prepare a graph with warrant value/exercise price on the vertical axis and common-stock price/exercise price on the horizontal. Plot the theoretical value relationship computed in (a).

(c) Given the market values of the warrants below, fit a curve to them on the graph constructed in (b).

Warrant	Market Value
A	$ 3
B	7
C	15
D	21
E	30

(d) Explain the relationship between the theoretical and the actual value of a warrant.

3. Max Murphy, Inc., has warrants outstanding which allow the holder to purchase three shares of stock for a total $60 for each warrant that is held. Currently, the market price per share of Max Murphy common is $18. However, investors hold the following probabilistic beliefs about the stock six months hence:

Market Price per Share	Probability
$16	0.15
18	0.20
20	0.30
22	0.20
24	0.15

(a) What is the present theoretical value of the warrant?
(b) What is the expected value of stock price six months hence?
(c) What is the expected value of theoretical value of the warrant six months hence?
(d) Would you expect the present market price of the warrant to equal its theoretical value? If not, why not?

4. The Beruth Company is contemplating raising $10 million by means of a debt
   issue. It has the following alternatives:

   659

   financing with options:
   the warrant and the
   convertible security

   (1) A 20-year, 6 percent convertible debenture issue with a $50 conversion price
       and $1,000 face value, or
   (2) A 20-year, 8 percent straight debt issue with a detachable warrant to pur-
       chase 4 shares for $50 a share attached to each $1,000 bond. The company
       has a 50 percent tax rate, and its stock is currently selling at $40 a share. Its
       earnings before interest and taxes are a constant 20 percent of its total
       capitalization, which currently appears as follows:

Common stock (par $5)	$ 5,000,000
Capital surplus	10,000,000
Retained earnings	15,000,000
Total	$30,000,000

   (a) Show the capitalizations resulting from each alternative, both before and
       after conversion or exercise (a total of four capitalizations).
   (b) Compute primary earnings per share currently and under each of the four
       capitalizations determined in (a).
   (c) If the price of Beruth stock went to $75, determine the theoretical value of
       each warrant issued under alternative (2) above.

5. The Charrier Boat Company has current earnings of $3 a share with 500,000
   shares outstanding. The company plans to issue 40,000 shares of 7 percent, $50
   par value convertible preferred stock at par. The preferred stock is convertible
   into two shares of common for each preferred share held. The common stock
   has a current market price of $21 per share.

   (a) What is the preferred stock's conversion value?
   (b) What is its conversion premium?
   (c) Assuming that total earnings stay the same, what will be the effect of the
       issue on earnings per share before conversion? After full conversion?
   (d) If profits after taxes increase by $1 million, what will be earnings per share
       before conversion? After full conversion?

6. The common stock of the Draybar Corporation earns $2.50 per share, has a
   dividend payout of ⅔, and sells at a P/E ratio of 16. Draybar wishes to offer $10
   million of 7 percent, 20-year convertible debentures with an initial conversion
   premium of 20 percent and a call price of 105. Draybar currently has 1 million
   common shares outstanding and has a 50 percent tax rate.

   (a) What is the conversion price?
   (b) What is the conversion ratio per $1,000 debenture?
   (c) What is the initial conversion value of each debenture?
   (d) How many new shares of common must be issued if all debentures are
       converted?
   (e) If Draybar can increase operating earnings by $1 million per year with the
       proceeds of the debenture issue, compute the new earnings per share and
       earnings retained before and after conversion.

7. Assume that the Draybar Corporation (see problem 6) raised the $10 million

through an issue of stock (total gross spread and expenses = 10 percent of gross proceeds of issue). How many new shares would have to be issued? If operating earnings were increased by $1 million through the use of the proceeds, compute the new earnings per share and earnings retention. Compare your answers with those obtained in 6(e) above.

8. Assume that the Draybar Corporation (see problem 6) could sell $10 million in straight debt at 9 percent as an alternative to the convertible issue. Compute the earnings per share and earnings retained after issuance of the straight debt under the assumption of a $1 million increase in operating earnings and compare your answers with those obtained in 6(e).

9. Sadfield Manufacturing Company is considering issuing $10 million in 7½ percent convertible subordinated debentures. Currently, the stock price is $36 per share, and the company believes it could obtain a conversion premium (issuing price in excess of conversion value) of approximately 12 percent. The call price of the debenture in the first ten years is $1,060 per bond, after which it drops to $1,030 in the next ten years and to $1,000 in the last ten years. To allow for fluctuations in the market price of the stock, the company does not want to call the debentures until their conversion value is at least 15 percent in excess of the call price. Earnings per share are expected to grow at an 8 percent compund annual rate in the foreseeable future, and the company envisions no change in its price/earnings ratio.

    (a) Determine the expected length of time that must elapse before the company is in a position to force conversion.
    (b) Is the issuance of a convertible security a good idea for the company?

10. Fujiwara Electronics Company has a warrant outstanding which enables the holder to acquire two shares of stock for $32 a share for each warrant held. The present market price of the stock is $39 a share, and the expected standard deviation of its continuously compounded return is 0.20. The warrant has three years until expiration. The current rate on short-term Treasury bills is 5 percent.

    (a) If one values the warrant as a "European" option and uses the Black-Scholes option pricing model, Eq. (4-2) in Chapter 4, what is the value of the warrant? (The calculations are possible with a reasonably sophisticated calculator or with an ordinary calculator and various tables.)
    (b) What would happen to the value of the warrant if the standard deviation were 0.40? Why does this occur?

SELECTED REFERENCES

ALEXANDER, GORDON J., ROGER D. STOVER, AND DAVID B. KUHNAU, "Market Timing Strategies in Convertible Debt Financing," *Journal of Finance,* 34 (March 1979), 143–55.

BACON, PETER W., AND EDWARD L. WINN, JR., "The Impact of Forced Conversion on Stock Prices," *Journal of Finance,* 24 (December 1969), 871–71.

BIERMAN, HAROLD, JR., "The Cost of Warrants," *Journal of Financial and Quantitative Analysis,* 8 (June 1973), 499–504.

BLACK, FISCHER, AND MYRON SCHOLES, "The Pricing of Options and Corporate Liabilities," *Journal of Political Economy,* 81 (May–June 1973), 637–54.

661

financing with options:
the warrant and the
convertible security

——, "The Valuation of Option Contracts and a Test of Market Efficiency," *Journal of Finance,* 27 (May 1972), 339–417.

BRENNAN, M. J., AND E. S. SCHWARTZ, "Convertible Bonds: Valuation and Optimal Strategies for Call and Conversion," *Journal of Finance,* 32 (December 1977), 1699–1715.

BRIGHAM, EUGENE F., "An Analysis of Convertible Debentures: Theory and Some Empirical Evidence," *Journal of Finance,* 21 (March 1966), 35–54.

CHEN, ANDREW H. Y., "A Model of Warrant Pricing in a Dynamic Market," *Journal of Finance,* 25 (December 1970), 1041–60.

FRANK, WERNER G., AND CHARLES O. KRONCKE, "Classifying Conversions of Convertible Debentures over Four Years," *Financial Management,* 3 (Summer 1974), 33–42.

FRANKLE, A. W., AND C. A. HAWKINS, "Beta Coefficients for Convertible Bonds," *Journal of Finance,* 30 (March 1975), 207–10.

GALAI, DAN, AND MIER I. SCHNELLER, "Pricing of Warrants and the Value of the Firm," *Journal of Finance,* 33 (December 1978), 1333–42.

HAYES, SAMUEL L. III, AND HENRY B. REILING, "Sophisticated Financing Tool: The Warrant," *Harvard Business Review,* 47 (January-February 1969), 137–50.

INGERSOLL, JONATHAN E., JR., "A Contingent-Claims Valuation of Convertible Securities," *Journal of Financial Economics,* 4 (January 1977), 289–321.

JENNINGS, EDWARD H., "An Estimate of Convertible Bond Premiums," *Journal of Financial and Quantitative Analysis,* 9 (January 1974), 33–56.

LEABO, DICK A., AND RICHARD L. ROGALSKI, "Warrant Price Movements and the Efficient Market Model," *Journal of Finance,* 30 (March 1975), 163–78.

LEWELLEN, WILBUR G., AND GEORGE A. RACETTE, "Convertible Debt Financing," *Journal of Financial and Quantitative Analysis,* 7 (December 1973), 777–92.

MEHTA, DILEEP, "The Impact of Outstanding Convertible Bonds on Dividend Policy," *Journal of Finance,* 31 (May 1976), 489–506.

MERTON, ROBERT C., "A Rational Theory of Option Pricing," *Bell Journal of Economics and Management Science,* 4 (Spring 1973), 141–83.

MILLER, ALEXANDER B., "How to Call Your Convertible," *Harvard Business Review,* 49 (May-June 1971), 66–70.

PINCHES, GEORGE E., "Financing with Convertible Preferred Stocks, 1960–1967," *Journal of Finance,* 25 (March 1970), 53–64.

PIPER, THOMAS R., AND JASPAR H. ARNOLD III, "Warrants and Convertible Debt as Financing Vehicles in the Private Placement Market," *Explorations in Economic Research of the National Bureau of Economic Research,* 4 (Spring 1977), 277–302.

RUBINSTEIN, MARK, with the assistance of JOHN C. COX, *Option Markets.* Englewood Cliffs, N.J.: Prentice-Hall, 1979.

RUSH, DAVID F., AND RONALD W. MELICHER, "An Empirical Examination of Factors Which Influence Warrant Prices," *Journal of Finance,* 29 (December 1974), 1449–66.

SAMUELSON, PAUL A., "Rational Theory of Warrant Pricing," *Industrial Management Review,* 6 (Spring 1965), 13–31.

SAMUELSON, PAUL A., AND ROBERT C. MERTON, "A Complete Model of Warrant Pricing That Maximizes Utility," *Industrial Management Review,* 10 (Winter 1969), 17–46.

SCHWARTZ, EDUARDO S., "The Valuation of Warrants: Implementing a New Approach," *Journal of Financial Economics,* 4 (January 1977), 79–93.

SHELTON, JOHN P., "The Relation of the Price of a Warrant to the Price of Its Associated Stock," *Financial Analysts Journal,* 23 (May-June and July-August 1967), 143–51 and 88–99.

SMITH, CLIFFORD W., JR., "Option Pricing: A Review," *Journal of Financial Economics,* 3 (January-March 1976), 3–51.

STONE, BERNELL K., "Warrant Financing," *Journal of Financial and Quantitative Analysis,* 11 (March 1976), 143–53.

VAN HORNE, JAMES C., "Warrant Valuation in Relation to Volatility and Opportunity Costs," *Industrial Management Review,* 10 (Spring 1969), 19–32.

WALTER, JAMES E., AND AGUSTIN V. QUE, "The Valuation of Convertible Bonds," *Journal of Finance,* 28 (June 1973), 713–32.

WEIL, ROMAN L., JR., JOEL E. SEGALL, AND DAVID GREEN, JR., "Premiums on Convertible Bonds," *Journal of Finance,* 23 (June 1968), 445–63.

———, "Reply," *Journal of Finance,* 25 (September 1970), 931–33.

WEYGANDT, JERRY J., "Valuation of Stock Option Contracts," *Accounting Review,* 52 (January 1977), 40–51.

part **VII**

expansion and contraction

23

mergers
and acquisitions

In Chapters 6 and 8, we considered the acquisition of another company as a capital-budgeting decision. Like an internally generated investment proposal, the acquisition requires an initial outlay, which is expected to be followed by future benefits. Our purpose in those chapters was to develop a conceptual framework for analyzing and evaluating the likely effect of an acquisition on the value of the firm in both firm-risk and market-risk contexts. In this chapter, we deal with some of the more practical aspects of external growth. Nonetheless, the economic framework developed in Chapters 6 and 8 underlies our discussion here. The basic difference is that we deal primarily with earnings per share in this chapter, whereas our concern before was with cash flows. We turn now to some basic definitions.

A *merger* is a combination of two corporations where only one survives. The merged corporation goes out of existence, leaving its assets and liabilities to the acquiring corporation. A merger must be distinguished from a *consolidation,* which involves the combination of two or more corporations whereby an entirely new corporation is formed. All of the old companies cease to exist, and shares of their common stock are exchanged for shares in the new company. When two companies of about the same size combine, they usually consolidate. When the two companies differ significantly in size, usually a merger is involved. Though it is important to understand the distinction, the terms *merger* and *consolidation* tend to be used interchangeably to describe the combination of two companies.

COMBINING TWO COMPANIES

A merger or consolidation often begins with negotiations between the managements of the two companies.[1] Usually, the boards of directors of the companies are kept up to date on the negotiations. When initial agreement is reached as to terms, the respective boards must ratify these terms. Upon ratification, the agreement is submitted to the common stockholders of both companies for approval. Depending upon the corporate charter, an established majority—usually two-thirds—of the total shares is required. After approval by the common stockholders, the merger or consolidation can take place once the necessary papers are filed with the states in which the companies are incorporated.

One hurdle remains, however—that neither the Antitrust Division of the Department of Justice nor the Federal Trade Commission brings suit to block the combination. In order to actually block a merger or consolidation, the government, under Section 7 of the Clayton Act, must prove that a "substantial lessening of competition" might occur on account of it. Because the costs in executive time, legal expenses, and other expenses of waging an antitrust battle are so great, most companies want to be reasonably sure that they will not be challenged before going ahead with a combination.

Accounting Treatment

From an accounting standpoint, a combination of two companies is treated either as a *purchase* or as a *pooling of interests*. With a purchase, the acquired company is treated as an investment by the buyer. If the buyer pays a premium above the fair market value of the assets, this premium must be reflected as goodwill on the buyer's balance sheet. Moreover, goodwill must be written off against future income, the logic being that it will be reflected in such income. Like any asset, an estimate must be made of its life; and goodwill is amortized over this period, which cannot exceed forty years. Thus earnings are reduced by the amount of the charge. It is important to recognize that goodwill charges are not deductible for tax purposes. Therefore the reduction of reported future earnings associated with this accounting treatment generally is viewed as a disadvantage by the acquiring firm.

---

[1]We defer consideration of a tender offer until later in this chapter.

In a pooling of interests, the balance sheets of the two companies are combined, with assets and liabilities simply being added together. As a result, goodwill is not reflected in the combination, and there is no charge against future income. Because reported earnings will be higher with the pooling-of-interests accounting treatment than they will be with the purchase treatment, many acquiring companies prefer it when the goodwill being acquired is substantial.

However, the choice of accounting treatment does not rest entirely with the acquiring company, but rather is governed by the circumstances of the merger and the rules of the accounting profession. Only under the following rather restricted conditions can a merger be treated as a pooling of interests:[2]

1. Each of the combined companies must be autonomous for at least two years prior to the pooling and independent of the others in the sense that no more than 10 percent of the stock is owned.

2. The combination must be consummated in a single transaction *or* in accordance with a specific plan within one year after the plan is initiated. In this regard, no contingent payments are permitted.

3. The acquiring corporation can issue only common stock, with rights identical to those of the majority of outstanding voting stock, in exchange for *substantially* all of the voting common stock of another company. Here, "substantially" means 90 percent or more.

4. The surviving corporation must not later retire or reacquire common stock issued in connection with the combination, must not enter into an arrangement for the benefit of former stockholders, and must not dispose of a significant portion of the assets of the combining companies for at least two years.

The most important condition is number 3, which states that common must be exchanged for common. The next most important is the prohibition of contingent payments. The result of these conditions is a significant constraint on the number of poolings of interest. Although there may be certain inequities in the rules, their overall effect is to reduce distortions in reported earnings per share caused by the pooling-of-interests accounting method.

So far we have considered only the case where the acquiring company pays a price in excess of the fair market value of the assets. However, in many situations the fair market value of the assets of the acquired company differs from the book value of those assets. As a result, the accounting and tax treatments are different depending on whether the purchase or the pooling-of-interests accounting method is employed. Under the purchase method, the

---

[2]*Opinions of the Accounting Principles Board,* No. 16 (New York: American Institute of Certified Public Accountants, August 1970).

assets are carried on the books of the acquiring company at their fair market value, whereas with the pooling-of-interests method, the assets are carried at their previous book value.

To illustrate, suppose ABC Company acquires XYZ Company in an exchange of stock valued at $2 million. Furthermore, XYZ Company had debt of $1 million and a net worth of $1.2 million prior to the merger, with the net book value of its assets being $2.2 million. However, at the time of the merger the fair market value of the assets is $2.5 million. On the other hand, ABC Company, the acquirer, had a net worth of $10 million, debt of $5 million, and assets having a net book value of $15 million prior to the merger. The effect of the merger under the purchase and the pooling-of-interests methods of accounting treatment is as follows (in thousands):[3]

	Before Merger		After Merger	
	ABC Company	XYZ Company	Purchase	Pooling
Net tangible assets	$15,000	$2,200	$17,500	$17,200
Goodwill	0	0	500	0
Total assets	$15,000	$2,200	$18,000	$17,200
Debt	$ 5,000	$1,000	$ 6,000	$ 6,000
Net worth	10,000	1,200	12,000	11,200
Total liabilities and net worth	$15,000	$2,200	$18,000	$17,200

With the purchase method, we see that the assets of the acquired company are written up by $300,000 to their fair market value of $2.5 million. Moreover, the balance of the price paid in excess of book value, $500,000, is reflected as goodwill and must be amortized in the manner described before. Under the pooling-of-interests accounting treatment, the assets shown for the surviving company are simply the sum of the book values of assets shown for the two companies prior to the merger.

In situations where the fair market value of the acquired assets exceeds their book value, there is an important economic advantage to using the purchase as opposed to the pooling-of-interests method of accounting treatment. Because the net tangible assets are written up, the surviving company can claim a larger depreciation expense for tax purposes. In turn, this results in a greater after-tax cash flow compared with the pooling-of-interests method where, because of a lower book value, depreciation charges are less. This represents an advantage for purchase over pooling if the objective of the firm is to maximize the present value of after-tax cash flows. To the extent the objective is maximizing accounting earnings, however, the purchase method

---

[3]For purposes of illustration, we assume that the acquiring company can use either of the two methods.

loses some of its appeal the greater the amount of goodwill that must be recorded.

Purchase of Assets or Purchase of Stock

The acquisition of another company can take place either by the purchase of assets or by the purchase of the common stock of the company being acquired. Under the former arrangement, the buying company may purchase all or a portion of the assets of another company and pay for this purchase either with cash or with its own stock. Frequently, the buyer acquires only the assets of the other company and does not assume its liabilities. If all the assets are purchased, the selling company is but a corporate shell. After the sale, its assets are composed entirely of cash or the stock of the buying company. The selling company can either hold the cash or stock or it can distribute the cash or stock to its stockholders as a liquidating dividend, after which the company is dissolved.

Thus, when its assets are purchased, the selling company can continue to exist if it holds the cash or stock arising from the sale. If it has cash, it may invest in other assets, such as a division of another company. Obviously, if only a portion of its assets are sold, the selling company will continue as a corporate entity. If paid in cash or with a debt instrument, the transaction is taxable to the selling company or its stockholders; that is, they must recognize the capital gain or loss on the sale of the assets at the time of the sale. If payment is made in preferred or common stock, however, the transaction is not taxable at the time of sale. The capital gain or loss is recognized only when the stock is sold. A purchase of assets is easier to effect than a purchase of stock, for all that is needed on the part of the buying company is approval by the board of directors. The selling company, however, needs the approval of its stockholders.

When an acquiring company purchases the stock of another company, the latter is merged into the acquiring company. The company that is acquired ceases to exist, and the surviving company assumes all its assets and liabilities. As with a purchase of assets, the means of payment to the stockholders of the company being acquired can be either cash or stock. If cash, the transaction is taxable to the stockholders of the acquired company at the time of the acquisition. If stock, the transaction is not taxable to the stockholders until the stock is sold.

Dissenting Stockholders

Although a combination generally depends only upon the approval of a required majority of the total number of shares outstanding, minority stockholders can contest the price paid for their stock. If a dissenting stockholder and the company fail to agree as to a just settlement on a voluntary basis, the stockholder can take his case to court and demand an appraisal of his shares and a settlement in cash. After a "fair market price" has been established by the court, the dissenting stockholder receives payment in cash for his shares. If the number of dissenting stockholders is large, they can cause considerable trouble. If the transaction is in stock, the demands for cash payments on the part of these stockholders may put a severe financial strain on the combination. Thus, most combinations depend not only upon obtaining approval of a required majority of stockholders but also upon minimizing the number of dissenting stockholders by making the offer attractive to all. Dissenting stockholders may be able to block the combination if they suspect that fraud is involved, even though the required majority of stockholders has approved it.

Holding Companies

Instead of actually acquiring another company, a firm may purchase a portion of its stock and act as a holding company. By definition, a *holding company* own sufficient voting stock to have a controlling interest in one or more other corporations. A holding company does not necessarily have to own 51 percent of the stock of another company in order to have control. For a widely held corporation, ownership of 20 percent or as little as 10 percent of the stock outstanding may constitute effective working control. The advantage of a holding company is that it allows a company to acquire control of another with a much smaller investment than would be necessary with a merger. Moreover, by acquiring only a portion of the stock, the holding company usually does not have to pay as high a price per share as it would if it sought to purchase all the stock. It may purchase the stock gradually without undue upward pressure on the market price of the stock. Another advantage of a holding company is the possibility that operating economies can be achieved through centralized management. One of the principal disadvantages of the holding company is that 15 percent of the dividends paid to it by the subsidiary is subject to taxation.[4] Thus the holding company must pay a partial tax on dividends, and stockholders of the holding company also must pay a tax on dividends they receive. The partial tax could be avoided, of course, if the stockholders owned the operating companies directly.

Through pyramiding a series of holding companies, it is possible to obtain considerable leverage with respect to assets controlled and earnings. For example, suppose holding Company A owns 20 percent of holding Companies B, C, and D, which, in turn, own 20 percent controlling interest in nine operating companies. Thus, for every dollar of capital in each of the operating companies—$9 in all—Company A is able to control them with an investment of $0.36 ($0.20 \times 0.20 \times \$9$), or 4 percent of the total capital of the operating companies. As long as the operating companies are profitable and able to pay dividends to the holding companies, all may go well. However, in the 1920s,

---

[4]If the holding company owns 80 percent or more of the voting stock of the subsidiary, the dividend is not subject to taxation.

there tended to be excessive pyramiding of holding companies, particularly

with respect to public utilities. In the 1930s, the leverage of these companies magnified the losses, and a number of the pyramids crumbled. Because of the many abuses of holding companies, the Public Utility Holding Company Act of 1935 was passed to restrict the operation of holding companies in the public utility field.

REASONS FOR COMBINATION

The reasons for a combination are many and complex. Moreover, they are not mutually exclusive; more than one usually is involved in a combination. The ultimate purpose, of course, is to increase the market value per share of the firm. From Chapter 2 we know that share price can be expressed as

$$P_0 = \sum_{t=1}^{\infty} \frac{D_t}{(1 + k_e)^t} \tag{23-1}$$

where D_t is the dividend expected at the end of period t, and k_e is the required rate of return of investors in a stock of the risk involved. The case for a higher valuation after a merger than before must be based upon raising the level of expected future dividends per share in the numerator of Eq. (23-1), or lowering the required rate of return, k_e, in the denominator. The former primarily involves increasing earnings per share over what they would otherwise be, while the latter involves reducing the risk to investors. The reasons for combination that we examine in this section can be evaluated in relation to these two factors.[5] Other more fundamental reasons were discussed in Chapter 8.

Operating Economies and Economies of Scale

Often, operating economies can be achieved through a combination of companies. Duplicate facilities can be eliminated, and marketing, accounting, purchasing, and other operations can be consolidated. For example, certain salesmen can be eliminated to avoid duplication of effort in a particular territory. The principal objective in a railroad merger is to realize economies of operation through elimination of duplicate facilities and runs. With an industrial company merger, a firm with a product that complements an existing product line can fill out that line and, hopefully, increase the total overall demand for the products of the acquiring company. The realization of

[5]For a comprehensive review of the empirical literature on mergers, see Dennis C. Mueller, "The Effects of Conglomerate Mergers," *Journal of Banking and Finance*, 4 (December 1977), 315–47.

such economies is known as *synergism;* the fused company is of greater value than the sum of the parts—that is, $2 + 2 = 5$.

In addition to operating economies, economies of scale may be possible with a merger of two companies. Economies of scale occur when average cost declines with increases in volume. Usually we think of economies of scale in production. However, economies of scale are possible in marketing, in purchasing, in distribution, in accounting, and even in finance. The idea is simply to concentrate a greater volume of activity into a given facility, into a given number of people, into a given distribution system, and so forth. In other words, increases in volume permit a more efficient utilization of resources. Like anything else, however, there are limits. Beyond a point, increases in volume may cause more problems than they remedy, and a company may actually become less efficient. Economists speak of an "envelope curve" with economies of scale possible up to some optimal point after which diseconomies occur.

Economies can perhaps best be realized with a *horizontal merger,* in which two companies in the same line of business are combined. The economies achieved by this means result primarily from eliminating duplicate facilities and offering a broader product line in the hope of increasing total demand. A *vertical merger,* whereby a company either expands forward toward the ultimate consumer or backward toward the source of raw material, may also bring about economies. This type of merger gives a company more control over its distribution and purchasing. In the formation of U.S. Steel Corporation in 1900, one of the purposes was a complete vertical integration of steel from extraction of ore to the final sale of the product. There are few operating economies in a *conglomerate merger,* where two companies in unrelated lines of business are combined.[6]

Some authors maintain that the possibility of economies is the only important justification for a merger when the objective is to maximize shareholder wealth.[7] Their reasons are essentially those discussed in Chapter 8—namely, that investors are able to achieve the other benefits associated with mergers on their own. In particular, conglomerate mergers are felt to lack economic justification unless the acquiring company can manage more productively the assets of the companies being acquired.

---

[6]For a different classification of acquisitions along the lines of financial, marketing, and manufacturing advantages as well as a framework for investigation, selection, negotiation, and integration, see Robert A. Howell, "Plan to Integrate Your Acquisitions," *Harvard Business Review,* 48 (November-December 1970), 66–76.

[7]In a test of 59 major industrial mergers, Robert A. Haugen and Terrence C. Langetieg, "An Empirical Test for Synergism in Merger," *Journal of Finance,* 30 (September 1975), 1003–14, find little evidence of synergism. Using a pairwise sample of merged firms and similar unmerged firms, the authors did not find that the merger altered the distribution of possible returns for the merged firm from that which existed before for the two separate firms.

Management Acquisition

Closely related to economies in the sense of raising expected future dividends per share over what they would otherwise be is the acquisition of management. If a firm finds that it is unable to hire top-quality management and that it has no one coming up through the ranks, it may seek a combination with another company having aggressive and competent management. The choice may be between gradual stagnation with an existing organization or combination with another company in order to obtain competent management. To foster the long-run wealth of stockholders, the latter may be the only realistic alternative.

Growth

A company may not be able to grow at a fast or balanced enough rate by internal expansion and may find that its only way of achieving a desired growth rate is by acquiring other companies. The cost of growth by acquisition may well be cheaper than the real cost of internal growth; the numerous costs and risks involved in developing and embarking upon a new product line or a new facility may be avoided through acquisition of a going concern. In addition, it usually is quicker to acquire new products and facilities through mergers than through internal development. An important aspect of external growth may be the acquisition of the research capabilities of another firm. Because research tends to be individually oriented, the acquiring company may be unable to develop such capabilities on its own. Closely related to research is the possession of basic patents. A company having certain patent rights may be extremely valuable for this reason alone.

Although these factors may lead to higher future earnings and growth, the critical factor is the price paid for the acquisition. If the company to be acquired is priced rationally in the market (that is, it is not undervalued or overvalued), its acquisition is unlikely to increase share price *unless* there is synergism. Unfortunately, in certain cases growth in sales, assets, and total earnings appears to have supplanted maximization of shareholder wealth as the primary goal of the firm. Under such circumstances, mergers obviously are attractive, because in most cases growth can be achieved more easily through external acquisitions than it can through internal development. As we discovered in Chapter 8, however, there is nothing magical about growth. More often than not growth can be obtained only through taking on greater risk. The combination of incremental growth and risk may actually result in a decline in share price. Financial markets equilibrate in terms of expected return and risk. It is not sufficient to consider only the numerator of Eq. (23-1); what happens to the denominator (the required rate of return) must be considered as well. Many a "growth" acquisition has fallen short of expectations because proper allowance was not made for risk.

Diversification

Diversification is the motive in some mergers. By acquiring a firm in a different line of business, a company may be able to reduce cyclical instability in earnings. Although it is virtually impossible to find two companies with negative correlation in earnings, it is possible to find situations in which there is only moderate correlation. Related to the argument for diversification is the notion of spreading risk. To the extent that investors in a company's stock are averse to risk and are concerned only with the total risk of the firm, a reduction in earnings instability would have a favorable impact upon share price. Unlike the previous reasons for merging, the effect here is to reduce the rate of return that investors require in the denominator of Eq. (23-1).

This argument assumes that investors evaluate risk solely in relation to the *total* risk of the firm. We know from Chapters 3 and 8, however, that investors are able to diversify risk on their own. If they evaluate risk in an overall market context, they will diversify at least as effectively on their own as the firm is able to do for them. Particularly when the stock of the company being acquired is publicly traded, there is no reason to believe that investors are not able to diversify their portfolios efficiently. Because the firm is unable to do something for them that they cannot do for themselves, diversification as a reason for merging usually is not a thing of value.[8] Consequently, it would not lead to an increase in share price. For the most part, the prospect for synergism is what is important when it comes to a merger.

Personal Reasons

In a tightly held company, the individuals who have controlling interest may want their company acquired by another company that has an established market for its stock. For estate tax purposes, it may be desirable for these individuals to hold shares of stock that are readily marketable and for which market-price quotations are available. The owners of a tightly held company may have too much of their wealth tied up in the company. By merging with a publicly held company, they obtain a marked improvement in their liquidity, enabling them to sell some of their stock and diversify their investments. Unlike the previous reasons we have investigated, this reason relates to specific stockholders as opposed to investors at large.

FINANCIAL TERMS OF EXCHANGE

When two companies are combined, a ratio of exchange occurs which denotes the relative weighting of the firms. In this section, we consider the ratio of exchange with respect to the earnings, the market prices, and the book

---

[8] In Chapter 8, we discussed certain conditions under which diversification through merging may have a positive effect on the total value of the firm. While these conditions may result in an effect, the effect is likely to be small relative to any synergistic effect.

values of the stocks of the two companies involved. We assume that the combination is consummated in stock rather than in cash or debt. The objective in any merger should be to maximize the wealth of existing stockholders. In Chapters 6 and 8, we developed a framework for analyzing a prospective acquisition's risk-return tradeoff in both firm-risk and market-risk contexts. With this information, one can assess the probable impact of the acquisition on share price. In this section, we consider the effect of a prospective acquisition on certain financial relationships. Though these relationships are embodied in the framework presented in Chapters 6 and 8, many companies prefer to analyze them separately. Whereas before we were concerned with the cash-flow impact of a merger, here we focus primarily on the earnings-per-share impact.

Earnings

In evaluating the possibility of an acquisition, it is important to at least consider the effect the merger has on the earnings per share of the surviving corporation. Suppose that Company A is considering the acquisition, by stock, of Company B. The financial data on the acquisition at the time it is being considered follow:

	Company A	Company B
Present earnings	$20,000,000	$5,000,000
Shares	5,000,000	2,000,000
Earnings per share	$ 4.00	$ 2.50
Price of stock	$64.00	$30.00
Price/earnings ratio	16	12

Assume that Company B has agreed to an offer of $35 a share to be paid in Company A stock. The exchange ratio, then, is $35/$64, or about 0.547 shares of Company A's stock for each share of Company B's stock. In total, 1,093,750 shares of Company A will need to be issued in order to acquire Company B. Assuming that the earnings of the component companies stay the same after the acquisition, earnings per share of the surviving company would be:

	Surviving Company A
Earnings	$25,000,000
Shares	6,093,750
Earnings per share	$4.10

Thus there is an immediate improvement in earnings per share for Company A as a result of the merger. Company B's former stockholders experience a reduction in earnings per share, however. For each share of B's stock they had held, they now hold 0.547 shares of A. Thus the earnings per share on each share of Company B's stock they had held is (0.547)(4.10), or $2.24, compared with $2.50 before.

Assume, however, that the price agreed upon for Company B's stock is $45 a share. The ratio of exchange, then, would be $45/$64, or about 0.703 shares of A for each share of B. In total, 1,406,250 shares would have to be issued, and earnings per share after the merger would be:

	Surviving Company *A*
Earnings	$25,000,000
Shares	6,406,250
Earnings per share	$3.90

In this case, there is initial dilution in Company A's earnings per share on account of the acquisition of Company B.[9] Dilution in earnings per share will occur anytime the price/earnings ratio paid for a company exceeds the price/earnings ratio of the company doing the acquiring. In our example, the price/earnings ratio in the first case was $35.00/$2.50, or 14, and in the second case, it was $45.00/$2.50, or 18. Because the price/earnings ratio of Company A was 16, there was an increase in earnings per share in the first case and a decrease in the second.

Thus both initial increases and decreases in earnings per share are possible. The *amount* of increase or decrease is a function of (1) the differential in price/earnings ratios, and (2) the relative size of the two firms as measured by total earnings.[10] The higher the price/earnings ratio of the acquiring company in relation to that of the company being acquired, and the larger the earnings of the acquired company in relation to those of the acquiring company, the greater the increase in earnings per share of the acquiring company. These relationships are illustrated in Figure 23-1 for three different earnings relationships. The *a* subscript for total earnings, T_a, and price/earnings ratio, P_a/E_a, denotes the acquiring company, while the *b* subscript for T_b and P_b/E_b denotes the company being acquired.

Future Earnings If the decision to acquire another company were based solely upon the initial impact on earnings per share, a company would never acquire another if there were an initial dilution in earnings per share. However, this type of analysis does not take into account the possibility of a future growth in earnings owing to the merger. If the earnings of Company B are expected to grow at a faster rate than those of Company A, a high ratio of exchange for the stock may be justified, despite the fact that there is initial dilution in earnings per share for stockholders of Company A. The superior

[9]Company B's former stockholders obtain an improvement in earnings per share. Earnings per share on each share of stock they had held is $2.74.

[10]See Walter J. Mead, "Instantaneous Merger Profit as a Conglomerate Merger Motive," *Western Economics Journal,* 7 (December 1969), 295–306.

figure 23-1
Earnings-per-share
change as a function
of the price/earnings
ratio differential and
relative earnings

growth in earnings of the acquired company may result eventually in higher earnings per share for these stockholders relative to earnings without the merger.

It is useful to graph likely future earnings per share with and without the acquisition. Figure 23-2 shows this for a hypothetical merger. The graph

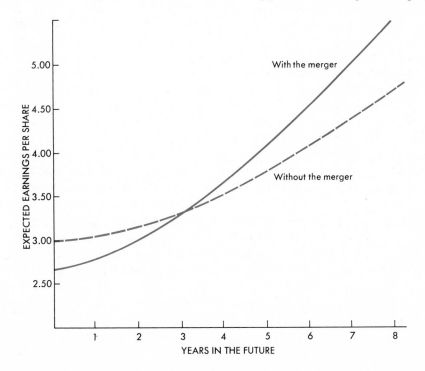

figure 23-2
Expected earnings per
share with and without
the merger

tells us how long it will take for the dilution in earnings per share to be eliminated, and for an accretion to take place. In this example, it is three years; earnings per share drop $0.30 initially, but this relative dilution is eliminated by the start of the fourth year. The greater the duration of dilution, the less desirable the acquisition is said to be from the standpoint of the acquiring company. Some companies set a ceiling on the number of years dilution will be tolerated, and this ceiling serves as a constraint in establishing the exchange ratio to be paid in the acquisition.

Another drawback to using the initial impact on earnings per share as the sole criterion for judging the value of a merger is that the earnings of the surviving company are not necessarily an additive affair, such that 2 + 2 = 4. In many cases, there are *synergistic* effects, such that 2 + 2 = 5. Because of economies, increases in demand, and so forth, earnings of the surviving company may be greater than the sum of the earnings of the two companies without the merger. In our example, suppose that total earnings three years after the merger are expected to be $36 million for the surviving company, whereas total earnings of Company A three years hence without the merger are expected to be $26 million. Assuming the price paid for Company B's stock is $45 a share, the expected earnings per share three years hence with with and without the merger are:

	With Merger	Without Merger
Expected earnings	$36,000,000	$26,000,000
Shares	6,406,250	5,000,000
Expected earnings per share	$5.62	$5.20

We see then that despite initial dilution, the acquisition of Company B produces a favorable effect upon future earnings per share over and above the expected growth in earnings per share for Company A without the merger. We can graph expected earnings per share, as in Figure 23-2, with and without the acquisition under the assumption of synergism. In fact, when an acquisition is being considered, graphs should be prepared under differing assumptions as to the exchange ratio. They also should be made under differing earnings assumptions for the combination; preparing multiple graphs gives management greater information on which to base negotiations.

Dividends per Share   The ratio of exchange of dividends per share sometimes is considered in the evaluation of a merger. However, the dividend decision really is separate from the merger decision. The important variable is prospective earnings, for dividends are a function of these earnings. The acquiring company can alter its dividend-payout ratio if the prospect of a higher total dividend is enticing to the stockholders of the company being acquired. Justification for this action, however, must be based upon an analysis of its effect upon shareholder wealth (see Chapters 11 and 12).

Market Value

The major emphasis in the bargaining process is on the ratio of exchange of market prices per share. The market price of a publicly held stock is the focal judgment of investors as to the "intrinsic" value of that company. Accordingly, it reflects the earnings potential of the company, dividends, business risk, capital structure, asset values, and other factors that bear upon valuation. The ratio of exchange of market prices is simply:

$$\frac{\text{Market price per share of acquiring company} \times \text{Number of shares offered}}{\text{Market price per share of acquired company}}$$

For example, if the market price of Company A is $60 per share and that of Company B is $30, and Company A offers a half share of its stock for each share of Company B, the ratio of exchange would be

$$\frac{\$60 \times 0.5}{\$30} = 1.00$$

In other words, the stocks of the two companies would be exchanged on a one-to-one market-price basis. If the market price of the surviving company is relatively stable at $60 a share, each set of stockholders is about as well off as before with respect to market value. However, there is little enticement to the company being acquired to accept a one-to-one market-value ratio of exchange. Consequently, the acquiring company usually must offer a price in excess of the current market price per share of the company it wishes to acquire. Instead of a half share of stock, Company A might have to offer 0.667 shares, or $40 a share in current market value.

Even when the acquiring company offers a price in excess of the current market price of the company being acquired, its own stockholders could be better off with respect to market price per share. The reason is that there may be a difference in the price/earnings ratios of the two companies. Suppose that Company B is a moderate-sized company whose stock is traded in the over-the-counter market. Because, among other reasons, its stock is not particularly marketable, its price/earnings ratio is 10. Company A, on the other hand, has a price/earnings ratio of 18. Assume the following financial information:

	Company A	Company B
Present earnings	$20,000,000	$6,000,000
Shares	6,000,000	2,000,000
Earnings per share	$ 3.33	$ 3.00
Market price per share	$60.00	$30.00
Price/earnings ratio	18	10

With an offer of 0.667 shares of Company A for each share of Company B, or $40 a share in value, the market-price exchange ratio for Company B is

$$\frac{\$60 \times 0.667}{\$30} = 1.33$$

Stockholders of Company B are being offered a stock with a market value of $40 for each share of stock they own. Obviously, they benefit from the acquisition with respect to market price, because their stock was formerly worth $30 a share. However, the stockholders of Company A also stand to benefit, *if the price/earnings ratio of the surviving company stays at 18.* The market price per share of the surviving company after the acquisition, all other things held constant, would be:

	Surviving Company
Total earnings	$26,000,000
Number of shares	7,333,333
Earnings per share	$3.55
Price/earnings ratio	18
Market price per share	$63.90

The reason for this apparent bit of magic whereby the stockholders of both companies benefit is the difference in price/earnings ratios.

Under the conditions described above, companies with high price/earnings ratios would be able to acquire companies with lower price/earnings ratios and obtain an immediate increase in earnings per share, despite the fact that they pay a premium with respect to the market value exchange ratio. The key factor, however, is what happens to the price/earnings ratio after the merger. If it stays the same, the market price of the stock will increase. As a result, an acquiring company would be able to show a steady growth in earnings per share if it acquired a sufficient number of companies over time in this manner.[11] Recognize that this increase is not the result of economies or underlying growth but is due to the "bootstrap" increase in earnings per share through acquisitions. To the extent the marketplace values this illusory growth, a company presumably could increase shareholder wealth through acquisitions alone. However, in reasonably efficient capital markets it seems unlikely that the market will hold constant the price/earnings ratio of a company that cannot demonstrate growth potential in ways other than acquiring companies with lower price/earnings ratios. The acquiring company must be able to manage the companies it acquires if the benefit of acquisitions is to be lasting.

[11]For further illustration of this process, see Mead, "Instantaneous Merger Profit," pp. 298–99.

Thus the acquiring company must consider the possibility that its price/earnings ratio will change with an acquisition. If the market is relatively free from imperfections and if synergism is not anticipated, we would expect the price/earnings ratio of the surviving firm to approach a weighted average of the two previous price/earnings ratios. Under these circumstances, the acquisition of companies with lower price/earnings ratios would not enhance shareholder wealth. In fact, if the market-price exchange ratio were more than one, shareholder wealth would decline. If synergism were expected, however, shareholder wealth could be increased through the acquisition. All of this is in keeping with our earlier discussion of the issue in Chapter 8.

Book Value

Book value per share is rather meaningless as a basis for valuation in most mergers. Whereas it was once the dominant factor, book value per share is important now only when it is significantly above market value. When the purpose of an acquisition is to obtain the liquidity of another company, book value per share and working capital per share become important in the terms of the exchange. For example, a number of years ago Textron acquired American Woolen primarily for the latter's liquidity. American Woolen's book value per share was approximately $60, its working capital per share was $24, and its market price per share was $16. Textron paid $25 a share in cash. The ratios of exchange of book value per share of two companies are calculated in the same manner as is the ratio for market values. The importance of this ratio in bargaining is usually restricted to situations in which a company is acquired for its liquidity and asset values rather than for its earning power.

TENDER OFFERS

In our hypothetical examples, it was assumed that negotiations were confined to the managements and boards of directors of the companies involved. However, the acquiring company can make its appeal directly to the stockholders of the company it wishes to acquire through a *tender offer*. A tender offer is an offer to purchase shares of stock of another company at a fixed price per share from any stockholder who "tenders" his shares. The tender price is usually set significantly above the present market price in order to provide an incentive to stockholders to tender their shares. Use of the tender offer allows the acquiring company to bypass the management of the company it wishes to acquire and, therefore, serves as a threat in any negotiations with that management. If management holds out for too high a price or otherwise balks at the offer of the acquiring company, that company can always make a tender offer.

The tender offer can also be used when there are no negotiations but when one company simply wants to acquire another. In a "surprise" tender offer, the acquiring company is careful not to reveal its intentions significantly in advance of the actual offer. However, when the tender offer involves a new issue of common stock, the securities must be registered in advance with the Securities and Exchange Commission. Such a registration, of course, eliminates the element of surprise and for this reason many tender offers are for cash. In both cash and stock tenders, the primary selling tool is the premium that is offered over the existing market price of the stock.[12] As a rule of thumb, a minimum premium of 20 percent may be required, which is adjusted up depending upon the circumstances. In addition, brokers are often given very attractive commissions for shares tendered through them. The tender offer itself is usually communicated through financial newspapers. Direct mailings are made to the stockholders of the company being bid for if the bidder is able to obtain a stockholders' list. Although a company is legally obligated to provide such a list, it usually is able to delay delivery long enough to frustrate the bidder.

From the standpoint of the company being bid for, a number of defensive tactics are available. First, management may try to persuade its stockholders that the offer is not in their best interests. Usually, the argument is that the bid is too low in relation to the true, long-run value of the firm. However, in the face of an attractive premium, the long run may be too distant. Some companies raise the cash dividend or declare a stock split in hopes of gaining stockholder support. Legal actions are often undertaken, more to delay and frustrate the bidder than with the expectation of winning. To the extent that the two firms are competitors, an antitrust suit may prove a powerful deterrent to the bidder. As a last resort, management of the company being bid for may seek a merger with a "friendly" company. Some of the strategies involved in tender offers are depicted in Figure 23-3.

Although the use of tender offers increased dramatically in the sixties, it declined in importance in the seventies. In part, this decline was due to coinciding changes in security regulations and accounting rules that tended to restrict the prospective acquirer. There are many who oppose such restrictions because they believe tender offers contribute to corporate "democracy" and, thereby, serve a socially useful function. If management does not behave so as to maximize the value of the firm to its shareholders, there is always the danger of a tender offer from another company. Whereas stockholders may not have enough control to effect a change otherwise, a tender offer may bring about a change and increase shareholder wealth.[13] In

---

[12]For an extended discussion of these and other issues involving tender-offer takeovers, see "Corporate Takeovers—The Unfriendly Tender Offer and the Minority Stockholder Freezeout," special issue of *The Business Lawyer,* 32 (May 1977).

[13]For a study of the stock-return performance of target companies and of bidder companies before and after tender offers, see Donald R. Kummer and J. Ronald Hoffmeister, "Valua-

A bidder takes pains to keep his intentions secret until the last minute.
"Claude; Courtesy of *Fortune Magazine.*"

Management often seeks to foil a bidder by quickly arranging a merger with another company.
"Claude; Courtesy of *Fortune Magazine.*"

Determined management opposition can usually fend off an unwanted take-over bid.
"Claude; Courtesy of *Fortune Magazine.*"

figure 23-3
Tender-offer strategies

tion Consequences of Cash Tender Offers," *Journal of Finance,* 33 (May 1978), 505–16. For an empirical study of the per share transaction costs involved in a tender offer, see Robert Smiley, "Tender Offers, Transaction Costs and the Firm," *Review of Economics and Statistics,* 58 (February 1976), 22–32.

recent years, the tender offer has largely displaced the proxy contest as a means of obtaining control of a company.

SUMMARY

A company may grow internally, or it may grow externally through acquisitions. The objective of the firm in either case should be to maximize existing shareholder wealth. Another company can be acquired through the purchase of either its assets or its stock. In turn, the means of payment can be cash, or it can be stock. When two companies combine and one loses its corporate existence, the combination is known as a merger; if two companies combine and form a new corporation, the combination is known as a consolidation. Other than merging or consolidating, one company can purchase effective working control of another company and act as a holding company. Accounting considerations come into play in that the merger must be treated either as a purchase or as a pooling of interests. With a purchase, any goodwill arising from the merger must be amortized against future earnings. The accounting method used depends on the circumstances of the merger and the constraints imposed by rules of the accounting profession.

There are a number of reasons for acquiring another company, all of which relate to expected return and risk. Among the more important are operating economies, economies of scale, acquisition of management, diversification, growth potential, and personal motives of the owners. Each was explored, and some of the common fallacies in reasoning were examined. In cases where the acquiring company does not wish to negotiate with the management of the prospective company, it can make a tender offer to purchase shares directly from the stockholders of that company.

Whenever there is an exchange of stock between two companies, certain financial relationships become important. Many companies focus on the impact on earnings per share. When the price/earnings ratio of the company being acquired is lower than the price/earnings ratio of the acquiring company, there is an initial improvement in earnings per share of the latter company; a dilution occurs when the price/earnings ratio is higher. Instead of looking only at the effect on initial earnings per share, it is desirable to look at the effect on expected future earnings per share as well. In efficient financial markets and in the absence of synergism, we would expect the price/earnings ratio of the surviving company to be a weighted average of the price/earnings ratios of the two premerger companies. For the most part, wealth cannot be created simply by merging with companies with low price/earnings ratios.

The basic economic foundation for mergers is the cash flows expected to be realized with the fusion of two companies, together with the incremental impact on systematic risk of the combined entity. This foundation was presented in Chapters 6 and 8. Our attention in this chapter was directed to the more practical considerations that arise in any merger. Most of these considerations are embodied in the more fundamental economic foundation, but at times they can exert an independent influence.

1. The following data are pertinent for Companies A and B:

	Company A	Company B
Present earnings (in millions)	$20	$ 4
Shares (in millions)	10	1
Price/earnings ratio	18	10

   (a) If the two companies were to merge and the exchange ratio were one share of Company A for each share of Company B, what would be the initial impact on earnings per share of the two companies? What is the market value exchange ratio? Is a merger likely to take place?
   (b) If the exchange ratio were two shares of Company A for each share of Company B, what happens with respect to the above?
   (c) If the exchange ratio were 1.5 shares of Company A for each share of Company B, what happens?
   (d) What exchange ratio would you suggest?

2.

	Net Income	Number of Shares	Market Price per Share	Tax Rate
Nimbus Company	$5,000,000	1,000,000	$100	50%
Noor Company	1,000,000	500,000	20	50

   The Nimbus Company wishes to acquire the Noor Company. If the merger were effected through an exchange of stock, Nimbus would be willing to pay a 25 percent premium for the Noor shares. If done for cash, the terms would have to be as favorable to the Noor shareholders; to obtain the cash, Nimbus would have to sell its own stock in the market.

   (a) Compute the exchange ratio and the combined earnings per share if an exchange of stock were accomplished.
   (b) If we assume that all Noor shareholders have held their stock for more than one year, have a 20 percent marginal capital gains tax rate, and paid an average of $14 for their shares, what cash price would have to be offered to be as attractive as the terms in (a) above?

3. Assume the exchange of Nimbus shares for Noor shares as outlined in problem 2 above.

   (a) What is the ratio of exchange?
   (b) Compare the earnings per Noor share before and after the merger. Compare the earnings per Nimbus share. On this basis alone, which group fared better? Why?
   (c) Why do you imagine that old Nimbus commanded a higher P/E than Noor? What should be the change in P/E ratio resulting from the merger?
   (d) If the Nimbus Company is in a high-technology growth industry and Noor makes cement, would you revise your answers?

(e) In determining the appropriate P/E ratio for Nimbus, should the increase in earnings resulting from this merger be added as a growth factor?

(f) In light of the above discussion, do you feel that the Noor shareholders would have approved the merger if Noor stock paid a $1 dividend and Nimbus paid $3? Why?

4. Instead of an exchange of stock (see problem 2 (b)), suppose that Nimbus offered Noor shareholders a 5 percent preferred stock, $100 par value, convertible 20 percent above the market, at the same exchange ratio proposed for the common stock. Assume the common-stock dividend payments of problem 3 (f).

(a) If this transaction were viewed as an exchange of common stock, what is the effective exchange ratio?

(b) Compute the change in dividend income per Noor share after the exchange for Nimbus convertible preferred. Compute the change in dividend income after conversion into Nimbus common.

(c) Compute earnings per share for new Nimbus before and after conversion.

(d) Compute earnings retention before and after conversion, assuming the dividend remains the same.

5. Copper Tube Company currently has annual earnings of $10 million, with 4 million shares of common stock outstanding and a market price per share of $30. In the absence of any mergers, Copper Tube's annual earnings are expected to grow at a compound rate of 5 percent per annum. Brass Fitting Company, whom Copper Tube is considering acquiring, has present annual earnings of $2 million, 1 million shares of common outstanding, and a market price per share of $32. Its annual earnings are expected to grow at a compound annual rate of 10 percent per annum. Copper Tube is considering offering 1.2 shares of its stock for each share of Brass Fitting Company. No synergistic effects are expected from the merger.

(a) What is the immediate effect on the surviving company's earnings per share?

(b) Would you want to acquire Brass Fitting Company? If it is not attractive now, when will it be attractive from the standpoint of earnings per share?

6. The shares of the Navigation Company and the Matson Company have the following characteristics:

	Navigation	Matson
EPS	$ 4	$ 2
Growth in EPS expected forever	5%	10%
Number of shares (in millions)	10	3
Price per share	$40	$30

(a) If Navigation acquires Matson with an exchange of stock on the basis of their market values, what will be the new EPS?

(b) Graph Navigation EPS into the future with and without the acquisition (assume no synergism).

(c) How long would it take to eliminate the dilution?

7. Let it be assumed that a holding company can always be set up with 50 percent debt at 8 percent and 20 percent preferred stock at 6 percent. Further assume

that all companies pay a tax rate of 50 percent, that the 85 percent intercorporate dividend exclusion applies in all cases, and that ownership of 40 percent of the stock of another company constitutes control. The shares of the Target Company can be obtained at their book value.

Target Company			
Total assets	$30,000,000	Debt (8%)	$15,000,000
		Preferred (6%)	5,000,000
		Common	10,000,000
			$30,000,000

(a) A group of investors has set up Holding Company A to acquire control of the Target Company. If the group holds all the equity of Holding Company A, how much money must they put up? If Target has operating earnings equal to 20 percent of total assets and pays all earnings in dividends, what return on investment will the group earn?

(b) Suppose the group sets up Holding Company B to acquire control of Holding Company A. If the group holds all the equity of B, how much money must they put up? If A pays all earnings in dividends, what return on investment will the group earn? How many dollars of operating assets does the group control per dollar of their own investment?

(c) How would your answers change if Target had operating earnings equal to 8 percent of total assets?

8. Collect data on situations where one company made a tender offer for the shares of another, and management hurriedly conducted negotiations with a third company. Compare the terms of the two offers, especially with regard to the price of the offer. Did the offer endorsed by management always bear the highest price? Should this not be the case under the theory? Examine the other terms of the offers, including employment contracts, options, bonuses, and retirement provisions. Correlate management's endorsement with

(a) Those offers having the highest price, and then

(b) Those having the most favorable employment terms.

Which correlation is higher? Why? Finally, determine which offer was accepted by the stockholders. Correlate this with (a) those having the highest price, and (b) those endorsed by management. Which correlation is higher? Why?

SELECTED REFERENCES

APPLEYARD, A. R., AND G. K. YARROW, "The Relationship between Take-over Activity and Share Valuation," *Journal of Finance*, 30 (December 1975), 1239–50.

AUSTIN, DOUGLAS V., "The Financial Management of Tender Offer Takeovers," *Financial Management*, 3 (Spring 1974), 37–43.

CONN, ROBERT L., AND JAMES F. NIEISEN, "An Empirical Test of the Larson-Gonedes Exchange Ratio Determination Model," *Journal of Finance*, 32 (September 1977), 749–59.

"Corporate Takeovers—The Unfriendly Tender Offer and the Minority Stockholder Freezeout," special issue of *The Business Lawyer*, 32 (May 1977).

CUNITZ, JONATHAN A., "Valuing Potential Acquisitions," *Financial Executive,* 39 (April 1971), 16–28.

DODD, PETER, AND RICHARD RUBACK, "Tender Offers and Stockholder Returns," *Journal of Financial Economics,* 5 (November 1977), 351–73.

HAUGEN, ROBERT A., AND TERRENCE C. LANGETIEG, "An Empirical Test for Synergism in Merger," *Journal of Finance,* 30 (September 1975), 1003–14.

HAYES, SAMUEL L. III, AND RUSSELL A. TAUSSIG, "Tactics in Cash Takeover Bids," *Harvard Business Review,* 45 (March-April 1967), 135–48.

HEATH, JOHN, JR., "Valuation Factors and Techniques in Mergers and Acquisitions," *Financial Executive,* 40 (April 1972), 34–44.

HIGGINS, ROBERT C., AND LAWRENCE D. SCHALL, "Corporate Bankruptcy and Conglomerate Merger," *Journal of Finance,* 30 (March 1975), 93–114.

HOGARTY, THOMAS F., "The Profitability of Corporate Mergers," *Journal of Business,* 43 (July 1970), 317–27.

HOWELL, ROBERT A., "Plan to Integrate Your Acquisitions," *Harvard Business Review,* 48 (November-December 1970), 66–76.

KIM, E. HAN, AND JOHN J. McCONNELL, "Corporate Merger and the Co-insurance of Corporate Debt," *Journal of Finance,* forthcoming.

KUMMER, DONALD R., AND J. RONALD HOFFMEISTER, "Valuation Consequences of Cash Tender Offers," *Journal of Finance,* 33 (May 1978), 505–16.

LARSON, KERMIT D., AND NICHOLAS J. GONEDES, "Business Combinations: An Exchange-Ratio Determination Model," *Accounting Review,* 44 (October 1969), 720–28.

LEV, BARUCH, AND GERSHON MANDELKER, "The Microeconomic Consequences of Corporate Mergers," *Journal of Business,* 45 (January 1972), 85–104.

LEWELLEN, WILBUR G., "A Pure Financial Rationale for the Conglomerate Merger," *Journal of Finance,* 26 (May 1971), 521–37.

MacDOUGAL, GARY E., AND FRED V. MALEK, "Master Plan for Merger Negotiations," *Harvard Business Review,* 48 (January-February 1970), 71–82.

MANDELKER, GERSHON, "Risk and Return: The Case of Merging Firms," *Journal of Financial Economics,* 1 (December 1974), 303–35.

MASON, HAL R., AND MAURICE B. GOUDZWAARD, "Performance of Conglomerate Firms: A Portfolio Approach," *Journal of Finance,* 31 (March 1976), 39–48.

MEAD, WALTER J., "Instantaneous Merger Profit as a Conglomerate Merger Motive," *Western Economic Review,* 7 (December 1969), 295–306.

MELICHER, RONALD W., AND DAVID F. RUSH, "Evidence on the Acquisition-Related Performance of Conglomerate Firms," *Journal of Finance,* 29 (March 1974), 141–50.

REINHARDT, UWE E., *Mergers and Consolidations: A Corporate-Finance Approach.* Morristown: General Learning Press, 1972.

SCOTT, JAMES H., JR., "On the Theory of Conglomerate Mergers," *Journal of Finance,* 32 (September 1977), 1235–50.

SHICK, RICHARD A., "The Analysis of Mergers and Acquisitions," *Journal of Finance,* 27 (May 1972), 495–502.

SHICK, RICHARD A., AND FRANK C. JEN, "Merger Benefits to Shareholders of Acquiring Firms," *Financial Management,* 3 (Winter 1974), 45–53.

SMALTER, DONALD J., AND RODERIC C. LANCEY, "P/E Analysis in Acquisition Strategy," *Harvard Business Review,* 44 (November-December 1966), 85–95.

SMILEY, ROBERT, "Tender Offers, Transactions Costs and the Firm," *Review of Economics and Statistics,* 58 (February 1976), 22–32.

STEVENS, DONALD L., "Financial Characteristics of Merged Firms: A Multivariate Analysis," *Journal of Financial and Quantitative Analysis,* 8 (March 1973), 149–58.

WESTON, J. FRED, KEITH V. SMITH, AND RONALD E. SHRIEVES, "Conglomerate Performance Using the Capital Asset Pricing Model," *Review of Economics and Statistics* (November 1972), 357–63.

24

business failure and reorganization

Our analysis throughout most of the book has assumed that the firm is a going concern; nevertheless, we must not lose sight of the fact that some firms fail. Recognition of this possibility is important both from the standpoint of internal management, and from the standpoint of a creditor with amounts owing from a company in financial distress. This point was brought into sharp focus in the 1970s with the bankruptcy of such large companies as Penn Central and W. T. Grant. Previously, bankruptcy was regarded as a phenomenon restricted to small firms—the Depression of the thirties being the last time major corporations had failed.

The word "failure" is vague, partly because there are varying degrees of failure. For example, a company is regarded as technically insolvent if it is unable to meet its current obligations. However, such insolvency may be only temporary and subject to remedy.[1] Insolvency in bankruptcy, on the other

---

[1]See James E. Walter, "Determination of Technical Insolvency," *Journal of Business,* 30 (January 1957), 30–43.

hand, means that the liabilities of a company exceed its assets; in other words, the net worth of the company is negative. Financial failure includes the entire range of possibilities between these extremes.

The remedies available to save a failing company vary in harshness according to the degree of financial difficulty. If the outlook is sufficiently hopeless, liquidation may be the only feasible alternative. However, many failing firms can be rehabilitated to the gain of creditors, stockholders, and society. Although the major purpose of a liquidation or rehabilitation is to protect creditors, the interests of the owners also are considered. (In the thirties, they were all but neglected.) Still, legal procedures favor creditors. Otherwise, they would hesitate to extend credit, and the allocation of funds in the economy would be less than efficient.

PREDICTION OF FINANCIAL DISTRESS

Although the causes of financial difficulty are numerous, many failures are attributable either directly or indirectly to management. Usually, nonfinancial problems lead to losses, which, in turn, lead to financial strain and eventual failure. Very seldom is one bad decision the cause of the difficulty; usually the cause is a series of errors, and the difficulty evolves gradually. Because with most companies the signs of potential distress are evident prior to actual failure, a creditor may be able to take corrective actions before failure finally occurs.

In an extensive research study, William H. Beaver used financial ratios to predict failure.[2] The study encompassed a sample of seventy-nine relatively large firms that failed.[3] For each of these companies, another firm was selected that did not fail but was in the same industry and was of approximately the same size as the firm that failed. The data collected for the nonfailed companies were for the same years as those for the failed firms. These samples were used to test the predictive ability of thirty financial ratios. The mean values of the ratios for the two samples were compared over the five-year period prior to failure. An example of such a comparison, using the cash-flow/total-debt ratio, is shown in Figure 24-1. We see that the mean ratio for the failed firms differs significantly from that for the nonfailed firms. Not only is it lower, but it deteriorates markedly as failure approaches.

In addition to a comparison of mean values, Beaver tested the samples using a form of discriminant analysis and then went on to analyze the evidence using likelihood ratios. Although not all of the financial ratios examined predicted failure equally well, many showed excellent predictive power. In a companion article, Beaver investigated the ability to predict

---

[2]"Financial Ratios as Predictors of Failure," *Empirical Research in Accounting: Selected Studies*, supplement to *Journal of Accounting Research* (1966), pp. 71–111.

[3]*Failure* was defined as the inability of a firm to meet its financial obligations.

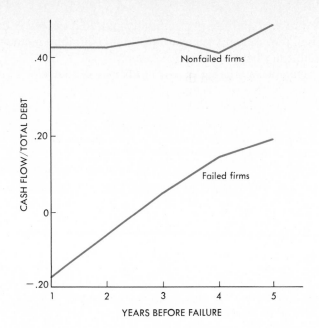

figure 24-1
Comparison of
mean values for failed
and nonfailed firms

failure from the changes in market prices of stocks.[4] He found that the median market price of the failed companies declined at an increasing rate as failure approached, relative to that for the nonfailed companies. The largest price decline occurred in the final year. Beaver concluded that investors adjust stock prices to the deteriorating condition of failing companies. Moreover, he found the evidence to be consistent with investors assessing the likelihood for failure on the basis of financial ratios.

In a similar type of study, Edward I. Altman employed multiple discriminant analysis to predict bankruptcy, using various financial ratios.[5] This statistical technique is described in the Appendix to Chapter 15. Altman worked with a sample of thirty-three corporations that filed for bankruptcy during the 1946–65 period. Like Beaver, he collected a paired sample of thirty-three nonbankrupt firms on a stratified random basis. Starting with twenty-two financial ratios, he selected the five that did the best combined job of predicting bankruptcy. These ratios were used to discriminate between bankrupt and nonbankrupt firms, using data from one to five years prior to

[4]William H. Beaver, "Market Prices, Financial Ratios, and the Prediction of Failure," *Journal of Accounting Research*, 6 (Autumn 1968), 179–92.

[5]"Financial Ratios, Discriminant Analysis and the Prediction of Corporate Bankruptcy," *Journal of Finance*, 23 (September 1968), 589–609. For a discussion of discriminant analysis as it applies to finance problems as well as an analysis of Altman's approach, see O. Maurice Joy and John O. Tollefson, "On the Financial Application of Discriminant Analysis," *Journal of Financial and Quantitative Analysis*, 10 (December 1975), 723–39; and Robert A. Eisenbeis, "Pitfalls in the Application of Discriminant Analysis in Business Finance and Economics," *Journal of Finance*, 32 (June 1977), 875–900.

bankruptcy. As expected, the predictive accuracy of the multiple discriminant model declined with the number of years prior to bankruptcy. However, the model was able to forecast failure quite well up to two years before bankruptcy. Altman also tested the model with secondary samples of bankrupt and nonbankrupt firms. Using the parameter estimates obtained in the original sample, he found the model to have considerable predictive accuracy when used in conjunction with the secondary samples. In his investigation, Altman, like Beaver, found that the financial ratios of bankrupt firms deteriorated as bankruptcy approached, the greatest deterioration occurring between the third and the second year. Altman concluded that through discriminant analysis, a creditor can predict potential bankruptcy successfully.

In a study similar to those of Beaver and Altman, Edward B. Deakin used a paired sample of thirty-two failed and nonfailed firms over the 1964–70 period.[6] Using discriminant analysis in conjunction with fourteen financial ratios, he found that bankruptcy could be predicted with a fairly high degree of accuracy as far ahead as three years. (The error rates increased sharply in the fourth and fifth years.) In essence, Deakin replicated Beaver's sampling method and found that discriminant analysis did a better job of predicting.

R. Charles Moyer also tested the usefulness of discriminant analysis in predicting bankruptcy.[7] In first testing Altman's discriminant function for five financial ratios, where the parameters were generated using 1946–65 data, Moyer found that predictive ability dropped dramatically when this function was used to predict bankruptcies during 1965–75. He concluded that caution was necessary when applying the original Altman model parameters to new data. However, when the model's parameters were reestimated using a stepwise routine that excluded superfluous variables, predictive accuracy was high. Like the other studies, accuracy declined as the number of years prior to failure was increased. In comparing the Altman model with alternative predictive models of failure, Moyer concluded that it stood up rather well with respect to discriminatory ability.

In a recent study, Edward I. Altman, Robert G. Haldeman, and P. Narayanan extended the original Altman discriminant function model and updated its application to the 1969–75 period.[8] A sample of fifty-three bankrupt firms and a matched sample of fifty-eight nonbankrupt firms were employed. Included in the samples were both manufacturing and retailing companies; this study represents the first to include retailing firms. On the

---

[6]"A Discriminant Analysis of Predictors of Business Failure," *Journal of Accounting Research,* 10 (Spring 1972), 167–79. For another study of this sort involving failure prediction, see Marc Blum, "Failing Company Discriminant Analysis," *Journal of Accounting Research,* 12 (Spring 1974), 1–25.

[7]"Forecasting Financial Failure: A Re-examination," *Financial Management,* 6 (Spring 1977), 11–17.

[8]"Zeta Analysis: A New Model to Identify Bankruptcy Risk of Corporations," *Journal of Banking and Finance,* 1 (June 1977). Both quadratic and linear models were tested, with the linear function winning out.

basis of discriminatory ability, twenty-seven original variables were reduced to seven: the return on assets ratio; the stability of earnings; the interest coverage ratio; the retained earnings to total assets ratio; the current ratio; the common equity to total capital ratio; and the size of total assets. Using a linear discriminant model, the authors were successful in predicting bankruptcy up to five years prior to failure. Successful classification ranged from 96 percent one year before failure to 70 percent five years before failure. In comparing their model with alternative models, including the original Altman model, the authors found it to be more accurate.

In yet another study, Jarrod W. Wilcox used a stochastic model in conjunction with a paired sample of matched failed and nonfailed companies of similar size and industry characteristics.[9] In total, fifty-two bankrupt firms over the 1949–71 period were studied. Accounting data were used to derive the adjusted cash position and the adjusted cash flow of the failed and non-failed firms, together with the variances of these measures, for each of the five years prior to failure. Using a gambler's ruin model, Wilcox ranked the risk of bankruptcy between the failed and the paired nonfailed firms. A high degree of correct predictions was found: 0.94, 0.90, 0.88, 0.90, and 0.76 for one to five years before failure, respectively.

Robert O. Edmister tested the usefulness of financial ratio analysis for predicting the failure of small businesses.[10] Similar to the others, he employed multiple discriminant analysis and found it to be an accurate predictor of failure if ratios were averaged over a three-year span. Unlike the results of Beaver and Altman, however, an analysis based upon one year's financial statements was not sufficient to discriminate failing from nonfailing firms. Consecutive financial statements were necessary for the successful analysis of small-business failures.

On the basis of the empirical studies described above, it would appear that signs of potential failure are evident well before actual failure occurs. For the creditor, the lag allows time to take corrective actions.

VOLUNTARY SETTLEMENTS

Despite difficulties caused by past mistakes, many companies can be preserved as going concerns and can make an economic contribution to society. Sometimes the rehabilitation is severe, in keeping with the degree of financial

---

[9]"A Prediction of Business Failure Using Accounting Data," *Empirical Research in Accounting: Selected Studies,* 1973, supplement to Volume 11 of the *Journal of Accounting Research,* See also Wilcox, "A Simple Theory of Financial Ratios as Predictors of Failure," *Journal of Accounting Research,* 9 (1971), 389–95.

[10]"An Empirical Test of Financial Ratio Analysis for Small Business Failure Prediction," *Journal of Financial and Quantitative Analysis,* 7 (March 1972), 1477–93. For an excellent overall discussion of this type of research, see Baruch Lev, *Financial Statement Analysis: A New Approach* (Englewood Cliffs, N.J.: Prentice-Hall, 1974), Part II.

difficulty. Nevertheless, these measures may be necessary if the firm is to obtain a new lease on life. In this chapter, we consider the remedies available to a company in financial distress, beginning with remedies that are voluntary on the part of creditors and the company and then examining legal actions that can be taken in connection with a failing company. It is important to recognize that at the time this chapter was being written, Congress was in the process of passing a major reform of the Bankruptcy Act. In what follows, we describe the remedies available to a failing firm under the existing Bankruptcy Act. In the last section of the chapter, we examine the major features of the new legislation.

Extensions

An extension involves nothing more than creditors extending the maturity of their obligations. In cases of temporary insolvency of a basically sound company, creditors may prefer to work the problem out with the company. By not forcing the issue with legal proceedings, creditors avoid considerable legal expense and the possible shrinkage of value in liquidation. Obviously, no one creditor is going to extend his obligation unless others do likewise. Consequently, the major creditors usually form a committee whose function is to negotiate with the company and to formulate a plan mutually satisfactory to all concerned.

We must point out, however, that no one creditor is obligated to go along with the plan. If there are dissenting creditors and they have small amounts owing, they may be paid off in order to avoid legal proceedings. The number of dissenters cannot be too large, for the remaining creditors must, in essence, assume their obligations. Obviously, the remaining creditors do not want to be left "holding the bag." If an extension is worked out, the creditors can institute controls over the company to assure proper management and to increase the probability of speedy recovery. In addition, they may elect to take security if marketable assets are available. The ultimate threat on the part of creditors is to initiate bankruptcy proceedings against the company and to force it into liquidation. By making an extension, however, they show an inclination to cooperate with the company.

Composition

A composition involves a pro rata settlement of creditors' claims in cash or in cash and promissory notes. The creditors must agree to accept a partial settlement in discharge of their entire claim. For example, a debtor may propose a settlement of sixty cents on the dollar. If creditors feel that the settlement is more than they could obtain in liquidation after legal expenses, they will probably accept. Even if it is somewhat less, they may still accept, because no company likes to be responsible for forcing another into bankruptcy. The settlement is a "friendly" one in the sense that legal proceedings are avoided.

As in an extension, however, the settlement must be agreed to by all creditors. Dissenting creditors must be paid in full, or they can force the company into bankruptcy. These creditors can be a considerable nuisance and may all but preclude a voluntary settlement. Overall, voluntary settlements can be advantageous to creditors as well as to the debtors, for they avoid legal expenses and complications.

Liquidation by Voluntary Agreement

In certain circumstances, creditors may feel that the company should not be preserved, because further financial deterioration seems inevitable. When liquidation is the only realistic solution, it can be accomplished either through a private settlement or through bankruptcy proceedings. An orderly private liquidation is likely to be more efficient and result in a significantly higher settlement. Such a voluntary liquidation is known as an *assignment*. A private settlement can also be through a formal assignment of assets to an appointed trustee. The trustee liquidates the assets and distributes the proceeds to creditors on a pro rata basis. Because the voluntary settlement must be agreed to by all creditors, it usually is restricted to companies with a limited number of creditors and securities outstanding that are not publicly held.

LEGAL PROCEDURES

Most legal procedures undertaken in connection with failing companies fall under the Bankruptcy Act of 1898, as amended by the Chandler Act of 1938. This act provides both for the liquidation of a company and for its reorganization. In most cases, the courts take over the operation of the company and preserve the *status quo* until a decision is reached whether to liquidate the company or keep it alive through reorganization.

Liquidation

If there is no hope for the successful operation of a company, liquidation is the only feasible alternative. The federal district court, then, declares the firm bankrupt and proceeds with a plan for orderly liquidation. Bankruptcy proceedings may be either voluntary or involuntary. With a voluntary bankruptcy, the company files a petition of bankruptcy with a federal district court. In an involuntary bankruptcy where there are more than twelve creditors, three or more of them with claims in excess of $500 may initiate the action by filing a petition with the court. However, the total debts of the company involved must be $1,000 or more. If the total number of creditors is less than twelve, any one creditor may file a petition. The federal court will declare the company an involuntary bankrupt if it violates one of the six acts of bankruptcy in the four months preceding the petition.[11]

Upon the declaration of bankruptcy, the court usually appoints a *referee* to take over the operation of the company temporarily and call a meeting of the creditors. The referee in bankruptcy is usually an outside lawyer who is appointed for a specific term. At the meeting of creditors, claims are proven, and the creditors are given the opportunity to appoint the *trustee in bankruptcy*. The trustee has the responsibility of liquidating the assets of the company and distributing liquidating dividends to the creditors. The conduct of the trustee in carrying out these responsibilites is under the supervision of the court. Until the trustee is appointed, the referee has full control of the situation.

In the distribution of the proceeds of a liquidation, the priority of claims must be observed. The administrative costs involved in the bankruptcy, unpaid wages up to $600 per employee earned within the previous three months, and taxes must be paid before creditors are entitled to receive any settlement. Secured creditors are entitled to the proceeds realized from the liquidation of specific assets on which they have a lien. If any balance of the claim is not realized from the sale of the collateral, these creditors become general creditors. General creditors are paid liquidating dividends on a pro rata basis from the total liquidation of unencumbered assets. If all of these claims are paid in full, liquidating dividends can then be paid to subordinated debtholders, to preferred stockholders, and, finally, to common stockholders. It is unlikely, however, that common stockholders will receive any distribution from a liquidation.

Upon the payment of all liquidating dividends, the bankrupt is discharged, thereby being relieved of any further claim. The principal objective of bankruptcy proceedings is an orderly liquidation of assets and an equitable distribution to creditors on a formal basis. The disadvantage of these proceedings is that they are slower and usually more expensive than a private liquidation. Some court-appointed officials are inefficient, being more concerned with their remuneration than with the proceeds available to creditors. As a result, a liquidation in bankruptcy may be less efficient than a private liquidation, providing creditors with a lower settlement. However, when creditors cannot come together in a voluntary manner, bankruptcy proceedings are the only recourse.

---

[11]The first act involves the concealment or removal of the bankrupt's property with the intent of defrauding creditors. The second act is the transfer of cash or other assets to one creditor in preference to others. The third act is the insolvent debtor's giving any creditor a lien on his property. The fourth act involves a general assignment by the debtor for the benefit of creditors. The fifth act occurs if the debtor, while insolvent, appoints a receiver or trustee to take charge of his property. The sixth act is an admission in writing by the debtor that he is unable to pay his debt and that he is willing to be adjudged a bankrupt.

Reorganization

It may be in the best interests of all concerned to reorganize a company rather than liquidate it. A reorganization is an effort to keep a company alive by changing its capital structure. The rehabilitation involves the reduction of fixed charges by substituting equity and limited-income securities for fixed-income securities.

Procedure   Most reorganizations of industrial and public utility companies occur under Chapter X of the Bankruptcy Act. Reorganization procedures are initiated in the same general manner as a liquidation in bankruptcy. The federal district court appoints an impartial *trustee* to operate the debtor's business until a reorganization plan is put into effect.[12] If the debts of the company are in excess of $250,000, the court must appoint a "disinterested" trustee—that is, a party independent of the debtor. In addition to managing the operations of the debtor temporarily, the trustee must compile all the essential information required by the court and creditors, and if the securites are publicly held, by the Securities and Exchange Commission (SEC). Included is information pertaining to the value of assets, the nature of the liabilities, and the operating potential of the debtor from the standpoint of profitability.

Most important, the trustee is charged with the responsibility of drawing up a plan of reorganization. This plan is proposed after a thorough review of the situation and discussions with creditors and stockholders. Committees may be formed by the various classes of creditors and stockholders to represent and protect the interests of each class. The plan then is submitted to the court for hearings and approval. If liabilities exceed $3 million, and the securities are publicly held, the plan must also be submitted to the SEC. The SEC acts only in an advisory capacity to the court; it prepares a report on the proposed plan and submits it to the court. The final decision is that of the court.

If the court feels the reorganization plan is "fair, equitable, and feasible," it will approve the plan. All parties must be treated fairly and equitably; moreover, the plan must be workable with respect to the earning power and financial structure of the reorganized company. The reorganized company cannot have too great an amount of fixed financial charges in relation to its expected earning power. Upon approval by the court, the plan is submitted to the creditor and stockholder groups for approval. In order to become effective, it must be accepted by a two-thirds majority of each class of debtholders and by a simple majority of each class of stockholders. Upon approval by the majority of a particular class of security holders, the plan is binding on dissenters in that class.

---

[12]The company is declared a "debtor" in a reorganization as opposed to a "bankrupt" in a liquidation.

The reorganization procedure for railroads is similar, except that the Interstate Commerce Commission plays an active role in the reorganization. Railroad reorganizations occur under Section 77 of the Bankruptcy Act and the Mahaffe Act of 1948. The reorganization plan must be submitted to the ICC, which approves the trustee. The ICC holds hearings and then either approves the proposed reorganization plan or submits its own plan to the court. The concern of the ICC is that the reorganization plan be compatible with the public's interest. The court, however, must approve the plan on the basis of whether it is fair, equitable, and feasible.

Reorganization Plan   The difficult aspect of a reorganization is the recasting of the company's capital structure to reduce the amount of fixed charges. In formulating a reorganization plan, the trustee must carry out three steps. First, he must determine the total valuation of the reorganized company. This step, perhaps, is the most difficult and the most important. The technique favored by trustees is a capitalization of prospective earnings. For example, if future annual earnings of the reorganized company are expected to be $2 million, and the overall capitalization rate of similar companies averages 10 percent, a total valuation of $20 million would be set for the company. The valuation figure is subject to considerable variation owing to the difficulty of estimating prospective earnings and determining an appropriate capitalization rate. Thus the valuation figure represents nothing more than a best estimate of potential value. Although the capitalization of prospective earnings is the generally accepted approach of valuing a company in reorganization, the valuation may be adjusted upward if the assets have substantial liquidating value. The common stockholders of the company, of course, would like to see as high a valuation figure as possible. If the valuation figure the trustee proposes is below the liquidating value of the company, common stockholders will argue for liquidation rather than reorganization.

Once a valuation figure has been determined, the next step is to formulate a new capital structure for the company to reduce fixed charges so that there will be an adequate coverage margin. To reduce these charges, the total debt of the firm is scaled down by being partly shifted to income bonds, preferred stock, and common stock. In addition to being scaled down, the terms of the debt may be changed. The maturity of the debt can be extended to reduce the amount of annual sinking-fund obligation. If it appears that the reorganized company will need new financing in the future, the trustee may feel that a more conservative ratio of debt to equity is in order to provide for future financial flexibility.

Once a new capital structure is established, the last step involves the valuation of the old securities and their exchange for new securities. Under an *absolute priority rule,* which is required in reorganization under Chapter X, all senior claims on assets must be settled in full before a junior claim can be settled. For example, in the exchange process, a bondholder must receive the par value of his bond in another security before there can be any distribution to preferred stockholders. The total valuation figure arrived at in step one sets an upper limit on the amount of securities that can be issued. Suppose that the existing capital structure of a company undergoing reorganization is as follows:

Debentures	$ 9 million
Subordinated debentures	3 million
Preferred stock	6 million
Common-stock equity (at book value)	10 million
	$28 million

If the total valuation of the reorganized company is to be $20 million, the trustee might establish the following capital structure in step two:

Debentures	$ 3 million
Income bonds	6 million
Preferred stock	3 million
Common stock	8 million
	$20 million

Having established the "appropriate" capital structure for the reorganized company, the trustee then must allocate the new securities. In this regard, he may propose that the debenture holders exchange their $9 million in debentures for $3 million in new debentures and $6 million in income bonds; that the subordinated debenture holders exchange their $3 million in securities for preferred stock; and that preferred stockholders exchange their securities for $6 million of common stock in the reorganized company. The common stockholders would then be entitled to $2 million in stock in the reorganized company, or 25 percent of the total common stock of the reorganized company. Before, these stockholders held 100 percent of the stock. It is easy to see why common stockholders would like to see as high a valuation figure as possible. To encourage high valuation, they may attempt to discount the troubles of the company as temporary and argue that the earning potential of the company is favorable.

Thus each claim is settled in full before a junior claim is settled. The example above represents a relatively "mild" reorganization. In a "harsh" reorganization, debt instruments may be exchanged entirely for common stock in the reorganized company and the old common stock eliminated completely. Had the total valuation figure in the example been $12 million, the trustee might have proposed a new capital structure consisting of $3 million in preferred stock and $9 million in common stock. Only the straight and subordinated debenture holders would receive a settlement in this case. The preferred and the common stockholders of the old company would receive nothing.

These examples serve to show that the common stockholders of a company undergoing reorganization suffer under an absolute priority rule, whereby claims must be settled in the order of their legal priority. From their standpoint, they would much prefer to see claims settled on a *relative priority basis*. Under this rule, new securities are allocated on the basis of the relative market prices of the securities. The common stockholders could never obtain senior securities in a reorganization, but they would be entitled to some common stock if their present stock had value. Because the company is not actually being liquidated, common stockholders argue that a rule of relative priority is really the fairest. However, the absolute priority rule has been upheld by the Supreme Court (*Case* v. *Los Angeles Lumber Products Company*, 1939). Their only recourse is to question whether the reorganization plan is fair and equitable to all security holders and not whether the absolute priority of claims is valid.

Chapter XI Procedures

Chapter XI of the Bankruptcy Act permits a failing company to seek an *arrangement*. In essence, an arrangement is a "legal" extension or composition. Only the company itself can initiate an arrangement, by filing a voluntary petition with a federal district court, attesting to the fact that it is unable to pay unsecured creditors and proposing a plan of action. Once the petition is filed, creditors cannot push for collection while an arrangement is being worked out. The court appoints a referee to call a meeting of creditors and discuss the plan proposed by the debtor. In addition, the court may appoint a receiver or trustee if the situation so warrants. The plan proposed by the debtor is subject to amendments by the creditors. Once a plan is approved by the majority of creditors and is judged by the court to be fair, equitable, and feasible, however, it becomes binding on all. In this respect, the arrangement has an advantage over a voluntary extension or composition, wherein creditors do not necessarily have to accept the plan. A large creditor can easily prevent a voluntary settlement from working.

The arrangement applies only to unsecured creditors, however. The claims of secured creditors are left intact; the debtor must pay secured creditors according to the terms of the obligations. An arrangement is usually a cheaper and quicker form of settlement than are other types of legal settlements. The method is well suited for the company whose creditors are mostly trade creditors and that has no publicly held fixed-income securities. If a company has publicly held securities and substantial changes in its capital structure are required, these changes will usually be effected under Chapter X, rather than under Chapter XI, of the Bankruptcy Act.

BANKRUPTCY REFORM

At the time of this writing, Congress was involved in a substantive revision of the bankruptcy laws of the United States. After many years of work, a comprehensive bill to overhaul the bankruptcy system was passed. This overhaul was felt to be necessary because (1) the substantial increase in the number of consumer bankruptcy cases severely strained the system; (2) the funding of the system was inefficient, counterproductive, and, at times, inequitable; and (3) existing laws were not uniformly applied across the system. As the last substantial revision of the Bankruptcy Act was made in 1938, the system simply was obsolete and administratively inefficient.

The new bill calls for setting up a network of bankruptcy courts with jurisdiction over all matters involving bankruptcy. The network would be independent of the present court system, and its judges would have the same rank as regular federal district judges. They would be appointed by the president with Senate confirmation, the same as with federal district judges. Thus, bankruptcy judges would have a high rank giving them broad powers. An administrative agency would be created to handle routine matters involved in a bankruptcy. Staffed with permanent employees, their duties would include many of those previously performed by outside parties in supervising the repayment plan and liquidation. However, the powers of this agency would be curtailed, with all important decisions to be made by the bankruptcy court.

In a number of smaller ways, the new bill would make bankruptcy somewhat less onerous for the debtor. Under the existing Bankruptcy Act, one of the six acts of bankruptcy must be proven. Frequently, this results in delays, during which time the debtor's assets are further depleted. Under the new bill, these acts would be eliminated and involuntary proceedings could be initiated by three creditors upon petition. The bill also provides for a number of changes designed to streamline the administration of a bankrupt estate. Certain red tape involved in the sale of property is eliminated so as to reduce administrative expenses and delays. Changes also are made in the treatment of the recovery of assets transferred before bankruptcy, so as to make it more equitable.

With respect to the distribution of assets, the bill proposes a major simplification of the provisions to make them more equitable among unsecured creditors. Wages to employees and claims for contributions to employee benefit plans are given substantial priority—in preference to all other creditors with the exception of administrative expenses, which come first. Third in priority come taxes accruing within one year prior to bankruptcy. This reduces the government's priority of claim, as the limit now is three years. All other outside claims are lumped together under the heading of general creditors, and the burden of proof of a legally enforceable and allowable claim is made less onerous.

In addition to these changes, Chapters X, XI, and XII of the present Bankruptcy Act, which deal with business rehabilitation, would be consolidated into a single chapter. The purpose here is to eliminate the overlap and confusion involved. Also, the new chapter would give creditors and stockholders a greater amount of flexibility in negotiating a reorganization plan. Finally, the new bill would make it easier for individuals and small-business owners to reschedule debts for a period up to three years, provided they have steady incomes. It is hoped that the changes mentioned, as well as other more detailed ones, will substantially improve the adjudication and administration of bankruptcy in the United States.[13] Only time will tell.

SUMMARY

Business failure encompasses a wide range of financial difficulty; it occurs whenever a company is unable to meet its current obligations. Usually the signs of failure are evident in advance of its actual occurrence. Discriminant analysis as well as other analytical tools have been used to predict business failure on the basis of various financial ratios. A number of empirical studies were reviewed, and the deterioration of financial ratios prior to failure was shown.

The remedies applied to a failing company vary in severity with the degree of financial difficulty. Voluntary settlements are informal and must be agreed to by all creditors and the company itself. The difficulty with a voluntary settlement is in obtaining agreement of all parties concerned. Included in voluntary settlements are extensions, compositions, a creditors' committee controlling the operations of the company, and a private liquidation.

Legal settlements are effected, for the most part, under Chapters X and XI of the Bankruptcy Act, as amended by the Chandler Act of 1938. Railroads are reorganized under Section 77 of the Bankruptcy Act. The least "harsh" of the legal procedures is an arrangement under Chapter XI. An arrangement is simply a formal extension or composition. Reorganizations and liquidations occur mostly under Chapter X. In a reorganization, the capital structure of the company is changed so as to reduce the total amount of fixed charges. The reorganized plan has to be fair, equitable, and feasible, as determined by the court and approved by a two-thirds majority of each class of debtholders and a majority of each class of stockholders. If the company cannot be rehabilitated, it will be declared bankrupt by the court and liquidated by a trustee in bankruptcy. Creditors receive liquidating dividends according to the priority of their claims.

In the last section, we described a new bill passed by Congress to reform the bankruptcy system. Depending upon the outcome, the act could be changed in a significant way.

[13]For an excellent comprehensive analysis of the reform proposal, see J. Ronald Trost and Lawrence P. King, "Congress and Bankruptcy Reform, Circa 1977," *Business Lawyer,* 33 (January 1978), 489–557.

1.

Fall Corporation Balance Sheet			
Cash	$ 1,000,000	Note payable	$ 1,000,000
Accounts receivable	2,000,000	Accounts payable	4,000,000
Inventories	5,000,000	Accrued wages	3,000,000
Prepaid expenses	1,000,000	Accrued taxes	1,000,000
Total current assets	$ 9,000,000	Total current liabilities	$ 9,000,000
Fixed assets, net	8,000,000	Long-term debt	12,000,000
Goodwill	5,000,000	Equity	1,000,000
Total assets	$22,000,000		$22,000,000

(a) Do you feel that it is likely that the Fall Corporation either is now or will soon be technically insolvent? Why? What steps could management take to correct this situation?

(b) Answer (a) with respect to the bankruptcy concept of insolvency.

(c) Compare and contrast these two concepts of insolvency.

(d) Is it possible that attempts to alleviate one form of insolvency could aggravate the other? How?

(e) Is the balance sheet the best tool for determining technical or fundamental insolvency? Can you suggest better ones?

2. Merry Land, an amusement park in Atlanta, has experienced increased difficulty in paying its bills. Although the park has been marginally profitable over the years, the current outlook is not encouraging, as profits during the last two years have been negative. However, the park is located on reasonably valuable real estate and has an overall liquidating value of $5 million. After much discussion with creditors, management has agreed to a voluntary liquidation. A trustee, who is appointed by the various parties to liquidate the properties, will charge $200,000 for his services. The Merry Land Company owes $300,000 in back property taxes. It has a $2 million mortgage on certain amusement park equipment which can be sold for only $1 million. Creditor claims are as follows:

Party	Book Value Claim
General creditors	$1,750,000
Mortgage bonds	2,000,000
Long-term subordinated debt	1,000,000
Common stock	-5,000,000

What amount is each party likely to receive in liquidation?

3. The Vent Corporation has been liquidated under bankruptcy proceedings. The book and liquidation values are as follows:

	Book	Liquidation
Cash	$ 700,000	$ 700,000
Accounts receivable	2,000,000	1,600,000
Inventory	3,500,000	2,000,000
Office building	5,000,000	3,000,000
Plant	8,000,000	5,000,000
Equipment	7,000,000	3,000,000
Total	$26,200,000	$15,300,000

The liability and equity accounts at the time of liquidation were as follows:

Accounts payable	$ 2,000,000
Accrued federal taxes	500,000
Accrued local taxes	200,000
Notes payable	1,000,000
Accrued wages	500,000
Total current liabilities	$ 4,200,000
Mortgage on office building	$ 3,000,000
First mortgage on plant	3,000,000
Second mortgage on plant	2,000,000
Subordinated debentures	5,000,000
Total long-term debt	$13,000,000
Preferred stock	$ 5,000,000
Common stock	7,000,000
Retained earnings	(3,000,000)
Total	$ 9,000,000
Total	$26,200,000

Expenses of liquidation (lawyers' fees, court costs, etc.) came to 20 percent of the proceeds. The debentures are subordinated only to the two first mortgage bonds. All of the accrued wages are less than three months old and less than $600 per employee. Determine the appropriate distribution of the proceeds of liquidation.

4. The Greenwood Corporation is in bankruptcy. The trustee has estimated that the company can earn $1.5 million before interest and taxes (50 percent) in the future. In the new capitalization, he feels that debentures should bear a coupon of 6 percent and have coverage of five times, income bonds (6 percent) should have overall coverage of two times, preferred stock (6.25 percent) should have after-tax coverage of three times, and common stock should be issued on a P/E basis of twelve times. Determine the capital structure that conforms to the trustee's criteria.

5. Assume that the Greenwood Corporation (see problem 4) originally had the following capital structure:

	Book Value	Market Value
Senior debentures	$10,000,000	$ 9,000,000
Subordinated debentures	15,000,000	12,000,000
Junior subordinated debentures	5,000,000	2,000,000
Preferred stock (par $100)	5,000,000	1,000,000
Common stock (1,000,000 shares, par value $10)	−10,000,000	1,000,000
	$25,000,000	$25,000,000

Determine which of the new securities each class of old securities holders would get under:

(a) The absolute priority rule

(b) The relative priority rule

6. *Research Project*

Compile data on recent bankruptcy cases involving fairly large companies. Learn as much as you can about "stockholder protective committees"; discover how many of these committees there are for each bankruptcy case you study. Finally, compare the amount of money going for legal fees, court costs, etc., as opposed to the amount the creditors finally receive. Do you begin to feel that there might be "self-interest" as well as "friendly" motives behind the creditors' acceptance of a composition? Whom do stockholder protective committees really protect? Can you find any parallels between bankruptcy law and probate law?

SELECTED REFERENCES

ALTMAN, EDWARD I., *Corporate Bankruptcy in America,* Lexington, Mass.: Heath Lexington Books, 1971.

———, "Corporate Bankruptcy Potential, Stockholder Returns and Share Valuation," *Journal of Finance,* 24 (December 1969), 887–900.

———, "Financial Ratios, Discriminant Analysis and the Prediction of Corporate Bankruptcy," *Journal of Finance,* 23 (September 1968), 589–609.

ALTMAN, EDWARD, I., ROBERT G. HALDEMAN, AND P. NARAYANAN, "Zeta Analysis: A New Model to Identify Bankruptcy Risk of Corporations," *Journal of Banking and Finance,* 1 (June 1977).

ALTMAN, EDWARD, I., AND ARNOLD W. SAMENTZ, EDS., *Financial Crises.* New York: John Wiley, 1977.

BEAVER, WILLIAM H., "Financial Ratios as Predictors of Failure," *Empirical Research in Accounting: Selected Studies,* supplement to *Journal of Accounting Research* (1966), pp. 71–111.

———, "Market Prices, Financial Ratios, and the Prediction of Failure," *Journal of Accounting Research,* 6 (Autumn 1968), 179–92.

COOGAN, PETER F., RICHARD BROUDE, AND HERMAN GLATT, "Comments on Some Reorganization Provisions of the Pending Bankruptcy Bills," *Business Lawyer,* 30 (July 1975).

CYR, CONRAD K., "Setting the Record Straight for a Comprehensive Revision of the Bankruptcy Act of 1898," *American Bankruptcy Law Journal,* 49 (Spring 1975).

DEAKIN, E. B., "A Discriminant Analysis of Predictors of Business Failure," *Journal of Accounting Research,* 10 (Spring 1972), 167–79.

DONALDSON, GORDON, "Strategy for Financial Emergencies," *Harvard Business Review,* 47 (November-December 1969), 67–79.

EDMISTER, ROBERT O., "An Empirical Test of Financial Ratio Analysis for Small Business Failure Prediction," *Journal of Financial and Quantitative Analysis,* 7 (March 1972), 1477–93.

GORDON, MYRON J., "Towards a Theory of Financial Distress," *Journal of Finance,* 26 (May 1971), 347–56.

MOYER, R. CHARLES, "Forecasting Financial Failure: A Re-examination," *Financial Management,* 6 (Spring 1977), 11–17.

MURPHY, PATRICK A., "Restraint and Reimbursement: The Secured Creditor in Reorganization and Arrangement Proceedings," *Business Lawyer,* 30 (November 1974).

MURRAY, ROGER F., "The Penn Central Debacle: Lessons for Financial Analysis," *Journal of Finance,* 26 (May 1971), 327–32.

STANLEY, DAVID T., AND MARJORIE GIRTH, *Bankruptcy: Problem, Process, Reform.* Washington, D.C.: Brookings Institution, 1971.

TROST, J. RONALD, AND LAWRENCE P. KING, "Congress and Bankruptcy Reform, Circa 1977," *Business Lawyer,* 33 (January 1978), 489–557.

VAN HORNE, JAMES C., "Optimal Initiation of Bankruptcy Proceedings by Debt Holders," *Journal of Finance,* 31 (June 1976), 897–910.

WALTER, JAMES E., "Determination of Technical Insolvency," *Journal of Business,* 30 (January 1957), 30–43.

WILCOX, JARROD W., "A Prediction of Business Failure Using Accounting Data," *Empirical Research in Accounting: Selected Studies,* 1973, supplement to Volume 11 of the *Journal of Accounting Research.*

part VIII

tools
of financial
analysis
and control

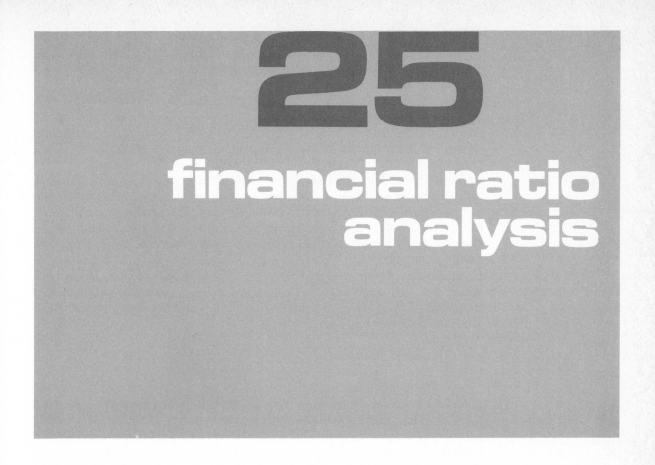

25

financial ratio analysis

INTRODUCTION TO FINANCIAL ANALYSIS

In order to make rational decisions in keeping with the objectives of the firm, the financial manager must have at his disposal certain analytical tools. The purpose of this chapter and of the next two is to examine the more important tools of financial analysis. Financial analysis is undertaken by outside suppliers of capital—creditors and investors—and also by the firm itself. The latter's purpose is not only for internal control but also for better understanding what capital suppliers seek in the way of financial condition and performance from it. The type of analysis varies according to the specific interests of the party involved. A trade creditor is interested primarily in the liquidity of a firm. His claim is short-term, and the ability of a firm to pay this claim is best judged by means of a thorough analysis of its liquidity. The claim of a bondholder, on the other hand, is long-term. Accordingly, he would be more interested in the cash-flow ability of the firm to service debt over the long run. The bondholder may evaluate this ability by analyzing the capital structure of the firm, the major sources and uses of funds, its profitability over time, and projections of future profitability.

An investor in a company's common stock is concerned principally with present and expected future earnings and the stability of these earnings about a trend, as well as their covariance with the earnings of other companies. As a result, the investor might concentrate his analysis on the profitability of the firm. He would be concerned with its financial condition insofar as it affects the ability of the firm to pay dividends and to avoid bankruptcy. In order to bargain more effectively for outside funds, the management of a firm should be interested in all aspects of financial analysis that outside suppliers of capital use in evaluating the firm. Management also employs financial analysis for purposes of internal control. In particular, it is concerned with profitability on investment in the various assets of the company and in the efficiency of asset management. In addition to suppliers of capital and the firm itself, various government regulators may use financial analysis. In particular, regulatory agencies are concerned with the rate of return a company earns on its assets as well as with the proportion of nonequity funds employed in the business. Thus the type of financial analysis undertaken varies according to the specific interests of the analyst. Financial statement analysis is part of a larger information-processing system on which informed decisions can be based.

Use of Financial Ratios

To evaluate the financial condition and performance of a firm, the financial analyst needs certain yardsticks. The yardstick frequently used is a ratio, or index, relating two pieces of financial data to each other. Analysis and interpretation of various ratios should give an experienced and skilled analyst a better understanding of the financial condition and performance of the firm than he would obtain from analysis of the financial data alone.[1]

The analysis of financial ratios involves two types of comparison. First, the analyst can compare a present ratio with past and expected future ratios for the same company. For example, the current ratio (the ratio of current assets to current liabilities) for the present year-end could be compared with the current ratio for the preceding year-end. When financial ratios are arrayed on a spread sheet over a period of years, the analyst can study the composition of change and determine whether there has been an improvement or a deterioration in the financial condition and performance of the firm over time. Financial ratios also can be computed for projected, or pro forma, statements and compared with present and past ratios. In the comparisons over time, it is best to compare not only financial ratios but also the raw figures.

The second method of comparison involves comparing the ratios of one firm with those of similar firms or with industry averages at the same point in time. Such a comparison gives insight into the relative financial condition and performance of the firm. Financial ratios for various industries

---

[1]For an excellent discussion of the history of ratio analysis, see James O. Horrigan, "A Short History of Financial Ratio Analysis," *Accounting Review,* 43 (April 1968), 284–94.

are published by Robert Morris Associates, Dun & Bradstreet, Prentice-Hall (*Almanac of Business and Industrial Financial Ratios*), the Federal Trade Commission–Securities and Exchange Commission, and various credit agencies and trade associations.[2] The analyst should avoid using "rules of thumb" indiscriminately for all industries. For example, the criterion that all companies should have at least a 2-to-1 current ratio is inappropriate. The analysis must be in relation to the type of business in which the firm is engaged and to the firm itself. Many sound companies have current ratios of less than 2 to 1. Only by comparing the financial ratios of one firm with those of similar firms can one make a realistic judgment.

In this regard, the analysis of the deviation of the company being analyzed from the overall norm should be based on some knowledge of the distribution of ratios for the companies involved. If the company being studied has a current ratio of 1.4 and the industry norm is 1.8, one would like to know the proportion of companies whose ratios are below 1.4. If it is only 2 percent, we are likely to be much more concerned than if it is 25 percent. Therefore we need information on the dispersion of the distribution in order to judge the significance of the deviation of a financial ratio for a particular company from the industry norm.[3] Several studies have shown that distributions of financial ratios for nonfinancial corporations deviate from the normality assumption typically imposed when making probabilistic statements.[4] Many distributions are skewed to the right. This is due to the fact that most financial ratios are bounded at zero on the low side but are unbounded on the upside. To the extent that the distribution of financial ratios for an industry deviates significantly from normal, the use of standardized deviations from the industry norm is not appropriate for making probabilistic statements. For asymmetric distributions, it may be better to express the relative standing of a particular company's financial ratio in terms of deciles. For example, a company's financial ratio might be described as being in the seventh decile for all the companies in the industry. In cases of asymmetry,

[2]Robert Morris Associates, an association of bank credit and loan officers, publishes industry averages based upon financial statements supplied to banks by borrowers. Eleven ratios are computed annually for 156 lines of business. In addition, each line of business is broken down according to four size categories. Dun & Bradstreet calculates annually fourteen important ratios for 125 lines of business. The *Almanac of Business and Industrial Financial Ratios* (Englewood Cliffs, N.J.: Prentice-Hall, 1977) shows industry averages for some twenty-two financial ratios. Approximately 170 businesses and industries are listed, covering the complete spectrum. The data for this publication come from U.S. corporate tax filings with the Internal Revenue Service. *The Quarterly Financial Report for Manufacturing Corporations* is published jointly by the Federal Trade Commission and the Securities and Exchange Commission. This publication contains balance-sheet and income-statement information by industry groupings and by asset size categories.

[3]For further discussion of this point, see Baruch Lev, *Financial Statement Analysis: A New Approach* (Englewood Cliffs, N.J.: Prentice-Hall, 1974), 62–64.

[4]See Edward B. Deakin, "Distributions of Financial Accounting Ratios: Some Empirical Evidence," *Accounting Review,* 51 (January 1976), 90–96; and J. Louis Heck, "Nonparametric Tests on the Normality Assumption of Selected Financial Ratios" (paper presented at the Financial Management Association Meetings, Seattle, October 14, 1977).

table 25-1
Aldine Manufacturing Company balance sheet

Assets		
	March 31, 1980	March 31, 1979
Cash and marketable securities	$ 177,689	$ 175,042
Accounts receivable	678,279	740,705
Inventories, at lower of cost (Fifo) or market	1,328,963	1,234,725
Prepaid expenses	20,756	17,197
Accumulated tax prepayments	35,203	29,165
Current assets	$2,240,890	$2,196,834
Fixed assets at cost	$1,596,886	$1,538,495
Less accumulated depreciation	856,829	791,205
Net fixed assets	$ 740,057	$ 747,290
Investment—long-term	65,376	—
Other assets	205,157	205,624
	$3,251,480	$3,149,748

this expression is more accurate and meaningful than expressing relative standing as a deviation from the industry norm.

Also, comparisons with the industry must be approached with caution. It may well be that the financial condition and performance of the entire industry is less than satisfactory. Just because a company is above average may not be sufficient. The company may have a number of problems on an absolute basis, and refuge should not be taken in a favorable comparison relative to the industry. In addition, the analyst should realize that the various companies within an industry grouping may not be homogeneous. Companies with multiple product lines often defy precise industry categorization. While such companies may be placed in the most "appropriate" industry grouping, the comparison of such a company with other companies in that industry may not be consistent. Also, companies in an industry may differ substantially in size. In these circumstances, it may be best to subdivide the industry so as to compare companies of similar size. All of these things make caution important when approaching the comparison of the financial ratios of a given company with those of other companies in the industry.

Because reported financial data and the ratios computed from these data are numerical, there is a tendency to regard them as precise portrayals of a firm's true financial status. For some firms, the accounting data may closely approximate economic reality. On many occasions, however, it is necessary to go beyond the reported figures in order to analyze properly the financial condition and performance of the firm. Such accounting data as depreciation, reserve for bad debts, and other reserves at best are estimates and may not reflect economic depreciation, bad debts, and other losses. To the extent

table 25-1 (con't.)

Liabilities and Net Worth		
	March 31, 1980	March 31, 1979
Bank loans and notes payable	$ 448,508	$ 356,511
Accounts payable	148,427	136,793
Accrued taxes	36,203	127,455
Other accrued liabilities	190,938	164,285
Current liabilities	$ 824,076	$ 785,044
Long-term debt	630,783	626,460
Stockholders' equity		
Common stock, $1.00 par value	420,828	420,824
Capital surplus	361,158	361,059
Retained earnings	1,014,635	956,361
Total stockholders' equity	$1,796,621	$1,738,244
	$3,251,480	$3,149,748

possible, accounting data from different companies should be standardized. It is important to compare apples with apples and oranges with oranges. Even with standardized figures, however, the analyst should use caution in interpreting the comparisons.

Types of Ratios

For our purposes, financial ratios can be divided into four types: liquidity, debt, profitability, and coverage ratios. The first two types are ratios computed from the balance sheet; the last two are ratios computed from the income statement and, sometimes, from both the income statement and the balance sheet. It is important to recognize from the outset that no one ratio gives us sufficient information by which to judge the financial condition and performance of the firm. Only when we analyze a group of ratios are we able to make reasonable judgments. In addition, it is very important to take into account any seasonal character in a business. Underlying trends may be assessed only through a comparison of raw figures and ratios at the same time of year. For example, we would not compare a December 31 balance sheet with a May 31 balance sheet but would compare December 31 with December 31.

Although the number of financial ratios that might be computed increases geometrically with the amount of financial data, we concentrate only upon the more important ratios in this chapter. Actually, the ratios needed to assess the financial condition and performance of a company are relatively few in number. To compute unneeded ratios adds both complexity and confusion to the problem. In order to illustrate the ratios discussed in this chapter, we use the balance sheet and income statements of the Aldine Manufacturing Company shown in Tables 25–1 and 25–2.

table 25-2
Aldine Manufacturing Company statement of earnings

	Year Ended March 31, 1980	Year Ended March 31, 1979
Net sales	$3,992,758	$3,721,241
Cost of goods sold	2,680,298	2,499,965
Selling, general, and administrative expenses	801,395	726,959
Depreciation	111,509	113,989
Interest expense	85,274	69,764
Earnings before taxes	$ 314,282	$ 310,564
Income taxes	163,708	172,446
Earnings after taxes	$ 150,574	$ 138,118
Cash dividends	92,300	88,634
Retained earnings	$ 58,274	$ 49,484

LIQUIDITY RATIOS

Liquidity ratios are used to judge a firm's ability to meet short-term obligagations. From them, much insight can be obtained into the present cash solvency of the firm and its ability to remain solvent in the event of adversities. Essentially we wish to compare short-term obligations with the short-term resources available to meet these obligations.

Current Ratio

One of the most general and most frequently used of these ratios is the *current ratio*:

$$\frac{\text{Current assets}}{\text{Current liabilities}}$$

For Aldine, the ratio for the 1980 year-end is

$$\frac{\$2,240,890}{\$824,076} = 2.72$$

The higher the ratio, supposedly, the greater the ability of the firm to pay its bills. However, the ratio must be regarded as a crude measure of liquidity because it does not take into account the liquidity of the individual components of the current assets.[5] A firm having current assets composed prin-

---

[5]For a thorough analysis of the shortcomings of the current ratio, see Kenneth W. Lemke, "The Evaluation of Liquidity: An Analytical Study," *Journal of Accounting Research,* 8 (Spring 1970), 47–77. Lemke shows that changes in the current ratio do not necessarily indicate a change in liquidity, and, therefore, the ratio cannot be interpreted in a consistent manner.

cipally of cash and current receivables is generally regarded as more liquid
than a firm whose current assets consist primarily of inventories.[6] Consequently, we must turn to "finer" tools of analysis if we are to evaluate crit-
ically the liquidity of the firm.

Acid-Test Ratio

A somewhat more accurate guide to liquidity is the *quick,* or *acid-test, ratio:*

$$\frac{\text{Current assests less inventories}}{\text{Current liabilities}}$$

For Aldine, this ratio is

$$\frac{\$2,240,890 - \$1,328,963}{\$824,076} = 1.11$$

This ratio is the same as the current ratio, except that it excludes inventories—presumably the least liquid portion of current assets—from the numerator. The ratio concentrates on cash, marketable securities, and receivables in relation to current obligations and thus provides a more penetrating
measures of liquidity than does the current ratio.

Liquidity of Receivables

To the extent that there are suspected imbalances or problems in
various components of the current assets, the financial analyst will want
to examine these components separately in his assessment of liquidity. Receivables, for example, may be far from current. To regard all receivables
as liquid, when in fact a sizable portion may be past due, overstates the
liquidity of the firm being analyzed. Receivables are liquid assets only insofar as they can be collected in a reasonable amount of time. For our analysis of receivables, we have two basic ratios, the first of which is the *average
collection period ratio:*

$$\frac{\text{Receivables} \times \text{Days in year}}{\text{Annual credit sales}}$$

For Aldine, this ratio is

$$\frac{\$678,279 \times 365}{\$3,992,758} = 62 \text{ days}$$

---

[6]We have defined *liquidity* as the ability to realize value in money—the most liquid of
assets. Liquidity has two dimensions: (1) the time required to convert the asset into money, and (2)
the certainty of the price realized. To the extent that the price realized on receivables is as
predictable as that realized on inventories, receivables would be a more liquid asset than
inventories, owing to the shorter time required to convert the asset into money. If the price
realized on receivables is more certain than that on inventories, receivables would be regarded as
being even more liquid.

The average collection period tells us the average number of days receivables are outstanding; that is, the average time it takes to convert them into cash.

The second ratio is the *receivable turnover ratio*:

$$\frac{\text{Annual credit sales}}{\text{Receivables}}$$

For Aldine, this ratio is

$$\frac{\$3{,}992{,}758}{\$678{,}279} = 5.89$$

Actually, these two ratios are inverses of each other. The number of days in the year, 365, divided by the average collection period, 62 days, gives the receivable turnover ratio, 5.89. The number of days in the year divided by the turnover ratio gives the average collection period. Thus, either of these two ratios can be employed.

When credit sales figures for a period are not available, we must resort to the total sales figures. The receivable figure used in the calculation ordinarily represents year-end receivables. However, when sales are seasonal or have grown considerably over the year, using the year-end receivable balance may not be appropriate. With seasonality, an average of the monthly closing balances may be the most appropriate figure to use. With growth, the receivable balance at the end of the year will be deceptively high in relation to sales. In this case, an average of receivables at the beginning and at the end of the year might be appropriate, if the growth in sales was steady throughout the year.

The average collection period ratio or the receivable turnover ratio indicates the slowness of receivables. Either ratio must be analyzed in relation to the billing terms given on the sales. For example, if the average collection period is forty-five days and the terms are 2/10, net 30[7], the comparison would indicate that a sizable proportion of the receivables is past due beyond the final due date of thirty days. On the other hand, if the terms are 2/10, net 60, the typical receivable is being collected before the final due date. A comparison of the average collection period and terms given by a specific company with those of other companies in the industry gives us additional insight into the investment in receivables. Too low an average collection period may suggest an excessively restrictive credit policy. The receivables on the books may be of prime quality and yet sales may be curtailed unduly—and profits less than they might be—because of this policy. In this situation, credit standards for an acceptable account should be relaxed somewhat. On the other hand, too high an average collection period may

---

[7]The notation means that the supplier gives a 2 percent discount if the receivable invoice is paid within ten days and that payment is due within thirty days if the discount is not taken.

indicate too liberal a credit policy. As a result, a large number of receivables may be past due, with some uncollectible. Here, too, profits may be less than those possible on account of bad-debt losses and the need to finance a large investment in receivables. In this case, credit standards should be raised.

Another means by which we can obtain insight into the liquidity of receivables is through an *aging of accounts*. With this method, we categorize the receivables at a moment in time according to the proportions billed in previous months. For example, we might have the following hypothetical aging of accounts receivable at December 31:

Proportion of Receivables Billed					
December	November	October	September	August and Before	Total
67%	19%	7%	2%	5%	100%

If the billing terms are 2/10, net 30, this aging tells us that 67 percent of the receivables at December 31 are current, 19 percent are up to one month past due, 7 percent are one to two months past due, and so on. Depending upon the conclusions drawn from our analysis of the aging, we may want to examine more closely the credit and collection policies of the company. In the example above, we might be prompted to investigate the individual receivables that were billed in August and before, in order to determine if any should be charged off. The receivables shown on the books are only as good as the likelihood that they will be collected. An aging of accounts receivable gives us considerably more information than the calculation of the average collection period, because it pinpoints the trouble spots more specifically.

It is important to recognize that both the average collection period and the aging of accounts receivable are affected by the pattern of sales. With rising sales, the average collection period and the aging will be more current than if sales are level, all other things the same. The reason is that a greater portion of sales is billed currently. On the other hand, when sales are declining over time, the average collection period and the aging will be less current than if sales are level. Here the reason is that a smaller portion of sales is billed currently. While the average collection period and the aging measures will not be significantly affected if there is only a modest and steady trend in sales, they will be affected if there is a rapid change in the pattern of sales or if there is a fluctuating pattern of sales behavior over time. For these situations, the average collection period and the aging schedule are not realistic portrayals of the liquidity of receivables. Adjustments in analysis should be made. For seasonal sales patterns, it is useful to compare the average collection period and aging at one point with the average collection period and aging at the same point in another year. For example, we might compare the average collection period and an aging at the end of May with those at the end of May in another year.

The important thing is to try to separate changes in the payment behavior of customers from changes in the pattern of sales. One way to do so is with a conversion matrix of receivables into cash.[8] Such a matrix is illustrated in Table 25-3. As we see, the matrix tells us the amount of credit sales in a given month and the months when the receivables so generated are collected. At the right of each collection amount, the percentage that amount represents in relation to total credit sales is shown. At the bottom of the table, total collections are shown for each month. The advantage of this type of calculation is that it permits the financial analyst to concentrate on the payment pattern of customers month by month as opposed to the combined payment and sales patterns. By tracing the collections in a month to when the sales occur, one can determine if the firm's collection experience is improving or deteriorating over time. In the case of sales that change significantly over time, this isolation of payments behavior from sales behavior is of critical importance. The principal limitation to the use of a conversion matrix is that such information is available only from the company and cannot be derived from financial statements. However, the same limitation applies to an aging of accounts receivable. In fact, the same information necessary to prepare an aging schedule can be used to derive a conversion matrix.

table 25-3

Conversion matrix of credit sales to cash

Month	Credit Sales	Monthly Collections (in thousands of dollars)					
		Jan.	Feb.	Mar.	Apr.	May	June
Oct.	$6,000	600(10%)					
Nov.	4,000	900(23%)	300(8%)	125(3%)			
Dec.	3,000	1,400(47%)	700(23%)	400(13%)			
Jan.	5,000	700(14%)	2,500(50%)	1,200(24%)	600(12%)		
Feb.	6,000		900(15%)	3,200(53%)	1,500(25%)	400(7%)	
Mar.	7,000			1,200(17%)	3,300(47%)	1,900(27%)	600(9%)
Apr.	8,000				1,100(14%)	4,100(51%)	1,900(24%)
May	7,000					1,300(19%)	3,300(47%)
June	5,000						700(14%)
Total collections		3,600	4,400	6,125	6,500	7,700	6,500

Note: The percentages are in relation to credit sales shown in the second column.

[8]Similar approaches have been proposed by W. G. Lewellen and R. W. Johnson, "Better Way to Monitor Accounts Receivable," *Harvard Business Review*, 50 (May-June 1972), 101–9; W. G. Lewellen and R. O. Edmister, "A General Model for Accounts Receivable Analysis and Control," *Journal of Financial and Quantitative Analysis*, 8 (March 1973), 195–206; and Bernell K. Stone, "The Payments-Pattern Approach to the Forecasting and Control of Accounts Receivable," *Financial Management*, 5 (Autumn 1976), 65–82. In all three articles, there is a detailed analysis of the problem as it relates in particular to the average collection period and the aging of accounts receivable.

Duration of Payables

From a creditor's point of view, it is desirable to obtain an *aging of accounts payable* or a *conversion matrix for payables*. These measures, combined with the less exact turnover of payables (annual purchases divided by payables), allows us to analyze payables in much the same manner as we do receivables. Also, one can compute the average age of a firm's accounts payable. The *average age of payables* is

$$\frac{\text{Accounts payable} \times 365}{\text{Purchase of raw materials}}$$

where accounts payable is the average balance outstanding for the year, and the denominator is the purchase of raw material during the year. This information is valuable in evaluating the probability that a credit applicant will pay on time. If the average age of payables is forty-eight days, and the terms in the industry are net 30, we know that a portion of the applicant's payables are not being paid on time. A credit check of other suppliers will give insight into the severity of the problem.

Liquidity of Inventories

We may compute the *inventory turnover ratio* as an indicator of the liquidity of inventory:

$$\frac{\text{Cost of goods sold}}{\text{Average inventory}}$$

For Aldine, the ratio is

$$\frac{\$2,680,298}{\$1,281,844} = 2.09$$

The figure for cost of goods sold used in the numerator is for the period being studied—usually one year; the average inventory figure used in the denominator typically is an average of beginning and ending inventories for the period. As was true with receivables, however, it may be necessary to compute a more sophisticated average when there is a strong seasonal element. The inventory turnover ratio tells us the rapidity with which the inventory is turned over into receivables through sales. This ratio, like other ratios, must be judged in relation to past and expected future ratios of the firm and in relation to ratios of similar firms, the industry average, or both.

Generally, the higher the inventory turnover, the more efficient the inventory management of a firm. However, a relatively high inventory turnover ratio may be the result of too low a level of inventory and frequent stockouts. It might also be the result of too many small orders for inventory replacement. Either of these situations may be more costly to the firm than carrying a larger investment in inventory and having a lower turnover ratio. Again, caution is necessary in interpreting the ratio. When the inventory turnover ratio is relatively low, it indicates slow-moving inventory or obsolescence of some of the stock. Obsolescence may necessitate substantial write-downs, which, in turn, would negate the treatment of inventory as a liquid asset. Because the turnover ratio is a somewhat crude measure, we would want to investigate any perceived inefficiency in inventory management. In this regard, it is helpful to compute the turnover of the major categories of inventory to see if there are imbalances, which may indicate excessive investment in specific components of the inventory. Once we have a hint of a problem, we must investigate it more specifically to determine its cause.

DEBT RATIOS

Extending our analysis to the long-term liquidity of the firm (that is, its ability to meet long-term obligations), several debt ratios may be used. The *debt-to-net-worth* ratio is computed by simply dividing the total debt of the firm (including current liabilities) by its net worth:

$$\frac{\text{Total debt}}{\text{Net worth}}$$

For Aldine, the ratio is

$$\frac{\$1,454,859}{\$1,796,621} = 0.81$$

When intangible assets are significant, they frequently are deducted from net worth to obtain the tangible net worth of the firm. Depending upon the purpose for which the ratio is used, preferred stock sometimes is included as debt rather than as net worth. Preferred stock represents a prior claim from the standpoint of the investor in common stock; consequently, he might include preferred stock as debt when analyzing a firm. The ratio of debt to equity will vary according to the nature of the business and the volatility of cash flows. An electric utility, with very stable cash flows, usually will have a higher debt ratio than will a machine tool company, whose cash flows are far less stable.

A comparison of the debt ratio for a given company with those of similar firms gives us a general indication of the credit-worthiness and financial risk of the firm. The reason that it is a general indication is that the assets and cash flows of the firm provide the wherewithal for payment of debt. To the extent that the asset totals are either overstated or understated with respect to their economic and liquidating values, the measure is faulty.

Much more is said about the analysis of financial risk in Chapters 9 and 10.

In addition to the ratio of total debt to equity, we may wish to compute the following ratio, which deals with only the long-term capitalization of the firm:

$$\frac{\text{Long-term debt}}{\text{Total capitalization}}$$

where total capitalization represents all long-term debt and net worth. For Aldine, the ratio is

$$\frac{\$630,783}{\$2,427,404} = 0.26$$

This measure tells us the relative importance of long-term debt in the capital structure. The ratios computed above have been based upon book value figures; it is sometimes useful to calculate these ratios using market values. The use of debt ratios is considered in Chapter 9, where we take up the problem of capital structure. Again, it is important to compare ratios for the same company over time and also to compare the ratios of one firm with those of similar companies. In summary, debt ratios tell us the relative proportions of capital contributed by creditors and by owners. They represent one means by which to judge the financial risk of the firm, the other being coverage ratios.

COVERAGE RATIOS

Coverage ratios are designed to relate the financial charges of a firm to its ability to service them. Such bond-rating services as Moody's Investors Service and Standard & Poor's make extensive use of these ratios. One of the most traditional of the coverage ratios is the *interest coverage ratio,* simply the ratio of earnings before interest and taxes for a particular reporting period to the amount of interest charges for the period. It is important to differentiate which interest charges should be used in the denominator. The *overall coverage method* stresses the importance of a company's meeting all fixed interest, regardless of the seniority of the claim. Suppose that we have the following financial data for a hypothetical company:

Average earnings before interest and taxes	$2,000,000
Interest on senior 7% bonds	−400,000
	$1,600,000
Interest on junior 8% bonds	160,000

The overall interest coverage would be $2,000,000/$560,000, or 3.57. This method implies that the credit-worthiness of the senior bonds is only as good as the firm's ability to cover all interest charges.

Of the various coverage ratios, the most objectionable is the *prior deductions method*. Using this method, we deduct interest on the senior bonds from average earnings and then divide the residual by the interest on the junior bonds. We find that the coverage on the junior bonds in our example is ten times ($1,600,000/$160,000). Thus the junior bonds give the illusion of being more secure than the senior obligations. Clearly, this method is inappropriate. The *cumulative deduction method,* perhaps, is the most widely used method of computing interest coverage. Under this method, coverage for the senior bonds would be five times. However, coverage for the junior bonds is determined by adding the interest charges on both bonds and relating the total to average earnings. Thus the coverage for the junior bonds would be $2,000,000/$560,000 = 3.57 times.

One of the principal shortcomings of an interest coverage ratio is that a firm's ability to service debt is related to both interest and principal payments. Moreover, these payments are not met out of earnings *per se*, but out of cash. Hence a more appropriate coverage ratio relates the cash flow of the firm (approximated by earnings before interest and taxes plus depreciation) to the sum of interest and principal payments. The *cash-flow coverage ratio* may be expressed as

$$\frac{\text{Annual cash flow before interest and taxes}}{\text{Interest} + \text{Principal payments } [1/(1-t)]}$$

where t is the federal income tax rate. Because principal payments are made after taxes, it is necessary to adjust this figure by $[1/(1-t)]$ so that it corresponds to interest payments, which are made before taxes.[9] If the rate were 50 percent and annual principal payments $100,000, before-tax earnings of $200,000 would be needed to cover these payments.[10]

A broader type of analysis would evaluate the ability of the firm to cover all charges of a fixed nature in relation to its cash flow. In addition to interest and principal payments on debt obligations, we would include preferred-stock dividends, lease payments, and possibly even certain essential capital expenditures. As taken up in Chapter 10, an analysis of this type is a far more realistic gauge than is a simple interest coverage ratio in determining whether a firm has the ability to meet its long-term obligations.[11]

---

[9]For an analysis of various approaches to coverage ratios when principal payments are involved, see M. Chapman Findlay III and Edward E. Williams, "Toward More Adequate Debt Service Coverage Ratios," *Financial Analysts Journal*, 31 (November-December 1975), 58–61.

[10]This statement assumes that earnings before taxes are in excess of $200,000.

[11]Donaldson argues also that the firm's ability to service debt is related to its cash-flow coverage of a number of fixed charges. He develops a probability approach to the problem and proposes that the probability of cash "insolvency" or cash "inadequacy" should be judged in

In assessing the financial risk of a firm, then, the financial analyst should first compute the debt ratios as a rough measure of financial risk. Depending upon the payment schedule of the debt and the average interest rate, however, debt ratios may or may not give an accurate picture of the ability of the firm to meet its financial obligations. Therefore he should analyze additionally the cash-flow ability of the firm to service debt. In this way, the financial analyst is able to get an accurate idea of the financial risk of the firm. Neither debt ratios nor coverage ratios are sufficient by themselves.

PROFITABILITY RATIOS

Profitability ratios are of two types: those showing profitability in relation to sales, and those showing profitability in relation to investment. Together these ratios give us indication of the firm's efficiency of operation. We do not take up the calculation of earnings per share or the effect of leverage on earnings per share in this chapter. These topics are considered in Chapter 27.

Profitability in Relation to Sales

The first ratio we consider is the *gross profit margin:*

$$\frac{\text{Sales less cost of goods sold}}{\text{Sales}}$$

For Aldine, the gross profit margin is

$$\frac{\$1,312,460}{\$3,992,758} = 32.9 \text{ percent}$$

This ratio tells us the profit of the firm relative to sales after we deduct the cost of producing the goods sold. It indicates the efficiency of operations as well as how products are priced. A more specific ratio of profitability is the *net profit margin:*

$$\frac{\text{Net profits after taxes}}{\text{Sales}}$$

For Aldine, this ratio is

$$\frac{\$150,574}{\$3,992,758} = 3.77 \text{ percent}$$

periods of recessions. We examine his approach in more detail in Chapter 10. Gordon Donaldson, "New Framework for Corporate Debt Capacity," *Harvard Business Review,* 40 (March-April 1962), 117–31.

The net profit margin tells us the relative efficiency of the firm after taking into account all expenses and income taxes, but not extraordinary charges.

By considering both ratios jointly, we are able to gain considerable insight into the operations of the firm. For example, if the gross profit margin is essentially unchanged over a period of several years, but the net profit margin has declined over the same period, we know that the cause is either higher expenses relative to sales or a higher tax rate. Therefore we would analyze these factors more specifically to determine the cause of the problem. On the other hand, if the gross profit margin falls, we know that the cost of producing the goods relative to sales has increased. This occurrence, in turn, may be due to lower prices or to lower operating efficiency in relation to volume. If expenses are constant in relation to sales, we would know that the lower net profit margin is due entirely to the higher cost of producing the goods relative to sales.

There are any number of combinations of changes possible in the gross and net profit margins. Indications of the sort illustrated above tell us where we should investigate further. In our analysis, it is useful to examine over time each of the individual expense items as a percentage of sales. By so doing, we can pick out specific areas of deterioration or improvement.

Profitability in Relation to Investment

The second group of profitability ratios relates profits to investments. One of these measures is the *rate of return on common-stock equity:*

$$\frac{\text{Net profits after taxes} - \text{Preferred-stock dividend}}{\text{Net worth} - \text{Par value of preferred stock}}$$

For Aldine, the rate of return is

$$\frac{\$150,574}{\$1,796,621} = 8.38 \text{ percent}$$

This ratio tells us the earning power on shareholders' book investment and is frequently used in comparing two or more firms in an industry. The figure for net worth used in the ratio may be expressed in terms of market value instead of book value. When we use market value, we obtain the earnings/price ratio of the stock.

A more general ratio used in the analysis of profitability is the *return on assets ratio:*

$$\frac{\text{Net profits after taxes}}{\text{Total assets}}$$

For Aldine, the ratio is

$$\frac{\$150,574}{\$3,251,480} = 4.63 \text{ percent}$$

This ratio is somewhat inappropriate, inasmuch as profits are taken after interest is paid to creditors. Because these creditors provide means by which part of the total assets are supported, there is a fallacy of omission. When financial charges are significant, it is preferable, for comparative purposes, to compute a net operating profit rate of return instead of a return on assets ratio. The *net operating profit rate of return* may be expressed as

$$\frac{\text{Earnings before interest and taxes}}{\text{Total assets}}$$

Using this ratio, we are able to abstract from differing financial charges (interest and preferred-stock dividends). Thus the relationship studied is independent of the way the firm is financed.

Turnover and Earning Power

Frequently, the financial analyst relates total assets to sales to obtain the *turnover ratio:*

$$\frac{\text{Sales}}{\text{Total assets}}$$

Aldine's turnover for the 1980 fiscal year was

$$\frac{\$3,992,758}{\$3,251,480} = 1.23$$

This ratio tells us the relative efficiency with which the firm utilizes its resources in order to generate output. It varies according to the type of company being studied. A food chain has a considerably higher turnover, for example, than does an electric utility. One shortcoming of the turnover ratio is that it places a premium on using old equipment. A firm with equipment that is almost fully depreciated and highly inefficient may show a high turnover but actually lose money. Consequently, the ratio should be used in conjunction with other measures of efficiency.

When we multiply the asset turnover of the firm by the net profit margin, we obtain the return on assets ratio, or *earning power* on total assets.

$$\text{Earning power} = \frac{\text{Sales}}{\text{Total assets}} \times \frac{\text{Net profits after taxes}}{\text{Sales}}$$
$$= \frac{\text{Net profits after taxes}}{\text{Total assets}}$$

For Aldine, we have

$$\frac{\$3,992,758}{\$3,251,480} \times \frac{\$150,574}{\$3,992,758} = 4.63 \text{ percent}$$

Neither the net profit margin nor the turnover ratio by itself provides an adequate measure of operating efficiency. The net profit margin ignores the utilization of assets, whereas the turnover ratio ignores profitability on sales. The return on assets ratio, or earning power, resolves these shortcomings. An improvement in the earning power of the firm will result if there is an increase in turnover on existing assets, an increase in the net profit margin, or both. Two firms with different asset turnovers and net profit margins may have the same earning power. For example, Firm A, with an asset turnover of 4 to 1 and a net profit margin of 3 percent, has the same earning power—12 percent—as Firm B, with an asset turnover of 1½ to 1 and a net profit margin of 8 percent.

With all the profitability ratios, comparisons of a company with similar companies are extremely valuable. Only by comparison are we able to judge whether the profitability of a particular company is good or bad, and why. Absolute figures provide some insight, but it is relative performance that is most important.

PREDICTIVE POWER OF FINANCIAL RATIOS

In the previous sections, we presented the important ratios used in financial analysis. Which ratios an analyst relies on depends upon his perception of their predictive power relative to the problem at hand—a perception based upon either subjective beliefs or empirical analysis. In helping him predict the future value of a stock, for example, an investor might feel that the return on investment ratio and various profit margin ratios were the most important. Most estimates of the predictive power of financial ratios are based upon the analyst's past experience with them. By their very nature, then, these estimates tend to be subjective and to differ from one analyst to the next.

A number of empirical studies have been undertaken that test the predictive power of financial ratios.[12] In one, William H. Beaver tested the ability of financial ratios to predict failure.[13] Because this study is described

---

[12]For an excellent overall discussion of this type of research see, George Foster, *Financial Statement Analysis* (Englewood Cliffs, N.J.: Prentice-Hall, 1978), Part IV; and Lev, *Financial Statement Analysis: A New Approach,* Part II.

[13]"Financial Ratios as Predictors of Failure," *Empirical Research in Accounting: Selected Studies in Journal of Accounting Research* (1966), pp. 71–111. For further testing in this regard where capitalized lease data are included, see Rick Elam, "The Effect of Lease Data on the Predictive Ability of Financial Ratios," *Accounting Review,* 50 (January 1975), 25–43. Elam found that the inclusion of these data did not increase the power of financial ratios to predict bankruptcy.

in the preceding chapter, we note here only that many of the thirty ratios studied showed considerable power to detect failure before it actually occurred. Not only did the financial ratios of failed firms differ significantly from those of nonfailed firms, but they deteriorated considerably during the five years prior to failure. Because the ratios were examined individually, with no attempt to test the joint predictive power of various combinations of ratios, it was not possible to select the best group of ratios for predicting failure. However, Beaver found that the best single predictor was the ratio of cash flow to total debt.

In another empirical study, Edward I. Altman employed financial ratios to predict corporate bankruptcy through multiple-discriminant analysis.[14] Because his studies also are described in the preceding chapter, we shall mention only the important results. Out of the twenty-two financial ratios examined, Altman selected the five that did the best combined job in predicting bankruptcy. These ratios were working capital to total assets, retained earnings to total assets, earnings before interest and taxes to total assets, market value of equity to book value of total debt, and sales to total assets. Using these ratios, Altman found the discriminant model to be an accurate predictor of bankruptcy.

In a follow-up study, Edward I. Altman, Robert G. Haldeman, and P. Narayanan extended the original Altman discriminant model and updated its application to newer evidence on bankruptcies.[15] In the new model, seven variables were employed: the return on assets ratio, the stability of earnings, the interest coverage ratio, the retained earnings to total assets ratio, the current ratio, the common equity to total capital ratio, and the size of total assets. The authors found this model to be an even more accurate predictor of bankruptcy up to five years in advance. In two other studies, Edward B. Deakin[16] and R. Charles Moyer[17] also tested the usefulness of discriminant analysis in predicting corporate failure and found it to do well. As these studies are described in the preceding chapter, the discussion will not be repeated here.

Like Altman and others, Robert O. Edmister employed discriminant analysis successfully to predict failure.[18] However, he analyzed small businesses as opposed to large corporations, lending additional credence to the technique. Edmister used a three-year average of the following financial

[14]"Financial Ratios, Discriminant Analysis and the Prediction of Corporate Bankruptcy," *Journal of Finance,* 23 (September 1968), 589–609.

[15]"Zeta Analysis: A New Model to Identify Bankruptcy Risk of Corporations," *Journal of Banking and Finance,* 1 (June 1977).

[16]"A Discriminant Analysis of Predictors of Business Failure," *Journal of Accounting Research,* 10 (Spring 1972), 167–79.

[17]"Forecasting Financial Failure: A Re-examination," *Financial Management,* 6 (Spring 1977), 11–17.

[18]"An Empirical Test of Financial Ratio Analysis for Small Business Failure Prediction," *Journal of Financial and Quantitative Analysis,* 7 (March 1972), 1477–93.

ratios: funds flow to current liabilities, equity to sales, working capital to sales, current liabilities to equity, inventory to sales, and the trend of the quick ratio relative to the industry average. This study also is described in the preceding chapter.

In contrast to predicting business failure, James O. Horrigan tested the power of financial ratios to predict corporate bond ratings.[19] With these ratings as the dependent variable, he regressed them against various financial ratios, using a sample of companies. The multiple-regression analysis revealed that working capital to sales, net worth to total debt, sales to net worth, and net operating profit to sales were best for predicting bond ratings. Horrigan concluded that a handful of ratios can be used in combination to predict the long-term credit standing of a firm.

Various models based on financial data have been used to predict good and bad commercial bank loans. Yair E. Orgler used a multiple-regression model to predict which loans would be criticized by bank examiners.[20] The principal financial ratio he used was the ratio of working capital to current assets. The model was only moderately successful in predicting criticized loans. In a study of French commercial loans, Edward I. Altman, Michel Margaine, Michel Schlosser, and Pierre Vernimmen used discriminant analysis in connection with forty-one financial ratios and data on 134 firms.[21] The authors found that their model was relatively effective in predicting loans with repayment problems (14 percent type I errors and 1 percent type II errors).

On the basis of these studies, it appears that financial ratios can be used as predictors of various events. In particular, the prediction of business failure has been successful, and this event is of key concern to suppliers of capital as well as to the firm itself. To the extent that the probability of failure can be approximated prior to its occurrence, corrective steps can be taken to reduce it to a tolerable level. As a result of the empirical testing of financial ratios, we have a better understanding of which ratios are important in predicting certain types of events. Rather than analyze a host of ratios indiscriminately, the financial analyst can home in on those ratios that are really

[19]"The Determination of Long-term Credit Standing with Financial Ratios," *Empirical Research in Accounting: Selected Studies*, in *Journal of Accounting Research* (1966), pp. 44–62. Richard R. West, "An Alternative Approach to Predicting Corporate Bond Ratings," *Journal of Accounting Research*, 8 (Spring 1970), 118–25, used a somewhat different model for predicting ratings and found the predictive accuracy to be about the same as Horrigan's. In yet another study, George E. Pinches and Kent A. Mingo, "A Multivariate Analysis of Industrial Bond Ratings," *Journal of Finance*, 28 (March 1973), 1–18, jointly applied factor analysis and M-group multiple-discriminant analysis to predict industrial bond ratings. Testing the 1967–68 period, they found that variables related to earnings stability, size, financial leverage, debt coverage stability, return on investment, and subordination to be the best for predictive purposes.

[20]"A Credit Scoring Model for Commercial Loans," *Journal of Money, Credit, and Banking*, 2 (November 1970), 435–45.

[21]"Financial and Statistical Analysis for Commercial Loan Evaluations: A French Experience," *Journal of Financial and Quantitative Analysis*, 9 (March 1974), 195–211.

important with respect to the problem at hand. These are the ratios that have underlying predictive ability. In addition to telling us which ratios are important, empirical testing can show us how these ratios can best be combined so that the analysis is most meaningful with respect to prediction of a future event. As a result of this work, financial ratio analysis has become more scientific and objective than ever before.

INFLATION AND FINANCIAL ANALYSIS

In financial ratio analysis, it is important to recognize that inflationary forces may mask the results. Part of the financial performance of a company for a period of time may be due to management decisions, but part may be attributable to external factors over which management has little control. In particular, inflation may give rise to holding period gains which are not attributable to management decisions involved in running the enterprise. The problem with holding period gains is that they vary with inflation and this clouds the analysis of the overall results. To the extent that the financial analyst wishes to differentiate performance based on conventional accounting data from economic profitability, he will need to adjust the accounting numbers.

The Problem Illustrated

To illustrate the problem with a simple example, suppose that Foster Tool Company, a wholesaler of tools, began business on December 31, 19X1, and had the following balance sheet at that time:

Assets		Liabilities and Net Worth	
Cash	$ 40,000	Common stock	$240,000
Inventory	100,000		
Net fixed assets	100,000		
	$240,000		$240,000

The fixed assets are assumed to have a depreciable life of ten years and inventory is assumed to be reported on a first-in–first-out (FIFO) basis.[22] Also, assume that sales occur entirely at the end of the first year of operation and that inflation for that year was 20 percent. For ease of understanding, we

[22]"This example draws on Lawrence Revsine, *Accounting in an Inflationary Environment* (New York: Laventhol & Horwath, 1977).

assume that inflation occurred at the beginning of 19X2 and that we live in a world of no taxes.

Operations for the first year are reported on a historical cost basis and are as follows:

Income		
Sales		$170,000
Cost of goods sold		
Beginning inventory	$100,000	
Purchases	120,000	
Ending inventory	(120,000)	100,000
Depreciation ($100,000/10)		10,000
Selling and administrative expenses		30,000
Net profit		$ 30,000

Note that the company's ending inventory is higher than its beginning inventory by the percentage increase in prices, namely 20 percent. The balance sheet of the company at December 31, 19X2, would be:

Assets		Liabilities and Net Worth	
Cash	$ 60,000		
Inventory	120,000	Common stock	$240,000
Net fixed assets	90,000	Retained earnings	30,000
	$270,000		$270,000

If we compute two of the more widely used profitability ratios, we find them to be:

$$\text{Net profit margin } (\$30,000/\$170,000) = 17.65\%$$
$$\text{Return on assets } (\$30,000/\$240,000) = 12.50\%$$

In both cases, the underlying economic profitability of the company is overstated. For one thing, with the FIFO method inventories that are sold are assumed to have been purchased at the prices prevailing when the oldest items in the inventory were purchased. With inflation, these prices will be considerably below their replacement costs. In the case of Foster Tool Company, the inventories sold are valued at $100,000 for accounting purposes, whereas their replacement cost at the time they were sold was $120,000. The costing of inventories in this manner tends to understate economic costs and to overstate economic profits. In addition to inventory valuation, depreciation charges are based on the original cost of the fixed assets, less accumulated depreciation. Again with inflation, the original cost is less than the current replacement cost of these assets. If these assets increase in value by

20 percent, their replacement value is $120,000 and economic depreciation would be $12,000 instead of the $10,000 used for accounting depreciation purposes.

Restating the income statement of Foster Tool Company on a replacement cost basis, we have for 19X2:

Income	
Sales	$170,000
Cost of goods sold (replacement cost)	120,000
Depreciation ($120,000/10)	12,000
Selling and administrative expenses	30,000
Net profit	$ 8,000

The profitability ratios are as follows when economic profits as opposed to profits on a historical cost basis are used:

$$\text{Net profit margin } (\$8,000/\$170,000) = 4.70\%$$
$$\text{Return on assets } (\$8,000/\$240,000) = 3.33\%$$

We see, then, that the economic performance results are substantially lower than those originally supposed when accounting data were used.

Suppose that in 19X3 no inflation occurs and that the income statement of the company is as follows on a historical cost basis:

Income		
Sales		$170,000
Cost of goods sold		
Beginning inventory	$120,000	
Purchases	120,000	
Ending inventory	(120,000)	120,000
Depreciation ($100,000/10)		10,000
Selling and administrative expenses		30,000
Net profit		$ 10,000

Therefore the profits of the company drop substantially from the $30,000 reported the preceding year, again using historical costs to compute the profit figure.

However, this "worsening" of the profit performance is primarily attributable to inflation, not to management. If we look at the income statement on a replacement cost basis for 19X3, we find:

Income	
Sales	$170,000
Cost of goods sold	120,000
Depreciation ($120,000/10)	12,000
Selling and administrative expenses	30,000
	$ 8,000

This profit figure is exactly the same as that for 19X2, again on a replacement cost basis.

To compute the return on assets ratio on this basis, we need to recast the 19X2 balance sheet to reflect replacement costs. This balance sheet becomes:

Assets		Liabilities and Net Worth	
Cash	$ 60,000	Common stock	$240,000
Inventories	120,000	Retained earnings	8,000
Net fixed assets	108,000	Holding period gain	40,000
	$288,000		$288,000

The gross fixed assets are adjusted upward for inflation by 20 percent to $120,000. When we subtract first-year economic depreciation of $12,000, we obtain net fixed assets of $108,000. The holding period gain of $40,000 is comprised of the inventory profit of $20,000, which arises from the FIFO method, together with the increase in value of the fixed assets of $20,000.[23] Both of these gains are attributable to inflation during 19X2. With $288,000 as the asset value, the profitability ratios for 19X3 using replacement cost data are:

$$\text{Net profit margin } (\$8,000/\$170,000) = 4.70\%$$
$$\text{Return on assets } (\$8,000/\$288,000) = 2.78\%$$

While the net profit margin is the same as in 19X2, the return on assets is lower. This is due to the denominator, beginning total assets, being larger than that for the preceding year.

Implications

The example illustrates the problems involved when the analyst tries to compare the financial ratios of a company over time in the face of differing rates of inflation. We see that historical cost accounting data are distorted

---

[23]"This treatment is the same as that of Revsine, *Accounting in an Inflationary Environment,* pp. 14–15.

from year to year as a result of the inflation influence. Financial ratios, particularly those dealing with profitability, likewise are distorted. Part of the operating results is due to inflation, which is beyond management's control. What may appear to be a significant change in profitability may simply be due to the vagaries of inflation upon closer examination. In most cases it is important that the financial analyst not only recognize the underlying cause of the distortion but make appropriate modifications in his assessment of the financial performance of the company over time.

In addition to a company's financial ratios being distorted over time, intercompany comparisons may be distorted. When historical costs are used, the company with older fixed assets will often show a higher return on investment in an inflationary environment than will a company whose fixed assets were acquired more recently. Not only will the depreciation charges for the former company be less, which, in turn, will result in greater reported profits, but total assets will be lower. This combination of higher profits and lower investment will result in a higher return on investment ratio, all other things the same. However, the difference in return performance may be due entirely to assets being purchased at different times, and not to the relative efficiency of management. The danger is that the company with older fixed assets may be much less efficient in an economic sense, but that its return on investment, as based on conventional accounting data, is as good as if not better than that of a more efficient producer. As a result, comparisons of return on investment ratios based on historical costs may lead to incorrect conclusions being drawn.

For both types of comparisons—financial ratios of a given company over time and intercompany—inflation can result in faulty economic assessments being derived by the financial analyst. In periods of rapidly changing inflation, particular caution is necessary. Under these circumstances, it is desirable to recompute financial ratios using replacement cost accounting data. This can be done in the manner illustrated. By doing so, the financial analyst is able to differentiate that portion of overall performance attributable to inflation from that which is more directly under management's control. Only in this way is the analyst able to get a handle on economic return as opposed to accounting return. Oranges must be compared with oranges and apples with apples if the inferences derived are to be meaningful.

SUMMARY

Financial ratios can be divided into four types: liquidity, debt, profitability, and coverage. Each of these types has a special use for the financial analyst. The ratios taken up in this chapter are employed extensively by outside creditors, investors, and government regulators. These ratios are also helpful for managerial control and for providing a better understanding of what outside suppliers of capital expect in the way of financial condition and performance. The usefulness of the ratios depends upon the ingenuity and experience of the financial analyst who employs them. By themselves, financial ratios are fairly meaningless; they must be analyzed on a comparative basis.

A comparison of ratios of the same firm over time is important in evaluating changes and trends in the firm's financial condition and profitability. This comparison may be historical; it may also include an analysis of the future based upon projected financial statements. Ratios may also be judged in comparison with those of similar firms in the same line of business and, when appropriate, with an industry average. Caution is necessary in such comparisons, however, because the distributions of financial ratios for an industry typically are not normal. Other caveats involved in intercompany comparisons were discussed and the various sources of industry financial ratio information presented.

From empirical testing in recent years, it appears that financial ratios can be used to predict certain events successfully, bankruptcy in particular. With this testing, financial ratio analysis has become more scientific and objective than ever before and we can look to further progress in this regard. In the last section, inflation was seen to distort financial ratio analysis. Both comparisons of a company's financial ratios over time and intercompany comparisons are subject to faulty economic interpretation in periods of changing inflation. Changes in the reported performance of a company may be due entirely to inflation and not to management. To differentiate the causes, the analyst must recompute financial ratios on the basis of replacement cost accounting data as opposed to historical cost data.

PROBLEMS

1. High-Low Plumbing Company sells plumbing fixtures on terms of 2/10, net 30. Its financial statements over the last three years follow.

	19_1	19_2	19_3
Cash	$ 30,000	$ 20,000	$ 5,000
Accounts receivable	200,000	260,000	290,000
Inventory	400,000	480,000	600,000
Net fixed assets	800,000	800,000	800,000
	$1,430,000	$1,560,000	$1,695,000
Accounts payable	230,000	300,000	380,000
Accruals	200,000	210,000	225,000
Bank loan—short term	100,000	100,000	140,000
Long-term debt	300,000	300,000	300,000
Common stock	100,000	100,000	100,000
Retained earnings	500,000	550,000	550,000
	$1,430,000	$1,560,000	$1,695,000
Sales	$4,000,000	$4,300,000	$3,800,000
Cost of goods sold	3,200,000	3,600,000	3,300,000
Net profit	300,000	200,000	100,000

Using the ratios taken up in the chapter, analyze the company's financial condition and performance over the last three years. Are there any problems?

2. A company has total annual sales (all credit) of $400,000, and a gross profit margin of 20 percent. Its current assets are $80,000; current liabilities, $60,000; inventories, $30,000; and cash, $10,000.

    (a) How much average inventory should be carried if management wants the inventory turnover to be 4? (Assume a 360-day year for calculations.)

    (b) How rapidly (in how many days) must accounts receivable be collected if management wants to have only an average of $50,000 invested in receivables? (Assume a 360-day year.)

3. The data for various companies in the same industry and of about the same size follow.

Company	A	B	C	D	E	F
Sales (in millions)	$ 10	$20	$ 8	$ 5	$ 12	$17
Total assets (in millions)	8	10	6	2.5	4	8
Net income (in millions)	0.7	2	0.8	0.5	1.5	1

Determine the asset turnover, net profit margin, and earning power for each of the companies.

4. Using the following information, complete the balance sheet below.

Long-term debt to net worth	.5 to 1
Total asset turnover	2.5 times
Average collection period*	18 days
Inventory turnover	9 times
Gross profit margin	10 percent
Acid-test ratio	1 to 1

*Assume a 360-day year, and all sales on credit.

Cash	$ _____	Notes and payables	$100,000
Accounts receivable	_____	Long-term debt	_____
Inventory	_____	Common stock	$100,000
Plant and equipment	_____	Retained earnings	100,000
Total assets	$ _____	Total liabilities and worth	$ _____

5. The long-term debt section of the balance sheet of the Diters Corporation appears as follows:

$7\frac{1}{4}$% Mortgage bonds of 1998	$2,500,000
$7\frac{5}{8}$% Second-mortgage bonds of 1993	1,500,000
$8\frac{3}{8}$% Debentures of 1991	1,000,000
$9\frac{1}{8}$% Subordinated debentures of 1995	1,000,000
	$6,000,000

(a) If the average earnings before interest and taxes of the Diters Corporation are $1.5 million, what is the overall interest coverage?

(b) Using the cumulative deduction method, determine the coverage for each issue.

6.

U.S. Republic Corporation balance sheet, Dec. 31, 19X3

Assets		Liabilities and Stockholders' Equity	
Cash	$ 500,000	Notes payable	$ 2,000,000
Accounts receivable	2,500,000	Accounts payable	1,000,000
Inventory*	3,500,000	Accrued wages	
Fixed assets, net	7,500,000	and taxes	1,000,000
Excess over book value		Long-term debt	6,000,000
of assets acquired		Preferred stock	2,000,000
(Intangible assets)	1,000,000	Common stock	1,000,000
Total assets	$15,000,000	Retained earnings	2,000,000
		Total liabilities	
		and equity	$15,000,000

*Inventory at 12/31/X2 = $1,500,000.

U.S. Republic Corporation statement of income
and retained earnings

Year Ended Dec. 31, 19X3		
Net sales:		
Credit		$ 8,000,000
Cash		2,000,000
Total		$10,000,000
Costs and expenses:		
Cost of goods sold	$6,000,000	
Selling, general, and administrative expenses	1,000,000	
Depreciation	700,000	
Interest on long-term debt	300,000	8,000,000
Net income before taxes		$ 2,000,000
Taxes on income		1,000,000
Net income after taxes		$ 1,000,000
Less: Dividends on preferred stock		120,000
Net income available to common		880,000
Add: Retained earnings at 1/1/X3		1,300,000
Subtotal		$ 2,180,000
Less: Dividends paid on common		180,000
Retained earnings at 12/31/X3		$ 2,000,000

(a) Fill in the 19X3 column.

U.S. Republic Corporation

Ratio	19X1	19X2	19X3	Industry 19X3
1. Current ratio	250%	200%		225%
2. Acid-test ratio	100%	90%		110%
3. Receivables turnover	5.0x	4.5x		6.0x
4. Inventory turnover	4.0x	3.0x		4.0x
5. Long-term debt/total capitalization	35%	40%		33%
6. Gross profit margin	39%	41%		40%
7. Net profit margin	17%	15%		15%
8. Rate of return on equity	15%	20%		20%
9. Return on tangible assets	15%	12%		10%
10. Tangible asset turnover	0.9x	0.8x		1.00x
11. Overall interest coverage	11x	9x		10x

(b) Evaluate the position of the company from the above table. Cite specific ratio levels and trends as evidence.

(c) Indicate which ratios would be of most interest to you and what your decision would be in each of the following situations:

   (1) U.S. Republic wants to buy $500,000 worth of raw materials from you, with payment to be due in ninety days.

   (2) U.S. Republic wants you, a large insurance company, to pay off its note at the bank and assume it on a ten-year maturity basis at the current coupon of 9 percent.

   (3) There are 100,000 shares outstanding and the stock is selling for $80 a share. The company offers you an opportunity to buy 50,000 additional shares at this price.

7. Stella Stores Inc. has sales of $6 million, an asset turnover ratio of 6 for the year, and net profits of $120,000.

   (a) What is the company's return on assets or earning power?

   (b) The company is considering the installation of new point-of-sales cash registers throughout its stores. This equipment is expected to increase efficiency in inventory control, reduce clerical errors, and improve record keeping throughout the system. The new equipment will increase the investment in assets by 20 percent and is expected to increase the net profit margin from 2 to 3 percent. No change in sales is expected. What is the effect of the new equipment on the return on assets ratio or earning power?

8. *Research Project*
Altman developed the following discriminant function using financial ratios:[24]

$$Z = 0.012X_1 + 0.014X_2 + 0.033X_3 + 0.06X_4 + 0.99X_5$$

$$\text{where } X_1 = \text{working capital/total assets}$$
$$X_2 = \text{retained earnings/total assets}$$

---

[24]See E. I. Altman, "Financial Ratios, Discriminant Analysis and the Prediction of Corporate Bankruptcy," *Journal of Finance,* September 1968, p. 594.

X_3 = earnings before interest and taxes/total assets
X_4 = market value equity/book value of total debt
X_5 = sales/total assets

and where X_1 through X_4 are expressed as whole percents (10 percent = 10) and X_5 is expressed normally (10 percent = .10). Altman concluded from his sample that all firms with a Z score above 2.99 were "nonbankrupt," while all with a Z score below 1.81 were "bankrupt." He further decided that a Z of 2.675 was the cutoff point providing the least misclassifications. *Required:* Obtain the annual reports for several firms in a given industry with asset size between $1 and $25 million (another of Altman's restrictions). Try to separate the strong from the weak on the basis of the above analysis. Then attempt to support your findings with other evidence (declining stock price, rising interest costs, poor earnings trend, and so on).

SELECTED REFERENCES

Almanac of Business and Industrial Ratios. Englewood Cliffs, N.J.: Prentice-Hall, 1977.

ALTMAN, EDWARD I., "Financial Ratios, Discriminant Analysis and the Prediction of Corporate Bankruptcy," *Journal of Finance,* 23 (September 1968), 589–609.

ALTMAN, EDWARD I., ROBERT G. HALDEMAN, AND P. NARAYANAN, "Zeta Analysis: A New Model to Identify Bankruptcy Risk of Corporations," *Journal of Banking and Finance,* 1 (June 1977).

ALTMAN, EDWARD I., MICHEL MARGAINE, MICHEL SCHLOSSER, AND PIERRE VERNIMMEN, "Financial and Statistical Analysis for Commercial Loan Evaluation: A French Experience," *Journal of Financial and Quantitative Analysis,* 9 (March 1974), 195–212.

ALTMAN, EDWARD, I., AND ARNOLD W. SAMETZ, EDS., *Financial Crises.* New York: John Wiley, 1977.

BEAVER, WILLIAM H., "Financial Ratios as Predictors of Failure," *Empirical Research in Accounting: Selected Studies in Journal of Accounting Research* (1966), pp. 71–111.

DEAKIN, EDWARD B., "A Discriminant Analysis of Predictors of Business Failure," *Journal of Accounting Research,* 10 (Spring 1972), 167–79.

———, "Distributions of Financial Accounting Ratios: Some Empirical Evidence," *Accounting Review,* 51 (January 1976), 90–96.

EDMISTER, ROBERT O., "An Empirical Test of Financial Ratio Analysis for Small Business Failure Predictions," *Journal of Financial and Quantitative Analysis,* 7 (March 1972), 1477–93.

FINDLAY, M. CHAPMAN III, AND EDWARD E. WILLIAMS, "Toward More Adequate Debt Service Coverage Ratios," *Financial Analysts Journal,* 31 (November–December 1975), 58–61.

FOSTER, GEORGE, *Financial Statement Analysis.* Englewood Cliffs, N.J.: Prentice-Hall, 1978.

HELFERT, ERICH A., *Techniques of Financial Analysis,* Chap. 2. Homewood, Ill.: Richard D. Irwin, 1977.

HORRIGAN, JAMES C., "The Determination of Long-Term Credit Standing with Financial Ratios," *Empirical Research in Accounting: Selected Studies in Journal of Accounting Research* (1966), pp. 44–62.

———, "A Short History of Financial Ratio Analysis," *Accounting Review,* 43 (April 1968), 284–94.

JAEDICKE, ROBERT K., AND ROBERT T. SPROUSE, *Accounting Flows: Income, Funds, and Cash,* Chap. 7. Englewood Cliffs, N.J.: Prentice-Hall, 1965.

KENNEDY, HENRY A., "A Behavioral Study of the Usefulness of Four Financial Ratios," *Journal of Accounting Research*, 13 (Spring 1975), 97–116.

LEMKE, KENNETH W., "The Evaluation of Liquidity: An Analytical Study," *Journal of Accounting Research*, 8 (Spring 1970), 47–77.

LEV, BARUCH, *Financial Statement Analysis: A New Approach.* Englewood Cliffs, N.J.: Prentice-Hall, 1974.

LEWELLEN, W. G., AND R. O. EDMISTER, "A General Model for Accounts Receivable Analysis and Control," *Journal of Financial and Quantitative Analysis*, 8 (March 1973), 195–206.

LEWELLEN, W. G., AND R. W. JOHNSON, "Better Way to Monitor Accounts Receivables," *Harvard Business Review*, 50 (May–June 1972), 101–9.

O'CONNOR, MELVIN C., "On the Usefulness of Financial Ratios to Investors in Common Stock," *Accounting Review*, 48 (April 1973), 339–52.

PINCHES, GEORGE E., AND KENT A. MINGO, "A Multivariate Analysis of Industrial Bond Ratings," *Journal of Finance*, 28 (March 1973), 1–18.

REVSINE, LAWRENCE, *Accounting in an Inflationary Environment.* New York: Laventhol and Horwath, 1977.

STONE, BERNELL K., "The Payments-Pattern Approach to the Forecasting of Accounts Receivable," *Financial Management*, 5 (Autumn 1976), 65–82.

WEST, RICHARD R., "An Alternative Approach to Predicting Corporate Bond Ratings," *Journal of Accounting Research*, 8 (Spring 1970), 118–25.

26
funds analysis and financial forecasting

The second portion of our examination of the tools of financial analysis and control deals with the analysis of funds flows and financial forecasting. A funds-flow statement is a valuable aid to a financial manager or a creditor in evaluating the uses of funds by a firm and in determining how these uses are financed. In addition to studying past flows, the analyst can evaluate future flows by means of a funds statement based upon forecasts. Such a statement provides an efficient method for the financial manager to assess the growth of the firm and its resulting financial needs and to determine the best way to finance those needs. In particular, funds statements are very useful in planning intermediate- and long-term financing. Closely related to the use of funds statements are common size and index analyses. In the former, we express the various balance sheet items as a percentage of total assets and the income statement items as a percentage of total sales. In the latter, balance sheet and income statement items are expressed as an index relative to an initial base year. The combination of these two approaches provides additional insights into the funds flows of a firm.

In the analysis of future funds flows, we have the cash budget and *pro forma* statements. The cash budget is indispensable to the financial manager in determining the short-term cash needs of the firm and, accordingly, in planning its short-term financing. When cash budgeting is extended to include a range of possible outcomes, the financial manager can evaluate the business risk and liquidity of the firm and plan a realistic margin of safety. This margin of safety might come from adjusting the firm's liquidity cushion, rearranging the maturity structure of its debt, arranging a line of credit with a bank, or a combination of the three. Cash budgets prepared for a range of possible outcomes are valuable also in appraising the ability of the firm to adjust to unexpected changes in cash flows. The preparation of *pro forma* balance sheets and income statements enables the financial manager to analyze the effect of various policy decisions on the future financial condition and performance of the firm. We examine each of these tools in turn.

SOURCE AND USE OF FUNDS

The flow of funds in a firm may be visualized as a continuous process. For every use of funds, there must be an offsetting source. In a broad sense, the assets of a firm represent the net uses of funds; its liabilities and net worth represent net sources. A funds-flow cycle for a typical manufacturing company is illustrated in Figure 26-1. For the going concern, there is really no starting or stopping point. A finished product is produced with a variety of inputs—namely, raw material, fixed assets, and labor. These inputs ultimately are paid for in cash. The product then is sold either for cash or on credit. A credit sale involves a receivable, which, when collected, becomes cash. If the selling price of the product exceeds all costs (including depreciation on assets) for a period of time, there is a profit for the period; if not, there is a loss. The reservoir of cash, the focal point in the figure, fluctuates over time with the production schedule, sales, collection of receivables, capital expenditures, and financing. On the other hand, reservoirs of raw materials, work in process, finished goods inventory, accounts receivable, and trade payables fluctuate with sales, the production schedule, and policies with respect to managing receivables, inventories, and trade payables.

The funds statement is a method by which we study the net funds flow between two points in time. These points conform to beginning and ending financial statement dates for whatever period of examination is relevant—a quarter, a year, or five years. It is important to emphasize that the funds statement portrays net rather than gross changes between two comparable financial statements at different dates. For example, gross changes might be thought to include all changes that occur between the two statement dates rather than the sum of these changes—the net change as defined. Although an analysis of the gross funds flow of a firm over time would be much more revealing than an analysis of net funds flow, we are usually constrained by the financial information available—namely, balance sheets and income statements that span particular periods of time. Funds may be defined in several different ways, depending upon the purpose of the analysis. Although they are often defined as cash, many analysts treat funds as working

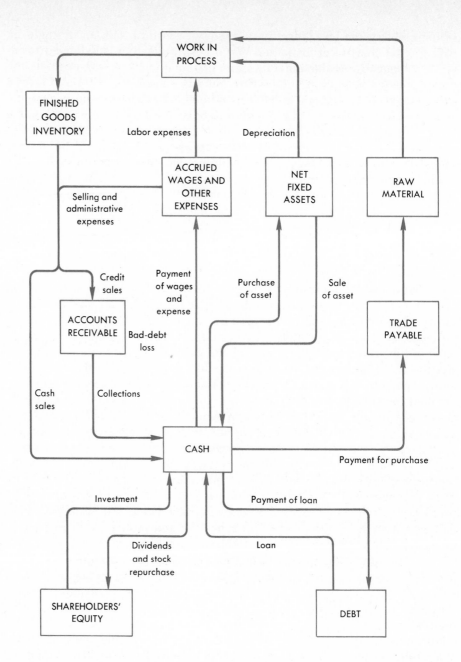

figure 26-1
Funds flow within
the firm

capital—a somewhat broader definition. Other definitions are possible, although the two described are the most common by far. Depending upon the analyst's objective, the definition can be broadened or narrowed. Because a funds-flow analysis on a cash basis serves as a building block for analyses using broader definitions of funds, we begin by defining funds as cash.

Funds Statement on a Cash Basis

Basically, one prepares a funds statement on a cash basis by (1) classifying net balance sheet changes that occur between two points in time into changes that increase cash and changes that decrease cash; (2) classifying, from the income statement and the surplus statement, the factors that increase cash and the factors that decrease cash; and (3) consolidating this information in a source and use of funds statement form. The first of these steps simply involves placing one balance sheet beside the other and computing the changes in the various accounts.

Sources of funds that increase cash are

1. A net decrease in any asset other than cash or fixed assets
2. A gross decrease in fixed assets
3. A net increase in any liability
4. Proceeds from the sale of preferred or common stock
5. Funds provided by operations

Funds provided by operations usually are not expressed directly on the income statement. To determine them, one must add back depreciation to net income after taxes. For Aldine Manufacturing Company, our example in the preceding chapter, we have

Net income after taxes	$150,574
Add noncash expenses: depreciation	111,509
Funds provided by operations	$262,083

Thus the net income of Aldine understates funds provided by operations by $111,509. Depreciation is not a source of funds, for funds are generated only from operations.[1] If operating losses before depreciation are sustained, funds are not provided regardless of the magnitude of depreciation charges.

Uses of funds include

1. A net increase in any asset other than cash or fixed assets
2. A gross increase in fixed assets
3. A net decrease in any liability
4. A retirement or purchase of stock
5. Cash dividends

To avoid double counting, we compute gross changes in fixed assets by adding depreciation for the period to net fixed assets at the ending financial

---

[1]For an extensive discussion of this concept, see Robert K. Jaedicke and Robert T. Sprouse, *Accounting Flows: Income, Funds, and Cash* (Englewood Cliffs, N.J.: Prentice-Hall, 1965), pp. 80–86.

table 26-1

Aldine Manufacturing Company sources and uses of
funds March 31, 1979 to March 31, 1980 (in
thousands)

Sources		Uses	
Funds provided by operations:			
Net profit	$150	Dividends	$ 92
Depreciation	112	Additions to fixed assets	104
		Increase—inventories	94
Decrease—accounts receivable	62	Increase—prepaid expenses	4
Increase—bank loans	92	Increase—tax prepayments	6
Increase—accounts payable	12	Increase—investments	65
Increase—other accruals	27	Decrease—accrued taxes	91
Increase—long-term debt	4	Increase—cash position	3
	$459		$459

statement date, and subtract from this amount net fixed assets at the beginning financial statement date. The residual represents the gross change in
fixed assets for the period. If the residual is positive, as is usually the case, it
represents a use of funds; if negative, it represents a source.

Once all sources and uses are computed, they may be arranged in
statement form so that we can analyze them better. Table 26-1 shows a source
and use of funds statement for the Aldine Manufacturing Company for the
fiscal year ended March 31, 1980. The balance sheet and income statement for
this corporation, on which the funds statement is based, are shown in Tables
25-1 and 25-2 of Chapter 25. When we subtract the total uses of funds in Table
26-1 from the total sources, the difference should equal the actual change in
cash between the two statement dates. If it does not, then the analyst must
search for the cause of the discrepancy. Frequently, discrepancies will be due
to surplus adjustments; and the analyst should be alert to this possibility.

In Table 26-1, we see that the principal uses of funds for the 1980 fiscal
year were additions to fixed assets, increases in inventories and in investments, and a sizable decrease in taxes payable. These uses were financed
primarily by funds provided by operations in excess of dividends; a decrease
in accounts receivable; and by increases in bank loans, payables, and accruals. As sources exceeded slightly the uses of funds, the cash balance rose
by $3,000. In a sources and uses of funds analysis, it is useful to place cash
dividends opposite net profits and additions to fixed assets opposite depreciation. Doing this allows the analyst to evaluate easily both the amount of
dividend payout and the net increase in fixed assets.

Funds as Working Capital

Financial analysts frequently prepare a source and use of working
capital statement. This statement is very similar to the source and use of
funds statement on a cash basis, but it takes into account working capital

table 26-2

**Aldine Manufacturing Company sources and uses
of working capital March 31, 1979
to March 31, 1980 (in thousands)**

Sources		Uses	
Funds provided by operations:			
Net profit	$150	Dividends	$ 92
Depreciation	112	Additions to fixed assets	104
Increase—long-term debt	4	Increase—investments	65
		Increase—working capital	5
	$266		$266

instead of cash. A source and use of working capital statement for Aldine Manufacturing Company for the year ended March 31, 1980, is shown in Table 26-2.

We see that the only difference between this statement and a funds statement on a cash basis is the omission of changes in the various components of current assets and current liabilities. This statement is analyzed much as the source and use of funds statement is. A source and use of working capital statement is used frequently by bankers, for they often require a borrower to maintain some sort of minimum working capital. It is used also by other lenders and by management for purposes of internal control.

Implications

The analysis of cash and working-capital funds statements gives us a rich insight into the financial operations of a firm—an insight that is especially valuable to the financial manager in analyzing past and future expansion plans of the firm and the impact of these plans on liquidity. He can detect imbalances in the uses of funds and undertake appropriate actions. For example, an analysis spanning the past several years might reveal a growth in inventories out of proportion with the growth of other assets and with sales. Upon analysis, he might find that the problem was due to inefficiencies in inventory management. Thus a funds statement alerts the financial manager to problems that he can analyze in detail and take proper actions to correct. When a company has a number of divisions, individual funds statements may prove useful. These statements enable top management to appraise the performance of divisions in relation to the funds committed to them.

Another use of funds statements is in the evaluation of the firm's financing. An analysis of the major sources of funds in the past reveals what portion of the firm's growth was financed internally and what portion externally. In evaluating the firm's financing, the analyst will wish to evaluate the ratio of dividends to earnings relative to the firm's total need for funds. Funds statements are useful also in judging whether the firm has expanded at too fast a rate and whether financing is strained. For example, we can determine if trade credit has increased out of proportion to increases in current assets and sales. If trade credit has increased at a significantly faster rate, we would wish to evaluate the consequences of increased slowness in trade payments on the credit standing of the firm and its ability to finance in the future. It is also revealing to analyze the mix of short- and long-term financing in relation to the funds needs of the firm. If these needs are primarily for fixed assets and permanent increases in working capital, we might be disturbed if a significant portion of total financing came from short-term sources.

An analysis of a funds statement for the future is extremely valuable to the financial manager in planning the intermediate- and long-term financing of the firm. It tells him the firm's total prospective need for funds, the expected timing of these needs, and their nature—that is, whether the increased investment is primarily for inventories, fixed assets, and so forth. Given this information, along with the expected changes in trade payables and the various accruals, he can arrange the firm's financing more effectively. In addition, he can determine the expected closing cash position of the firm simply by adjusting the beginning cash balance for the change in cash reflected on the projected source and use statement. In essence, the projected change in cash is a residual.

COMMON SIZE AND INDEX ANALYSES

In addition to the funds statement, it is often useful to express balance sheet and income statement items as percentages. The percentages can be related to totals, such as total assets or total sales, or to some base year. Called common size analysis and index analysis, respectively, the evaluation of trends in financial statement percentages over time affords the analyst insight into the underlying movement of funds. While a good portion of this insight is revealed in source and use of funds statements, a deeper and broader under-standing of a firm's funds flows is possible when the analysis is extended to include the above considerations. In order to illustrate these two types of analysis, we shall use the balance sheet and income statements of Riker Electronics Company for the 1977 through 1980 fiscal years. These statements are shown in Tables 26-3 and 26-4.

Statement Items as Percents of Totals

In common size analysis, we express the various components of a balance sheet as percentages of the total assets of the company. In addition, this can be done for the income statement, but here items are related to sales. The gross and net profit margins, which we took up in Chapter 25, are examples of this type of expression; and it can be extended to all the items on the income statement. The expression of individual financial statement items as percentages of totals usually permits insights not possible from a review of the raw figures themselves.

table 26-3
Riker Electronics Corporation balance sheet
(in thousands)

Assets				
	1977	1978	1979	1980
Cash	$ 2,507	$ 4,749	$ 11,310	$ 19,648
Accounts receivable	70,360	72,934	85,147	118,415
Inventory	77,380	86,100	91,378	118,563
Other current assets	6,316	5,637	6,082	5,891
Current assets	$156,563	$169,420	$193,917	$262,517
Fixed assets—net	$ 79,187	$ 91,868	$ 94,652	$115,461
Other long-term assets	4,695	5,017	5,899	5,491
Total assets	$240,445	$266,305	$294,468	$383,469
Liabilities and Net Worth				
Accounts payable	$ 35,661	$ 31,857	$ 37,460	$ 62,725
Notes payable	20,501	25,623	14,680	17,298
Other current liabilities	11,054	7,330	8,132	15,741
Current liabilities	$ 67,216	$ 64,810	$ 60,272	$ 95,764
Long-term debt	888	979	1,276	1,917
Total liabilities	$ 68,104	$ 65,789	$ 61,548	$ 97,681
Preferred stock	0	0	0	2,088
Common stock	$ 12,650	$ 25,649	$ 26,038	$ 26,450
Capital surplus	36,134	33,297	45,883	63,049
Retained earnings	123,557	141,570	160,999	194,201
Net worth	$172,341	$200,516	$232,920	$285,788
Total liabilities and net worth	$240,445	$266,305	$294,468	$383,469

To illustrate, common size balance sheet and income statements are shown in Tables 26-5 and 26-6 for Riker Electronics Company for the fiscal years 1977 through 1980. In the first of the two tables, we see that over the four-year time span the percentage of current assets increased and that this was particularly true of cash. In addition, we see that accounts receivable showed a relative increase from 1979 to 1980. On the liability and net worth side of the balance sheet, the debt of the company declined on a relative basis from 1977 to 1980. However, with the large absolute increase in assets that occurred in 1980, the debt ratio increased from 1979 to 1980. This is particularly apparent in accounts payable, which increased substantially in both absolute and relative terms.

The common size income statement in Table 26-6 shows the gross profit margin fluctuating from year to year. When this is combined with selling, general and administrative expenses, which also fluctuate over time, the end result is a net profit picture which varies from year to year. While

table 26-4

Riker Electronics Corporation income statement
(in thousands)

	1977	1978	1979	1980
Sales	$323,780	$347,322	$375,088	$479,077
Cost of goods sold	148,127	161,478	184,507	223,690
Gross Profit	$175,653	$185,844	$190,581	$255,387
Selling expenses	$ 79,399	$ 98,628	$103,975	$125,645
General and administrative expenses	43,573	45,667	45,275	61,719
Total expenses	$122,972	$144,295	$149,250	$187,364
Earnings before interest and taxes	$52,681	$41,549	$41,331	$68,023
Other income	1,757	4,204	2,963	3,017
Earnings before taxes	$54,438	$45,753	$44,294	$71,040
Taxes	28,853	22,650	20,413	32,579
Earnings after taxes	$ 25,585	$ 23,103	$ 23,881	$ 38,461

1980 shows a sharp improvement over 1979 and 1978, it still is not as good as 1977 on a before-tax relative basis.

Statement Items as Indexes Relative to a Base Year

The common size balance sheet and income statement can be supplemented by the expression of items as trends from a base year. In the case of Riker Electronics Corporation, the base year is 1977 and all financial statement items are 100.0 for that year. Items for the three subsequent years are expressed as an index relative to that year. For example, if a statement item were $22,500 compared with $15,000 in the base year, the index would be 150. In Tables 26-7 and 26-8, indexed balance sheet and income statements are shown. In the first of these two tables, the buildup in cash from the base year is particularly apparent, and this agrees with our previous assessment. Note also the large increase in accounts receivable and inventories from 1979 to 1980. The latter was not apparent in the common size analysis. To a lesser extent, there was a sizable increase in fixed assets. On the liability side of the balance sheet, we note the large increase in accounts payable as well as in other current liabilities which occurred from 1979 to 1980. This, coupled with retained earnings and the sale of common stock, financed the large increase in assets that occurred between these two points in time.

The indexed income statement in Table 26-8 gives much the same picture as the common size income statement, namely, fluctuating behavior. However, the sharp improvement in 1980 profitability is more easily distin-

table 26-5
Riker Electronics Corporation common size balance sheet

Assets				
	1977	1978	1979	1980
Cash	1.0	1.8	3.8	5.1
Accounts receivable	29.3	27.4	28.9	30.9
Inventory	32.2	32.3	31.0	30.9
Other current assets	2.6	2.1	2.1	1.5
Current assets	65.1	63.6	65.9	68.5
Fixed assets—net	32.9	34.5	32.1	30.1
Other long-term assets	2.0	1.9	2.0	1.4
Total assets	100.0	100.0	100.0	100.0
Liabilities and Net Worth				
Accounts payable	14.8	12.0	12.7	16.4
Notes payable	8.5	9.6	5.0	4.5
Other current liabilities	4.6	2.8	2.8	4.1
Current liabilities	28.0	24.3	20.5	25.0
Long-term debt	0.4	0.4	0.4	0.5
Total liabilities	28.3	24.7	20.9	25.5
Preferred stock	0.0	0.0	0.0	0.5
Common stock	5.3	9.6	8.8	6.9
Capital surplus	15.0	12.5	15.6	16.4
Retained earnings	51.4	53.2	54.7	50.6
Net worth	71.7	75.3	79.1	74.4
Total liabilities and net worth	100.0	100.0	100.0	100.0

guished. Moreover, the indexed statement gives us information on the magnitude of absolute change in profits and expenses. With the common size statement, we have no information about how total assets or total sales change over time.

In summary, the standardization of balance sheet and income statement items as percentages of totals and as indexes to a base year often gives us insights additional to those obtained from analyses of financial ratios and source and use of funds statements. This supplemental information can be valuable in providing a better understanding of a company's underlying uses of funds and how those uses are financed over time. While the expressions of balance sheet and income statement items as percentages of totals and as indexes relative to a base year are not a substitute for the source and use statement, they provide us with a deeper and more extended knowledge of a company's funds movements over time. In addition, a deeper understanding of changes in a company's profitability is possible.

table 26-6

Riker Electronics Corporation common size
income statement

	1977	1978	1979	1980
Sales	100.0	100.0	100.0	100.0
Costs of goods sold	45.7	46.5	49.2	46.7
Gross profit	54.3	53.5	50.8	53.3
Selling expenses	24.5	28.4	27.7	26.2
General and administrative expenses	13.5	13.1	12.1	12.9
Total expenses	38.0	41.5	39.8	39.1
Earnings before interest, and taxes	16.3	12.0	11.0	14.2
Other income	0.5	1.2	0.8	0.6
Earnings before taxes	16.8	13.2	11.8	14.8
Taxes	8.9	6.5	5.4	6.8
Earnings after taxes	7.9	6.7	6.4	8.0

CASH BUDGETING

A cash budget involves a projection of future cash receipts and cash disbursements of the firm over various intervals of time. It reveals to the financial manager the timing and amount of expected cash inflows and outflows over the period studied. With this information, he is better able to determine the future cash needs of the firm, plan for the financing of these needs, and exercise control over the cash and liquidity of the firm.

Cash budgets may be for almost any period of time. For near-term forecasts, monthly periods probably are the ones used most frequently, because they take into account seasonal variations in cash flows. When cash flows are extremely volatile but predictable, budgets at more frequent intervals may be necessary for determining peak cash requirements. By the same token, when cash flows are relatively stable, budgeting at quarterly or even longer intervals may be justified. Generally, the further in the future the period for which one is trying to predict cash flows, the more uncertain the forecast. The expense of preparing monthly cash budgets usually is warranted only for predictions concerning the near future.

The cash budget is only as useful as the accuracy of the forecasts that are used in its preparation.[2] The greater the possible dispersion of actual results from those estimated, the more the allowance that must be made for unexpected swings in cash flow. A firm whose cash flows are subject to much

---

[2]For an excellent analysis of cost of inaccuracy versus the cost of the forecast itself, see John C. Chambers, Satinder K. Mullick, and Donald D. Smith, "How to Choose the Right Forecasting Technique," *Harvard Business Review*, 49 (July-August 1971), 45–74.

table 26-7
Riker Electronics Corporation indexed balance sheet

Assets			
	1977	1978	1979	1980
Cash	100.0	189.4	451.1	783.7
Accounts receivable	100.0	103.7	121.0	168.3
Inventory	100.0	111.3	118.1	153.2
Other current assets	100.0	89.2	96.3	93.3
Current assets	100.0	108.2	123.9	167.7
Fixed assets—net	100.0	116.0	119.5	145.8
Other long-term assets	100.0	106.9	125.6	117.0
Total assets	100.0	110.8	122.5	159.5

Liabilities and Equities			
Accounts payable	100.0	89.3	105.0	175.9
Notes payable	100.0	125.0	71.6	84.4
Other current liabilities	100.0	66.3	73.6	142.4
Current liabilities	100.0	96.4	89.7	142.5
Long-term debt	100.0	110.2	143.7	215.9
Total liabilities	100.0	96.6	90.4	143.4
Preferred stock	0.0	0.0	0.0	100.0
Common stock	100.0	202.8	205.8	209.1
Capital surplus	100.0	92.1	127.0	174.5
Retained earnings	100.0	114.6	130.3	157.2
Net worth	100.0	116.3	135.2	165.8
Total liabilities and net worth	100.0	110.8	122.5	159.5

uncertainty should provide for either a cash cushion, ready borrowing power, or both to tide it over in periods of adverse cash developments.

Preparation of the Cash Budget

Receipts   The key to the accuracy of most cash budgets is the forecast of sales. This forecast can be based upon an internal analysis, an external one, or both. With an internal approach, salesmen are asked to project sales for the forthcoming period. The product sales managers screen these estimates and consolidate them into sales estimates for product lines. The estimates for the various product lines then are combined into an overall sales estimate for the firm. The basic problem with an internal approach is that it can be too myopic. Often, important trends in the economy and in the industry are overlooked.

table 26-8

Riker Electronics Corporation indexed
income statement

	1977	1978	1979	1980
Sales	100.0	107.3	115.8	148.0
Cost of goods sold	100.0	109.0	124.6	151.0
Gross profit	100.0	105.8	108.5	145.4
Selling expenses	100.0	124.2	131.0	158.2
General and administrative expenses	100.0	104.8	103.9	141.6
Total expenses	100.0	117.3	121.4	152.4
Earnings before interest and taxes	100.0	78.9	78.5	129.1
Other income	100.0	239.3	168.6	171.7
Earnings before taxes	100.0	84.0	81.4	130.5
Taxes	100.0	78.5	70.7	112.9
Earnings after taxes	100.0	90.3	93.3	150.3

For this reason, many companies use an external analysis as well. With an external approach, economic analysts make forecasts of the economy and of industry sales for several years to come. In this regard, regression analysis may be used to estimate the association between industry sales and the economy in general. Given these basic predictions of business conditions and industry sales, the next step is to estimate market share by individual products, prices that are likely to prevail, and the expected reception of new products. Usually, these estimates are made in conjunction with marketing managers. However, the ultimate responsibility should lie with the economic forecasting department. Given this information, an external forecast of sales can be prepared.

When the internal forecast of sales differs from the external one, as it is likely to do, a compromise must be reached. Past experience will show which of the two forecasts is more accurate. In general, the external forecast should serve as the foundation for the final sales forecast. However, it often will need to be modified by the internal forecast. For example, the firm might expect to receive several large orders from customers, and these orders might not show up in the external forecast. By basing the final sales forecast on both internal and external analyses, it usually is more accurate than is either an internal or an external forecast by itself. The final sales forecast should be based upon prospective demand and not be modified initially by internal constraints such as physical capacity. The decision to remove these constraints will depend upon the forecast. The importance of accurate sales forecasts cannot be overestimated, for most of the other forecasts, in some measure, are based upon expected sales.

Given the sales forecast, the next job is to determine the cash receipts from these sales. With cash sales, cash is received at the time of the sale; with credit sales, however, the receipts do not come until later. How much later will depend upon the billing terms given, the type of customer, and the credit and collection policies of the firm. Suppose, for purposes of illustration, that the terms offered by Continental Sheetmetal Company are net 30, meaning that payment is due within thirty days after the invoice date. Assume also that in the company's experience, 90 percent of receivables are collected, on the average, one month from the date of the sale, and that 10 percent are collected two months from the date of the sale, with no bad-debt losses. Moreover, on the average, 10 percent of total sales are cash sales.

If the sales forecast are those shown in the first line of Table 26-9, we can compute a schedule of the expected sales receipts based upon the above assumptions. This schedule appears in Table 26-9. For January, we see that total sales are estimated to be $250,000, of which $25,000 are cash sales. Of the $225,000 in credit sales, 90 percent, or $202,500, are expected to be collected in February; and 10 percent, or $22,500, are expected to be collected in March. Similarly, sales in other months are broken down according to the same percentages. The firm should be alert to change its assumptions with respect to collections when there is an underlying shift in the payment habits of its customers. For example, if there is a slowdown in the economy, certain customers are likely to become slower in their trade payments. The firm must take account of this change if its cash budget is to be realistic.

From this example, it is easy to see the effect of a variation in sales upon the magnitude and timing of cash receipts, all other things held constant. For most firms, there is a degree of correlation between sales and collection experience. In times of recession and sales decline, the average collection period is likely to lengthen and bad-debt losses increase. Thus the collection experience of a firm may reinforce a decline in sales, magnifying the downward impact upon total sales receipts.

Cash receipts may arise from the sale of assets, as well as from sales of the product. Suppose, for example, that the firm intends to sell $40,000 in fixed assets in February. Total cash receipts in February, then, would be

table 26-9
Schedule of sales receipts (in thousands)

	Nov.	Dec.	Jan.	Feb.	Mar.	Apr.	May	June
Total sales	$300.0	$350.0	$250.0	$200.0	$250.0	$300.0	$350.0	$380.0
Credit sales	270.0	315.0	225.0	180.0	225.0	270.0	315.0	342.0
Collections—one month		243.0	283.5	202.5	162.0	202.5	243.0	283.5
Collections—two months			27.0	31.5	22.5	18.0	22.5	27.0
Total collections			$310.5	$234.0	$184.5	$220.5	$265.5	$310.5
Cash sales			25.0	20.0	25.0	30.0	35.0	38.0
Total sales receipts			$335.5	$254.0	$209.5	$250.5	$300.5	$348.5

$294,000. For the most part, the sale of assets is planned in advance and, therefore, is easily predicted for purposes of cash budgeting.

Disbursements Next comes a forecast of cash disbursements. Given the sales forecast, a production schedule may be established. Management may choose either to gear production closely to sales or to produce at a relatively constant rate over time. With the former production strategy, inventory carrying costs generally are lower, but total production costs are higher than with the latter strategy. With steady production, the opposite usually occurs. If sales fluctuate, finished goods inventories build up during certain periods and require storage. Because storage is uneven throughout the year, inventory carrying costs are generally higher than they would be if production were geared to sales. On the other hand, production typically is more efficient. Which alternative is better will depend upon the added cost of carrying inventory when production is geared to sales relative to the savings available if production is steady. The final production schedule embodies decisions with respect to inventory management, a topic taken up in Chapter 16.

Once a production schedule has been established, estimates can be made of the materials that will need to be purchased, the labor that will be required, and any additional fixed assets the firm will need to acquire. As with receivables, there is a lag between the time a purchase is made and the time of actual cash payment. If the average billing terms given by suppliers are net 30, and the firm's policy is to pay its bills at the end of this period, there is approximately a one-month lag between a purchase and the payment. If the production program of Continental Sheetmetal calls for the manufacture of goods in the month preceding forecasted sales, we might have a schedule of expenses like that in Table 26-10. As we see, there is a one-month lag between the time of purchase and the payment for the purchase.

Wages are assumed to increase with the amount of production. Generally, wages are more stable over time than are purchases. When production dips slightly, workers usually are not laid off. When production picks up, labor becomes more efficient with relatively little increase in total wages. Only after a certain point is overtime work required or do new workers have to be hired to meet the increased production schedule. Included in other expenses are general, administrative, and selling expenses; property taxes; interest expenses; power, light, and heat expenses; maintenance expenses;

table 26-10

Schedule of expenses (in thousands)

	Dec.	Jan.	Feb.	Mar.	Apr.	May	June
Purchases	$100	$ 80	$100	$120	$140	$150	$150
Cash payment for purchases		100	80	100	120	140	150
Wages		80	80	90	90	95	100
Other expenses		50	50	50	50	50	50
Total cash expenses		$230	$210	$240	$260	$285	$300

table 26-11
Schedule of cash disbursements (in thousands)

	Jan.	Feb.	Mar.	Apr.	May	June
Total cash expenses	$230	$210	$240	$260	$285	$300
Capital expenditures		150	50			
Dividend payments			20			20
Income taxes	30			30		
Total cash disbursements	$260	$360	$310	$290	$285	$320

and indirect labor and material expenses. These expenses tend to be reasonably predictable over the short run.

In addition to cash expenses, we must take into account capital expenditures, dividends, federal income taxes, and any other cash outflows. Because capital expenditures are planned in advance, they usually are predictable for the short-term cash budget. As the forecast becomes more distant, however, prediction of these expenditures becomes less certain. Dividend payments for most companies are stable and are paid on specific dates. Estimation of federal income taxes must be based upon projected profits for the period under review. Other cash outlays might consist of the repurchase of stock or payment of long-term debt. These outlays are combined with total cash expenses to obtain the schedule of total cash disbursements shown in Table 26-11.

Net Cash Flow and Cash Balance   Once we are satisfied that we have taken into account all foreseeable cash inflows and outflows, we combine the cash receipts and cash disbursements schedules to obtain the net cash inflow or outflow for each month. The net cash flow may then be added to beginning cash in January, which is assumed to be $100,000, and the projected cash position computed month by month for the period under review. This final schedule is shown in Table 26-12.

The cash budget shown indicates that the firm is expected to have a cash deficit in April and May. This deficit is caused by a decline in collections through March, capital expenditures totaling $200,000 in February and March, and a cash dividend of $20,000 in March. With the increase in collec-

table 26-12
Net cash flow and cash balance (in thousands)

	Jan.	Feb.	Mar.	Apr.	May	June
Total cash receipts	$335.5	$294.0*	$209.5	$250.5	$300.5	$348.5
Total cash disbursements	260.0	360.0	310.0	290.0	285.0	320.0
Net cash flow	$ 75.5	$ (66.0)	$(100.5)	$ (39.5)	$ 15.5	$ 28.5
Beginning cash without financing	100.0	175.5	109.5	9.0	(30.5)	(15.0)
Ending cash without financing	175.5	109.5	9.0	(30.5)	(15.0)	13.5

*Includes sales receipts of $254,000 and cash sales of assets of $40,000.

tions in May and June, the cash balance without financing rises to $13,500 in June. The cash budget indicates that peak cash requirements occur in April. If the firm has a policy of maintaining a minimum cash balance of $75,000 and of borrowing from its bank to maintain this minimum, it will need to borrow an additional $66,000 in March. Additional borrowings will peak at $105,500 in April, after which they will decline to $61,500 in June, if all goes according to prediction.

Alternative means of meeting the cash deficit are available. The firm may be able to delay its capital expenditures or its payments for purchases. Indeed, one of the principal purposes of a cash budget is to determine the timing and magnitude of prospective financing needs so that the most appropriate method of financing can be arranged. A decision to obtain long-term financing should be based upon long-range funds requirements and upon considerations apart from a cash forecast. In addition to helping the financial manager plan for short-term financing, the cash budget is valuable to him in managing the firm's cash position. On the basis of a cash budget, he can plan to invest excess funds in marketable securities. The result is an efficient transfer of funds from cash to marketable securities and back.

Deviations from Expected Cash Flows

Often, there is a tendency to place considerable faith in the cash budget simply because it is expressed in numbers. It is important to stress again that a cash budget represents merely an *estimate* of future cash flows. Depending upon the care devoted to preparing the budget and the volatility of cash flows resulting from the nature of the business, actual cash flows will deviate more or less widely from those that were expected. In the face of uncertainty, we must provide information about the range of possible outcomes. To analyze cash flows only under one set of assumptions, as is the case with conventional cash budgeting, results in a faulty perspective of the future.

To take into account deviations from expected cash flows, it is desirable to work out additional cash budgets. For example, we might want to base one cash forecast upon the assumption of a maximum probable decline in business, and another upon the assumption of the maximum probable increase in business. By bringing possible events into the open for discussion, management is better able to plan for contingencies. Not only will such discussion sharpen its perspective on the probability of occurrence of a particular event, but it will give management a better understanding of the magnitude of its impact on the firm's cash flows.[3]

Given the preparation of a cash budget based upon expected cash flows, it is often a simple matter to trace through a change in one or a series of figures in order to take into account a large number of possibilities. In determining the spectrum of possible outcomes, simulation techniques can be

[3]See Gordon Donaldson, "Strategy for Financial Emergencies," *Harvard Business Review,* 47 (November-December 1969), 69.

useful. The computer can be programmed to calculate a cash budget under
varying assumptions. With a time-sharing system, the analyst can type in a
change in assumptions; and the computer will recompute and print out a new
cash budget in a matter of minutes. Examples of a change in assumptions
include a decline in sales or an increase in the average collection period. For
each set of assumptions and resulting cash budget, a probability of occurrence should be attached. The ease with which reruns can be made with a
computer time-sharing system allows extensive analysis of the sensitivity of
the firm's expected cash position to changes in assumptions.

The expected cash position plus the probability distribution of possible outcomes gives us a considerable amount of information. We can see the
additional funds required or the funds released under various possible outcomes. This information enables us to determine more accurately the minimum cash balance, maturity structure of debt, and borrowing power necessary to give the firm a margin of safety. It enables the financial manager to
anticipate sharp changes in the firm's cash position.

We also can analyze the ability of the firm to adjust to deviations
from the expected outcomes. For example, if sales should fall off, how flexible
are our expenses? What can be cut? By how much? How quickly? How much
effort should be devoted to the collection of receivables? In the case of an
unexpected increase in business, what additional purchases will be required,
and when? Can labor be expanded? Can the present plant handle the additional demand? How much in funds will be needed to finance the buildup?
Answers to these questions provide valuable insight into the efficiency and
flexibility of the firm under a variety of conditions.[4] In addition, an analysis of
this sort helps answer the important question of the costs of various deviations from expected outcomes. Again, simulation is a useful method for
evaluating these costs.

The final product might be a series of distributions of end-of-the-
month cash without financing. An example of relative frequency distributions for the months of January through June is shown in Figure 26-2. Bar
graphs are used, as these are usually the product of a simulation. The most
likely values of ending cash are depicted by the highest bar; these conform
with the values shown in Table 26-12. We note that while several of the
distributions are reasonably symmetrical, others are skewed. In particular,
the distributions for March and April are skewed to the left. As a result, the
need for cash during these months might be considerably greater than that
depicted in Table 26-12. It is clear that the type of information portrayed in
Figure 26-2 better enables management to plan for contingencies than does
information giving only single-point estimates of monthly cash flows.

From the standpoint of internal planning, it is far better to allow for a
range of possible outcomes than to rely solely upon the expected outcome.
This allowance is particularly important for firms whose business is relatively unstable in character. If the plans of the firm are based only upon

[4]Donaldson, "Strategy for Financial Emergencies," pp. 71–79, develops a framework
for evaluating the resources available to meet adverse financial contingencies.

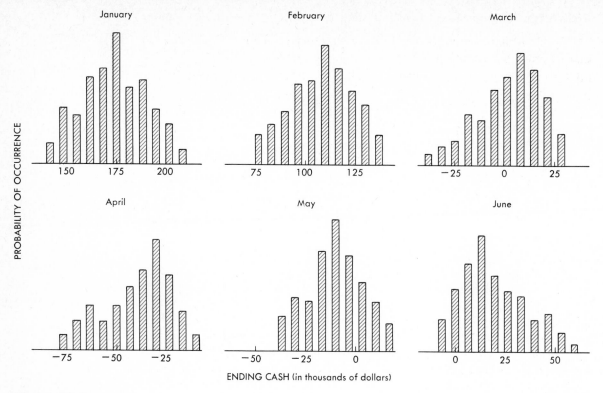

figure 26-2
Distributions of ending cash

expected cash flows, the firm is likely to be caught flat-footed in the case of a significant deviation from the expected outcome, and have difficulty making an adjustment. An unforeseen deficit in cash may be difficult to finance on short notice. Therefore it is extremely important for the firm to be honest with itself and attempt to minimize the costs associated with deviations from expected outcomes by taking the steps necessary to assure accuracy and by preparing additional cash budgets so as to take into account the range of possible outcomes.

PRO FORMA STATEMENTS

In addition to projecting the cash flow of a firm over time, it often is useful to prepare a projected, or *pro forma*, balance sheet and income statement for selected future dates. A cash budget gives us information only as to the prospective future cash positions of the firm, whereas *pro forma* statements embody forecasts of all assets and liabilities as well as of income statement items. Much of the information that goes into the preparation of the cash budget, however, can be used to derive a *pro forma* statement. As before, the key to accuracy is the sales forecasts.

Pro Forma Balance Sheet

To illustrate the preparation of a *pro forma* balance sheet, suppose that we wish to prepare a *pro forma* statement for Continental Sheetmetal for June 30 and that the company has the following balance sheet at December 31:

Assets (in thousands)		Liabilities (in thousands)	
Cash	$ 100	Bank borrowings	$ 50
Receivables	342	Accounts payable	200
Inventory	350	Accrued wages and expenses	250
Current assets	$ 792	Accrued income taxes	70
		Current liabilities	$ 570
Net fixed assets	800	Net worth	1,022
Total assets	$1,592	Total liabilities and net worth	$1,592

Receivables at June 30 can be estimated by adding to the receivable balance at December 31 the total projected credit sales from January through June, less total projected credit collections for the period. On the basis of the information in the cash budget, receivables at June 30 would be $342,000 + $31,500, or $373,500.

If a cash budget is not available, the receivable balance may be estimated on the basis of a turnover ratio. This ratio, which depicts the relationship between credit sales and receivables, should be based upon past experience. To obtain the estimated level of receivables, projected sales simply are divided by the turnover ratio. If the sales forecast and turnover ratio are realistic, the method will produce a reasonable approximation of the receivable balance. The estimated investment in inventories at June 30 may be based upon the production schedule, which, in turn, is based upon the sales forecast. This schedule should show expected purchases, the expected use of inventory in production, and the expected level of finished goods. On the basis of this information, together with the beginning inventory level, a *pro forma* estimate of inventory can be made. Rather than use the production schedule, estimates of future inventory can be based upon a turnover ratio of cost of goods sold to inventory. This ratio is applied in the same manner as for receivables. Suppose that on the basis of a turnover ratio, we estimate inventory to be $420,000 on June 30, a figure that represents a moderate increase over the inventory level of December 31, in keeping with the buildup in sales.

Future net fixed assets are estimated by adding planned expenditures to existing net fixed assets and subtracting from this sum depreciation for the period, plus any sale of fixed assets at book value. From the cash budget, we note that capital expenditures are estimated at $200,000 over the period and that $40,000 in fixed assets will be sold at what we assume to be their depreciated book values. If depreciation for the period is expected to be $110,000, the expected net addition to fixed assets would be $50,000, ($200,000 − $40,000 − $110,000), and projected net fixed assets at June 30 would be $850,000. Because capital expenditures are planned in advance, fixed assets generally are fairly easy to forecast.

Turning now to the liabilities, accounts payable are estimated by adding total projected purchases for January through June, less total projected cash payments for purchases for the period, to the December 31 balance. Our estimate of accounts payable, therefore, is $200,000 + $50,000, or $250,000. The calculation of accrued wages and expenses is based upon the production schedule and the historic relationship between these accruals and production. We assume the estimate of accrued wages and expenses to be $240,000. Accrued income taxes are estimated by adding to the current balance taxes on forecasted income for the six-month period, less the actual payment of taxes. If income taxes for the period are forecast at $60,000, and the firm is scheduled to make $60,000 in actual payments, estimated accrued income taxes at June 30 would be $70,000.

Net worth at June 30 would be the net worth at December 31 plus profits after taxes for the period, less the amount of cash dividends paid. If profits after taxes are estimated at $65,000, net worth at June 30 would be $1,022,000 plus $65,000 minus dividends of $40,000, or $1,047,000. Two items remain: cash and bank loans. We see from the cash budget that estimated cash at June 30 would be $13,500 without additional financing. If the firm has the policy of maintaining a minimum cash balance of $75,000 and borrowing from its bank to maintain this balance, cash at June 30 would be $75,000, and bank borrowings would increase by $61,500 to $111,500. In general, cash and notes payable serve as balancing factors in the preparation of *pro forma* balance sheets, whereby assets and liabilities plus net worth are brought into balance.

Once we have estimated all the components of the *pro forma* balance sheet, they are combined into a balance sheet format. The *pro forma* balance sheet at June 30 is:

Assets (in thousands)		Liabilities (in thousands)	
Cash	$ 75.0	Bank borrowings	$ 111.5
Receivables	373.5	Accounts payable	250.0
Inventories	420.0	Accrued wages and expenses	240.0
Current assets	$ 868.5	Accrued income taxes	70.0
		Current liabilities	$ 671.5
Net fixed assets	850.0	Net worth	1,047.0
Total assets	$1,718.5	Total liabilities and net worth	$1,718.5

The cash-budget method is but one way to prepare a *pro forma* statement; one also can make direct estimates of all of the items on the balance sheet by projecting financial ratios into the future and then making estimates on the basis of these ratios. Receivables, inventories, accounts payable, and accrued wages and expenses frequently are based upon a historical relationship to sales and production when a cash budget is not available.

Pro Forma Income Statement

The *pro forma* income statement is a projection of income for a period of time in the future. As was true with our other projections, the sales forecast is the key input. Given this forecast, production schedules can be formulated and estimates made of production costs for the product or products. The analyst may wish to evaluate each component of the cost of goods sold. A detailed analysis of purchases, production wages, and overhead costs is likely to produce the most accurate forecasts. Often, however, costs of goods sold are estimated on the basis of past ratios of cost of goods sold to sales.

Selling and administrative expenses are estimated next. Because both of these expenses usually are budgeted in advance, estimates of them are fairly accurate. Typically, these expenses are not overly sensitive to changes in sales in the very short run, particularly to reductions in sales. Next, we estimate other income and expenses as well as interest expenses to obtain net income before taxes. Income taxes are then computed based upon the applicable tax rate and deducted, to arrive at estimated net income after taxes. All of these estimates are then combined into an income statement.

Pro forma statements allow us to study the composition of expected future balance sheets and income statements. Financial ratios may be computed for analysis of the statements; these ratios and the raw figures may be compared with those for present and past balance sheets. Using this information, the financial manager can analyze the direction of change in the financial condition and performance of the firm over the past, the present, and the future. If the firm is accustomed to making accurate estimates, the preparation of a cash budget, *pro forma* statements, or both, literally forces it to plan ahead and to coordinate policy in the various areas of operation. Continual revision of these forecasts keeps the firm alert to changing conditions in its environment and in its internal operations. Again, it is useful to prepare more than one set of *pro forma* statements in order to take into account the range of possible outcomes.

SUMMARY

In this chapter, we continued our examination of the analytical tools of the financial manager; we looked at source and use of funds statements, common size and index analyses, the cash budget, and *pro forma* statements. The source and use of funds statement gives the financial analyst considerable insight into the uses of funds and how these uses are financed over a specific period of time. Funds-flow analysis is valuable in analyzing the commitment of funds to assets and in planning the firm's intermediate- and long-term financing. The flow of funds studied, however, represents net rather than gross transactions between two points in time.

Additional insight often is obtained when balance sheet and income statement items are expressed as percentages. The percentages can be in relation to total assets or total sales, or in relation to some base year. Called common size analysis and index analysis, respectively, the idea is to study trends in financial statement items over time. In this regard, a rich understanding of the underlying funds movement of the firm as well as of its profitability is possible with these two types of analysis.

A cash budget is a forecast of the future cash receipts and cash disbursements of a firm. This forecast is particularly useful to the financial manager in determining the probable cash balances of the firm over the near future and in planning for the financing of prospective cash needs. In addition to analyzing expected cash flows, the financial manager should take into account possible deviations from the expected outcome. An analysis of the range of possible outcomes enables management to better assess the efficiency and flexibility of the firm and to determine the appropriate margin of safety.

Finally, we considered the preparation of *pro forma* balance sheets and income statements. These statements give the financial manager insight into the prospective future financial condition and performance of the firm, giving him yet another tool for financial planning and control.

PROBLEMS

1. Galow Fish Canning Company reports the following changes from the preceding year-end. Categorize these changes as either a source of funds or a use of funds.

Item	Change
Cash	$-$100
Accounts receivable	700
Inventory	$-$ 300
Gross fixed assets	900
Depreciation	1,000
Accounts payable	300
Accruals	$-$ 100
Long-term debt	$-$ 200
Net profit	600
Dividends	400

2. Serap-Jones, Inc., had the following financial statements for 1979 and 1980. Prepare a source and use of funds statement and evaluate your findings.

	1979	1980
Assets:		
Cash	$ 53,000	$ 31,000
Marketable securities	87,000	0
Accounts receivable	346,000	528,000
Inventories	432,000	683,000
Current assets	$ 918,000	$1,242,000
Net fixed assets	1,113,000	1,398,000
Total	$2,031,000	$2,640,000

	1979	1980
Liabilities and Equity:		
Accounts payable	$ 413,000	$ 627,000
Accruals	226,000	314,000
Bank borrowings	100,000	235,000
Current liabilities	$ 739,000	$1,176,000
Common stock	100,000	100,000
Retained earnings	1,192,000	1,364,000
Total	$2,031,000	$2,640,000

Note: Depreciation was $189,000 for 1980 and no dividends were paid.

3.

Kohn Corporation comparative balance sheets at Dec. 31 (in millions)

Assets	19_1	19_2	Liabilities and Net Worth	19_1	19_2
Cash	$ 5	$ 3	Notes payable	$20	$ 0
Accounts receivable	15	22	Accounts payable	5	8
Inventories	12	15	Accrued wages	2	2
Fixed assets, net	50	55	Accrued taxes	3	5
Other assets	8	5	Long-term debt	0	15
Total assets	$90	$100	Common and surplus	60	70
			Total liabilities and net worth	$90	$100

Kohn Corporation statement of income and retained earnings year ended Dec. 31, 19_2

Net sales		$50,000,000
Expenses		
Cost of goods sold	$25,000,000	
Selling, general, and administrative expenses	5,000,000	
Depreciation	5,000,000	
Interest	1,000,000	36,000,000
Net income before taxes		$14,000,000
Less: Taxes		7,000,000
Net income		$ 7,000,000
Add: Retained earnings at 12/31/_1		40,000,000
Subtotal		$47,000,000
Less: Dividends		3,000,000
Retained earnings at 12/31/_2		$44,000,000

(a) Prepare a source and use of funds statement on a cash basis for 19_2 for the Kohn Corporation.

(b) Prepare a source and use of working capital statement for 19_2 for the Kohn Corporation.

4. Financial statements for the Sennet Corporation follow.

Sennet Corporation balance sheet at Dec. 31
(in millions)

	19_1	19_2		19_1	19_2
Cash	$ 4	$ 5	Accounts payable	$ 8	$10
Accounts receivable	7	10	Notes payable	5	5
Inventory	12	15	Accrued wages	2	3
Current assets	$23	$30	Accrued taxes	3	2
Net plant	40	40	Current liabilities	$18	$20
			Long-term debt	20	20
			Common stock	10	10
			Retained earnings	15	20
Total assets	$63	$70	Total liabilities and net worth	$63	$70

Sennet Corporation income statement
19_2 (in millions)

Sales		$100
Cost of goods sold	$50	
Selling, general, and administrative expenses	15	
Depreciation	3	
Interest	2	70
Net income before taxes		$ 30
Taxes		15
Net income		$ 15

(a) Prepare a source and use of funds statement for Sennet.

(b) Prepare a source and use of working capital statement.

5. At December 31, the balance sheet of Rodriguez Malting Company was the following (in thousands):

Cash	$ 50	Accounts payable	$360
Accounts receivable	530	Bank loan	400
Inventories	545	Accruals	212
Current assets	$1,125	Current liabilities	$972
Net fixed assets	1,836	Long-term debt	450
		Common stock	100
		Retained earnings	1,439
Total assets	$2,961	Total liabilities and net worth	$2,961

The company has received a large order and anticipates the need to go to its

bank in order to increase its borrowings. As a result, it needs to forecast its cash requirements for January, February, and March.

Typically, the company collects 20 percent of its sales in the month of sale, 70 percent in the subsequent month, and 10 percent in the second month after the sale. All sales are credit sales.

Purchases of raw materials to produce malt are made in the month prior to the sale and amount to 60 percent of sales in the subsequent month. However, payments for these purchases occur in the month after the purchase. Labor costs, including overtime, are expected to be $150,000 in January, $200,000 in February, and $160,000 in March. Selling, administrative, taxes, and other cash expenses are expected to be $100,000 per month for January through March. Actual sales in November and December and projected sales for January through April are as follows (in thousands):

November	$ 500
December	600
January	600
February	1,000
March	650
April	750

On the basis of this information:

(a) Prepare a cash budget for the months of January, February, and March.
(b) Determine the amount of additional bank borrowings necessary to maintain a cash balance of $50,000 at all times.
(c) Prepare a *pro forma* balance sheet for March 31.

6. Prepare a cash budget for the Ace Manufacturing Company, indicating receipts and disbursements for May, June, and July. The firm wishes to maintain, at all times, a minimum cash balance of $20,000. Determine whether or not borrowing will be necessary during the period and, if it is, when and for how much. As of April 30, the firm had a balance of $20,000 in cash.

Actual Sales		Forecasted Sales	
January	$50,000	May	$ 70,000
February	50,000	June	80,000
March	60,000	July	100,000
April	60,000	August	100,000

Accounts Receivable: 50 percent of total sales are for cash. The remaining 50 percent will be collected equally during the following two months (the firm incurs a negligible bad-debt loss).

Cost of Goods Manufactured: 70 percent of sales. 90 percent of this cost is paid during the first month after incurrence, the remaining 10 percent is paid the following month.

Sales and Administrative Expenses: $10,000 per month plus 10 percent of sales. All of these expenses are paid during the month of incurrence.

Interest Payments: A semiannual interest payment of $18,000 is paid during July. An annual $50,000 sinking-fund payment is also made at that time.

Dividends: A $10,000 dividend payment will be declared and made in July.

Capital Expenditures: $40,000 will be invested in plant and equipment in June.

Taxes: Income tax payments of $1,000 will be made in July.

7. Downeast Nautical Company expects sales of $2.4 million next year and expects sales of the same amount the following year. Sales are spread evenly throughout the year. On the basis of the following information, prepare a *pro forma* balance sheet and income statement for year-end:

Cash = Minimum of 4% of annual sales.

Accounts receivable = 60-day average collection period based on annual sales.

Inventories = Turnover of 8 times a year.

Net fixed assets = $500,000 now. Capital expenditures equal to depreciation.

Accounts payable = One month's purchases.

Accruals = 3% of sales.

Bank borrowings = $50,000 now. Can borrow up to $250,000.

Long-term debt = $300,000 now; $75,000 payable at year-end.

Common stock = $100,000. No additions planned.

Retained earnings = $500,000 now.

Net profit margin = 8 percent of sales.

Dividends = None.

Cost of goods sold = 60% of sales.

Purchases = 50 percent of costs of goods sold.

Income taxes = 50 percent of before-tax profits.

---

8. Given the information that follows, prepare a cash budget for the Central City Department Store for the first six months of 19_2.

   (a) All prices and costs remain constant.

   (b) Sales are 75 percent for credit and 25 percent for cash.

   (c) In terms of credit sales, 60 percent are collected in the month after the sale, 30 percent in the second month, and 10 percent in the third. Bad-debt losses are insignificant.

   (d) Sales, actual and estimated, are:

October, 19_1	$300,000	March, 19_2	$200,000
November, 19_1	350,000	April, 19_2	300,000
December, 19_1	400,000	May, 19_2	250,000
January, 19_2	150,000	June, 19_2	200,000
February, 19_2	200,000	July, 19_2	300,000

   (e) The store has a gross margin of 20 percent and purchases and pays for each month's anticipated sales in the preceding month.

(f) Wages and salaries are:

January	$30,000	April	$50,000
February	40,000	May	40,000
March	50,000	June	35,000

(g) Rent is $2,000 a month.

(h) Interest on $500,000 of 6 percent bonds is due at the end of the calendar quarter.

(i) A tax prepayment on 19_2 income of $50,000 is due in April.

(j) A capital investment of $30,000 is planned in June.

(k) The company has a cash balance of $100,000 at December 31, 19_1, which is the minimum desired level for cash. Funds can be borrowed in multiples of $5,000 on a monthly basis. (Ignore interest on such borrowings.)

9. Use the cash budget worked out in problem 8 and with the following additional information prepare a *pro forma* income statement for the first half of 19_2 for the Central City Department Store.

(a) Inventory at 12/31/_1 was $200,000.

(b) Depreciation is taken on a straight-line basis on $250,000 of assets with an average remaining life of ten years and no salvage value.

(c) The tax rate is 50 percent.

10. Tic Tac Homes has had the following balance sheet statements during the past four years (in thousands):

	19X1	19X2	19X3	19X4
Cash	214	93	42	38
Receivables	1,213	1,569	1,846	2,562
Inventories	2,102	2,893	3,678	4,261
Net fixed assets	2,219	2,346	2,388	2,692
Total assets	5,748	6,901	7,954	9,553
Accounts payable	1,131	1,578	1,848	2,968
Notes payable	500	650	750	750
Accruals	656	861	1,289	1,743
Long-term debt	500	800	800	800
Common stock	200	200	200	200
Retained earnings	2,761	2,812	3,067	3,092
Total liabilities and net worth	5,748	6,901	7,954	9,553

Using index analysis, what are the major problems in the company's financial condition?

SELECTED REFERENCES

CHAMBERS, JOHN C., SATINDER K. MULLICK, AND DONALD D. SMITH, "How to Choose the Right Forecasting Technique," *Harvard Business Review*, 49 (July-August 1971), 45–74.

HELFERT, ERICH A., *Techniques of Financial Analysis*, 4th ed., Chaps. 1 and 3. Homewood, Ill.: Richard D. Irwin, 1977.

JAEDICKE, ROBERT K., AND ROBERT T. SPROUSE, *Accounting Flows: Income, Funds, and Cash*, Chaps. 5 and 6. Englewood Cliffs, N.J.: Prentice-Hall, 1965.

PAN, JUDY, DONALD R. NICHOLS, AND O. MAURICE JOY, "Sales Forecasting Practices of Large U.S. Industrial Firms," *Financial Management*, 6 (Fall, 1977) 72–77.

PAPPAS, JAMES L., AND GEORGE P. HUBER, "Probabilistic Short-Term Financial Planning," *Financial Management*, 3 (Autumn 1973), 36–44.

PARKER, GEORGE G. C., AND EDILBERTO L. SEGURA, "How to Get a Better Forecast," *Harvard Business Review*, 49 (March-April 1971), 99–109.

STAUBUS, G. J., "Alternative Asset Flow Concepts," *Accounting Review*, 41 (July 1966), 397–412.

TRUMBULL, WENDELL, P., "Developing the Funds Statement as the Third Major Financial Statement," *N.A.A. Bulletin*, 45 (April 1963), 21–31.

27
operating and financial leverage

Leverage may be defined as the employment of an asset or funds for which the firm pays a fixed cost or fixed return. The fixed cost or return may be thought of as the fulcrum of a lever. With a lever, one force is transformed, or magnified, into another force that is larger. This concept applies to mechanical leverage, such as that which occurs with a wrench, as well as to operating and financial leverage. In this chapter, we explore the principles of operating and financial leverage. The former is due to fixed costs associated with the production of a good or service, whereas the latter is due to the existence of fixed financing costs—in particular, interest on a loan. Both types of leverage affect the level and variability of after-tax earnings and, hence, the overall risk of a company.

OPERATING LEVERAGE

Operating leverage occurs any time a firm has fixed costs that must be met regardless of volume. In the very long run, of course, all costs are variable.

Consequently, our analysis necessarily involves the short run. We employ assets with a fixed cost in the hope that volume will produce revenues more than sufficient to cover all fixed and variable costs. One of the more dramatic examples of operating leverage is in the airline industry, where a large portion of total costs are fixed. Beyond a certain break-even load factor, each additional passenger represents essentially straight profit to the airline.

The essential thing is that fixed costs do not vary as volume changes. These costs include such things as depreciation of buildings and equipment, insurance, property taxes, part of the overall utility bills, and part of the cost of management. On the other hand, variable costs vary directly with the level of output. These costs include raw materials, direct labor costs, part of the overall utility bills, direct selling commissions, and certain parts of general and administrative expenses. With fixed costs, the percentage change in profits accompanying a change in volume is greater than the percentage change in volume. This phenomenon is known as operating leverage.

It is important to recognize that operating leverage is but one component of the overall business risk of the firm. The principal factors giving rise to business risk are uncertainty with respect to sales demand and uncertainty with respect to the costs of production. Operating leverage magnifies the impact of these factors on the variability of profits. However, operating leverage is not the source of the variability. Consequently, the degree of operating leverage of a firm should not be taken to represent its business risk. Given the underlying variability of sales and costs of a firm, however, increases in operating leverage will increase the total variability of profits and, hence, increase the company's business risk. Operating leverage may be studied by means of a break-even or cost-volume-profit analysis.

Break-Even Analysis

To illustrate break-even analysis, consider a firm that produces a quality testing machine that sells for $50 a unit. The company has annual fixed costs of $100,000 and variable costs are $25 a unit regardless of the volume sold. We wish to study the relationship between total costs and total revenues. One means for doing so is with the break-even chart in Figure 27-1, which shows the relationship between profits, fixed costs, variable costs, and volume. By *profits,* we mean operating profits before taxes. This definition purposely excludes interest on debt and preferred-stock dividends. These costs are not part of the total fixed costs of the firm when it comes to analyzing operating leverage. They are taken into account when we analyze financial leverage in the next section.

The intersection of the total cost line with the total revenue line represents the break-even point. The fixed costs that must be recovered from the sales dollar after the deduction of variable costs determines the volume necessary to break even. In Figure 27-1, this break-even point is 4,000 units of output. At the break-even point, variable costs plus fixed costs equal total revenue:

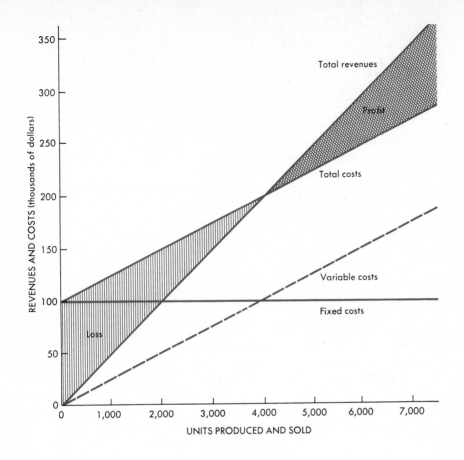

figure 27-1
Break-even analysis:
original conditions

$$F + V(X) = P(X) \qquad (27\text{-}1)$$

where F = fixed costs
V = variable costs per unit
X = volume of output (in units)
P = price per unit

Rearranging Eq. (27-1), the break-even point is

$$X = F/(P - V)$$
$$= 100{,}000/(50 - 25) = 4{,}000 \qquad (27\text{-}2)$$

For each additional increment of volume above the break-even point, there is increasing profit represented by the dotted area in the figure. Likewise, as volume falls below the break-even point, there are increasing losses, represented by the lined area. Table 27-1 shows the profit for various levels of volume. We see that the closer the volume to the break-even point, the greater the percentage change in profit in relation to a percentage change in volume.

table 27-1

Relation between profit and volume

Volume (in thousand units)	0	1	2	3	4	5	6	7
Operating profit (in thousands)	−$100	−$75	−$50	−$25	0	$25	$50	$75

The degree of operating leverage of a firm at a particular level of output is simply the percentage change in profits over the percentage change in output that causes the change in profits. Thus,

$$\text{Degree of operating leverage at X units} = \frac{\text{Percentage change in profits}}{\text{Percentage change in output}} \qquad (27\text{-}3)$$

Rather than calculate the percentages involved directly, a simple formula is available for expressing the relationship:

$$\text{DOL at X units} = \frac{X(P - V)}{X(P - V) - F} \qquad (27\text{-}4)$$

Suppose that we wished to determine the degree of operating leverage for 5,000 units of output for our hypothetical example firm:

$$\text{DOL at 5,000 units} = \frac{5,000(50 - 25)}{5,000(50 - 25) - 100,000} = 5$$

For 6,000 units of output, we have

$$\text{DOL at 6,000 units} = \frac{6,000(50 - 25)}{6,000(50 - 25) - 100,000} = 3$$

We see, then, that the further the level of output is from the break-even point, the lower the degree of operating leverage. The greater the degree of operating leverage for a given level of output, the more that profits vary with variations in output.

A break-even chart, like that in Figure 27-1, tells us the relationship between operating profits and volume. The greater the ratio of price to variable costs per unit, the greater the absolute sensitivity of profits to volume and the greater the degree of operating leverage for all levels of output. However, a change in volume is not the only factor that affects profits. Indeed, a change in the selling price, in variable cost per unit, or in fixed costs will affect profits. In the light of Figure 27-1, we examine a favorable change in each of these factors, with all other factors being held constant.[1]

[1]For a mathematical analysis of the effect of changes in these factors on profits, as well as an analysis of the risk associated with such changes, see Thomas A. Morrison and Eugene Kaczka, "A New Application of Calculus and Risk Analysis to Cost-Volume-Profit Changes," *Accounting Review*, 44 (April 1969), 330–43.

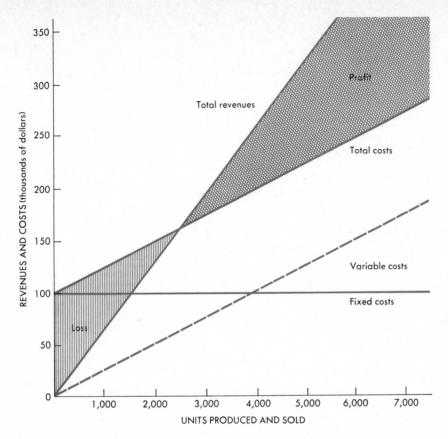

figure 27-2
Break-even analysis:
price increase

Increase in Price Figure 27-2 shows the change for an increase in price from $50 to $65 per unit. We see that the break-even point is reduced from 4,000 units to 2,500 units as a result of this price increase; and, of course, profits are $15 per unit greater for each level of volume.

Decrease in Fixed Costs For a decrease in fixed costs from $100,000 to $50,000, with the original $50 per unit price, the break-even point is reduced even further. Figure 27-3 illustrates this case. The break-even point now is 2,000 units, and total profits are increased by $50,000 for all levels of volume.

Decrease in Variable Costs Finally, Figure 27-4 shows the change when variable costs per unit are lowered from $25 to $20. The break-even point is lowered to 3,333 units, and profit is $5 greater per unit of output. Table 27-2 summarizes the profits for various levels of volume under the alternatives cited. The last column of the table shows the relationship between profit and volume if all three of the changes occur simultaneously.

Despite a number of limitations that we shall take up shortly, break-even analysis gives management a good deal of information about the operating risk of the company. Given an approximate break-even point, management can compare fluctuations in expected future volume with this point to ascertain the stability of profits. Knowledge of this stability is important to

775

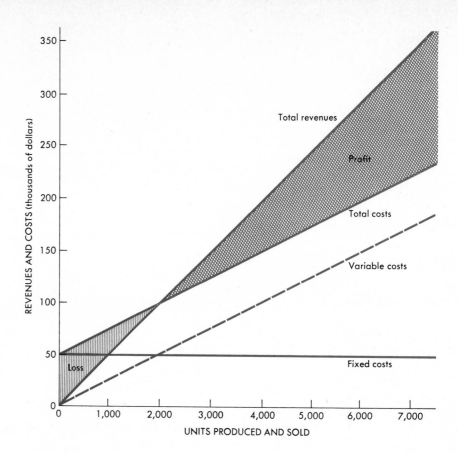

figure 27-3
Break-even analysis:
decrease in fixed costs

the financial manager in determining the ability of the firm to service debt, as we shall see shortly.

Such an analysis is important also when planning the acquisition of assets that will require additional fixed costs. In general, the greater the fixed costs of a firm, the greater the degree of operating risk. Therefore a firm will not wish to undertake an increase in fixed costs unless there are sufficient benefits to be derived. In this regard, the expected future trend and stability of volume, together with the ratio of expected price to expected variable costs per unit, will bear heavily upon the decision to increase fixed costs. As we saw in the previous discussion, break-even analysis is useful in determining the change in profits that accompanies a change in pricing and costs. Depending upon the elasticity of demand and the ratio of price to variable costs, price cutting to boost volume may or may not be worthwhile. Break-even analysis provides us with a means for deciding.

Limitations

Although break-even analysis seems simple enough in concept—and this simplicity is one of its virtues—its effectiveness is limited in several ways.

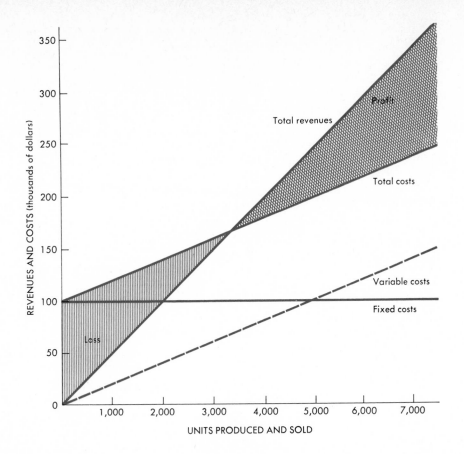

figure 27-4
Break-even analysis:
decrease in variable
costs

These limitations must be recognized and the method modified if it is to provide meaningful results. One assumption of the method is that there is a constant price and variable cost per unit, irrespective of volume. In many cases, the firm's sales volume may influence the market price of a product. For example, increased output may lead to a decline in market price. Moreover,

table 27-2
Relation between profits and volume

Volume (in units)	Profits (in thousands)				
	Original Case	Price ($65)	Fixed Costs ($50,000)	Variable Costs ($20)	All Three
0	−$100	−$100	−$ 50	−$100	−$ 50
2,000	−50	−20	0	−40	40
4,000	0	60	50	20	130
6,000	50	140	100	80	220
8,000	100	220	150	140	310

variable costs are likely to increase as the firm approaches full capacity; for example, less efficient labor or costly overtime help may have to be used. These shortcomings of break-even analysis can be remedied by making the relationships between total sales and volume, and total costs and volume, nonlinear, to correspond with economic reality.

Another difficulty with break-even analysis is the classification of costs as fixed or variable. In practice, many costs defy clear categorization because they are partly fixed and partly variable. These costs are known as semivariable costs. Moreover, we assume that costs classified as fixed remain unchanged over the entire volume range, but this range is limited by the immediate physical capacity of the firm. A steel company may have an idle marginal plant that it can put into operation if it needs additional output, but putting the plant into operation may increase fixed costs. If the range of volume considered includes this plant, fixed costs would not be constant but would increase in a step function manner at the point in volume at which the plant was to be reopened. For most situations, however, new physical capacity must be constructed if volume is to be increased beyond some critical point. Consequently, a break-even analysis is relevant only for volume up to that point.

Another problem relates to multiple products. Break-even analysis perhaps is best suited for a one-product analysis. When there are multiple products, a single break-even analysis cannot be used unless the product mix remains unchanged. When the product mix does change, it may be necessary to prepare a separate break-even analysis for each product. Here, allocating expenses that are common to all product lines may present a problem.

The information inputs for break-even analysis are usually based upon historical relationships. However, these relationships may not be particularly stable over time. For extreme volume changes, there may be no historical precedent. Moreover, it is not past relationships of costs, volume, and profits that we are trying to judge but, rather, future ones. These estimates are subject to uncertainty and risk—elements that are not taken into account in traditional break-even analysis.

Finally, we must note that the short-term horizon in break-even analysis is a limitation for longer-range planning. The benefits realized from certain expenditures, such as capital expenditures and research and development outlays, are not likely to be realized during the period of time encompassed by most break-even analyses. A break-even analysis would not justify these expenditures, but they may well be necessary to the continued life of the firm. Despite the many limitations of break-even analysis, however, it can be an important tool to the financial manager if it is employed properly and if it is reasonably appropriate to the situation.[2]

---

[2]For an empirical analysis of operating leverage and risk for samples of electrical utilities, steel companies, and oil companies, see Baruch Lev, "On the Association between Operating Leverage and Risk," *Journal of Financial and Quantitative Analysis,* 9 (September 1974), 627–41.

Financial leverage, as defined before, involves the use of funds obtained at a fixed cost in the hope of increasing the return to common stockholders. Favorable or positive leverage is said to occur when the firm earns more on the assets purchased with the funds than the fixed cost of their use. Unfavorable or negative leverage occurs when the firm does not earn as much as the funds cost. The favorability of financial leverage, or "trading on the equity" as it is called, is judged in terms of the effect upon earnings per share to common stockholders. We are interested in determining the relationship between earnings per share and earnings before interest and taxes (EBIT) under various financing alternatives and the indifference points between these alternatives.

Calculation of Earnings per Share

To illustrate a break-even analysis of leverage, suppose Cherokee Tire Company with long-term capitalization of $10 million, consisting entirely of common stock, wishes to raise another $5 million for expansion through one of three possible financing plans. The company may finance with (1) all common stock; (2) all debt, at 9 percent interest; or (3) all preferred stock with a 7 percent dividend. Present annual earnings before interest and taxes (EBIT) are $1,400,000, the income tax rate is 50 percent, and 200,000 shares of stock are now outstanding. Common stock can be sold at $50 per share under financing option 1, or 100,000 additional shares of stock.

In order to determine the EBIT break-even, or indifference, points between the various financing alternatives, we begin by caluclating earnings per share for some hypothetical level of EBIT. Suppose we wished to know what earnings per share would be under the three financing plans if EBIT were $2 million. The calculations are shown in Table 27-3. We note that interest on debt is deducted before taxes, while preferred-stock dividends are deducted after taxes. As a result, earnings available to common stockholders are higher under the debt alternative than they are under the preferred-stock alternative, despite the fact that the interest rate on debt is higher than the preferred-stock dividend rate.

Break-Even, or Indifference, Analysis

Given the information in Table 27-3, we are able to construct a "break-even" or indifference chart similar to what we did for operating leverage. On the horizontal axis we plot earnings before interest and taxes (EBIT) and on the vertical axis, earnings per share (EPS). For each financing alternative, we must draw a straight line to reflect EPS for all possible levels of EBIT. To do so, we need two datum points for each alternative. The first is the EPS calculated for some hypothetical level of EBIT. For $2 million in EBIT, we see in Table 27-3 that earnings per share are $3.33, $3.88, and $3.25

table 27-3

Calculations of earnings per share under three financing
alternatives

	All Common	All Debt	All Preferred
Earnings before interest and taxes (hypothetical)	$2,000,000	$2,000,000	$2,000,000
Interest	—	$ 450,000	—
Earnings before taxes	$2,000,000	$1,550,000	$2,000,000
Income taxes	$1,000,000	$ 775,000	$1,000,000
Earnings after taxes	$1,000,000	$ 775,000	$1,000,000
Preferred-stock dividend	—	—	$ 350,000
Earnings available to common stockholders	$1,000,000	$ 775,000	$ 650,000
Number of shares	300,000	200,000	200,000
Earnings per share	$3.33	$3.88	$3.25

for the common, debt, and preferred-stock financing alternatives. We simply plot these earnings per share at the $2 million mark in EBIT. It is important to recognize that it does not matter which hypothetical level of EBIT we choose for calculating EPS. Assuming good graph paper, one level is as good as the next.

The second datum point is simply the EBIT necessary to cover all fixed financial costs for a particular financing plan, and it is plotted on the horizontal axis. For the common-stock alternative, there are no fixed costs, so the intercept on the horizontal axis is zero. For the debt alternative, we must have EBIT of $450,000 to cover interest charges; so $450,000 becomes the horizontal axis intercept. For the preferred-stock alternative, we must divide total annual dividends by one minus the tax rate in order to obtain the EBIT necessary to cover these dividends. Thus we need $700,000 in EBIT to cover $350,000 in preferred-stock dividends, assuming a 50 percent tax rate. Again, preferred dividends are deducted after taxes, so it takes more in before-tax earnings to cover them than it does to cover interest. Given the horizontal axis intercepts and earnings per share for some hypothetical level of EBIT, we draw a straight line through the two sets of points. The break-even or indifference chart for Cherokee Tire Company is shown in Figure 27-5.

We see from the figure that the earnings-per-share indifference point between the debt and common-stock financing alternatives is $1,350,000 in EBIT. If EBIT is below that point, the common-stock alternative will provide higher earnings per share; above that point the debt alternative is best. The indifference point between the preferred-stock and the common-stock alternatives is $2,100,000 in EBIT. Above it, the preferred-stock alternative is favored with respect to earnings per share; below it, the common-stock alternative is best. We note that there is no indifference point between the debt and preferred-stock alternatives. The debt alternative dominates for all levels of EBIT and by a constant amount of earnings per share, namely $0.63.

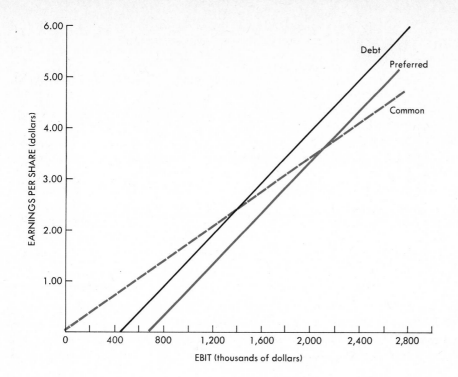

figure 27-5
Indifference chart for three financing alternatives

The indifference point between two methods of financing can be determined mathematically by

$$\frac{(\text{EBIT}^* - C_1)(1 - t)}{S_1} = \frac{(\text{EBIT}^* - C_2)(1 - t)}{S_2}$$

(27-5)

where EBIT* = the EBIT indifference point between the two methods of financing
for which we solve

C_1, C_2 = annual interest expenses or preferred-stock dividends on a before-tax basis for financing methods 1 and 2

t = corporate tax rate

S_1, S_2 = number of shares of common stock to be outstanding after financing for methods 1 and 2

Suppose we wished to determine the indifference point between the common-stock and the debt-financing alternative in our example. We would have

$$\frac{(\text{EBIT}^* - 0)(0.5)}{300,000} = \frac{(\text{EBIT}^* - 450,000)(0.5)}{200,000}$$

(27-6)

Rearranging, we obtain

$$0.5(\text{EBIT}^*)(200,000) = 0.5(\text{EBIT}^*)(300,000) \\ - 0.5(450,000)(300,000)$$

$$100,000 \text{ EBIT}^* = 135,000,000,000$$
$$\text{EBIT}^* = \$1,350,000$$

The indifference point in EBIT, where earnings per share for the two methods of financing are the same, is $1,350,000. This amount can be verified graphically in Figure 27-5. Thus, indifference points for financial leverage can be determined either graphically or mathematically.

The degree of financial leverage at a particular level of EBIT is simply the percentage change in earnings per share in relation to a percentage change in EBIT. To illustrate, suppose EBIT were $2 million in our example. A $1 million increase would raise earnings per share from $3.88 to $6.38, or by approximately 64.4 percent. When this percentage increase is taken over the percentage increase in EBIT, 50 percent, the degree of financial leverage is found to be 1.29. An easier method for determining the degree of financial leverage is

$$\text{Degree of financial leverage at EBIT of } y = \frac{\text{EBIT}}{\text{EBIT} - C} \qquad (27\text{-}7)$$

where C as before is the annual interest expense or preferred-stock dividend on a before-tax basis. For our example, using the debt-financing alternative at $2 million in EBIT, we have

$$\text{DFL at \$2 million} = \frac{2,000,000}{2,000,000 - 450,000} = 1.29$$

For the preferred-stock financing alternative, the degree of financial leverage is

$$\text{DFL at \$2 million} = \frac{2,000,000}{2,000,000 - 700,000} = 1.54$$

Through an EBIT–EPS analysis, we can evaluate various financing plans or degrees of financial leverage with respect to their effect upon earnings per share. The presentation in this chapter has been devoted primarily to the construction of indifference charts as well as to providing other tools for analyzing financial leverage.[3] In Chapter 10, the use of this information is considered in the overall context of determining an appropriate capital structure.

However, certain limitations to the use of these tools of analysis should be pointed out at this time. The type of analysis presented implies that the firm should raise capital by the cheapest means possible—usually

[3]For a mathematical analysis of the relationship between financial leverage and the return on equity, see Sol S. Shalit, "On the Mathematics of Financial Leverage," *Financial Management*, 4 (Spring 1975), 57–66.

debt—as long as the expected return from investment of these funds exceeds their explicit cost. It is important, however, to recognize that this procedure usually is inappropriate if the objective of the firm is to maximize shareholder wealth. Implicit costs, represented by a decline in the price/earnings ratio of the common stock because of increased financial risk, are ignored. A decline in the price/earnings ratio may partially or wholly offset the earning-per-share advantage of using debt. Moreover, there is a tendency in such a static analysis to regard the explicit costs of debt and preferred stock as constant, regardless of the degree of leverage. However, we know that beyond a certain point, lenders require higher and higher rates of interest as leverage increases. In Part III, where we studied both the explicit and the implicit costs of financing, these limitations were analyzed in considerably more detail. We point to the various limitations at this time only so the reader will not be tempted to make a conclusion with respect to financing based solely upon an EBIT–EPS analysis.

COMBINED EFFECT OF TWO TYPES OF LEVERAGE

When financial leverage is combined with operating leverage, the effect of a change in revenues on earnings per share is magnified. The combination of the two increases the dispersion and risk of possible earnings per share. To determine the effect of a change in units of output on earnings per share, we combine the equation for the degree of operating leverage, Eq. (27-4), with that for the degree of financial leverage, Eq. (27-7). Because EBIT is simply $X(P - V) - F$, whereas before X is the units of output, P is price per unit, V is variable cost per unit, and F is fixed costs, Eq. (27-7) can be expressed as

$$\frac{\text{EBIT}}{\text{EBIT} - C} = \frac{X(P - V) - F}{X(P - V) - F - C} \tag{27-8}$$

Combining this equation with that for the degree of operating leverage, Eq. (27-4), we obtain

$$\begin{aligned} \text{Degree of operating and financial leverage at X units} &= \frac{X(P - V)}{X(P - V) - F} \cdot \frac{X(P - V) - F}{X(P - V) - F - C} \\ &= \frac{X(P - V)}{X(P - V) - F - C} \end{aligned} \tag{27-9}$$

We see that the amount of fixed financial costs, C, increases the degree of combined leverage over what it would be with operating leverage alone.

Suppose that our hypothetical example firm used to illustrate operating leverage had $200,000 in debt at 8 percent interest. Recall that the selling price was $50 a unit, variable cost $25 a unit, and annual fixed costs were

$100,000. Assume that the tax rate is 50 percent, the number of shares of common stock outstanding is 10,000 shares, and that we wish to determine the combined degree of leverage at 8,000 units of output. Therefore,

$$\text{DO \& FL at 8,000 units} = \frac{8,000(50 - 25)}{8,000(50 - 25) - 100,000 - 16,000}$$

$$= 2.38$$

Thus a 10 percent increase in the number of units produced and sold would result in a 23.8 percent increase in earnings per share. Earnings per share at the two levels of output are:

	8,000 units	8,800 units
Sales less total variable costs	$200,000	$220,000
Fixed costs	$100,000	$100,000
EBIT	$100,000	$120,000
Interest	$ 16,000	$ 16,000
Profit before taxes	$ 84,000	$104,000
Taxes	$ 42,000	$ 52,000
Profit after taxes	$ 42,000	$ 52,000
Shares outstanding	10,000	10,000
Earnings per share	$4.20	$5.20

This degree of combined leverage compares with 2.00 for operating leverage alone. We see, then, the relative effect of adding financial leverage on top of operating leverage.

Operating and financial leverage can be combined in a number of different ways to obtain a desirable degree of overall leverage and risk of the firm. High operating risk can be offset with low financial risk and vice versa. The proper overall level of risk involves a tradeoff between total risk (the product of operating and financial risk) and expected return. This tradeoff must be made in keeping with the objective of the firm, and it is discussed in Parts I through III. The discussion here is meant to show how certain tools can be employed to provide information on the two types of leverage and their combined effect.

SUMMARY

Operating leverage may be defined as the employment of an asset with a fixed cost in the hope that sufficient revenue will be generated to cover all fixed and variable costs. We can study the operating leverage of a firm by using a break-even graph. This graph enables us to analyze the relationship between

profits, volume, fixed costs, variable costs, and prices. By varying these factors, management may determine the sensitivity of profits and, in so doing,
obtain a better understanding of the operating risk of the firm. Whereas
break-even analysis is a very useful tool, certain limitations to its
effectiveness must be recognized.

  Financial leverage is defined as the use of funds with a fixed cost in
order to increase earnings per share. By using an indifference chart, we can
study the relationship between earnings before interest and taxes (EBIT) and
earnings per share under various alternative methods of financing. The degree of sensitivity of earnings per share to EBIT is dependent upon the
explicit cost of the method of financing, the number of shares of common
stock to be issued, and the nearness to the indifference point. Although an
EBIT–EPS chart is useful in analyzing the explicit costs of various methods of
financing, it does not take into account any implicit costs inherent in the use
of a specific method of financing.

  For both operating and financial leverage, we can determine the
degree of leverage. In the first case, we relate the change in profits that
accompanies a change in output; in the second, the change in earnings per
share that accompanies a change in earnings before interest and taxes. By
combining the two formulas, we can determine the effect of a change in
output upon earnings per share. In this way, we can better depict the relative
influence of the two types of leverage.

PROBLEMS

1. What effect will a change in a firm's sales volume have on its break-even point,
   assuming that price remains constant?

2. The Centrex Company is contemplating the purchase of a new machine. The
   machine will cost $10,000, will be depreciated on a straight-line basis, and will
   have a life of five years (no salvage). If the firm has a variable cost ratio (variable
   costs/sales) of .75, how much added annual revenue must the new machine
   generate so that the firm can maintain the same annual profit (in dollars) as
   before the purchase?

3. What effect would each of the following have on the degree of operating leverage
   possessed by a firm?

   (a) The firm becomes more capital-intensive (uses more capital inputs relative
       to labor inputs).
   (b) The firm has recently initiated a guaranteed annual wage.

4. The Madison Company earns an after-tax monthly profit of $2,400 on monthly
   sales of $88,000. The average tax rate of the company is 40 percent. The only
   product of the company sells for $20, of which $15 is variable cost.

   (a) What is the monthly fixed cost of the Madison Company?
   (b) What is its break-even point in units? In dollars?

5. What would be the effect of the following on the break-even point of the Madison
   Company (problem 4)?

(a) An increase in price of $5 per unit (assume that volume is constant)
(b) A decrease in fixed costs of $2,000
(c) A decrease in variable costs of $1 per unit and an increase in fixed costs of $6,000

6. The Botts Corporation is a new firm that wishes to determine an appropriate capital structure. It can issue 8 percent debt and 6 percent preferred and has a 50 percent tax rate. The total capitalization of the firm will be $5 million, and common will be sold at $20 per share. The possible capital structures are:

Plan	Debt	Preferred	Equity
1	0	0	100%
2	30%	0	70%
3	30%	20%	50%
4	50%	0	50%
5	50%	20%	30%

(a) Construct an EBIT–EPS chart for the five plans.
(b) Determine the indifference points.
(c) Is the maximization of EPS at a given EBIT the sole function of a firm's capital structure? If not, are the points determined in (b) truly "indifference" points?

7. Using Eq. (27-5), compute the indifference point between financial plans #1 and #5 in problem 6. Does it correspond with that plotted on your graph?

8. Several Texas tycoons have decided to organize a new airline that will provide service from Dallas to New York City. All arrangements, including regulatory approval, have been made except the plan of financing. Tycoon A, a conservative type, has suggested that the $10 million needed to organize the corporation should be derived solely from the sale of common stock (1 million shares @ $10). Tycoon B, who is a bit less conservative, feels that some debt should be included in the capital structure. He argues that half the needed investment should be raised by selling bonds. Currently, such financing can be obtained at a 6 percent coupon rate. Tycoon C, who tends toward the speculative side, believes that only 25 percent of the needed investment should be raised from the sale of common stock, the remainder from the sale of bonds. The investment bankers of the new firm have indicated that C's proposal would require at least a 7 percent coupon rate for the bonds.

(a) Assuming the firm earns $200,000 (EBIT), with an average tax rate of 40 percent, what are the earnings per share (EPS) for each proposal? What is the rate of return on total capital (EBIT/Total Capital) for each? What is the rate of return on equity capital (Net Income/Equity Capital) for each? Which alternative provides the highest EPS and the highest return?
(b) Answer the questions outlined in (a), assuming an EBIT of $1 million.
(c) Answer the questions outlined in (a), assuming an EBIT of $2 million.
(d) What arguments might you raise against the use of B's or C's proposal, even if EBIT were anticipated to be high?

9. Gallatin Quarter Company makes saddles. During the preceding calendar year it earned $200,000 after taxes. The company is in a 40 percent tax bracket, had no

debt outstanding at year-end, and has 100,000 shares of common stock outstanding. At the beginning of the current year it finds that it needs to borrow $300,000 at an interest rate of 10 percent in order to expand its operations.

(a) What is the degree of financial leverage if EBIT stays the same as last year?

(b) What are earnings per share before and after financing if EBIT stays the same?

(c) What is the degree of financial leverage if EBIT should increase by 50 percent? (Compute on the basis of the new level.)

(d) What are the absolute and percentage increases in earnings per share if EBIT increases by 50 percent?

10. The Last Gasp Water Company sells distilled water by the gallon. The price per gallon is 75 cents and variable costs are 40 cents per gallon. Fixed costs involved in production are $1 million. The company has $5 million of 8 percent bonds outstanding.

(a) Compute the degree of operating leverage at 3 million gallons of water produced and sold, at 4 million gallons, at 5 million gallons, at 6 million gallons, and at 7 million gallons.

(b) Compute the degree of financial leverage at the above gallons of water produced and sold. Assume that EBIT is price minus variable cost per gallon times the number of gallons, less the amount of fixed costs.

(c) Compute the degree of combined operating and financial leverage at the above gallons of water produced and sold.

(d) What generalizations can you make?

SELECTED REFERENCES

ADAR, ZVI, AMIR BARNEA, AND BARUCH LEV, "A comprehensive Cost-Volume-Profit Analysis under Uncertainty," *Accounting Review*, 52 (January 1977), 137–49.

HASLEM, JOHN A., "Leverage Effects on Corporate Earnings," *Arizona Review*, 19 (March 1970), 7–11.

HELFERT, ERICH A., *Techniques of Financial Analysis*, 4th ed., Chap. 2. Homewood, Ill.: Richard D. Irwin, 1977.

JAEDICKE, ROBERT K., AND ALEXANDER A. ROBICHEK, "Cost-Volume-Profit Analysis under Conditions of Uncertainty," *Accounting Review*, 39 (October 1964), 917–26.

LEV, BARUCH, "On the Association between Operating Leverage and Risk," *Journal of Financial and Quantitative Analysis*, 9 (September 1974), 627–42.

MORRISON, THOMAS A., AND EUGENE KACZKA, "A New Application of Calculus and Risk Analysis to Cost-Volume-Profit Changes," *Accounting Review*, 44 (April 1969), 330–43.

PERCIVAL, JOHN R., "Operating Leverage and Risk," *Journal of Business Research*, 2 (April 1974), 223–27.

RAUN, D. L., "The Limitations of Profit Graphs, Break-even Analysis, and Budgets," *Accounting Review*, 39 (October 1964), 927–45.

REINHARDT, U. E., "Break Even Analysis for Lockheed's Tri Star: An Application of Financial Theory," *Journal of Finance*, 28 (September 1973), 821–38.

SHALIT, SOL S., "On the Mathematics of Financial Leverage," *Financial Management*, 4 (Spring 1975), 57–66.

table A-1
Present value of one dollar due at the end of *n* years

N	1%	2%	3%	4%	5%	6%	7%	8%	9%	10%	N
01	0.99010	0.98039	0.97007	0.96154	0.95238	0.94340	0.93458	0.92593	0.91743	0.90909	01
02	.98030	.96117	.94260	.92456	.90703	.89000	.87344	.85734	.84168	.82645	02
03	.97059	.94232	.91514	.88900	.86384	.83962	.81630	.79383	.77218	.75131	03
04	.96098	.92385	.88849	.85480	.82270	.79209	.76290	.73503	.70843	.68301	04
05	.95147	.90573	.86261	.82193	.78353	.74726	.71299	.68058	.64993	.62092	05
06	.94204	.88797	.83748	.79031	.74622	.70496	.66634	.63017	.59627	.56447	06
07	.93272	.87056	.81309	.75992	.71068	.66506	.62275	.58349	.54703	.51316	07
08	.92348	.85349	.78941	.73069	.67684	.62741	.58201	.54027	.50187	.46651	08
09	.91434	.83675	.76642	.70259	.64461	.59190	.54393	.50025	.46043	.42410	09
10	.90529	.82035	.74409	.67556	.61391	.55839	.50835	.46319	.42241	.38554	10
11	.89632	.80426	.72242	.64958	.58468	.52679	.47509	.42888	.38753	.35049	11
12	.88745	.78849	.70138	.62460	.55684	.49697	.44401	.39711	.35553	.31863	12
13	.87866	.77303	.68095	.60057	.53032	.46884	.41496	.36770	.32618	.28966	13
14	.86996	.75787	.66112	.57747	.50507	.44230	.38782	.34046	.29925	.26333	14
15	.86135	.74301	.64186	.55526	.48102	.41726	.36245	.31524	.27454	.23939	15
16	.85282	.72845	.62317	.53391	.45811	.39365	.33873	.29189	.25187	.21763	16
17	.84438	.71416	.60502	.51337	.43630	.37136	.31657	.27027	.23107	.19784	17
18	.83602	.70016	.58739	.49363	.41552	.35034	.29586	.25025	.21199	.17986	18
19	.82774	.68643	.57029	.47464	.39573	.33051	.27651	.23171	.19449	.16351	19
20	.81954	.67297	.55367	.45639	.37689	.31180	.25842	.21455	.17843	.14864	20
21	.81143	.65978	.53755	.43883	.35894	.29415	.24151	.19866	.16370	.13513	21
22	.80340	.64684	.52189	.42195	.34185	.27750	.22571	.18394	.15018	.12285	22
23	.79544	.63416	.50669	.40573	.32557	.26180	.21095	.17031	.13778	.11168	23
24	.78757	.62172	.49193	.39012	.31007	.24698	.19715	.15770	.12640	.10153	24
25	.77977	.60953	.47760	.37512	.29530	.23300	.18425	.14602	.11597	.09230	25

table A-1
Present value of one dollar due at the end of n years (cont.)

N	11%	12%	13%	14%	15%	16%	17%	18%	19%	20%	N
01	0.90090	0.89286	0.88496	0.87719	0.86957	0.86207	0.85470	0.84746	0.84034	0.83333	01
02	.81162	.79719	.78315	.76947	.75614	.74316	.73051	.71818	.70616	.69444	02
03	.73119	.71178	.69305	.67497	.65752	.64066	.62437	.60863	.59342	.57870	03
04	.65873	.63552	.61332	.59208	.57175	.55229	.53365	.51579	.49867	.48225	04
05	.59345	.56743	.54276	.51937	.49718	.47611	.45611	.43711	.41905	.40188	05
06	.53464	.50663	.48032	.45559	.43233	.41044	.38984	.37043	.35214	.33490	06
07	.48166	.45235	.42506	.39964	.37594	.35383	.33320	.31392	.29592	.27980	07
08	.43393	.40388	.37616	.35056	.32690	.30503	.28478	.26604	.24867	.23257	08
09	.39092	.36061	.33288	.30751	.28426	.26295	.24340	.22546	.20897	.19381	09
10	.35218	.32197	.29459	.26974	.24718	.22668	.20804	.19106	.17560	.16151	10
11	.31728	.28748	.26070	.23662	.21494	.19542	.17781	.16192	.14756	.13459	11
12	.28584	.25667	.23071	.20756	.18691	.16846	.15197	.13722	.12400	.11216	12
13	.25751	.22917	.20416	.18207	.16253	.14523	.12989	.11629	.10420	.09346	13
14	.23199	.20462	.18068	.15971	.14133	.12520	.11102	.09855	.08757	.07789	14
15	.20900	.18270	.15989	.14010	.12289	.10793	.09489	.08352	.07359	.06491	15
16	.18829	.16312	.14150	.12289	.10686	.09304	.08110	.07078	.06184	.05409	16
17	.16963	.14564	.12522	.10780	.09293	.08021	.06932	.05998	.05196	.04507	17
18	.15282	.13004	.11081	.09456	.08080	.06914	.05925	.05083	.04367	.03756	18
19	.13768	.11611	.09806	.08295	.07026	.05961	.05064	.04308	.03669	.03130	19
20	.12403	.10367	.08678	.07276	.06110	.05139	.04328	.03651	.03084	.02608	20
21	.11174	.09256	.07680	.06383	.05313	.04430	.03699	.03094	.02591	.02174	21
22	.10067	.08264	.06796	.05599	.04620	.03819	.03162	.02622	.02178	.01811	22
23	.09069	.07379	.06014	.04911	.04017	.03292	.02702	.02222	.01830	.01509	23
24	.08170	.06588	.05322	.04308	.03493	.02838	.02310	.01883	.01538	.01258	24
25	.07361	.05882	.04710	.03779	.03038	.02447	.01974	.01596	.01292	.01048	25

table A-1
Present value of one dollar due at the end of *n* years (cont.)

N	21%	22%	23%	24%	25%	26%	27%	28%	29%	30%	N
01	0.82645	0.81967	0.81301	0.80645	0.80000	0.79365	0.78740	0.78125	0.77519	0.76923	01
02	.68301	.67186	.66098	.65036	.64000	.62988	.62000	.61035	.60093	.59172	02
03	.56447	.55071	.53738	.52449	.51200	.49991	.48819	.47684	.46583	.45517	03
04	.46651	.45140	.43690	.42297	.40960	.39675	.38440	.37253	.36111	.35013	04
05	.38554	.37000	.35520	.34111	.32768	.31488	.30268	.29104	.27993	.26933	05
06	.31863	.30328	.28878	.27509	.26214	.24991	.23833	.22737	.21700	.20718	06
07	.26333	.24859	.23478	.22184	.20972	.19834	.18766	.17764	.16822	.15937	07
08	.21763	.20376	.19088	.17891	.16777	.15741	.14776	.13878	.13040	.12259	08
09	.17986	.16702	.15519	.14428	.13422	.12493	.11635	.10842	.10109	.09430	09
10	.14864	.13690	.12617	.11635	.10737	.09915	.09161	.08470	.07836	.07254	10
11	.12285	.11221	.10258	.09383	.08590	.07869	.07214	.06617	.06075	.05580	11
12	.10153	.09198	.08339	.07567	.06872	.06245	.05680	.05170	.04709	.04292	12
13	.08391	.07539	.06780	.06103	.05498	.04957	.04472	.04039	.03650	.03302	13
14	.06934	.06180	.05512	.04921	.04398	.03934	.03522	.03155	.02830	.02540	14
15	.05731	.05065	.04481	.03969	.03518	.03122	.02773	.02465	.02194	.01954	15
16	.04736	.04152	.03643	.03201	.02815	.02478	.02183	.01926	.01700	.01503	16
17	.03914	.03403	.02962	.02581	.02252	.01967	.01719	.01505	.01318	.01156	17
18	.03235	.02789	.02408	.02082	.01801	.01561	.01354	.01175	.01022	.00889	18
19	.02673	.02286	.01958	.01679	.01441	.01239	.01066	.00918	.00792	.00684	19
20	.02209	.01874	.01592	.01354	.01153	.00983	.00839	.00717	.00614	.00526	20
21	.01826	.01536	.01294	.01092	.00922	.00780	.00661	.00561	.00476	.00405	21
22	.01509	.01259	.01052	.00880	.00738	.00619	.00520	.00438	.00369	.00311	22
23	.01247	.01032	.00855	.00710	.00590	.00491	.00410	.00342	.00286	.00239	23
24	.01031	.00846	.00695	.00573	.00472	.00390	.00323	.00267	.00222	.00184	24
25	.00852	.00693	.00565	.00462	.00378	.00310	.00254	.00209	.00172	.00142	25

table A-1
Present value of one dollar due at the end of *n* years (cont.)

N	40%	39%	38%	37%	36%	35%	34%	33%	32%	31%	N
01	0.71429	0.71942	0.72464	0.72993	0.73529	0.74074	0.74627	0.75188	0.75758	0.76336	01
02	.51020	.51757	.52510	.53279	.54066	.54870	.55692	.56532	.57392	.58272	02
03	.36443	.37235	.38051	.38890	.39754	.40644	.41561	.42505	.43479	.44482	03
04	.26031	.26788	.27573	.28387	.29231	.30107	.31016	.31959	.32939	.33956	04
05	.18593	.19272	.19980	.20720	.21493	.22301	.23146	.24029	.24953	.25920	05
06	.13281	.13865	.14479	.15124	.15804	.16520	.17273	.18067	.18904	.19787	06
07	.09486	.09975	.10492	.11040	.11621	.12237	.12890	.13584	.14321	.15104	07
08	.06776	.07176	.07603	.08058	.08545	.09064	.09620	.10214	.10849	.11530	08
09	.04840	.05163	.05509	.05882	.06283	.06714	.07179	.07680	.08219	.08802	09
10	.03457	.03714	.03992	.04293	.04620	.04973	.05357	.05774	.06227	.06719	10
11	.02469	.02672	.02893	.03134	.03397	.03684	.03998	.04341	.04717	.05129	11
12	.01764	.01922	.02096	.02287	.02498	.02729	.02984	.03264	.03574	.03915	12
13	.01260	.01383	.01519	.01670	.01837	.02021	.02227	.02454	.02707	.02989	13
14	.00900	.00995	.01101	.01219	.01350	.01497	.01662	.01845	.02051	.02281	14
15	.00643	.00716	.00798	.00890	.00993	.01109	.01240	.01387	.01554	.01742	15
16	.00459	.00515	.00578	.00649	.00730	.00822	.00925	.01043	.001177	.01329	16
17	.00328	.00370	.00419	.00474	.00537	.00609	.00691	.00784	.00892	.01015	17
18	.00234	.00267	.00304	.00346	.00395	.00451	.00515	.00590	.00676	.00775	18
19	.00167	.00192	.00220	.00253	.00290	.00334	.00385	.00443	.00512	.00591	19
20	.00120	.00138	.00159	.00184	.00213	.00247	.00287	.00333	.00383	.00451	20
21	.00085	.00099	.00115	.00135	.00157	.00183	.00214	.00251	.00294	.00345	21
22	.00061	.00071	.00084	.00098	.00115	.00136	.00160	.00188	.00223	.00263	22
23	.00044	.00051	.00061	.00072	.00085	.00101	.00119	.00142	.00169	.00201	23
24	.00031	.00037	.00044	.00052	.00062	.00074	.00089	.00107	.00128	.00153	24
25	.00022	.00027	.00032	.00038	.00046	.00055	.00066	.00080	.00097	.00117	25

table A-2

Present value of one dollar per year. *n* years at *r*%

Year	1%	2%	3%	4%	5%	6%	7%	8%	9%	10%	Year
1	0.9901	0.9804	0.9709	0.9615	0.9524	0.9434	0.9346	0.9259	0.9174	0.9091	1
2	1.9704	1.9416	1.9135	1.8861	1.8594	1.8334	1.8080	1.7833	1.7591	1.7355	2
3	2.9410	2.8839	2.8286	2.7751	2.7232	2.6730	2.6243	2.5771	2.5313	2.4868	3
4	3.9020	3.8077	3.7171	3.6299	3.5459	3.4651	3.3872	3.3121	3.2397	3.1699	4
5	4.8535	4.7134	4.5797	4.4518	4.3295	4.2123	4.1002	3.9927	3.8896	3.7908	5
6	5.7955	5.6014	5.4172	5.2421	5.0757	4.9173	4.7665	4.6229	4.4859	4.3553	6
7	6.7282	6.4720	6.2302	6.0020	5.7863	5.5824	5.3893	5.2064	5.0329	4.8684	7
8	7.6517	7.3254	7.0196	6.7327	6.4632	6.2098	5.9713	5.7466	5.5348	5.3349	8
9	8.5661	8.1622	7.7861	7.4353	7.1078	6.8017	6.5152	6.2469	5.9852	5.7590	9
10	9.4714	8.9825	8.5302	8.1109	7.7217	7.3601	7.0236	6.7101	6.4176	6.1446	10
11	10.3677	9.7868	9.2526	8.7604	8.3064	7.8868	7.4987	7.1389	6.8052	6.4951	11
12	11.2552	10.5753	9.9539	9.3850	8.8632	8.3838	7.9427	7.5361	7.1607	6.8137	12
13	12.1338	11.3483	10.6349	9.9856	9.3935	8.8527	8.3576	7.9038	7.4869	7.1034	13
14	13.0038	12.1062	11.2960	10.5631	9.8986	9.2950	8.7454	8.2442	7.7861	7.3667	14
15	13.8651	12.8492	11.9379	11.1183	10.3796	9.7122	9.1079	8.5595	8.0607	7.6061	15
16	14.7180	13.5777	12.5610	11.6522	10.8377	10.1059	9.4466	8.8514	8.3125	7.8237	16
17	15.5624	14.2918	13.1660	12.1656	11.2740	10.4772	9.7632	9.1216	8.5436	8.0215	17
18	16.3984	14.9920	13.7534	12.6592	11.6895	10.8276	10.0591	9.3719	8.7556	8.2014	18
19	17.2261	15.6784	14.3237	13.1339	12.0853	11.1581	10.3356	9.6036	8.9501	8.3649	19
20	18.0457	16.3514	14.8774	13.5903	12.4622	11.4699	10.5940	9.8181	9.1285	8.5136	20
21	18.8571	17.0111	15.4149	14.0291	12.8211	11.7640	10.8355	10.0168	9.2922	8.6487	21
22	19.6605	17.6580	15.9368	14.4511	13.1630	12.0416	11.0612	10.2007	9.4424	8.7715	22
23	20.4559	18.2921	16.4435	14.8568	13.4885	12.3033	11.2722	10.3710	9.5802	8.8832	23
24	21.2435	18.9139	16.9355	15.2469	13.7986	12.5503	11.4693	10.5287	9.7066	8.9847	24
25	22.0233	19.5234	17.4131	15.6220	14.0939	12.7833	11.6536	10.6748	9.8226	9.0770	25

table A-2
Present value of one dollar per year. n years at r% (cont.)

Year	11%	12%	13%	14%	15%	16%	17%	18%	19%	20%	Year
1	0.9009	0.8929	0.8850	0.8772	0.8696	0.8621	0.8547	0.8475	0.8403	0.8333	1
2	1.7125	1.6901	1.6681	1.6467	1.6257	1.6052	1.5852	1.5656	1.5465	1.5278	2
3	2.4437	2.4018	2.3612	2.3216	2.2832	2.2459	2.2096	2.1743	2.1399	2.1065	3
4	3.1024	3.0373	2.9745	2.9137	2.8550	2.7982	2.7432	2.6901	2.6386	2.5887	4
5	3.6959	3.6048	3.5172	3.4331	3.3522	3.2743	3.1993	3.1272	3.0576	2.9906	5
6	4.2305	4.1114	3.9976	3.8887	3.7845	3.6847	3.5892	3.4976	3.4098	3.3255	6
7	4.7122	4.5638	4.4226	4.2883	4.1604	4.0386	3.9224	3.8115	3.7057	3.6046	7
8	5.1461	4.9676	4.7988	4.6389	4.4873	4.3436	4.2072	4.0776	3.9544	3.8372	8
9	5.5370	5.3282	5.1317	4.9464	4.7716	4.6065	4.4506	4.3030	4.1633	4.0310	9
10	5.8892	5.6502	5.4262	5.2161	5.0188	4.8332	4.6586	4.4941	4.3389	4.1925	10
11	6.2065	5.9377	5.6869	5.4527	5.2337	5.0286	4.8364	4.6560	4.4865	4.3271	11
12	6.4924	6.1944	5.9176	5.6603	5.4206	5.1971	4.9884	4.7932	4.6105	4.4392	12
13	6.7499	6.4235	6.1218	5.8424	5.5831	5.3423	5.1183	4.9095	4.7147	4.5327	13
14	6.9819	6.6282	6.3025	6.0021	5.7245	5.4675	5.2293	5.0081	4.8023	4.6106	14
15	7.1909	6.8109	6.4624	6.1422	5.8474	5.5755	5.3242	5.0916	4.8759	4.6755	15
16	7.3792	6.9740	6.6039	6.2651	5.9542	5.6685	5.4053	5.1624	4.9377	4.7296	16
17	7.5488	7.1196	6.7291	6.3729	6.0472	5.7487	5.4746	5.2223	4.9897	4.7746	17
18	7.7016	7.2497	6.8399	6.4674	6.1280	5.8178	5.5339	5.2732	5.0333	4.8122	18
19	7.8393	7.3658	6.9380	6.5504	6.1982	5.8775	5.5845	5.3162	5.0700	4.8435	19
20	7.9633	7.4694	7.0248	6.6231	6.2593	5.9288	5.6278	5.3527	5.1009	4.8696	20
21	8.0751	7.5620	7.1016	6.6870	6.3125	5.9731	5.6648	5.3837	5.1268	4.8913	21
22	8.1757	7.6446	7.1695	6.7429	6.3587	6.0113	5.6964	5.4099	5.1486	4.9094	22
23	8.2664	7.7184	7.2297	6.7921	6.3988	6.0442	5.7234	5.4321	5.1668	4.9245	23
24	8.3481	7.7843	7.2829	6.8351	6.4338	6.0726	5.7465	5.4509	5.1822	4.9371	24
25	8.4217	7.8431	7.3300	6.8729	6.4641	6.0971	5.7662	5.4669	5.1951	4.9476	25

table A-2

Present value of one dollar per year. n years at $r\%$ (cont.)

Year	21%	22%	23%	24%	25%	26%	27%	28%	29%	30%	Year
1	0.8264	0.8197	0.8130	0.8065	0.8000	0.7937	0.7874	0.7813	0.7752	0.7692	1
2	1.5095	1.4915	1.4740	1.4568	1.4400	1.4235	1.4074	1.3916	1.3761	1.3609	2
3	2.0739	2.0422	2.0114	1.9813	1.9520	1.9234	1.8956	1.8684	1.8420	1.8161	3
4	2.5404	2.4936	2.4483	2.4043	2.3616	2.3202	2.2800	2.2410	2.2031	2.1662	4
5	2.9260	2.8636	2.8035	2.7454	2.6893	2.6351	2.5827	2.5320	2.4830	2.4356	5
6	3.2446	3.1669	3.0923	3.0205	2.9515	2.8850	2.8210	2.7594	2.7000	2.6427	6
7	3.5079	3.4155	3.3270	3.2423	3.1611	3.0833	3.0087	2.9370	2.8682	2.8021	7
8	3.7256	3.6193	3.5179	3.4212	3.3289	3.2407	3.1564	3.0758	2.9986	2.9247	8
9	3.9054	3.7863	3.6731	3.5655	3.4631	3.3657	3.2728	3.1842	3.0997	3.0190	9
10	4.0541	3.9232	3.7993	3.6819	3.5705	3.4648	3.3644	3.2689	3.1781	3.0915	10
11	4.1769	4.0354	3.9018	3.7757	3.6564	3.5435	3.4365	3.3351	3.2388	3.1473	11
12	4.2785	4.1274	3.9852	3.8514	3.7251	3.6060	3.4933	3.3868	3.2859	3.1903	12
13	4.3624	4.2028	4.0530	3.9124	3.7801	3.6555	3.6381	3.4272	3.3224	3.2233	13
14	4.4317	4.2646	4.1082	3.9616	3.8241	3.6949	3.5733	3.4587	3.3507	3.2487	14
15	4.4890	4.3152	4.1530	4.0013	3.8593	3.7261	3.6010	3.4834	3.3726	3.2682	15
16	4.5364	4.3567	4.1894	4.0333	3.8874	3.7509	3.6228	3.5026	3.3896	3.2832	16
17	4.5755	4.3908	4.2190	4.0591	3.9099	3.7705	3.6400	3.5177	3.4028	3.2948	17
18	4.6079	4.4187	4.2431	4.0799	3.9279	3.7861	3.6536	3.5294	3.4130	3.3037	18
19	4.6346	4.4415	4.2627	4.0967	3.9424	3.7985	3.6642	3.5386	3.4210	3.3105	19
20	4.6567	4.4603	4.2786	4.1103	3.9539	3.8083	3.6726	3.5458	3.4271	3.3158	20
21	4.6750	4.4756	4.2916	4.1212	3.9631	3.8161	3.6792	3.5514	3.4319	3.3198	21
22	4.6900	4.4882	4.3021	4.1300	3.9705	3.8223	3.6844	3.5558	3.4356	3.3230	22
23	4.7025	4.4985	4.3106	4.1371	3.9764	3.8273	3.6885	3.5592	3.4384	3.3254	23
24	4.7128	4.5070	4.3176	4.1428	3.9811	3.8312	3.6918	3.5619	3.4406	3.3272	24
25	4.7213	4.5139	4.3232	4.1474	3.9849	3.8342	3.6943	3.5640	3.4423	3.3286	25

table A-2

Present value of one dollar per year. *n* years at *r*% (cont.)

Year	31%	32%	33%	34%	35%	36%	37%	38%	39%	40%	Year
1	0.7634	0.7576	0.7519	0.7463	0.7407	0.7353	0.7299	0.7246	0.7194	0.7143	1
2	1.3461	1.3315	1.3172	1.3032	1.2894	1.2760	1.2627	1.2497	1.2370	1.2245	2
3	1.7909	1.7663	1.7423	1.7188	1.6959	1.6735	1.6516	1.6302	1.6093	1.5889	3
4	2.1305	2.0957	2.0618	2.0290	1.9969	1.9658	1.9355	1.9060	1.8772	1.8492	4
5	2.3897	2.3452	2.3021	2.2604	2.2200	2.1807	2.1427	2.1058	2.0699	2.0352	5
6	2.5875	2.5342	2.4828	2.4331	2.3852	2.3388	2.2939	2.2506	2.2086	2.1680	6
7	2.7386	2.6775	2.6187	2.5620	2.5075	2.4550	2.4043	2.3555	2.3083	2.2628	7
8	2.8539	2.7860	2.7208	2.6582	2.5982	2.5404	2.4849	2.4315	2.3801	2.3306	8
9	2.9419	2.8681	2.7976	2.7300	2.6653	2.6033	2.5437	2.4866	2.4317	2.3790	9
10	3.0091	2.9304	2.8553	2.7836	2.7150	2.6495	2.5867	2.5265	2.4689	2.4136	10
11	3.0604	2.9776	2.8987	2.8236	2.7519	2.6834	2.6180	2.5555	2.4956	2.4383	11
12	3.0995	3.0133	2.9314	2.8534	2.7792	2.7084	2.6409	2.5764	2.5148	2.4559	12
13	3.1294	3.0404	2.9559	2.8757	2.7994	2.7268	2.6576	2.5916	2.5286	2.4685	13
14	3.1522	3.0609	2.9744	2.8923	2.8144	2.7403	2.6698	2.6026	2.5386	2.4775	14
15	3.1696	3.0764	2.9883	2.9047	2.8255	2.7502	2.6787	2.6106	2.5457	2.4839	15
16	3.1829	3.0882	2.9987	2.9140	2.8337	2.7575	2.6852	2.6164	2.5509	2.4885	16
17	3.1931	3.0971	3.0065	2.9209	2.8398	2.7629	2.6899	2.6206	2.5546	2.4918	17
18	3.2008	3.1039	3.0124	2.9260	2.8443	2.7668	2.6934	2.6236	2.5573	2.4941	18
19	3.2067	3.1090	3.0169	2.9299	2.8476	2.7697	2.6959	2.6258	2.5592	2.4958	19
20	3.2112	3.1129	3.0202	2.9327	2.8501	2.7718	2.6977	2.6274	2.5606	2.4970	20
21	3.2147	3.1158	3.0227	2.9349	2.8519	2.7734	2.6991	2.6285	2.5616	2.4979	21
22	3.2173	3.1180	3.0246	2.9365	2.8533	2.7746	2.7000	2.6294	2.5623	2.4985	22
23	3.2193	3.1197	3.0260	2.9377	2.8543	2.7754	2.7008	2.6300	2.5628	2.4989	23
24	3.2209	3.1210	3.0271	2.9386	2.8550	2.7760	2.7013	2.6304	2.5632	2.4992	24
25	3.2220	3.1220	3.0279	2.9392	2.8556	2.7765	2.7017	2.6307	2.5634	2.4994	25

table B-1
Area of normal distribution that is X standard deviations
to the left or right of the mean

Number of Standard Deviations from Mean (X)	Area to the Left or Right (One tail)	Number of Standard Deviations from Mean (X)	Area to the Left or Right (One tail)
0.00	.5000	1.55	.0606
0.05	.4801	1.60	.0548
0.10	.4602	1.65	.0495
0.15	.4404	1.70	.0446
0.20	.4207	1.75	.0401
0.25	.4013	1.80	.0359
0.30	.3821	1.85	.0322
0.35	.3632	1.90	.0287
0.40	.3446	1.95	.0256
0.45	.3264	2.00	.0228
0.50	.3085	2.05	.0202
0.55	.2912	2.10	.0179
0.60	.2743	2.15	.0158
0.65	.2578	2.20	.0139
0.70	.2420	2.25	.0122
0.75	.2264	2.30	.0107
0.80	.2119	2.35	.0094
0.85	.1977	2.40	.0082
0.90	.1841	2.45	.0071
0.95	.1711	2.50	.0062
1.00	.1577	2.55	.0054
1.05	.1469	2.60	.0047
1.10	.1357	2.65	.0040
1.15	.1251	2.70	.0035
1.20	.1151	2.75	.0030
1.25	.1056	2.80	.0026
1.30	.0968	2.85	.0022
1.35	.0885	2.90	.0019
1.40	.0808	2.95	.0016
1.45	.0735	3.00	.0013
1.50	.0668		

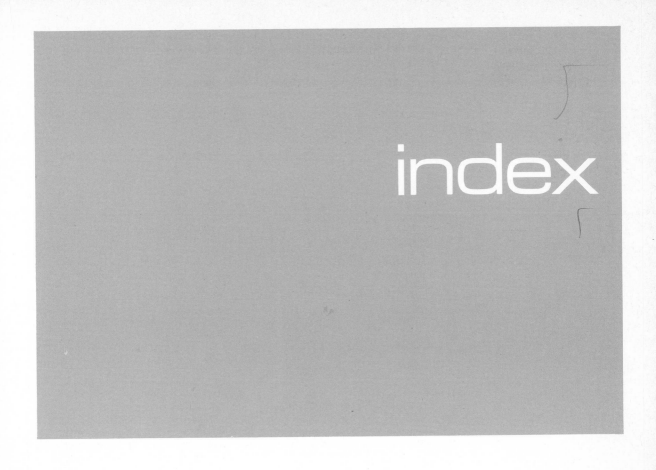

index